# Kenya

Matthew D Firestone
Stuart Butler, Paula Hardy, Adam Karlin

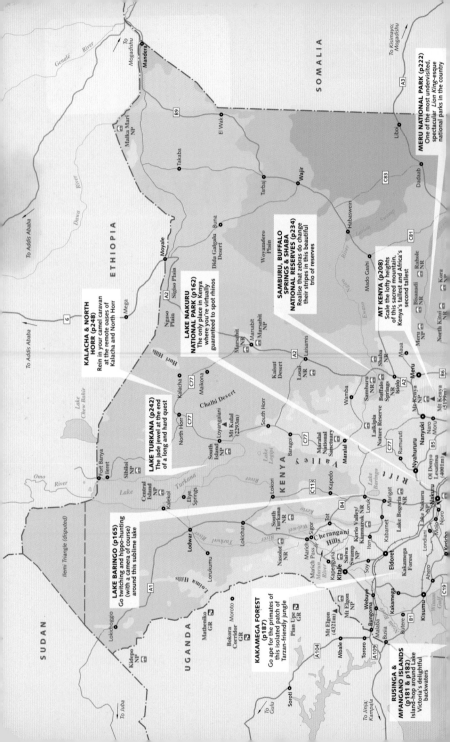

**MERU NATIONAL PARK (p222)**
One of the most underrated, spectacular *Lion King*-esque national parks in the country

**SAMBURU, BUFFALO SPRINGS & SHABA NATIONAL RESERVES (p234)**
Realise that zebras do change their stripes in this beautiful trio of reserves

**MT KENYA (p208)**
Scale the lofty heights of this sacred mountain, Kenya's tallest and Africa's second tallest

**LAKE NAKURU NATIONAL PARK (p162)**
The only place in Kenya where you're virtually guaranteed to spot rhinos

**KALACHA & NORTH HORR (p248)**
Rein in your camel caravan at the remote oases of Kalacha and North Horr

**LAKE TURKANA (p242)**
The jade jewel at the end of a long and hard quest

**LAKE BARINGO (p165)**
Go twitching and hippo-hunting (with a camera of course) around this sublime lake

**KAKAMEGA FOREST (p187)**
Go ape for the primates of this isolated patch of Tarzan-friendly jungle

**RUSINGA & MFANGANO ISLANDS (p181 & p182)**
Island-hop around Lake Victoria's delightful backwaters

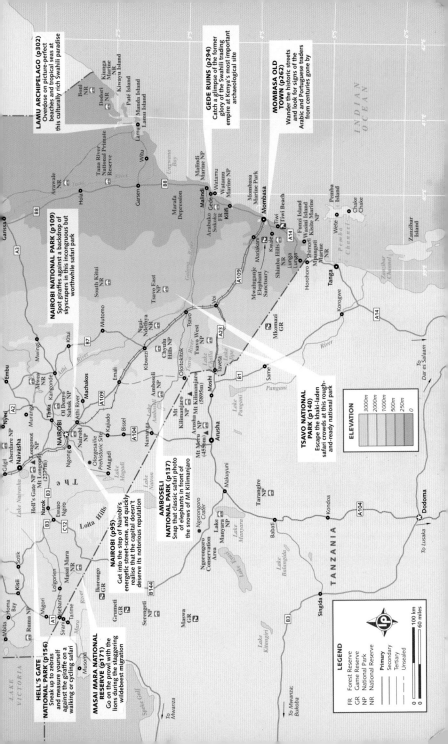

**LAMU ARCHIPELAGO (p302)**
Overdose on picture-perfect beaches and tropical seas at this culturally rich Swahili paradise

**GEDE RUINS (p294)**
Catch a glimpse of the former glory of the Swahili trading empire at Kenya's most important archaeological site

**MOMBASA OLD TOWN (p262)**
Wander the historic streets and look for signs of the Arabic and Portuguese traders from centuries gone by

**NAIROBI NATIONAL PARK (p109)**
Spot giraffes against a backdrop of skyscrapers in this incongruous but worthwhile safari park

**NAIROBI (p95)**
Get into the step of Nairobi's energetic street-scene, and quickly realise that the capital doesn't deserve its notorious reputation

**AMBOSELI NATIONAL PARK (p137)**
Snap that classic safari photo of elephants in front of the snows of Mt Kilimanjaro

**TSAVO NATIONAL PARK (p140)**
Escape the khaki-laden safari crowds at this rough-and-ready national park

**HELL'S GATE NATIONAL PARK (p156)**
Sneak up to zebras and measure yourself against the giraffe on a walking or cycling safari

**MASAI MARA NATIONAL RESERVE (p171)**
Go on the prowl with the lions during the staggering wildebeest migration

**ELEVATION**

| | |
|---|---|
| | 3000m |
| | 2000m |
| | 1000m |
| | 500m |
| | 250m |
| | 0 |

**LEGEND**

FR Forest Reserve
GR Game Reserve
NP National Park
NR National Reserve

Primary
Secondary
Tertiary
Unsealed

0 — 100 km
0 — 60 miles

# On the Road

**MATTHEW D FIRESTONE Coordinating Author**
This picture was taken after a sunrise balloon ride over the Masai Mara National Reserve (p171). Note that the shot was carefully cropped to remove the nearby hippo- and croc-lined banks of the Mara River, which was narrowly missed by our fearless captain after an unexpected gust of wind kicked up during our final descent.

**STUART BUTLER** This photo was taken on a walking safari (p171) on the edge of the Masai Mara. As you can see my two guides are trying their hardest to look like brave Maasai warriors whilst I'm trying my hardest (and succeeding) to look like a typical tourist.

**ADAM KARLIN** This is me with a merry crew of Swahili sailors on the day we explored the mangrove islands of the Lamu archipelago (p302) by dhow. We tacked up the Manda Channel, unsuccessfully fished, consumed much food and generally slipped into the syrup-slow pace – too slow for me, but God bless these guys for living the dream – of island life.

*For full author biographies see p373.*

# Kenya Highlights

Kenya may well be Africa-in-microcosm. It offers bustling cities, lofty mountains, colourful tribal cultures, beaches and coral reefs, stretches of desert and vast savannas, and some of Africa's best wildlife attractions. There are countless reasons to come here, and picking just one highlight is nigh on impossible. We've asked around and selected some favourite sights and attractions to get you inspired but we're sure you'll soon have Kenyan highlights of your own...

TOM COCKREM

## 1 HEADING NORTH

Getting on a bus, or hitching on a truck, heading north from Maralal (p242) into the red dust of the northern deserts gives you a real taste of adventure. Here the roads are patchy, the thorn trees are sparse and the wind is relentlessly hot. Rugged mountains reach skyward, the Jade Sea offers respite from the desert and Samburu, Turkana and Gabbra people move their camels on as they have for centuries.

**Will Gourlay, Lonely Planet Staff**

## BAREFOOT IN LAMU

The best way to get around Lamu (p302) is barefoot in the late afternoon. The narrow streets come alive as the heat of the day subsides. Kids gather on doorsteps and little girls play with skipping ropes. Old men in *kikois* (cotton wraparounds) greet passing friends and discuss the issues of the day. Donkeys groan under their loads, and a cool breeze pushes the dhows across the harbour.

**Will Gourlay, Lonely Planet Staff**

ARIADNE VAN ZANDBERGEN

## 2 MWALUGANJE ELEPHANT SANCTUARY

Watching elephants for a whole afternoon in the Mwaluganje Elephant Sanctuary (p271) is just magical: whole families of jumbos rumble down to splash and spray at the waterhole. Continue watching them later with a (Tusker) beer on the terrace and your cash goes to the local community – perfect!

**Geoff & Barbara Welford, Travellers, England**

MARK DAF

## 4 MERU NATIONAL PARK

ARIADNE VAN ZANDBERGEN

After so much safari exposure, it can take a lot to get excited. But some things, like seeing elephants and giraffes in the wild – in this case in Meru National Park (p222) – will always make my eyes pop out like a kid. What makes the moment cooler? Seeing said animals from a 4WD I was driving myself over rutted tracks and open savanna.

**Adam Karlin, Lonely Planet Author**

## MAASAI MARKET, NAIROBI

Walking through the narrow paths at the Maasai market in Nairobi (p131), where creativity and Kenyan culture come together, the joyful sellers call out, attracting attention for you to buy their wooden and stone handicrafts, *kiondos* (woven baskets) and jewellery – I not only came out with a rare piece of art, but also a piece of their rich traditional culture.

**Dipin Chhabra, Lonely Planet Staff**

**5**

TOM COCKREM

## NAIROBI

Nairobi (p95) is vilified as one of the most dangerous cities in the world, so there is a bizarre sense of satisfaction you get after spending a month living there without so much as having your wallet lifted. Ignore the hype and check it out as Nairobi really is one of the continent's great capitals, and there is so much more to do here than you'd imagine.

**Matthew D Firestone,
Lonely Planet Author**

ELLIOT DANIEL

**6**

© TERRY WALL / ALAMY

**7**

## LEOPARD-SPOTTING AT DAWN, LAKE NAKURU NATIONAL PARK

We barely allowed ourselves to imagine seeing Africa's almost mythical beast, but luck was more than on our side on our dawn safari in Lake Nakuru National Park (p162) – we turned a corner and there he was, strolling at ease down the road! We watched in awed silence as he scent-marked a fallen tree then melted away, his spots perfect camouflage in the long grass.

**Anna Welford, Lonely Planet Staff**

DOUGLAS STEARLEY

## TEA BENEATH THE TREES, KAKAMEGA FOREST

For refreshment with a twist, take your afternoon tea Kenyan style – such as in the gardens of Rondo Retreat at the unique Kakamega Forest (p187), where noisy hornbills and elegant colobus monkeys play in the trees above while you sip.

**Stuart Butler,
Lonely Planet Author**

**9**

© GARY COOK / ALA

**8**

## MAN-EATERS OF TSAVO

While I'd heard about the famed 'man-eaters of Tsavo' (p147), I had seen enough lions on safari to not be scared by a few overgrown cats. Of course, my attitude quickly changed after we got a flat tyre in lion country. It's one thing to stare down the king of the jungle inside a 4WD, but it's quite another to see one prowling around in the distance at eye-level.

**Matthew D Firestone,
Lonely Planet Author**

ARIADNE VAN ZANDBERGE

**10**

## PATÉ ISLAND

A great moment of discovery is walking across the red path that worms its way over the island of Paté (p314), under palms, and over the scutter of wind-blown grass, then wading into a mangrove jungle, past dark vines and brown tides, until emerging in the ruins of Shanga, one of the great city states of the Swahili coast.

**Adam Karlin, Lonely Planet Author**

# Contents

# Regional Map Contents

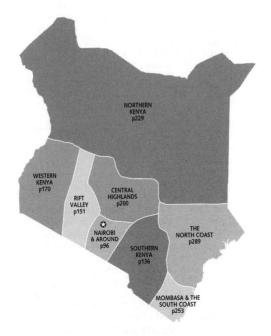

# Destination Kenya

Few destinations in the world can evoke such powerful imagery as Kenya, one of East Africa's premier safari destinations. Indeed, the acacia-dotted savannas of Kenya are inhabited by classic African animals, from towering elephants and prancing gazelles to prides of lions and stalking leopards. The country also plays host to the annual wildebeest migration, the largest single movement of herd animals on the planet.

However, what makes Kenya truly stand out as a travel destination is the vast palette of landscapes that comprise this visually stunning country. While the flaunted image of the savannas of Masai Mara is perhaps the single key selling point for Kenya's tourist industry, intrepid travellers can also explore the barren expanses of the Rift Valley, the glacial ridges of Mt Kenya and the beaches of the Swahili coast. This rich diversity of quintessential African environments presents opportunities for hiking, trekking, diving, sailing and so much more.

But to simply focus on Kenya's wildlife and nature is to ignore the people that make this country so dynamic. Kenya is a thriving multi-cultural country with a wide cross-section of everything that is classic and contemporary Africa. Everyday life brings together traditional tribes and urban families, ancient customs and modern sensibilities. And, while much of East Africa has suffered from bitter feuds between divided ethnic groups, Kenya has usually been regarded as an island of stability in a troubled region.

Yet, following the disputed elections of 27 December 2007, Kenya was crippled by a wave of violence that scarred the national conscience, and threatened to collapse the country's lucrative tourism industry. While incumbent President Mwai Kibaki and opposition leader Raila Odinga debated the accuracy of the voting results, the world watched in horror as conflict erupted in the streets. In a few short weeks, a reported 1000 Kenyans were brutally killed, another 350,000 were internally displaced, and the image of Kenya as a safe and peaceful destination was instantaneously shattered.

In February 2008, former UN Secretary-General Kofi Annan brokered a power-sharing agreement between the warring factions, and in April 2008, President Kibaki named a grand coalition cabinet of 41 ministers, which included the newly elected Prime Minister Odinga and his two deputies. At the time of writing, it was difficult to say if the peace accords will weather the impending storm of change. However, it is within the nature of the Kenyan people to be optimistic.

While internal political life is at times tumultuous, it seems that Kenyans retain an innate self-confidence, a belief that things are improving, and a desire to see their homeland take a prominent place on the world stage. Indeed, now that Kenya's 'native son' sits in the White House, perhaps this vision isn't so grandiose after all. Furthermore, Kenya is a regional heavy hitter, especially since it has finally joined hands with Tanzania and Uganda in a long-sought-after customs union. In addition to paving the way for full revival of the defunct East African Community (EAC), the customs union has been extremely beneficial for travellers, who can now pass relatively unhindered between these neighbouring countries.

Kenya may be a somewhat more intimidating destination than it once was, but it remains one of the undisputed highlights of Africa. Check your inhibitions, ignore the hype, bring your sense of adventure, and get ready for some truly inspiring and life-changing travel.

## FAST FACTS

Population: 37.9 million

Total fertility rate: 4.7 children per woman

Population growth rate: 2.7%

HIV/AIDS adult prevalence rate: 6.7%

Workforce engaged in agriculture: 75%

Highest point: Mt Kenya 5199m

Lowest point: Indian Ocean 0m

Land boundaries: 3477km

Oldest town: Lamu (established 15th century)

Number of times Kenya has not won the Olympic steeplechase: none

# Getting Started

Planning a trip to Kenya is a pleasure in itself: the country is so versatile that it's virtually a blank canvas, catering equally for thrill-seekers and sun-seekers, budget backpackers and high-end high rollers, those who like it tough and those who just want to get going. Whatever you want to do here, you'll discover that it's pretty straightforward to sort yourself out on the ground, and, in many cases, more reliable than trying to make advance plans.

## WHEN TO GO

The main tourist season is in January and February, when the weather is hottest and driest. At this time, the animals in the wildlife parks tend to congregate more around the watercourses, making them easier to spot. However, the parks can get crowded and rates for accommodation soar – also make sure you avoid Christmas and Easter unless you want to pay much higher prices.

See Climate Charts for more information (p325).

From June to October, the annual wildebeest migration takes place, with thousands of animals streaming into the Masai Mara National Reserve from the Serengeti.

During the long rains (the low season, spanning from March to the end of May) things are much quieter. Wildlife is harder to spot and mosquitoes are rife, a combination that keeps most tourists away.

See also the Directory (p329) for information on festivals and events.

## COSTS & MONEY

Travelling in Kenya can cost as much or as little as you like, depending on what kind of standards you're happy with. In general, for the midrange

---

### DON'T LEAVE HOME WITHOUT...

- Checking the latest visa situation (p338) and government travel advisories (p326)
- Vaccination card, insect repellent and malaria prophylaxis
- Learning at least a few basic phrases in Kiswahili
- Antidiarrhoeal medicine, in case you get a bad dose of the runs
- Sunblock and a hat, so you don't get cooked by the tropical sun
- Clothes that you don't mind getting absolutely filthy or wet
- A swimsuit and a beach towel
- A poncho for rainy days and wet boat trips
- A pair of river sandals or reef walkers and sturdy hiking boots
- An alarm clock for catching early-morning matatus
- A waterproof, windproof jacket and warm layers for highland hiking and camping
- A flashlight (torch)
- Binoculars and a field guide
- Miscellaneous necessities: compact umbrella, padlock, matches, pocket knife
- An appetite for fresh fruit
- A thirst for cold lager
- Your sense of adventure

traveller staying in small hotels with a decent level of comfort, eating the occasional Western meal, using matatus and taxis, taking in the odd museum, and treating yourself to a beer in the evening should cost around KSh3500 per day. Budget travellers could get this down to as little as KSh1000 by foregoing private bathrooms, eating in Kenyan canteens, walking or taking local buses and skipping the booze, while top-end types can find themselves paying anything from US$300 upwards for a taste of the high life. Accommodation is the biggest single expense, and staying in Nairobi or on the coast will push costs up sharply (see p317).

On top of this, you'll probably want to allow some extra cash for more expensive tourist activities such as trekking, diving and other excursions. The biggest outlay for most visitors will be visiting the national parks, whether on a safari or independently. For more information, see the Safaris chapter, p65.

## TRAVEL RESPONSIBLY

When backpackers first started blazing the hippie trail across the old Silk Road during the 1960s and 1970s, sustainability was an implicit concept that few people needed to give much thought. Travel at the time was nearly always slow, overland and utterly dependent on local economies. In fact, Nairobi was a famous staging point on the Cape to Cairo trail (which gave birth to the actual Thorn Tree that inspired Lonely Planet's online community).

But things change, and sometimes in dramatic ways. Today, travel is one of the world's fastest-growing industries, and in recent years Kenya has enjoyed higher tourism growth rates than many European and Asian destinations. Even in light of the 2007 election violence, Kenya maintains a relatively positive image abroad as one of the safest safari destinations in Africa.

The continuous growth of the travel industry has brought incredible economic success to Kenya. However, this growth has also placed enormous stress on both the environment and local cultures, and threatens to destroy the very destinations that tourists are seeking out. For instance, national parks have suffered rapid erosion due to errant 4WD vehicles, and hot showers at bush hotels are a strain on already scant local resources.

In recent years, the term 'sustainable tourism' has emerged as a buzz word in the industry, though few people have a clear idea of exactly what this

---

### HOW TO TRAVEL GREEN IN KENYA

Here are some tips for protecting the environment in Kenya and beyond:

- Recycle – ask at your hotel if they have a recycling system in place.
- Pick up rubbish – while walking along a beach or a trail, pick up any rubbish you see as your actions might inspire others to do the same.
- Respect the land – stick to the trails as they lessen the erosion caused by human transit. Likewise, don't damage plants, and always observe wildlife from a distance.
- Respect the sea – always follow the basic snorkel and scuba guidelines, keep garbage out of the water, and remember not to eat or purchase endangered or undersized seafood.
- Don't feed animals – feeding the animals interferes with their natural diets and makes them susceptible to bacteria transferred by humans or pesticides contained within fruit.
- Shop smart – avoid souvenirs made from threatened species, such as ebony and mahogany, by asking carvers and vendors about the source of their materials.

# TOP 10

## BOOKS

Get a deeper sense of what makes Kenya tick through these standout fiction and nonfiction reads. For more on local literature, see p48.

1  *Mzungu Boy* (2005) Meja Mwangi

2  *Wizard of the Crow* (2006) Ngũgĩ wa Thiong'o

3  *Flame Trees of Thika* (2000) Elspeth Huxley

4  *I Laugh so I Won't Cry: Kenya's Women Tell the Stories of Their Lives* (2005) ed Helena Halperin

5  *A Primate's Memoir* (2004) Robert M Sapolsky

6  *The In-Between World of Vikram Lall* (2005) MG Vassanji

7  *Tick Bite Fever* (2004) David Bennun

8  *The Green Belt Movement: Sharing the Approach and the Experience (2005)* Wangari Maathai

9  *Wildlife Wars: My Battle to Save Kenya's Elephants* (2002) Richard Leakey

10  *The Tree Where Man Was Born* (1972) Peter Matthiessen

## FILMS

See the many shades of Kenya on the big (or small) screen for some pre-trip inspiration. For more on the Kenyan film industry, see p50.

1  *Nowhere in Africa* (2002) Director: Caroline Link

2  *Enough is Enough* (2005) Director: Kibaara Kaugi

3  *Safari ya Jamhuri* (Road to Freedom; 2003) Director: Wanjiru M Njendu

4  *Africa, the Serengeti* (1994) Director: George Casey

5  *The Constant Gardener* (2005) Director: Fernando Meirelles

6  *Babu's Babies* (2003) Director: Christine Bala

7  *The Oath* (2004) Director: Nathan Collett

8  *14 Million Dreams* (2003) Director: Miles Roston

9  *Born Free* (1966) Director: James Hill

10  *Out of Africa* (1985) Director: Sydney Pollack

## PHOTO BOOKS

Given its stunning national parks and wildlife, vibrant cities and diverse people, it's no surprise photo opportunities abound in Kenya. Check out how these books beautifully make the most of them.

1  *Africa Adorned* (1984) Angela Fisher

2  *Shootback* (2000) ed Lana Wong

3  *African Ark* (1990) Carol Beckwith and Angela Fisher

4  *Maasai* (1990) Tepilit Ole Saitoti Carol Beckwith

5  *Turkana: Kenya's Nomads of the Jade Sea* (1997) Nigel Pavitt

6  *African Visions: Diary of an African Photographer* (2001) Mirella Ricciardi

7  *This Is Kenya* (2005) Jean Hartley

8  *Journey Through Kenya* (1994) Mohammed Amin, Duncan Willets and Brian Tetley

9  *Through Open Doors: A View of Asian Cultures in Kenya* (1983) Cynthia Salvadori

10  *African Ceremonies* (1999) Carol Beckwith and Angela Fisher

concept entails. Put simply, though, sustainable tourism refers to striking the ideal balance between the traveller and their surrounding environment. For ways to do this on your travels in Kenya, see the boxed text, p14.

## TRAVEL LITERATURE

Already a firm favourite among animal lovers and conservationists, *A Primate's Memoir: Love, Death and Baboons in East Africa*, by Robert M Sapolsky, is an engaging account of a young primatologist's years working in Kenya.

Equally personal and a bit less serious at heart, David Bennun's entertaining *Tick Bite Fever* tells of the author's accident-prone childhood in Africa, complete with suicidal dogs and Kenya Cowboys.

For a more serious look at social and cultural issues, read *No Man's Land: An Investigative Journey Through Kenya and Tanzania*, by George Monbiot, which follows the fortunes of the region's nomadic tribes.

Bill Bryson turns his social conscience and trademark gentle humour on the region in his *African Diary*, concentrating on a seven-day trip to Kenya.

Londoner Daisy Waugh provides a city girl's take on the thoroughly untouristy town of Isiolo in *A Small Town in Africa*, giving a more modern alternative to the many settlers' tales in print.

Increasingly hard to find but worth the effort, *Journey to the Jade Sea*, by John Hillaby, recounts this prolific travel writer's epic trek to Lake Turkana in the days before the Kenyan tourist boom.

Finally, while some of her observations are far from politically correct by today's standards, the heartfelt *Out of Africa,* by Karen Blixen (Isak Dinesen), remains perhaps the single definitive account of the colonial experience in Africa.

## INTERNET RESOURCES

**Artmatters** (www.artmatters.info) Information on arts and culture from Kenya and East Africa.

**Kenya Association of Tour Operators** (www.katokenya.org) Contains the full list of KATO-approved member companies.

**Kenya Wildlife Service** (www.kws.org) Up-to-date conservation news and detailed information on national parks and reserves.

**Lonely Planet** (www.lonelyplanet.com) Travel news and summaries, the Thorn Tree bulletin board and links to more web resources.

**Magical Kenya** (www.magicalkenya.com) The official website of the Kenya Tourism Board; has some good information on sights and activities.

**Nation Newspaper** (www.nationmedia.com) Kenya's foremost newspaper.

# Itineraries
## CLASSIC ROUTES

### SAFARI NJEMA

**One to Two Weeks /
Nairobi to Amboseli National Park**

This classic route will put you face to face with the continent's most charismatic creatures. *Safari njema* – have a good trip!

Departing from **Nairobi** (p95), Kenya's (in)famous rough-and-ready capital city, the first port of call is the world-renowned **Masai Mara National Reserve** (p171). Between July and October, the Mara plays host to the annual wildebeest migration, which offers a definitive slice of safari Africa. Even if you can't time your visit to coincide with this epic event, the Mara is still worth visiting as the most famous national park in Kenya.

From here the trail leads northeast to the **Samburu National Reserve** (p234), a dusty, red, desert habitat that shelters several species of animals not found elsewhere in Kenya.

The safari trail continues down to **Amboseli National Park** (p137), which is regarded as one of the best places in Africa to get up close and personal with herds of grazing elephants.

For those who want to see the jewels in Kenya's tourist crown, this short but sweet tour takes in the country's top three national parks.

## IN SEARCH OF THE BIG FIVE

**Three to Four Weeks /
Lake Nakuru to Mombasa**

The ultimate goal of any safari-goer is to spot the Big Five, namely lion, leopard, rhino, buffalo and elephant. While you're going to have to put in a lot of hours to spot them all – particularly the elusive leopard – this itinerary will have you ticking them off the list in no time.

Start your search at **Lake Nakuru National Park** (p162), an alkaline lake in the Rift Valley, which is home to many thousands of pink flamingos and pelicans. This vitally important national park also protects the country's largest population of endangered black rhinos, as well as large herds of buffalo.

From Lake Nakuru, your next stop is the obligatory safari in **Masai Mara National Reserve** (p171), which is veritable lion country. With a little luck, you can also occasionally spot leopards lounging in trees, and cheetahs prowling around the savannas. From Masai Mara, head south to **Amboseli National Park** (p137) for a wildlife drive through Kilimanjaro's court. Against a backdrop of Africa's tallest peak, you'll see dozens and dozens of elephants.

From Amboseli it's a straightforward drive to **Tsavo West National Park** (p140) and **Tsavo East National Park** (p144), Kenya's largest wildlife parks. As they are relatively undeveloped, Tsavo West and East are where you can have a truly wild safari experience.

From here you can head down the highway to the ancient Swahili port of **Mombasa** (p255), where you can either fly straight home, or start a whole new journey exploring the Kenyan coast.

Indeed, it's just a short trip southwest to the **Mwaluganje Elephant Sanctuary** (p271), a small but important reserve that protects elephant migratory routes, and on to the densely forested **Shimba Hills National Reserve** (p270), home to the rare sable antelope.

**This wildlife-focused journey takes in all of the major safari parks, ending up on the coast for a change of scene.**

## SUN, SURF & SWAHILI

**Two to Three Weeks /
Mombasa to Lamu**

Whether you're interested in exploring the remaining vestiges of Swahili culture, or simply kickin' it on the beach for days on end, don't miss the chance to explore Kenya's sun-drenched coast.

From the coastal gateway of **Mombasa** (p255), the first stop heading south is **Tiwi Beach** (p271), a tranquil white-sand paradise that is popular with independent travellers. Just down the road, you can head on to the package-holiday destination of **Diani Beach** (p273) for a taste of the more full-on resort experience.

Near the Tanzanian border, **Funzi** (p279) and **Wasini** (p279) islands provide a dose of real, unspoilt coastal life, and also afford easy access to the excellent **Kisite Marine National Park** (p280). Whether you spot crocs along the banks of mangrove-lined rivers or dolphins crashing through the surf, a visit to the marine park is a wonderful complement to Kenya's terrestrial wildlife destinations.

Back now on the coastal trail, make a quick stop in the charming town of **Kilifi** (p286) before pressing on to the **Arabuko Sokoke Forest Reserve** (p293), one of the largest remaining tracts of indigenous coastal forest in East Africa.

Further north are the **Gede ruins** (p294), an ancient Swahili city that dates back to the 13th century. Another historic destination along the Swahili coast is **Malindi** (p296), a 14th-century trading post that is now one of the country's leading beach destinations for Italian holiday makers.

This itinerary ends (and peaks) at the wonderful **Lamu archipelago** (p302), a veritable tropical paradise and Swahili heritage gem.

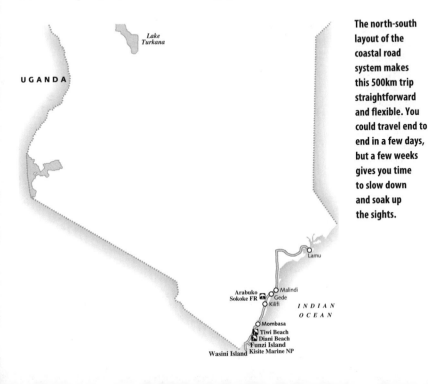

**The north-south layout of the coastal road system makes this 500km trip straightforward and flexible. You could travel end to end in a few days, but a few weeks gives you time to slow down and soak up the sights.**

# ROADS LESS TRAVELLED

## DESERT FRONTIERS

**Two to Three Weeks /
Isiolo to Lokichoggio**

This unbeaten trail winds through the harsh and barren landscape around Lake Turkana, which dominates the northwest corner of the country.

The eastern gateway to this region is the small town of **Isiolo** (p230), just north of Mt Kenya. There are several good national parks and wildlife reserves in this area, and a side trip out to **Matthews Range** (p237) is great for walkers. Alternatively, you can plough straight in to the desert route and head up the rough road to **Marsabit** (p237), the dusty tribal centre of this remote area, which boasts a fine national park.

Assuming you're not tempted to hop over the border to Ethiopia at **Moyale** (p240), a real wild frontier, take the western loop to Turkana via **North Horr** (p248), heading for the tiny lakeside settlement of **Loyangalani** (p246), a base for trips into even more remote parts of the country.

From here the trail leads south again, passing all kinds of scenic zones and the stopover towns of **South Horr** (p245) and **Baragoi** (p245). It's worth stopping for a couple of days in **Maralal** (p242), to replenish supplies and sample the joys of camel-trekking.

You could end the trip here but, for the full effect, head up to the other side of Turkana, passing through the lush western area around **Marich** (p249) to reach sweltering **Lodwar** (p250) and the lovely lake shore at **Eliye Springs** (p251).

**This wilderness trip will take you deep into the desert, though plan on a couple of weeks to complete the route as the going can get tough in this far-flung corner of Kenya.**

# WESTERN WETLANDS

**Two to Three Weeks /
Naivasha to Narok**

To the west of Nairobi lie some of the country's most fertile and scenic spots, characterised by still and tranquil bodies of water.

An excellent place to start is **Lake Naivasha** (p153) in the Rift Valley, a popular freshwater lake with easy access to several national parks and beautiful scenery. Then it's an easy hop to **Lakes Nakuru** (p162), **Bogoria** (p164) and **Baringo** (p165), all of which support a wealth of birdlife.

From here, the road west leads past the **Lake Kamnarok** and **Kerio Valley National Reserves** (p193), perfect and little-explored territory for trekkers. Depending on time, you can take the more direct Eldoret road or the longer Cherangani Hills loop to reach the agricultural town of **Kitale** (p193) and the lovely **Saiwa Swamp National Park** (p197), which is a real wetland treat.

Heading south now, you'll come across the **Kakamega Forest Reserve** (p187), an essential stop for walkers and bird-lovers alike. Then continue down the road to the region's main city **Kisumu** (p175), on the shore of Lake Victoria, for a few urban comforts.

Skirting the Winam Gulf, you'll reach the busy service town of **Kisii** (p183), a handy hub for Lake Victoria's small islands, and the tiny **Ruma National Park** (p181), a rarely visited gem.

At the far end of this south road is **Isebania** (p346), where you could cross into Tanzania. Otherwise, if you have a 4WD you can travel the hard way through **Masai Mara National Reserve** (p171), ending up in **Narok** (p169). From here you can head back to Nairobi or start the whole circuit again.

**This circuit takes in the best of Kenya's temperate western zone, in a round trip of around 1500km. From the Rift Valley to Lake Victoria, this route provides a nice complement to some of the more tourist-trodden areas of the country.**

# TAILORED TRIPS

## ACTIVE KENYA

Fans of an active lifestyle are spoilt for choice in Kenya, and sampling all the options across the country could easily take several weeks.

**Diani Beach** (p273), south of Mombasa, offers the full range of water sports, as well as other pastimes including quad-biking and forest walks.

Seaborne activities are also popular along most of the Swahili coast – **Malindi** (p296) is the region's major deep-sea fishing centre, while **Wasini Island** (p279) offers superb scuba-diving. The stunningly beautiful **Lamu archipelago** (p302) is best explored in a traditional dhow, though the more hard core can explore the island chain by windsurfing.

Due south of Nairobi, **Lake Magadi** (p115) makes an interesting detour to investigate the hot springs and picnic in the arid wastes.

Over to the west, **Hell's Gate National Park** (p156) is the best spot in the country for mountain biking, while the **Masai Mara National Reserve** (p171) specialises in balloon safaris. You can also take to the air in the Central Highlands, at the gliding club in **Nyeri** (p321).

Finally, real adrenaline junkies can hit the rapids for some white-water rafting on the **Ewaso Ngiro River** (p323).

## FOOTSTEPS ACROSS THE LANDSCAPE

This circuit, which should take you a few weeks depending on your pace, allows intensive exploration of some of the country's best hiking trails.

On the coast, **Arabuko Sokoke Forest Reserve** (p293) is criss-crossed with walking tracks, and is especially popular with birders. Off the main Nairobi–Mombasa road, **Taita Hills** (p148) also offers a plethora of outdoor activities away from the usual tourist routes.

In the Rift Valley, **Longonot National Park** (p151) offers trekkers the chance to wander up Mt Longonot, while craggy **Hell's Gate National Park** (p156) is great for exploring.

Western Kenya has huge potential for serious trekkers, particularly on **Mt Elgon** (p195), by the Ugandan border. The **Cherangani Hills** (p198) are another prime area to get lost in for a couple of days or more.

Heading north, the **Ndoto Mountains** (p237) is a great remote mountain range, while Mt Marsabit provides the exercise in **Marsabit National Park** (p239).

And of course, there's the granddaddy of them all, **Mt Kenya** (p208), which is the second-highest peak in Africa.

# History

Africa is the oldest and most stable land mass on earth. Consider: 5 million years spans all of human evolution; 670 million years encompasses the evolutionary history of all animal life; 3,600 million years goes back to the beginnings of life itself. Africa has seen it all, and preserves the evidence. It is hardly surprising then that our own human ancestry should have evolved so dramatically on the continent. The earliest evidence of their existence consisting of fossil fragments, stone tools and, most poignant of all, a trail of footprints preserved in the petrified surface of a mud pan in East Africa.

## THE CRADLE OF MANKIND

The Tugen Hills, west of Lake Baringo, are a product of the tectonic uplift and fracture which created the Great Rift Valley (p150). Here palaeontologists have discovered one of the most diverse and densely packed accumulations of fossil bone in Africa bedded down in lava flows dating back more than 16 million years.

The hills represent a unique archaeological record in Africa, for the fossil beds incorporate that most elusive period of human history between 14 and 4 million years ago when the largely primate *Kenyapithecus* evolved into our earliest bipedal ancestor *Australopithecus afarensis*. What's more, the proximity of the hills to other fossil-rich sites like Laetoli and the Olduvai Gorge (Tanzania), Hadar (Ethiopia) and Lake Turkana (Kenya), makes them especially relevant.

Get to grips with the history of the continent with John Reader's *Africa: A Biography of a Continent*, a definitive piece of research.

Throughout the 1960s and 1970s the Tugen Hills were the subject of intense interest, following the Leakey discoveries of hominid fossils at Olduvai Gorge in 1959. In the sandy clay, seven of the 18 hominoid specimens known from that period were found. The jaw fragment at 5 million years old represents the closest ancestor of *A afarensis*, that family band that left their footprints on the Laetoli mud pan (Tanzania), while a fragment of skull, dating from 2.4 million years ago, represents the earliest-known specimen of our own genus, *Homo*.

Richard Leakey – son of veteran archaeologists Louis and Mary – made his first independent excavation in the Tugen Hills in 1967. But new finds at Lake Turkana (p245) in 1969 quickly had him transferring his focus to the north of the country, turning up dozens of fossil sites. Discoveries here were to turn accepted archaeological thought on its head with the surprise find of a completely new hominid specimen – *Homo habilis* (able man).

Prior to the Leakey discovery it was thought that there were only two species of proto-humans: the 'robust' hominids and the 'gracile' hominids, which eventually gave rise to modern humans. However, the Turkana finds

## TIMELINE

| 3,700,000 BC | 1,600,000 BC | 100,000 BC |
|---|---|---|
| A group of early hominids walk across the Laetoli pan, moving away from the volcano which puffs clouds of fine ash over the landscape. Their footsteps take them to the grasslands of the Serengeti plains. | In 1984, Kamoya Kimeu discovers the Turkana Boy (fossil KNM-WT 15000), a nearly complete skeleton of an 11- or 12-year-old hominid boy who lived 1.6 million years ago and died at Nariokotome near Lake Turkana. | *Homo sapiens* strike out to colonise the world, moving into the eastern Mediterranean. By 40,000 years ago they reach Asia and Australia and 10,000 years later they are settled across Europe. |

demonstrated that the different species lived at the same time and even shared resources – advancing the Leakey theory that evolution was more complex than a simple linear progression.

For more on Kenya's fossil finds look up www.leakeyfoundation .org. Members can even sign up for trips with the Leakeys themselves.

In 1984, Kamoya Kimeu (a member of the Leakey expedition) uncovered the spectacular remains of a young boy's skeleton dating back 1.6 million years. Standing at a height of 1.6m tall, the boy was appreciably bigger than his *H habilis* contemporary. His longer limbs and striding gait were also more characteristic of modern human physiology, and his larger brain suggested greater cognitive ability. *H erectus* was the biggest and brainiest hominid to date and was the longest surviving and most widely dispersed of all the ancestral toolmakers, disappearing from the fossil records a mere 200,000 years ago. From this remarkable evolutionary leap it was but a small step to our closest ancestors, *H sapiens,* who made an appearance around 130,000 years ago.

Prehistory buffs can soak up the atmosphere and check out the myriad animal fossils left on site at the Sibiloi National Park (p247).

## A PASTORAL SCENE

By 10,000 BC the Sahara was widely populated. A lush climatic wet phase meant the dune fields of today were covered with fertile wooded grasslands. African cereals were domesticated in the region and the beginnings of a farming lifestyle emerged. Southward expansion was limited by a band of tropical forest and swamp inhabited by the deadly tsetse fly, which is fatal to cattle and people.

Over the next 5000 years climatic change dramatically altered the environment. Increasing aridity drove people south in all directions, and eventually shaped the environment into what we know today. The tsetse belt dropped south, leaving in its wake a belt of grassland known as the Sahel – the largest pastoral zone in Africa.

The first arrivals of North Africans in East Africa were a Cushitic-speaking population, who moved south with their domestic stock from Ethiopia. At the same time a population of Nilote-speakers from the Sudan moved into the western highlands of the Rift Valley (the Maasai, Luo, Samburu and Turkana tribes are their modern-day descendents). These pastoralists shared the region with the indigenous Khoikhoi (ancestors of the modern-day San), who had occupied the land for thousands of years.

Africa's fourth linguistic family, the Bantu-speakers, arrived from the Niger Delta around 1000 BC. Soon they became East Africa's largest ethno-linguistic family, which they remain today. Kenya's largest tribe, the Kikuyu, along with the Gusii, Akamba and Meru tribes are all descended from them.

African agriculture developed over a wide area as a mosaic of different crops, traditions and techniques. The generally hostile environment of sub-Saharan Africa inspired a conservative approach to the business of making a living – to endure, communities focused on minimising the risk of failure,

| 2000 BC–1000 | 200 | 200–300 |
|---|---|---|
| Immigrant groups start to colonise sub-Saharan Africa. First Cushites from Ethiopia move south into central Kenya, followed by Nilote-speakers from the Sudan. Finally, these groups are joined by Bantu-speakers from Nigeria and the Cameroon. | It is estimated that by the year 200 there are 20 million people living in Africa. More than half live in North Africa, leaving only 10 million people in sub-Saharan Africa. | With the introduction of the camel, trans-Saharan journeys become practicable and profitable. The news of large gold deposits undoubtedly spur Arab ambitions and interests in the continent. |

not maximising returns. Such an approach inevitably led to a conservative social structure, and a political structure uniquely suited to the conditions of sub-Saharan Africa evolved: the age-grade system. The system worked by dividing all males and, in some cases, females into age-sets with their own range of social and political duties. With its respect for the wisdom of the elders, the age-group system established a gerontocracy as the dominant political organisation in sub-Saharan Africa. This system still influences African politics and culture today.

Another significant factor of early African development was the almost total absence of long-range trade. Long-distance trade was feasible only if it involved rare items of high value or volume, as it required people to collect and carry goods to distant markets – people that communities could ill-afford to lose. The demand for salt eventually broke through these barriers.

The salt routes are generally recognised as the earliest and most highly trafficked routes in Africa, sufficiently well defined by the 16th century for the Portuguese to use them as the main gateway to the interior of the continent. The production and distribution of salt stimulated economic activity as never before, and had a profound effect on the Sahelian grasslands.

The increased demand for labour stimulated a growth in population and a major shift in social and economic relationships. A vertical stratification of society came into being, culminating in the centralisation of authority. Power was exercised most coercively by traders who not only sold their goods to distant markets, but also sold the porters who had carried them. From such modest beginnings began one of the most lucrative and damaging commercial enterprises the continent would ever see: the slave trade.

Thousands of fragments of Chinese porcelain have been discovered at Gede and elsewhere along the East African coast - testament to old trade routes between Africa and the Far East.

## THE LAND OF ZANJ

It is no accident that the development of the first indigenous African states coincides with the rising importance of gold as a medium of exchange in the economies of the Mediterranean and beyond. Gold was never a feature of indigenous African culture but in Egypt, Greece and Rome gold was highly prized. As early as 400 BC, Azania (as the East African coast was then known) was an important trading post for the Greeks.

By the 8th century, Arab dhows were docking in East African ports as part of their annual trade migration. Arabs set up trading posts long the seaboard, intermarrying with Africans and creating a cosmopolitan culture that became known as Swahili. Before long there were Arab-Swahili city states all along the coast from Somalia to Mozambique; the remains of many of these settlements can be still be seen, most notably at Gede (p294).

By the 10th century the 'Land of Zanj' (the present-day coastal region of Kenya and Tanzania) was exporting leopard skins, tortoiseshell, rhino horns, ivory and, most importantly, slaves and gold to Arabia and India.

| 300s | 800 | 1415 |
|---|---|---|
| Minted in Carthage, gold coinage starts to circulate throughout North Africa. Romans are obliged to pay taxes in gold; this indicates a substantial trans-Saharan trade as no other source could have sufficed. | Muslims from the Arabian peninsula and Persia start to dock in East African ports. Soon they establish Arab-Swahili states all along the coast from Somalia to Mozambique. These operate as trading depots. | Chinese fleets visit East Africa in the early 15th century, captained by Zheng He. In 1415 a giraffe is transported to Beijing and presented by Malindi envoys to the emperor himself. |

Ports included Shanga, Gede, Lamu and Mombasa as well as Zanzibar (Tanzania). Kilwa, 300km south of Zanzibar, marked the southern-most limit of travel for Arab dhows. For over 700 years, up to 1450, the Islamic world was virtually the only external influence on sub-Saharan Africa.

## BLACK GOLD

The word *Swahili* originates from the Arabic word *sawahil*, which means 'of the coast'. It refers both to the Swahili language as well as the Islamic people of the coast.

Arab-Swahili domination on the coast received its first serious challenge with the arrival of the Portuguese in the 15th century. In 1497, while on his pioneering voyage along the coastline of South and East Africa, Vasco da Gama found Arab dhows at the Zambezi delta loaded with gold dust.

Portugal's exploration of Africa was spurred on by the tales of gold and riches that traders brought back from their travels. During the same period Europe was desperately short of labour as it struggled to recover from the effects of the Black Death (1347–51). Demand was especially high in southern Europe – nowhere more so than in the newly cultivated sugar plantations of Lebanon, Syria, Cyprus, Sicily, the Canaries and Madeira. These plantations were initially worked by captive Muslims and Slavic peoples (hence the word 'slaves'), but with access to Africa a whole new labour market opened up.

Relations between the Portuguese and the native population were not easy. The Swahili coast was rich and Islamised; by comparison the Portuguese sea-farers were devoutly Christian and largely impoverished. Their fear provoked suspicion among the Arabs, which in turn led to conflict.

The Portuguese consolidated their position on the East African coast by the blatant use of force and terror – justifying their actions as battles in a Christian war against Islam. They sailed their heavily armed vessels into the harbours of important Swahili towns, demanding submission to the rule of Portugal and payment of large annual tributes. Towns that refused were attacked, their possessions seized and resisters killed. Zanzibar was the first Swahili town to be taken in this manner (in 1503). Malindi formed an alliance with the Portuguese, which hastened the fall of Mombasa in 1505. Although the cultural impact of Portuguese colonisation was minimal, the wider impact of the commercial trade routes was to have an irrevocable effect.

By 1800, more than 8000 slaves were passing through the Swahili slave markets every year. Perhaps four times as many died before ever reaching the markets.

The ensuing four centuries drastically altered the social, political and economic systems that had previously provided a relatively peaceful equilibrium. The slave trade diverted resources towards the coast, where the exchange for European goods represented a net loss to the continent. Africans brought gold, slaves, ivory, beeswax, gum arabic, dyes, timber and foodstuffs, and exchanged them for goods for which they previously had no need: textiles, metal goods, alcohol and, most influential of all, guns and gun powder.

Slaves left Africa via the Sahara, the Red Sea, the Atlantic and the East African coast. The total estimated number of slaves exported from tropical Africa between 1500 and the late 1800s is put at 18 million; 2 million from East Africa. By the height of the slave trade in the 18th century, the ramifica-

| 1441–46 | 1492–1505 | 1593 |
|---|---|---|
| By the 15th century Portuguese caravels begin exploring West Africa. They look for gold, but find slaves. Between 1441 and 1446 the first 1000 slaves were shipped to Portugal. | Dom Francisco de Almeida's armada begins the Portuguese conquest of Kenya. Mombasa falls in 1505 followed by towns like Barawa (Somalia), Kilwa, Moçambique and Sofala, up and down the coast. | The Portuguese construct the coral Fort Jesus in Mombasa. Accounts from the garrison at Mombasa record the first evidence of maize production in Africa. |

tions of the business had touched every region on the continent and commercialised indigenous economies, creating a demand for imported goods, which, ultimately, could only be supplied by the export of slaves.

The East African plantation economy reached its peak between 1875 and 1884, driven by demand from European sugar and coffee plantations on Mauritius and Réunion. Around 50,000 slaves passed through the markets every year – nearly 44% of the total population of the coast. In fact, the spice business was so profitable that Sultan Seyyid Said of Oman moved his entire court to Zanzibar in 1832.

Overall, close to 600,000 slaves were sold through the Zanzibar market between 1830 and 1873, when a treaty with Britain paved the way for the end of the trade. It is true that slavery was already an established fact of African life before the advent of the slave trade. But enslavement for sale and the importation of foreign goods were radical departures from everything that had gone before, and the social, psychological and economic impact changed the fate of the continent forever.

For a first-hand account of the suffering of the slave trade, pick up a copy of *The Life of Olaudah Equiano*. Sold into slavery, he later became an important part of the abolitionist cause.

## BRITISH EAST AFRICA

In 1884 European powers met in Germany for the Berlin conference. Here behind closed doors they decided the fate of the African continent. No African leaders were invited to attend, nor were they consulted. What's more, the new national terrain may have satisfied political ambitions but it hid a multitude of potential problems; the newly defined nation states cut through at least 177 ethnic 'culture areas', while some new countries, such as the Gabon with a population of 500,000 people, were hardly viable economic units.

The colonial settlement of Kenya dates from 1885, when Germany established a protectorate over the sultan of Zanzibar's coastal possessions. In 1888 Sir William Mackinnon received a royal charter and concessionary rights to develop trade in the region under the aegis of the British East Africa Company (BEAC). Seeking to consolidate their East African territories, Germany traded its coastal holdings in return for sole rights over Tanganyika (Tanzania) in 1890. Still, it was only when the BEAC ran into financial difficulties in 1895 that the British government finally stepped in to establish formal control through the East African Protectorate.

In order to force the indigenous population into the labour market, the British introduced a hut tax in 1901. This could only be paid in cash so Africans had to seek paid work.

Initially, British influence was confined to the coastal area. Large parts of the interior were inaccessible due to the presence of warrior tribes like the Maasai. However, the Maasai front began to crack following a brutal civil war between the Ilmaasai and Iloikop groups and the simultaneous arrival of rinderpest (a cattle disease), cholera, smallpox and famine. The British were able to negotiate a treaty with the Maasai, allowing the British to drive the Mombasa–Uganda railway line through the heart of Maasai grazing lands.

The completion of the railway enabled the British administration to relocate from Mombasa to the more temperate Nairobi. Although the Maasai

| 1729 | 1807–73 | 1884–85 |
|---|---|---|
| The Portuguese grip on East Africa comes to an end in 1698, when Mombasa falls to Baluchi Arabs from Oman after a 33-month siege. In 1729 the Portuguese leave the Kenyan coast for good. | Legislation abolishing the slave trade is enacted in Britain in 1807. Another 65 years pass before Sultan Barghash of Zanzibar bans the slave trade on the East African coast. | The Berlin Conference convenes and Africa is divided into colonial territories. Today the continent is divided into 53 states; more than four times the number in South America. |

suffered the worst annexations of land, being restricted to designated reserves, the Kikuyu from Mt Kenya and the Aberdares (areas of white settlement), came to nurse a particular grievance about their alienation from the land.

By 1912, settlers like Lord Delamere (see boxed text, p126) had established themselves in the highlands and set up mixed agricultural farms, turning a profit for the colony for the first time and spurring other Europeans to follow suit. These first outposts, Naivasha (p153) and the Ngong Hills (p114), are still heavily white-settled areas today.

For an intriguing glimpse at life in precolonial Kenya, hunt down a copy of Khadambi Asalache's *A Calabash Life*.

The colonial process was interrupted by WWI, when two thirds of the 3000 white settlers in Kenya formed impromptu cavalry units and marched against Germans in neighbouring Tanganyika. Colonisation resumed after the war, under a scheme by which veterans of the European campaign were offered subsidised land in the highlands around Nairobi. The net effect was a huge upsurge in the white Kenyan population, from 9000 in 1920 to 80,000 in the 1950s.

After 1918, as Europe struggled to rebuild in a postwar world of harsh economic realities, one of the overriding foreign policies of colonial governments was to make the African colonies pay their way.

## INDEPENDENCE

Although largely peaceful and a period of economic growth, the interwar years were to see the fomenting of early nationalist aspirations. Grievances over land appropriation and displacement were only exacerbated in 1920, when, after considerable lobbying from white settlers, Kenya was transformed into a Crown Colony. A Legislative Council was established but Africans were barred from political participation (right up until 1944). In reaction to their exclusion, the Kikuyu tribe, who were under the greatest pressure from European settlers, founded the Young Kikuyu Association, led by Harry Thuku. This was to become the Kenya African Union (KAU), a nationalist organisation demanding access to white-owned land.

One passionate advocate for the movement was a young man called Johnstone Kamau, later known as Jomo Kenyatta. When this early activism fell on deaf ears he joined the more outspoken Kikuyu Central Association; the association was promptly banned.

In 1929, with money supplied by Indian communists, Kenyatta sailed for London to plead the Kikuyu case with the British colonial secretary, who declined to meet with him. While in London, Kenyatta met with a group called the League Against Imperialism, which took him to Moscow and Berlin, back to Nairobi and then back to London, where he stayed for the next 15 years. During this time, he studied revolutionary tactics in Moscow and built up the Pan-African Federation with Hastings Banda (who later became the president of Malawi) and Kwame Nkrumah (later president of Ghana).

| 1888 | 1901 | 1890 |
|---|---|---|
| Sir William Mackinnon is granted a 50-year concession. He establishes the British East Africa Company (BEAC) in Mombasa. Its focus is the exportation of goods and agriculture and the construction of the East African Railway. | The East African Railway links the coast with Uganda. The construction of the line sees a huge influx of Indians from Ismaili Muslim and Sikh communities, who provide the bulk of skilled manpower. | Waiyaki Wa Henya, a Kikuyu chief who signed a treaty with Frederick Lugard of the BEAC under considerable pressure, burns down Lugard's Fort. Waiyaki is abducted two years later and murdered. |

Although African nationalists made impressive headway, it was the advent of WWII that was to ultimately bring about the rapid demise of colonialism in Africa. The war demonstrated that Africa was an invaluable member of the world community, contributing significant numbers of men and indispensable mineral resources to the war effort.

In 1941, in a desperate bid for survival, British premier Winston Churchill crossed the Atlantic to plead for American aid. The resulting Atlantic Charter (1942), which Churchill negotiated with President Roosevelt, enshrined the end of colonialism in the third clause, which stated self-determination for all colonies as one of the postwar objectives.

In October 1945 the sixth Pan-African Congress was convened in Manchester, England. For the first time this was predominantly a congress of Africa's young leaders. Kwame Nkrumah and Jomo Kenyatta were there, along with trade unionists, lawyers, teachers and writers from all over Africa. By the time Kenyatta returned to Kenya in 1946, he was the leader of a bona fide Kenyan liberation movement. Using his influence as leader, he quickly assumed the top spot of the proindependence KAU, a group with considerable support from African war veterans.

Although Kenyatta appeared willing to act as the British government's accredited Kenyan representative within a developing constitutional framework, militant factions among the KAU had a more radical agenda. When in 1951 Ghana became the first African country to achieve independence, it raised the stakes even higher.

Starting with small-scale terror operations, bands of guerrillas began to intimidate white settlers, threaten their farms and anyone deemed to be a collaborator. Their aim: to drive white settlers from the land and reclaim it. Kenyatta's role in the Mau Mau uprising, as it came to be known, was equivocal. At a public meeting in 1952, he denounced the movement. But he was arrested along with other Kikuyu politicians and sentenced to seven years' hard labour for 'masterminding' the plot.

Four years of intense military operations ensued. The various Mau Mau units came together under the umbrella of the Kenya Land Freedom Army, led by Dedan Kimathi, and outright guerrilla warfare followed with the British declaring a state of emergency in 1952.

By 1956, the Mau Mau had been quelled and Dedan Kimathi was publicly hanged on the orders of Colonel Henderson (who was later deported from Kenya for crimes against humanity). But Kenyatta was to continue the struggle following his release in 1959. Soon even white Kenyans began to feel the winds of change, and in 1960 the British government officially announced their plan to transfer power to a democratically elected African government. Independence was scheduled for December 1963, accompanied by grants and loans of US$100 million to enable the Kenyan assembly to buy out European farmers in the highlands and restore the land to local tribes.

Africans played a key role in WWII. The East African Carrier Corps consisted of over 400,000 men, and the development of the atom bomb was utterly dependent on uranium from the Congo.

*Red Strangers: The White Tribe of Kenya* (CS Nicholls) has a different, unusually sympathetic perspective on colonialism, examining the history of Kenya's white settler population before and after independence.

| 1918–39 | 1920 | 1930s |
|---|---|---|
| The interwar period facilitates economic activity and social and physical mobility. Famine relief and campaigns against epidemic diseases are established in the colonies stimulating a 37.5% increase in the population of Africa. | Kenya is declared a Crown Colony. Africans are disbarred from the Legislative Council. The next year the first nationalist organisation, the Kenya African Union, is established and presses for land rights. | Thousands of European settlers occupy the Central Highlands, farming tea and coffee. The area was already home to over a million members of the Kikuyu tribe, whose land claims are not recognised in European terms. |

## HARAMBEE

The political handover began in earnest in 1962 with Kenyatta's election to a newly constituted parliament. To ensure a smooth transition of power, Kenyatta's party, the Kenya African National Union (KANU), which advocated a unitary, centralised government, joined forces with the Kenya African Democratic Union (KADU), which favoured *majimbo*, a federal set-up. *Harambee*, meaning 'pulling together', was seen as more important than political factionalism, and KADU voluntarily dissolved in 1964, leaving Kenyatta and KANU in full control.

*Weep Not, Child,* written by Kenya's most famous novelist, Ngũgĩ wa Thiong'o, tells the story of British occupation and the effects of the Mau Mau on the lives of black Kenyans.

The early days of postcolonial independence were full of optimism. Kenyatta took pains to allay the fears of white settlers, declaring 'I have suffered imprisonment and detention; but that is gone, and I am not going to remember it. Let us join hands and work for the benefit of Kenya'. But the nascent economy was vulnerable and the political landscape was barely developed. As a result the consolidation of power by the new ruling elite nurtured an authoritarian regime, the effect of which would reverberate 45 years later in the 2008 elections.

Although considered an African success story, the Kenyatta regime failed to undertake the essential task of deconstructing the colonial state in favour of a system with greater relevance to the aspirations of the average Kenyan. The *majimbo* (regionalist) system – advocated by KADU and agreed upon in the run-up to independence – was such a system. But with their dissolution in 1964 it was abandoned.

Consolidation of power was then buttressed by a series of constitutional amendments, culminating in the Constitutional Amendment Act No 16 of 1969, which empowered the president to control the civil service. The effects were disastrous. Subsequent years saw widespread discrimination in favour of Kenyatta's own tribe, the Kikuyu. The Trade Union Disputes Act illegalised industrial action and when KADU tried to reassemble as the Kenya People's Union (KPU) they were banned. Corruption soon became a problem at all levels of the power structure and the political arena contracted.

The first major Kenyan film to tackle the thorny subject of the Mau Mau uprising, Kibaara Kaugi's *Enough is Enough* is a fictionalised biopic of Wamuyu wa Gakuru, a Kikuyu woman who became a famed guerrilla fighter.

## ONE-PARTY STATE

Kenyatta was succeeded in 1978 by his vice-president, Daniel arap Moi. A Kalenjin, Moi was regarded by establishment power brokers as a suitable front man for their interests, as his tribe was relatively small and beholden to the Kikuyu.

On assumption of power, Moi sought to consolidate his regime by marginalising those who had campaigned to stop him from succeeding Kenyatta. Lacking a capital base of his own upon which he could build and maintain a patron–client network, and faced with shrinking economic opportunities, Moi resorted to a politics of exclusion. He reconfigured the financial, legal, political and administrative institutions. For instance, a constitutional

| 1942 | 1946 | 1952–56 |
| --- | --- | --- |
| The Atlantic Charter, signed by Winston Churchill and President Roosevelt, guarantees self-determination for the colonies as a postwar objective. The charter also gives America access to African markets. | Jomo Kenyatta completes his degree in anthropology and returns to Kenya as the head of the Kenya African Union (KAU). The British government view him as their accredited representative in the independence handover. | The British declare a state of emergency and mobilise to quell the Mau Mau uprising. By 1956 nearly 2000 Kikuyu loyalists have been killed, while the death toll among the Mau Mau is 11,500. Thirty-two white settlers die. |

amendment in 1982 made Kenya a de jure one-party state, while another in 1986 removed the security of tenure for the attorney-general, comptroller, auditor general and High Court judges, making all these positions personally beholden to the president. These developments had the effect of transforming Kenya from an 'imperial state' under Kenyatta to a 'personal state' under Moi.

By the early 1990s, foreign aid donors were looking askance at state-led development and increasingly chose to redirect their funds to CSOs (civil society organisations), such as the Kenya Human Rights Commission. With this new policy agenda, CSOs were thrust into the centre of the political economy of development, with a specific agenda to mediate state–society relations and empower people socially, economically and politically. External donors all began to channel their resources into this sector.

The stories of some of the torture victims held at Nyayo House during Moi's regime are told in the haunting 2004 documentary *Walking Shadows*, directed by Ndungi Githuki.

Following the widely contested 1988 elections, Charles Rubia and Kenneth Matiba joined forces to call for the freedom to form alternative political parties and stated their plan to hold a political rally in Nairobi on 7 July without a licence. Though the duo was detained prior to their intended meeting, people turned out anyway, only to be met with brutal police retaliation. Twenty people were killed and police arrested a slew of politicians, human-rights activists and journalists.

The rally, known thereafter as *Saba Saba* ('seven seven' in Kiswahili), was a pivotal event in the push for a multiparty Kenya. The following year, the Forum for the Restoration of Democracy (FORD) was formed, led by Jaramogi Oginga Odinga, a powerful Luo politician who had been vice-president under Jomo Kenyatta, and had played an important role in the independence movement – first as a member of KANU and then, after an ideological split, as leader of his own party, the KPU. FORD was initially banned and Odinga was arrested, but the resulting outcry led to his release and, finally, a change in the constitution that allowed opposition parties to register for the first time.

Faced with a foreign debt of nearly US$9 billion and blanket suspension of foreign aid, Moi was pressured into holding multiparty elections in early 1992, but independent observers reported a litany of electoral inconsistencies. Just as worrying, about 2000 people were killed during ethnic clashes in the Rift Valley, widely believed to have been triggered by government agitation. Nonetheless, Moi was overwhelmingly reelected.

Against these political realities, Kenya's first-past-the-post electoral system was extremely vulnerable. In 1992 Moi secured only 37% of the votes cast against a combined opposition tally of 63%. The same results were replicated in the 1997 elections, when Moi once again secured victory with 40% of the votes cast against 60% of the combined opposition.

Nevertheless, after the 1997 elections, KANU was forced to bow to mounting pressure and initiate some changes under the aegis of the Inter-Parties

| **1963** | **1966** | **1978** |
|---|---|---|
| Kenya gains independence; Jomo Kenyatta becomes president. In the same year the Organisation of African Unity is established, aimed at providing Africa with an independent voice in world affairs. | The Kenya People's Union is formed by Jaramogi Oginga Odinga, a Luo elder. Following unrest at a presidential visit to Nyanza Province the party is banned and Kenya becomes a de facto one-party state. | Kenyatta is succeeded by his vice-president Daniel arap Moi, who goes on to become one of the most enduring 'Big Men' of Africa, ruling a virtual autocracy for the next 25 years. |

MUNGIKI: A NEW MAU MAU?

Established in 1995 by Maina Njenga, the *Mungiki* (literally 'multitude') refer to themselves as *thuna cia Mau Mau* (Mau Mau offshoot). Just as the Mau Mau garnered support from Kikuyu squatters oppressed by the colonial agrarian system, so *Mungiki* draws its support from the poorest of the poor displaced by the ethnic clashes in the wake of the 1992–93 and 1997–98 elections. Njenga claimed to have had a vision from Ngai (God), who commanded him to liberate his people from oppression.

The fundamental principles of *Mungiki* are cultural self-determination, self-pride and self-reliance. In the poorest slums of Nairobi they provide jobs and hope in an otherwise bleak economic landscape. They also advocate a return to traditional beliefs and practices.

Although initially a movement with a religious, political and cultural agenda, since 1997 the *Mungiki* have become increasingly entangled with urban vigilantism. With mounting running costs, they started to levy 'taxes' from its members for the supply of basic services, and vied for control of the city's lucrative matatu routes. As a result the group was outlawed in 2000. As the government began to crack down on *Mungiki* (the Kenya Human Rights Commission alleged the government killed 500 *Mungiki* members prior to the 2007 elections), they responded by procuring weapons and organising themselves into militia, ostensibly to defend their communities. Insecure conditions in Nairobi further facilitated and empowered the movement, and by 2007 the group was engaged in gang wars with rival groups.

Economic exploitation and exclusion from politics are huge contributors to the ease with which *Mungiki* attracts its members. *Mungiki* offers support and a sense of community to many disenchanted young people, especially those whose lives have been affected by crime, drug abuse and prostitution. In *Mungiki* many young men have found an opportunity to express themselves and acquire leadership roles that are denied to them in the current political landscape.

Despite all this, many Kenyans loathe and fear *Mungiki* because of its atavistic nature. Others condemn it as parochial and tribalist. Moreover, its recent associations with violence have left many Kenyans convinced that it is a terror gang, and many fear that if the organisation ever breaches its narrow base, the country will have a serious problem to deal with.

Parliamentary Group (IPPG). Some Draconian colonial laws were repealed, as well as the requirement for licences to hold political rallies. In addition, in 1998 parliament passed an act that sought to review the constitution, although little has been achieved with this and it resurfaced as a major bone of contention in the 2007 elections.

## A NEW ERA?

Having been beaten twice in the 1992 and 1997 elections, 12 opposition groups united to form the National Alliance Rainbow Coalition (NARC). With Moi's presidency due to end in 2002, many feared that he would alter the constitution again to retain his position. This time, though, he announced his intention to retire.

**1982**

The Universities Academic Staff Union (UASU) is one of the few credible opposition groups remaining. They are banned in 1982. This leads to a short-lived coup by the airforce. The following crackdown drives opposition underground.

**1984**

The medical community learns of the first reported case of AIDS in an article published in the *East African Medical Journal*. By 2005 the estimated number of people living with HIV/AIDS in Kenya is 1.3 million.

**1991**

The collapse of the Soviet Union changes the face of African politics. Foreign pressure is now brought to bear on the government. In 1991 parliament repeal the one-party state section of the constitution.

Moi put his weight firmly behind Uhuru Kenyatta, the son of Jomo Kenyatta, as his successor, but the support garnered by NARC ensured a resounding victory for the party, with 62% of the vote. Mwai Kibaki was inaugurated as Kenya's third president on 30 December 2002.

When Kibaki assumed office in January 2003, donors were highly supportive of the new government. During its honeymoon period, the Kibaki administration won praise for a number of policy initiatives, especially a crackdown on corruption. In 2003–04, donors – including the US, the UK, Germany and the World Bank – contributed billions of dollars to the fight against corruption, including support for the office of a newly appointed anticorruption 'czar', and the International Monetary Fund resumed lending in November 2003.

Despite initially positive signs, it became clear by mid-2004 that large-scale corruption was still a considerable problem in Kenya. Western diplomats alleged that corruption had cost the treasury US$1 billion since Kibaki took office. In February 2005, the British High Commissioner Sir Edward Clay denounced the 'massive looting' of state resources by senior government politicians, including sitting cabinet ministers. Within days, Kibaki's anticorruption 'czar', John Githongo, resigned and went into exile amid rumours of death threats related to his investigation of high-level politicians. The UK, the US and Germany rapidly suspended their anticorruption lending. With Githongo's release of a damning detailed dossier on corruption in the Kibaki regime in February 2006, Kibaki was forced to relieve three ministers of their cabinet positions.

At the root of the difficulties of fighting corruption were the conditions that brought Kibaki to power. To maximise his electoral chances his coalition included a number of KANU officials who were deeply implicated in the worst abuses of the Moi regime. Indebted to such people for power, Kibaki was only ever able to affect a half-hearted reshuffle of his cabinet. He also allowed his ministers a wide margin of manoeuvre to guarantee their continued support.

The slow march to democratisation in Kenya has been attributed to the personalised nature of politics, where focus is placed on individuals with ethnic support bases rather than institutions. Even after the 2002 NARC victory, the prospects for institutionalisation remained slim. Indeed, one of NARC's key campaign planks was a new constitutional dispensation for the country. But on assumption of power in January 2003, the NARC regime reneged on this promise and resorted to stonewalling the review process. At the end of the day, the government heavily edited the draft constitution before subjecting it to a referendum. Politicians Raila Odinga, of the Orange Democratic Movement (ODM), and Kalonzo Musyoka (of the Orange Democratic Movement-Kenya) – both former Kibaki allies – led the opposition to the draft. It was resoundingly rejected by Kenyans in November 2005.

*The Constant Gardener, directed by Fernando Meirelles, shot numerous scenes in Nairobi's infamous Kibera slum. The novel was banned in Kenya for its depiction of corrupt African officials.*

*Just in case he was in any doubt about his popularity by the end of his regime, outgoing president Moi was pelted with mud during his final presidential speech!*

| 1993 | 1998 | 2002 |
|---|---|---|
| In August 1993 inflation reaches a record 100% and the government's budget deficit is over 10% of GDP. Donors suspend aid to Kenya and insist on wide-ranging economic reforms to stabilise the economy. | Terrorist attacks shake US embassies in Nairobi and Dar es Salaam, killing more than 200 people. The effect on the Kenyan economy is devastating. It takes the next four years to rebuild the shattered tourism industry. | Mwai Kibaki wins the 2002 election as the leader of the National Alliance Rainbow Coalition. For the first time in Kenyan history the ballot box succeeds in electing a president by popular vote. |

## A POLITICAL AWAKENING

On 27 December 2007, Kenya held presidential, parliamentary and local elections. While the parliamentary and local government elections were largely considered credible, the presidential elections were marred by serious irregularities, reported by both Kenyan and international election monitors, and by independent nongovernmental observers. Nonetheless, the Electoral Commission declared Mwai Kibaki the winner, triggering a wave of violence across the country.

The Rift Valley, Western Highlands, Nyanza Province and Mombasa – areas afflicted by years of political machination, previous election violence and large-scale displacement – exploded in ugly ethnic confrontations. The violence left more than 1000 people dead and over 600,000 people homeless.

Fearing the stability of the most stable linchpin of East Africa, then UN Secretary-General Kofi Annan and a panel of 'Eminent African Persons' flew to Kenya to mediate talks. A power-sharing agreement was signed on 28 February 2008 between President Kibaki and Raila Odinga, the leader of the ODM opposition. The coalition provided for the establishment of a prime ministerial position (to be filled by Raila Odinga), as well as a division of cabinet posts according to the parties' representation in parliament. Key to the negotiations was the constitutional amendment stating that the prime minister can only be sacked by parliament and not by the president.

The fragile coalition government has started the complex task of long-term reform. If they are to succeed in any measure they have to address the key issues of constitutional reform (a new constitution is now slated for April 2009), land tenure reform, judicial reform and, more importantly, the poverty and inequality that plagues the country. Analysts stress that personal politics must be institutionalised and an effective system of checks and balances be put in place to curb corruption and injustice. Local economists also estimate that Kenya needs to achieve growth of at least 12% if the country is to achieve any trickle-down effect – although election violence has caused an estimated US$1 billion loss in the tourism industry alone.

The challenge is huge. Inflation is on the rise, fuel and food price rises are cutting deep, while the manufacturing sector was forced to cut back operations by 70% due to insecurity. But the main key to success will be the relationship between Kibaki and Odinga. It remains to be seen whether they can transition Kenya safely into a new era of political maturity and maximise the huge potential of this vibrant and vital country.

The postelection violence is expected to have a significant impact on economic growth, reducing the projected 8% growth to around 4% to 6%.

To keep abreast of the changing political landscape, log on and read reports from Kenya's most popular daily, www.nation.co.ke.

## 2006

Chinese President Hu Jintao signs an oil exploration contract with Kenya; the deal allows China's state-controlled CNOOC Ltd to prospect for oil on the borders of Sudan and Somalia and in coastal waters.

## 2007

In 2007 Kenyans go to the polls again. The outcome is contested amid bloody clashes. International mediation finally brings about a power-sharing agreement in April 2008.

## 2030

Vision 2030 is Kenya's blueprint for structural reform, which promises massive investment in tourism, agriculture, trade and manufacturing. Its aim is to boost growth and address the economic challenges faced by the country.

# The Culture

## THE NATIONAL PSYCHE

Dynamic, down-to-earth, resourceful and respectful, Kenyans are proud of the country and identity that they have forged for themselves since independence. Despite a crumbling colonial infrastructure, years of turbulent political change, a mosaic of tribes and a rapidly growing population, Kenyans have worked, hustled, struggled and strained to deliver impressive economic growth (7% in 2007) and to finally make their voices heard in the political arena – and they've managed it in a largely peaceful fashion.

Sure, it hasn't been an easy journey, and detractors will point to the postelection violence of 2007/2008 and shake their heads, muttering dark tales of tribalism and the fragile veneer of national identity. True, there isn't a great sense of national consciousness (although it is growing), but this focus on tribe often distracts observers from the positive features of Kenyan society and culture.

In general, Kenyans approach life with great exuberance and an admirable live-and-let-live attitude. Be it on a crowded matatu, in a buzzing marketplace or enjoying a drink in a bar, you cannot fail to notice that Kenyans are quick to laugh and are never reluctant to offer a smile. Theirs is a very joyful approach to life, despite the fact that many of them live in dire economic circumstances.

Kenyans are also extremely gregarious – rare is the occasion when you will see a lone Kenyan. At the slightest sign of activity a crowd will gather, from the smallest child to the most self-important businessman who happens along. Passers-by become onlookers – events are observed and participated in and, before long, pundits will be offering their version of the proceedings and their opinions on all and sundry. This inclusiveness often extends to outsiders – any willing traveller is sure to be asked to participate in a spontaneous dance or a game of football.

'any willing traveller is sure to be asked to participate in a spontaneous dance or a game of football'

Education, too, has had a unifying effect. Kenya continues to send more students to the US to study than any other African country, including giants such as Nigeria and South Africa, and literacy stands at an impressive 85%. The positive effects of a generation of educated Kenyans who came of age in the 1980s are now everywhere to be seen. Kenyans abroad have started to invest seriously in the country and Nairobi's business landscape is changing rapidly. The informal hustle of the market has started to converge with the formal business community to create a dynamic, entrepreneurial environment. Likewise a new middle class demands new apartment blocks and cars, and small manufacturing businesses, call centres and IT start-ups are defining new business horizons. However, beneath the buzz Kenyans remain quite conservative, and are still concerned with modesty in the way they dress and socialise.

Undoubtedly as Kenya modernises, pressures are brought to bear on traditional lifestyles and competing cultural systems, especially in poorer rural communities where the people drain continues apace. It is hoped the current coalition government (bloated as it is) can mitigate some of these pressures, given that it now represents a broader spectrum of tribes and interests. However, this tension produces some intriguing sights – Samburu nomads in the arid north sporting digital watches along with their traditional beads, young men in traditional Lamu donning nylon dreads and Rasta caps amid the *bui-buis* (cover-all worn by some Islamic women) and headscarves, and middle-class businessmen with tribal tattoos or scars. It is a chaotic and captivating evolution.

Kenya certainly has its fair share of poverty, alienation and urban over-crowding, but even in the dustiest shantytowns life is lived to the full.

## LIFESTYLE

Traditional culture provides strong societal glue in Kenya. Respect for one's elders, firmly held religious beliefs, traditional gender roles and the tradition of *ujamaa* (literally 'familyhood') create a well-defined social structure with some stiff moral mores at its core. But despite some heavyweight social responsibilities, Kenyans have an easygoing approach to life and a wicked sense of humour, as their rich store of proverbs illustrate.

What's more, the emotional framework of the extended family makes for an inclusive and supportive network. As the pace and demands of modern life increase, this support is becoming ever more vital as parents migrate to cities for lucrative work, leaving their children with grandparents or aunts and uncles to be cared for. This fluid system has also enabled many to deal with the devastation wreaked by the HIV/AIDS epidemic.

Historically, the majority of Kenyans were either farmers or cattle herders with family clans based in small interconnected villages. Even today, as traditional rural life gives way to a frenetic urban pace, this strong sense of community remains and the importance of social interactions like greetings should not be underestimated; nor should the generally conservative nature of the majority of Kenyans. With most people following some form of Christianity or Islam, modesty in dress and manner remain very important. Keeping up appearances extends to dressing well, behaving modestly (and respectfully to one's elders and social superiors), performing religious and social duties and fulfilling all essential family obligations. Education, too, is important and the motivation to get a good education is high.

As Kenya gains a foothold in the 21st century it is grappling with ever-increasing poverty. At least 46% of the population are living below the poverty line with nearly 80% of these in rural areas. Unemployment is estimated at 23%, although there is a large body of people who, while employed, are significantly underemployed. Although showing some gains since 2005, the Human Development Report Index (which measures the well-being of a country taking into account life expectancy, education and standard of living) still ranked Kenya at a dismal 148 out of 177 countries in 2007, while the country's income gap between rich and poor remains within the 10 worst in the world.

## ECONOMY

Kenya's economy is fairly broad-based and is bolstered by the resilience, resourcefulness and improved confidence of the private sector. The growth in the private sector has also reinforced Nairobi's position as the primary communication and financial hub of East Africa. It enjoys the region's best transport links, communications infrastructure and trained personnel, and following the enactment of the Privatisation Law (2005), parastatals like KenGen (Kenya Electricity), Kenya Railways, Telkom Kenya and Kenya Re (insurance) have been privatised. Accelerating growth to reduce the poverty is the top priority of the new government.

However, barely 3 million out of 38 million people hold a bank account. In such a context the vast majority of Kenyan's are excluded from the benefits of savings accounts and small-loan facilities – the lack of financial structures impeding the much-vaunted 'trickle-down' effect. Here technology may provide a life-saving bridge to the future.

Kenya has 1.1 million AIDS orphans, and an estimated 140,000 to 170,000 children living with HIV/AIDS.

In 2007, horticulture exports rose 65% to US$1.12 billion, overtaking tourism as the country's largest foreign-exchange earner.

Evidence of this can be seen with Safaricom's (Kenya's mobile phone giant) pioneering M-pesa scheme, which allows mobile-phone owners to transfer money between their phones. Although it offers no access to credit, it provides the beginnings of a credit history to customers who would otherwise struggle to obtain an account or loan in a traditional bank.

Despite that postelection violence has forced the government to scale back the projected growth for next year (from 8% to between 4% and 6%), in general the economy seems to have weathered the political storm, although local economists posit that the country needs to see double-digit growth for there to be any real trickle-down effect. More worrying is the rise of inflation over the last five years. In May 2008 the Bank of Kenya announced inflation had hit a dizzying 31.5% (up from 11.8% in November 2007). However, tightening monetary policy will have an impact on that much-needed growth. Balancing the two will be a tricky business for Kenya's new government.

Since 2002 the Nairobi Stock Exchange has risen over 700% in dollar terms, making it one of the best-performing markets in the world.

### A Common Market

In 1996, Kenya, Tanzania and Uganda reestablished the East African Community (EAC). The objective of this trade agreement is to harmonise tariffs and customs, free movement of people and goods, and improve infrastructure. In 2007, Rwanda and Burundi also joined the community.

Although little of real note has materialised from the agreement to date, its existence and stated objectives are a positive step for Kenya and its neighbours. For example, before the revival of the EAC, Kenya's recorded trade with Tanzania and Uganda was too insignificant to measure. It has since grown to almost 30% of Kenya's total trade. Furthermore, a Common Market for Eastern and Southern Africa (COMESA) was endorsed in May 2007, agreeing to an expanded free-trade zone in 2008.

## POPULATION

Kenya's population in 2008 was estimated at 37,953,840. Life expectancy is 56 years and the infant-mortality rate is 56 per 1000 births. Males aged between 15 and 29 represent almost exactly 30% of Kenya's population, and almost 70% of the country's unemployed are people under 30 years of age.

Along with other developing countries in Africa and the Middle East, Kenya is experiencing unprecedented growth rates. Currently at around 2.75%, the growth rate has slowed in the last few years due to the prevalence of HIV/AIDS, which, according to the UN, affects 7% to 8% of adults. However, this still represents a significant growth rate and one that brings with it worrying concerns. Throughout the industrial revolution Britain's population never expanded at more than 1.5% per year, and America's century-changing baby boom peaked at 2.05% in 1950. By contrast Kenya's population growth rate has broken the 4% mark in the past, and with its current rate the population is set to double in 23 years. To be as rich (or just merely as poor) as their parents, children today will require an economy twice as large.

Since 1968, Kenya has won gold in the steeple-chase in every Olympic Games the country has competed in. In the 2008 Olympics Kenya took out 14 gold, silver and bronze medals.

## SPORT

Football (soccer) is a big deal in Kenya. People are nuts about it, and the big teams draw big crowds. Harambee Stars, AFC Leopards and Mathare United are among the best teams in the Kenyan premiership, which increasingly attracts foreign players from across the continent. Check out the *Daily Nation* for fixtures. Kenyans, too, seem to have a national obsession with the English premiership league. Every Kenyan supports Arsenal, Manchester United or Liverpool, even if they can't name a single Kenyan player.

Kenyan long-distance runners are among the world's best, with current competitors including Moses Masai, Joyce Chepchumba and Henry

Kipchirchir. However, much of their competitive running takes place outside the country; even trials and national events in Kenya sometimes fail to attract these stars, despite these events being flagged in the press well in advance. **Moi Stadium** (Thika Rd), outside Nairobi, is a popular venue for events.

The annual **East African Safari Rally** (www.eastafricansafarirally.com) is a rugged 3000km rally – which has been held annually since 1953 – passing through Kenya, Uganda and Tanzania along public roadways, and attracting an international collection of drivers with their vintage (pre-1971) automobiles. If you're here, the spectacle is worth seeking out.

For the latest on the Kenyan football scene, log on to www .kenyapremierleague .com, which also features a league table and results of recent matches.

## MULTICULTURALISM

Kenya is home to over 40 tribal groups (this number becomes much larger if counting the various 'subgroups'). They break down into three distinct linguistic groups: Bantu-speakers (who include the Kikuyu, Meru, Embu, Akamba and Luyha), Nilotic-speakers (the Maasai, Turkana, Samburu, Pokot, Luo and Kalenjin) and the minority Cushitic-speakers (El Molo, Somali, Rendille and Galla). See also below.

On the coast, Swahili is the name given to the local people who, although they have various tribal ancestries, have intermarried with Arab settlers over the centuries, giving rise to the Kiswahili language and a predominantly Arabic culture (see also p257).

Although most tribal groups have coexisted relatively peacefully since independence, the increasingly ethnocentric bias of government and civil service appointments has led to escalating unrest and disaffection. During the hotly contested elections of 1992, 1997 and 2007, clashes between two major tribes, the Kikuyu and Luo, bolstered by allegiances with other smaller tribes like the Kalenjin, have resulted in death and mass displacement (see p34). This has certainly led to an increasing anxiety among the middle- and upper-classes that the country may be riven along ethnic lines if something isn't done to address major inequalities. Local analysts point out that election violence is more to do with economic inequality than with tribalism – they insist that there are only two tribes in Kenya: the rich and the poor.

Bordered by five neighbours, Kenya has also been subject to an influx of refugees from time to time, namely from Uganda, Somalia, Sudan and Burundi. However, this represents only a fraction of the population at 1%, with current estimates of refugees numbering only 345,000.

Other minorities include about 80,000 Indians (see also opposite), 30,000 Arabs and 30,000 Europeans.

## TRIBES OF KENYA

The tribe is an important aspect of a Kenyan's identity: upon meeting a fellow Kenyan, the first question on anyone's lips is: 'What tribe do you come from?' However, distinctions between many tribal groups are slowly being eroded as people move to major cities for work, and intermarry.

### Akamba (also Kamba)
**11% of population**

Many Akamba lost their lives during WWI fighting for the British Army.

The region east of Nairobi towards Tsavo National Park is the traditional homeland of the Bantu-speaking Akamba. Great traders in ivory, beer, honey, iron weapons and ornaments, they traditionally plied their trade between Lake Victoria all the way to the coast and north to Lake Turkana. In particular, they traded with the Maasai and Kikuyu for food stocks. Highly regarded by the British for their fighting ability, they were drafted in large numbers into the British Army. After WWI the British tried to limit their cattle stocks and settled more Europeans in their tribal territories. In response, the Akamba

**THE INDIAN INFLUENCE**

India's connections with East Africa go back to the days of the spice trade, but the first permanent settlers from the Indian subcontinent were indentured workers, brought here from Gujarat and the Punjab by the British to build the Uganda Railway. After the railway was finished, the British allowed many workers to stay and start up businesses, and hundreds of *dukas* (small shops) were set up across the country.

Asian numbers were augmented after WWII and the Indian community came to control large sectors of the East African economy. However, few gave their active support to the black nationalist movements in the run-up to independence, despite being urged to do so by India's prime minister, and many were hesitant to accept local citizenship after independence. This earned the distrust of the African community, who felt the Indians were simply there to exploit African labour.

Fortunately, Kenya escaped the anti-Asian pogroms that plagued Uganda, and the Asian community continues to be a driving force in the economy, dominating the retail, construction and manufacturing industries. One of the most successful entrepreneurs of recent years is the Atul Shah family, who own the supermarket superbrand, Nakumatt. In 2006 they reported a turnover of $300 million, a 150% increase on the previous year. They plan to expand their Kenyan portfolio to 30 stores across the country, along with planned investment of $20 million to expand their operations into Uganda, Rwanda and Tanzania.

marched en masse to Nairobi to squat peacefully at Kariokor Market in protest, forcing the administration to relent. Nowadays, they are more famous for their elegant *makonde*-style (ebony) carving. Akamba society is clan-based with all adolescents going through initiation rites at about the age of 12. Subgroups of the Akamba include the Kitui, Masaku and Mumoni.

## Borana
### less than 0.1% of population
The Borana are one of the cattle-herding Oromo peoples, indigenous to Ethiopia, who migrated south into northern Kenya. They are now concentrated around Marsabit and Isiolo. The Borana observe strict role segregation between men and women – men being responsible for care of the herds while women are in charge of children and day-to-day life. Borana groups may pack up camp and move up to four times a year, depending on weather conditions and available grazing land. As a nomadic group their reliance on oral history is strong, with many traditions passed on through song.

## El Molo
### less than 0.1% of population
This tiny tribal group has strong links with the Rendille, their close neighbours. The El Molo rely on Lake Turkana for their existence, living on a diet mainly of fish and occasionally crocodiles, turtles and other wildlife. Hippos are hunted from doum-palm rafts, and great social status is given to the warrior who kills a hippo. An ill-balanced, protein-rich diet and the effects of too much fluoride have taken their toll on the tribe. Intermarriage with other tribes and abandonment of the nomadic lifestyle has helped to raise their numbers to about 4000, who now live on the mainland near Loyangalani.

Like the Rendille, the El Molo worship a god called Wak and bury their dead under stone cairns.

## Gabbra
### less than 0.1% of population
This small pastoral tribe lives in the far north of Kenya, from the eastern shore of Lake Turkana up into Ethiopia. Many Gabbra converted to Islam during the time of slavery. Traditional beliefs include the appointment of an *abba-olla* (father of the village), who oversees the moral and physical

well-being of the tribe. Fathers and sons form strong relationships, and marriage provides a lasting bond between clans. Polygamy is still practised by the Gabbra, although it is becoming less common. Gabbra men usually wear turbans and white cotton robes, while women wear *kangas,* thin pieces of brightly coloured cotton. The Gabbra are famous for their bravery, hunting lions, rhinos and elephants.

### Gusii (also Kisii)
**7% of population**

The Gusii traditionally consider death the work of 'witchcraft' rather than a natural occurrence.

The Gusii occupy the Western Highlands, east of Lake Victoria, forming a small Bantu-speaking island in a mainly Nilotic-speaking area. Primarily cattle-herders and crop-cultivators, they farm Kenya's cash crops – tea, coffee and pyrethrum – as well as market vegetables. They are also well known for their basketry and distinctive, rounded soapstone carvings, which have a cubist air about them. In fact, Picasso was heavily influenced by African art during his cubist period. Like many other tribal groups, Gusii society is clan based, with everyone organised into age-sets. Medicine men *(abanyamorigo)*, in particular, hold a highly respected and privileged position, performing the role of doctor and social worker. One of their more peculiar practices is trepanning: the removal of sections of the skull or spine to aid maladies such as backache or concussion.

### Kalenjin
**11% of population**

Many Kenyan athletes are Nandi or Kipsigis.

The Kalenjin comprise the Nandi, Kipsigis, Eleyo, Marakwet, Pokot and Tugen (former president Moi's people) and occupy the western edge of the central Rift Valley area. They first migrated to the area west of Lake Turkana from southern Sudan around 2000 years ago, but gradually filtered south as the climate became harsher. More recent times have seen them band together to form a larger power base, although frictions still exist. For example, the Kipsigis have a love of cattle rustling. which continues to cause strife between them and neighbouring tribes. However, the tribe are most famous for producing Kenya's Olympic runners (75% of all the top runners in Kenya are Kalenjin). As with most tribes, the Kalenjin are organised into age-sets. Administration of the law is carried out at the *kok* (an informal court led by the clan's elders).

### Kikuyu (also Gikikuyu)
**22% of population**

The Kikuyu are renowned for their entrepreneurial skills and for popping up everywhere in Kenya (the Kikuyu name Kamau is as common as Smith is in Britain).

The Kikuyu are Kenya's largest and most influential tribe, and contributed the country's first president, Jomo Kenyatta. Famously warlike, the Kikuyu overran the lands of the Athi and Gumba tribes, becoming hugely populous in the process. Now their heartland surrounds Mt Kenya, although they also represent the largest proportion of people living in Kenya's major cities. With territory bordering that of the Maasai, the tribe shares many cultural similarities due to intermarriage. The administration of the clans *(mwaki)* was originally taken care of by a council of elders, with a good deal of importance being placed on the role of the witchdoctor, the medicine man and the blacksmith. Initiation rites for both boys and girls consist of ritual circumcision for boys and genital mutilation for girls (although the latter is slowly becoming less common). Each group of youths of the same age belongs to a *riikaan* (age-set) and passes through the various stages of life, and their associated rituals, together. Subgroups of the Kikuyu include the Embu, Ndia and Mbeere.

## Luhya
**14% of population**
Made up of 18 different groups (the largest being the Bukusu), the Bantu-speaking Luhya are the second-largest group in Kenya. They occupy a relatively small, high-density area of the country in the Western Highlands centred on Kakamega. In the past, the Luhya were skilled metal workers, forging knives and tools that were traded with other groups, but today most Luhya are agriculturists, farming groundnuts, sesame and maize. Smallholders also grow large amounts of cash crops such as cotton and sugar cane. Many Luhya are superstitious and still have a strong belief in witchcraft, although to the passing traveller this is rarely obvious. Traditional costume and rituals are becoming less common, due mostly to the pressures of the soaring Luhya population.

## Luo
**12% of population**
The tribe of US president Barack Obama's father, the Luo live on the shores of Lake Victoria and are Kenya's third-largest tribal group. Though originally a cattle-herding people like the Maasai, their herds suffered terribly from the rinderpest outbreak in the 1890s so they switched to fishing and subsistence agriculture. During the struggle for independence, many of the country's leading politicians and trade unionists were Luo, including Tom Mboya (assassinated in 1969) and the former vice-president Oginga Odinga, who later spearheaded the opposition to President Moi. Kenya's current prime minister, Raila Odinga, is also a Luo. Socially, the Luo are unusual among Kenya's tribes in that they don't practise circumcision for either sex. The family unit is part of a larger grouping of *dhoot* (families), several of which in turn make up an *ogandi* (group of geographically related people), each led by a *ruoth* (chief). The Luo, like the Luhya, have two major recreational passions, soccer and music, and there are many distinctive Luo instruments made from gourds and gut or wire strings.

Few Luo today wear traditional costume - they have a reputation for 'flashiness', often carrying two mobile phones.

## Maasai
**2% of population**
Despite representing only a small proportion of the total population, the Maasai are, for many, the definitive symbol of Kenya. With a reputation (often exaggerated) as fierce warriors, the tribe has largely managed to stay outside the mainstream of development in Kenya and still maintains large cattle herds along the Tanzanian border. The British gazetted the Masai Mara National Reserve in the early 1960s, displacing the Maasai, and they slowly continued to annex more and more Maasai land. Resettlement programs have met with limited success as the Maasai scorn agriculture and land ownership. The Maasai still have a distinctive style and traditional age-grade social structure, and circumcision is still widely practised for both men and women. Women typically wear large platelike bead necklaces, while the men typically wear a red-checked *shuka* (blanket) and carry a distinctive ball-ended club. Blood and milk is the mainstay of the Maasai diet, supplemented by a drink called *mursik*, made from milk fermented with cow's urine and ashes, which has been shown to lower cholesterol.

*The Worlds of a Maasai Warrior: An Autobiography*, by Tepilit Ole Saitoti, presents an intriguing perspective on the juxtaposition of traditional and modern in East Africa.

## Meru
**5% of population**
Originally from the coast, the Meru now occupy the northeastern slopes of Mt Kenya. Up until 1974 the Meru were led by a chief (the *mogwe*), but on his death the last incumbent converted to Christianity. Strangely, many of

their tribal stories mirror the traditional tales of the Old Testament, which has led some to theorise that they might be a lost tribe of Israel. The practice of ancestor worship, however, is still widespread. They have long been governed by an elected council of elders *(njuuri)*, making them the only tribe practising a structured form of democratic governance prior to colonialism. The Meru now live on some of the most fertile farmland in Kenya and grow numerous cash crops. Subgroups of the Meru include the Chuka, Igembe, Igoji, Tharaka, Muthambi, Tigania and Imenti.

The Meru are active in the cultivation of *miraa*, the stems of which contain a stimulant similar to amphetamines and are exported to Somalia and Yemen.

## Pokot
### less than 0.1% of population
The pastoral Pokot (who are Kalenjin by language and tradition but less urbanised than other Kalenjin groups) herd their cattle and goats across the waterless scrub north of Lake Baringo and the Cherangani Hills. Cattle-raiding, and the search for water and grazing, has often brought them into conflict with the Turkana, Samburu and the Ugandan Karamojong. Pokot warriors wear distinctive headdresses of painted clay and feathers. Flat, aluminium nose ornaments shaped like leaves and lower-lip plugs are common among men. Circumcision is part of the initiation of men and many Pokot women undergo female genital mutilation at around age 12. Pokot hill farmers are a separate and distinct group who grow tobacco and keep cattle, sheep and goats in the hills north of Kitale, on the approaches to Marich Pass. These hill farmers have a strong craft tradition, producing pottery and metalwork, as well as snuff boxes from calabashes or horns.

## Rendille
### less than 0.1% of population
The Rendille are pastoralists who live in small nomadic communities in the rocky Kaisut Desert in Kenya's northeast. They have strong economic and kinship links with the Samburu and rely heavily on camels for many of their daily needs, including food, milk, clothing, trade and transport. The camels are bled by opening a vein in the neck with a blunt arrow or knife. The blood is then drunk on its own or mixed with milk. Rendille society is strongly bound by family ties centred on monogamous couples. Mothers have a high status and the eldest son inherits the family wealth. It is dishonourable for a Rendille to refuse a loan, so even the poorest Rendille often has claims to at least a few camels and goats. Rendille warriors often sport a distinctive visorlike hairstyle, dyed with red ochre, while women may wear several kilos of beads.

After giving birth to their first child, Rendille women adopt a clay head-decoration known as a *doko*, resembling a rooster's comb.

## Samburu
### 0.5% of population
Closely related to the Maasai, and speaking the same language, the Samburu occupy an arid area directly north of Mt Kenya. It seems that when the Maasai migrated to the area from Sudan, some headed east and became the Samburu. Like the Maasai, they too have retained their traditional way of life as nomadic pastoralists, depending for their survival on their livestock. They live in small villages of five to eight families, divided into age-sets, and they continue to practise traditional rites like male and female circumcision and polygamy. After marriage, women traditionally leave their clan, so their social status is much lower than that of men. Samburu women wear similar colourful bead necklaces to the Maasai. Like the Maasai and Rendille, Samburu warriors paste their hair with red ochre to create a visor to shield their eyes from the sun. Due to conflicts with the Somalis, they regard Islam with great suspicion and some Samburu have converted to Christianity.

## Swahili
**0.6% of population**
Although the people of the coast do not have a common heritage, they do have a linguistic link: Kiswahili (commonly referred to as Swahili), a Bantu-based language that evolved as a means of communication between Africans and the Arabs, Persians and Portuguese who colonised the East African coast (the word *swahili* is a derivative of the Arabic word for coast – *sawahil*). The cultural origins of the Swahili come from intermarriage between the Arabs and Persians with African slaves from the 7th century onwards. In fact, many anthropologists consider the Swahili a cultural tribe brought together by trade routes rather than a tribe of distinct biological lineage. A largely urban tribe, they occupy coastal cities like Mombasa, Malindi, Lamu and Stone Town (Zanzibar); and given the historical Arab influence, the Swahili largely practise Islam. Swahili subgroups include Bajun, Siyu, Pate, Mvita, Fundi, Shela, Ozi, Vumba and Amu (residents of Lamu).

The website www .bluegecko.org/kenya is a great source of information about the various peoples of Kenya and the arts.

## Turkana
**1.5% of population**
Originally from Karamojong in northeastern Uganda, the Turkana live in the virtual desert country of Kenya's northwest. Like the Samburu and the Maasai (with whom they are linguistically linked), the Turkana are primarily cattle herders, although fishing on the waters of Lake Turkana and small-scale farming is on the increase. Traditional costume and practices are still commonplace, although the Turkana are one of the few tribes to have voluntarily given up the practice of circumcision. Men typically cover part of their hair with mud, which is then painted blue and decorated with ostrich and other feathers and, despite the intense heat, their main garment is a woollen blanket. A woman's attire is dictated by her marital and maternal status; the marriage ritual itself is quite unusual and involves kidnapping the bride. Tattooing is also common. Men were traditionally tattooed on the shoulders for killing an enemy – the right shoulder for killing a man, the left for a woman. Witchdoctors and prophets are held in high regard and scars on someone's lower stomach are usually a sign of a witchdoctor's attempt to cast out an undesirable spirit using incisions.

A surprising number of Turkana men still wear markings on their shoulders to indicate they have killed another man.

## MEDIA
Kenya has one of the most diverse media scenes in Africa with some lively broadcast output. The key independent print media are the Nation Media Group, the Standard Group, People Ltd and the Times Media group, of which the Nation Media Group have the largest circulation and the only two Swahili publications. In addition, around 120 foreign correspondents representing 100 media organisations report from Nairobi.

Overall the press have a good deal of independence, although in the past most newspapers have practised some form of self-censorship, especially during the Moi era. In 2008, following the contested elections, the government imposed a ban on some live broadcast output. It was met with outrage from local and international journalists.

Although newspapers are widespread in the major cities, most Kenyans still rely on the radio for news and information. There are hundreds of FM stations broadcasting in English, Kiswahili and other indigenous languages. KBC (the state-owned Kenya Broadcasting Corporation) is the largest, although Citizen FM is the local radio station of choice. Capital and Kiss are popular private music channels, while East FM caters for Nairobi's Asian

**CONNECTIONS**

In a country of nearly 38 million people, only 2.77 million have access to the internet. If the last great revolution was mobile phones, the next will surely be access to the web. In January 2007 the Kenyan government signed a US$2.7 million contract with Tyco Telecommunications to construct a fibre-optic cable to Fujairah in the United Arab Emirates called the East African Marine System (TEAMS). Two other fibre-optic cables are being considered, which would link Kenya with India.

Initially slated for construction in 2008, the TEAMS project was delayed by the postelection violence although it has now been rescheduled for 2009. Once online, the government expects the cable to have a significant and positive effect on the economy. Currently East Africa pays up to US$7000 per megabite of data, one of the highest prices in the world. Once the fibre-optic cables are in place, this price should come down to around US$500 per megabite.

If the mobile-phone industry is anything to go by (the World Bank estimates that a 10% rise in mobile use gives a 0.6% rise in GDP growth), the benefits could be significant and timely, given the pressures on the Kenyan economy to deliver tangible results.

listeners. BBC, Voice of America and Radio France International service the local expatriate community.

KBC is the only national radio and television network, although the independent TV sector is growing with both the Nation and Standard groups operating a broadcast service.

## RELIGION

As a result of intense missionary activity, the majority of Kenyans outside the coastal and eastern provinces are Christians (including some home-grown African Christian groups that do not owe any allegiance to the major Western groups). Street preachers are common throughout the country, and their fire-and-brimstone sermons normally attract a large crowd. Unsurprisingly, hard-core evangelism has made some significant inroads and many TV-style groups from the US have a strong following. It's worth visiting a church to attend a service while you're in Kenya, even if it is just to enjoy the unaccompanied choral singing.

In the east of the country and along the coast, the majority of Kenyans are Muslims. They make up about 10% of the population. Most Muslims in Kenya belong to the Sunni branch of the faith, although Wahabi fundamentalism is on the rise due to the numerous *madrassas* (religious schools) built here by Saudi Arabia.

Only a small minority of Kenyans belong to the Shi'a branch of Islam, and most are found among people from the Indian subcontinent. The most influential sect are the Ismailis – followers of the Aga Khan. They represent a very liberal version of Islam and are strongly committed to the education of women.

In 2002, two schoolgirls took their father to court and won the right not to be circumcised.

A minority of people observe animist African religions, which link people with the natural environment through the belief that trees and animals have their own spirits. Respect and fear of the natural environment resulting from such beliefs long acted as a successful means of managing and understanding an often unruly and hostile environment. There are also small communities of Hindus, Sikhs and Jains.

## WOMEN IN KENYA

During Kenya's struggle for independence, women fought hard alongside men. Many, such as Me Katilili and Mary Muthoni Nyanjiru, were instrumental in Kenya's fight for freedom as well as in advancing women's rights and interests. Unfortunately, these efforts did not translate into greater political participation following independence. At the Lancaster House conference, where Kenya's independence constitution was negotiated, there was only one woman present out of around 70 Kenyan delegates. As a result, there is no provision in the constitution for discrimination on the basis of gender, although there are provisions for race, tribe, place of origin, colour and creed. In Ngũgĩ wa Thiong'o's *Petals of Blood*, Wanja the barmaid sums it up, '…with us girls the future seemed vague…it was as if we knew that no matter what efforts we put into our studies, our road lead to the kitchen or the bedroom'.

*I Laugh So I Won't Cry: Kenya's Women Tell the Stories of Their Lives,* edited by Helena Halperin, offers fascinating glimpses into the lives of Kenyan women.

Since the mushrooming of feminist lobby groups and civic associations in the 1990s, things have moved on somewhat. However, there is still a major discrepancy in the ways in which women and men have access to essential services and resources like land and credit, while traditional gender roles still largely prevail. It is not uncommon to hear conservative views of the a-woman's-place-is-in-the-kitchen variety espoused. What's more, women still face huge obstacles in the political arena, with only 10% representation in parliament.

That said, Kenyan women are increasingly gaining more educational opportunities and, particularly in the cities, are coming to play a more prominent role in business and politics. And although in rural areas typical gender roles are observed, there is still a significant degree of flexibility as women are accorded status and respect in their capacity as mothers, wives, healers, teachers and members of extended lineages. Also, if food provision is regarded as the primary role of the breadwinner, then women are the major breadwinners – the majority of small-scale farming in Kenya is undertaken by women.

One of the most notable Kenyan women in the media is Professor Wangari Maathai, an environmentalist and human rights activist (see also p62), who became the first African woman to win the Nobel Peace Prize in 2004. Although she has campaigned tirelessly against government oppression and advocated for women's rights, she is most famous for the Green Belt Movement, which she founded in 1977.

---

### FEMALE GENITAL MUTILATION

The controversial practice of female genital mutilation (FGM), often termed 'female circumcision', is still widespread across Africa, including throughout Kenya. In some parts of tribal Kenya more than 90% of women and girls are subjected to FGM in some form.

The term *FGM* covers a wide range of procedures from a small, mainly symbolic cut, to the total removal of the clitoris and external genitalia (known as infibulation); the open wound is then stitched up.

The effects of FGM can be fatal. Other side effects, including chronic infections, the spread of HIV, infertility, severe bleeding and lifelong pain during sex, are not uncommon.

Thanks to decades of work by international and local human rights groups, FGM is now banned in Kenya for girls under 17, but the ritual still has widespread support in parts of the community and continues clandestinely. Despite backing from the World Health Organisation, attempts to stamp out FGM are widely perceived as part of a Western conspiracy to undermine African cultural identity. Many local women's groups, such as the community project Ntanira na Mugambo (Circumcision Through Words), are working towards preserving the rite of passage aspect of FGM without any surgery. It seems likely that it will be African initiatives such as this, rather than Western criticism, that will finally put an end to FGM.

## ARTS

Kenya has a dynamic and burgeoning arts scene, running the gamut from music and literature to art, theatre, dance and a wealth of material crafts such as basketry, pottery, textile production and sculpture. It provides not only a powerful medium for expressing African culture but is also a means for expressing the dreams and frustrations of the poor and disenfranchised.

www.artmatters.info is a fabulous resource covering many aspects of the arts scene throughout Kenya and the rest of East Africa.

Most interestingly, during the 2008 postelection crisis, Kenyan writers, artists and musicians rallied to help people, reporting on hundreds of stories, broadcasting programs urging calm and unity, and offering workshops and courses aimed at helping people deal with their traumas while opening the way for reconciliation.

### Music

With its diversity of indigenous languages and culture, Kenya has a rich and exciting music scene. Influences, most notably from the nearby Democratic Republic of Congo and Tanzania, have also had an effect in diversifying the sounds, and more recently reggae and hip hop have permeated the pop scene.

Despite this creative outpouring local musicians face a tough time making their voices heard over competing American and European sounds. Local production houses, like Sync Sound Studios, have gone some way to supporting and promoting home-grown talent and helping them distribute to overseas markets. Of these, Ted Josiah is probably Kenya's most ambitious music producer. In 1999, he moved from Sync Sound Studios to set up his own company, Blue Zebra Records, and has since backed leading names like Necessary Noize, Suzanna Owiyo and Gidi Gidi Maji Maji. He also founded the Kisima Awards in 1994 and was reportedly behind the ODM's 2007 election commercials.

According to local belief, lurking inside many carvings are the spirits they represent, thus giving them supernatural powers.

The live-music scene in Nairobi is fluid and a variety of clubs cater for traditional and contemporary musical tastes. A good reference is the *Daily Nation*, which publishes weekly top-10 African, international and gospel charts and countrywide gig listings on Saturday. Live-music venues are listed under Entertainment headings throughout this book.

#### AFRICAN MUSICAL STYLES

The Congolese styles of rumba and *soukous,* known collectively as *lingala,* were first introduced into Kenya by artists such as Samba Mapangala (who is still playing) in the 1960s and have come to dominate most of East Africa. This upbeat party music is characterised by clean guitar licks and a driving *cavacha* drum rhythm.

Kenyan bands were also active during the 1960s, producing some of the most popular songs in Africa, including Fadhili William's famous *Malaika* (Angel), and *Jambo Bwana,* Kenya's unofficial anthem, written and recorded by the hugely influential Them Mushrooms.

Music from Tanzania was influential in the early 1970s, when the band Simba Wanyika helped create Swahili rumba, which was taken up by bands such as the Maroon Commandos and Les Wanyika.

*Benga* is the contemporary dance music of Kenya. It refers to the dominant style of Luo pop music, which originated in western Kenya, and spread throughout the country in the 1960s being taken up by Akamba and Kikuyu musicians. The music is characterised by clear electric guitar licks and a bounding bass rhythm. Some well-known exponents of *benga* include DO Misiani (a Luo) and his group Shirati Jazz, which has been around since the 1960s and is still churning out the hits. You should also look out for Globestyle, Victoria Kings and Ambira Boys.

**PLAYLIST**

- *Amigo* – classic Swahili rumba, with an interesting horn and saxophone combination, from one of Kenya's most influential bands, Les Wanyika
- *Guitar Paradise of East Africa* – an old album, but one that ranges through Kenya's various musical styles including the classic hit 'Shauri Yako'
- *Journey* – dedicated to Jabali Afrika's stirring acoustic sounds complete with drums, congas, shakers and bells
- *Kenyan: The First Chapter* – a collection of pioneering groups experimenting with Kenya's home-grown blend of African lyrics with R&B, house, reggae and dancehall genres
- *Mama Africa* – Suzanna Owiyo is considered the Tracy Chapman of Kenya, and this album of acoustic Afropop showcases her compelling and powerful voice beautifully
- *Nuting but de Stone* – phenomenally popular compilation by Kisima Award–winning Hardstone; combines African lyrics with American urban sounds and Caribbean *ragga*
- *Rumba is Rumba* – infectious Congolese *soukous* with Swahili lyrics, produced by Sync Sound Studios with great production values
- *Nairobi Beat: Kenyan Pop Music Today* – a great mix showcasing a variety of regional sounds including Luo, Kikuyu, Kamba, Luhya, Swahili and Congolese
- *Virunga Volcano* – from Orchestre Virunga, this album hums with the creative energy of samba, with sublime guitar licks, a bubbling bass and rich vocals

Contemporary Kikuyu music often borrows from *benga*. Stars include Sam Chege, Francis Rugwati and Daniel 'Councillor' Kamau, who was popular in the 1970s and is still going strong. Joseph Kamaru, the popular musician and notorious nightclub owner of the late 1960s, converted to Christianity in 1993 and now dominates the gospel music scene.

*Taarab,* the music of the East African coast, originally only played at Swahili weddings and other special occasions, has been given a new lease of life by coastal pop singer Malika.

Popular bands today are heavily influenced by *benga, soukous* and also Western music, with lyrics generally in Kiswahili. These include bands such as Them Mushrooms (now reinvented as Uyoya) and Safari Sound. For upbeat dance tunes, Ogopa DJs, Nameless, Redsan and Deux Vultures are recommended acts.

## RAP, HIP HOP & OTHER STYLES
Having arrived in Kenya in the 1990s, American-influenced gangster rap and hip hop are also on the rise, including such acts as Necessary Noize, Poxi Presha and Hardstone. The similarities between the slums of Nairobi and the ghettos of North America may be few, but both have proved cauldrons in which potent rap music has developed. In Nairobi, you're unlikely to miss seeing Snoop Dogg and 50 Cent emblazoned on the side of a matatu, or hearing their music blaring. Admiration for these big names has translated into a home-grown industry. In 2004, Dutch producer Nynke Nauta gathered rappers from the Eastlands slums of Nairobi and formed a collective, Nairobi Yetu. The resultant album, *Kilio Cha Haki* (A Cry for Justice), featuring raps in Sheng (a mix of Kiswahili, English and ethnic languages), has been internationally recognised as a poignant fusion of ghetto angst and the joy of making music.

Rapper Emmanuel Jal, a former south-Sudanese child soldier and former Nairobi resident, topped the Kenyan charts in 2005 and later that year

The Homeboyz Academy (www.africanhiphop .com) in Nairobi aims to give budding artists and producers a head start; it's said you need to crack it in Nairobi if you're going to make it in East Africa.

performed to great acclaim at Live8 in Britain. He subsequently recorded an album, *Ceasefire,* with the Sudanese *oud* (a form of lute or mandolin) maestro Abdel Gadir Salim. In 2008 he released the album *Warchild* (a documentary film about Jal's life was also released the same year, and his memoir published early in 2009 – both entitled *War Child*).

Kenya pioneered the African version of the Reggaeton style (a blend of reggae, hip hop and traditional music), which is now becoming popular in the US and UK. Dancehall is also huge here – Shaggy has a third home in Kenya and Sean Paul visits regularly.

Other names to keep an eye or ear out for include Prezzo (Kenya's king of bling), Nonini (a controversial women-and-booze rapper), Nazizi (female MC from Necessary Noize) and Mercy Myra (Kenya's biggest female R&B artist).

## Literature

There are plenty of novels, plays and biographies by contemporary Kenyan authors, but they can be hard to find outside the country, despite being published by the African branches of major Western publishing companies. The Heinemann's African Writers Series offers a major collection of such works, but they are generally only available in Nairobi and Mombasa.

Two of Kenya's best authors are Ngũgĩ wa Thiong'o and Meja Mwangi. Ngũgĩ is uncompromisingly radical, and his harrowing criticism of the neocolonialist politics of the Kenyan establishment landed him in jail for a year (described in his *Detained: A Prison Writer's Diary*), lost him his job at Nairobi University and forced him into exile. Meja Mwangi sticks more to social issues and urban dislocation, but has a mischievous sense of humour that threads its way right through his books.

Titles by Ngũgĩ wa Thiong'o include *Petals of Blood, Matigari, The River Between, A Grain of Wheat, Devil on the Cross* and *Wizard of the Crow,* which was shortlisted for the 2007 Commonwealth Writers' Prize. All offer insightful portraits of Kenyan life and will give you an understanding of the daily concerns of modern Kenyans. He has also written extensively in his native language, Gikuyu. Notable titles by Meja Mwangi include *The Return of Shaka, Weapon of Hunger, The Cockroach Dance, The Last Plague* and *The Big Chiefs*. His *Mzungu Boy,* winner of the Children's Africana Book Award in 2006, depicts the friendship of white and black Kenyan boys at the time of the Mau Mau uprising.

One of Kenya's rising stars on the literary front is Binyavanga Wainaina, who won the Caine Prize for African Writing in July 2002. The award-winning piece was the short story *Discovering Home*, about a young Kenyan working in Cape Town who returns to his parents' village in Kenya for a year. Since then he has gone on to write for international magazines and newspapers such as *National Geographic*, *Granta*, the *New York Times* and the *Guardian*. *Vanity Fair* also ran an interesting piece by him in 2007, which gives a great insight into the contemporary Kenyan cityscape.

More recently, Wainaina, along with fellow Caine nominee, Muthoni Garland, has been reflecting on the postelection violence. With other writers and journalists they formed the Concerned Kenyan Writers (CKW) group, which aims to inspire and unite people and show them that there is a pay off in peace and nationhood. In the wake of the violence they penned more than 160 news and analytical reports as well as poems and short stories. Not only did they hope to heal some of Kenya's internal divisions but they also sought to correct what they saw as the 'Dark Continent' reporting that the international media indulged in, in the wake of the violence.

*Facing the Lion* is Joseph Lekuton's beautifully crafted memoir of how he grew up as a poor Maasai boy, who, through a series of incredible twists and turns, ends up in the US studying for an MBA.

Read Wangari Maathai's autobiography, *Unbowed: One Woman's Story,* for an inspirational tale of how one person really can make a difference.

To follow their work, and the work of contemporary writers, look out for *Kwani?*, Kenya's first literary journal established by Wainaina in 2003. Nairobi based, it facilitates the production and distribution of Kenyan literature and hosts an annual literary festival that attracts a growing number of international names. Their website (http://kwani.org) is a great way to stay up to date with the contemporary scene.

To get a taste of writing by Kenyan women look for *Unwinding Threads*, a collection of short stories by many authors from all over Africa. The first female Kenyan writer of note is Grace Ogot, who worked initially for the BBC as an overseas broadcaster and became the first woman to have her work published by the East African Publishing House. Her work includes *Land Without Thunder, The Strange Bride, The Graduate* and *The Island of Tears*. Born in Nyanza Province, she sets many of her stories against the scenic background of Lake Victoria, and offers an insight into Luo culture in precolonial Kenya. Another interesting writer is Margaret Atieno Ogola, the author of the celebrated novel *The River and the Source* and its sequel, *I Swear by Apollo*, which follow the lives of four generations of Kenyan women in a rapidly evolving country. Other books of note are Marjorie Magoye's *The Present Moment*, which follows the life of a group of elderly women in a Christian refuge, and *The Man from Pretoria* by Kenyan conservationist and journalist Hilary Ngweno.

Elspeth Huxley's *Flame Trees of Thika* remains an enduring classic - the story of early-20th-century Kenya where cultures collide with all the grace of runaway trains.

## Painting

Given the diverse artistic heritage of Kenya, it is unsurprising to learn that there is a wealth of artistic talent in the country, practising both traditional painting and all manner of sculpture, printing, mixed media and graffiti.

However, it can be hard to get a good overview of the scene, given that there are few professional galleries, and artworks are largely displayed and sold through local galleries in the shopping malls of Nairobi. One of the best private galleries is Gallery Watatu (p131), which has regular exhibitions and a good permanent display.

The newly established Rahimtulla Museum of Modern Art (p109) is trying to take a more professional approach to promoting the work of Kenyan artists, although compared with international galleries it is small scale. Larger and more established is the Go-Down Arts Centre (p108), located in the hectic Industrial Area. Bringing together both art and the performing arts, it acts as a hub for Nairobi's contemporary arts scene.

Check out www.art4peace.org to see some of the grass-roots efforts that local artists have engineered to help people come to terms with their election experiences.

## Dance, Theatre & Performance

There are a number of contemporary dance troupes and theatre groups in Kenya, although the majority of performances take place in Nairobi. The Phoenix and Miujiza Players, Mbalamwezi Theatre Group, plus the La Campagnie Gaara and Bakututu dance groups, and Sigana Troupe, are all names to look out for. Other than in purpose-built theatres, plays and performances are often held in the various foreign cultural centres in Nairobi, Mombasa and Kisumu.

For more details on the Kenyan scene contact the Mzizi Arts Centre (p108), which hosts a variety of art, craft, dance, literature and performance events. They also host *sigana* performances here, which offer travellers an insight into an authentic African performance form. It contains elements of all the major African cultural forms – narration, song, music, dance, chant, ritual, mask, movement, banter and poetry – blending them into one long, wonderful storytelling performance.

The dance troupes of the Bomas of Kenya offer an interesting, if touristy, overview of various tribal dances (see p114).

To see what's on across the country, pick up a copy of Saturday's *Daily Nation*.

## Cinema

Kenya has always been a popular location for film production, starting in the 1930s with Hollywood classics like *The Snows of Kilimanjaro, King Solomon's Mines* and *Mogambo*, which were all filmed in Kenya. Later *Born Free*, adapted from Joy Adamson's book about rehabilitating lions back into the wild, and Sydney Pollack's *Out of Africa*, which details the story of Karen Blixen's life in colonial Kenya, brought Kenya to life for millions of viewers. The latter went on to win the Academy Award for Best Picture in 1986.

Since then Kenya has served as a location for Bob Rafelson's historical drama *Mountains of the Moon*, which won critical acclaim for its vivid retelling of the Burton/Speke expedition; and more recently Caroline Link crafted the sympathetic *Nowhere in Africa*, which paints a portrait of Jewish refugees struggling to create a new life in wartime Kenya. The film was a major success and won over 14 international awards, including the 2002 Academy Award for Best Foreign Language Film. The year 2005 brought a final hit with Fernando Meirrelles' *The Constant Gardener*, which was shot on location in Loiyangalani (a small town on Lake Turkana) and the enormous Kibera slum in Nairobi (see also p116).

Despite these international successes, the local Kenyan industry has struggled to establish itself, plagued, as it is, by underfunding. In 1998, it received a major boost with the opening of the Zanzibar International Film Festival (ZIFF), which is now one of the region's premier cultural events. The festival serves as a venue for artists from the Indian Ocean basin and beyond and has stimulated home-grown talents. One such auteur is Kibaara Kaugi, whose *Enough is Enough* (2004), a brave exploration of the Mau Mau uprising, garnered critical praise.

Galvanised into action, the government established the **Kenya Film Commission** (KFC; www.kenyafilmcommission.com) in 2005. The aim of the commission is to support and promote the Kenyan film industry locally as well as internationally. One notable success since its inception is *Kibera Kid*, a short film set in the Kibera slum, written and directed by Nathan Collett. It tells the story of 12-year-old Otieno, an orphan living with a gang of thieves, who must make a choice between gang life and redemption. Featuring a cast of children, all of whom live in Kibera, the film won a Student EMMY and played at film festivals worldwide including the Berlin Film Festival.

One of the indisputable highlights of *Nowhere in Africa* was the interaction of veteran Kenyan actor Sidede Onyulo and five-year-old German actress Lea Kurka, bantering all the while in Kiswahili.

The ZIFF website (www.ziff.or.tz) is the best jumping-off point into the world of East African cinema.

# Food & Drink

The Kenyan culinary tradition has generally emphasised feeding the masses as efficiently as possible, with little room for flair or innovation. Indeed, most meals are centred on *ugali*, a thick, doughlike mass made from maize and/or cassava flour, and is something of an acquired taste for foreigners (to say the least). While traditional fare may veer towards the bland but filling, if you hunt around, there are some treats to be found.

For starters, Kenya is blessed with a cornucopia of natural produce. Markets are bursting with crisp vegetables and the steamy coast provides abundant tropical fruit. The Indian Ocean provides Kenyans with plentiful fresh seafood, and meat – be it beef, goat, mutton or even camel – is consumed throughout the country with incredible gusto. And of course, there is nothing quite like the experience of dining on five-star cuisine at a luxury safari camp, surrounded by the sights and sounds of the African bush.

## STAPLES & SPECIALITIES
### Counting Carbs

Kenyan cuisine has few culinary masterpieces and is mainly survival food, offering the maximum opportunity to fill up at minimum cost. As you might imagine, most meals in Kenya largely consist of heavy starches, the most ubiquitous being *ugali*. *Ugali* is made from boiled grains cooked into a thick porridge until it sets hard, then served up in flat slabs. It's incredibly stodgy and tends to sit in the stomach like a brick, but most Kenyans swear by it – it will fill you up after a long day's safari, but it won't set your taste buds atingle.

In general, good *ugali* should be neither too dry nor too sticky, which makes it easy to enjoy as a finger food. Take some with the right hand from the communal pot (your left hand is used for wiping – and we don't mean your mouth!), roll it into a small ball with the fingers, making an indentation with your thumb, and dip it into the accompanying sauce. Eating with your hand is a bit of an art, but after a few tries it starts to feel natural. Don't soak the *ugali* too long (to avoid it breaking up in the sauce), and keep your hand lower than your elbow (except when actually eating) so the sauce doesn't drip down your forearm.

In addition to *ugali*, Kenyans also rely on potatoes, rice, chapati and *matoke*. The rice-based dishes, biriani and pilau, are clearly derived from Persia – they should be delicately spiced with saffron and star anise and liberally sprinkled with carrot and raisins. The chapati is identical to its Indian

Pilau flavoured with spices and stock is the signature dish at traditional Swahili weddings. The expression 'going to eat pilau' means to go to a wedding.

---

**WE DARE YOU**

If you're lucky (!) and game, you may be able to try various cattle-derived products beloved of the pastoral tribes of Kenya. Samburu, Pokot and Maasai warriors have a taste for cattle blood. The blood is taken straight from the jugular, which does no permanent damage to the cattle, but it is certainly an acquired taste. *Mursik* is made from milk fermented with grass ash, and is served in smoked gourds. It tastes and smells pungent, but it contains compounds that reduce cholesterol, enabling the Maasai to live quite healthily on a diet of red meat, milk and blood. Don't expect it to turn up at your typical Kenyan watering hole, though you may be able to sample it at villages in the Masai Mara National Reserve.

predecessor, while *matoke* is mashed green plantains, which when well prepared can taste like buttery, lightly whipped mashed potato. Also look out
for *irio* (or *kienyeji),* made from mashed greens, potato and boiled corn or
beans; *mukimo,* a kind of hash made from sweet potatoes, corn, beans and
plantains; and *githeri,* a mix of beans and corn.

## Flesh & Bone

Make no mistake about it – Kenyans are enthusiastic carnivores and their
unofficial national dish, *nyama choma* (barbecued meat), is a red-blooded,
hands-on affair. Most places have their own on-site butchery, and *nyama
choma* is usually purchased by weight, often as a single hunk of meat. Half
a kilogram is usually enough for one person (taking into account bone and
gristle), and it'll be brought out to you chopped into small bite-sized bits
with vegetable mash and greens.

For the lowdown on various Kenyan recipes, including the ubiquitous *ugali* and *sukuma wiki,* check out www.blissites .com/kenya/culture /recipes.html.

Goat is the most common meat, but you'll see chicken, beef and some
game animals (ostrich and crocodile) in upmarket places. Don't expect *nyama
choma* to melt in the mouth – its chewiness is probably indicative of the
long and eventful life of the animal you are consuming. You'll need a good
half-hour at the end of the meal to work over your gums with a toothpick.
Copious quantities of Tusker beer also tend to help it go down.

In addition to *nyama choma,* Kenyans are also fond of meat-based stews,
which help make their carb-rich diet more palatable. Again, goat, chicken
and beef, as well as mutton, are the most common cuts on the menu, though
they tend to be pretty tough, despite being cooked for hours on end.

## Fruit & Veg

*Ugali* (and most Kenyan dishes for that matter) is usually served with *sukuma wiki*
(braised or stewed spinach). *Sukuma wiki* in Kiswahili means, literally, 'stretch the
week', the implication being that it's so cheap it allows the householder to stretch
the budget until the next weekly pay cheque. Despite its widespread availability,
a dish of well-cooked *sukuma wiki* with tomatoes, stock and capsicum makes a
refreshing change from the abundance of meat in other recipes.

Because of the country's varied climate, there is often an excellent array
of fruit to be found. Depending on the place and the season, you can buy
mangoes, papayas, pineapples, passionfruit, guavas, oranges, custard
apples, bananas (of many varieties), tree tomatoes and coconuts. Chewing
on a piece of sugar cane is also a great way to end a meal. Prices are low and
the quality is very high.

---

### KENYA'S TOP FIVE EATERIES

- **Carnivore** (p125), Nairobi – while you can no longer eat game meat here, Kenya's most
  famous restaurant is still a boisterous affair, attracting tourists and flush locals.
- **Ali Barbour's Cave Restaurant** (p277), Diani beach – a truly unique setting for one of the
  coast's top eateries, peeking out of a coral cave at starry skies and a silky beach.
- **Railway Beach** (p179), Kisumu – wade into the smoke, sink into a chair and enjoy fried fish
  with the locals on the shores of Lake Victoria.
- **Tamarind Restaurant** (p267), Mombasa – this romantic, open-terraced restaurant overlooks
  the harbour, and serves up Swahili-style seafood that highlights the region's history in the
  spice trade.
- **Haandi** (p127), Nairobi – undisputed top dog among Kenya's many Indian restaurants, this
  classy curry-house provides an authentic taste of South Asia.

## Kenyan Classics

Breakfast in Kenya is generally a simple affair consisting of chai (tea; see below) accompanied by a *mandazi* (semisweet doughnut). *Mandazi* are best in the morning when they're freshly made – they become rubbery and less appetising as the day goes on. Another traditional breakfast dish is *uji* (a thin, sweet porridge made from bean, millet or other flour), which is similar to *ugali* and best served warm, with lashings of milk and brown sugar

The most distinctive Kenyan food is found on the coast. Swahili dishes reflect the history of contact with Arabs and other Indian Ocean traders, and incorporate the produce of the region – the results can be excellent. Grilled fish or octopus will be a highlight of any menu, while coconut and spices such as cloves and cinnamon feature prominently.

The large South Asian presence in East Africa means that Indian food commonly appears on menus throughout Kenya. Most restaurants serve curries and Indian-inspired dishes such as masala chips (ie chips with a curry sauce), while authentic Indian restaurants along the coast and elsewhere dish up traditional dishes from the subcontinent.

Western dishes such as roast chicken and steak are staples in upmarket restaurants found in the bigger towns. In addition, international-style buffets at luxury hotels and safari lodges can be extremely lavish affairs, especially when served by candlelight at a rural bush camp.

## DRINKS
### Nonalcoholic Drinks

Despite the fact that Kenya grows some excellent tea and coffee, getting a decent cup of either can be difficult. Quite simply, the best stuff is exported.

Chai is the national obsession, and although it's drunk in large quantities, it bears little resemblance to what you might be used to. As in India, the tea, milk and masses of sugar are boiled together and stewed for ages and the result is milky and very sweet – it may be too sickly for some, but the brew might just grow on you. Spiced masala chai with cardamom and cinnamon is very pleasant and rejuvenating. For tea without milk ask for chai *kavu*.

As for coffee, it is often sweet and milky, and made with a bare minimum of instant coffee. However, in Nairobi and in other larger towns, there are a steadily increasing number of coffee houses serving very good Kenyan coffee, and you can usually get a good filter coffee at any of the big hotels. With all the Italian tourists who visit the coast, you can now get a decent cappuccino or espresso pretty much anywhere between Diani Beach and Lamu.

All the old favourites are also here in Kenya, including Coca-Cola, Sprite and Fanta – they go under the generic term of 'soda' and are available everywhere. Stoney's Ginger Ale (known just as Stoney's) and Bitter Lemon are hugely popular, as is Vimto, a fizzy fruity concoction that quenches your thirst while settling the stomach.

With all the fresh fruit that's available in Kenya, the juices on offer are breathtakingly good. All are made using modern blenders, so there's no point asking for a fruit juice during a power cut. Although you can get juices made from almost any fruit, the nation's favourite is passionfruit. It is known locally just as 'passion', although it seems a little odd asking a waiter or waitress whether they have passion and how much it costs!

## Alcohol

Kenya has a thriving local brewing industry, and formidable quantities of beer are consumed throughout the day and night. You'll usually be given a choice of 'warm' or 'cold' beer. 'Why warm?', you might well ask.

Tap water is best avoided, though bottled water is widely available. Be wary of ice and fruit juices diluted with unpurified water. With fruit and vegetables, it's best to follow the adage: 'cook it, peel it, boil it or forget it'.

Curiously, most Kenyans appear to prefer it that way, despite the fact that room temperature in Kenya is a lot hotter than room temperature in the USA or Europe.

The local beers are Tusker, Pilsner and White Cap, all manufactured by Kenya Breweries and sold in 500mL bottles. Tusker comes in three varieties: Tusker Export, Tusker Malt Lager and just plain Tusker. Tusker Export is a stronger version of ordinary Tusker, while Tusker Malt has a fuller taste, for more discerning palettes. Locally produced foreign labels include Castle (a South African beer) and Guinness, though the Kenyan version is nothing like the genuine Irish article.

Kenya has a fledgling wine industry, and the Lake Naivasha Colombard wines are generally quite good. This is something that cannot be said about the most commonly encountered Kenyan wine – papaya wine. Quite how anyone came up with the idea of trying to reproduce a drink made from grapes using papaya is a mystery, but the result tastes foul and smells unbearable. On the other hand, you can get cheap South African, European and even Australian wine by the glass in upmarket restaurants in major cities and tourist areas.

A popular Kenyan cocktail is *dawa,* which translates from the Kiswahili as 'medicine'. Clearly based on the Brazilian *caipirinha,* it's made with vodka, lime and honey. We suggest you enjoy a tipple at sunset in a bar overlooking the coast, which can certainly have a therapeutic effect on your mind and body.

Although it is strictly illegal for the public to brew or distil liquor, it remains a way of life for many Kenyans. *Pombe* is the local beer, usually a fermented brew made with bananas or millet and sugar. It shouldn't do you any harm. The same cannot be said for the distilled drinks known locally as *chang'a,* which are laced with genuine poisons. See below for more on the perils of drinking *chang'a.*

*In restaurants catering to tourists, tip about 10%, assuming service warrants it. Tipping isn't expected in small, local establishments, though rounding up the bill is always appreciated.*

## WHERE TO EAT & DRINK

The most basic local eateries are usually known as *hotels* or *hotelis,* and they often open only during the daytime. You may find yourself having dinner at 5pm if you rely on eating at these places. However, even in smaller towns it's usually possible to find a restaurant that offers a more varied menu at a higher price. Often these places are affiliated with the town's midrange and top-end hotels, and are usually open in the evening. You'll find that many of the big nightclubs also serve food until late into the night. Menus, where they exist in the cheaper places, are usually just a chalked list on a board. In more upmarket restaurants, they are usually written only in English.

### LETHAL BREW

Kenya has a long tradition of producing its own bootleg liquor, but you should steer well clear of *chang'a*. In 2005, 48 people died near Machakos after drinking a bad batch of *chang'a*. A further 84 were hospitalised and treated with vodka to reduce the effects of methyl alcohol poisoning – such incidents are not uncommon.

In fact the drink, Sorghum Baridi, from Central Province, contains so much methyl alcohol that the bottles are actually cold to the touch! Perhaps the most dangerous *chang'a* comes from Kisii, and is fermented with marijuana twigs, cactus mash, battery alkaline and formalin. Needless to say these brews can have lethal effects, and we don't recommend that you partake unless you're really looking to lose your mind, your eyesight and possibly your life.

**DOS & DON'TS**

For Kenyans, a shared meal and eating out of a communal dish are expressions of solidarity between hosts and guests: here are a few tips to help you get into the spirit of things.

- If you're invited to eat and aren't hungry, it's OK to say that you've just eaten, but try to share a few bites of the meal in recognition of the bond with your hosts.
- Leave a small amount on your plate to show your hosts that you've been satisfied.
- Don't take the last bit of food from the communal bowl – your hosts may worry that they haven't provided enough.
- Never, ever handle food with the left hand!
- If others are eating with their hands, do the same, even if cutlery is provided.
- Defer to your hosts for customs that you aren't sure about.

## Quick Eats

Eating fast food has taken off in a big way and virtually every town has a place serving greasy-but-cheap chips, burgers, sausages, pizzas and fried chicken. Lashings of tomato and chilli sauces are present to help lubricate things. A number of South African fast-food chains have taken hold in Nairobi, such as the ubiquitous Steers.

On the streets in Kenya, you may encounter roasted corn cobs and deep-fried yams, which are eaten hot with a squeeze of lemon juice and a sprinkling of chilli powder. *Sambusas,* deep-fried pastry triangles stuffed with spiced mincemeat, are good for snacking on the run, and are obvious descendants of the Indian samosa.

Something you don't come across often, but which is an excellent snack, is *mkate mayai* (literally 'bread eggs'), a wheat dough pancake, filled with minced meat and egg and fried on a hotplate. On the coast street food is more common and you will find cassava chips, chapatis and *mishikaki* (marinated grilled meat kebabs, usually beef).

The most long-lasting impact that Portuguese explorers had on Kenya was in the culinary field. Portuguese travellers introduced maize, cassava, potatoes and chillies from South America - all of which are now staples of the Kenyan diet.

## Self-catering

Preparing your own food is a viable option if you are staying in a place with a kitchen, or if you're camping and carrying cooking gear. Every town has a market, and there's usually an excellent range of fresh produce. Western-style supermarkets are found in major towns, with the Nakumatt chain setting the standard for quality and range.

## VEGETARIANS & VEGANS

Vegetarian visitors are likely to struggle, as meat features in most meals and many vegetable dishes are cooked in meat stock. But, with a bit of scouting around, you will be able to find something. You may find yourself eating a lot of *sukuma wiki* (p52), while other traditional dishes such as *githeri* are hearty, if not particularly inspiring, options. Beans and avocado will also figure prominently in any vegetarian's culinary encounters in Kenya. Many Indian restaurants will provide a vegetarian *thali* (an all-you-can-eat meal) that will certainly fill you up. Buying fresh fruit and vegetables in local markets can help relieve the tedium of trying to order around the meat on restaurant menus.

Note that most tour operators are willing to cater to special dietary requests, such as vegetarian, vegan, kosher or halal, with advance notice.

## EATING WITH KIDS

Kenyans are family-friendly, and dining out with children is no problem. Hotel restaurants occasionally have high chairs, and while special children's meals aren't common, it's easy enough to find items that are suitable for young diners. Avoid curries and other spicy dishes, uncooked, unpeeled fruit and vegetables, meat from street vendors (as it's sometimes undercooked) and unpurified water. Supermarkets stock boxes of fresh juice, and fresh fruit (tangerines, bananas and more) is widely available.

## EAT YOUR WORDS

Want to know *mayai* from *mandazi*? *Samaki* from *sukari*? Make the most of the cuisine scene by getting to know the language. For pronunciation guidelines, see the Language chapter.

### Useful Phrases

| | |
|---|---|
| I'm a vegetarian. | *Nakula mboga tu.* |
| I don't eat meat. | *Mimi sili nyama.* |
| I'm starving! | *Nina njaa kali!* |
| Is there a restaurant near here? | *Je, kuna hoteli ya chakula hapo jirani?* |
| Can you recommend a ...? | *Unaweza kupendekeza ...?* |
|   bar | *baa* |
|   cafe/coffee house | *mgahawa* |
|   restaurant | *hoteli kula* |
| Do you serve food here? | *Mnauza chakula hapa?* |
| Can you cook for us? | *Unaweza kutupikia chakula?* |
| What would you recommend? | *Chakula gani ni kizuri?* |
| What's in that dish? | *Chakula hicho kinapikwaje* |
| I'll have that. | *Nataka hicho* |
| I'd like ... | *Natoka ...* |
| I'd like ..., please. | *Naomba ...* |
|   a childrens menu | *menyu kwa watoto* |
|   the drink list | *orodha ya vinywaji* |
|   a half portion | *nusu* |
|   a menu (in English) | *menyu (kwa Kiingereza)* |
| Without chilli pepper, please. | *Bila pilipili, tafadhali.* |
| Please bring me the bill. | *Lete bili tafadhali.* |
| This isn't very good. | *Chakula hiki si kizuri sana.* |
| This is too spicy. | *Chakula hiki ni mno chenye viungo.* |
| That was delicious! | *Chakula kitamu sana!* |

### Menu Decoder

**biriani** – casserole of rice and spices with meat or seafood
**mchuzi** – sauce, sometimes with bits of beef and very well cooked vegetables
**mishikaki** – kebab
**nyama choma** – barbecued meat
**pilau** – spiced rice cooked in broth, with seafood or meat and vegetables
**supu** – soup; usually somewhat greasy, and served with a piece of beef, pork or meat fat in it
**ugali** – thick, porridgelike maize- or cassava-based staple, served in a solid form and sold everywhere
**wali na kuku/samaki/nyama/maharagwe** – cooked white rice with chicken/fish/meat/beans

## Food Glossary

### BASICS
**baridi** – cold
**joto** – hot
**kijiko** – spoon
**kikombe** – cup
**kisu** – knife
**kitambaa cha mikono** – napkin
**sahani** – plate
**tamu** – sweet
**uma** – fork

### STAPLES
**chipsi** – chips
**kiazi** – potato
**maharagwe** – beans
**mkate** – bread
**matoke** – cooked and mashed plantains
**ndizi ya kupika** – plantains
**wali** – rice (cooked)

### MEAT & SEAFOOD
**kaa** – crab
**kuku** – chicken
**nyama mbuzi** – goat
**nyama ng'ombe** – beef
**nyama nguruwe** – pork
**pweza** – octopus
**samaki** – fish

### FRUIT & VEGETABLES
**chungwa** – orange
**dafu** – coconut (green)
**embe** – mango
**kiazi** – potato
**kitunguu** – onion
**mboga** – vegetables
**nanasi** – pineapple
**nazi** – coconut (ripe)
**ndizi** – banana
**nyanya** – tomato
**papai** – papaya
**sukuma wiki** – spinach (braised or stewed)
**tunda** – fruit

### OTHER DISHES & CONDIMENTS
**chumvi** – salt
**mayai (yaliyochemshwa)** – eggs (boiled)
**maziwa ganda** – yoghurt
**sukari** – sugar

### DRINKS
**bia (baridi/yamoto)** – beer (cold/warm)
**maji (ya kuchemsha/ya kunywa/ya madini)** – water (boiled/drinking/mineral)
**maji ya machungwa** – orange juice

# Environment

## THE LAND

Straddling the equator and covering an area of some 583,000 sq km, including around 13,600 sq km of Lake Victoria, Kenya is undeniably beautiful. Oh yes is she beautiful! The country, which is bordered to the north by Ethiopia and Sudan, to the east by the Indian Ocean and the deserts of Somalia, to the west by Uganda and Lake Victoria, and to the south by Tanzania, contains almost every possible landscape. There are golden deserts of epic expanse, jungles of creepy-crawlies, snowman-friendly ice caps, sultry beaches lapped by warm waters full of fish far too pretty to eat, farmers' fantasy agricultural land, lush lakes and, of course, the undulating savannas of safari legend. Whatever you want, this beauty's got it.

Probably the most important geological feature is the Rift Valley, a vast range of valleys rather than a single valley, following a 5000km-long crack in the earth's crust. Within the Rift Valley are numerous dips and troughs and there are some huge volcanoes including Mt Kenya, Mt Elgon and Mt Kilimanjaro (across the border in Tanzania).

The main rivers in Kenya are the Athi/Galana River, which empties into the Indian Ocean near Malindi, and the Tana River, which makes love to the coast midway between Malindi and Lamu. Aside from Lake Victoria in the west, Kenya has numerous small volcanic lakes, as well as a sea of jade, otherwise known by the more boring name of Lake Turkana, which straddles the Ethiopian border in the north.

For an evocative picture of Kenya's physical, environmental and cultural make-up, track down Peter Matthiessen's classic, *The Tree Where Man Was Born*, an account of the author's epic journey through East Africa in the 1960s.

## WILDLIFE
### Animals

For most people Kenya means animals. The Big Five (lion, buffalo, elephant, leopard and rhino) and a huge variety of other less famous but equally impressive animals can be seen in at least two of the major parks.

The birdlife is equally varied and includes such flagship species as the ostrich, vulture and marabou stork, whose ugliness you don't want disturbing your dreams. Around bodies of water, you may see flamingos, exotic cranes and storks, while the forests are home to huge hornbills and rare species such as the sunbird and touraco. Even the starlings get a makeover here, with the superb starling being everything it's cracked up to be. There are also dozens of species of weaver bird, which make the distinctive baglike nests seen hanging from acacia trees.

Having trouble telling your dikdik from your serval? Try the hand-illustrated *Kingdon Field Guide to African Mammals* (Jonathon Kingdon), widely considered to be the definitive guide to the continent's fauna. It's also available in a pocket edition.

### ENDANGERED SPECIES

Many of Kenya's major predators and herbivores have become endangered over the past few decades, because of the continuous destruction of their natural habitat and merciless poaching for ivory, skins, horn and bush meat.

The black rhino is probably Kenya's most endangered large mammal. It's commonly poached for its horn and, faced with relentless poaching by heavily armed gangs in the 1980s, the wild rhino population plummeted from 20,000 in 1969 to just 539 today. **Rhino Ark** (☎ 020-609866; www.rhinoark .org) is one organisation that raises funds to create rhino sanctuaries and donations are always appreciated.

While the elephant is not technically endangered, it is still often the target of poachers. A number of elephants are killed every year, especially in the area around Tsavo East National Park. Current elephant numbers are estimated at 35,000.

**DUDUS**

Because of its lush climate, Kenya has some huge tropical bugs, known as *dudus* in Kiswahili. Arachnophobes should watch out for the plum-sized golden orb spider, with its famously strong web, and the delightfully named Mombasa golden starburst baboon spider, regarded as a 'small' tarantula, as it reaches only 12cm in diameter! There are also several large species of scorpion, often seen after rain.

Perhaps Kenya's most notorious *dudu* is the safari ant. These huge red ants sweep across the countryside in endless columns, consuming everything that lies in their path. Locally they're often known as 'army' or 'crazy' ants for their brutal search-and-destroy tactics. Tribespeople use the pincers of safari ants as improvised stitches for wounds – don't believe they work? Stick your finger into the middle of a column and see what happens!

An altogether friendlier species is the *jongo* (giant millipede). Although these insect behemoths can reach 20cm in length, they eat only decaying wood and will roll themselves up into a defensive coil if approached. One of the more entertaining bugs is the dung beetle, which has the unenviable task of acting as the savanna's sewage disposal expert. It does this by rolling small amounts of dung into a ball and then, like David Beckham at his best, dribbling it across the plains to its burrow, where its young chew on it!

## Plants

Romantics will certainly find no end of pretty flowers to inspire poetry for that someone special and the country's flora is notably diverse because of the wide range of physiographic regions. The vast plains of the south are characterised by distinctive flat-topped acacia trees, interspersed with the equally recognisable baobab trees and savage whistling thorn bushes.

The savanna grassland of the Masai Mara supports a huge variety of animal life. The grass grows tremendously fast after the rains, and provides food for an enormous range of herbivores and insects. The trampling and grazing of the various herbivores that call the Mara home promotes the growth of grasses, rather than broadleaf plants, which are more vulnerable to damage from grazing, drought and fire.

On the slopes of Mt Elgon and Mt Kenya the flora changes as the altitude increases. Thick evergreen temperate forest grows between 1000m and 2000m, giving way to a belt of bamboo forest that reaches as high as about 3000m. Above this height is mountain moorland, characterised by the amazing groundsel tree and giant lobelias (see also p210). In the semidesert plains of the north and northeast the vegetation cover is thorny bush, which can seem to go on forever. In the northern coastal areas mangroves are prolific, and there are still a few small pockets of coastal rainforest.

The biggest consumers of ivory are the Chinese and Japanese - most of it is used to produce chopsticks and bangles.

## NATIONAL PARKS & RESERVES

Kenya's national parks and reserves rate among the best in Africa, and around 10% of the country's land area is protected by law. Despite the ravages of human land exploitation and poaching, there is still an incredible variety of birds and mammals in the parks.

Going on safari is an integral part of the Kenyan experience, and more popular parks such as Masai Mara National Reserve and Amboseli National Park can become so overcrowded in the high season (January to February) that you'll struggle to get a wildlife photo without a crowd of vans in the background.

Fortunately, the smaller and more remote parks, such as Saiwa Swamp National Park, see only a handful of visitors at any time of year. In addition

Kenya's national bird is the lilac-breasted roller, which can be seen in many national parks, including the Masai Mara National Reserve, Lake Nakuru and Meru National Parks.

## NATIONAL PARKS & RESERVES

| Park/Reserve | Features | Activities | Best time to visit |
|---|---|---|---|
| Aberdare National Park (p204) | dramatic highlands, waterfalls and rainforest; elephants, black rhinos, bongo antelope, black leopards | trekking, fishing, gliding | year-round |
| Amboseli National Park (p137) | dry plains and scrub forest; elephants, buffaloes, lions, antelope | wildlife drives | Jun-Oct |
| Arabuko Sokoke Forest Reserve (p293) | coastal forest; Sokoke scops owls, Clarke's weavers, elephant shrews, Amani sunbirds, butterflies, elephants | bird tours, walking, running, cycling | year-round |
| Hell's Gate National Park (p156) | dramatic rocky outcrops and gorges; lammergeiers, eland, giraffes, lions | cycling, walking | year-round |
| Kakamega Forest Reserve (p187) | virgin tropical rainforest; red-tailed monkeys, flying squirrels, 330 bird species | walking, bird-watching | year-round |
| Lake Bogoria National Reserve (p164) | scenic soda lake; flamingos, greater kudu, leopards | bird-watching, walking, hot springs | year-round |
| Lake Nakuru National Park (p162) | hilly grassland and alkaline lakeland; flamingos, black rhinos, lions, warthogs, over 400 bird species | wildlife drives | year-round |
| Masai Mara National Reserve (p171) | savanna and grassland; Big Five, antelope, cheetahs, hyenas | wildlife drives, ballooning, wildebeest migration | Jul-Oct |
| Meru National Park (p222) | rainforest, swamplands and grasslands; white rhinos, elephants, lions, cheetahs, lesser kudu | wildlife drives, fishing | year-round |
| Mt Elgon National Park (p195) | extinct volcano and rainforest; elephants | walking, trekking, fishing | Dec-Feb |
| Mt Kenya National Park (p208) | rainforest, moorland and glacial mountain; elephants, buffaloes, mountain flora | trekking, climbing | Jan-Feb, Aug-Sep |
| Nairobi National Park (p109) | open plains with urban backdrop; black rhinos, birdlife, rare antelope | wildlife drives, walking | year-round |
| Saiwa Swamp National Park (p197) | swamplands and riverine forest; sitatunga antelope, crowned cranes, otters, black-and-white colobus | walking, bird-watching | year-round |
| Samburu, Buffalo Springs & Shaba National Reserves (p234) | semiarid open savanna; elephants, leopards, gerenuks, crocodiles | wildlife drives | year-round |
| Shimba Hills National Reserve (p270) | densely forested hills; elephants, sable antelope, leopards | walking, forest tours | year-round |
| Tsavo East & West National Parks (p140 & p144) | sweeping plains and ancient volcanic cones; Big Five | rock climbing, walking, wildlife drives | year-round |

to protecting wildlife, some parks have been created to preserve the landscape itself – Mt Kenya, Mt Elgon, Hell's Gate, Mt Longonot and Kakamega Forest are all worth investigating.

A number of marine national parks have also been established, providing excellent diving and snorkelling (see p280, p282, p291 and p298).

## NATIONAL PARK ENTRY FEES

Admission to parks in Kenya is being converted to a 'smartcard' system for payment of fees. The cards must be charged with credit in advance and can be topped up at certain locations. Remaining credit is not refundable. Note that Kenya Wildlife Service (KWS) now also accepts euros and UK pounds.

At the time of writing the smartcard system was in use at Nairobi, Lake Nakuru, Aberdare, Amboseli and Tsavo National Parks. The other parks still work on a cash system. Smartcards are available at the KWS headquarters in Nairobi and Mombasa, at the main gates of the participating parks, and at the Malindi Marine National Park office.

The KWS has a number of categories for parks and reserves. These include the following:

| Category | Park |
| --- | --- |
| Premium | Amboseli, Lake Nakuru |
| Wilderness | Aberdare, Chyulu Hills, Meru, Tsavo East & Tsavo West |
| Scenic & special interest | Arabuko Sokoke, Kakamega, Shimba Hills & all other parks |
| Marine | Kiunga, Malindi, Mombasa & Watamu |

Entry is US$20/10 per nonresident adult/child for Hell's Gate and Mt Elgon National Parks, US$20/10 for Kisite Marine National Park, US$55/20 for Mt Kenya National Park, and US$40/20 for Nairobi National Park. Non-KWS reserves including Masai Mara and Buffalo Springs have entry fees comparable to the Wilderness parks (see individual park reviews for more details).

Entry and camping fees to the parks per person per day are as follows:

| Category | Nonresident adult/child (US$) | Resident adult/child (KSh) | Camping adult nonresident (US$)/resident (KSh) |
| --- | --- | --- | --- |
| Premium | 60/30 | 1000/500 | 25/500 |
| Wilderness | 50/25 | 1000/500 | 25/200 |
| Scenic & special interest | 20/10 | 500/250 | 15/150 |
| Marine | 15/10 | 300/150 | n/a |

Take US$5 off the camping fees for nonresident children. The land-based parks and reserves charge KSh300 for vehicles with fewer than six seats and KSh1000 for vehicles seating six to 12. 'Special' campsites cost from US$15 to US$40 per adult nonresident, plus a KSh7500 weekly reservation fee. Guides are available in most parks for an additional fee.

All fees cover visitors for a 24-hour period, but if you leave and re-enter you must pay a re-entry fee at some parks, which will be between US$5 and US$20 less than the full entry fee.

Be aware that at some non-smartcard parks and reserves (not always KWS run) ticket guards will ask if you require a receipt. If not, they take your money (often with a discount) and then pocket the cash. Note that many unscrupulous drivers and safari guides are wise to this and just split your fee with the park guides without you being any the wiser.

See www.kws.org for further fee informaton for special activities, services and packages.

The most important national parks and reserves are shown in the accompanying table (opposite).

Entry fees to national parks are controlled by the **KWS** (Kenya Wildlife Service; ☎ 020-600800; www.kws.org; PO Box 40241, Nairobi), while some reserves, such as Masai Mara, are administered by the relevant local authority. See above for park categories and prices.

## ENVIRONMENTAL ISSUES

As a country with some of Africa's most spectacular national parks and reserves, and with some of the most amazing animals on earth, it is fortunate that environmental issues have grown in importance over the past few decades.

Four sites in Kenya are included on the Unesco World Heritage list: Mt Kenya, the Lake Turkana national parks, Lamu's Old Town and the Mijikenda *kayas* (sacred forests).

## Wildlife Conservation
### KENYA WILDLIFE SERVICE (KWS)
With a total ban on hunting imposed in the country in 1977, the KWS was free to concentrate solely on conserving Kenya's wildlife. This came just in time, as the 1970s and '80s were marred by a shocking amount of poaching, linked to the drought in Somalia, when hordes of poachers were driven across the border into Kenya by a lack of success in their own country. A staggering number of Kenya's rhinos and elephants were slaughtered and many KWS officers were in league with poachers, until the famous palaeontologist Dr Richard Leakey cleaned up the organisation in the 1980s and '90s. A core part of his policy was arming KWS rangers with modern weapons and high-speed vehicles and allowing them to shoot poachers on sight, which seems to have dramatically reduced the problem.

The East African Wildlife Society (www.eawildlife .org), based in Nairobi, is the most prominent conservation body in the region and a good source of information.

However, there have been several raids on elephant and rhino populations since 2001. As a result, there is now open talk of abandoning some of the more remote parks (such as those parks that are close to the Ethiopian or Somali borders) and concentrating resources in the parks that receive most visitors and where results can be achieved. At the same time, community conservation projects are being encouraged, and many community-owned ranches are now being opened up as private wildlife reserves, with the backing of both the KWS and international donors.

### PRIVATE CONSERVATION
It has been claimed that more than 75% of Kenya's wildlife lies outside the country's national parks and reserves, and there is little doubt that

### WANGARI MAATHAI, NOBEL LAUREATE
On Earth Day in 1977 Professor Wangari Maathai planted seven trees in her backyard, setting in motion the grass-roots environmental campaign that later came to be known as the Green Belt Movement. Since then, more than 40 million trees have been planted throughout Kenya and the movement has expanded to more than 30 other African countries. The core aim of this campaign is to educate women – who make up some 70% of farmers in Africa – about the link between soil erosion, undernourishment and poor health, and to encourage individuals to protect their immediate environment and guard against soil erosion by planting 'green belts' of trees and establishing tree nurseries.

Maathai, who served as Assistant Minister for the Environment between 2003 and 2005, has worked extensively with various international organisations to exert leverage on the Kenyan government, and was awarded the Nobel Peace Prize in 2004 (the first African woman to receive one) for her tireless campaigning on environmental issues. However, the Moi regime consistently vilified her as a 'threat to the order and security of the country', due to her demands for free and fair multiparty elections, and throughout the years her public demonstrations have been met with acts of violence and she has spoken of receiving death threats.

In addition to environmental issues she is also heavily involved in women's rights (her first husband divorced her because she was 'too strong-minded for a woman'; the judge in the divorce case agreed and then had her imprisoned for speaking out against him!), and in 2006 she was one of the founders of the Nobel Women's Initiative, which aims to bring justice, peace and equality to women. Maathai's personal views have also attracted controversy in some circles, particularly on the subject of AIDS, about which it's claimed that she said the syndrome was created by scientists for use in 'biological warfare' against blacks. However, she has denied making this statement.

Whatever her beliefs, Maathai is certainly a fascinating figure, and the Green Belt Movement is still one of the most significant environmental organisations in Kenya. Maathai's book *Unbowed: One Woman's Story* was published in 2006.

---

**THE START OF A BEAUTIFUL FRIENDSHIP?**

While other countries have been fighting a losing battle to preserve wildlife by separating animals and humans, local communities in parts of northern Kenya, like the Maasai of Il Ngwesi, Laikipia Maasai of Lekurruki and the Samburu within the Matthews Range, are actually increasing animal populations (and their own standard of living) by embracing peaceful cohabitation.

These communities treat wildlife as a natural resource and take serious action to protect the animals' well-being, whether by combating poaching with increased security or by modifying their herding activities to minimise human–animal conflict and environmental damage. With financial and logistical support from many sources, including Lewa Wildlife Conservancy (LWC), Laikipia Wildlife Forum (LWF) and the Northern Ranchlands Trust (NRT), these communities have built the magical ecolodges whose income now provides much-needed funds for their education, health and humanitarian projects.

The pioneering doesn't stop there. The LWF and NRT also coordinate wildlife conservancy on large private ranches and small farms (in northern Kenya and on the Laikipia Plateau), hoping to spark more sustainable development projects and further improve local standards of living. If these brave projects continue to prove that humans and wildlife can not only live in the same environment but actually thrive from the mutual relationship, an amazing precedent will be set.

---

the future of conservation in Kenya lies in private hands. Lewa Wildlife Conservancy (p232), near Isiolo, is probably the best known, and most successful, private reserve. Private wildlife reserves often have the resources to work more intensively on specific conservation issues than national parks and reserves can, and it is no accident that some of the largest concentrations of rhinos are within these areas.

The **Laikipia Wildlife Forum** (LWF; ☎ 0726500260; www.laikipia.org) is an umbrella organisation that represents many lodges and conservation areas in Laikipia, the large slab of ranch land northwest of Mt Kenya. Ranches in this area are particularly active in wildlife conservation, and the LWF is a good source of up-to-date information about projects and accommodation in the region. Other private game ranches and conservation areas can be found around the Tsavo (East and West, though mainly West) and Amboseli National Parks.

## Deforestation

More than half of Africa's forests have been destroyed over the last century, and forest destruction continues on a large scale in parts of Kenya – today, less than 3% of the country's original forest cover remains. Land grabbing, charcoal burning, agricultural encroachment, as well as illegal logging, have all taken their toll over the years. However, millions of Kenyans still rely on wood and charcoal for cooking fuel, so travellers to the country will almost certainly contribute to this deforestation, whether they like it or not.

The degazetting of protected forests is another contentious issue, sparking widespread protests and preservation campaigns. On the flipside, locals in forest areas can find themselves homeless if the government does enforce protection orders.

Despite these problems, some large areas of protected forest remain. The Mt Kenya, Mt Elgon and Aberdare National Parks, Kakamega Forest Reserve and Arabuko Sokoke Forest Reserve are all tremendous places to visit, packed with thousands of species of fauna and flora.

Native hardwood such as ebony and mahogany is often used to make the popular carved wooden statue souvenirs sold in Kenya. Though this industry supports thousands of local families who may otherwise be without

Want to be really green? Forget about flying to Kenya; go overland on public transport! Admittedly you'll need more than a fortnight but as well as reducing your carbon footprint you also get an adventure thrown in!

For a list of the disappointingly small number of Kenyan ecofriendly tour companies, contact the Ecotourism Society of Kenya (www.ecotourism kenya.org).

**KILLING THE GOOSE THAT LAID THE GOLDEN EGG**

Tourism is one of the biggest industries in Kenya and the vast majority of tourists come to see unsullied wild places and wildlife. So you might think that the Kenyan tourism industry would be a world leader when it comes to best environmental practices – sadly that is not the case. On the ecotourism of Kenya website (www.ecotourismkenya.org) only 29 establishments are listed as having been awarded an ecofriendly status (though a business does have to request that they are assessed), and in the course of research for this book only a handful of establishments were felt to be truly ecofriendly.

Few lodges and camps display sensitivity towards the environment in the running of their businesses. One especially bad example witnessed was workmen digging quantities of sand out of the banks of the Ewaso Ngiro River to be used in lodge construction! You will also find that very few lodges and camps have recycling systems, alternative energy sources or other environmental initiatives in place. Most also have gardens filled with beautiful, but non-native, plants, which can cause devastation to the local environment. There are, of course, exceptions and these have been noted in the text, though most of these top-end lodges suggest that you travel to them by air – not the most environmentally sound way of travelling, though often the easiest.

Bad practice isn't just limited to accommodation, as many safari companies and guides have questionable environmental records – don't be at all surprised to see your driver dropping rubbish out of the window. And then there are the tourists themselves – many people chase and harass animals in the pursuit of better photographs. Some scientists actually believe that many animals are now changing their habits in order to avoid the minibus circus in the national parks – cheetahs are starting to hunt in the middle of the day, when they have the least chance of making a kill but will encounter fewer people causing distractions.

As a visitor, the best way to help combat these problems is to be very selective about who you do business with and very vocal about the kind of standards you expect – see p93 for tips on minimal-impact safaris. The more that tourists insist on responsible practices, the more safari operators and hotels will take notice, and, while you may end up paying more for an ecofriendly trip, in the long term you'll be investing in a sustainable tourist industry and the preservation of Kenya's delicate environment.

We've included a GreenDex (p390) this book listing some of the more environmentally or socially aware businesses.

an income, it also consumes an estimated 80,000 trees annually. The WWF and Unesco campaigned to promote the use of common, faster-growing trees, and many handicraft cooperatives now use wood taken from forests managed by the Forest Stewardship Council. If you buy a carving, ask if the wood is sourced from managed forests.

## Tourism

The tourist industry, as well as being a saviour of Kenya's animals, is also the cause of some environmental problems, most notably the heavy use of firewood by tourist lodges and erosion caused by safari minibuses, which creates virtual dust bowls in parks such as Amboseli, Samburu and Masai Mara. A number of operators were recently banned from the Mara for misdemeanours ranging from nonpayment of rent for tented camps to harassment of wildlife, but there are few signs that the ban is being enforced.

The KWS now insists that every new lodge and camp be designed in an ecofriendly manner. However, most lodges tend to be anything but environmentally sound. See the boxed text above for more.

# Safaris

*Safari* has to be one of the most evocative words ever to infiltrate the English language. In Kiswahili, safari quite literally means 'journey', though to eager visitors flocking to the Kenyan national parks, it means so much more. From inspiring visions of wildebeests fording raging rivers, and lions stalking their heedless prey through the savanna grass, to iridescent flamingos lining a salty shore at sunset, and the guilty thrill of watching vultures tear flesh and hyenas crunch through bone, a safari into the wild is untamed Africa at its finest.

Compared to other countries on the continent, Kenya is not always the cheapest destination for safaris. However, with its huge diversity of natural attractions, it is undeniably one of the most appealing. The well-developed travel industry also allows access to even the remotest areas with a minimum amount of effort. The biggest problem you're likely to face is simply choosing a trip, and the hardest thing you'll have to do is return to so-called civilisation afterwards.

With that said, there are quite literally hundreds of companies vying for your tourist buck, and it's worth remembering that not all the predators in Kenya walk on four legs. However, thanks in part to the number, variety and accessibility of its wildlife, Kenya's safari industry has become highly competitive, and caters to penny-pinching shoestringers, posh jet-setters and just about everyone else in between. While there is certainly no substitute for your own hard research, this chapter provides an overview to consider when planning a Kenyan safari.

> 'The hardest thing you'll have to do is return to so-called civilisation afterwards'

## PLANNING A SAFARI

### BOOKING

Many travellers prefer to get all the hard work done before they arrive in Kenya by booking from abroad, either through travel agents or directly with safari companies. This fairly common practice also ensures that you'll be able to secure a spot at the more famous lodges, especially during peak seasons when places start filling up months in advance. However, while most safari operators will take internet bookings, making arrangements with anyone other than a well-established midrange or top-end operator can be a risky business. If you're going for a budget option, you should certainly wait and do your research on the ground when you arrive.

If you want to book a safari once in Kenya, a good starting point is to visit one of the travel agents in Nairobi or Mombasa. However, allow at least a day to shop around, don't rush into any deals, and steer clear of any attempts of intimidation by touts or dodgy operators. The best way to ensure you get what you pay for is to decide exactly what you want, then visit the various companies in person and talk through the kind of package you're looking for. Unfortunately, more than a few travellers book the first safari that fits their budget, and end up feeling that they should have chosen something else.

### COSTS

Most safari operator quotes include park entrance fees, the costs of accommodation or tent rental, transport costs from the starting base to the park, and the costs of fuel plus a driver/guide for wildlife drives. However,

---

**WARNING: SAFARI SCAMS**

Every year we get numerous letters from readers complaining about bad experiences on safari, such as dodging park fees and ignoring client requests, to pure rip-offs and outright criminal behaviour. For the most part, these incidents are perpetrated by Nairobi's budget companies, which shave every possible corner to keep their costs down. With this in mind, we can only reinforce just how important it is to take care when booking a safari, particularly at the budget level.

One persistent feature of Kenya's safari scene is the street tout, who will approach you almost as soon as you step out of your hotel in the streets of Nairobi and Mombasa. They're not all bad guys, and the safari you end up with may be fine, but you'll pay a mark-up to cover their commission, and the constant hard sell can be exasperating. On the plus side, many will take you around to several companies, and if you want to do a quick circuit of the budget operators, they can actually be quite helpful.

We can't stress enough how important it is to not rush your booking. Talk to travellers, do as much research as possible, insist on setting out every detail of your trip in advance, don't be pressured into anything and don't pay any substantial amounts of cash up front. If in doubt, think seriously about stretching your budget to use a reputable midrange firm. The budget companies listed in this chapter are 'reliable' in that they have been operating under the same name for years, but satisfaction is by no means guaranteed whoever you go with.

Of course, we receive plenty of positive feedback as well, so don't let potential problems put you off entirely. Indeed, one of the highlights of any trip to Africa is a wildlife safari, so it's certainly worth making the effort to book one – just keep your wits about you, and make it clear from the start that you won't take any crap from anyone!

---

this varies enough that it's essential to clarify before paying. Drinks (whether alcoholic or not) are generally excluded, and budget camping safari prices usually exclude sleeping-bag hire. Prices quoted by agencies or operators usually assume shared (double) room/tent occupancy, with supplements for single occupancy ranging from 20% to 50% of the shared-occupancy rate.

If you are dealing directly with lodges and tented camps rather than going through a safari operator, you may be quoted 'all-inclusive' prices. In addition to accommodation, full board and sometimes park fees, these usually include two 'activities' (usually wildlife drives, or sometimes one wildlife drive and one walk) per day, each lasting about two to three hours. They generally exclude transport costs to the park. Whenever accommodation-only prices apply, you'll need to pay extra to actually go out looking for wildlife. Costs for this vary considerably, and can range from about US$30 per person per day per 'activity' to US$200 per vehicle per day for a wildlife drive.

## Budget Safaris

Most safaris at the lower end of the price range are camping safaris. In order to keep costs to a minimum, groups often camp outside national park areas (thereby saving park admission and camping fees) or – alternatively – stay in budget guest houses outside the park. Budget operators also save costs by working with larger groups to minimise per-person transport costs, and by keeping to a no-frills set-up with basic meals and a minimum number of staff. For most safaris at the budget level, as well as for many midrange safaris, daily kilometre limits are placed on the vehicles.

For any budget safari, the bare minimum cost for a registered company is about US$75 to US$100 per person per day, which should include transport, food (three meals per day), park entry and camping fees, tents and cooking equipment. Sleeping-bag hire will cost you an additional US$10 to US$15 for the duration of the trip.

## Midrange Safaris

Most midrange safaris use lodges, where you'll have a comfortable room and eat in a restaurant. Overall, safaris in this category are reliable and reasonably good value. A disadvantage is that they may have somewhat of a packaged-tour or production-line feel. This can be minimised by selecting a safari company and accommodation carefully, by giving attention to who and how many other people you travel with, and by avoiding the large, popular lodges during peak season.

The prices for staying in lodges or tented camps are considerably higher on the whole. In high season you're looking at US$150 to US$200 per person per night in the lodges, though these prices do drop a bit in the low season. Again, if you want a room to yourself there's usually a supplement of around 25%, although it can be as high as 50%.

## Top-End Safaris

Private lodges, luxury tented camps and even private fly-in camps are used in top-end safaris, all with the aim of providing guests with as 'authentic' and personal a bush experience as possible without foregoing the creature comforts. For the price you pay (from US$200 up to US$600 or more per person per day), expect a full range of amenities, as well as top-quality guiding. Even in remote settings without running water you will be able to enjoy hot, bush-style showers, comfortable beds and fine dining. Also expect a high level of personalised attention and an intimate atmosphere – many places at this level have fewer than 20 beds.

In addition to the 'Big Five' (elephants, lions, leopards, buffaloes and rhinos), there's also the 'Little Five' (elephant shrews, ant lions, leopard tortoises, buffalo weavers and rhino beetles).

## Tipping

Assuming service has been satisfactory, tipping is an important part of the safari experience, especially to the driver/guides, cooks and others whose livelihoods depend on tips. Many operators have tipping guidelines, though in general you can expect to tip about US$3 to US$5 per staff member per day from each traveller. This value should increase substantially if you're on a top-end safari, part of a large group or if an especially good job has been done.

Also, it's never a mistake to err on the side of generosity while tipping. Remember that other travellers are going to follow you and the last thing anyone wants to find is a disgruntled driver/guide who couldn't care less whether you see wildlife or not.

## WHAT TO BRING

Any organised safari will provide camping gear or accommodation and all meals. You may have to provide your own drinking water, and alcohol is almost always extra; bringing your own can reduce costs. Sleeping bags can usually be hired from your safari company or local outfitters. If you're planning to attempt the Mt Kenya trek, it's probably worth bringing a decent bag from home.

You'll need enough clothing and footwear for hot days and cold nights, but the amount of baggage you'll be allowed will be limited. Excess gear can usually be stored at the safari company's offices. Don't forget to bring a pocket knife and a torch (flashlight) – the company will provide kerosene lanterns for the camp, but it's unlikely they'll be left on all night.

'Luxury' items such as toilet paper and mosquito nets are generally not provided. Mosquito nets can often be hired and insect repellent, skin cream and mosquito coils are always a good idea. There are few shops in the bush, so sanitary products, medicines and other important items should all be brought with you.

---

**SAFARI STYLE**

While price can be a major determining factor in safari planning, there are other considerations that are just as important:

- **Ambience** Will you be staying in or near the park? (If you stay well outside the park, you'll miss the good early-morning and evening wildlife-viewing hours.) Are the surroundings atmospheric? Will you be in a large lodge or an intimate private camp?

- **Equipment** Mediocre vehicles and equipment can significantly detract from the experience, and, in remote areas, lack of quality and appropriate back-up arrangements can be a safety risk.

- **Access and activities** If you don't relish the idea of hours in a 4WD on bumpy roads, consider areas offering walking and boat safaris.

- **Guides** A good driver/guide can make or break your safari. Staff at reputable companies are usually knowledgeable and competent. Staff at operators trying to cut corners are possibly unfairly paid, and are not likely to be knowledgeable or motivated.

- **Community commitment** Look for operators who do more than just give lip service to ecotourism principles, and who have a commitment to the communities where they work.

- **Setting the agenda** Some drivers feel that they have to whisk you from one good 'sighting' to the next. If you prefer to stay in one strategic place for a while to experience the environment and see what comes by, discuss this with your driver.

- **Extracurriculars** It's not uncommon for drivers to stop at souvenir shops. While this does give the driver an often much-needed break from the wheel, most shops pay drivers commissions to bring clients, which means you may find yourself spending more time souvenir shopping than you'd bargained for. If you're not interested, discuss this with your driver at the outset.

- **Less is more** If you'll be teaming up with others to make a group, find out how many people will be in your vehicle, and try to meet your travelling companions before setting off.

- **Special interests** If bird-watching or other special interests are important, arrange a private safari with a specialised operator.

---

## WHEN TO GO

Wildlife can be seen at all times of year, but the migration patterns of the big herbivores (which in turn attract the big predators) are likely to be a major factor in deciding when to go. From July to October, huge herds of wildebeest and zebras cross from the Serengeti in Tanzania to the Masai Mara, and Amboseli also receives huge herds at this time. This is probably prime viewing time as the land is parched, the vegetation has died back and the animals are obliged to come to drink at the ever-shrinking waterholes. However, most safari companies increase their rates at this time.

The long rains (from March to June) and short rains (from October to November) transform the national parks into a lush carpet of greenery. It's very scenic, but it does provide much more cover for the wildlife to hide behind, and the rain can turn the tracks into impassable mush. Safaris may be impossible in the lowland parks during either rainy season.

## ITINERARIES

Most itineraries offered by safari companies fall into one of three loosely defined 'circuits', which can all be combined for longer trips. Treks up Mt Kenya (p211) are a fourth option, sold separately or as an add-on, and the majority of firms now also offer trips into Tanzania and Uganda. A few tour operators also take in Kenya's western circuit, which includes Kakamega Forest Reserve (p187) and Mt Elgon (p195).

When planning your safari, don't be tempted to try to fit too much in to your itinerary. Distances in Kenya are long, and hopping too quickly from park to park is likely to leave you at the end tired, unsatisfied and feeling that you haven't even scratched the surface. Try instead to plan longer periods at just one or two parks – exploring in depth what each has to offer, and taking advantage of cultural and walking opportunities in park border areas.

### The Mara Circuit

The standard itineraries pushed on visitors by most companies are three- to seven-day safaris from Nairobi to the Masai Mara (p171). The shorter versions generally involve two nights in the park and two half-days travelling, while the longer trips include stops at Lake Nakuru (p162) and Samburu National Reserve (p234). You also have the option of visiting Lakes Baringo (p165) and Bogoria (p164) while in this region.

### The Southern Circuit

Offered as the main alternative to the Mara, southern itineraries make a beeline for Amboseli National Park (p137) and its famous Kilimanjaro backdrop. Anything longer than a three-day trip here should allow you to also visit Tsavo West (p140), with a couple more days required to add on Tsavo East (p144) as well. Most companies will give you the option of being dropped in Mombasa at the end of this route rather than heading back to Nairobi, which saves you a bit of travelling, and has the added benefit of allowing you time to explore the marine parks and other attractions of the coast.

Although weighty, *The Safari Companion - A Guide to Watching African Mammals*, by Richard Estes, is an excellent and indispensable guide to many of the animals you'll see on safari.

### The Northern Circuit

The focal point of any northern safari is Lake Turkana (p245), which requires at least a week to visit effectively due to the long distances involved. Depending on how long you take, and which side of the lake you visit, possible stops include Lake Bogoria (p164), Lake Baringo (p165), Marsabit National Park (p239), Samburu National Reserve (p234) and Maralal (p242) – a two-week safari could even cover all of these.

# BOOKING A SAFARI

## SERVICE & FEEDBACK

The service provided by even the best safari companies can vary, depending on the driver, the itinerary, the behaviour of the wildlife, flat tyres and breakdowns and, of course, the attitude of the passengers themselves. It's possible for a good company to provide a bad safari and for bad companies to shine occasionally. It's also a volatile market and a company that has a good reputation one year can go to the dogs the next. We've tried to recommend some of the better companies later in this chapter, but this shouldn't take the place of hands-on research once you arrive in the country.

It's worth getting in touch with the **Kenyan Association of Tour Operators** (KATO; ☎ 020-713348; www.katokenya.org) before making a booking. It may not be the most powerful regulatory body in the world, but most reputable safari companies subscribe, and going with a KATO member will give you *some* recourse in case of conflict. Accreditation by the **Kenya Professional Safari Guides Association** (KPSGA; ☎ 020-609355; www.safariguides.org; PO Box 24397, Nairobi) is also a good indicator of quality. On the ethical side, the **Ecotourism Society of Kenya** (ESOK; ☎ 020-2724755;

---

**ANIMAL-SPOTTING**

When you visit Kenya's parks and reserves, you'll be spending a lot of time craning your neck and keeping watchful eyes out for animals and birds. There are a few telltale signs to note, as well as a few things you can do to maximise your chances of spotting the Big Five. Most are just common sense.

The best time to see wildlife is between 6.30am and 9.30am, and from 3.30pm to 6.30pm. Make sure your safari company takes you out during these times. Wildlife drives in the middle of the day are unlikely to turn up much, although there are signs that in the popular parks (such as Amboseli and Masai Mara), animals are actually changing their normal hunting habits to avoid the tourists. When the tourists head back to the lodges for lunch, the carnivores go out hunting – in peace.

In wooded country, agitated and noisy monkeys or baboons are often a sign that there's a big cat (probably a leopard) around. Vultures circling are not necessarily an indication of a kill below. But if they are gathering in trees, and seem to be watching something, you can reasonably assume they are waiting their turn for a go at a carcass.

One final note – taking a longer safari is great, but endless long days peering out of a sunroof, on bumpy roads, in the heat, eating the same food, stuck with the same people, can take its toll quicker than you might think. Any animal you see on the first day will be exciting, though sooner or later most travellers will experience safari fatigue, that jaded feeling of 'not another zebra, I wanna see a freaking leopard!' If this happens, a few cultural activities, an afternoon's relaxation or even just a quick swim can do wonders for keeping things fresh.

---

www.ecotourismkenya.org) also maintains a list of member companies who subscribe to its code of conduct for responsible, sustainable safaris.

One thing to look out for whichever company you book with is client swapping. Quite a few companies shift clients on to other companies if they don't have enough people to justify running the trip themselves. This ensures that trips actually depart on time, and saves travellers days of waiting, but it does undermine consumer trust. Reputable companies will usually inform you before they transfer you. In any case, it may not be the end of the world if you end up taking your safari with a different company; just make sure the safari you booked and paid for is what you get.

The brochures for some safari companies may give the impression that they offer every conceivable safari under the sun, but in fact, many companies also advertise trips run by other companies. While it's not the most transparent way to do business, again, it needn't be the end of the world. A reliable company will normally choose reliable partners, and you're only really likely to come unstuck at the budget end of the market. Sadly, the only way some of the shoddier operators can get business is through touts, and these companies employ all sorts of tricks to cut costs, including not maintaining their vehicles, entering national parks through side entrances to avoid fees, and employing glorified matatu 6drivers with little knowledge of the wildlife as guides.

Be particularly careful of safari companies in Nairobi. Some of these guys don't actually run *any* of their own safaris, and are basically just travel agents. If you book with one of these operators and anything goes wrong, or the itinerary is changed without your agreement, you have very little comeback, and it'll be virtually impossible to get a refund. Unfortunately, it's often hard to tell which are genuine safari companies and which are agents. If you want to know who you're dealing with throughout, go with one of the more expensive agents and confirm exactly who will be operating which parts of the trip, particularly if you are detouring to Tanzania or Uganda.

We welcome all feedback on your safari experiences and will try to incorporate it into future editions of this book.

## CAMPING SAFARIS

Camping safaris cater for budget travellers, the young (or young at heart) and those who are prepared to put up with a little discomfort to get the authentic bush experience. At the bottom of the price range, you'll have to forgo luxuries such as flush toilets, running water and cold drinks, and you'll have to chip in to help with chores such as putting up the tents and helping prepare dinner. Showers are provided at some but not all campsites, although there's usually a tap where you can scrub down with cold water. The price of your safari will include three meals a day cooked by the camp cook(s), although food will be of the plain-but-plenty variety.

There are more comfortable camping options, where there are extra staff to do all the work, but they cost more. A number of companies have also set up permanent campsites in the Masai Mara and Samburu National Reserves where you can just drop into bed at the end of a dusty day's drive. At the top end of this market are some very plush luxury campsites offering hot showers and big permanent tents fitted with mosquito nets, beds and sheets, about as far from real camping as five-star hotels are from youth hostels. See p72 for companies using these kinds of sites.

'Few things can match the thrill of waking up in the middle of the African bush'

Whatever you pay, you'll end up hot, tired and dusty at the end of the day, but you'll sleep well, and if you're lucky, your travelling companions should be like-minded independent souls with a sense of adventure. Few things can match the thrill of waking up in the middle of the African bush with nothing between you and the animals except a sheet of canvas and the dying embers of last night's fire. Be aware, however, that it's not unusual for elephants or hippos to trundle through the camp at night, and people have been maimed or killed in the past in Kenya's national parks.

Reliable companies offering camping safaris at the time of writing included the following:

**Basecamp Explorer** (off Map pp100–1; ☎ 020-577490; www.basecampexplorer.com; Ole Odume Rd, Hurlingham, Nairobi) An excellent Scandinavian-owned ecotourism operator offering comprehensive camping itineraries in Samburu, Lake Nakuru and the Masai Mara, with walking at Mt Kenya, Lake Bogoria and Lake Baringo. The firm also has its own luxury site in the Masai Mara and runs plenty of high-end conservation-based safaris, including trips to Lamu, Tanzania, Mt Kenya and Kilimanjaro.

**Best Camping Tours** (Map pp104–5; ☎ 020-229667; www.bestcampingkenya.com; I&M Towers, Kenyatta Ave, Nairobi) This company offers budget camping safaris on all the main routes, including Amboseli, Masai Mara and Tsavo West (four days). Longer safaris visit various combinations of Amboseli, Tsavo West, the Rift Valley lakes, Masai Mara, Mt Kenya, Samburu and Lake Nakuru. It also runs trips into Tanzania.

**Bushbuck Adventures** (off Map pp100–1; ☎ 020-7121505; www.bushbuckadventures.com; Peponi Rd, Westlands, Nairobi) Bushbuck is a small company specialising in personalised safaris. It has a private, semipermanent camp in the northwest corner of the Masai Mara. As a result, it's relatively expensive, though company profits are put into conservation projects. The company is also strong on walking safaris throughout the country.

**Eastern & Southern Safaris** (Map pp104–5; ☎ 020-242828; www.essafari.co.ke; Finance House, Loita St, Nairobi) A classy and reliable outfit aiming at the midrange and upper end of the market, with standards to match. Classic Kenyan trips as well as safaris in Tanzania and Uganda are available. Departures are guaranteed with just two people for some itineraries.

**Gametrackers** (Map pp104–5; ☎ 020-338927; www.gametrackersafaris.com; Nginyo Towers, cnr Koinange & Moktar Daddah Sts, Nairobi) Long established and very reliable, this company offers a full range of camping and lodge safaris around Kenya, including routes in the remote Lake Turkana, short excursions to Nairobi National Park, walking treks in Aberdare National Park, Mt Kenya treks and numerous long-haul trips to Tanzania, Uganda and further afield.

**Let's Go Travel** (Map pp104–5; ☎ 020-340331; www.lets-go-travel.net; Caxton House, Standard St, Nairobi) This popular travel agent runs its own safaris and excursions, and also sells on an amazing range of trips from other companies, covering Tanzania, Uganda, Ethiopia and even the

Seychelles, as well as plenty of specialist and remote options in Kenya itself. Prices are on the high side for camping, but the scope justifies the expense, and it's also a good port of call for unusual lodge safaris and car hire. Note, however, that we have received mixed reports from travellers, so it might be worth checking around before you part with your cash.

**Safari Seekers** (www.safari-seekerskenya.com) Mombasa (Map p260; ☎ 041-220122; Diamond Trust Arcade, Moi Ave); Nairobi (Map pp104–5; ☎ 020-652315/6; Jubilee Insurance Exchange Bldg, Kaunda St) This budget company, which has been operating for a number of years now, has its own permanent campsites in Amboseli, Samburu and Masai Mara, and runs camping and lodge safaris in Kenya, Tanzania and Uganda. Departures are at least once a week, or any time with at least four people. Safari Seekers also offers air safaris to Amboseli and Masai Mara with accommodation at luxury lodges or tented camps.

**Safe Ride Tours & Safaris** (Map pp104–5; ☎ 020-253129; www.saferidesafaris.com; Ave House, Kenyatta Ave, Nairobi) A relatively new budget operator consistently recommended by readers for its camping excursions. This operator can also arrange minor conveniences such as airport transfers, car rentals and flight tickets to East African destinations as far flung as Zanzibar.

**Sana Highlands Trekking Expeditions** (Map pp104–5; ☎ 020-227820; www.sanatrekking kenya.com; Contrust House, Moi Ave, Nairobi) A big budget player that has had a good reputation in the past for walking safaris and trekking trips to some of Kenya's more remote parks. It also offers the usual camping and lodge itineraries.

**Savuka Tours & Safaris** (Map pp104–5; ☎ 020-225108; www.savuka-travels.com; Pan African House, Kenyatta Ave, Nairobi) Another big-budget operator with tented camps on the edges of the national parks. Mara, Amboseli, Lake Nakuru and Samburu itineraries are available.

**Special Camping Safaris Ltd** ( ☎ 020-3540720; scs@iconnect.co.ke; Whistling Thorns, Isinya/ Kiserian Pipeline Rd, Kiserian) This small family-run company offers good trips to Masai Mara, the Rift Valley, Lakes Naivasha, Nakuru, Bogoria and Baringo, Maralal, Samburu and the Mt Kenya foothills. Group sizes are small and manageable, which leads to a personalised experience.

## LODGE & TENTED-CAMP SAFARIS

'there's a world of luxurious lodges with swimming pools and bars overlooking waterholes'

If you can't do without luxuries, there's another side to the safari business – a world of luxurious lodges with swimming pools and bars overlooking waterholes, and remote tented camps that re-create the way wealthy hunters travelled around Kenya a century ago. Some of the lodges are beautifully conceived and the locations are to die for, perched high above huge sweeps of savanna or water holes teeming with African wildlife. Most are set deep within the national parks, so the safari drives offer maximum wildlife-viewing time. And thankfully, most of the environmental bad habits of the previous decades (such as leopard baiting) have fallen out of favour.

In the lodges you can expect rooms with bathrooms or cottages with airconditioning, international cuisine, a terrace bar beneath a huge *makuti* (palm-thatched) canopy with wonderful views, a swimming pool, wildlife videos and other entertainments, and plenty of staff on hand to cater for all your requirements. Almost all lodges have a waterhole, and some have a hidden viewing tunnel that leads right to the waterside. Some also put out salt to tempt animals to visit, a dubious habit that really shouldn't be encouraged.

The luxury-tented camps tend to offer semipermanent tents with fitted bathrooms (hot showers come as standard), beds with mosquito nets, proper furniture, fans and gourmet meals served alfresco in the bush. The really exclusive ones are even more luxurious than the lodges, and tend to be *very* expensive: many of the guests fly in on charter planes, which should give you some impression of the kind of budget we're talking about.

Some camping safari companies also provide lodge-based safaris. The following are reliable and have been around for years. Most are members of KATO. In and around Mombasa, most bookings are done through hotels.

*(Continued on page 89)*

# WILDLIFE & HABITAT David Lukas

When you think of East Africa the word *safari* comes to mind – and Kenya is where it all began. From the year-long safari undertaken by US President Theodore Roosevelt in 1909, to Joy Adamson's portrayal of the lioness Elsa in *Born Free*, to Karen Blixen's sweeping tale *Out of Africa*, Kenya forms the centrepiece of our popular image of Africa. And for good reason – it is one of the top places in the world to see wildlife. You will never forget the shimmering carpets of zebras and wildebeest, the ferocious explosion of cheetahs springing from cover, or the spine-tingling roars of lions at night. Even better, Kenya offers unlimited opportunities for independent travellers.

# Cats

In terms of behaviour, the six common cats of Kenya are little more than souped-up housecats; it's just that some weigh half as much as a horse and others jet along as fast as a speeding car. With their excellent vision and keen hearing, cats are superb hunters. And some of the most stunning scenes in Africa are the images of big cats making their kills. If you happen across one of these events you won't easily forget the energy and ferocity of these life-and-death struggles.

### ① Cheetah
Weight 40-60kg; length 200-220cm Less cat than greyhound, the cheetah is a world-class sprinter. Although it reaches 112km/h, the cheetah runs out of steam after 300m and must cool down for 30 minutes before hunting again. This speed comes at another cost – the cheetah is so well adapted for running that it lacks the strength and teeth to defend its food or cubs from attack by other large predators.

### ② Lion
Weight 120-150kg (female), 150-225kg (male); length 210-275cm (female), 240-350cm (male) Those lions sprawled out lazily in the shade are actually Africa's most feared predators. Equipped with teeth that tear effortlessly through bone and tendon they can take down an animal as large as a bull giraffe. Each group of adults (a pride) is based around generations of females who do all the hunting; the swaggering males fight amongst themselves and eat what the females catch.

### ③ Caracal
Weight 8-19kg; length 80-120cm The caracal is a gorgeous tawny cat with extremely long, pointy ears. This African version of the northern lynx has jacked-up hind legs like a feline dragster. These beanpole kickers enable this slender cat to make vertical leaps of 3m and swat birds out of the air.

### ④ Leopard
Weight 30-60kg (female), 40-90kg (male); length 170-300cm More common than you realise, the leopard relies on expert camouflage to stay hidden. During the day you might only spot one reclining in a tree after it twitches its tail, but at night there is no mistaking their bone-chilling groans, which sound like wood being sawn at high volume.

### ⑤ Wildcat
Weight 3-6.5kg; length 65-100cm If you see what looks like a tabby wandering the plains of Kenya you're likely seeing a wildcat, the direct ancestor of our domesticated housecat. Occurring wherever there are abundant mice and rats, the wildcat is readily found on the outskirts of villages, where it can be best identified by its unmarked rufous ears and longish legs.

### ⑥ Serval
Weight 6-18kg; length 90-130cm Twice as large as a housecat but with long legs and very large ears, the beautifully spotted serval is adapted for walking in tall grass and making prodigious leaps to catch rodents and birds. More diurnal than most cats, it may be seen tossing food in the air and playing with it.

# Primates

East Africa is the evolutionary cradle of primate diversity, giving rise to over 30 species of monkeys, apes and prosimians (the 'primitive' ancestors of modern primates). Somewhere along the way, one branch of the family tree apparently teetered onto the path that gave rise to humans – a controversial hypothesis supported by Leakey's famous excavations at Olduvai Gorge. No matter what you believe, it is possible to see hints of human society in the complex social lives of Kenya's many primates.

### ❶ Vervet Monkey
Weight 4-8kg; length 90-140cm If any monkey epitomises the African savanna it would be the widespread and adaptable vervet monkey. Each troop of vervets is composed of females who defend a home range passed down from generation to generation, while males fight each other for bragging rights and access to females. If you think their appearance too drab, check out the extraordinary blue and scarlet colours of their sexual organs when aroused.

### ❷ Black-and-White Colobus
Weight 10-23kg; length 115-165cm Also known as the guereza, the black-and-white colobus is one of Kenya's most popular primates, due to the flowing white bonnets of hair arrayed across its black body. Like all colobus, this agile primate has a hook-shaped hand, so it can swing through the trees with the greatest of ease. When two troops run into each other expect to see a real show.

### ❸ Olive Baboon
Weight 11-30kg (female), 22-50kg (male); length 95-180cm Although the formidable olive baboon has 5cm-long fangs and can kill a leopard, its best defence may consist of running up trees and showering intruders with liquid excrement. Either way, you won't want to alarm this animal. Intelligent and opportunistic, troops of these greenish baboons are common in western Kenya, while much paler yellow baboons range over the eastern half of the country.

### ❹ De Brazza's Monkey
Weight 4-8kg; length 90-135cm Riverside forests of west-central Kenya are home to this rare and colourful monkey, one of the country's many types of arboreal monkeys. Despite glaring red eyebrows and big bushy white beards, de Brazza's monkeys are surprisingly inconspicuous, due to their grizzled upperparts and habit of sitting motionless for up to eight hours. In the early morning and late afternoon they ascend to higher branches to eat fruit and sunbathe.

### ❺ Lesser Galago
Weight 100-300g; length 40cm A squirrel-sized nocturnal creature with doglike face and huge eyes, the lesser galago belongs to a group of prosimians that have changed little in 60 million years. Best known for its frequent bawling cries (hence the common name 'bushbaby'), the galago would be rarely seen except that it readily visits feeding stations at many popular safari lodges. Living in a world of darkness, galagos communicate with each other through scent and sound.

# Cud-chewing Mammals

Africa is arguably most famous for its astounding variety of ungulates – hoofed mammals that include everything from buffaloes to giraffes and rhinos. Many of these animals live in herds, in order to protect themselves from the continent's formidable predators, with some herds numbering in the millions. Ungulates who ruminate (chew their cud) and have horns are called bovines. Among this family, antelope are particularly numerous, with about 40 amazingly different species in East Africa alone.

### ❶ Waterbuck

Weight 160-300kg; length 210-275cm If you're going to see any antelope on safari, it's likely to be the big, shaggy and, some say, smelly waterbuck. Dependent on waterside vegetation, waterbuck numbers fluctuate dramatically between wet and dry years.

### ❷ Wildebeest

Weight 140-290kg; length 230-340cm Few animals evoke the spirit of the African plain as much as the wildebeest. Over a million gather on the Masai Mara alone, where they form vast, constantly moving herds accompanied by a host of predators and gaggles of wide-eyed tourists.

### ❸ Gerenuk

Weight 30-50kg; length 160-200cm The gerenuk is one of the strangest creatures you'll ever see – a tall slender gazelle with a giraffelike neck. Adapted for life in semi-arid brush, the gerenuk stands on its hind legs to reach 2m-high branches.

### ❹ Greater Kudu

Weight 120-315kg; length 215-300cm The oxen-sized greater kudu is a study in elegance. One of the tallest antelope, it relies on white pinstripes to conceal it in brushy thickets. The very long spiralling horns of the male are used in ritualised combat.

### ❺ Kirk's Dikdik

Weight 4-5kg; length 35-40cm When you're scarcely larger than a hare you need some clever ways to protect yourself from your many predators. This tiny savanna antelope with an inflated nose lives in dense thickets and marks out escape routes with the scent glands on its face.

### ❻ Gazelle

Weight 15-35kg; length 95-150cm Lanky and exceptionally alert, Thomson's and Grant's gazelles are two extremely similar long-legged antelope built for speed. In southern Kenya an estimated 400,000 migrate in great herds, along with zebras and wildebeest. Look for their attractive black flank stripes.

### ❼ Hartebeest

Weight 120-220kg; length 190-285cm Yes the long face of the hartebeest (kongoni) is an odd sight, but it helps this short-necked antelope reach grass to graze on. Commonly seen on open plains, the hartebeest is easily recognised by its set of backward-twisted horns.

### ❽ African Buffalo

Weight 250-850kg; length 220-420cm Imagine a cow on steroids then add a particularly fearsome set of curling horns and you get the massive African buffalo. Thank goodness they're usually docile because an angry or injured buffalo is an extremely dangerous animal.

### ❾ Oryx

Weight 120-200kg; length 200-230cm With towering 1m-long straight horns and a boldly patterned face, this elegant creature is one of Kenya's most dramatic antelope. Exquisitely adapted for desert living, they can survive for months on the scant water in the plants they eat.

# Hoofed Mammals

A full stable of Africa's mega-charismatic animals can be found in this group of ungulates. Other than the giraffe, these ungulates are not ruminants and can be seen over a much broader range of habitats than bovines. They have been at home in Africa for millions of years and are among the most successful mammals to have ever wandered the continent. Without human intervention, Africa would be ruled by elephants, zebras, hippos and warthogs.

### ① Giraffe

Weight 450-1200kg (female), 1800-2000kg (male); height 3.5-5.2m The 5m-tall giraffe does such a good job with upward activity – reaching up to grab high branches, towering above the competition – that stretching down to get a simple drink of water is difficult. Though they stroll along casually, a healthy giraffe can outrun any predator.

### ② African Elephant

Weight 2200-3500kg (female), 4000-6300kg (male); height 2.4-3.4m (female), 3-4m (male) No one stands around to argue when a towering bull elephant rumbles out of the brush. Though the elephant is commonly referred to as 'the king of beasts', elephant society is actually ruled by a lineage of elder females.

### ③ Hippopotamus

Weight 510-3200kg; length 320-400cm The hippopotamus is one strange creature. Designed like a floating beanbag with tiny legs, the 3000kg hippo spends its time in or very near water chowing down on aquatic plants. Placid? No way! Hippos have tremendous ferocity and strength when provoked.

### ④ Plains Zebra

Weight 175-320kg; length 260-300cm My oh my, those plains zebras sure have some wicked stripes. Although each animal is as distinctly marked as a fingerprint, scientists still aren't sure what function these patterns serve. Do they help zebras recognise each other?

### ⑤ Rock Hyrax

Weight 1.8-5.5kg; length 40-60cm It doesn't seem like it, but those funny tail-less squirrels you see lounging around on rocks are an ancient cousin to the elephant. You won't see some of the features that rock hyraxes share with their larger kin, but look for tusks when one yawns.

### ⑥ Black Rhinoceros

Weight 700-1400kg; length 350-450cm Pity the black rhinoceros for having a horn worth more than gold. Once widespread and abundant south of the Sahara, the rhino has been poached to the brink of extinction. Unfortunately, females may only give birth every five years.

### ⑦ Warthog

Weight 45-75kg (female), 60-150kg (male); length 140-200cm Despite their fearsome appearance and sinister tusks, only the big males are safe from lions, cheetahs and hyenas. To protect themselves when attacked, warthogs run for burrows and reverse in while slashing wildly with their tusks.

# Carnivores

It is a sign of Africa's ecological richness that the continent supports a remarkable variety of predators. In addition to six common cats, Kenya's other two dozen carnivores range from slinky mongooses to social hunting dogs. All are linked in having carnassial (slicing) teeth, but visitors may be more interested in witnessing the superb prowess of these amazingly efficient hunters. When it comes to predators, expect the unexpected and you'll return home with a lifetime of memories!

### ❶ Spotted Hyena

Weight 40-90kg; length 125-215cm The spotted hyena is one of Kenya's most unusual animals. Living in packs ruled by females that grow penislike sexual organs, these savage fighters use their bone-crushing jaws to disembowel terrified prey on the run or to do battle with lions. The sight of maniacally giggling hyenas at a kill, piling on top of each other in their eagerness to devour hide, bone and internal organs, is unsettling.

### ❷ Common Genet

Weight 1-2kg; length 80-100cm Though nocturnal, these slender agile hunters are readily observed slinking along roadsides or scrambling among the rafters of safari lodges. Looking like a cross between a cat and a raccoon, genets are easily recognised by their cream-coloured bodies and leopard-like spotting. Genets mark their territories with urine and anal secretions up to 60 times an hour.

### ❸ Banded Mongoose

Weight 1.5-2kg; length 45-75cm Kenya's eight species of mongoose may be difficult to separate, but the common banded mongoose is easily recognised by its finely barred pattern and social nature. Bounding across the savanna on their morning foraging excursions, family groups are a delightful sight when they stand up on their hind legs for a better view of the world. Not particularly speedy, they find delicious snacks in toads, scorpions and slugs.

### ❹ Hunting Dog

Weight 20-35kg; length 100-150cm Uniquely patterned so that individuals recognise each other, hunting dogs run in packs of 20 to 60 to chase down antelope and other animals. Organised in complex hierarchies with strict rules of conduct, these social canids are incredibly efficient hunters. However, disease and persecution has pushed them into near-extinction and they now rank as one of Africa's foremost must-see animals.

### ❺ Golden Jackal

Weight 6-15kg; length 85-130cm It barks and yelps like a dog and looks like a mangy mutt but the golden jackal is one of Africa's scrappiest critters. Despite its trim, diminutive form, the jackal fearlessly stakes a claim at the dining table of the African plain. If not through sheer fierceness and bluff, then through tact and trickery, a jackal manages to fill its belly while holding hungry vultures and much stronger hyenas at bay.

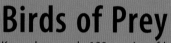

# Birds of Prey

Kenya has nearly 100 species of hawks, eagles, vultures and owls, ranging from the songbird-sized pygmy kestrel to the massive lammergeier, making this one of the best places in the world to see an incredible variety of birds of prey. Look for them perching on trees, soaring high overhead, or gathered around a carcass, though the scolding cries of small birds harassing one of these feared hunters may be your first clue to their presence.

4

### ❶ Lappet-faced Vulture

Length 115cm Seven of Kenya's eight vultures can be seen mingling with lions, hyenas and jackals around carcasses. Through sheer numbers they compete, often successfully, for scraps of flesh and bone. It's not a pretty sight when gore-encrusted vultures take over a carcass that no other scavenger wants, but it's the way nature works. The monstrous lappet-faced vulture, a giant among vultures, gets its fill before other vultures move in.

### ❷ Bateleur

Length 60cm The bateleur is an attractive serpent-eagle with a funny name. French for 'acrobat' or 'tumbler', the name refers to its distinctive low-flying aerial acrobatics. When it is in flight, look for this eagle's white wings and odd tail-less appearance; close up look for the bold colour pattern and scarlet face.

### ❸ Secretary Bird

Length 100cm In a country full of strange birds, the secretary bird literally stands head and shoulders above the masses. With the body of an eagle and the legs of a crane, the secretary bird stands 1.3m tall and walks up to 20km a day in search of vipers, cobras and other snakes, which it kills with lightning speed and agility. This idiosyncratic, grey-bodied raptor is commonly seen striding across the savanna.

### ❹ African Fish Eagle

Length 75cm Given its name, don't be surprised to see the African fish eagle hunting for fish around water. With a wingspan over 2m this replica of the American bald eagle presents an imposing appearance, but it is most familiar for its loud ringing vocalisations, which have become known as 'the voice of Africa'.

### ❺ Augur Buzzard

Length 55cm Perhaps Kenya's commonest raptor, the augur buzzard occupies a wide range of wild and cultivated habitats. Virtually identical to the red-tailed hawk of the Americas, this buzzard is sometimes called the African red-tailed hawk. One of their most successful hunting strategies is to float motionlessly in the air by riding the wind then swooping down quickly to catch unwary critters.

# Birds

Bird-watchers from all over the world travel to Kenya in search of the country's 1100 species of birds – an astounding number by any measure – including birds of every shape and colour imaginable. No matter where you travel in the country you will be enchanted and amazed by the ever-changing avian kaleidoscope.

### ❶ Ostrich

Height 200-270cm If you think the ostrich looks prehistoric, you're not far off. Standing 270cm and weighing upwards of 130kg, these ancient flightless birds escape predators by running away at 70km/h or lying flat on the ground to resemble a pile of dirt.

### ❷ Red-billed Oxpecker

Length 18cm The odd little red-billed oxpecker is a starling that sits on the backs of large mammals, where it eats 100 ticks a day. Any benefit to the animal is cancelled out, as the oxpecker keeps old wounds open in order to drink blood and pus.

### ❸ Superb Starling

Length 18cm The superb starling is a stellar example of the many birds in Kenya that slap together bright colours and call it a day. With black face, yellow eyes and metallic blue-green upper parts contrasting sharply with its red-orange belly, it seems like an exotic rarity, but is actually surprisingly abundant.

### ❹ Lilac-breasted Roller

Length 40cm Nearly everyone on safari gets to know the gorgeously coloured lilac-breasted roller. Related to the kingfisher, the roller gets its name from its tendency to 'roll' from side to side in flight as a way of showing off its iridescent blues, purples and greens.

### ❺ Lesser Flamingo

Length 1m Coloured deep rose-pink and gathering by the hundreds of thousands on shimmering salt lakes, the lesser flamingo creates some of the most dramatic wildlife spectacles found in Africa, especially when they all fly at once or perform synchronised courtship displays.

### ❻ Hamerkop

Length 60cm The hamerkop is a relative of the stork, with an oddly crested, cartoonish, woodpecker-like head. Nicknamed the 'hammerhead', it is frequently observed hunting frogs and fish at the water's edge. Look for its massive 2m-wide nests in nearby trees.

### ❼ Saddle-billed Stork

Height 150cm; wingspan 270cm Not only is the saddle-billed stork the most stunning of Kenya's eight stork species, it is also one of the more remarkably coloured of all the country's birds. As if the 270cm wingspan wasn't impressive enough, check out its brilliant red kneecaps and bill.

### ❽ Speckled Mousebird

Length 35cm Not every bird in Kenya is the biggest, best or most colourful. The gregarious speckled mousebird is none of those things, but it does attract attention due to its comical habit of hanging from branches and wires while resting or sleeping.

### ❾ Vulturine Guineafowl

Length 71cm Take an electric-blue chicken, drape black-and-white speckled feathers over its body and place an elegant ruff around its neck and you have a pretty flamboyant bird. Look for guineafowl walking around in large groups in semiarid areas.

# Habitats

Nearly all of Kenya's wildlife occupies a specific type of habitat, and you will hear rangers and fellow travellers refer to these habitats repeatedly as they describe where to search for animals. Your wildlife-viewing experience will be greatly enhanced if you learn how to recognise these habitats and the animals you might expect to find in each one.

### ❷ High Mountains

Kenya is remarkable for having extensive high-mountain habitats, including unexpected snowy crags and glaciers on the equator. The massive extinct volcanoes of Mt Elgon and Mt Kenya are islands of montane forest, bog, giant heather and moorland soaring above the surrounding lowlands. The few animals that survive here are uniquely adapted to these bizarre landscapes.

### ❶ Savanna

Savanna is *the* classic East African landscape – broad rolling grasslands dotted with lone acacia trees. The openness of this landscape makes it a perfect home for large herds of grazing zebras and wildebeest, in addition to fast-sprinting predators like cheetahs. Shaped by fire and grazing animals, savanna is a dynamic habitat in constant flux with adjacent woodlands.

### ❸ Semiarid Desert

Much of eastern and northern Kenya sees so little rainfall that shrubs and hardy grasses, rather than trees, are the dominant vegetation. Lack of water limits larger animals such as zebras, gazelles and antelope to waterholes but when it rains this habitat explodes with plant and animal life. During the dry season many plants shed their leaves to conserve water and grazing animals move on in search of food and water.

*(Continued from page 72)*

**Abercrombie & Kent** (Map p111; ☎ 020-6950000; www.abercrombiekent.com; Abercrombie & Kent House, Mombasa Rd, Nairobi) For more than five decades, Abercrombie & Kent has been regarded by international jet-setters as the world's premiere luxury travel company. You're going to have to pay to play with these guys, though A & K has a reputation for incredible luxury that is balanced with authenticity.

**Micato Safaris** (Map pp104–5; ☎ 020-220743; www.micato.com; View Park Towers, Monrovia St, Nairobi) A five-year winner of *Travel & Leisure*'s top safari operator, Micato is another big player on the top-end circuit. Check out its website, which lists high-end safari trips throughout East Africa that will pretty much blow your mind.

**Pollman's Tours & Safaris** (Map p111; ☎ 020-337234; www.pollmans.com; Pollman's House, Mombasa Rd, Nairobi) A Kenyan-based operator that specialises in individually catered safaris in its fleet of 4WDs. In addition to the heavy-hitting national parks, it also runs trips along the Mombasa coast and down into Tanzania.

**Private Safaris** (www.privatesafaris.co.ke) Mombasa ( ☎ 041-476000; Safari House, Kaunda St); Nairobi (Map p111; ☎ 020-554150; Twinstar Tower, Mombasa Rd) Another highly customisable safari agent, Private can book trips all throughout Sub-Saharan Africa. If you want to link your East African travels to another trip, let's say, Botswana and Namibia, these are your go-to guys.

**Somak Travel** (www.somak-nairobi.com) Mombasa ( ☎ 041-487349; Somak House, Nyerere Ave); Nairobi (Map p111; ☎ 020-535508; Somak House, Mombasa Rd) A Kenyan-based operator with more than 30 years of experience on the safari circuit, Somak is a home-grown favourite. It offers the usual in Kenyan classics as well as a few interesting Tanzanian options.

**Southern Cross Safaris** (www.southerncrosssafaris.com) Malindi (Map p297; ☎ 042-30547; Malindi Centre, Lamu Rd); Mombasa ( ☎ 041-475074; Kanstan Centre, Nyali Bridge, Malindi Rd); Nairobi (Map p109; ☎ 020-884712; Symbion House, Karen Rd) An extremely professional Kenyan-specialist company, Southern Cross is a good choice for individually designed safaris. You can choose from its suggested tours, or design one that meets your specific needs.

**United Touring Company** (UTC; www.utc.co.ke) Mombasa ( ☎ 041-316333; Moi Ave); Nairobi (Map pp104–5; ☎ 020-331960; Fedha Towers, Kaunda St) With more than five decades of experience in the Kenyan market, UTC has expanded its operations into Tanzania, Uganda and even Ethiopia. However, its bread and butter remains specialised safaris throughout its Kenyan homelands.

## SPECIALIST SAFARIS
### Bird-Watching Safaris

Most of the safari companies listed in this chapter offer some kind of bird-watching safaris, though the quality is not always up to par for serious birders. For the very best Kenya has to offer, contact **Origins Safaris** (Map pp104–5; ☎ 020-312137; www.originsafaris.info; Fedha Towers, Standard St, Nairobi), originally set up as East African Ornithological Safaris by one of the best ornithologists in Kenya. The company offers one- to two-week specialist bird-watching extravaganzas that take in Mt Kenya, the Rift Valley lakes, Kakamega Forest Reserve, the Masai Mara National Reserve and Lake Victoria. Top-class lodges are used throughout this trip, and there are monthly departures throughout the year.

*Birds of Kenya and Northern Tanzania,* by Dale Zimmerman, Donald Turner & David Pearson, is an essential field guide for birders.

### Camel Safaris

This is a superb way of getting right off the beaten track and into areas where vehicle safaris don't or can't go. Most camel safaris go to the Samburu and Turkana tribal areas between Isiolo and Lake Turkana, and you'll have a chance to experience nomadic life and mingle with tribal people. Wildlife is also plentiful, although it's the journey itself that is the main attraction.

You have the choice of riding the camels, or walking alongside them, and most caravans are led by experienced Samburu *moran* (warriors), and accompanied by English-speaking tribal guides who are well versed in bush lore, botany, ornithology and local customs. Most travelling is done as early as possible in the cool of the day, and a campsite established around noon. Afternoons are time for relaxing, guided walks and showers before drinks and dinner around the campfire.

All companies provide a full range of camping equipment (generally including two-person tents) and ablution facilities, but they vary in what they require you to bring. Some even provide alcoholic drinks, although normally you pay extra for this. The typical distance covered each day is 15km to 18km so you don't have to be superfit to survive this style of safari.

The following companies offer camel safaris of varying lengths:

**Bobong Camp** ( ☎ 062-32718) This remote camp offers Kenya's best self-catered camel safaris – you can create your own package and pretty much roam where you want to throughout Turkana and Samburu country. Bookings can be made through any of the safari operators previously mentioned in this chapter.

**Desert Rose** ( ☎ 0722638774; www.desertrosekenya.com; PO Box 44801-00100, Nairobi) These walking camel-train safaris leave from the remote Desert Rose lodge just north of Baragoi in northern Kenya. A wide variety of safaris are available, ranging from simple trips with no ice or meat to more luxurious trips with chilled wine and three-course meals. All trips are led by experienced guides and you have the Matthews Range, Ndoto Mountains and Ol Doinyo Nyiro (near South Horr) as your playground.

**Yare Safaris** (Map pp104–5; ☎ 020-214099; www.yaresafari.co.ke; Windsor House, University Way, Nairobi) This well-established independent operator offers trips to its signature Yare Camel Club & Camp ( ☎ 065-62295) in Maralal, picking up the camels at the Ewaso Ngiro River. Packages are highly customisable in length, comfort and scope.

## Cultural Safaris

See www.tourism concern.org.uk for more on fair trade in tourism and travellers' guidelines

With ecofriendly lodges now springing up all over Kenya, remote population groups are becoming increasingly involved with tourism. There are also a growing number of companies offering cultural safaris, allowing you to interact with locals in a far more personal way than the rushed souvenir stops that the mainstream tours make at Maasai villages. The best of these combine volunteer work with more conventional tour activities, and provide accommodation in tents, eco-lodges and village houses.

Reliable and interesting companies include the following:

**Eco-Resorts** ( ☎ 042-32191; www.eco-resorts.com) This US-based company offers a variety of activity-based volunteer and cultural packages and customised safaris around Kenya. A proportion of profits go to community and conservation projects, so you can feel good about spending your big safari bucks in the areas where it counts the most.

**IntoAfrica** ( ☎ 0114-2555610; www.intoafrica.co.uk; 40 Huntingdon Cres, Sheffield, S11 8AX, UK) One of the most highly praised safari companies in East Africa, IntoAfrica specialises in 'fair-traded' trips providing insights into African life and directly supporting local communities. The company's commendable safaris explore cultures *and* offer wildlife viewing, and offers accommodation in a good mix of hotels, bush camps and permanent tented camps. Trips leave on scheduled dates, though if you're a small group, you can pay a bit more and begin the trip when you want.

**Origins Safaris** ( ☎ 020-312137; www.originsafaris.info) Origins also offers a superb range of exclusive cultural safaris around the country, including such rare sights as Samburu circumcision ceremonies and tribal initiation rites in southern Ethiopia.

## Fishing Safaris

Kenya offers some wonderful fishing safaris, though keep in mind that organised trips are very much geared towards wealthier visitors.

Perhaps the grandest option is a flying trip to **Rutundu Log Cabins** ( ☎ 020-340331) in Mt Kenya National Park. Both Lake Rutundu and Lake Alice, a two-hour drive to the south, are well stocked with rainbow trout, while nearby Kazita Munyi River is stocked with brown trout. Rods, flies, boats and guides are all available. Accommodation is in comfortable and well-equipped self-catering cabins, and half- and full-board options are also available. Bookings can be made through any of the safari operators previously mentioned in this chapter.

For shorter fishing excursions, several top-end lodges in the Masai Mara offer short flying trips to Lake Victoria for Nile perch fishing. Half-day river and lake trout-fishing trips can also be arranged from the Mt Kenya Safari Club (p218) in Nanyuki. Deep-sea fishing off the Kenyan coast can be arranged with just about any travel agent or top-end resort along the coast.

## Flying Safaris

These safaris essentially cater for the well off who want to fly between remote airstrips in the various national parks, and stay in luxury tented camps. If money is no object, you can get around by a mixture of charter and scheduled flights and stay in some of the finest camps in Kenya – arrangements can be made with any of the lodge and tented-camp safari operators. Flying safaris to Lake Turkana and Sibiloi National Park are common, and most safari companies will be able to sort out a countrywide itinerary. Quite a few special-interest safari operators use light aircraft to save time.

## Motorcycle Safaris

Operating out of Diani Beach, **Fredlink Tours** (Map p272; ☎ 040-3202647; www.motor bike-safari.com; Diani Plaza, Diani Beach) runs motorcycle safaris to the Taita Hills and the Kilimanjaro foothills. Large 350cc trail bikes are used and the full six-day trips include a wildlife drive in Tsavo West National Park and two nights' lodge accommodation. Trips include meals, camping, guides, fuel and support vehicles. Fredlink also rents out motorcycles and scooters and can arrange custom-guided motorcycle tours around the coastal area.

## Truck Safaris

Overlanding is a common element of many people's travels through Africa. Although most are bound for elsewhere in Africa – Cape Town is a particularly popular destination – a few Kenya-only trips are available in converted flat-bed trucks that can carry up to 24 passengers.

Following are popular outfits with tours within Kenya. For more on companies that include Kenya as part of an overland trip, see p347.

**Acacia Expeditions** ( ☎ 020-7706 4700; www.acacia-africa.com) As well as overland trips, Acacia runs shorter tours within Kenya that include stops at Masai Mara, Lake Nakuru and Mt Kenya. The company also runs specialist tours for disabled clients.

**Guerba Expeditions** Kenya ( ☎ 020-553056; guerba@africaonline.co.ke; PO Box 43935, Nairobi); UK ( ☎ 01373-826611; www.guerba.co.uk) This excellent outfit has deep Kenyan roots. Truck safaris take in a good breadth of domestic destinations including Masai Mara, Nakuru, Naivasha, Tsavo West and Diani Beach.

## Walking & Cycling Safaris

For the keen walker or cyclist and those who don't want to spend all their time in a safari minibus, there are a number of options. For information on treks in Mt Kenya National Park, see p211.

ResponsibleTravel.com (www.responsibletravel.com) is a good place to start planning a culturally and environmentally responsible safari.

**Bike Treks** (off Map p108; ☎ 020-446371; www.biketreks.co.ke; Kabete Gardens, Westlands, Nairobi) This company offers just about every possible combination of walking and cycling safaris that range from quick three-day jaunts to full-on expeditions. A minimum of three people guarantees departure, and trips can easily be combined with more traditional safari options.

**Ontdek Kenya** ( ☎ 061-2030326; www.ontdekkenya.com; PO Box 2352, Nyeri) This small operator has been recommended by several readers for its unique tailor-made trips. In addition to the usual safari outings, Ontdek really pulls out the speciality cards by offering walking trips catered specifically to women, vegetarians and bird-watchers.

**Samburu Trails Trekking Safaris** (UK ☎ 0131-6256635; www.samburutrails.com) A small British specialist outfit offering a range of foot excursions in some less-visited parts of the Rift Valley. Excursions range from easy multiday walks to weeklong hard-core treks that tackle some of the country's most stunning terrain.

**Savage Wilderness Safaris** (Map p108; ☎ 020-521590; www.whitewaterkenya.com; Sarit Centre, Westlands, Nairobi) Kenya's premier white-water rafting company also offers organised and custom walking safaris in the Loita and Chyulu Hills. A number of readers have also recommended the company for climbing and mountaineering trips to Mt Kenya and elsewhere.

## DO-IT-YOURSELF SAFARIS

A DIY safari is a viable and enticing proposition in Kenya if you have some camping equipment, and can get a group together to share the costs of renting a vehicle (see p350). With that said, it's not a good idea to go on a do-it-yourself safari by yourself. Not counting the everyday risks of bush driving, if you have to change a tyre in lion country, you'll want someone to watch your back.

Doing it yourself has several advantages over organised safaris, primarily total flexibility, independence and being able to choose your travelling companions. However, as far as costs go, it's generally true to say that organising your own safari will cost at least as much, and usually more, than going on a cheap organised safari to the same areas.

Apart from the cost, vehicle breakdowns, accidents, security and a lack of local knowledge are also major issues. Maps are hard to find, particularly for remote areas, and if you do break down in the wild, you're well and truly on your own. Not to mention the fact that whoever is driving is going to be too busy concentrating on the road to notice much of the wildlife.

If you want to hire camping equipment, the best place to go is **Atul's** (Map pp104-5; ☎ 020-225935; Biashara St) in Nairobi. Identification, such as a passport, is required and advance booking is recommended if you want to save a bit of time. Expect to pay KSh250 per day for a sleeping bag with liner, KSh500 for a two-person dome tent and KSh120 per day for a gas stove (gas canisters are extra). On most items there is a deposit of KSh2000 to KSh3000. For longer trips it may work out cheaper to buy some things at the big Nakumatt supermarkets in Nairobi, which sell cheap plastic plates, stoves, chairs etc.

It's also possible to hire a vehicle and camping equipment as one package: **Tough Tracks** ( ☎ 050-2030329; www.toughtracks.com) offers the rather unusual option of renting a fully fitted 4WD with roof-mounted tent and everything else you might need for a long self-service safari for up to four people, including mobile phone, fridge, gas cooker and cooking utensils. The firm is based in Naivasha, but will deliver your vehicle to Nairobi or Mombasa and pick it up from an agreed point such as an airport with prior arrangement.

Regular wildlife drives can cause other shifts in animal behaviour patterns - in Tsavo West leopards apparently now lurk in roadside ditches during the day, waiting for dikdik (small antelope) scared by cars.

## Bush Driving

Although there is an extensive network of both sealed and unsealed roads throughout Kenya, the thrill and adventure of bush driving is unequalled. Not surprisingly, the country is a favourite destination of veteran off-road enthusiasts. However, just because you've read a survival manual doesn't mean that you're ready to head out into the wilds. Four-wheel driving is serious business, and tourists have died in the past due to careless mistakes. Remember – real (and safe) four-wheel driving is nothing like you see on the TV. The following paragraphs contain some road-tested tips that should help you in planning a safe and successful 4WD expedition.

## MINIMAL-IMPACT SAFARIS

However much you pride yourself on your environmental awareness, there's one wild card on every safari: the driver. The person who controls the car controls the impact your trip makes on the country you're passing through, and with massive professional and financial pressure on them, most drivers will habitually break park rules to get you closer to the action. In the interests of the animals and the people around you, please observe the following:

- Never get out of your vehicle, except at designated points where this is permitted. Certain species may look harmless enough, but the animals are wild and you should treat them as such.

- Never get too close to the animals and back off if they are getting edgy or nervous. Stress can alter the animals' natural behaviour patterns and could make the difference between this year's lion cubs surviving or getting killed by other predators.

- Animals always have the right of way. Slow down if you see animals on the road ahead, and leave them plenty of space.

- Don't follow predators as they move off – you try stalking something when you've got half a dozen minibuses in tow!

- Keep to the tracks. One of the biggest dangers in the parks is land degradation from vehicles criss-crossing the countryside. The tyre tracks act as drainage channels for the rain and erode the soil, which affects the grasses that attract the herbivores, which attract the predators.

- Don't light fires except at campsites, and dispose of cigarettes carefully. An old film case is the best place for cigarette butts, which can then be disposed of outside the park.

- Don't litter the parks and campsites. Unfortunately, the worst offenders are safari drivers and cooks who toss everything and anything out the window.

- Many safaris feature side trips to *manyattas* (livestock camps), which provide an opportunity for local people to make a bit of income from tourism, either posing for photographs or selling souvenirs. Guides and drivers usually levy a fee of around US$10 per head for this, but often this money goes into the driver's pocket. Ensure that the driver gives local people their fare due.

- There isn't necessarily a relationship between the price paid and the likelihood of the local community benefiting from your visit. Find out as much as you can about an operator's social and cultural commitment before booking.

Although a good map and a compass may be sufficient for navigating in your own country, it is strongly advisable to invest in a good Global Positioning System (GPS) before travelling in East Africa. Although GPS units are *not* a substitute for a map and a compass, they are useful for establishing waypoints, and helping you determine which direction you're heading. As a general rule, you should always be able to identify your location on a map, even if you're navigating with a GPS unit.

Stock up on emergency provisions, even if you're sticking to the main highways. Distances between towns can be long, and you never know where you're going to break down (or when someone might pick you up). Petrol and diesel tend to be available in most major towns, though it's wise to never pass a station without filling up. If you're planning a long expedition, carry the requisite amount of fuel in metal jerry cans, and remember that engaging 4WD burns nearly twice as much fuel as highway driving. As for water and food, a good rule is to carry 5L of water per person per day, as well as a good supply of high-calorie, nonperishable emergency food items.

Garages throughout Kenya are surprisingly well stocked with basic 4WD parts, and you haven't truly experienced Africa until you've seen the ingenuity of a bush mechanic. The minimum you should carry is a tow rope, shovel, extra fan belt, vehicle fluids, spark plugs, baling wire, jump leads,

## DRIVING TIPS & TRICKS

Still keen to give bush driving a go? Here are a few tips from past readers:

- When driving through high grass, seeds can quickly foul radiators and cause overheating. If the temperature gauge begins to climb, stop and remove plant material from the grille.

- If the road is corrugated, gradually increase your speed until you find the correct speed – it'll be obvious when the rattling stops.

- If you have a tyre blow-out, do not hit the brakes or you'll lose control. Steer straight ahead as best you can, and let the car slow itself down before you attempt to bring it to a complete stop.

- When you meet other cars it's like dust clouds passing in the night. When a vehicle approaches from the opposite direction, reduce your speed and keep as far left as possible. On remote roads, it's customary to wave at the other driver as you pass.

- In rainy weather, gravel roads can turn to quagmires, and desert washes may fill with water. If you're uncertain about the water depth in a wash, get out and check (unless it's a raging torrent, of course!), and only cross when it's safe for the type of vehicle you're driving.

- Look out for animals. Antelope, in particular, often bound onto the road unexpectedly.

- Avoid swerving sharply or braking suddenly on an unsealed road or you risk losing control. If the rear wheels begin to skid, steer gently in the direction of the skid until you regain control. If the front wheels skid, take a firm hand on the wheel and steer in the opposite direction of the skid.

- Dust permeates everything on dirt roads – wrap your food, clothing and camera equipment in dust-proof plastic or keep them in sealed containers. To minimise dust inside the vehicle, pressurise the interior by closing the windows and turning on the blower.

- Overtaking (passing) can be extremely dangerous because your view may be obscured by dust kicked up by the car ahead. Try to gain the attention of the driver in front by flashing your high beams, which indicates that you want to overtake. If someone behind you flashes their lights, move as far to the left as possible.

fuses, hoses, a good jack and a wooden plank (to use as a base in sand and salt), several spare tyres and a pump. A good Swiss Army knife or Leatherman tool combined with a sturdy roll of duct tape can also save your vehicle's life in a pinch.

Although 4WD exploration and bush camping go hand in hand, Kenya offers a remarkably extensive network of well-maintained campsites, even in the remotest of places. Camping equipment varies according to personal preference, though essentials include a waterproof tent, a three-season sleeping bag (you will need a warmer bag in the winter), a ground mat or Therm-a-Rest, fire-starting supplies, firewood, a basic first-aid kit and a torch with extra batteries. Although seasoned hikers stick to the adage 'less is best', again, it's best to ere on the side of caution, especially if you have extra room in your 4WD.

Sand tracks are most easily negotiated, and least likely to bog vehicles in the cool mornings and evenings, when air spaces between sand grains are smaller. To further prevent bogging or stalling, move as quickly as possible and keep the revs up, but avoid sudden acceleration. Shift down gears in advance of deep sandy patches or the vehicle may stall and bog.

When negotiating a straight course through rutted sand, allow the vehicle to wander along the path of least resistance. Anticipate corners and turn the wheel slightly earlier then you would on a solid surface – this allows the vehicle to ski smoothly round – then accelerate gently out of the turn. Driving on loose sand may be facilitated by lowering the air pressure in the tyres, thereby increasing their gripping area.

# Nairobi & Around

One of the most vilified cities in Africa, Nairobi has a reputation amongst foreign tourists as being an incredibly dangerous place racked by violent crime and extreme poverty. Indeed, the city has garnered the unfortunate nickname of 'Nairobbery', and most first-timers are keen on holing up in their hotel rooms, and counting down the minutes until their safari departure. While the crime statistics are unsettling, it's easy enough to sidestep the worst dangers here, and although you might not believe it at first glance, Nairobi is actually an extremely dynamic and cosmopolitan city full of tourist attractions.

The central business district has more going for it than any other Kenyan conurbation: there's a comprehensive range of shops, the matatus are the funkiest around, most safari companies are based here, the cultural scene is thriving, the nightlife is unbridled and it's virtually the only place in the country where you can get a truly varied diet. Even cafe culture has reached the downtown area, adding a soupçon of sophistication to the supposed urban badlands.

Even if the inner city does terrify you, a quick matatu ride can whisk you into another world for that much-needed rural escape. From the secluded suburbs of Karen and Langata to the lush walking trails of the Ngong Hills, there's no need to forego all the creature comforts of urban living. And speaking of creatures, the outskirts of Nairobi can thrust you firmly into the domain of Kenyan wildlife, whether you're snogging giraffes at the Giraffe Centre, or watching lions prowl at Nairobi National Park.

Moral of the story: stop complaining about Nairobi, drop your pretences, and get out there and explore it – you might be surprised by what you find.

## HIGHLIGHTS

- Spotting wildlife in the most incongruous of surroundings at the **Nairobi National Park** (p109)
- Watching a gleeful group of baby elephants being bottle-fed at the **David Sheldrick Wildlife Trust** (p112)
- Tangling tongues with a rubber-necked ungulate at Langata's **Giraffe Centre** (p113)
- Broadening your appreciation of all things cultural and environmental at the **National Museum** (p103)
- Surveying the cityscape from the grand heights of the **Kenyatta Conference Centre** (p107)
- Making the essential foodie pilgrimage to **Carnivore** (p125) and dancing it off at **Simba Saloon** (p130)
- Striking out for some proper exercise, walking through the incredibly scenic **Ngong Hills** (p114)

National Museum ★★ Kenyatta Conference Centre
Ngong Hills ★
        ★ Carnivore & Simba Saloon
    Giraffe ★
    Centre      ★ Nairobi National Park
        ★
    David Sheldrick
    Wildife Trust

| ■ TELEPHONE CODE: 020 | ■ POPULATION: OVER 3 MILLION | ■ AREA: 680 SQ KM |

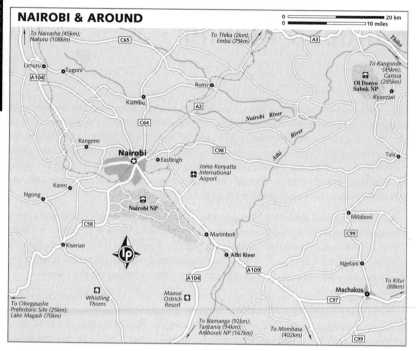

**NAIROBI & AROUND**

## HISTORY

Nairobi is a completely modern creation, and almost everything here has been built in the last 100 years. In fact, until the 1890s, the whole area was just an isolated swamp. But, as the tracks of the East Africa railway were laid down between Mombasa and Kampala, a depot was established on the edge of a small stream known to the Maasai as *uaso nairobi* (cold water). Sadly, the Maasai were quickly and forcibly removed from the land as the British East Africa protectorate had ambitious plans to open up the interior to white colonial settlement.

In addition to its central position between the coast and British holdings in Uganda, Nairobi benefited from its extremely hospitable environment. Its proximity to a network of rivers meant that water was abundant, and its high elevation and cool temperatures were conducive to comfortable residential living without fear of malaria. Although Nairobi did struggle in its early years with frequent fires and an outbreak of the plague, by 1907 the booming commercial centre replaced Mombasa as the capital of British East Africa.

Even when the first permanent buildings were constructed, Nairobi remained a real frontier town, with rhinos and lions freely roaming the outskirts. As a result, the colonial government built some grand hotels to accommodate the first tourists to Kenya – big-game hunters, lured by the attraction of shooting the country's almost naively tame wildlife. In 1946, Nairobi National Park was established as the first national park in East Africa – it remains the only wildlife reserve in the world bordering a capital city.

After achieving independence in 1963, Nairobi grew too rapidly by most accounts, putting a great deal of pressure on the city's infrastructure. Power cuts and water shortages became a common occurrence, and enormous shanty towns of tin-roofed settlements sprung up on the outskirts of the capital. In the name of modernisation, almost all of the colonial-era buildings were replaced by concrete office buildings, which today characterise much of the modern city.

However, Nairobi has been successful in establishing itself as East Africa's largest city and main transport hub. The capital is also situated firmly at the centre of national life and politics, though this position did the city no favours in 1998 when the US embassy on Moi Ave was bombed by militants with links to Al Qaeda. More than 200 Kenyans were killed in the attack, and although four suspects were convicted and sentenced to life without parole, many locals were angered by what they considered lenient sentences (they had wanted the death penalty) and meagre compensation. Even today, resentment still lingers in certain quarters of the city.

In recent years, the growth of the city has put tremendous pressure on the government to develop protected lands such as the Nairobi National Park. But the government has so far resisted, as these lands continue to support traditional migration routes for herd animals.

In December 2007, the shanty towns of Nairobi were set ablaze as riots broke out following the disputed presidential election. Hundreds of homes were burnt to the ground by protestors, and many suffered violent attacks. At the time of writing, order had been restored to the city, though deep scars remain, especially amongst those who were internally displaced.

## ORIENTATION

The compact city centre is bounded by Uhuru Hwy to the west, Haile Selassie Ave to the south, Tom Mboya St at the east, and University Way at the north end. Northeast of the centre, on the eastern side of Tom Mboya St, is the rougher River Rd area where most of the bus offices are found.

Various suburbs surround the downtown area. Southwest of the centre, beyond Uhuru and Central Parks, are Nairobi Hill, Milimani and Hurlingham, with several hostels, campsites and hotels. Further out are Wilson Airport, Nairobi National Park and the expat enclaves of Langata and Karen. The country's main airport, Jomo Kenyatta International Airport, is southeast of the centre.

North of the centre you will find the expat-dominated suburbs of Westlands and Parklands, home to large European and Indian communities. The suburbs further out, such as Kibera, Kayole and Githurai, are mainly poverty-stricken shanty towns with terrible reputations for violent crime.

## Maps

Many hotels and travel companies give out free promotional maps, which serve as rudimentary guides to the downtown area,

For more detailed coverage, the best option is the *City of Nairobi: Map & Guide* produced by Survey of Kenya, available at bookshops around the city. It covers the suburbs and has a detailed map of the central area.

Also adequate, with some hotels and places of interest marked, is the 1:15,000 *Map Guide of Nairobi City Centre* (KSh200) published by Interland Maps.

Much better, though bulkier, is *Nairobi A to Z* (KSh510) by RW Moss. Like the equivalents in other countries, the *A to Z* covers the whole city in detail.

## INFORMATION
### Bookshops

For newspapers and magazines, there are dozens of street vendors and hawkers selling current editions of the daily papers and old editions of Western publications.

**Book Villa** (Map pp104–5; ☎ 337890; Standard St) New, discounted and secondhand books. Also runs a borrowing scheme.

**Bookpoint** (Map pp104–5; ☎ 211156; Moi Ave)

**Text Book Centre** Westlands (Map p108; ☎ 3747405; Sarit Centre); Kijabe St (Map p100–1; ☎ 330340) One of the best bookshops in East Africa. The sister shop on Kijabe St isn't as big or well stocked.

**Westland Sundries Bookshop** Downtown (Map pp104–5; ☎ 212776; New Stanley Hotel, Kenyatta Ave); Westlands (Map p108; ☎ 446406; Ring Rd)

### Camping Equipment

**Atul's** (Map pp104–5; ☎ 225935; Biashara St) Hires out everything from sleeping bags to folding toilet seats – see p92.

**Kenya Canvas Ltd** (Map pp104–5; ☎ 343262; Muindi Mbingu St)

**X-treme Outdoors** (off Map p100–1; ☎ 2722224; Yaya Centre, Hurlingham)

### Clubs & Societies

**East African Wild Life Society** (EAWLS; off Map pp100–1; ☎ 574145; www.eawildlife.org; Riara Rd, Kilimani, PO Box 20110) This society is at the forefront of conservation efforts in East Africa.

**Friends of Nairobi National Park** (FoNNaP; Map p111; ☎ 500622; http://fonnap.wordpress.com; Kenya Wildlife

**NAIROBI IN...**

**Two Days**
Start by heading out to the suburbs of Karen and Langata, where you can get up-close-and-personal with wildlife at the Langata **Giraffe Centre** (p113) and the **David Sheldrick Wildlife Trust** (p112). A visit to the **Karen Blixen Museum** (p113) is recommended for fans of the book *Out of Africa*, which can also be paired with a shopping trip to the **Kazuri Beads & Pottery Centre** (p114). In the evening, dinner at **Carnivore** (p125) and dancing at the **Simba Saloon** (p130) is a must.

On the second day, head downtown to visit the **National Museum** (p103), view the city from the **Kenyatta Conference Centre** (p107), and browse contemporary art at the **National Archives** (p107). In the evening, you can eat posh at **Tamarind Restaurant** (p125) and dance dirty at **Simmers** (p129).

**Four Days**
With another two days, you can safari in **Nairobi National Park** (p109), and have dinner and catch a movie at the **Village Market** (p132).

For your final 24 hours, do a bit of shopping in the **curio markets** (p131), eat at Kenya's best Indian restaurant, namely **Haandi** (p127), and work off the calories at the massive club that is **Pavement** (p130).

---

Service Headquarters, Langata Rd) The society aims to protect migration routes between the Masai Mara and the national park.

**Mountain Club of Kenya** (MCK; ☎ 602330; www .mck.or.ke; Wilson Airport) The club meets at 8pm every Tuesday at the clubhouse at Wilson Airport (Map p111). Members organise frequent climbing and trekking weekends around the country and have a huge pool of technical knowledge about climbing in Kenya.

**Nature Kenya** ( ☎ 3749957; www.naturekenya.org; National Museum) Located just off Museum Hill Rd at the museum, it runs a variety of local outings – see p115.

## Cultural Centres

All the foreign cultural organisations have libraries (opposite) open to the public.

**Alliance Française** (Map pp104–5; ☎ 340054; www .ambafrance-ke.org; cnr Moktar Daddah & Loita Sts; ⏰ 8.30am-6.30pm Mon-Fri, to 5pm Sat) Has the best events program of all the centres, showcasing Kenyan and other African performing arts.

**British Council** (Map pp100–1; ☎ 334855; www .britishcouncil.org; Upper Hill Rd; ⏰ 9.30am-5.30pm Mon-Fri, to 1pm Sat)

**Cultural Council of the Islamic Republic of Iran** (Map pp104–5; ☎ 214352; Ambank House, Monrovia St; ⏰ 9am-5pm Mon-Fri, 9.30am-4.30pm Sat) Hosts exhibitions and displays on Islam.

**Goethe Institut** (Map pp104–5; ☎ 224640; www .goethe.de/nairobi; Maendeleo House, cnr Monrovia & Loita Sts; ⏰ 10am-12.30pm Thu-Tue, 2-5pm Mon-Fri)

**Japan Information & Culture Centre** (Map pp100–1; ☎ 2898515; www.ke.emb-japan.go.jp; Mara Rd, Upper Hill; ⏰ 8.30am-5pm Mon-Fri) Free video shows and Japanese cinema screenings.

**Nairobi Cultural Institute** (Map pp100–1; ☎ 569205; Ngong Rd) Holds lectures and other functions of local cultural interest.

## Emergency

**AAR Health Services** (Map pp100–1; ☎ 271737; Fourth Ngong Ave)

**Aga Khan Hospital** (Map pp100–1; ☎ 3662000; Third Parklands Ave) A reliable hospital with 24-hour emergency services.

**Emergency services** ( ☎ 999) The national emergency number to call for fire, police and ambulance assistance. A word of warning, though – don't rely on prompt arrival.

**Flying Doctors Service** ( ☎ 602495, emergency 315454)

**Police** (Map pp100-1 & pp104–5; ☎ 240000) Phone for less-urgent police business.

**St John's Ambulance** ( ☎ 2100000)

**Tourist helpline** ( ☎ 020-604767) Twenty-four hour service.

## Internet Access

There are hundreds of internet cafes in downtown Nairobi – most of them tucked away in anonymous office buildings in the town centre. Connection speed is decent assuming you're not streaming YouTube, though machine quality varies wildly. Rates range from KSh1 to KSh4 per minute.

**AGX** (Map pp104–5; Barclays Plaza, Loita St; per min KSh1; ⏰ 8am-8pm Mon-Sat) Best connections in town, with a choice of browsers.

**Avant Garde e-centre** (Map pp104-5; Fedha Towers, Kaunda St; 7.30am-9pm Mon-Sat, 11am-6pm Sun)

**Capital Realtime** (Map pp104-5; ☎ 247900; Lonhro House, Standard St; 8.30am-7.30pm Mon-Fri, 10am-4pm Sat)

**Dallas Communications** (Map pp104-5; ☎ 223655; 20th Century Plaza, Mama Ngina St)

**EasySurf** (Map p108; ☎ 3745418; Sarit Centre, Westlands; 9am-8pm Mon-Sat, 10am-2pm Sun)

## Libraries

Many of Nairobi's cultural centres (opposite) also have libraries available to the public.

**Kenya National Library** (Map pp100-1; ☎ 2725550; www.knls.or.ke; Ngong Rd; 8am-6.30pm Mon-Thu, to 4pm Fri, 9am-5pm Sat)

**McMillan Memorial Library** (Map pp104-5; ☎ 221844; Banda St; 9am-6pm Mon-Fri, 9.30am-4pm Sat) A smaller collection in a lovely colonial-era building.

## Medical Services

Nairobi has plenty of healthcare facilities used to dealing with travellers and expats, which is a good thing as you're going to want to avoid the Kenyatta National Hospital (Map pp100-1) – although it's free, stretched resources mean you may come out with something worse than what you went in with.

**AAR Health Services** (Map pp100-1; ☎ 2715319; Williamson House, Fourth Ngong Ave) Westlands (Map p108; ☎ 446201; Sarit Centre) Probably the best of a number of private ambulance and emergency air-evacuation companies. It also runs a private clinic in Westlands.

**Acacia Medical Centre** (Map pp104-5; ☎ 212200; ICEA Bldg, Kenyatta Ave; 7am-7pm Mon-Fri, to 2pm Sat)

**Aga Khan Hospital** (Map pp100-1; ☎ 740000; Third Parklands Ave; 24hr)

**KAM Pharmacy** (Map pp104-5; ☎ 251700; Executive Tower, IPS Bldg, Kimathi St) A one-stop shop for medical treatment, with a pharmacy, doctor's surgery and laboratory.

**Medical Services Surgery** (Map pp104-5; ☎ 317625; Bruce House, Standard St; 8.30am-4.30pm Mon-Fri)

**Nairobi Hospital** (Map pp100-1; ☎ 722160; off Argwings Kodhek Rd; 24hr)

**Transcom Medical Centre** (Map pp104-5; ☎ 217564; Tsavo Rd)

## Money

Jomo Kenyatta International Airport has several exchange counters in the baggage reclaim area and a **Barclays Bank** ( 24hr) with an ATM outside in the arrivals hall.

There are Barclays branches with guarded ATMs on Mama Ngina St (Map pp104–5), Muindi Mbingu St (Map pp104–5) and on the corner of Kenyatta and Moi Aves (Map pp104–5). There are also branches in the Sarit Centre (Map p108) and on Woodvale Grove (Map p108) in Westlands, and the Yaya Centre (off Map pp100–1) in Hurlingham.

The other big bank is Standard Chartered Bank, which has numerous downtown branches.

Foreign-exchange bureaus offer slightly better rates for cash than the banks. There are dozens of options in the town centre, so it's worth strolling around to see who is currently offering the best deal.

**American Express** (Map pp104-5; ☎ 222906; Hilton Hotel, Mama Ngina St; 8.30am-4.30pm Mon-Fri)

**Cosmos Forex** (Map pp104-5; ☎ 250582; Rehema House, Standard St)

**Goldfield Forex** (Map pp104-5; ☎ 244554; Fedha Towers, Kaunda St)

**Mayfair Forex** (Map pp104-5; ☎ 226212; Uganda House, Standard St)

**Postbank** (Map pp104-5; 13 Kenyatta Ave) For Western Union money transfers.

**Travellers Forex Bureau** (Map p108; ☎ 447204; The Mall Shopping Centre, Westlands)

## Photography Equipment

Shops selling and developing film are still common across Nairobi, and most can also do instant passport-size photographs. Digital printing, however, is slowly becoming the norm and most places can burn images from your memory card onto a DVD.

**Elite Camera House** (Map pp104-5; ☎ 224521; Kimathi St)

**Expo Camera Centre** Downtown (Map pp104-5; ☎ 226846; Mama Ngina St); Westlands (Map p108; ☎ 441253; Mpaka Rd) Hires out SLR cameras and lenses.

**Fedha Foto Studio** (Map pp104-5; ☎ 220515; Fedha Towers, Kaunda St)

**Fotoland** (Map pp104-5; ☎ 343042; Moi Ave)

## Post

The vast **main post office** (Map pp104-5; ☎ 243434; Kenyatta Ave; 8am-6pm Mon-Fri, 9am-noon Sat) is a well-organised edifice close to Uhuru Park. Around the back of the main building is the **EMS office** ( 8am-8pm Mon-Fri, 9am-12.30pm Sat), for courier deliveries (see p334), and there's a Telkom Kenya office upstairs.

If you just want stamps, head to the post offices on Haile Selassie Ave (Map pp104–5), Moi Ave (Map pp104–5) and Tom Mboya St (Map pp104–5), or in the Sarit Centre (Map p108)

# NAIROBI

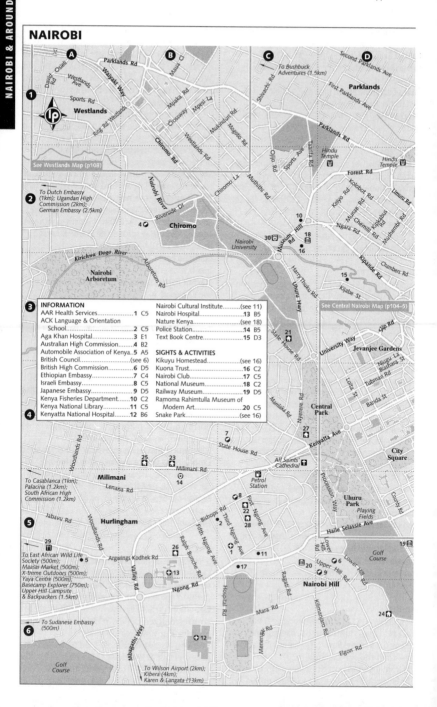

See Westlands Map (p108)

See Central Nairobi Map (p104–5)

**INFORMATION**

| | |
|---|---|
| AAR Health Services | **1** C5 |
| ACK Language & Orientation School | **2** C5 |
| Aga Khan Hospital | **3** E1 |
| Australian High Commission | **4** B2 |
| Automobile Association of Kenya | **5** A5 |
| British Council | (see 6) |
| British High Commission | **6** D5 |
| Ethiopian Embassy | **7** C4 |
| Israeli Embassy | **8** C5 |
| Japanese Embassy | **9** D5 |
| Kenya Fisheries Department | **10** C2 |
| Kenya National Library | **11** C5 |
| Kenyatta National Hospital | **12** B6 |
| Nairobi Cultural Institute | (see 11) |
| Nairobi Hospital | **13** B5 |
| Nature Kenya | (see 18) |
| Police Station | **14** B5 |
| Text Book Centre | **15** D3 |

**SIGHTS & ACTIVITIES**

| | |
|---|---|
| Kikuyu Homestead | (see 16) |
| Kuona Trust | **16** C2 |
| Nairobi Club | **17** C5 |
| National Museum | **18** C2 |
| Railway Museum | **19** D5 |
| Ramoma Rahimtulla Museum of Modern Art | **20** C5 |
| Snake Park | (see 16) |

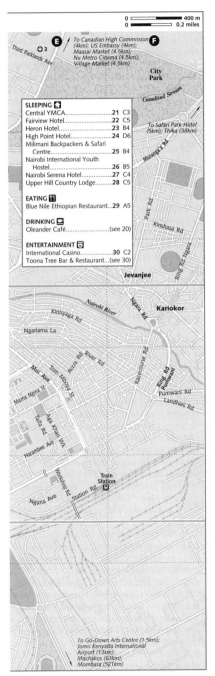

and on Mpaka Rd (Map p108) in Westlands. The Moi Ave office is a good place for sending parcels – packing boxes are available for KSh50 to KSh100.

**DHL** Downtown (Map pp104–5; ☎ 534988; www.dhl.co .ke; International House, Mama Ngina St); Westlands (Map p108; ☎ 6925120; Sarit Centre) Reliable private courier.

## Telephone & Fax

Public phones are common in Nairobi, but many just don't work. **Telkom Kenya** (Map pp104–5; ☎ 232000; Haile Selassie Ave; ✆ 8am-6pm Mon-Fri, 9am-noon Sat) has dozens of payphones and you can buy phonecards. Many stands downtown sell Telkom Kenya phonecards and top-up cards for prepaid mobiles. Alternatively, there are numerous private agencies in the centre of town offering international telephone services.

**Lazards** (Map pp104–5; Kenya Cinema Plaza, Moi Ave; ✆ 7am-10pm; ) International phone calls from as little as KSh10 per minute to North America or Europe and international faxes from KSh40 per page. You may need ID to get into the building.

## Toilets

It may come as a shock to regular travellers to African, but Nairobi now has a handful of manned public toilets around the downtown area offering flush toilets with a basic level of cleanliness. Signs will indicate you need to pay to do your business (about KSh5). Some central shopping centres, such as Kenya Cinema Plaza, have free public conveniences.

## Tourist Information

Despite the many safari companies with signs saying 'Tourist Information', there is still no official tourist office in Nairobi. For events and other listings you'll have to check the local newspapers or glean what you can from a handful of magazines, which take a bit of effort to hunt down. *Go Places* (free) and the *Going Out Guide* (KSh150) are probably the most widespread, available from travel agents, airline offices and some hotels.

The vast noticeboards found at the **Sarit Centre** (Map p108; Westlands) and **Yaya Centre** (off Map pp100–1; Hurlingham) are good places to look for local information. All sorts of things are advertised here, including language courses, vehicles for sale and houses for rent.

**Langata Link** (Map p109; ☎ 891314; www.langatalink .com; Langata South Rd; ) Aimed mainly at residents, the travel desk here has plenty of information about hotels and restaurants in Langata and Karen as well as further afield.

NAIROBI & AROUND

## Travel Agencies

**Bunson Travel** (Map pp104-5; ☎ 248371; www.bunson
kenya.com; Pan Africa Insurance Bldg, Standard St) A good
upmarket operator with offices around Africa and the
Indian Ocean islands.

**Flight Centre** (Map pp104-5; ☎ 210024; Lakhamshi
House, Biashara St) This company has been doing discounted air tickets for years and is totally switched on to
the backpacker market. It also acts as a broker for camping
safaris and runs overland trips across Africa.

**Let's Go Travel** Downtown (Map pp104-5; ☎ 340331;
www.lets-go-travel.net; Caxton House, Standard St); Westlands (off Map p108 ☎ 447151; ABC Place, Waiyaki Way);
Karen (Map p109; ☎ 882505; Karen shopping centre,
Langata Rd) Highly recommended, Let's Go is very good for
flights, safaris and pretty much anything else you might
need. It publishes an excellent price list of hotels, lodges,
camps and bandas (thatched-roofed huts) in Kenya (also
searchable on its website), and acts as main booking agent
for many off-the-beaten-track and unusual travel options.

**Tropical Winds** (Map pp104-5; ☎ 341939; www
.tropical-winds.com; Barclays Plaza, Loita St) Nairobi's STA
Travel representative.

## DANGERS & ANNOYANCES

First-time visitors to Nairobi are understand-
ably daunted by the city's unenviable reputation. 'Nairobbery', as it has been nicknamed
by jaded residents and expats, is commonly
regarded as the most dangerous city in Africa,
beating stiff competition from Johannesburg
and Lagos. Carjacking, robbery and violence
are daily occurrences, and the social ills behind them are unlikely to disappear in the
near future.

However, shell-shocked first-timers should
take comfort in the fact that the majority of
problems happen in the shanty towns, far
from the main tourist zones. The downtown
area bound by Kenyatta Ave, Moi Ave, Haile
Selassie Ave and Uhuru Hwy is unthreaten-
ing and comparatively trouble-free as long
as you use a bit of common sense. There are
also plenty of *askaris* (security guards) about
in case you need assistance.

In fact, compared to Johannesburg and
Lagos, where armed guards, razor-wired
compounds and patrol vehicles are the norm
rather than the exception, Nairobi's Central
Business District (CBD) is quite relaxed and
hassle-free. As long as you stay alert, walk with
confidence, keep a hand on your wallet and
avoid wearing anything too flashy, you should
encounter nothing worse than a few persistent
safari touts and the odd con artist.

But there are a few places where you do
need to employ a slightly stronger self-preser-
vation instinct. Potential danger zones include
the area around Latema and River Rds (east of
Moi Ave), which is a hotspot for petty theft.
This area is home to the city's bus terminals,
so keep an eye on your bags and personal
belongings at all times if passing through here.
Uhuru Park is a very pleasant place during the
daylight hours, though it tends to accumulate
all kinds of dodgy characters at night.

Nairobi's infamous reputation is largely the
result of its horrific shanty towns, which lie
on the outskirts of the city. These expansive
areas, largely devoid of electricity, plumbing
and fresh water, are tense places where op-
portunism can quickly lead to violent crime.
If you want to visit these places to get a better
sense of how Nairobi's less fortunate inhabitants live, do so with a reliable local friend
or as part of an organised tour (see boxed
text, p116).

Once the shops in the CBD have shut,
the streets empty rapidly, and the whole
city centre takes on a deserted and slightly
sinister air. After sunset, mugging is a risk
anywhere on the streets, and you should always take a taxi, even if you're only going
a few blocks. This will also keep you safe
from the attentions of Nairobi's street prostitutes, who flood into town in force for a
bit of moonlighting.

The most likely annoyance for travellers
is petty theft, which is most likely to occur
at budget hotels and campsites around the
city. As a general rule, you should take advantage of your hotel's safe and never leave
your valuables out in the open. While you're
walking around town, don't bring anything
with you that you wouldn't want to lose. As
an extra safety precaution, it's best to only
carry money in your wallet, and hide your
credit and bank cards elsewhere.

In the event that you are mugged, never,
ever resist – simply give up your valuables
and, more often than not, your assailant
will flee the scene rapidly. Remember that a
petty thief and a violent aggressor are very
different kinds of people, so don't give your
assailant any reason to do something rash.

Finally – the majority of foreign visitors
and resident expats in Nairobi never experience any kind of problem, so try not to be
paralysed with fear. Again, it's important to
understand the potential dangers and annoy-

ances that are present, though you shouldn't let fear exile you to your hotel room. Exude confidence, practise street smarts, and chances are you'll actually end up really enjoying your time in Nairobi.

## Scams

Nairobi's active handful of confidence tricksters seem to have relied on the same old stories for years, and it's generally easy to spot the spiels once you've heard them a couple of times.

It is almost a certainty that at some point during your time in Nairobi you will be approached on the street by a safari tout. Most of these persistent guys are hoping to drag you into an operator's office, where they can expect to receive a small commission. A small minority are hoping to distract you with their glossy brochures while they deftly lift your wallet.

This is not to say that safari touts are bad people – a good number of them really do want to help you make a booking. With that said, it's better to err on the side of caution and work directly with a reliable operator. For more information, see the Safaris chapter (p65).

Apart from the regular safari rip-offs, you should be careful of something known as the 'Nairobi bump'. The usual tactic is for a scammer to bump into you in the street, and then try to strike up a small conversation. If this happens, keep walking, as it's probably the most effective way of preventing your wallet or backpack from being stolen.

You should also be wary of anyone who says they work at your hostel/hotel/campsite, even if they actually know the names of the staff there. We have received countless letters from travellers who have been duped into handing over money on the street for seemingly valid reasons, such as buying groceries for the evening's dinner. If someone claiming to be from your accommodation asks for money, be sceptical and just walk away.

Given the continuing severity of the conflicts in Sudan, another local speciality is the Sudanese refugee scam (see boxed text, p107).

In short, always exercise caution while talking to anyone on the streets of Nairobi. While there are genuinely good people out there, the reality is that foreign tourists are an easy target for scamming.

# SIGHTS
## City Centre

Nairobi's most popular tourist attractions are out in the suburbs, though there are a handful of museums and cultural institutions scattered around the city that can easily occupy a full day.

### NATIONAL MUSEUM

A grand alternative to the dozens of poky little local museums around the country, Kenya's **National Museum** (Map pp100-1; ☎ 742131; www .museums.or.ke; Museum Hill Rd; adult/child KSh800/400; ⏲ 9.30am-6pm) is housed in an imposing building amid lush leafy grounds just outside the centre, and has a good range of cultural and natural history exhibits. The gardens are peppered with random sculptures, including a large dinosaur, and the inner courtyard has a life-size fibreglass model of pachyderm celebrity Ahmed, the massive elephant who became a symbol of Kenya at the height of the 1980s poaching crisis, and was placed under 24-hour guard by Jomo Kenyatta.

Inside, one of the major attractions is the Peoples of Kenya series of tribal portraits by *Born Free* author Joy Adamson, a fantastic record of the country's cultural diversity. Upstairs are huge galleries of stuffed birds (at least 900 specimens) and animals, and good ethnographical displays on the various Kenyan tribal groups. Downstairs, there are re-creations of rock art from Tanzania, an exhibition of hominid fossils from Lake Turkana and various geological displays. The outlying gallery hosts temporary exhibits, covering topics such as Swahili and South Asian culture in Kenya and wildlife in the Masai Mara. Volunteer guides offer tours in English, Dutch and French; it's worth booking them in advance. There's no charge for their services, but a donation to the museum is appropriate.

The 1st floor also contains the excellent **Gallery of Contemporary East African Art**, where local artists exhibit their work; as all the items are for sale, the displays change regularly, and it's always an interesting cross-section of the contemporary scene. For a look at the artists in action, visit the **Kuona Trust** (Map pp100-1), a nonprofit art studio just by the museum, where Kenyan artists can gather and express themselves. You're welcome to wander around but ask before taking photos.

# CENTRAL NAIROBI

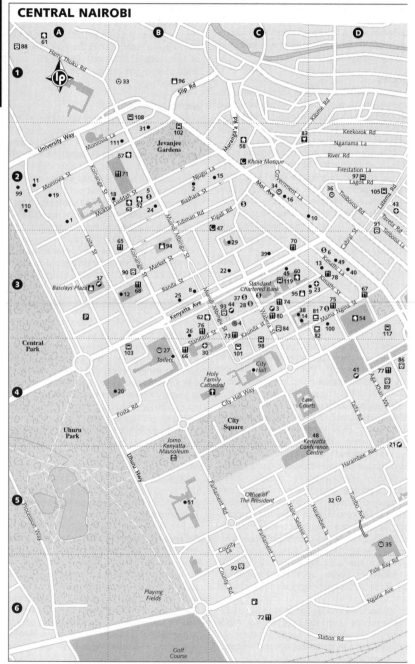

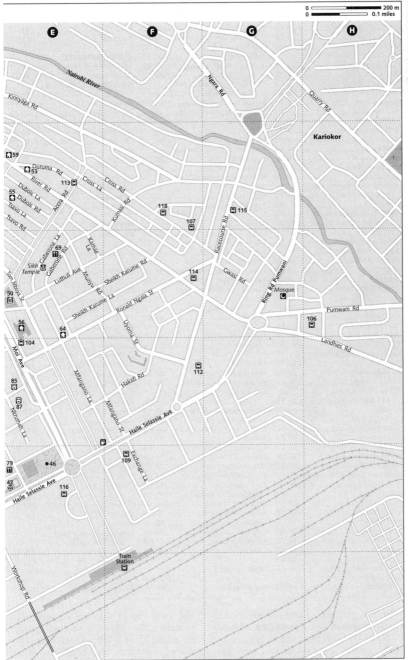

In the grounds, there's a re-created **Kikuyu homestead** and a **snake park** (adult/child KSh200/100; ☉ 9.30am-6pm), where you can see black mambas, some sad-looking crocodiles and giant creepy-crawlies known locally as *dudus*, though some visitors will find the whole affair is a bit too zoolike. There is a guided nature trail nearby but it isn't

---

### SUDANESE SCAMMERS

One classic Nairobi con trick that you'll likely be subjected to is the Sudanese refugee story, commonly combined with the equally well-worn university scam. In this gambit, it turns out that your interlocutor has coincidentally just won a scholarship to a university in your country (the amount of research they do is quite astounding), and would just love to sit down and have a chat with you about life there.

Then at some point you'll get the confidential lowering of the voice as the Sudanese portion of the story kicks in with 'You know, I am not from here…', leading into an epic tale of woe that involves them having walked barefoot all the way from Juba or Darfur to flee the war.

Of course, once you've shown due sympathy they'll come to the crux of the matter: they have to get to Mombasa or Dar es Salaam or elsewhere to confirm their scholarship and fly out for their studies, and all they need is a few thousand shilling – not that they could ask you, their new friend, for that much money, though anything you could spare to help them out would be greatly appreciated…(you get the idea).

---

particularly exciting as it skirts alongside two main roads.

### KENYATTA CONFERENCE CENTRE

Towering over City Square on City Hall Way, Nairobi's signature building (Map pp104–5) was designed as a fusion of modern and traditional African styles, though the distinctive saucer tower looks a little dated next to some of the city's flashier glass edifices. Staff will accompany you up to the **viewing platform** (adult/child KSh400/200; 9.30am-6pm) and helipad on the roof for wonderful views over Nairobi. The sightline goes all the way to the suburbs and on clear days you can see aircraft coming in to land over the Nairobi National Park. You're allowed to take photographs from the viewing level but not elsewhere in the building. Access may be restricted during events and conferences.

### RAILWAY MUSEUM

The main collection at this interesting little **museum** (Map pp100-1; Station Rd; adult/child KSh200/100; 8.15am-4.45pm) is housed in an old railway building and consists of relics from the East African Railway. There are train and ship models, photographs, tableware and oddities from the history of the railway, such as the engine seat that allowed visiting dignitaries like Theodore Roosevelt to take potshots at unsuspecting wildlife from the front of the train.

In the grounds are dozens of fading locomotives in various states of disrepair, dating from the steam days to independence (which puts the newer trains on a par with those still being used on the Nairobi–Mombasa line). You can walk around the carriages at your leisure. At the back of the compound is the steam train used in the movie *Out of Africa*. It's a fascinating introduction to this important piece of colonial history.

The museum is reached by a long lane beside the train station, or you can cut across the vacant land next to the Shell petrol station on Haile Selassie Ave.

### NATIONAL ARCHIVES

Right in the bustling heart of Nairobi is the distinctive **National Archives** (Map pp104-5; 749341; Moi Ave; admission free; 8.30am-5pm Mon-Fri, to 1pm Sat), the 'Memory of the Nation', a vast collection of documents and reference materials housed in the fine former Bank of India building. It's mainly used by students and researchers, but the ground-floor atrium and gallery display an eclectic selection of contemporary art, historical photos of Nairobi, cultural artefacts, furniture and tribal objects, giving casual visitors a somewhat scattergun glimpse of East African heritage.

### UHURU PARK

A huge expanse of manicured green edging on the concrete expanse of the CBD, this attractive **park** (Map pp104-5; admission free; dawn-dusk) is a popular respite from the mean city streets. During the day, it attracts picnicking families, businessmen stepping out of the office and just about anyone in need of a little green. During the night, you're going to want to steer clear as it's popular with the kinds of people you'd be happier not to meet face-to-face.

Interestingly, Uhuru Park largely owes its existence to Wangari Maathai, the Kenyan Nobel Peace Prize winner who started the Green Belt Movement to plant more trees

NAIROBI & AROUND

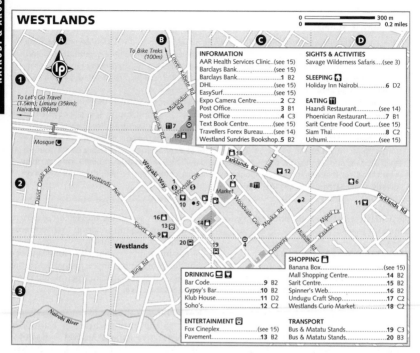

## WESTLANDS

0 ———— 300 m
0 ———— 0.2 miles

**INFORMATION**
AAR Health Services Clinic..(see 15)
Barclays Bank....................(see 15)
Barclays Bank..................**1** B2
DHL...............................(see 15)
EasySurf..........................(see 15)
Expo Camera Centre............**2** C2
Post Office.......................**3** B1
Post Office ......................**4** C3
Text Book Centre................(see 15)
Travellers Forex Bureau......(see 14)
Westland Sundries Bookshop.**5** B2

**SIGHTS & ACTIVITIES**
Savage Wilderness Safaris....(see 3)

**SLEEPING**
Holiday Inn Nairobi..............**6** D2

**EATING**
Haandi Restaurant.............(see 14)
Phoenician Restaurant..........**7** B1
Sarit Centre Food Court....(see 15)
Siam Thai.......................**8** C2
Uchumi............................(see 15)

**SHOPPING**
Banana Box.....................(see 15)
Mall Shopping Centre........**14** B2
Sarit Centre....................**15** B2
Spinner's Web..................**16** B2
Undugu Craft Shop............**17** C2
Westlands Curio Market........**18** C2

**DRINKING**
Bar Code..........................**9** B2
Gypsy's Bar......................**10** B2
Klub House......................**11** D2
Soho's............................**12** C2

**ENTERTAINMENT**
Fox Cineplex....................(see 15)
Pavement.......................**13** B2

**TRANSPORT**
Bus & Matatu Stands.........**19** C3
Bus & Matatu Stands.........**20** B3

across the continent. In the late 1980s, she fought to save the park from the bulldozers of the former Moi government. Moi had famously suggested that she should be more of a proper woman in the 'African tradition'. Since then, Maathai has emerged as a prominent public figure, pushing for peace, rights for women and sustainable development (see also p62).

### PARLIAMENT HOUSE
If you fancy a look at how democracy works (or doesn't) in Kenya, it's possible to obtain a free permit for a seat in the public gallery at **parliament house** (Map pp104-5; ☎ 221291; Parliament Rd) – just remember, applause is strictly forbidden! If parliament is out of session, you can tour the buildings by arrangement with the serjeant-at-arms.

### JAMIA MOSQUE
Nairobi's main **mosque** (Map pp104-5; Banda St) is a lovely building in typical Arabic Muslim style, with all the domes, marble and Quranic inscriptions you'd expect from an important Islamic site, plus the traditional row of shops

down one side to provide rental income for its upkeep. Sadly non-Muslims are very rarely allowed to enter, but you can happily examine the appealing exterior from the street.

### AMERICAN EMBASSY MEMORIAL GARDEN
This well-tended walled **garden** (Map pp104-5; Moi Ave; admission KSh40; ☻ 8am-8pm) occupies the former site of the American embassy, which was destroyed by the terrorist bombings of 1998. It's a lovely little spot despite being right between busy Moi and Haile Selassie Aves – the entrance fee pays for maintenance.

### ARTS CENTRES
The **Go-Down Arts Centre** (off Map pp100-1; ☎ 5552227; Dunga Rd; admission free), a converted warehouse in the Industrial Area, just south of the CBD, contains 10 separate art studios, and is rapidly becoming a hub for Nairobi's burgeoning arts scene, bringing together visual and performing arts with regular exhibitions, shows, workshops and open cultural nights.

The **Mzizi Arts Centre** (Map pp104-5; ☎ 574372; Sonalux House, Moi Ave; admission free), a smaller centre in a central office building, is a good place to view contemporary Kenyan art, craft, dance, literature and performance art. 'Cultural Personality Evenings', when Kenyan cultural stars give lectures, and *sigana* performances are held here (see p49 for more information on the performing arts).

### ART GALLERIES

There are few public art galleries in Nairobi, but plenty of shops sell work by local artists and they welcome browsers.

In Upper Hill, the impressive-sounding **Ramoma Rahimtulla Museum of Modern Art** (Map pp100-1; ☎ 729181; Rahimtulla Tower, Upper Hill Rd; admission free) is actually a small gallery situated in a large skyscraper, promoting and selling work by Kenyan artists.

Of the private galleries, the longest established is the central **Gallery Watatu** (p131), which has regular exhibitions and a good permanent display.

Work by many contemporary Kenyan and other African artists is often displayed in the foreign cultural centres (see p98) and in various museums.

## Karen & Langata

These posh suburbs to the south of Nairobi, while still technically within the city limits, bear little resemblance to the urban sprawl of the capital. Inhabited mainly by the descendants of white settlers and foreign expats, these leafy environs conceal extensive ranks of houses and villas designed to recall provincial England, all discreetly set in their own colonial grounds. The genteel atmosphere and a relative wealth of attractions make Karen and Langata appealing destinations for a quick and easy escape from city life.'

### NAIROBI NATIONAL PARK

The incongruous suburban location of this **national park** (Map p111; adult/child/student US$40/20/15, smartcard required), makes it unique in Africa, and adds an intriguing twist to the usual safari experience. Indeed, abundant wildlife plays out the drama of mother nature against a backdrop of looming skyscrapers, speeding matatus and jets coming in to land at the nearby airport.

Remarkably, the animals seem utterly unperturbed by all the activity around them, and you stand a good chance of seeing gazelles, warthogs, zebras, giraffes, ostriches,

buffaloes, lions, cheetahs and even leopards. The landscape is mixture of savanna and swampland, and is home to the highest concentration of black rhinos (over 50) in the world. The wetland areas also sustain approximately 400 recorded species of bird, which is more than in the whole of the UK!

Nairobi National Park is fenced in parts to keep the wildlife out of the city, though it is not a closed system; it is kept open to allow animals to migrate along a narrow wildlife corridor to the Rift Valley. Concentrations of wildlife are higher in the dry season as water is almost always available in the park. Sadly, this traditional migration route is

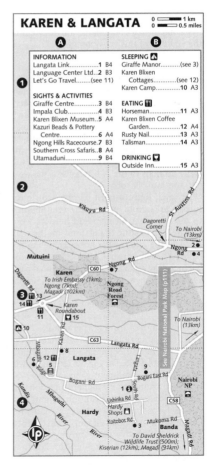

**KAREN & LANGATA**

0 — 1 km
0 — 0.5 miles

**INFORMATION**
Langata Link.................1 B4
Language Center Ltd...2 B3
Let's Go Travel........(see 11)

**SIGHTS & ACTIVITIES**
Giraffe Centre.............3 B4
Impala Club................4 B3
Karen Blixen Museum...5 A4
Kazuri Beads & Pottery
Centre...................6 A4
Ngong Hills Racecourse.7 B3
Southern Cross Safaris..8 A4
Utamaduni................9 B4

**SLEEPING**
Giraffe Manor..........(see 3)
Karen Blixen
Cottages............(see 12)
Karen Camp.............10 A3

**EATING**
Horseman.................11 A3
Karen Blixen Coffee
Garden.................12 A4
Rusty Nail................13 A3
Talisman.................14 A3

**DRINKING**
Outside Inn..............15 A3

**NAIROBI & AROUND**

---

### KAREN BLIXEN

The suburb of Karen takes its name from Karen Blixen, aka Isak Dinesen, a Danish coffee planter and aristocrat who went on to become one of Europe's most famous writers on Africa. Although she lived a life of genteel luxury on the edge of the Ngong Hills, her personal life was full of heartbreak. After her first marriage broke down, she began a love affair with the British playboy Denys Finch Hatton, who subsequently died in a plane crash during one of his frequent flying visits to Tsavo National Park.

Blixen then returned to Denmark, where she began her famous memoir *Out of Africa*. The book is one of the definitive tales of European endeavour in Africa, but Blixen was passed over for the 1954 Nobel Prize for Literature in favour of Ernest Hemingway. She died from malnutrition at her family estate in Denmark in 1962.

*Out of Africa* was later made into a movie starring Meryl Streep, Robert Redford and one of the retired trains from Nairobi's Railway Museum. Needless to say, the final production was terrific from a Hollywood perspective, but leaves out enough of the colonial history to irk historians and Kenyan nationalists alike.

---

under threat as spiralling population densities along the park boundaries are threatening the viability of this ecosystem.

### History

As Nairobi boomed in the early 20th century, conflicts between humans and animals became a major inhibitor of growth. Early residents of the capital were forced to carry guns at night to protect themselves from lions, while herd animals routinely raided country farms. As a result, the colonial government of British East Africa set about confining the game animals to the Athi plains to the west and south of Nairobi.

In 1932, Kenyan-born Mervyn Cowie returned to Nairobi after a nine-year absence to discover that farmers and herders were threatening wildlife populations on the outskirts of the city. In the hopes of saving his beloved urban retreat, Cowie started to campaign for the establishment of a national park system in Kenya. In 1946, Nairobi National Park became the first national park in British East Africa, though the event was not without controversy, as the Maasai pastoralists were forcibly removed from the parklands.

At the same time, Cowie was named director of Nairobi National Park, a position he held until 1966. During his tenure, Cowie emerged as a prominent Kenyan conservationist, instrumental in wildlife protection and the development of tourism throughout East Africa. He is known in popular accounts for having chased an elephant away from the then Princess Elizabeth's party during their visit to the Treetops Hotel in Aberdare National Park in 1952.

In 1989, Nairobi National Park was thrust into the international spotlight when Kenyan President Daniel arap Moi burnt 12 tons of ivory at a site near the main gate. This dramatic event improved Kenya's conservation image at a time when East African wildlife was being decimated by relentless poaching.

### Orientation & Information

Nairobi National Park is easily the most accessible of all Kenya's wildlife parks, located just 7km south of the CBD. At just 117 sq km, the park is also one of the smallest in Africa.

The headquarters of the **Kenya Wildlife Service** (KWS; ☎ 600800; www.kws.org) is also located at the park entrance.

Keeping the wildlife migration pathway open is one of the principal aims of the Friends of Nairobi National Park (p97).

### Sights & Activities

Despite its unusual location next to one of East Africa's largest cities, Nairobi National Park is all about the **safari**.

The annual wildebeest and zebra migration that takes place in July and August can be seen here (albeit in significantly less concentrations than in Masai Mara), and there are generally large aggregations of antelope and buffaloes here year-round. Lions and hyenas are also commonly sighted within the park, though you will need a bit of patience and a lot of luck to spot the resident cheetahs and leopards.

Nairobi National Park has acquired the nickname 'Kifaru Ark', a testament to its success as a rhinoceros (*kifaru* in Kiswahili) sanctuary. In fact, the park is one of the only

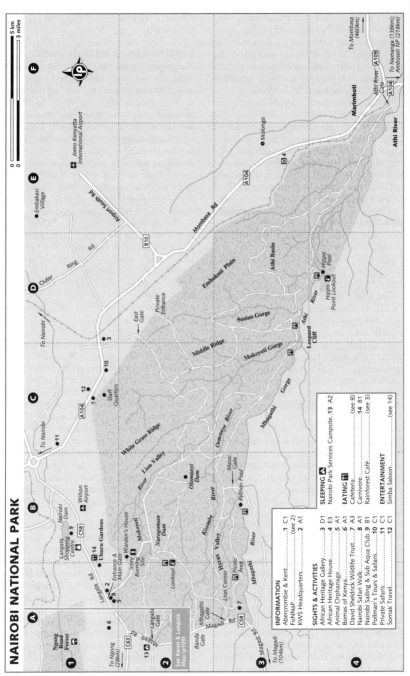

NAIROBI NATIONAL PARK

0 — 5 km
0 — 3 miles

To Namanga (138km);
Amboseli NP (218km)

To Mombasa
(460km)

Marimboti

Athi River

Athi River
Gate

A104

A109

Jomo Kenyatta
International Airport

Molongo

A104

Mombasa Rd

Embakasi
Village

Embakasi Plain

Athi Basin

Hippo
Pool

Airport South Rd

B10

Sosian Gorge

Hippo
Point Lookout

Outer    Ring    Rd

Private
Entrance

Leopard    Athi    River
Cliff

East
Gate

Middle Ridge

Mokoyeti Gorge

To Nairobi

3

Staff
Quarters

10

12

1

Mbagathi    Gorge

White Grass Ridge

Lion Valley

Ormoney River

Masai
Gate

A104

To Nairobi

11

Nairobi
Dam

Wilson
Airport

River

Olmanyi
Dam

River

Python Pool

9

C58

Uhuru Gardens

Mokoyeti

Kisembe    River

Langata
Shopping
Centre

14

Warden's House

Entrance &
Main Gate

Narogoman
Dam

Hyrax    Valley

River

Banda
Gate

Langata    Rd

2

Ivory
Burning
Site

Lookout

Lion Corner

Picnic
Area

Nairobi
Dam

Magadi    Rd

See Karen & Langata
Map (p109)

5

Ngong
Road
Forest

6

C63

Langata
Gate

Mbagathi
Gate

C58

Magadi    Rd

Mbagathi    Gate

7

13

To Ngong
(28km)

To Magadi
(104km)

places in Kenya where you are almost guaranteed to spot a black rhino in the wild.

The cheapest way to see the park is on the Park Shuttle, a big KWS bus that leaves the main gate at 3pm Sundays for a 2½-hour tour (adult/child US$20/5). You'll need to book in person at the main gate by 2.30pm.

Alternatively, most Nairobi-based safari companies (p65) offer various tours of the park. The half-day packages usually depart twice a day, at 9.30am and 2pm, and cost around US$75 per person. Combined trips including the Bomas of Kenya (p114) and lunch at the famed Carnivore restaurant (p125) are also popular, costing upwards of US$125 per person.

Also on the park grounds is the **Nairobi Safari Walk** (adult/child US$20/5; 8.30am-5.30pm), a sort of zoo-meets-nature boardwalk with lots of birds as well as other wildlife, including a pygmy hippo and a white rhino. This is a good spot to bring the kiddies, who will undoubtedly enjoy the critter close-ups.

The nearby **Animal Orphanage** (adult/child US$15/5; 8.30am-5.30pm) houses formerly wild animals that have been recovered by park rangers for various reasons. Although it's something of a glorified zoo, the orphanage does protect animals that would have died without human intervention. It also serves as a valuable education centre for Nairobi-ites and school children who might not otherwise have the chance to interact with wildlife.

### Sleeping & Eating
Nairobi Park Services has a fine **campsite** on the edge of the park – see p121 for more information. There is also a small **cafeteria** on the park grounds, which serves cold drinks and hot Kenyan standards.

### Getting There & Away
The main entrance to the park is on Langata Rd, but there are also public gates on Magadi Rd. The Athi River Gate at the far end of the park is handy if you're planning to continue on to Mombasa, Amboseli or the Tanzanian border.

The roads in the park are passable for 2WDs, but travelling in a 4WD is never a bad idea, especially if the rains have been heavy.

Matatus 125 and 126 pass right by the park entrance; departing from the train station, the ride (KSh40) should take about 30 to 45 minutes depending on traffic. A taxi should cost between KSh800 and KSh1000 from the city centre.

### DAVID SHELDRICK WILDLIFE TRUST
Occupying a plot within Nairobi National Park, this nonprofit **trust** (Map p111; 891996; www.sheldrickwildlifetrust.org) was established in 1977 shortly after the death of David Sheldrick, who served as the antipoaching warden of Tsavo National Park. Together with his wife Daphne, David pioneered techniques of raising orphaned black rhinos and elephants and reintroducing them back into the wild, and the trust retains close links with Tsavo for these and other projects. Rhinos and elephants are still reared on site, and can be viewed daily between 11am and noon.

There's no official charge for visiting, but a donation of KSh300 per person is requested. There's a gift shop and information centre, and usually someone around to answer questions. Be advised that visiting times are strictly regulated, so do not try and stop by at other times.

After opening its doors, visitors are escorted over to a small viewing area centred on a muddy watering hole. A few moments later, much like a sports team marching out onto the field in a scene from an epic sports film, the animal handlers come in alongside a dozen or so baby elephants. For the first part of the viewing, the handlers bottle-feed the baby elephants while explaining the tragic backgrounds of each of the animals.

Once the little guys have drunk their fill, they proceed to romp around like big babies, though it's serious business keeping them in line as they each weigh a few hundred kilos. The elephants seem to take joy in misbehaving in front of their masters, so don't be surprised if a few break rank and start rubbing up against your leg!

The baby elephants also use this designated timeslot for their daily mud bath, which, needless to say, makes for some great photos. Of course, if you're travelling with an expensive digital SLR, you might want to keep your guard up as these little devils have been known to spray a tourist or two with a trunkful of mud.

Once the show ends, you're permitted to check out the orphaned rhinos, which are a bit feistier and a whole lot more dangerous than the elephants. Although it can be a little depressing to see these majestic animals in cages, remember that they are being rehabilitated, and will eventually be released into the wild.

To get here by bus or matatu, take 125 or 126 from Moi Ave and ask to be dropped off at the KWS central workshop on Magadi Rd (KSh40, 50 minutes). It's about 1km from the workshop gate to the Sheldrick centre – it's signposted and KWS staff can give you directions. Be advised that at this point you'll be walking in the national park, which does contain lions, so stick to the paths. A taxi should cost between KSh800 and KSh1000 from the city centre.

### GIRAFFE CENTRE

This vitally important **breeding centre** (Map p109; ☎ 891568; www.giraffecenter.org; Koitobos Rd; adult/child nonresident KSh500/250, resident KSh100/20; ☿ 9am-5.30pm), run by the African Fund for Endangered Wildlife (AFEW), was started in 1979 by Jock Leslie-Melville, the Kenyan grandson of a Scottish earl. Jock and his wife Betty started by raising a baby giraffe in their Langata home, though the late couple was successful in introducing several breeding pairs of Rothschild giraffes into Kenyan national parks.

Unlike the more common reticulated and Masai giraffes, the Rothschild giraffe is an endangered species, having suffered severe habitat loss in western Kenya. In 1979, when this nongovernmental, nonprofit organisation was just getting off the ground, there were no more than 130 Rothschild giraffes in the wild. Today, the population numbers more than 300, and the centre has successfully released these charismatic creatures into Lake Nakuru National Park, Mwea National Reserve, Ruma National Park and Nasalot National Reserve.

The mission statement of the centre is to create awareness and provide environmental education aimed at encouraging visitors to appreciate and conserve Kenya's biodiversity. Despite this serious take-home message, there is plenty of fun and games at this highly recommended attraction. At the centre you can observe, hand-feed or even kiss Rothschild giraffes from a raised wooden structure, which is quite an experience, especially for children or children at heart. There's also an interesting self-guided forest walk through the adjacent Gogo River bird sanctuary.

If you can't get enough of mother nature's vertically enhanced mammals, you might like to stay at the phenomenal Giraffe Manor on the grounds here, one of Nairobi's grandest accommodation options. For more information, see p121.

To get here from central Nairobi by public transport, take matatu 24 via Kenyatta Ave to the Hardy shops, and walk from there. Alternatively, take matatu 26 to Magadi Rd, and walk through from Mukoma Rd. A taxi should cost between KSh800 and KSh1000 from the city centre.

### UTAMADUNI

A charitable organisation set in a large colonial house near the Giraffe Centre, **Utamaduni** (Map p109; ☎ 890464; Bogani East Rd; admission free; ☿ 9.30am-6pm) is essentially a large crafts emporium, with more than a dozen separate rooms selling all kinds of excellent African artworks and souvenirs. You can visit the workshops in the garden, and there's a playground and restaurant. It's a regular stop for the more upmarket tour companies, so prices start relatively high, but there's none of the hard sell you'd get in town. A portion of all proceeds goes to the Kenya Wildlife Foundation.

### KAREN BLIXEN MUSEUM

This **museum** (Map p109; ☎ 882779; www.museums.or.ke; Karen Rd; adult/child nonresident KSh200/100, resident KSh50/20; ☿ 9.30am-6pm) is the farmhouse where Karen Blixen, author of *Out of Africa*, lived between 1914 and 1931. She left after a series of personal tragedies, but the lovely colonial house has been preserved as a museum. It, along with the adjacent agricultural college, was presented by the Danish government to the Kenyan government at independence.

The museum is set in lovely gardens, and is an interesting place to wander around, especially if you're a fan of the Hollywood classic. With that said, the movie was *actually* shot at a nearby location, so don't be surprised if things don't look entirely right!

Just down the road you'll find the Karen Blixen Coffee Garden (p127) and the Karen Blixen Cottages (p121), just in case you want to make the most of your *Out of Africa* experience.

The museum is about 2km from Langata Rd. The easiest way to get here is by matatu 24 via Kenyatta Ave, which passes right by the entrance. A taxi should cost between KSh800 and KSh1000 from the city centre.

## KAZURI BEADS & POTTERY CENTRE

An interesting diversion in Karen is this **craft centre** (Map p109; ☎ 883500; www.kazuri.com; Mbagathi Ridge; ⏰ 8am-4:30pm Mon-Sat, 11am-4:30pm Sun), which was started by an English expat in 1975 as a place where single mothers could learn a marketable skill and achieve self-sufficiency. Starting with just two employees, the workforce has burgeoned to over 100, including several disabled women who work from home. A knowledgeable foreman provides a tour (free of charge) of the various factory buildings, where you can observe the process from the moulding of raw clay to the glazing of the finished products. A tasteful gift shop is right on the premises, with prices considerably cheaper than at other retail locations. It's located on Karen Rd near the Karen Blixen Museum.

## BOMAS OF KENYA

A cultural centre at Langata, the **Bomas of Kenya** (Map p111; ☎ 891801; Langata Rd; adult/child nonresident KSh600/300, resident KSh100/25; ⏰ performances 2.30pm Mon-Fri, 3.30pm Sat & Sun) is near the main gate to Nairobi National Park. The talented resident artists perform traditional dances and songs taken from the country's various tribal groups, including Arabic-influenced Swahili *taarab* music, Kalenjin warrior dances, Embu drumming and Kikuyu circumcision ceremonies. It's touristy, of course, but it's still a spectacular afternoon out, and the centre itself has such a high profile that the first meeting of the National Constitutional Conference was held here in 2003, producing the so-called Bomas Draft of the new constitution.

Bus or matatu 125 or 126 runs here from Nairobi train station (KSh30, 30 minutes). Get off at Magadi Rd, from where it's about a 1km walk, clearly signposted on the right-hand side of the road. A taxi should set you back between KSh800 and KSh1000.

## AFRICAN HERITAGE HOUSE

Designed by Alan Donovan, an African heritage expert and gallery owner, this stunning **exhibition house** (Map p111; ☎ 0721-518389; www .africanheritagebook.com; off Mombasa Rd; admission free) overlooking Nairobi National Park can be visited by prior arrangement only. The mud architecture combines a range of traditional styles from across Africa, and the interior is furnished exclusively with tribal artefacts and artworks. For those with a bit of money to burn, it's possible to negotiate overnight stays, formal meals and luxurious transfers by steam train or helicopter.

For more information, you can drop in at the **African Heritage Gallery** (Map p111; ☎ 890528; Libra House, Mombasa Rd), which sells the same kind of upmarket *objets d'art* you'll see in the house.

## Ngong Hills

The green and fertile Ngong Hills were where many white settlers set up farms in the early colonial days. It's still something of an expat enclave, and here and there in the hills are perfect reproductions of English farmhouses with country gardens full of flowering trees – only the acacias remind you that you aren't rambling around the Home Counties of England.

Close to Pt Lamwia, the summit of the range, is the **grave of Denys Finch Hatton**, the famous playboy and lover of Karen Blixen. A large obelisk east of the summit on the lower ridges marks his grave, inscribed with a line from 'The Rime of the Ancient Mariner', one of his favourite poems. The hills still contain plenty of wildlife (antelope and buffaloes are common) and there are legends about a lion and lioness standing guard at Finch Hatton's graveside.

The hills provide some excellent **walking**, but robbery has been a risk in the past; ask locals for the latest information. If you're worried, take an organised tour or an escort from the Ngong police station or KWS office.

Several Sundays a month, hundreds of Nairobi residents flee the noise and bustle of the city for the much more genteel surroundings of the **Ngong Hills Racecourse** (Map p109; ☎ 573923; Ngong Rd), just east of Karen. In the past, races had to be cancelled because of rogue rhinos on the track, but the biggest danger these days is stray balls from the golf course in the middle!

The public enclosure is free to enter; entry to the grandstand is KSh100, or you can pay KSh250 for a platinum pass, which gives you access to the cushioned members' seating and the restaurant overlooking the course. A race card costs KSh30 and you can bet as little as KSh20 with some bookies (minimum KSh100 with the course Tote). There are usually three races every month during the season, which runs from October to July.

You can get here on the Metro Shuttle bus (KSh40, 30 minutes) and matatus 24 or 111 (KSh20), all from Haile Selassie Ave.

## Lake Magadi

The most southerly of the Kenya's Rift Valley lakes, this **soda lake** (off Map p96) is rarely visited by tourists because of its remoteness. However, if you have your own vehicle, it makes an easy day trip from Nairobi, and is one of the more unusual diversions from the city.

The most mineral-rich of the soda lakes, it is almost entirely covered by a thick encrustation of soda that supports flamingos and other waterbirds, and gives the landscape a bizarre lunar appearance. A causeway leads across the most visually dramatic part of this strange landscape to a viewpoint on the western shore. It's worth a drive if you have a 4WD, otherwise you can head to the hot springs further south. The springs aren't particularly dramatic, but you can take a dip in the deeper pools, and there are large numbers of fish that have adapted to the hot water. You may run into local tribespeople, particularly Maasai, who will offer to show you the way and 'demonstrate' everything for you for a small fee.

The thick soda crust is formed when the mineral-rich water, pumped up from hot springs deep underground, evaporates rapidly in the 38°C temperature to leave a mineral layer. A soda-extraction factory 'harvests' this layer and extracts sodium chloride (common salt) and sodium carbonate (soda), which are put straight onto trains to Mombasa. Not surprisingly, Magadi is purely a company town, run by the unimaginatively named Magadi Soda Co, for factory staff and their families.

On your way back to Nairobi, don't miss the chance to stop at the famous **Olorgasailie Prehistoric Site** (off Map p96). Several important archaeological finds were made at this site, 40km north of Magadi, by the Leakeys in the 1940s, including hand axes and stone tools thought to have been made by *Homo erectus* about half a million years ago.

Fossils have also been discovered and some are still there, protected from the elements by shade roofs. A guided tour (KSh200) is available, and there are numerous noticeboards and displays.

If you want to stay out here, camping is your only option. The **Olorgasailie campsite** (Hwy C58; camping KSh200, bandas s/d KSh500/800) is not a bad place to stay for the night; you'll need to bring your own food, bedding and drinking water. It can get pretty windy out here, but you'll certainly feel like you're properly in the bush and it's likely you'll have the place to yourself.

The C58 road from Nairobi is in good condition, although there is very little traffic on it after Kiserian. There is also at least one matatu a day to Nairobi (KSh200), leaving in the morning and returning to Magadi in the evening.

## ACTIVITIES

**Nature Kenya** organises a variety of outings, including half-day bird walks that depart from the National Museum – contact them for more information (p98).

Most international tourist hotels have **swimming pools** that can be used by nonguests for a daily fee of between KSh200 and KSh500. Hotels with heated pools near the city centre are all of the top-end variety – see p118.

A number of private **sports clubs** in the suburbs offer facilities for nonmembers. All are out in the posher suburbs, and tend to be rather exclusive, so it's probably best to come here with either nice clothes or thick skin. Temporary daily membership fees apply.

**Impala Club** (Map p109; ☎ 565684; Ngong Rd, Karen)
**Nairobi Club** (Map pp100-1; ☎ 725726; Ngong Rd, Nairobi Hill)
**Nairobi Sailing & Sub Aqua Club** (Map p111; ☎ 501250; Nairobi Dam, Langata Rd)

## TOURS

There's not much to see in downtown Nairobi, but most travel agents and safari operators can take you on a tour of the National and Railway Museums, parliament and the city market for a small fee. Also popular are trips to suburban attractions such as Nairobi National Park, the Bomas of Kenya, the Karen Blixen Museum and the Giraffe Centre – prices are negotiable depending on the size of your party and your intended itinerary. See p109 for more on these attractions. Also see p65 for tour companies and details of longer trips.

For an introduction to the world of *jua kali,* Kenya's open-air manufacturing industry, **People to People Tourism** ( ☎ 786193; www.peopletopeopletourism.com) combines tours of the usual tourist sights with visits to *jua kali* workshops producing crafts and other goods.

## KIBERA

Home to an estimated one million residents, the shanty town of Kibera (off Map pp100–1) is second in size only to Soweto in Johannesburg, South Africa. Kibera, which is derived from a Nubian word *kibra*, meaning forest, is a sprawling urban jungle of shanty town housing. The neighbourhood was thrust into the Western imagination when it was featured prominently in the Fernando Meirelles film *The Constant Gardener,* which is based on the book of the same name by John le Carré. With the area heavily polluted by open sewers, and lacking even the most basic infrastructure, residents of Kibera suffer from poor nutrition, violent crime and disease.

Although it's virtually impossible to collect accurate statistics on shanty towns, which change their demographics almost daily, the rough estimates for Kibera are shocking enough. According to local aid workers, Kibera is home to one pit toilet for every 100 people, suffers from an HIV/AIDS infection rate of more than 20%, and four out of every five people living here are unemployed. These stark realities are compounded by the fact that the social services needed to address the situation are largely absent from governmental policies.

### History

The British established Kibera in 1918 for Nubian soldiers as a reward for service in WWI. However, following Kenyan independence in 1963, housing in Kibera was rendered illegal by the government on the basis of land tenure. But this new legislation inadvertently allowed the Nubians to rent out their property to a greater number of tenants than legally permitted and, for poorer tenants, Kibera was perceived as affordable despite the legalities. Since the mid-1970s, though, control of Kibera has been firmly in Kikuyu hands, who now comprise the bulk of the population.

### Orientation

Kibera is located southwest of the CBD. Although it is 2.5 sq km in area, it's home to somewhere between a quarter and a third of Nairobi's population, and has a density of an estimated 300,000 people per sq km.

## FESTIVALS & EVENTS

**Kenya Fashion Week** ( ☎ 0733636300; Sarit Centre, Westlands) An expo-style fashion event held in June, bringing together designers and manufacturers from all over the country.

**Tusker Safari Sevens** (www.safarisevens.com; Impala Club, Ngong Rd, Karen) A high-profile international seven-a-side rugby tournament held every June. It's always hotly contested and the Kenyan team has a strong record in the tournament.

**Kenya Music Festival** ( ☎ 2712964; Kenyatta Conference Centre) Held over 10 days in August, Kenya's longest-running music festival was established almost 80 years ago by the colonial regime. African music now predominates, but Western and expat musicians still take part.

## SLEEPING

It shouldn't come as too much of a surprise that Nairobi, being the capital, has the largest breadth of accommodation in the country. The strength of Nairobi's sleeping scene is clearly its variety – from rough-and-ready cheapies on the wrong side of the tracks to palatial country estates out in the verdant suburbs. As a result, your experience bedding down in the capital will be largely dependent on where you choose to lie, since each of Nairobi's neighbourhoods varies considerably in character.

The heart and soul of Nairobi is the city centre, so if you want to go to bed and wake up in the centre of it all, then look no further. The main budget area is between Tom Mboya St and River Rd, where you'll find dozens of small hotels and guest houses, though most of the rock-bottom cheapies are usually brothels or dosshouses for drunks. A much better option is to spring for a midrange or top-end crash pad, several of which have prominent locations in the CBD and offer surprisingly comfortable surrounds.

Of the outlying areas, the eastern districts of Nairobi Hill and Milimani have the most promising selection, catering for all budgets. This is where you'll find Nairobi's preferred backpacker spots, as well as a clutch of reliable business hotels and upmarket lodges. If you want to be a bit further out, there are also a handful of comfortable spots in the expat-friendly Westlands and Parklands.

For a decidedly different take on Nairobi, consider heading out into the 'burbs, namely

The railway line heading to Kisumu intersects Kibera, though the shanty town doesn't actually have a station. However, this railway line does serve as main thoroughfare through Kibera, and you'll find several shops selling basic provisions along the tracks.

### Visiting Kibera

An increasing number of tourists to Kenya are interested in visiting Kibera, though the jury is still out on whether or not these trips are constructive. On the one hand, it does lead to awareness, and many Kibera residents want their story to be told to the outside world. On the other hand, going to see humanity living in depraved conditions has a zoolike quality to it that is impossible to dismiss, and some residents don't appreciate these kinds of visitors.

With that said, visiting Kibera with a trustworthy local resident or with an NGO worker who knows the scene can be a wonderfully eye-opening experience. After all, there is nothing quite like the enjoyment of playing a bit of footy with street children aspiring to be the next Pelé. But be aware that a number of establishments in Nairobi are starting to offer 'cultural tours' to Kibera – many of which visitors may feel are not much more than organised voyeurism promoting little human interaction.

If you are considering a visit to Kibera, ask questions about the nature of your trip, and consider the potential positive and negative impact that it may have on the community.

### Getting There & Away

If you're not visiting Kibera as part of an organised tour, you can get there by taking bus 32 or matatu 32c from the Kencom building along Moi Ave. Be advised that this route is notorious for petty theft, so be extremely vigilant and pay attention to your surroundings. Again, it is highly recommended that if you visit Kibera, you do so under the supervision of a local resident or NGO worker.

Karen, Langata or Ngong Hills. For the most part, accommodation out here is at the top of the top end, though the bucolic charm exuded by many of these properties is worth every shilling. If that's out of your price range, however, there are a couple of campsites out here that are worth checking out.

Regarding budget, you can expect to pay a bit more in Nairobi than you would for the same facilities elsewhere in Kenya, especially in the midrange and top-end categories. However, in a city where personal safety is something of an issue, it's worth shelling out more for secure surroundings, especially if you're travelling with expensive gear. The majority of midrange and top-end places also tend to throw in a hearty buffet breakfast, which can certainly keep you going throughout the day.

In this section, accommodation is broken down by neighbourhood and then by budget. Keep in mind that economic inflation and political instability in Kenya can have drastic consequences, and prices are likely to change – use the prices here as general comparisons as opposed to fixed and non-negotiable rates. Also, rates vary considerably at the top-end properties, so it's best to contact them in advance as you can usually secure slight discounts.

This is by no means a comprehensive laundry list, but following are a selection of the better options.

## City Centre

Budget accommodations in the city centre are extremely bare bones and can be a bit intimidating to unseasoned travellers, though they'll do in a pinch. Midrange accommodation options offer a significant step up in quality. At the top end are several of Nairobi's most storied hotels, which occupy some of the choicest locations around.

### BUDGET

**New Kenya Lodge** (Map pp104-5; ☎ 222202; River Rd; dm/r KSh500/1000) Staff here are very friendly, and there's hot water in the evening (or so they claim) at this long-standing shoe-stringer's haunt. This spot has seen better decades, though it's got an aged charm if you're not too fussy about things like, well, cleanliness.

**Eva May Lodge** (Map pp104-5; ☎ 216218; cnr River & Duruma Rds; s/d KSh1000/1300) Low standards here don't quite do the rather lovely-sounding name justice, but it's a decent guest house with small, perfectly reasonable rooms. When there is water, it comes courtesy of the electric shower attachment, so make sure you're not wearing any metal jewellery before you jump in.

**Hotel Africana** (Map pp104-5; ☎ 220654; Dubois Rd; s/d KSh1000/1500) The Africana has clean, bright rooms, and is better looked after than many places in its class, with a TV room and a roof garden offering a bird's-eye view of the busy streets. The plain but convenient onsite restaurant specialises in tasty Indian grub.

**Central YMCA** (Map pp100-1; ☎ 2724116; State House Rd; s/d 1000/1500) While it might not inspire the Village People to dedicate a song to it, this central spot has a decent range of passable rooms. Note that you don't need to be a man or a Christian to stay at the YMCA, though you'll certainly be in the majority here if you're either.

**Terrace Hotel** (Map pp104-5; ☎ 221636; Ronald Ngala St; s/d KSh1000/1500) One of the better deals you'll get at the budget end, the hotel wears its worn atmosphere like a badge of honour. While it compares very favourably to some of the cell-like establishments around, it's still spartan by most standards.

### MIDRANGE

**Terminal Hotel** (Map pp104-5; ☎ 228817; Moktar Daddah St; s/d KSh2000/2500) Although it's lacking in quality compared to other midrange offerings, the Terminal Hotel is preferable to budget crash pads in the city centre. The emphasis here is on doing the basics well, with no overblown attempts at tourist frills, and the clean and adequate rooms speak for themselves.

**Down Town Hotel** (Map pp104-5; ☎ 310485; Moktar Daddah St; s/d KSh2000/2500) Just down the road from the Terminal, Down Town doesn't have quite the personality of its neighbour, but provides much the same kind of standards for much the same kind of price. If the Terminal's full, chances are this is where they'll send you for alternative accommodation, and you're unlikely to hold it against them.

**Sixeighty Hotel** (Map pp104-5; ☎ 332680; www .680-hotel.co.ke; Muindi Mbingu St; s/d KSh2400/3200; P ▢) A significant step up from cheaper offerings, this central hotel is aimed squarely at local and international businesspeople.

There's little inspired about the place, though facilities are adequate, it's very secure and there's even the occasional wi-fi signal.

**Kenya Comfort Hotel** (Map pp104-5; ☎ 317606; www.kenyacomfort.com; cnr Muindi Mbingu & Monrovia Sts; s/d from US$38/56; P ▢) This cheerily painted place is kept in top nick, offering a fine selection of modern tiled rooms and a lift for easy access. Meals are also available in the popular 24-hour Sokoni bar-restaurant, and the rooftop guest-lounge is a nice place to survey the city.

**Hotel Ambassadeur Nairobi** (Map pp104-5; ☎ 246615; Tom Mboya St; s/d from US$60/70; P ▢) Believe it or not this big hotel opposite the National Archives once belonged to the posh Sarova chain, and structurally not much has changed. We do suspect room standards were rather more exacting in those days, though it's still a very attractive place to post up for a few nights.

**Meridian Court Hotel** (Map pp104-5; ☎ 313991; Muranga'a Rd; s/d from KSh5250/6750; P ▢ ▨) The elaborate lobby here is rather more prepossessing than the grey concrete blocks above it, but it's hardly worth complaining when you're essentially getting a suite for the price of a standard room. There's no great luxury involved, but the pool, bar and restaurants make it good value in this price range.

### TOP END

**Hilton Nairobi Hotel** (Map pp104-5; ☎ 250000; www.hilton.com; Mama Ngina St; s/d from US$135/150; P ▨ ▢ ▨) A distinct Nairobi landmark, the Hilton dominates the centre of town with its round tower, occupying virtually an entire block with rooms, restaurants, shops and a whole slew of business facilities. Although its overwhelming modernity isn't as atmospheric as some of Nairobi's more seasoned top-end hotels, the Hilton remains one of the best deals in town for upmarket travellers.

**New Stanley Hotel** (Map pp104-5; ☎ 316377; www .sarovahotels.com/stanley; cnr Kimathi St & Kenyatta Ave; s/d from US$225/250; P ▨ ▢ ▨) A Nairobi classic: the original Stanley Hotel was established in 1902, though the latest version is a very smart and modern construction run by the sophisticated Sarova Hotels. Colonial decor prevails inside, with lashings of green leather, opulent chandeliers and old-fashioned fans, though the real highlight (at least from our perspective!) is the Thorn Tree Café (see p124), which inspired Lonely Planet's online community.

**Norfolk Hotel** (Map pp104–5; ☎ 216940; www.fair mont.com/NorfolkHotel; Harry Thuku Rd; s/d from US$275/300; **P** ❄ **▣** ☎) Built in 1904, Nairobi's oldest hotel was *the* place to stay during colonial days – the hotel remains the traditional starting point for elite safaris, and the Lord Delamere Terrace (see p124) is still Nairobi's most famous meeting place. Thanks to the leafy grounds, it has an almost rustic feel, providing an appealing contrast to the modern bent of more central options, and it is by far the best spot in town for those looking for a bit of historical authenticity. To learn more about the colourful antics of Lord Delamere, one of the Norfolk's legendary patrons, see the boxed text, p126.

**ourpick Nairobi Serena Hotel** (Map pp100–1; ☎ 2822000; www.serenahotels.com; Central Park, Procession Way; r/ste from US$400/500; **P** ❄ **▣** ☎) Consolidating its reputation as one of the best top-flight chains in East Africa, this entry in the Serena canon has a fine sense of individuality, with its international-class facilities displaying a touch of safari style. A member of the prestigious 'Leading Hotels of the World' group, the Nairobi Serena is considered by many to be the capital's most elegant accommodation. Of particular note is the onsite Maisha health spa, which offers a wide range of holistic cures aimed at soothing your travel-worn bones and balancing your wanderlust-ridden mind. Given the choice, opt for one of the amazing garden suites, where you can take advantage of your own private patio garden, complete with minipergola for eating outside. As the hotel is right opposite Uhuru Park, avoid walking anywhere from here at night.

## Milimani & Nairobi Hill

Milimani and Nairobi Hill really do have it all – the city's top three backpacker spots are all here, pleasantly removed from the congestion of the city centre. If you're a midrange traveller looking for more stable digs, there are a number of hotels out here that will provide biz amenities without breaking the bank. And these two tranquil neighbourhoods are also home to their fair share of upmarket lodges, all of which provide copious amounts of luxury and style.

### BUDGET

**ourpick Upper Hill Campsite & Backpackers** (off Map pp100–1; ☎ 6750202; www.upperhillcampsite.com; Othaya Rd, Kileleshwa; camping KSh350, dm KSh500, banda 1200,

d with/without bathroom 2000/1500; **P** **▣**) An attractive, secure compound and an oasis from the mean city streets, Upper Hill offers a range of accommodation, attracting a loyal following of overland trucks and an international mix of backpackers and budget travellers. It is centred on a restored colonial house that rests elegantly on a sprawling estate in the embassy district of Kileleshwa. Competing for the title of Nairobi's top backpacker spot, Upper Hill organises just about every kind of safari and outdoor excursion you can imagine, and they'll even take the time to tune up your ride if you're on a self-drive expedition.

This spot is not actually in Upper Hill, though it's easy enough to access by public transport from the city centre – take matatu or bus 46 along Othaya Rd until you pass the Egyptian embassy on the left-hand side; the entrance to the property is just past here on the right-hand side. It's a long and not too recommendable walk from the city centre, but you can take a taxi out here for between KSh400 and KSh1000, depending on the time of day and your bargaining skills.

**Milimani Backpackers & Safari Centre** (Map pp100–1; ☎ 2724827; www.milimanibackpackers.com; Milimani Rd, Milimani; camping KSh350, dm KSh600, permanent tent KSh450, s/d cabin KSh1300/1500; **P** **▣**) Formerly known as Nairobi Backpackers, this up-and-coming spot has great potential. At the time of writing, things were still getting started, though it looks like the new owners are going to do a great job with the place. Whether you camp out back, cosy up in the dorms or splurge on your own cabin, you'll end up huddled around the fire at night, swapping travel stories and dining on home-cooked meals with fellow travellers. The friendly staff can also help you book a safari, organise onward travel or simply get your bearings. Any matatu or bus going down either Valley or Ngong Rds from the train station will drop you off near the hostel, though you can walk here from the city centre in about 30 minutes (assuming of course that you're not carrying all of your heavy bags, which might also make you a target for theft).

**Nairobi International Youth Hostel** (Map pp100–1; ☎ 2723012; www.hihostels.com; Ralph Bunche Rd, Milimani; dm/d from US$10/25; **P** **▣**) A well-looked-after budget option, Nairobi's Hostelling International branch isn't as atmospheric as the Upper Hill Campsite and Milimani Backpackers though it's a comfortable and relaxed spot to meet other travellers. Kenya's HI instalment offers the usual range of hosteller-catered amenities including an activity centre, booking desk, cybercafe, bar-restaurant and a communal lounge. Any matatu or bus going down either Valley or Ngong Rds will get you here. Note that many people have been robbed returning to the youth hostel by foot after dark, so it's best to always take a taxi at night.

### MIDRANGE

**our pick** **Upper Hill Country Lodge** (Map pp100-1; ☎ 2881600; www.countrylodge.co.ke; Second Ngong Ave, Milimani; s/d from KSh5100/7800; (P) (🖳)) This brand-spanking-new property was constructed by the owners of the adjacent Fairview Hotel, though rather than striving for over-the-top opulence, the focus here is on affordable luxury for business travellers. With prices starting at around KSh5000 a room, the Country Lodge is one of the best-value midrange options in Nairobi, though its minimalist yet stylish living quarters can compete with the best of them. The big news here for anyone travelling with their laptop is that free wi-fi is available throughout the premises, and it is strong and reliable enough to actually get some work done. Travellers can also unwind in the small gym, relax in the rock garden or take advantage of the bars and restaurants at the Fairview next door.

**Heron Hotel** (Map pp100-1; ☎ 2720740; www.heron hotel.com; Milimani Rd, Milimani; s/d from US$75/110; (P) (🖳) (🖭)) Anyone who can remember Buffalo Bill's will be astounded at the transformation: management is obviously *very* keen to shake the reputation garnered in the days not so long ago, when the bar here doubled as a notorious brothel! Today it's a model of respectability, changed beyond all recognition, and is a good choice for business travellers or comfort queens looking for a bit of affordable privacy.

**High Point Hotel** (Map pp100-1; ☎ 2724312; www .highpointcourt.com; Lower Hill Rd, Nairobi Hill; r from KSh6000; (P) (🖳) (🖭)) If you're looking for space and seclusion without laying out a fortune, this World Bank–affiliated suite and apartment complex is an excellent choice that provides ample eye-candy for view vultures – you can supposedly see both Mts Kenya and Kilimanjaro from the penthouse balcony (though it would have to be an incredibly smog-free day!). The split-level rooms have

kitchenettes and living rooms, and the range of onsite facilities adds to the great value offered here.

### TOP END

**Fairview Hotel** (Map pp100-1; ☎ 2711321; www.fair viewkenya.com; Bishops Rd, Milimani; s/d from KSh7500/11,000; (📶) (🖳) (🖭) (👶)) An excellent top-end choice that is nicely removed from the central hubbub, the Fairview is defined by its winding paths and green-filled grounds, which create a refined atmosphere, especially around the charming courtyard restaurant. Rooms of varying degrees of luxury are helpfully classified like airline seating, ranging from Economy to First Class.

**Palacina** (off Map pp100-1; ☎ 2715517; www.palacina .com; Kitale Lane, Milimani; ste 1-/2-person US$210/360, penthouses US$550; (P) (🖳) (🖭)) The fabulous collection of stylish suites, at what is possibly the first genuine boutique hotel in Kenya, is perfect for well-heeled sophisticates who still like the personal touch. Intimate rooms are awash with calming tones, boldly accented by rich teak woods, lavish furniture and private jacuzzis – on that note, there's a separate apartment complex for long-term renters, just in case you don't want to leave.

## Westlands & Parklands

Considering the number of restaurants and shopping centres in Westlands and Parklands, it's surprising how little accommodation there is in the area. However, there are two noteworthy upmarket properties worth checking out.

**Holiday Inn Nairobi** (Map p108; ☎ 3740920; www.holi dayinn.com; Parklands Rd, Parklands; s/d from US$200/250; (P) (📶) (🖳) (🖭)) Forget everything you think you know about the Holiday Inn, especially if you've stayed at any one of these generic properties in North America. The Nairobi instalment of this hotel chain is housed in a 1930s Edwardian-style hotel that exudes timeless class and colonial ambiance.

**Safari Park Hotel** (off Map pp100-1; ☎ 3633000; www.safaripark-hotel.com; Thika Rd; s/d from US$250/300; (P) (📶) (🖳) (🖭)) A huge complex done out in mock traditional decor worthy of a real safari lodge – perfect if you don't want your luxury experience to end when you leave the national parks. The *boma*-style lobby is quite spectacular, particularly the chandelier, and there are so many facilities we won't even try to list them all (five different restaurants, casino and what is dubbed as 'the largest swimming pool in Africa' for starters). Note that Safari Park is located on the outskirts of Parklands, so you're better off choosing the Holiday Inn if you want to be closer to the city centre.

## Karen & Langata

Staying in Karen and Langata puts you pretty far from the city centre, though that's precisely the point. These leafy suburbs are a welcome respite from the grit of the CBD, and you'll be within easy striking distance of some of Nairobi's top tourist attractions. Accommodation in these parts gravitates towards either basic campsites or hedonistic luxury, though you're spoilt for choice at either extreme.

**Karen Camp** (Map p109; ☎ 8833475; www.karen camp.com; Marula Lane; camping/dm/r US$4/6/20; [P] ) You wouldn't expect to find a backpacker-friendly option out here in affluent Karen, which is why we like this friendly little spot so much. The quiet location and smart facilities are reason enough to make the trek out to the shady campsites, spic-and-span dorms and permanent safari-style tents.

**Nairobi Park Services Campsite** (Map p111; ☎ 890661; www.nairobicampsite.com; Magadi Rd; camping/dm/r US$4/6/20; [P] ) Located on the edge of Nairobi National Park, this campsite is set in a garden complete with a great wood-finished bar and restaurant with satellite TV, cold beers and cheap meals. The vehicle work-bays make it a good pit stop for overland trucks and self-drivers, so you can expect to have some good company here.

**Karen Blixen Cottages** (Map p109; ☎ 882130; www.blixencoffeegarden.co.ke; 336 Karen Rd; per person US$175; [P] [🚗] ) Located near the Karen Blixen Museum, this lovely clutch of cottages is centred on a formal garden, and adjacent to a small coffee plantation and a country restaurant. If you're keen on having an *Out of Africa* experience, then look no further as this country charmer is for you.

**our pick** **Giraffe Manor** (Map p109; ☎ 891078; www .giraffemanor.com; Mukoma Rd; s/d half board US$375/580, full board US$425/625; [P] ) Built in 1932 in the typical English style, this elegant manor is situated on 56 hectares, much of which is given over to the adjacent Giraffe Centre (p113). As a result, you may have a Rothschild giraffe peering through your bedroom window first thing in the morning, which is, needless to say, just about one of the most surreal experiences you could imagine!

As if that wasn't enough of a hard sell, the real appeal of the Giraffe Manor is that you're treated as a personal guest of the owners, which means you can use their chauffeur, sample their wines and dine in lavish excess. Literary buffs should ask for the Karen Blixen room, decked out with furniture the famous author gave the owners when she left Africa for the last time.

## Ngong Hills & Athi River

If Karen and Langata aren't far enough away from the city centre for you, then consider bedding down amongst the famed Ngong Hills. Arguably one of the most stunning parts of the greater Nairobi area, the Ngong Hills are home to a popular ranch a world away from the urban bump and grind. Near the Athi River, also on the south side of the city, is another recommended spot, especially good if you want to get up-close-and-personal to some fine, feathered friends.

**Whistling Thorns** (Map p96; ☎ 072-721933; www .whistlingthorns.com; Isinya/Kiserian Pipeline Rd, near Kiserian; camping KSh250, cottage per person KSh2500-3500; [P] [🚗] ) This scenic ranch located in the Maasai foothills of the Ngong is a wonderfully rural spot to launch or wind down your Kenyan holiday. While the owners specialise in offering horse-riding safaris through the area, less active guests are contented by walking the trails, bird-watching on the open plains or just feasting on the delicious home cooking. To get here by public transport, take bus or matatu 111 or 126 from Moi Ave to Kiserian (KSh50, one hour) and change to an Isinya/Kajiado matatu. Ask to be dropped at Whistling Thorns, which is 200m from the roadside. Count on a two-hour trip from central Nairobi.

**Maasai Ostrich Resort** (Map p96; ☎ 020-350014; www.mericagrouphotels.com; off A104; camping adult/child KSh400/250, s/d from US$60/82; [P] [🚗] ) Combining an ostrich farm and a hotel is a fairly unusual idea, but, then again, why not? Certainly the luxury farmhouse accommodation and gardens provide a nice setting, and there's a range of activities to keep you busy in an otherwise unpromising area, from tennis to ostrich rides. To get out here, take the road towards Namanga (A104) and turn left at the sign – southbound public transport can get you to the turn-off, but it's another 7km to the farm itself.

---

**CAN KENYA BOUNCE BACK?** *Kennedy O Opalo*

Before December 2007, Kenya was famous for being an oasis of peace in the volatile East African region. With troubles in Somalia, southern Sudan and northern Uganda, Kenya served as a safe haven for refugees fleeing from violence back home. But that is not all that Kenya was famous for. With its unique blend of tourist attractions, Kenya remained a favoured destination for tourists from all over the world.

But all this was to be put on the line after a disputed presidential election on 27 December 2007. The election was a close call, and was marred by various misdeeds on the part of the two leading parties. In the end, the electoral commission proclaimed the incumbent president, Mwai Kibaki, the winner, sparking riots from opposition supporters who were convinced that their man, Raila Odinga, had won the election. The riots soon degenerated into all-out violence that very nearly plunged the country into civil war. The images on TV screens across the world were both shocking and disappointing. Kenyans turned on each other with machetes and all manner of crude weapons.

Unfortunately the local and international news reporting of the violence did not get the entire picture. While it is true that most of the fighting was along tribal lines, the real causes were economic and political.

Economic causes included perceived historical injustices in the distribution of land in the Rift Valley province (where casualties were highest) and the unequal distribution of government resources. The political causes were obvious – supporters of the opposition fought against supporters of the government. Most of those killed for political reasons died from bullet wounds as police forcefully quelled protests over the disputed election in cities and major towns all across country.

Although the media erroneously labelled the the clashes as tribal, most analysts agree that the violence was not inherently tribal. After all, Kenyans had coexisted peacefully for over four

---

# EATING

Nairobi is well stocked with places to eat, particularly in the city centre, where you can choose anything from the cheap workers' canteens around River Rd to Chinese feasts and full-on splurges off Kenyatta Ave. For dinner it's worth heading out to the suburbs, which offer dozens of choices of cuisine from all over the world – Karen and Langata have the best range, though there are some good choices in Westlands and Parklands and in Milimani and Upper Hill.

Like in the rest of the country, lunch is the main meal of the day, and city workers flock to the numerous canteens dishing up simple, classic Kenyan and Swahili dishes along with Western staples like chicken and chips. Any of the Kenyan and Swahili places listed here can whip you up a feed in next to no time. There are also innumerable indistinguishable fast-food joints around town following the Western model – Kimathi St and Moi Ave have particularly high concentrations.

Kenyans tend to give short shrift to vegetarianism – *nyama choma* (barbecued meat) is the national dish, and just about every pub-restaurant in town will throw a goat leg on the coals for you any time of day. For a more exotic take on things, there are some amazing restaurants where you can really do *nyama* in style. The law now limits what game meat can be served, but should the fancy take you, you can still sample ostrich, camel and even crocodile (think sweet, slightly fishy chicken).

Nairobi has plenty of upmarket restaurants serving internationally inspired cuisine. In fact, first-timers to Nairobi are often surprised by the cosmopolitan nature of the capital's dining scene, especially out in the well-heeled suburbs. The capital is also famous for its Indian cuisine, which makes an appearance in some form or another on just about every menu.

At budget and some midrange eateries, it's recommend that you pay in cash, especially if you haven't racked up too large a bill. However, all of the upmarket places listed in this section do accept credit cards, though be advised that most add 17% VAT to the bill. As in just about anywhere else, be sure to check your bill carefully before signing your name.

Note that in this section, eating options are broken down by neighbourhood and then by budget. Also be advised that restaurants come

decades in one state. However, for many people the disputed election served as an opportunity to seek redress for the various injustices they had endured since Kenya achieved independence in 1963.

Luckily for the people of Kenya, the international community acted to prevent the country from descending into the mess that some other African countries have found themselves in over the last few decades. A concerted effort on the part of the UN, the US and the EU ensured that the president and the opposition reached an agreement, resulting in the formation of a unity government. Since then, the situation in the country has returned to normal, although a section of those displaced by the violence are yet to return home.

The brief crisis had enormous human and material costs. More than 1000 people died, and hundreds of thousands were displaced from their homes. Government estimates put the economic cost at KSh60 billion (around US$770 million). Tourism, a mainstay of the Kenyan economy, was particularly affected. With the sector contributing about 12% of GDP and 9% of wage employment, the decline in visits was devastating.

The new unity government has tried to woo back tourists. The charismatic tourism minister, Najib Balala, has spearheaded an effort to rebrand Kenya as a safe tourist destination – most recently with a swanky commercial on CNN, the first ever of its kind about Kenya. To the ministry's credit, tourists have been trickling back, and the country's wounds seem to be healing.

This is should not come as a surprise. Kenya's wildlife, beautiful beaches, geographical features and cultural diversity remain attractive to tourists from all over the globe. From the annual wildebeest migration in Masai Mara to the picture-perfect beaches of the Swahili coast, Kenya remains one of Africa's most alluring destinations.

*Kennedy O Opalo is a Kenyan currently studying economics at Yale University in the US.*

and go quickly in the fickle capital, though these popular spots have thus far stood the test of time.

## City Centre

Nairobi's lifeblood flows through the CBD, which is why you'll find the lion's share of restaurants here. Cheap canteens and fast-food eateries fuel a good number of Nairobi's office workers, though there are several upmarket places that can set the scene for that crucial business lunch. If you're planning on having dinner anywhere in the city centre, be sure to take a taxi back to your accommodation as the streets empty out once the sun goes down.

### BUDGET

**Beneve Coffee House** (Map pp104-5; ☎ 217959; cnr Standard & Koinange Sts; dishes KSh50-150; ☒ lunch & dinner Mon-Fri) A small self-service cafe that has locals queuing outside in the mornings waiting for it to open. Food ranges from African- and Indian-influenced stews to curries, fish and chips, samosas, pasties and a host of other choices, all at low, low prices.

**Nyama choma stalls** (Map pp104-5; Haile Selassie Ave; lunch around KSh200) A definite step down the scale,

but worth it for the atmosphere, are the back-street stalls near the Railway Museum, behind the Shell petrol station. Foreigners are a rare sight, but you'll be warmly welcomed and encouraged to sample other Kenyan dishes such as *matoke* (cooked mashed plantains).

**Malindi Dishes** (Map pp104-5; Gaberone Rd; mains KSh100-250; ☒ lunch & dinner) A nice, little Swahili canteen – as the name suggests, this place serves great food from the coast, including pilau (curried rice with meat), birianis (spicy rice casseroles) and coconut fish, with side dishes such as *ugali* (maize- or cassava-based staple), naan and rice. You'll get a grand halal feed here, but true to its Muslim roots, it's closed for prayer at lunchtime on Friday.

**Dancing Spoon Café & Wine Bar** (Map pp104-5; ☎ 227581; 20th Century Plaza, Mama Ngina St; dishes KSh200-350; ☒ lunch & dinner) Next to the 20th Century Cinema, this bright canteen serves good Western and Kenyan food well into the evening hours. If you're planning on a night out that the cinema, stop by – there is nothing quite like a sizzling steak and a frothy beer before you take in a movie.

**Seasons Restaurant** (Map pp104-5; mains KSh250-300, buffets KSh450; ☒ lunch & dinner); Nairobi Cinema

( ☎ 227697; Uchumi House, Aga Khan Walk); Kimathi St ( ☎ 0720846276; Mutual Bldg) Whatever the season, the cafeteria vats here always brim with cheap Kenyan and Western favourites, which is probably why this local chain has taken on a strong following. The Nairobi Cinema outlet has a popular bar and beer garden, where you can even bring your own bottle and pay a small corkage fee.

**Etouch Food Court** (Map pp104-5; Union Towers, cnr Moi Ave & Mama Ngina St; meals KSh350-500; ☺ lunch & dinner) We all need a bit of greasy comfort food from time to time, and Nairobi-ites are certainly no exception. If you find yourself craving a quick fix, head to the Etouch Food Court, a central collection of cheap 'n' easy fast-food joints such as Nando's, Chicken Inn, Creamy Inn, Pizza Inn…you get the idea.

### MIDRANGE

**Lord Delamere Terrace & Bar** (Map p260; ☎ 216940; www.fairmont.com/NorfolkHotel; Harry Thuku Rd; light meals KSh300-600; ☺ lunch & dinner) Since 1904, this popular rendezvous spot at the Norfolk Hotel has existed as the unofficial starting and ending point for East African safaris. While it has been patronised by almost all of the first European pioneer settlers, it is named after the colourful character that is Lord Delamere (see boxed text, p126). While atmosphere may be a bit too colonial for some people's taste, there's no denying the palatable sense of history that ebbs from the walls.

**Pasara Café** (Map pp104-5; ☎ 338247; Lonrho Bldg, Standard St; dishes KSh300-750; ☺ 7am-6pm Mon-Fri, from 8am Sat) At the forefront of Nairobi's burgeoning cafe culture, this stylish modern bar-brasserie never fails to impress with its nifty selection of snacks, sandwiches, grills and breakfasts, always offering something that bit more ambitious than the usual cafeteria fare. The atmosphere equals that of any European coffeehouse, making it a fine place to relax with a newspaper away from all the stresses of the capital's streets.

**Fiesta Restaurant & Bar** (Map pp104-5; ☎ 240326; Koinange St; mains KSh500-750; ☺ 7am-midnight) Despite the Latin resonances of the name and the bright adobe-style decor, the Fiesta doesn't have anything remotely Tex-Mex on offer, concentrating instead on a fine selection of upmarket international dishes. Staff are smiley and almost unnervingly eager, and the chefs do themselves particular credit with some very un-Kenyan recipes, such as *nasi*

*goreng* (Indonesian rice dish) and pork chops with a honey and mustard glaze.

**Panda Chinese Restaurant** (Map pp104-5; ☎ 213018; Fedha Towers, Kaunda St; mains KSh500-750; ☺ noon-2.30pm & 6-10pm) A spacious, very classy restaurant hidden away on Kaunda St, this is where you should head if you have a sudden and incurable craving for beef and broccoli. The staff are attentive to the point of overzealousness, especially when it's quiet, and the food is some of the best Chinese chow you'll find in these parts.

**Thorn Tree Café** (Map pp104-5; ☎ 228030; New Stanley Hotel, Kimathi St; mains KSh500-850; ☺ lunch & dinner) The Stanley's legendary cafe still serves as a popular meeting place for travellers of all persuasions, and caters to most tastes with a good mix of food. The original thorn-tree notice-board in the courtyard gave rise to the general expression, and inspired Lonely Planet's own online Thorn Tree Travel Forum. While the cafe is now on its third acacia and the notice-board's not quite the paperfest it once was, a little nostalgia is *de rigueur,* even if only to pause and recognise an original landmark on the Cape to Cairo overland trail.

**Restaurant Akasaka** (Map pp104-5; ☎ 220299; Standard St; mains KSh550-900; ☺ noon-2.30pm & 6-10pm Mon-Sat) A wonderful Japanese restaurant next to the Sixeighty Hotel, the Akasaka is always a little quiet, but this befits the stylish Japanese decor. The food is surprisingly very authentic – there's even a *tatami* room (reservations required), where you can eat at traditional low tables. Akasaka runs the full gamut of Japanese cuisine including udon noodles, miso soups, sushi sets, tempura, teriyaki, sukiyaki and even great value bento boxes for lunch on the go.

**Porterhouse Restaurant** (Map pp104-5; ☎ 221829; Mama Ngina St; mains KSh550-1000; ☺ 5-10.30pm) Steak-lovers should make this discreetly swish 1st-floor restaurant their first port of call: apart from a few token dishes such as chicken Kiev, the menu here is entirely dedicated to the art of carving chunks of cow, and with a two-person chateaubriand for just under a thousand shillings, it's easy to get into the moo-d (ahem).

**Trattoria** (Map pp104-5; ☎ 340855; cnr Wabera & Kaunda Sts; mains KSh650-1000; ☺ 7.30am-midnight) A very popular downtown Italian restaurant swathed in trellises and plants, offering excellent pizzas, pasta, varied mains and a whole page of desserts. The atmosphere and food are excellent, and it's packed every night, especially the upstairs balcony section, where you can lord it over the city streets like a wannabe Mafioso.

## TOP END
**Alan Bobbé's Bistro** (Map pp104-5; ☎ 226027; Cianda House, Koinange St; mains KSh750-1000; ☻ lunch & dinner)
The talented Mr Bobbé established this superb French bistro in 1962, and Nairobi gourmets and gourmands alike have been worshipping at his culinary altar ever since. Even reading the chatty handwritten menu is enough to send the palate into raptures. The interior, doused in red velvet, adds perfectly to the recherché ambience. Reservations and smart dress are encouraged, cigars and pipes are not. Look for the poodle above Koinange St.

**ourpick Tamarind Restaurant** (Map pp104-5; ☎ 251811; www.tamarind.co.ke; Aga Khan Walk; mains KSh1000-2000; ☻ 2.30-4.30pm & 8.30pm-midnight)
Kenya's most prestigious restaurant chain runs Nairobi's best seafood restaurant, located in the monumental National Bank Building. The splendid menu offers all manner of exotic flavours, and the lavish dining room is laid out in a sumptuous modern Arabic-Moorish style. Starters range from locally raised Kilifi oysters to red snapper in spicy harissa, though save room for the crustacean onslaught of flambéed lobster with cognac, sunset Pwani crab and tikka masala prawns. Smart dress is expected, and you'll need to budget at least

## FOR THE LOVE OF MEAT
Love it or hate it, **Carnivore** (Map p111; ☎ 605933; www.carnivore.co.ke; off Langata Rd; veg/meat buffet KSh1200/1550; ☻ lunch & dinner; P ) is hands down the most famous *nyama choma* in Kenya, beloved of tourists, expats and wealthier locals alike for the past 25 years. It is also something of an institution for overlanders on the Cape to Cairo route, who make the obligatory pilgrimage here for the purpose of consuming copious amounts of chargrilled meat.

Owned by the established Tamarind chain, Carnivore has twice been voted among the 50 best restaurants in the world. In the past, this honour was largely in recognition of the fact that you could dine here on exotic game meats. This was made all the more poignant by the fact that live versions of the dinner menu were prancing about in nearby Nairobi National Park.

In recent years, however, strict new laws mean that zebra, hartebeest, kudu and the like are now off the menu, which makes things distinctly less exotic. If this hampers your dinner plans, fret not, as you can still sample camel, ostrich and crocodile in addition to the more standard offerings of beef, pork and chicken. But if you're heading overland to South Africa, you can always dine at the Johannesburg instalment of Carnivore, which isn't affected by game-meat laws.

At the entrance to Carnivore is a huge barbecue pit laden with real swords of beef, pork, lamb, chicken and farmed game meats. As long as the paper flag on your table is flying, waiters will keep bringing the meat, which is carved right at the table with a healthy amount of bravado. While this blood-soaked feast will be off-putting to a good number of vegetarians, it might come as a surprise that the menu at Carnivore does cater for its animal-loving patrons.

While dinners at Carnivore ultimately devolve into hedonistic bingefests, you can tip the flag over temporarily to give yourself a break to digest everything. If you do manage to save some space, note that dessert and coffee are included in the set price. A hefty 26% tax and service charge is added to the bill, and alcoholic drinks are extra.

A healthy number of cynics, including both resident expats and jaded travellers, label Carnivore as a tourist circus worth skipping out on. Whatever the argument, it is a quarter-of-a-century-old Nairobi tradition that continues to thrive. And, while it's certainly not for everyone, a lot of fun can be had here, especially if you go with the right people, as well as a serious craving for hunks of dead animals.

At lunchtime, you can get to Carnivore by matatu 126 from the city centre – the turn-off is signposted just past Wilson Airport, from where it's a 1km walk. At night, it's best to hire a taxi, which should run to about KSh650 to KSh800 each way depending on your bargaining skills. While your driver will most likely offer to wait for you, it's not necessary, as plenty of taxis mill about in the hopes of scooping up a late-night fare.

One last thing – if you end up gorging yourself on absurd quantities of red meat, you can justify your excesses with an all-night danceathon at the adjacent Simba Saloon (p130).

**THE LORD OF HAPPY VALLEY**

During the colonial heyday, Happy Valley (the highland area outside Nairobi) played host to an eccentric cast of British elites, who had a reputation for fondness of drinking, drug abuse and wife swapping. However, few can rival Hugh Cholmondeley, third Baron of Delamere, one of the first Britons to settle in Kenya. Immortalised in history books and local lore, Lord Delamere was a controversial yet celebrated hunter, pioneer, farmer, soldier, socialite, statesmen and – quite frankly – a total nutter.

Lord Delamere first set foot on the African continent in 1891 to hunt lion in then British Somaliland. He is widely credited with coining the term 'white hunter', which came to describe the professional big-game hunters in British East Africa. Five years after his arrival, he led an expedition across the deserts of southern Somaliland into the verdant highlands of what is now central Kenya. By the early 1900s, Lord Delamere owned more than 300,000 acres of land, and was already one of Kenya's most influential colonists.

For more than twenty years, he doggedly farmed his vast country estates by mere trial and error, experimenting with various crop strains from around the British Empire. He is famous for stating, 'I started to grow wheat in East Africa to prove that though I lived on the equator, I was not in an equatorial country'.

Lord Delamere was also active in recruiting English landed gentry to buy up holdings in British East Africa, and helped put Happy Valley on the map. He was also reportedly something of a drunken lout, and was particularly fond of inciting emotions through his antics. At the Norfolk Hotel, which still bears a restaurant named his honour (p124), Lord Delamere once rode his horse through the dining room, wooing dinner guests with his ability to leap over banquet tables.

In his later years, Lord Delamere became fully convinced of white supremacy, and established himself as a firebrand politician determined to protect British holdings in Africa. Often described as the 'Cecil Rhodes of Kenya', he once wrote of his support for the 'extension of European civilisation', stating that the British were '…superior to heterogeneous African races only now emerging from centuries of relative barbarism…'

In 1931, Lord Delamere died at the age of 61, leaving behind a mixed legacy that still has prominent repercussions today. On the one hand, he helped build the foundations of Kenya's modern agricultural economy, while, on the other, he exemplified the deeply resented policies of the British colonial government that would ultimately drive Kenyans to seek their independence. Although Nairobi's main thoroughfare once bore the name Delamere Ave, it was immediately renamed Kenyatta Ave in 1963.

Even today, Lord Delamere's progeny continue to capture both Kenyan and British headlines. In April 2005 Lord Delamere's great-grandson, Baron Thomas Cholmondeley, was suspected of shooting and killing Samson ole Sisina, a Maasai game warden, though charges were dropped despite public outcry. One year later, Robert Njoya was shot and killed when caught poaching on Cholmondeley's property. Cholmondeley was arrested and charged with murder, though his case remained unresolved at the time of print. The police spokesman on the case was reported as saying, 'The Delameres used to be untouchable. But that's all changed now.'

KSh2500 for the full works – much more if you want wine or cocktails and lobster – though seafood gourmands the world over agree that it's money well spent.

## Milimani & Upper Hill

While not quite as restaurant-rich as other neighbourhoods of Nairobi, Milimani, Upper Hill and Hurlingham are still home to a few recommended spots.

**Yaya Centre** (off Map pp100-1; Argwings Kodhek Rd, Hurlingham) This expat favourite is home to a speciality food-court as well as a reasonable selection of cafes and kiosks. The Saffron restaurant upstairs (mains KSh400 to KSh800) does great Indian eat-in and takeaway food, as evidenced by the near-steady stream of diners coming and going.

**Blue Nile Ethiopian Restaurant** (Map pp100-1; ☎ 0722898138; bluenile@yahoo.com; Argwings Kodhek Rd, Hurlingham; mains KSh500-700; ☾ lunch & dinner) One of those rare places with a character all its own, Blue Nile's quirky lounge, painted with stories from Ethiopian mythology, couldn't be mistaken for anywhere else. For the full, communal, African eating experience, order the five- to seven-person *doro wat* (spicy traditional chicken stew, KSh3500) with a few glasses of *tej* (honey wine; KSh125).

## Westlands & Parklands

The preferred commercial areas for moneyed Kenyans and resident expats, Westlands and Parklands have eateries that cater for their wealthy clientele, offering up impressive international spreads. While there are fewer bargains here than in the city centre, you can expect a high level of quality, and the relaxed and pleasant surroundings are certainly preferable to the mayhem of the CBD.

**Sarit Centre food court** (Map p108; ☎ 3747408; www.saritcentre.com; Parklands Rd, Westlands; prices vary; ❤ lunch & dinner) This huge food court on the 2nd floor of this popular shopping mall has a great variety of small restaurants and fast-food places catering to discerning palates. Standard Kenyan and Indian offerings are available here, as are other international eats including Italian, Chinese and Continental cuisines.

**Phoenician Restaurant** (Map p108; ☎ 3741524; Karuna Rd, Westlands; mains KSh500-800; ❤ lunch & dinner Tue-Sun) This garden restaurant, tucked away behind the Sarit Centre, may well be the only dedicated Lebanese restaurant in Kenya. There's plenty here for veggies, and with more starters than main courses, assembling your own mixed meze offers plenty of scope for a Middle East feast.

**Siam Thai** (Map p108; ☎ 3751728; Unga House, Muthithi Rd, Westlands; mains KSh500-900; ❤ lunch & dinner) While Asian food in Kenya tends to gravitate towards greasy Chinese, this attractive restaurant has an extensive menu of actual Thai food (gasp!). Curries here are rich, thick and spicy, which is exactly the way they're supposed to be. Unga House can be reached from either Woodvale Grove or Muthithi Rd.

**our pick** **Haandi Restaurant** (Map p108; ☎ 4448294; The Mall Haandi Centre, Ring Rd, Westlands; mains KSh750-1250; ❤ noon-2.30pm & 7-10.30pm; ⚹ ) An international award-winner that is widely regarded as the best Indian restaurant in Kenya, Haandi has sister restaurants in Kampala, London and Middlesex, and even sells its own souvenir T-shirts. While you might not expect to find a restaurant of this calibre in a shopping mall, your doubts will disappear the moment the waiter brings the tome of a menu to your table. Indeed, it reads something like a

recipe book crossed with a guide to Indian cuisine, and includes wonderful Mughlai (North Indian) spreads, tandoori dishes and plenty of vegetarian curries. Be sure to come here with an empty stomach as it isn't exactly the lightest fare, especially when served with Haandi's signature stacks of naan and piles of basmati rice.

## Karen & Langata

Long regarded as ground zero for epicureans living in Nairobi, Karen and Langata are home to most of the city's finest and most famous eateries, including the legendary meat-lover's establishment that is Carnivore (see boxed text, p125). You're going to need to bring a heavy wallet (and an empty stomach) to get the most out of a meal in these parts, though Karen and Langata are arguably the best neighbourhoods for a dinner out on the town.

**Rainforest Café** (Map p111; ☎ 555872; Libra House, Mombasa Rd; meals KSh350-500, buffet KSh900; ❤ lunch & dinner) The fact that Rainforest is owned and operated by NAS Airport Services might ring alarm bells at first, but you won't find any pre-packed trays here. In fact, locals reckon this is one of the few places in town you can get a decent sandwich, and the all-encompassing buffets are good value. There's no à la carte menu, though you can order individual dishes from the display.

**Rusty Nail** (Map p109; ☎ 882461; Dagoretti Rd; mains KSh450-800; ❤ lunch & dinner) The combination Moroccan/Turkish styling of this pavilion restaurant belies the range of food on offer – lunch and dinner menus change every week, offering anything from felafel and kebabs to snapper and coronation chicken. Cream teas and traditional Sunday roasts cater for nostalgic English foodies, though diners in the know are quick to feast on the rotating Middle Eastern specialities.

**Horseman** (Map p109; ☎ 884560; Karen shopping centre, Langata Rd; mains 500-1000; ❤ lunch & dinner) Horseman is three restaurants in one, set in a leafy patio garden straight out of rural England, with a surprisingly authentic pub to match. One section specialises in roasted meats, one serves pizzas and the third offers Chinese, Indian and Kenyan food. There's even a takeaway section on the main road outside, offering fast-food versions of various dishes (KSh150 to KSh300).

**Karen Blixen Coffee Garden** (Map p109; ☎ 882138; www.blixencoffeegarden.co.ke; Karen Rd; mains KSh750-1200;

☼ 7am-10pm) Just down the road from the Karen Blixen Museum, this upmarket option offers diners and snackers five different areas in which to enjoy a varied menu, including the plush L'Amour dining room, the historic 1901 Swedo House and the main section, which is a smart restaurant set in a veritable English country garden. The food is excellent, especially the hand-thrown pizzas cooked in a stone oven; there's also a friendly and very popular pub for throwing down an *Out of Africa*–inspired nightcap.

**Talisman** (Map p109; ☎ 883213; 320 Ngong Rd; mains KSh800-1400; ☼ from 9am Tue-Sun) This classy cafe/bar/restaurant is incredibly fashionable with the Karen in-crowd, and rivals any of Kenya's top eateries for imaginative international food. The comfortable loungelike rooms mix modern African and European styles, the courtyard provides some welcome air, and specials such as *tajine* (Moroccan stew) perk up the palate no end. The cakes and desserts also come highly recommended, especially if your sweet tooth has been thus far neglected in Kenya.

### Self-Catering

There are very few places to stay with self-catering facilities, but you can buy supplies for snack lunches, safaris etc, as well as cooking ingredients, from the many supermarkets downtown and in the suburbs.

**Nakumatt** Downtown (Map pp104-5; ☎ 335011; Kenyatta Ave); Lifestyle (Map pp104-5; ☎ 340015; Moktar Daddah St); Village Market ( ☎ 522508; Village Market, Limuru Rd, Gigiri) The principal supermarket chain in Nairobi and Kenya as a whole, Nakumatt invariably has a huge selection of Kenyan and Western foods and other products. The new Lifestyle store spreads over several floors, with departments stocking all kinds of useful household and outdoor goods.

**Uchumi** (Map p108; Sarit Centre, Parklands Rd) Once the main supermarket chain in town, Uchumi has faded fast in Nakumatt's wake and several central branches have closed. They have a good range of items for sale.

## DRINKING
### Cafes

Western cafe culture has hit Nairobi big-style, seized upon enthusiastically by local expats and residents pining for a decent cup of Kenyan coffee. All these places offer at least some form of food, whether it's a few cakes or a full menu, but none serve alcohol.

### CITY CENTRE

**Dormans Café** (Map pp104-5; ☎ 0724238976; Mama Ngina St; coffee KSh100-190) Established in the 1960s, this venerable firm has only recently branched out into the cafe business, but has certainly made an aggressive Starbucks-style start, opening a shiny pine outlet right opposite its main rival, Nairobi Java. The coffee's good, the selection of teas is impressive, and the food definitely hits the spot.

**Kahawa** (Map pp104-5; ☎ 221900; Fedha Towers, Kaunda St; mains KSh200-400) Kahawa has an unusual coastal theme – the counter even resembles a traditional dhow (Arabic sailing vessel), complete with mast. The menu, however, is anything but old-fashioned, proffering an ever-changing cavalcade of unexpected specials to complement the grills and steaks, from frittata to a 'Mexican breakfast'.

**Nairobi Java House** (Map pp104-5; ☎ 313565; www.nairobijava.com; snacks KSh100-200, meals KSh300-750; ☼ 7am-8.30pm Mon-Sat) This fantastic coffeehouse is rapidly turning itself into a major brand, and you may see its logo on T-shirts as far afield as London and beyond. Aficionados say the coffee's some of the best in Kenya, and there are plenty of cakes and other sweet and savoury treats.

**Oleander Café** (Map pp100-1; Rahimtulla Tower, Upper Hill Rd, Nairobi Hill; drinks KSh40-100) This small elevated cafe has limited stocks of food and drink. However, the terrace is so surrounded by greenery that you barely even notice the busy road below, providing a perfect respite if you happen to be in the Nairobi Hill area.

### Bars

There are plenty of cheap but very rough-and-ready bars around Latema Rd and River Rd, though these places aren't recommended for female travellers, and even male drinkers should probably watch themselves. There are some safer and friendlier watering holes around Tom Mboya St and Moi Ave, and many of the restaurants and hotels listed previously are fine places for a drink. You can also head to Westlands and Karen, where the drinking scene brings in a lot more expats. Even in the 'burbs, however, foreign women without a man in tow will draw attention virtually everywhere.

### CITY CENTRE

**Hornbill Pub** (Map pp104-5; ☎ 246615; Hotel Ambassadeur Nairobi, Tom Mboya St) A large, dark but friendly bar stretching the width of the block between Moi Ave and Tom Mboya St, with lashings of cold Tusker and sizzling *nyama choma* on the hot coals.

**Roast House** (Map pp104-5; Kilome Rd) This split-level green bar-restaurant is one of the better specimens in the River Rd area, with regular DJ nights, but caution is still advised if coming here at night – bring a local friend if you want to take part in the action.

**Zanze Bar** (Map pp104-5; ☎ 222532; Kenya Cinema Plaza, Moi Ave) A lively and friendly top-floor bar with pool tables, a dance floor, cheap beer and reasonable food. During the week things are relatively quiet, but from Friday to Sunday it rocks until the early hours, with a much more relaxed vibe than the big clubs.

### WESTLANDS & PARKLANDS
**Bar Code** (Map p108; Westview Centre, Ring Rd) It's nowhere near as cool as it thinks it is, but this very modern late-opening lounge bar does at least have a good range of international spirits and cocktails, plus semicompetent DJs spinning R&B and hip hop for the tiny dance floor. The lurid painted toilets are probably the best bit, in keeping with the vague gangster theme.

**Gypsy's Bar** (Map p108; ☎ 4440836; Woodvale Grove) This is probably the most popular bar in Westlands, pulling in a large, mixed crowd of Kenyans, expats and prostitutes. Snacks are available, and there's decent Western and African music, with parties taking over the pavement in summer. This is also as close as you'll get to a gay-friendly venue in Kenya, though it's still best to be discreet.

**Klub House** (Map p108; ☎ 749870; Parklands Rd) Further west, past the large Holiday Inn complex, the Klub House is another old favourite. The spacious bar has more pool tables than anywhere else and is a good place to party until late. Music is predominantly Latin, Caribbean and home-grown Swahili.

**Soho's** (Map p108; ☎ 3745710; Parklands Rd) A lively and popular place that pulls in a smart Kenyan and expat crowd. As well as the crisp cold beers, there's a good selection of wines and cocktails.

### UPPER HILL & MILIMANI
**Casablanca** (off Map p100-1; ☎ 2723173; Lenana Rd, Hurlingham) This Moroccan-style lounge bar has been an instant hit with Nairobi's fastidious expat community, and you don't have to

spend much time here to become a convert. Shisha pipes, wines and cocktails conspire to ease you into what's bound to end up a late night.

### KAREN & LANGATA
**Outside Inn** (Map p109; ☎ 882110; Plains House, Karen Rd) Perfect for a bit of rowdy drinkage, this semiopen barn of a bar is a firm favourite with residents for its relaxed, boozy atmosphere, and stays friendly even when it's packed for televised football or rugby fixtures.

## ENTERTAINMENT
For information on all entertainment in Nairobi and for big music venues in the rest of the country, get hold of the *Saturday Nation*, which lists everything from cinema releases to live-music venues. There will also be plenty of suggestions run in the magazine *Going Out*.

### Nightclubs
There's a good selection of dance clubs in Nairobi's centre and there are no dress codes, although there's an unspoken assumption that males will at least wear a shirt and long trousers. Beer in all these places is reasonably priced at about KSh150, but imported drinks cost a lot more.

Due to the high numbers of female prostitutes, men will generally get the bulk of the hassle, though even women in male company are by no means exempt from approaches by either sex.

### CITY CENTRE
**Florida 2000** (Map pp104-5; ☎ 229036; Moi Ave; men/women KSh200/100) The original blueprint for the New Florida (below), this big dancing den near City Hall Way still works to exactly the same formula of booze, beats and tightly packed bodies.

**New Florida** (Map pp104-5; ☎ 215014; Koinange St; men/women KSh200/100; ☽ to 6am, later Sat & Sun) The 'Mad House' is a big, rowdy club housed in a bizarre blacked-out saucer building above a petrol station. The music policy ranges from jazz to the customary weekend mish-mash of Western pop. Whichever night you choose, it's usually mayhem, crammed with bruisers, cruisers, hookers, hustlers and curious tourists, but it's great fun if you're in the right mood (or just very drunk).

**ourpick Simmers** (Map pp104-5; ☎ 217659; cnr Kenyatta Ave & Muindi Mbingu St; admission free) If

NAIROBI & AROUND

---

**SIDEWALK STRIFE**

One recent trend in Nairobi has seen all kinds of bars and restaurants extending their seating areas onto the pavement, European cafe–style, often with brightly coloured awnings, plants and other trappings to jazz up the drab street surroundings. A positive development, surely? Apparently not, as far as the city council is concerned.

The first sign that all was not well came when an entire vanload of council *askaris* (security guards) descended on the Kengeles Bar & Restaurant on Koinange St, leaving a startled crowd of punters and passers-by in their wake. The council claimed the owners were warned repeatedly about new regulations banning street extensions and had been told to remove the offending structure; the restaurant, however, said this was the first time they'd heard anything about it at all.

In the wake of the incident, other cafes removed their own pavement patios with quite remarkable alacrity, fearful of further action from above. Several nearby rivals have a different take on matters – as one competitor suggested to the *Daily Nation* shortly after the event, Kengeles may well have been targeted for personal reasons, as it's rumoured that the proprietors have had wrangles with the council in the past.

Whatever the truth, only a handful of pavement restaurants have dared to hold their ground, and it seems we'll have to wait a while longer before Kenyan cafe culture finally hits the streets. Until it does, reach for the skies – Nairobi's many 1st-floor balcony restaurants are still the best places in town to catch and shoot the breeze.

---

you're tired of having your butt pinched to the strains of limp R&B in darkened discos, Simmers is the place to come to rediscover a bit of true African rhythm. The atmosphere at this open-air bar-restaurant is almost invariably amazing, with the ever-enthusiastic crowds turning out to wind and grind the night away to incessant parades of bands playing anything from Congolese rumba to Kenyan *benga* (contemporary dance). Refreshingly, the women here are more likely to be locals out for a giggle than working girls out for business, so for once men shouldn't have to worry too much about being hassled. And most people are very friendly should you feel the need to, say, compliment someone on their *lingala* (Congolese) dancing. With free-flowing Tusker, a separate shots bar and plenty of *nyama choma* to keep the lion from the door, it's no wonder the place always feels like a party.

### WESTLANDS & PARKLANDS
**Pavement** (Map p108; ☎ 4441711; Ring Rd; admission KSh500) Split between a relaxed ground-level bar and the big, modern basement club where the action happens, Pavement is the dance venue of choice for most resident expats, and isn't as messy as its counterparts in town. Leavening the usual mix of hip hop and chart pop, weekends here favour funky house, trance and techno you might get on a night out in your own country.

### KAREN & LANGATA
**Simba Saloon** (Map p111; ☎ 501706; off Langata Rd; admission KSh200-300; ☽ Wed-Sun) Next door to Carnivore, this large, partly open-air bar and nightclub pulls in a huge crowd, particularly on Wednesday, Friday and Saturday. There are video screens, several bars, a bonfire and adventure playground in the garden, and unashamedly Western music on the dance floor. It's usually rammed with wealthy Kenyans, expat teenagers, travellers and NGO workers, plus a fair sprinkling of prostitutes. You can also get a range of well-priced food at all hours, and there's a Dormans coffee-stall to keep those eyelids open til closing.

## Live Music
**Green Corner Restaurant & Cactus Pub** (Map pp104-5; ☎ 335243; Tumaini House, Nkrumah Lane; admission free) This very popular after-work bar and restaurant just opposite the Nairobi Cinema has live bands on Thursday and Sunday and DJs the rest of the week. Music is generally modern, East African and enthusiastically received.

**Toona Tree Bar & Restaurant** (Map pp100-1; ☎ 3740802; toonatree@africaonline.co.ke; International Casino, Museum Hill Rd; admission free) Part of the massive International Casino complex by the National Museum, Toona Tree has live bands on Friday and Saturday, playing jazz, blues and classic hits.

## Cinemas

Nairobi is a good place to take in a few films at a low price. The upmarket cinemas show a mix of Western blockbusters and even more popular Bollywood extravaganzas. Tickets range from KSh150 to KSh250, depending on the time and the cinema.

**Nu Metro Cinema** (off Map pp100-1; ☎ 522128; numetro@swiftkenya.com; Village Market, Gigiri) The first entry in a chain of modern multiplexes springing up around Nairobi, showing new Western films fairly promptly after their international release. Seats here are generally expensive, but still cheaper than the popcorn at a London picture house.

**Fox Cineplex** (Map p108; ☎ 227959; Sarit Centre, Westlands) Another good modern cinema in the same price bracket as Nu Metro, located on the 2nd floor of the Sarit Centre.

**20th Century Cinema** (Map pp104-5; ☎ 210606; 20th Century Plaza, Mama Ngina St), **Kenya Cinema** (Map pp104-5; ☎ 227822; Kenya Cinema Plaza, Moi Ave) and **Nairobi Cinema** (Map pp104-5; ☎ 338058; Uchumi House, Aga Khan Walk) are all owned by the same chain. The first two show mainly Western movies, while the Nairobi Cinema goes through phases of only screening Christian 'message' films.

**Odeon** (Map pp104-5; Latema Rd) is one of several local cinemas showing a mix of Indian, South African and Western films. Tickets are very cheap but reels are often scratched.

## Theatre

**Professional Centre** (Map pp104-5; ☎ 225506; www .phoenixplayers.net; Parliament Rd) Local theatre troupe the Phoenix Players put on regular performances at this venue with an unlikely name. Many of the plays are by foreign playwrights but a good proportion is by Kenyans, and new works are well represented.

**Kenya National Theatre** (Map pp104-5; ☎ 225174; Harry Thuku Rd; tickets from KSh200) Opposite the Norfolk Hotel, this is the major theatre venue in Nairobi. As well as contemporary and classic plays, there are special events such as beauty pageants, which are less highbrow but still culturally interesting.

For African theatre, the foreign cultural centres (p98) are often the places to head for. Also, check the *Daily Nation* to see what's on.

## SHOPPING

Nairobi is a good place to pick up souvenirs before heading home, though be warned as prices are usually higher than elsewhere in the country. With that said, there are loads of souvenir shops downtown and in the area northwest of Kenyatta Ave, so you're spoilt for selection.

Although most places sell exactly the same things, there are a few speciality shops with better-than-average crafts. The 'Little India' area around Biashara St is good for fabric, textiles and those all-important souvenir Tusker T-shirts. If you're interested in buying local music, just wander around the River Rd and Latema Rd area and listen out for the blaring CD kiosks.

**City Market** (Map pp104-5; Muindi Mbingu St) The city's souvenir business is concentrated in this covered market, which has dozens of stalls selling wood carvings, drums, spears, shields, soapstone, Maasai jewellery and clothing. It's a hectic place and you'll have to bargain hard (and we *mean* hard), but there's plenty of good stuff on offer. It's an interesting place to wander around in its own right, though you generally need to be shopping to make the constant hassle worth the bother.

**Gallery Watatu** (Map pp104-5; ☎ 228737; Lonhro House, Standard St) If you want fine Kenyan art and/or potential museum pieces, this is a reliable place to make a big purchase. There's a permanent display here, and many of the display items are for sale, though you need to be prepared to part with upwards of KSh20,000.

**Spinners Web** (Map p108; ☎ 4440882; Viking House, Waiyaki Way, Westlands) This place works with workshops and self-help groups around the country. It's a bit like a handicrafts version of Ikea, with goods displayed the way they might look in Western living-rooms, but there are some appealing items, including carpets, wall-hangings, ceramics, wooden bowls, baskets and clothing.

**Westland Curio Market** (Map p108; Parklands Rd, Westlands) Near the Sarit Centre in Westlands, this complex of stalls located at a road junction has the usual tourist kitsch as well some genuine tribal objects, such as Turkana wrist-knives and wooden headrests. Like at the City Market, you're going to need to bargain hard here, though the sales pressure is a bit softer.

**Maasai Market** Central Nairobi (Map pp104-5; off Slip Rd; ☺ Tue); Gigiri (off Map pp100-1; Village Market, Limuru Rd; ☺ Fri); Yaya Centre (off Map pp100-1; Argwings Kodhek; ☺ Sun) These busy curio markets are held every Tuesday on the waste ground near

---

**SHOPPING IN STYLE**

The beautifully conceived shopping centre, **Village Market** (off Map pp100-1; ☎ 522488; www.villagemarket-kenya.com; Limuru Rd, Gigiri; 👤), has a selection of entertainment activities to help you while away an afternoon, including the Nu Metro Cinema (p131), a bowling alley, pool hall, water slides, minigolf and a children's playground complete with toy-car rides and a minitrain circuit. You can get here with matatu 106 (KSh40) from near the train station.

---

Slip Rd in town, Friday in the rooftop car park at the Village Market shopping complex (above) and Sunday next to the Yaya Centre. The markets are open from early morning to late afternoon. Check with your accommodation as locations and schedules do change.

**Undugu Craft Shop** (Map p108; ☎ 4443525; Woodvale Grove, Westlands) A good charitable venture, this nonprofit organisation supports community projects in Nairobi and has top-quality crafts.

**Banana Box** (Map p108; ☎ 3743390; Sarit Centre, Westlands) Amid the rather less altruistic commercialism of the Sarit Centre, Banana Box works in conjunction with community projects and refugee groups and offers modern uses for traditional objects.

## GETTING THERE & AWAY

### Air

Nairobi is the main arrival and departure point for international flights, although some touch down in Mombasa as well. For information about international services to and from Nairobi, see p341.

**Kenya Airways** (Map pp104-5; ☎ 32074100; www .kenya-airways.com; Barclays Plaza, Loita St), the principal international and domestic carrier, has a booking office in the city centre, though their website is efficient and reliable. Fares are generally lower if you can book more than a week or two in advance.

**Airkenya** ( ☎ 605745; www.airkenya.com; Wilson Airport) services domestic airports throughout the country. As for Kenya Airways, it's best to book online, though you can always visit their office at Wilson Airport.

**Safarilink** ( ☎ 600777; www.safarilink-kenya.com; Wilson Airport) offers similar services as Airkenya,

though it's a much smaller player on the domestic scene.

Note that the check-in time for domestic flights is one to two hours before departure. Also be aware that the baggage allowance is only 15kg, as there isn't much space on the small turboprop aircraft.

Fares and frequency of flights vary considerably depending on availability and the season, so it's best to check the internet for current information.

### Bus

In Nairobi, most long-distance bus company offices are in the River Rd area, clustered around Accra Rd and the surrounding streets. Several companies go to Mombasa, including Akamba, Busscar, Busstar, Mash Express, Mombasa Raha and Falcon. Most services leave in the early morning or late evening; the trip takes eight to 10 hours with a meal break on the way. Buses leave from outside each company's office. Fares range from KSh500 to KSh100 and tickets can be purchased on the buses, at bus stops and at surrounding shops.

**Coastline Safaris** (Map pp104-5; ☎ 217592; cnr Latema & Lagos Rds) is the most comfortable and expensive service. **Akamba** (Map pp104-5; ☎ 340430; Lagos Rd) is the biggest private bus company in the country and has an extensive network. It's not the cheapest, but it's the safest and most reliable. It has buses to Eldoret, Kakamega, Kericho, Kisii, Kisumu, Kitale, Machakos, Mombasa, Kampala (Uganda) and Mwanza, Moshi and Dar es Salaam (Tanzania). Buses leave from Lagos Rd and there's a **booking office** (Map pp104-5; ☎ 222027; Wabera St), near City Hall.

The government-owned **KBS** (Kenya Bus Service; ☎ 229707) is a large, reliable operator, cheaper than Akamba but with slower buses. The main bus station is east of the centre on Uyoma St, but there's a downtown **booking office** (Map pp104-5; ☎ 341250; cnr Muindi Mbingu & Monrovia Sts). There are loads of buses to Kisumu and Kakamega and less frequent services to Busia, Eldoret, Kisii, Kitale and Malaba.

**Easy Coach** (Map pp104-5; ☎ 210711; easycoach@wananchi.com; Haile Selassie Ave) is a reliable company serving western Kenyan destinations on the Kisumu/Kakamega route with daily buses to Arusha in the other direction.

The **Country Bus Station** (Map pp104-5; Landhies Rd) is a hectic, disorganised place with buses to Machakos, Busia, Eldoret, Kakamega, Kisumu, Nyeri, Nakuru, Nanyuki, Malaba and Meru. Eldoret Express is the biggest operator with plenty of buses to Kisumu and the Ugandan border.

See p348 for details on other bus companies operating out of Nairobi.

## Matatu

Most matatus leave from Latema, Accra, River and Cross Rds and fares are similar to the buses. The biggest operator here is **Crossland Services** (Map pp104–5; ☎ 245377; Cross Rd), which serves destinations including Eldoret (KSh500, three hours), Kericho (KSh600, three hours), Kisii (KSh800, five hours), Kisumu (KSh800, four hours), Naivasha (KSh150, one hour), Nakuru (KSh250, two hours) and Nanyuki (KSh400, two hours). On the same road are **Molo Line Services** (Map pp104–5; ☎ 0724342966) with matatus to Eldoret, Naivasha, Nakuru and Kisumu, and **Narok Line** (Map pp104–5; ☎ 213020), which serves Kisii, Narok and Kericho.

Other companies are located on the surrounding streets. Head to the main bus and matatu area on Accra Rd (Map pp104–5) for matatus to Chogoria (KSh350, 2½ hours), Embu (KSh300, 1½ hours), Meru (KSh500, three hours) and Nanyuki (KSh400, 2½ hours). Matatus leave from Latema Rd for Nyahururu (KSh300, three hours) and Nyeri (KSh300, two hours). There are loads of matatus to Naivasha (KSh150, 1½ hours) and the Tanzanian border at Namanga (KSh300, three hours) from the corner of Ronald Ngala St and River Rd (Map pp104–5). For Thika (KSh100, 40 minutes), go to the Total petrol station on Racecourse Rd (Map pp100–1).

---

### WARNING – THINGS CHANGE

Transport information is extremely vulnerable to change. At the time of writing, fuel prices in Kenya were soaring and it is almost certain that prices for bus routes will increase.

You should get local opinions, quotes and advice before parting with your hard-earned cash – a good place to inquire is at your hotel. In addition, tickets for private buses should always be booked at least one day in advance given the uncertainty of the transport grid.

---

## Peugeot (Shared Taxi)

As with matatus, most of the companies offering Peugeot shared taxis have their offices around the Accra, River and Cross Rds area. One reliable company is **Crossland Services** (Map pp104–5; ☎ 245377; Cross Rd), which has cars to Eldoret, Kabarnet, Kericho, Kitale and Nakuru. Other companies serve Isiolo, Kisumu, Meru and Malaba. Fares are about 20% higher than the same journeys by matatu. Most services depart in the morning.

## Shuttle Minibus

Shuttle minibuses run from Nairobi to Kampala (Uganda), and to Arusha and Moshi in Tanzania (see p345 for details).

## Train

The train from Nairobi to Mombasa receives divided reviews – some acclaim it as a sociable and comfortable means of avoiding the highway while spotting some wildlife from the windows; for others it's too shabby and time-consuming. The latter isn't helped by inconsistent scheduling and lax timetable enforcement.

Nairobi train station has a small **booking office** (Map pp104–5; Station Rd; ✆ 9am–noon & 2-6.30pm), though don't bother trying to get in touch with them – you need to stop in person to book tickets a few days in advance of your intended departure. For Mombasa (1st/2nd class US$65/43, 14 to 16 hours), trains leave Nairobi at 7pm on Monday, Wednesday and Friday; arrive early.

## GETTING AROUND
### To/From Jomo Kenyatta International Airport

Kenya's main **international airport** (Map p111; ☎ 827638) is 15km out of town, off the road to Mombasa. There's now a dedicated airport bus run by Metro Shuttle (part of KBS, p134), which can drop you off at hotels in the city centre. Going the other way, the main departure point is across from the Hilton Nairobi Hotel. The journey takes about 40 minutes and costs US$5 per person. Buses run every half-hour from 8am to 8.30pm daily and stop at both air terminals.

A cheaper way to get into town is by city bus 34 (KSh30), but a lot of travellers get robbed on the bus or when they get off. Always hold onto valuables and have small change ready for the fare. Buses run from 5.45am to 9.30pm weekdays, 6.20am to 9.30pm Saturdays and 7.15am to 9.30pm Sundays, though the last few evening services may not operate. Heading to the airport, buses travel west along Kenyatta Ave.

A much safer method (and also your only option at night) is to take a taxi. The asking price is usually about KSh1500 in either direction, but you should be able to bargain down to KSh1000 from town. If you book at one of the 'information' desks at the airport, you'll still end up in a public taxi, but it isn't any more expensive.

### To/From Wilson Airport

To get to **Wilson Airport** (Map p111; ☎ 501941), for Airkenya services or charter flights, the cheapest option is to take bus or matatu 15, 31, 34, 125 or 126 from Moi Ave (KSh20, from 15 minutes depending on traffic). A taxi from the centre of town will cost you KSh600 to KSh800, depending on the driver. In the other direction, you'll have to fight the driver down from KSh1000. The entrance to the airport is easy to miss – it's just before the large BP petrol station.

### Bus

The ordinary city buses are run by **KBS** (☎ 229707) but hopefully you won't need to use them much. Forget about them if you're carrying luggage – you'll never get on, and even if you do, you'll never get off! Most buses pass through downtown, but the main KBS terminus is on Uyoma St, east of the centre.

Useful buses include 46 from Kenyatta Ave, for the Yaya Centre in Hurlingham (KSh20), and 23 from Jevanjee Gardens, for Westlands (KSh20). There are services about every 20 minutes from 6am to 8pm Monday to Saturday.

### Car

See p349 for comprehensive information on car hire, road rules and conditions. If you are driving, beware of wheel-clampers: parking in the centre is by permit only, available from the parking attendants who roam the streets in bright yellow or red jackets. If you park overnight in the street in front of your hotel, the guard will often keep an eye on your vehicle for a small consideration.

### Matatu

Nairobi's horde of matatus follows the same routes as buses and displays the same route numbers. For Westlands, you can pick up 23 on Moi Ave or Latema Rd. Matatu 46 to the Yaya Centre stops in front of the main post office, and 125 and 126 to Langata leave from in front of the train station. As usual, you should keep an eye on your valuables while on all matatus.

### Taxi

As people are compelled to use them due to Nairobi's endemic street crime, taxis here are overpriced and undermaintained, but you've little choice, particularly at night. Taxis don't cruise for passengers, but you can find them parked on every other street corner in the city centre – at night they're outside restaurants, bars and nightclubs.

Fares around town are negotiable but end up pretty standard. Any journey within the downtown area costs KSh300, from downtown to Milimani Rd costs KSh400, and for longer journeys such as Westlands or the Yaya Centre, fares range from KSh500 to KS650. From the city centre to Karen and Langata is around KSh850 one way.

You can also find a few Indonesian-style *tuk-tuks* operating from Kenyatta Ave, though they're slowly being phased out.

# Southern Kenya

Although this tiny region is straddled by Nairobi and Mombasa, southern Kenya is quite simply safari country par excellence. With the sole exceptions of Masai Mara and Lake Nakuru, Amboseli and Tsavo rank at the top of Kenya's national park offerings. Along the border with Tanzania, where the slopes of Mt Kilimanjaro meet the Amboseli plains, enormous herds of elephants roam the imperial court of Africa's highest peak. At Tsavo, a national park so massive it's divided into east and west sectors, you can bush camp in some of Kenya's wildest landscapes.

While the tourist trail definitely swings towards Amboseli and Tsavo, southern Kenya is also home to a number of natural wonders, including the extensive lava tubes of the Chyulu Hills, and the lush landscapes of the Taita Hills. The region also plays host to a number of community-run reserves and projects that are bringing the good conservation fight to the grass-roots level. Boasting a wide range of tented camps, lodges, bandas and campsites awaiting the weary traveller, it's certainly no hardship finding somewhere to wake up in the wilds of southern Kenya.

The majesty of nature aside, southern Kenya is a major transport route for anyone heading south to Tanzania's northern circuit. The Nairobi–Mombasa road also serves as the region's principal artery, which makes it easy to spend some time exploring the area before being seduced by the tropical climes of the coast. So, before you break out the beach blanket and the sunscreen, spend a bit more time on safari, and get to know a few more of Kenya's charismatic creatures.

**SOUTHERN KENYA**

---

## HIGHLIGHTS

- Snapping that quintessential safari photo of elephant herds framed by Mt Kilimanjaro at **Amboseli National Park** (p137)

- Spotting hippos and crocs in the pristine oasis of **Mzima Springs** (p141) at Tsavo West National Park

- Catching a rare glimpse of some of Kenya's last remaining black rhinos at the **Ngulia Rhino Sanctuary** (p141) in Tsavo West National Park

- Braving the country's scariest lions in the back country of **Tsavo East National Park** (p144)

- Spelunking in **Leviathan** (p140), the world's longest lava tube, part of the Chyulu Hills National Park

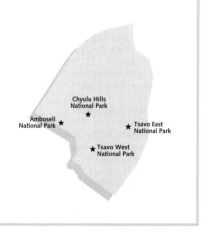

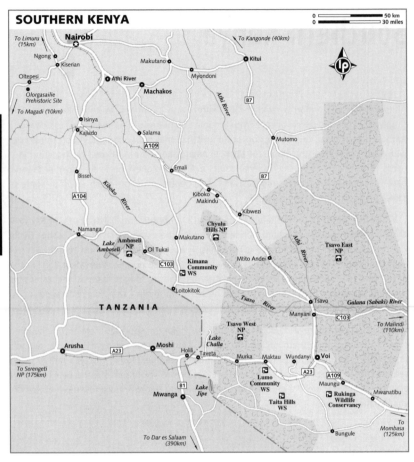

## Climate

Falling between central Kenya and the coast, this area tends to be hot and dry, with average temperatures around 30°C, but still experiences heavy rainfall from March to June and from October to November.

## National Parks & Reserves

Between Nairobi and Voi, you'll find Amboseli, Chyulu Hills, Tsavo West and Tsavo East National Parks, and the Ngai-Ndethya National Reserve. There are also a number of private conservation areas, including Kimana Community Wildlife Sanctuary, Lumo Community Wildlife Sanctuary, Taita Hills Wildlife Sanctuary and Rukinga Wildlife Conservancy.

## Getting There & Around

The main towns here are easily accessible by public transport, especially those strung out along the Nairobi–Mombasa road. However, trying to visit the national parks independently can be a logistical nightmare without your own transport. Most people take the easy option, and simply visit on an organised safari from Nairobi or Mombasa. For more information on organising a safari, see p65.

## THE ROAD TO ARUSHA

Heading south from Nairobi, the A104 runs straight to the Tanzanian border en route to the city of Arusha (Tanzania). This road will also take you to the border town of Namanga, which is a good place to stock up on fuel and supplies before entering Amboseli National Park.

The first point of interest along this route is **Bissel**, which is a vibrant Maasai township with a busy market where you can buy all sorts of tribal objects, as well as everyday goods. Facilities include a petrol station, a handful of *dukas* (small shops or kiosks), a freight container selling wholesale soft drinks and plenty of small bars and *hotelis* (eateries). You'll be a bit of a novelty as not many tourists stop along this route, but people are very friendly, and if you feel like stretching your legs, the hilly grasslands surrounding the town are good for a light walk.

If you're relying on public transport, there are matatus running from Bissel to Nairobi (KSh200, one hour) and Namanga (KSh100, one hour).

Continuing south, the border town of **Namanga** has a surprisingly relaxed atmosphere away from the frontier itself. The border crossing is open 24 hours, and the two posts are almost next to each other, so you can walk across. Moneychangers do a brisk trade on the Kenyan side of the border, though if you use them don't believe anyone who says you can't take Kenyan shillings into Tanzania or vice versa!

Numerous Maasai women come here to sell bead jewellery and other Maasai crafts, and will materialise like magic around tourist vehicles, especially at the petrol stations. There's some great stuff on offer, but you'll have to haggle like a pro to get a bargain.

If you want to break up your travels, consider spending a night at the **Namanga River Hotel** ( ☎ 5132070; camping KSh300; s/d from KSh1750/2500; P ), which offers a shady campsite, an attractive clutch of cabins of varying levels of luxury, and a decent bar-restaurant that is often frequented by overland trucks.

Buses between Nairobi and Arusha pass through daily (KSh250 to KSh500, two hours). Matatus and Peugeots (shared taxis) also run here from the junction of River Rd and Ronald Ngala St in Nairobi (KSh250 to KSh300).

Akamba has an office at the Kobil station, where you can book seats on the morning bus to Arusha. Several other companies also cover this route, as do matatus and Peugeots from the Tanzanian side of the border. For more details on getting to/from Tanzania see p345.

## AMBOSELI NATIONAL PARK

While it may lack the profusion of wildlife found at Masai Mara and Lake Nakuru, Kenya's third-most popular park boasts one of the country's most spectacular backdrops, namely Mt Kilimanjaro. Africa's highest peak broods over the southern boundary of the park, and while cloud cover can render the mountain's massive bulk invisible for much of the day, you'll be rewarded with some stunning vistas when the weather clears. Amboseli is also prime elephant country, so add this park to your safari itinerary if you want to shoot some pics of these monolithic beasts.

Although it's a prominent part of the country's tourist portfolio, Amboseli has been at the centre of some controversy since President Kibaki's 2005 attempt to downgrade it from a national park to a national reserve, which would have transferred its administration from the Kenya Wildlife Service (KWS) to local authorities. Supporters claim that the move would rightfully return control of the land to the local community, though conservation bodies argue that it was simply a political move, aimed at securing the crucial Maasai vote.

With that said, degazetting national parks theoretically could undermine Kenya's whole wildlife preservation system, and – constitutionally speaking – is illegal. At the time of writing, however, Amboseli remained a national park, though Kibaki's next move on this issue will doubtless come in for heavy scrutiny.

### Information

At 392 sq km, **Amboseli** ( ☎ 045-622251; www.kws .org/amboseli.html; adult/child nonresident US$60/30, smartcard required) is a small national park, though the landscape provides limited cover for wildlife. The vegetation here used to be much denser, but rising salinity, damage by elephants and irresponsible behaviour with safari vehicles has caused terrible erosion.

Sadly, these factors are having a dramatic effect on the park – the rains seem to provide less relief every season, and it may only be a matter of several years before the lack of food makes the animals move on.

It's therefore important for vehicles to stick to the defined tracks to avoid making the situation worse. Hopefully, others will follow suit, and the grasslands that drew all

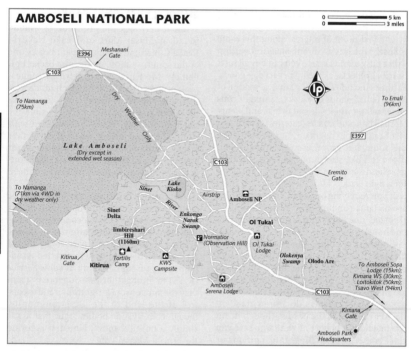

**AMBOSELI NATIONAL PARK**

0 — 5 km
0 — 3 miles

these animals here in the first place can be preserved for future generations.

## Sights & Activities

Amboseli's permanent swamps of **Enkongo Narok** and **Olokenya** create a marshy belt across the middle of the park. These spots are the centre of activity for elephants, hippos, buffaloes and waterbirds, while the surrounding grasslands are home to grazing antelope. Spotted hyenas are plentiful, and jackals, warthogs, olive baboons and vervet monkeys are all present. Lions can still be found in Amboseli, although the once-famous black-maned lions are no longer here. Black rhinos are also absent – the few that survived a sustained period of poaching were moved to Tsavo West in 1995.

**Normatior** (Observation Hill) provides an ideal lookout from which to orientate yourself to the plains, swamps and roads below. From the top, you can spot hundreds of dots on the plains, typically zebras, gazelles and wildebeest. Amboseli is also well known for its elephant herds, which can be seen raising

dust as they cross the plains to drink and feed at the swamps.

From Observation Hill, the northern route runs across the **Sinet Delta**, which is an excellent place for bird-watching. Commonly sighted species include jacanas, herons, egrets, ibises, geese, plovers, storks, ducks, fish eagles and flamingos.

If you leave Amboseli by way of **Kimana gate** on the way to Tsavo West National Park, then keep your eyes open for Masai giraffes in the acacia woodlands. This is also where you'll find gerenuks, an unusual breed of gazelle that 'browses' by standing on their hind legs and stretching their necks.

## Sleeping & Eating

All lodge prices given here are for full board. For nonguests, a buffet lunch at any of the upmarket lodges will cost around US$20 to US$25.

### CAMPING

**KWS campsite** (camping per adult/child US$10/2; (P) ) Just inside the southern boundary of the park, with toilets, an unreliable water supply (bring your own) and a small bar selling warm beer and soft drinks. It's fenced off from the wildlife, so you can walk around safely at night, though *don't* keep food in your tent, as baboons visit during the day looking for an uninvited feed.

### LODGES

**Amboseli Sopa Lodge** ( ☎ Nairobi 020-3750460; www .sopalodges.com/amboseli/home.html; s/d low season US$71/142, high season US$142/198; P ☎ ) Located just outside the park boundaries on the road to Tsavo National Park, the Sopa Lodge offers a clutch of clay huts that are decked out in lavish safari spreads and a healthy smattering of Kenyan curios. The cactus gardens are frequently visited by troops of marauding monkeys, which certainly adds to the thrill of being on safari.

**Ol Tukai Lodge** ( ☎ Nairobi 020-4445514; www.oltukai lodge.com; s/d low season US$150/180, high season US$210/255; P ☎ ) Lying at the heart of Amboseli on the edge of a dense acacia forest, Ol Tukai is a splendidly refined lodge with soaring *makuti* (thatched palm-leaved roofs) and tranquil gardens defined by towering trees. Accommodation is in wooden chalets, which are brought to life with vibrant zebra prints, while the split-level bar has sweeping view of Kili, and a pervading atmosphere of peace and luxury.

**Amboseli Serena Lodge** ( ☎ Nairobi 020-2710511; www .serenahotels.com; s/d low season US$155/255, high season US$285/385; P ☎ ) A classically elegant property in Amboseli, the Serena is comprised of fiery-red adobe cottages that overlook the wildlife-rich Enkongo Narok swamp, and fringed by lush tropical gardens of blooming flowers and manicured shrubs. The safari-chic bar-restaurant is accented by indigenous artwork, including hanging gourds and elaborate batiks, and the impeccable service and attention to detail are more reminiscent of a fine downtown bistro.

**our pick Tortilis Camp** ( ☎ Nairobi 020-604053; www .chelipeacock.com/camps/tortilis; s/d low season US$468/740, high season US$516/858; P ) This wonderfully conceived site is one of the most exclusive ecolodges in Kenya, commanding a superb elevated spot with perfect Kilimanjaro vistas. The name is derived from the *Acacia tortilis* trees that grow in thick concentrations around the intimate and overwhelmingly opulent canvas tents. Lavish meals, which are based on North Italian traditional recipes from the owner's family cookbook, feature herbs and vegetables from the huge on-site organic garden. And, just so you don't feel guilty about leaving behind an ecological footprint, take comfort in the fact that everything is cooked without firewood, and solar power is used exclusively to heat the water.

## Getting There & Away

### AIR

**Airkenya** (www.airkenya.com) has daily flights (around US$175) between Wilson Airport in Nairobi and Amboseli. You'll need to arrange with one of the lodges or a safari company for a vehicle to meet you at the airstrip.

### CAR & 4WD

The usual approach to Amboseli is via Namanga. The road is sealed and in surprisingly good condition from Nairobi to Namanga – the 75km dirt road to the Meshanani gate is pretty rough but passable (allow around four hours from Nairobi). In the dry season it's also possible to enter through Kitirua gate, but this is a bumpy old road and it's hard to follow. The track branches right off the main Amboseli road after about 15km. Some people also enter from the east via the Amboseli–Tsavo West road, although this track is in bad shape, and shouldn't be considered in a conventional vehicle.

During the 1990s there were bandit attacks in this area, so vehicles have to travel together, accompanied by armed guards. Convoys leave from the Tsavo turnoff near the Sopa Lodge at scheduled times – inquire at your lodge, as times change frequently. Allow approximately 2½ hours to cover the 94km from Amboseli to the Chyulu gate at Tsavo West.

Self-drivers will need a 4WD to make the most of the park. Petrol is available at the Serena and Sopa lodges.

## KIMANA COMMUNITY WILDLIFE SANCTUARY

While it's not as grand in scope as Southern Kenya's signature national parks, this 40-hectare **sanctuary** (admission US$20) protects an impressive concentration of wildlife, and any money spent here directly supports the local community. While the foundations of Kimana were established in 1996 by USAID and KWS, the sanctuary has since been owned and managed by local Maasai. Today, Kimana serves as an encouraging template for similar initiatives throughout the continent, particularly now that the prestigious African Safari Club has set up several upmarket properties within the sanctuary.

If you're sticking to a tight budget, there are three guarded **campsites** (camping per site US$10) within the sanctuary itself, though you'll have to be self-sufficient, as facilities are very basic.

Although a night here is an extremely expensive proposition, **Campi ya Kanzi** ( ☎ Nairobi 020-605349; www.campiyakanzi.com; s/d from US$600/980; **P** ) is a worthwhile Maasai-run initiative that directly supports education, health care and environmental conservation in local communities. Accommodation is in luxury tents scattered around an enormous ranch that is centred on a nostalgically decorated stone lodge.

Elsewhere in the sanctuary, Kimana Zebra Lodge, Leopard Lodge, Kilimanjaro Camp and Twiga Camp are all run by the private African Safari Club. For booking information, check out its website at www.africansafariclub.com.

Kimana is located about 30km east of Amboseli, just off the road heading to Tsavo West National Park. The only access to this area is the poorly maintained dirt track leading west from Emali (on the Nairobi–Mombasa road) to Loitokitok on the Tanzanian border, or the even more diabolical road between Amboseli and Tsavo West.

Note that while there's officially no need to join the Tsavo convoy if you're coming here from Amboseli, the area south of Kimana does have a reputation for banditry.

## CHYULU HILLS NATIONAL PARK

Just northwest of Tsavo West National Park are the dramatic **Chyulu Hills** (adult/child US$50/25), a collection of ancient volcanic cinder cones and elaborate underground caverns. The hills were gazetted as a national park in 1983 and have splendid views of Mt Kilimanjaro, as well as thriving populations of elands, giraffes, zebras and wildebeest, plus a small number of elephants, lions and buffaloes.

Within the Chyulu Hills is the aptly named **Leviathan**, believed to be the longest lava tube in the world, which was formed by hot lava flowing beneath a cooled crust. You'll need full caving equipment to explore it, and perhaps a bit of prior experience spelunking in claustrophobic conditions. Caving and trekking trips in the hills are possible with **Savage Wilderness**

**Safaris Ltd** (Map p108; ☎ Nairobi 020-2521590; www.whitewaterkenya.com; Sarit Centre, Westlands).

There is a lot to see in the park, though sadly Chyulu Hills has only the most basic of infrastructure, despite a serious drive in recent years to open up the park for tourism. Forced evictions in 1997 have still not removed the problems of local communities damaging the ecosystem, and poaching is still a big problem here. Hunters have taken such a large toll on the park's smaller animals, and they are now becoming increasingly confident at targeting larger game.

The park headquarters are 1.3km inside the northwest gate, not far from Kibwezi on the Nairobi–Mombasa road. For the time being, the best access is on the west side of the park, from the track between Amboseli and Tsavo West. Note that the track into the hills from the headquarters is extremely tough going, so you're going to need a durable 4WD vehicle to attempt this route.

If you're completely self-sufficient, you can spend the night at the extremely basic but perfectly functional **KWS campsite** (camping per adult/child US$25/20; **P** ), located near the park headquarters.

If you're travelling with a decidedly larger budget, **Ol Donyo Wuas** (Map p142; ☎ Nairobi 020-600457; www.richardbonhamsafaris.com; s/d from US$590/970; **P** **☎** ) is a well-established ecolodge constructed entirely of local materials and employs advanced water recycling and solar-power systems. While guests are treated to paramount luxury, the real highlights of this property are the wildlife drives and horse-riding excursions in the national park.

Until the road from Kibwezi is brought up to standard, your best bet to get here is the dirt track that branches off the Amboseli–Tsavo West road about 10km west of Chyulu gate. Ol Donyo Wuas can be reached via this track, although most guests fly in on air charters from Nairobi. The park headquarters is signposted just outside Kibwezi, about 41km northwest of Mtito Andei on the main Nairobi–Mombasa road.

## TSAVO WEST NATIONAL PARK

Tsavo West covers a huge variety of landscapes, from swamps, natural springs and rocky peaks to extinct volcanic cones, rolling plains and sharp outcrops dusted with greenery. But for all of its diversity, Tsavo West is not a park where you will see animals

---

### EXPLORING TSAVO NATIONAL PARK

At nearly 21,000 sq km, **Tsavo National Park** is by far the largest national park in Kenya. For administrative and practical purposes, it has been split into two areas: **Tsavo West National Park** (9000 sq km) and **Tsavo East National Park** (11,747 sq km), divided by the Nairobi–Mombasa road (A109).

Both parks feature some excellent scenery, but the undergrowth here is considerably higher than in Amboseli or Masai Mara, so it takes a little more effort to spot the wildlife, particularly the big predators. The compensation for this is that the landscapes are some of the most dramatic in Kenya, the animals are that little bit wilder and the parks receive comparatively few visitors, compared to the hordes that descend on Amboseli and the Masai Mara.

The northern half of Tsavo West is the most developed, with a number of excellent lodges, as well as several places where you can get out of your vehicle and walk. The landscape is also striking, and is largely comprised of volcanic hills and sweeping expanses of savanna. The southern part of the park, on the far side of the dirt road between Voi and Taveta on the Tanzanian border, is rarely visited.

Tsavo East is more remote, though most of the action here is concentrated along the Galana River – the north part of the park isn't truly secure due to the threat of banditry. The landscape here is drier, with rolling plains hugging the edge of the Yatta Escarpment, a vast prehistoric lava flow.

Tsavo had terrible problems with poachers during the 1980s, when the elephant population dropped from 45,000 to just 5000, and rhinos were almost wiped out entirely. Populations are slowly recovering, and there are close to 10,000 elephants in the two parks, but less than 100 rhinos, down from about 9000 in 1969 (for more on poaching, see p145).

Entry is US$50/25 per adult/child per day, and camping is US$25 per adult; as the two parks are administered separately you have to pay separate entrance fees for each. Both use the smartcard system – you'll need enough credit for your entry fee and any camping charges for as long as you're staying. Smartcards can be bought and recharged at the Voi gate to Tsavo East.

There's a small **visitor centre** (admission free; 8am-5pm) near the Mtito Andei gate to Tsavo West, with interesting displays on conservation issues and some of the animals and birds in the park.

All the track junctions in Tsavo East and Tsavo West have numbered and signposted cairns, which (in theory) makes navigation fairly simple. In practice, some signposts are missing, and the numbering system is often confusing, so a map is helpful.

Survey of Kenya publishes a *Tsavo East National Park* map and a newer *Tsavo West National Park* map. Both are available from the main entrance gates and the visitor centre at Tsavo West. Tourist Maps' *Tsavo National Parks* covers both parks.

Fuel is available at Kilaguni Serena and Ngulia Safari lodges in Tsavo West, and at Voi Safari Lodge in Tsavo East.

---

constantly. Indeed, much of its appeal lies in its dramatic scenery and sense of space. If possible, come here with some time to spare, rather than a need to dash about and tick off a list of animals seen – you could have it all to yourself.

## Orientation & Information
For the complete rundown on exploring Tsavo West, see above.

## Sights & Activities
The focus of Tsavo West is untouchably **Mzima Springs**, which produces an incredible 350 mil-lion litres of fresh water a day. The springs are the source of the bulk of Mombasa's fresh water, and you can walk down to a large pool that is a favourite haunt of hippos and crocodiles. There's an underwater viewing chamber, which gives a creepy view of thousands of primeval-looking fish. Be a little careful here though, as both hippos and crocs are potentially dangerous.

Just southeast of Kilaguni Serena Lodge are **Chaimu Crater**, and the **Roaring Rocks** viewpoint, which can be climbed in about 15 minutes. The views from either spot are stunning – falcons, eagles and buzzards whirl over the

# TSAVO EAST & WEST NATIONAL PARKS

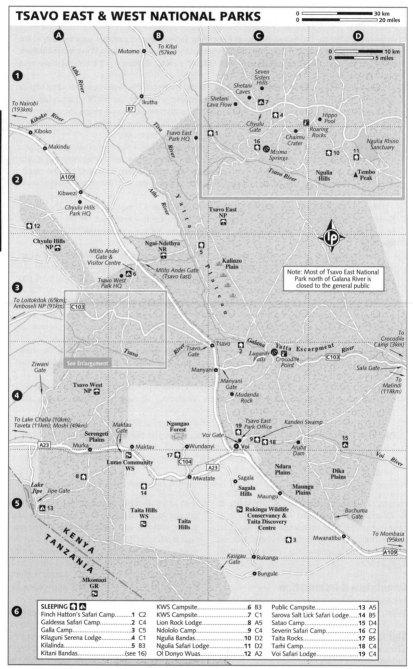

**Note:** Most of Tsavo East National Park north of Galana River is closed to the general public

plains. While there is little danger when walking these trails, be aware that the wildlife is still out there, so keep your eyes open.

Another attraction is the **Ngulia Rhino Sanctuary**, which is located at the base of Ngulia Hills and is part of the Rhino Ark program. It's close to Ngulia Safari Lodge but a long drive from anywhere else – with good reason. The 70-sq-km area is surrounded by a 1m-high electric fence, and provides a measure of security for the park's last 50-odd black rhinos. There are driving tracks and waterholes within the enclosed area, and there's a good chance of seeing one of these elusive creatures.

Some of the more unusual species to look out for in the park include the naked mole rat, which can sometimes be seen kicking sand from its burrows, and the enigmatically named white-bellied go-away bird, which is often seen perched in dead trees. Red-beaked hornbills and bateleur eagles are also common. Look out for dung beetles rolling huge balls of elephant poo along the tracks.

It's possible to go **rock-climbing** at Tembo Peak and the Ngulia Hills, but you'll need to arrange this in advance with the **park warden** ( ☎ 043-622483). This area is also fantastic for birdlife, and there's a very reliable hippo pool on the Mukui River, near the Ngulia Safari Lodge.

**Lake Jipe** (ji-*pay*), at the southwest end of the park, is reached by a desperately dusty track from near Taveta. You can hire boats at the campsite to take you hippo and crocodile spotting on the lake (US$5). Huge herds of elephants come to the lake to drink, and large flocks of migratory birds stop here from February to May.

About 4km west of the Chyulu gate of Tsavo West National Park, on the road to Amboseli, are the spectacular **Shetani lava flows**. This vast expanse of folded black lava spreads for 50 sq km across the savanna at the foot of the Chyulu Hills, looking strangely as if Vesuvius dropped its comfort blanket here. The last major eruption here is believed to have taken place around 200 years ago, but there are still few plants among the cinders. It's possible to follow the lava flows back from the Amboseli–Tsavo West road to the ruined cinder cone of Shetani (from the Kiswahili for 'devil'), at the foot of the Chyulu Hills. The views are spectacular, but you need to be wary of wildlife in this area, as there are predators about.

Nearby are the **Shetani Caves**, which are also a result of volcanic activity. You'll need a torch (flashlight) if you want to explore, but watch your footing on the razor-sharp rocks, and keep an eye out for the local fauna – we've heard rumours that the caves are sometimes inhabited by hyenas, who don't take kindly to being disturbed.

## Sleeping & Eating
### BUDGET & MIDRANGE
**KWS campsites** (camping per adult/child US$10/5; P ) The public sites are at Komboyo, near the Mtito Andei gate, and at Chyulu, just outside the Chyulu gate. Facilities are basic, so make sure you're prepared to be self-sufficient.

There are also some small independently run **public campsites** along the shores of Lake Jipa.

**Ngulia Bandas** ( ☎ Voi 043-30050; bandas from US$55, meals US$10-15; P ) This hillside camp is Tsavo's best luxury bargain, offering thatched stone cottages on the edge of the escarpment overlooking a stream, where leopards are known to hide out. All in all, the setting and standards outdo plenty of the more ambitious lodges, for a fraction of the price.

**Kitani Bandas** ( ☎ Mombasa 041-5485001; bandas from US$75, meals US$10-15; P ) Run by the same people as the top-end luxury Severin Safari Camp, Kitani is located next to a waterhole, about 2km past its sister site, and offers possiblu the cheapest Kili views in the park. Accommodation here is obviously much simpler than the flash tented kind, but it's great value, and there's a small shop providing supplies at not-too-inflated prices.

**Ngulia Safari Lodge** ( ☎ 043-30000; s/d low season US$59/118, high season US$118/165; P 🛋 ) Ngulia's more upmarket offering is a curiously unattractive block in a spectacular location, constructed in the bad old days of emerging mass tourism, when hotels made little effort to blend in. The surrounding Ngulia Hills attract loads of birds and there's a waterhole right by the restaurant, with sweeping views over the Ngulia Rhino Sanctuary on the other side.

### TOP END
**Severin Safari Camp** ( ☎ Mombasa 041-5485001; www .severin-kenya.com; s/d low season US$78/156, high season US$159/224; P ) This is a fantastic complex of thatched luxury tents with affable staff, Kilimanjaro views from the communal lounge area and nightly hippo visitations. Room

facilities are surprisingly luxurious (you even get a bidet!), given that it's much cheaper than some of Tsavo's more opulent spots.

**Kilaguni Serena Lodge** ( ☎ 045-340000; www.serena hotels.com; s/d/ste low season US$115/225/575, high season US$320/435/700; **P** 🖳 🏊 ) Although it's the oldest existing park lodge in Kenya, Kilaguni has recently been renovated, and is as attractive a place as ever. The centrepiece here is a splendid bar and restaurant overlooking a busy illuminated waterhole – the vista stretches all the way from Mt Kilimanjaro to the Chyulu Hills, though the extravagant suites are practically cottages in their own right, boasting chintzy living rooms and epic balconies.

**Finch Hatton's Safari Camp** ( ☎ Nairobi 020-553237; www.finchhattons.com; s/d low season US$315/415, high season US$355/585; **P** 🏊 ) This upmarket tented camp, which is distinguished by its signature bone china and gold shower taps (guests are requested to dress for dinner), was named after Denys Finch Hatton, the playboy hunter and lover of Karen Blixen, who died at Tsavo, despite his obsession with maintaining civility in the middle of the bush. It's situated among springs and hippo pools in the west of the park, in grounds so sprawling you have to take an escort at night to keep you safe from the animals.

## Getting There & Away

The main access to Tsavo West is through the Mtito Andei gate on the Mombasa–Nairobi road in the north of the park, where you'll find the park headquarters and visitor centre. The main track cuts straight across to Kilaguni Serena Lodge and Chyulu gate. Security is a problem here, so vehicles for Amboseli travel in armed convoys, leaving Kilaguni Serena Lodge at 8am and 10am.

Another 48km southeast along the main road is the Tsavo gate – it is handy for the Ngulia Hills lodges and the rhino sanctuary. Few people use the Maktau gate on the Voi–Taveta road in the south of the park.

The tracks here are only really suitable for 4WDs, and the roads in the south of the park are particularly challenging.

## TSAVO EAST NATIONAL PARK

Despite the fact that one of Kenya's largest rivers flows through the middle of the park, the landscape in Tsavo East is markedly flatter and drier than in Tsavo West. However, the contrast between the permanent greenery of the river and the endless grasses and thorn trees that characterise much of the park is visually arresting. In comparison to its more developed brother, Tsavo East doesn't see as many visitors, though it has an undeniable wild and primordial charm. The park is also home to some enormous elephant herds, particularly near the Voi gate, as well as the rare but striking melanistic (black) servals.

### Orientation & Information

For the complete rundown on exploring Tsavo East, see p141.

### Sights & Activities

Much of the wildlife is concentrated on the **Galana River**, which cuts a green gash across the dusty plains of the park, and supports plentiful crocs, hippos, kudus, waterbucks and dikdiks. There are several places along the flat-topped escarpments lining the river where you can get out of your vehicle (with due caution of course). Most scenic are **Lugards Falls**, a wonderful landscape of water-sculpted channels, and **Crocodile Point**, where you may see abundant crocs and hippos.

Towering over a natural dam near the Manyani gate is **Mudanda Rock**, which attracts elephants in the dry season, and is reminiscent of Australia's Uluru (Ayers Rock).

The rolling hills in the south of the park are also home to large herds of elephants, usually covered in thick orange dust (to keep the skin cool and prevent insect bites). The action is concentrated around the waterhole at Voi Safari Lodge, **Kanderi Swamp** and the public campsite.

Further into the park, about 30km east of Voi gate, is the **Aruba Dam**, which spans the Voi River, and attracts heavy concentrations of diverse wildlife.

The area north of the Galana River is dominated by the **Yatta Escarpment**, a vast prehistoric lava flow. However, much of this area is off limits to travellers because of the ongoing campaign against poachers (see also opposite).

Until their partial translocation to Tsavo East, the sole surviving population of **hirola antelope** was found near the Kenya–Somalia border in the south Tana River and Garissa districts. Intense poaching (for meat) and habitat destruction have reduced their numbers from an estimated 14,000 in 1976 to a pitiful 450 today. At the time of writing,

## POACHING & CULLING DEBATE

The most notorious environmental issue in Kenya is arguably poaching, which still occurs through-out the country. In one sense, it's not difficult to see why: according to the International Fund for Animal Welfare (IFAW), a kilogram of elephant ivory is worth upwards of an estimated US$750 wholesale, and rhino horn is valued at US$2000 per kilogram. This amounts to thousands of dollars for a single horn, up to 100 times what the average Kenya earns in a year.

Poaching is also difficult to control due to resource and personnel shortages and the vastness and inaccessibility of many areas. Entrenched interests are also a major contributing factor, with everyone from the poachers themselves (often local villagers struggling to earn some money), to ivory dealers, and government officials at the highest levels benefitting. Indeed, international bodies such as the IFAW were among the first to blow the whistle on the imbedded corruption that was systematically destroying wildlife.

In 1989, in response to the illegal trade and diminishing numbers of elephants, the Convention on International Trade in Endangered Species (CITES) banned the import and export of ivory. It also increased funding for antipoaching measures. When the ban was established, world raw ivory prices plummeted by 90%, and the market for poaching and smuggling was radically reduced.

Although elephant populations recovered in some ravaged areas, human populations contin-ued to grow, and another problem surfaced – elephants eat huge quantities of foliage, but in the past, herds would eat their fill then migrate to another area, allowing time for vegetation to regenerate. However, an increasing human population pressed the elephants into smaller and smaller areas – mostly around national parks – and the herds were forced to eat everything available. In many places, the bush began to look extremely sparse.

Increasingly across the region, park authorities are also facing elephant overpopulation. Proposed solutions include relocation (where herds are permanently transplanted to other areas) and contraception. The only other alternative is to cull herds, sometimes in large numbers; this seems a bizarre paradox, but illustrates the seriousness of the problem. In the West, people generally hold a preservationist viewpoint, that elephant herds should be protected for their own sake or for aesthetic reasons. While there are some opposing views, the general local sentiment maintains that the elephant must justify its existence on long-term economic grounds for the benefit of local people, or for the country as a whole.

This is an issue sure to generate much debate, with proponents of culling citing the health of the parks and wildlife, including the elephants themselves, while organisations such as the International Fund for Animal Welfare (IFAW) are appalled at such a solution, which they claim is cruel, unethical and scientifically unsound. IFAW believes aerial surveys of elephant numbers are inaccurate, population growth has not been accurately surveyed, and other solutions have not been looked at carefully enough.

Furthermore, there is much dispute about whether controlled ivory sales should be reintro-duced, with countries with excessive elephant populations and large ivory stockpiles pushing hard for a relaxation on the ban. Some argue that countries with large tracts of protected land are paying for the inability of other African countries to properly manage and protect their wildlife. Indeed, it remains to be seen whether a lift on the ban will occur, but meanwhile debate about the ivory trade, and the culling solution to overpopulation, rages on.

there were approximately 100 left within the park confines.

## Sleeping & Eating
### BUDGET & MIDRANGE
**Ndololo Camp** (camping US$10) There's a single public camping area with basic facilities near Kanderi Swamp. Note that elephants wan-der through here frequently, so be extremely aware of your surroundings.

**Tarhi Camp** ( ☎ Mombasa 041-5486378; www .camp-tarhi.de; s/d half-board US$65/120; **P** ) This German-run campsite is located on the edge of the Voi River about 14km east of Voi gate, and is a good compromise be-tween bare-bones camping and over-the-top luxury. It's a lovely, peaceful spot and the rates include authentic Deutschland-inspired meals as well as wildlife walks with a Maasai guide.

**Voi Safari Lodge** ( ☎ Mombasa 041-471861; s/d low season US$88/115, high season US$118/165; P ☒ ) Just 4km from Voi gate, this is a long, low complex perched on the edge of an escarpment overlooking an incredible sweep of savanna. There is an attractive rock-cut swimming pool, as well as a natural waterhole that draws elephants, buffaloes and the occasional predator – also check out the chubby rock hyraxes sunning themselves on ledges.

### TOP END

**Satao Camp** ( ☎ Mombasa 041-475074; www.sataocamp .com; s/d low season US$95/135, high season US$175/215; P ) Located on the banks of the Voi River, this luxury camp is run by the top-class operator Southern Cross Safaris. Intimacy is the theme here, with just 20 canopied tents, all of which are perfectly spaced around a private waterhole.

**Kilalinda** ( ☎ Nairobi 020-882598; www.privatewilderness .com; s/d low season US$350/550, high season US$400/650; P ☒ ) Proof that even top-end resorts can take environmental issues seriously – this very fine ecolodge was built without felling a single tree, and the owners are spearheading a campaign to reintroduce wildlife to areas that were depleted by poachers in previous decades. Accommodation is in lavish cottages adorned with oriental rugs, antique furnishings and other symbols of decadent living.

**Galdessa Safari Camp** ( ☎ Nairobi 020-7123156; www .galdessa.com; s/d from US$445/700; P ) Perched on the edge of the Galana River, approximately 15km west of Lugards Falls, this Italian-owned safari camp is by far the swishest property in Tsavo East, especially since it's often booked out entirely by private parties. For a healthy dose of European sophistication in your bush camping experience (fine wines, gourmet dining, fashionable decor and impeccable service) look no further (assuming of course you've got a whole pile of euros to burn!).

### Getting There & Away

The main track through the park follows the Galana River from the Tsavo gate to the Sala gate. Most tourist safaris enter Tsavo East via the Sala gate, where a good dirt road runs east for 110km to the coast. If you're coming from Nairobi, the Voi gate (near the town of same name) and the Manyani gate (on the Nairobi–Mombasa road) are just as accessible.

Roads within the park are decidedly rough, and a 4WD with decent ground clearance is recommended. Expect longish journey times however you're travelling.

## VOI
☎ 043

Voi is a key service town at the intersection of the Nairobi–Mombasa road, the road to Moshi in Tanzania and the access road to the Voi gate of Tsavo East National Park. While there is little reason to spend any more time here than is needed to get directions, fill up on petrol and buy some snacks for the road, you'll inevitably pass through here at some point.

In the town centre, you can find a **post office** ( ☎ 30253), and can pick up supplies from **Bafaigh Supermarket**. There is also a branch of **Kenya Commercial Bank** ( ☎ 30138) on the Nairobi–Mombasa road.

If you need to bed down for the night, and don't want to spend another night in Tsavo East, the centrally located **Tsavo Park Hotel** ( ☎ 30050; s/d from US$35/45; P ) is probably the best option in town. It's very much a spartan affair that isn't too inspiring, though it is a good place to stop for a hot meal if you want to break up the driving.

From Voi, frequent buses and matatus run to Mombasa (KSh400, three hours), and buses to Nairobi (KSh500 to KSh800, six hours) pass through town, usually in the morning and in the late evening. There are daily matatus to Wundanyi (KSh150, one hour) and Taveta (KSh300, two hours), on the Tanzanian border.

See p345 for information about travel to Tanzania.

### Rukinga Wildlife Conservancy

Just southeast of Voi, this private reserve covers 68,000 hectares of ranch land between Tsavo East and Tsavo West, and is operated as an exclusive tourist concession of **Savannah Camps & Lodges** ( ☎ Nairobi 020-331191; www.savannahcamps.com).

Accommodation is provided at **Galla Camp** (s/d from US$135/200), a luxury tented camp within the sanctuary, though the focus here is on conservation, as opposed to upmarket wildlife watching. Guests can access the **Taita Discovery Centre**, which offers an exciting range of environmental education and bush adventure courses.

If you're looking for a long-term commitment, the centre will provide basic food and

### MAN-EATERS OF TSAVO

Wild felines the world over are rightfully feared and respected, though the famed 'man-eaters of Tsavo' were probably the most dangerous lions to have ever roamed the planet. During the building of the Kenya–Uganda Railway in 1898, Engineer Lt Col John Henry Patterson led the construction of a railway bridge over the Tsavo River in Kenya. However, efforts soon came to a halt when railway workers started being dragged from their tents at night and devoured by two maneless male lions.

The surviving workers soon decided that the lions had to be ghosts or devils, which put the future of the railway in jeopardy. This drove Patterson to create a series of ever more ingenious traps, though each time the lions evaded them, striking unerringly at weak points in the camp defences. Patterson was finally able to bag the first man-eater by hiding on a flimsy wooden scaffold baited with the corpse of a donkey. The second one was dispatched a short time later, although it took six bullets to bring the massive beast down.

According to Patterson's calculations, the two lions killed and ate around 135 workers in less than one year. He detailed his experiences in the best-selling book *The Man-Eaters of Tsavo* (1907), which was later rather freely filmed as *Bwana Devil* (1952) and *The Ghost and the Darkness* (1996).

In a vengeful twist, Patterson turned the two man-eaters into floor rugs, which he kept for more than a quarter of a century. However, in 1924 he finally rid himself of the lions by selling their skins to the Chicago Field Museum for the sum of US$5000. The man-eaters of Tsavo were then stuffed and placed on permanent display, where they remain to this day.

To date, scientists have offered up a number of hypotheses to explain the ferocious behaviour of the man-eaters. Research has shown that Tsavo lions have noticeably elevated levels of the male sex hormone testosterone, which could have been responsible for their hair loss and increased territorial behaviour. The pair themselves had badly damaged teeth, which may have driven them to abandon their normal prey and become man-eaters.

It as also been suggested by historians that an outbreak of rinderpest (an infectious viral disease) might have decimated the lions' usual prey, forcing them to find alternative food sources. Alternatively, the man-eaters may have developed their taste for human flesh after growing accustomed to finding human bodies at the Tsavo River crossing, where slave caravans often crossed, en route to Zanzibar.

While the descendants of Tsavo's man-eaters aren't quite the indiscriminate killing machines that their forbears were, they still have a reputation for ferocity and are much wilder than the lazy kitty cats you come across in Masai Mara. On that note, be aware of your surroundings, sleep in closed campsites and give mother nature's predators a healthy amount of respect and distance.

lodging for volunteers, starting at around US$250 per week.

## Wundanyi

The provincial capital of Wundanyi is set high in the Taita Hills, and numerous trails criss-cross the cultivated terraced slopes around town leading to dramatic gorges, waterfalls, cliffs and jagged outcrops. It's easy to find someone to act as a guide, but stout walking boots and a head for heights are essential.

Other attractions in the hills include the butterflies of **Ngangao Forest**, a 6km matatu ride northwest to Werugha (KSh60); the huge granite **Wesu Rock** that overlooks Wundanyi; and the **Cave of Skulls** where the Taita people once put the skulls of their ancestors (and where the original African violets were discovered).

The best of Wundanyi's limited accommodation offerings, **Taita Rocks** ( ☎ 0735-651349; r KSh500-2000) is perched up a slope off the road on the way into town, with views towards Wesu Rock. The rooms are priced according to size and there's a small restaurant and bar here for getting your feed before hiking.

Frequent matatu services run between Wundanyi and Voi (KSh140, one hour). Leave Wundanyi by around 8.30am if you want to connect with the morning buses to Nairobi from Voi. There are also direct matatus to Mombasa (KSh350, four to five hours) and an irregular morning service to Nairobi (KSh700, seven hours).

lonelyplanet.com

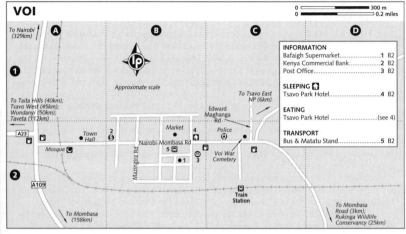

VOI

Map labels: To Nairobi (329km); To Taita Hills (40km); Tsavo West (45km); Wundanyi (50km); Taveta (112km); A23; Town Hall; Mosque; A109; To Mombasa (158km); Mazingira Rd; Nairobi-Mombasa Rd; Market; Edward Maghanga Rd; To Tsavo East NP (6km); Police; Voi War Cemetery; Train Station; To Mombasa Road (3km); Rukinga Wildlife Conservancy (25km); Approximate scale; 0 300 m; 0 0.2 miles

## Taita Hills Wildlife Sanctuary

The Taita Hills, a fertile area of verdant hills and scrub forest, is a far cry from the semi-arid landscape of Tsavo. Within the hills is the private **wildlife sanctuary** (adult US$25), covering an area of 100 sq km – the landscape is dramatic and all the plains wildlife is here in abundance.

The centrepiece of the sanctuary is the up-market **Sarova Salt Lick Safari Lodge** ( 30270; www.sarovahotels.com/saltlick; r from US$162; ), a visually striking complex of mushroom-like houses on stilts surrounding a water-hole. Since the Taita Hills are not an official national park, the sanctuary permits night drives, which provide good opportunities for spotting nocturnal animals, as well as watching hunting behaviour – you can organise everything through the Salt Lick.

The Taita Hills are located south of the dirt road from Voi to Taveta – you will need to arrange private transport to access the sanctuary.

## Lumo Community Wildlife Sanctuary

This innovative community-run **reserve** (adult/child US$20/10) of 657 sq km was formed from three community-owned ranches in 1996, but only opened to the public in 2003. It's partly funded by the EU, and involves local people at every stage of the project, from the park rangers to senior management.

Birdlife is plentiful and all the Big Five are here, as well as several war relics from WWI. For more information, call the **sanctuary**

**offices** ( 30936) in the village of Maktau, near Maktau gate. If you contact them in advance, the rangers may be able to arrange a wildlife drive or guide for a reasonable price.

Accommodation within the sanctuary is provided by the private **Lion Rock Lodge** ( 0735453089; d full board from US$120; ), a *makuti* and canvas compound that is owned and operated by the Tsavo Park Hotel in Voi (p146).

The sanctuary lies on the Voi–Taveta road, so you can get here by public bus or matatu, though a private car is helpful for moving around.

## THE ROAD TO MOSHI

Heading west from Voi, the A23 runs straight to the Tanzanian border en route to the city of Moshi. This road will also drop you off at the border town of Taveta, which is a good place to stock up on fuel and supplies before crossing.

Before entering Taveta, there is a worthwhile detour to the rarely visited **Lake Challa**, a deep, spooky crater lake about 10km north of the town. There are grand views across the plains from the crater rim, near the defunct Lake Challa Safari Lodge, with the mysterious waters shimmering hundreds of metres below.

The lake gained notoriety in early 2002, when a gap-year student was killed by crocodiles here. With that said, you can walk around the crater rim, and down to the water, but be very careful near the water's edge, and under no circumstances consider swimming. Those man-eating crocs haven't gone anywhere and a quick dip is not worth the risk.

The road to Challa turns off the Voi–Taveta road on the outskirts of Taveta, by the second police post. On Taveta market days (Wednesday and Saturday) there are local buses to Challa village (KSh50), passing the turn-off to the crater rim.

Continuing on to **Taveta**, this dusty little town sits on the Tanzanian border, and hosts a busy market on Wednesday and Saturday that attracts people from remote villages on both sides of the border.

A pastel orange building conveniently situated on the main road, **Tripple J Paradise** ( ☎ 5352463; r from KSh800; P ) is little more than a crash pad for drivers heading back and forth between Kenya and Tanzania, though it'll do in a pinch if you can't make it to Moshi in one go.

The Tanzania border is open 24 hours, but the border posts are 4km apart, so you'll have to take a *boda-boda* (bicycle taxi; KSh40) if you don't have your own wheels. From Holili on the Tanzanian side, there are matatus to Moshi (TSh1200), where you can change on to Arusha (TSh2000).

From Taveta, numerous matatus head to Voi (KSh300, 2½ hours) and Mombasa (KSh700, four hours) throughout the day.

# Rift Valley

Coming from Nairobi the first glimpses of the spectacular Rift Valley are breathtaking. The escarpment on which the city rests crashes sheer to the floor of a volcano-studded valley hundreds of metres below, across which savanna grasslands reach out beyond the horizons. If the view could speak it would surely say, 'Welcome to Africa', and what a welcome the Rift Valley provides.

The gouge in the planet that is the Rift Valley stretches thousands of kilometres from the salty shores of the Dead Sea to the palm trees of Mozambique, and was formed some eight million years ago, when mother earth tried to rip Africa in two. Africa bent, Africa buckled – but Africa never gave in.

This battle of geological forces has left Kenya's Rift Valley looking as if it were created by giants. There's a ribbon of steaming and bubbling soda lakes that scars the valley like the footprints of a massive hippopotamus, and numerous dried-out volcanic cones standing to attention like amplified termite mounds.

In places, giants continue to roam; towering giraffes peer over the heads of a million pink flamingos and rhinos look like something from the age of the dinosaurs in Lake Nakuru National Park. Not far away you can cycle right up to the Gates of Hell, where legend has it that a Maasai woman was turned to stone and buffaloes get hot under the collar.

It's not all monsters and violent eruptions, though; the calming panoramas over the freshwater lakes of Naivasha and Boringo, full of diva-voiced song birds and floppy-winged butterflies, are perfect places to wile away the days and be thankful to mother earth for trying to break Africa in two.

---

## HIGHLIGHTS

- Searching for rhino hiding amongst the blushing pink flamingos at **Lake Nakuru National Park** (p162)
- Being serenaded to sleep by snorting, hungry hippos and waking to the fish eagles' dawn chorus at **Lake Baringo** (p165)
- Huffing and puffing to the crater rim of **Mt Longonot** (opposite) to be rewarded with a glorious Rift Valley vista
- Watching a stressed mother earth let off steam at **Lake Bogoria National Reserve** (p164)
- Trying to out-sprint a buffalo in the scorching gorges of **Hell's Gate National Park** (p156)

## Geography

Kenya's Rift Valley is part of the Afro-Arabian rift system that stretches 6000km from the Dead Sea to Mozambique, passing through the Red Sea, Ethiopia, Kenya, Tanzania and Malawi. A western branch forms a string of lakes in the centre of the continent (Albert, Edward, Kivu and Tanganyika), joining the main system at the tip of Lake Malawi. The East African section of the rift failed and now only the Red Sea rift continues, slowly separating Africa from the Middle East.

In Kenya, the Rift Valley can be traced through Lake Turkana, the Cherangani Hills and lakes Baringo, Bogoria, Nakuru, Elmenteita, Naivasha and Magadi. A chain of volcanoes also lines the valley. While most are now extinct, no fewer than 30 remain active and, according to local legend, Mt Longonot erupted as recently as 1860. This continuing activity supports a considerable number of hot springs, and provides ideal conditions for geothermal power plants, which are increasingly important for Kenya's energy supply.

Besides providing fertile soil, the volcanic deposits have created alkaline waters in most Rift Valley lakes. These shallow soda lakes, formed by the valley's lack of decent drainage, experience high evaporation rates, which further concentrates the alkalinity. The strangely soapy and smelly waters are, however, the perfect environment for the growth of microscopic blue-green algae, which in turn feed lesser flamingos, tiny crustaceans (food for greater flamingos) and insect larvae (food for soda-resistant fish).

## Climate

Although slightly hotter than the Central Highlands, the Rift Valley enjoys a pleasant climate and temperatures typically don't surpass 28ºC. Like the highlands, rain usually falls in two seasons: March to the beginning of June (the 'long rains') and October to the end of November (the 'short rains').

## National Parks & Reserves

Lake Nakuru National Park (p162), with its sweeping pink shores of pecking flamingos, regular rhino sightings and abundance of other wildlife, is the region's heavy hitter. While Hell's Gate National Park (p156) sees much fewer visitors, it does offer the unique opportunity to walk unguided through striking landscapes and among African plains

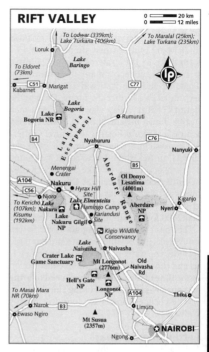

wildlife in all its natural glory. Standing in stunning contrast to these two national parks is the harsh and desolate beauty of Lake Bogoria National Reserve (p164). Steam plumes rise from its hydrothermal shores, which play second home to Lake Nakuru's massive flamingo population.

## Getting There & Away

The valley's close proximity to Nairobi means virtually everybody enters the region using the extensive road network. Regular buses and matatus link the towns to Nairobi, western Kenya and the Central Highlands.

## Getting Around

You'll have no trouble getting around this region. Convenient matatus and buses ply all major (and most minor) routes and most roads are in great shape.

## LONGONOT NATIONAL PARK

Few places offer better Rift Valley views than the serrated crater rim of **Mt Longonot**, rising 1000m above the baking valley floor. In dog years this dormant volcano is ancient, while in geological terms it's just a wee pup at 400,000 years of age.

Since the best vistas in the **park** (adult/child US$20/10) are only reached after a sweaty 1½-hour hike to the crater summit (2776m), peace and quiet accompany the panoramas. To dance and skip your way around the crater rim takes a further 2½ hours. Despite the bounty of Rift Valley views, your eyes may just be drawn inward to the 2km-wide **crater**, a little lost world hosting an entirely different ecosystem. Including time for gawking, this 11km trek should take about six hours.

It's a good idea to take a KWS (Kenya Wildlife Service) ranger as this would be a lonely old walk on your own. Guides, available at the gate, cost KSh1500 to the summit or KSh2000 for the full monty around the rim.

The basic **Oloongonot Campsite** (camping per person US$5) sits just beyond the gate and has basic facilities (no water or firewood), though a toilet and shower block were under construction at the time of research. You will need to bring all your own food and cooking supplies.

The cheapest hotels are found in nearby Naivasha.

### Getting There & Away

Driving, it's 75km northwest of Nairobi on the Old Naivasha Rd. If you're without a vehicle, take a matatu from Naivasha to Longonot village, from where there's a path (ask locals) to the park's access road.

## MT SUSUA

Less frequented than Longonot but more interesting, this unique volcano is well worth the effort of visiting. The steep outer crater protects a second inner crater, whose rim peaks at 2357m and begs to be trekked. There's also a network of unexplored caves on the east side of the mountain.

There's no designated route and all land is owned by local Maasai, so you'll have to find someone to guide you in the nearby villages that dot the B3 Nairobi–Narok road.

## NAIVASHA

☎ 050

Bypassed by the new A104 Hwy to Nairobi, Naivasha has become an agricultural backwater that now exists primarily to service the area's blossoming flower industry. Although a convenient base for visits to Longonot National Park it's hard to see why you would

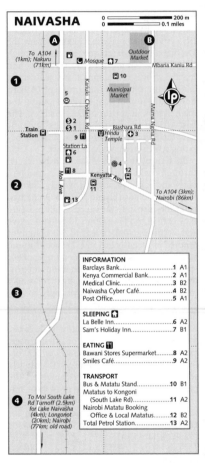

| INFORMATION | |
| --- | --- |
| Barclays Bank | 1 A1 |
| Kenya Commercial Bank | 2 A1 |
| Medical Clinic | 3 B2 |
| Naivasha Cyber Café | 4 B2 |
| Post Office | 5 A1 |

| SLEEPING 🏠 | |
| --- | --- |
| La Belle Inn | 6 A2 |
| Sam's Holiday Inn | 7 B1 |

| EATING 🍴 | |
| --- | --- |
| Bawani Stores Supermarket | 8 A2 |
| Smiles Café | 9 A2 |

| TRANSPORT | |
| --- | --- |
| Bus & Matatu Stand | 10 B1 |
| Matatus to Kongoni | |
| (South Lake Rd) | 11 A2 |
| Nairobi Matatu Booking | |
| Office & Local Matatus | 12 B2 |
| Total Petrol Station | 13 A2 |

choose to stay the night here rather than at the lake shore (opposite). It is, however, a good place to stock up on supplies for your lakeside adventure.

The town was badly affected by the post-election violence of 2008, though there are few signs of that today.

### Information

**Barclays Bank** (Moi Ave) With ATM.

**Naivasha Cyber Café** (per hr KSh50; ⏰ 7.30am-6pm) One of several internet cafes tucked away inside the Jubilee Mall. Open Sundays.

**Kenya Commercial Bank** (Moi Ave) With ATM (Visa only).

**Medical Clinic** (Biashara Rd; ⏰ 9am-7pm Mon-Sat, 11am-4pm Sun) Crude clinic and lab services.

**Post office** (Moi Ave)

## Sleeping

**Sam's Holiday Inn** ( ☎ 0720268469; Mbaria Kaniu Rd; s/tw KSh350/600) The beds might be back-bendingly saggy but they still represent the best budget digs in town. All rooms have private bathrooms with hot showers and there's a lively bar (so opt for a room further away from this).

**La Belle Inn** ( ☎ 020-3510404; Moi Ave; s/d KSh2500/2900) Naivasha's oldest hotel is a classic colonial-style option, with rooms of various sizes sporting dark wooden floors, local artwork and a refined atmosphere of times long past. Prices quoted include breakfast.

## Eating & Drinking

**Smiles Café** (Kariuki Chotarai Rd; meals KSh100-150; ☺ breakfast, lunch & dinner) As smiley as the name suggests, this little green-and-white treasure offers cholesterol-filled fried breakfasts, as well as hearty stews. It's always busy and conversations come easy.

**La Belle Inn** (Moi Ave; meals KSh200-400; ☺ lunch & dinner) Whether your stomach is rumbling for an Indian curry, steak, pork spare ribs, beef kebab, fresh tilapia from the lake or even apple pie, this great colonial verandah is for you. It's also a top place for drinks, with the Happy Valley bar worth propping up in the evenings.

**Bawani Stores Supermarket** (Moi Ave) This is the perfect place for self-caterers to stock up.

There's a cluster of cheap bars and butcheries on Kariuki Chotara Rd, although you'd have to be pretty brave to venture into most of them.

## Getting There & Away

The main bus and matatu station is off Mbaria Kaniu Rd, close to the municipal market. Frequent buses and matatus leave for Nakuru (KSh150, 1¼ hours), Nairobi (KSh150, 1½ hours), Nyahururu (KSh250, 1¾ hours) and places west. Frequent matatus plough down to the lake with Kongoni costing KSh100 and Fisherman's Camp area KSh70 (45 minutes). As well as the bus station you can also catch these from Kenyatta Ave.

## LAKE NAIVASHA
☎ 050

For many people Lake Naivasha is the first port of call after Nairobi, and with its shores fringed in papyrus and yellow-barked acacias, bulbous snorting hippos playing in the shal-lows, a cacophony of twittering birds and a gentle climate, there is no denying its appeal over the urban mayhem of Nairobi.

A vast range of plains animals and a plethora of birdlife have long called the verdant shoreline home, as have the Maasai, who considered it prime grazing land. Unfortunately for the Maasai, the splendour of the surroundings wasn't lost on early settlers, and it was one of the first areas they settled, eventually becoming the favourite haunt of Lord Delamere and the decadent Happy Valley set of the 1930s (see also p126). Amazingly, between 1937 and 1950, the lake was Kenya's main airport, with British Overseas Airways Corporation's Empire and Solent flying-boats landing here after their four-day journey from Southampton. Lake Naivasha still has one of the largest settler and expat communities in Kenya and can have a resort feel to it in high season, when it essentially becomes Kenya's St Tropez, but with Tusker beer rather than champagne.

Not only does Lake Naivasha's fresh water bestow it with a unique ecosystem (in comparison with the vast majority of Rift Valley lakes, which are highly alkaline), but it also means the lake can be used for irrigation purposes. While the surrounding countryside has historically been a major production area for beef cattle and fresh fruit and vegetables, today the flower industry rules the roost. Shade houses have proliferated in the hills recently, and Lake Naivasha is now the centre of Kenya's US$360 million flower industry. Astoundingly, flowers that are picked here in the early morning can be at Europe's flower auctions the same day.

However, it's this very beauty and fertility that threatens to destroy the lake. Anyone who visited the place a decade ago wouldn't recognise it if they returned. The wealth generated by the flower farms has spawned massive development. In addition, pesticides and fertilizers are seeping into the lake and wreaking havoc with the ecosystem. Irrigation has further destabilised erratic water levels, which had seen the lake almost dry up in the 1940s, before rebounding by the '60s. The lake is currently receding again, and now only spreads over 139 sq km.

The lake's ecology has been interfered with on a number of other occasions, notably with the introduction of foreign fish (for sports and commercial fisheries), crayfish,

RIFT VALLEY

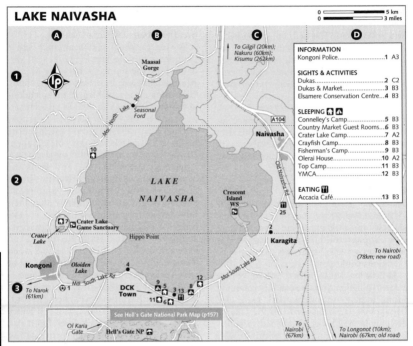

## LAKE NAIVASHA

| | | | | 0 ———— 5 km |
| | | | | 0 ———— 3 miles |

To Gilgil (20km);
Nakuru (60km);
Kisumu (262km)

Maasai
Gorge

Seasonal
Ford

Naivasha

A104

*LAKE*

*NAIVASHA*

Crescent
Island
WS

Crater Lake
Game Sanctuary

Hippo Point

Karagita

Crater
Lake

Kongoni

Oloiden
Lake

To Narok
(61km)

DCK
Town

To Nairobi
(78km; new road)

To Nairobi
(67km)

To Longonot (10km);
Nairobi (67km; old road)

Ol Karia
Gate

Hell's Gate NP

See Hell's Gate National Park Map (p157)

**INFORMATION**
Kongoni Police..........................1 A3

**SIGHTS & ACTIVITIES**
Dukas......................................2 C2
Dukas & Market.......................3 B3
Elsamere Conservation Centre...4 B3

**SLEEPING**
Connelley's Camp.....................5 B3
Country Market Guest Rooms...6 B3
Crater Lake Camp.....................7 A2
Crayfish Camp..........................8 B3
Fisherman's Camp....................9 B3
Olerai House...........................10 A2
Top Camp...............................11 B3
YMCA.....................................12 B3

**EATING**
Accacia Café...........................13 B3

RIFT VALLEY

the South American coypu (an aquatic rodent that initially escaped from a fur farm) and various aquatic plants, including the dreaded water hyacinth.

For these reasons Naivasha has been the focus of conservation efforts and in 1995, after years of lobbying from the Lake Naivasha Riparian Association (LNRA), the lake was designated a Ramsar site, officially recognising it as a wetland of international importance. Besides educating the locals dependent on the lake about the environmental issues involved, the LNRA, Elsamere Conservation Centre and other organisations work to establish a code of conduct among the local growers that will maintain the lake's biodiversity. The results are promising, but much remains to be done.

Despite all its problems the lake continues to draw visitors – half of Nairobi seems to decamp here at weekends, and they come for good reason. With plenty of things to see and do, a fun-loving atmosphere and, in the still morning mists, an undeniable beauty, Lake Naivasha remains the best place to get to grips with being in Kenya.

## Sights
### CRATER LAKE GAME SANCTUARY

Surrounding a beautiful volcanic crater lake is this small **sanctuary** (admission KSh700, car KSh200), with many trails, including one for hikers along the steep but diminutive crater rim. The sanctuary makes for a superb place for a cheap safari and, besides the impressive 150 bird species recorded here, giraffes, zebras and other plains wildlife are also regular residents on the more open plains surrounding the crater. While walking, remember that buffaloes lurk in the woods. The tiny jade-green crater lake is held in high regard by the local Maasai, who even believe its waters help soothe ailing cattle.

### CRESCENT ISLAND WILDLIFE SANCTUARY

The protruding rim of a collapsed volcanic crater forms this island on the eastern side of Lake Naivasha. It's a private **sanctuary** (adult/child US$20/10), where you can walk beneath acacias in search of giraffes, Thomson's and Grant's gazelles, elands, waterbucks and countless bird species. Oh, and there are some rather gigantic pythons too!

Almost all accommodation options rent boats for island trips (around KSh3000 per hour). **Fishermans Camp** (right) charge a set fee of KSh5000, plus entry fees for a tour of the island. It's technically possible to drive here along a small causeway, but the land owner charges extortionate fees for crossing his property.

### ELSAMERE CONSERVATION CENTRE

This **conservation centre** ( ☎ 2021055; www.elsamere .com; admission KSh600; ⊙ 8am-6.30pm) is the former home of the late Joy Adamson of *Born Free* fame. She bought the house in 1967 with a view to retiring here with her husband, George. Adamson did much of her writing from Elsamere, right up until her murder in 1980.

Now a conservation centre focused on lake ecology and environmental awareness programs, the site is open to the public and entry includes afternoon tea, complete with a mountain of biscuits on the hippo-manicured lawns (with a chance to see eastern black-and-white colobus monkeys), a visit to the memorial room and a showing of the weathered 40-minute *Joy Adamson Story*.

## Sleeping

### BUDGET & MIDRANGE

Due to its popularity, Lake Naivasha has the Rift Valley's best range of accommodation. To generalise, the further away you head from Naivasha town, along Moi South Lake Rd, the better the accommodation becomes and the more the countryside will make you smile.

**YMCA** ( ☎ 501009, 0720434497; dm KSh300, camping KSh400, bandas with/without bathroom per person KSh1000/ KSh600) You'll find scruffy and overpriced bandas and an equally unappealing, though far more sensibly priced, dorm here. It's a 15-minute walk to the lake but is handy for Hell's Gate. The camping pitches, in the shade of the acacias, are pleasant. Meals are also available (breakfast KSh250, lunch and dinner KSh300). It's popular with Kenyans and gets busy with school groups during the holidays.

**Top Camp** ( ☎ 0720550409; camping KSh300, bandas s/tw from KSh700/1400, cottages KSh2000-4000) It lacks Fisherman's Camp's lakeside location, but Top Camp boasts crazy lake views from its hill-top perch. It's a quiet place with various tin-roofed, bamboo-walled bandas (almost all have bathrooms). There are also cooking utensils, plates and a charcoal burner avail-

able for self-caterers, though if you're not feeling like Jamie Oliver someone might be persuaded to cook for you. There are a couple of large cosy cottages with full kitchens, books aplenty, privacy and views.

**Connelley's Camp** ( ☎ 50004; camping KSh300, dm KSh600, r per person KSh800, bandas Sun-Thu/Fri & Sat KSh3000/5000) Camping here is excellent value and even at weekends it remains slightly more tranquil than some of its neighbours, but the same cannot be said for the rest of the accommodation – KSh5000 for a banda (read: old caravan) with an outdoor toilet and shower?

**Fisherman's Camp** ( ☎ 50462, 0726870590; www.fisher manscampkenya.com; camping KSh300, tents from KSh400, ban-das Sun-Thu per person KSh1000, Fri & Sat per banda KSh4000) Spread along the grassy tree-laden southern shore and full of hungry hippos, Fisherman's is a perennial favourite of campers, overland companies and backpackers. While hippo movements have been restricted by electric fences for safety reasons, you still stand a real chance of seeing one of these great beasts graz-ing at night. The site is huge, but at weekends is very busy and has a beer-swilling, noisy party atmosphere more akin to Glastonbury than Africa! As at Glastonbury, you should keep an eye on your belongings when camping. During the week things are much calmer and, depend-ing on your point of view, more pleasant. Nonguests are charged KSh100 admission.

**Country Market Guest Rooms** (DCK Town; r KSh500) If not the best value then certainly the cheapest four-walls-and-a-roof-style accommodation is to be found at this peaceful lodging, run by a friendly local woman in the small hamlet of DCK Town. The 11 small, self-contained rooms are very clean and have hot-water show-ers. The beds are a little too small for an arguing couple but perfect for those still in love! Its only real drawback is its distance from the lake.

**Crayfish Camp** ( ☎ 2020239; www.crayfishcamp.com; camping KSh500, s without bathroom KSh1000, s/d with bathroom & breakfast KSh2500/3200; ▯ ) Following Fisherman's lead, the Crayfish Camp can seem more like a beer garden than a camp-site, but it's not a bad option. The pricey new rooms are a bit minimalist, but have some charm, while the petite rooms with shared facilities are very plain-Jane. The cottages all back up against a flower factory.

### TOP END

**Crater Lake Camp** ( ☎ 2020613; crater@africaonline.co.ke; camping KSh500, s/d full board US$187/280) A luxury

---

**THE STONE LADY**

Fischer's Tower (opposite) may look like nothing more than a needle of rock, but if that rock could talk, which it once could, it would tell you how it was actually a pretty young Maasai woman, sent from her home village against her wishes to marry a fearless warrior. As she left she was warned not to turn back, but in her sadness she couldn't resist one last longing glance at her old home. As soon as she did so, she was cast into stone and she remains rooted to the spot to this day.

---

tented camp nestled among trees and overlooking the tiny jade-green crater lake dotted with blushing pink flamingos. This is one of those ever-so-exclusive and romantic hideaways that Kenya excels at and, as if to reinforce that point, the Honeymoon tent contains a whirlpool bath and other romantic essentials. You can explore the whole of the surrounding sanctuary on foot (mind the buffaloes). You can also camp here and make use of the showers and toilets.

**Olerai House** ( ☎ Nairobi 020-891112; www.olerai .com; Moi North Lake Rd; s/d full board US$390/600) Lost under a blanket of tropical flowers, this beautiful house is like something from a fairy tale, where petals dust the beds and floors, the Maasai sing you to sleep on a Venetian gondola, zebras hang out with pet dogs and your every whim is attended to.

## Eating & Drinking

Since food and drinks can be had at most of the accommodation options mentioned previously, there's little in the way of independent wining and dining.

**Accacia Café** (meals KSh80-100; ☻ lunch & dinner) If the restaurants found at most of the camps just aren't 'Africa' enough for you (or cost too much) then slide on over to this immaculate little locals' cafe in DCK Town where you'll get beef stew for KSh80.

**Fisherman's Camp** (meals KSh250-425; ☻ lunch & dinner) Everything from fruit smoothies and chicken tikka to burgers and chilli con carne make their way onto plates at this atmospheric restaurant and bar. Be prepared to wait, and wait, and wait for your food. It's easily the most popular 'Saturday Night Fever' spot for well-to-do Kenyans.

A small market and some *dukas* (small shops or kiosks) are found in DCK Town, near Fisherman's Camp, for basic supplies.

## Getting There & Away

Frequent matatus (KSh100, one hour) run along Moi South Lake Rd between Naivasha town and Kongoni on the lake's western side, passing the turnoffs to Hell's Gate National Park and Fisherman's Camp (KSh70).

It's a 5km walk from Kongoni to Crater Lake, but don't do this alone, as there have been muggings in the past.

There's one daily matatu along Moi North Lake Rd, leaving from the Total petrol station in Naivasha around 3pm. Returning to town, you'll need to be on the road by about 7am, otherwise it's a long dusty walk.

## Getting Around

Most budget and midrange accommodation options rent reasonable boats for lake trips (KSh3000 per hour). Top-end lodges charge between KSh3000 and KSh4000 per hour for similar rides.

If you'd like to row-row-row your boat, Fisherman's Lodge can help you out (KSh300 per hour).

Most sites also hire mountain bikes; Fisherman's Camp charges KSh500 for a full day or KSh300 for a half-day. You'll find cheaper rides at various places signposted off Moi South Lake Rd, but check the contraptions carefully before paying. Whichever bike you choose you can get ready to say hello to a very bruised and saddle-sore arse after a day cycling through Hell's Gate!

## HELL'S GATE NATIONAL PARK

Looking at animals from the safety of your car seat is all well and good, but let's be honest – after a while who *doesn't* get the urge to get out of the vehicle and re-enter the food chain? Well, at Hell's Gate you really can do that, because this unique park actively encourages you to walk or, better still, cycle, through an African savanna-scape teeming with large animals. You'll find that senses become heightened ten-fold when a group of buffaloes start looking annoyed with you as you try to calmly cycle past and – wow, giraffes really are tall aren't they? – and even those previously soft-looking zebras and Thomson's gazelles start looking a little life-threatening when standing face to face with a group of them. The knowledge that cheetahs, lions and leopards aren't unheard of here only adds to the excitement of it all.

Keep an eye out for the massive lammergeiers (bearded vultures), which are slowly being reintroduced. Their wingspans can reach almost 3m and their favourite hobby is dropping bones from great heights in order to release the marrow within.

The scenery here is dramatic, with rich ochre soils and savanna grasses squeezed between looming cliffs of rusty columnar basalt – it's all aglow in the early morning.

Marking the eastern entrance to **Hell's Gate Gorge** is **Fischer's Tower**, a 25m-high volcanic column named after Gustav Fischer, a German explorer who reached here in 1882. Commissioned by the Hamburg Geographical Society to find a route from Mombasa to Lake Victoria, Fischer was stopped by territorial Maasai, who comprehensively and most efficiently kiboshed his campaign by slaughtering almost his entire party.

Rising from the gorge's southern end is the large **Central Tower**. A picnic site and ranger's post are close by, from where an excellent walk descends into the **Lower Gorge** (Ol Njorowa). This narrow sandstone ravine has been stunningly sculpted by water, and the incoming light casts marvellous shadows. You'd do well to spend a couple of hours exploring here. It's a steep and very slippery descent, but some steps have been cut into the rock and whole school parties manage it on a regular basis.

The park's western half is much less scenic and hosts the **Ol Karia Geothermal Station**, a power project utilising one of the world's hottest sources of natural steam. The plumes of rising steam can be seen from many of the park's viewpoints. It's usually possible to have a look around the site – ask the guards at Ol Karia II.

If walking with megafauna doesn't light your fire then get the adrenaline flowing with some technical rock climbing. The park's resident climber, **Simon Kiane** ( ☎ 0720909718), charges from US$10 to act as an instructor and guide to both beginners and the experienced on the gorges' sheer red walls.

## Information

The usual access point to the **park** (adult/child US$25/10, bicycle KSh50, guide KSh500) is through the main Elsa gate, 2km from Moi South Lake Rd, where there's an **information centre** ( ☎ 050-2020284). With the two gates on the northwest corner of the park closed, the only other gate is Ol Karia.

## Sleeping

Although it's convenient to sleep at Lake Naivasha's many lodges and camps (p155), the park's two gorgeous **public campsites** (adult/child US$15/10) can't be recommended enough.

**Naiburta**, sitting halfway up the Hell's Gate Gorge and looking west past Fischer's Tower, is the most scenic site, with basic

**RIFT VALLEY**

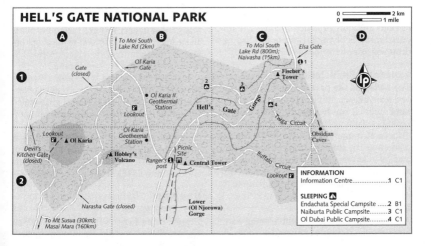

**HELL'S GATE NATIONAL PARK**

| INFORMATION | |
| --- | --- |
| Information Centre.................1 | C1 |

| SLEEPING | |
| --- | --- |
| Endachata Special Campsite .....2 | B1 |
| Naiburta Public Campsite.........3 | C1 |
| Ol Dubai Public Campsite.........4 | C1 |

---

**KIGIO WILDLIFE CONSERVANCY**

Many people believe that the future of conservation in Kenya is in the hands of private companies and individuals, and judging by the superb Kigio Wildlife Conservancy, they might just have a point. Situated along the Naivasha–Nakuru road, this 3500-acre reserve was started on a struggling dairy farm in 1997 and has met with phenomenal success; zebras, impalas, Thomson's gazelles, buffaloes and elands are all commonly sighted. In 2002 KWS translocated eight Rothschild giraffes here and the first white rhinos have recently been translocated.

Unfortunately, casual visitors are not encouraged to drop in: to visit you must be staying in the supremely comfortable colonial-style **Malewa Ranch House** ( ☎ Nairobi 020-3535878; from €384), which is rented exclusively to one group at a time.

---

toilets, an open banda for cooking and freshwater taps.

**Ol Dubai**, resting on the gorge's opposite side, offers identical facilities and views east to the orange bluffs and the puffs of steam from the power station.

The **Endachata Special Campsite** (adult/child US$10/5, plus set-up fee KSh5000) has no services, and besides absolute solitude, offers no more ambience than the cheaper public sites.

## Getting There & Around

The round trip from the park's turn-off on Moi South Lake Rd to the shore of Lake Naivasha via Elsa gate and Ol Karia gate is 22km; the distance between the two gates via Moi South Lake Rd is 9km. If you intend to walk through the park, allow a full day, and take plenty of supplies.

## NAIVASHA TO NAKURU

Besides the odd zebra and gangs of hardened road warriors (baboons) dotting the roadside between Naivasha and Nakuru, there are some obvious and not-so-obvious sights. The frequent matatus plying this route will happily drop you anywhere you like.

### Kariandusi Prehistoric Site

The **Kariandusi site** (adult/child KSh500/250; ⏰ 9am-6pm) is signposted off the A104 Hwy near Lake Elmenteita. It was here in the 1920s that the Leakeys (a family of renowned archaeologists) discovered numerous obsidian and lava tools made by early humans between 1.4 million and 200,000 years ago. Two excavations sites are preserved and there's a new gallery displaying a brief history of early human life.

### Lake Elmenteita

A major tourist attraction with passing water birds, though strangely less popular with passing humans, Lake Elmenteita's beautiful soda shoreline is often fringed in rainbow shades, thanks to hundreds of brilliant flamingos and other birds. It's not a national park, so there are no entry fees, and you can walk around parts of the shoreline that aren't privately owned. There is an **ostrich park** (admission KSh250; ⏰ 6am-5pm) not far from the lake shore, where you can get up close and personal with these oversized chickens. Children will love it.

Loved by both children and adults alike are the hot-air balloon safaris organised by **Go Ballooning Kenya** ( ☎ 0723702181; www.goballooningkenya.com). At US$365 per person for three hours it's cheaper than ballooning in the Masai Mara.

### SLEEPING

**Flamingo Camp** (Map p151; camping KSh300, safari tents s/d KSh1500/2000, cottages s/d KSh1500/2500) It's a little overpriced but you're paying for the setting and it's a setting worth paying for! Situated right on the western fringe of the lake it invites peaceful evenings of waterside dreaming. Bird-watchers will get their binoculars all steamed up in excitement at the avian life visible from your cottage terrace. Meals can be prepared with plenty of warning.

**Lake Elmenteita Lodge** ( ☎ 050-50648; s/d full board high season US$138/176; ⚟ ) Sitting around a maze-like bougainvillea garden, the slightly dated cottages here represent good value for money. The bar's terrace, with stunning lake views, is crying out for the company of you and a gin and tonic. Numerous activities are on offer, including horse riding (KSh1800 per hour) and nature walks (KSh500 per person).

## NAKURU

☎ 051 / pop 300,000

Despite being Kenya's fourth-largest centre, Nakuru doesn't feel like anything more than an overgrown country town and has a relaxed atmosphere, making it a pleasant base for a few days. It's on the doorstep of the delightful Lake Nakuru National Park and is only a few kilometres from the deep, dramatic Menengai Crater.

## Information

Changing cash and travellers' cheques in Nakuru is easy, with numerous banks and foreign exchange bureaus. Barclays Bank's ATMs are the most reliable. Plenty of cardphones are scattered around town.

**Aga Khan Satellite Laboratory** (off Court Rd) Various lab services including malaria tests.

**Crater Travel** ( ☎ 2215019; off Kenyatta Ave) One of the few reputable travel agencies in town.

**Dana Communications Services** (Kenyatta Ave; per hr KSh60; ☯ 7am-6.30pm) Fast connections and open Sunday.

**Petmary Cyber Café** (Kenyatta Ave; per hr KSh60; ☯ 8.30am-5.30pm) Nakuru's fastest internet connections.

**Post office** (Kenyatta Ave)

**Spoonbill Tours & Safaris** ( ☎ 0733502768; Carnation Hotel, Mosque Rd) Seems to have a monopoly on activities around Nakuru. Most travel agents, including Crater Travel, use their services.

## Sleeping

Many safari drivers will do everything in their power to get you to stay in the hotel of their choice by insisting that it's the best in town and that all the others have closed down after aliens abducted all the staff or

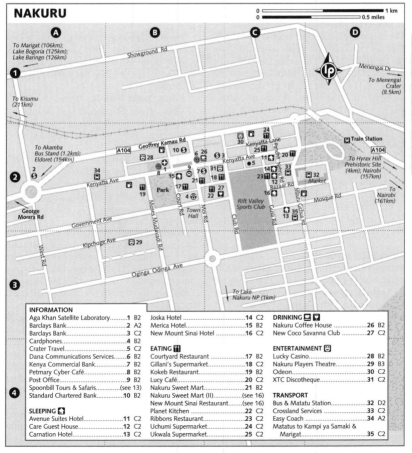

**NAKURU**

other such equally unlikely scenarios. Most of these places are well out of town, in a slightly rough neighbourhood not that far from the national park's main gates.

### BUDGET

Lurking within the maze of noisy and dirty budget options were these standouts.

**Joska Hotel** ( ☎ 2212546; Pandhit Nehru Rd; r KSh400) Foam mattresses have shag-carpet covers in these basic rooms. Everything is rather clean, but you'll have to be a porcelain jockey – the toilets lack seats. The double beds are small.

**Care Guest House** ( ☎ 0721636447; Pandhit Nehru Rd; s/tw KSh400/500) This is a surprise: at first glance you fear the worst, but the pokey pink rooms are actually very tidy and all have attached bathrooms with hot – OK warm – well alright, possibly tepid, showers.

**New Mount Sinai Hotel** (Bazaar Rd; s/tw KSh450/600) Foreigners are considered 'special' and therefore get the posh, and clean, rooms right up on the roof and with amazing views of Lake Nakuru. Staff can help organise trips to the lake (and just in case you forget they will remind often). If there was a fire the numerous padlocked security gates would be a right laugh to get past.

**Carnation Hotel** ( ☎ 2215360; Mosque Rd; s/tw KSh750/1300) The plastic-fantastic flower-filled Carnation Hotel is the town's prettiest budget rose. Rooms, with their multicoloured tiled floors and kitsch bed sheets, have plenty of character, as well as hot showers.

Campers can drop tent in nearby Lake Nakuru National Park (p162), and at Hyrax Hill Prehistoric Site (opposite).

### MIDRANGE & TOP END

**Avenue Suites Hotel** ( ☎ 2210607; avenuesuiteshotel @yahoo.co.uk; Kenyatta Ave; s/d KSh1500/2000) Easily the best value accommodation in town. All rooms are mini-suites with enticing bathrooms, TVs and comfy beds. Everything is spick and span and the friendly staff are dressed up as spiffily as the rooms – there's even a doorman in top hat.

**Merica Hotel** ( ☎ 2216013; merica@kenyaweb.com; Kenyatta Ave; s/d half board US$65/110; ⚅ ⚃ ) Opened in 2003, this contemporary tower hosts Nakuru's only top-end rooms. Ride the glass elevators up the sunlit atrium to well-appointed rooms large enough to host a wildebeest migration. Besides modern comfort,

there's classic fun in Nakuru's best swimming pool (nonguests KSh200).

## Eating

You'll have no trouble getting pleasantly stuffed in Nakuru.

**New Mount Sinai Restaurant** (Bazaar Rd; meals KSh80-100; ☽ lunch & dinner) Cheap, cheerful and spot-on local dishes at this popular place below the hotel of the same name.

**Lucy Café** (off Mburu Gichua Rd; meals KSh80-120; ☽ lunch & dinner) Close to the bus station and with a stunning line in sausage and chips, as well as a few much more boring, though healthier, items.

**Ribbons Restaurant** (Gusii Rd; meals KSh50-200; ☽ lunch & dinner) One of the best restaurants for cheap Kenyan dishes. There is a balcony overlooking the street and it's a pretty-in-pink colour.

**Planet Kitchen** (off Moi Rd; meals KSh75-200; ☽ lunch & dinner) The foliage-covered terrace here is a great place to hide from the noisy streets, and the food, especially the steak (KSh200), is pleasant.

**Nakuru Sweet Mart** (Moi Rd; meals KSh120-220; ☽ lunch & dinner) This Sweet Mart is more of a sit-down option than the canteen (below) and serves sandwiches, burgers, greasy fried chicken and chips.

**Nakuru Sweet Mart (II)** (Gusii Rd; meals KSh100-200; ☽ lunch & dinner) Spotless canteen serving old-fashioned Kenyan food, a few Indian treats and a magnificent range of sticky pieces of artwork. There is a useful noticeboard for long-term visitors.

**Kokeb Restaurant** (Moses Mudavadi Rd; meals KSh200-300; ☽ lunch & dinner) A relaxed garden restaurant serving an interesting mixture of Ethiopian and Italian fare. If you're not making the big adventure north and across the border to the real thing, try some *injera* (spongy flatbread) and *wat* (stew) here.

**Courtyard Restaurant** (off Court Rd; meals KSh250-500; ☽ lunch & dinner) This place scratches a variety of itches, from Indian to Italian and from beef stew to seafood, though you'd be lucky to find them all actually available. The paneer tikka (curry with cubes of curd cheese) is rather enjoyable. As the name suggests, there's a nice courtyard.

There are several well-stocked supermarkets for self-caterers, including Uchumi and Ukwala.

## Drinking

There are plenty of places pouring wobbly pops (beers), including the top-end hotels, and even one wee shop which brews great coffee.

**New Coco Savanna Club** (Government Ave; KSh50) A cavernous place with pounding music, the odd pool-shark and frequent ladies' nights. It also attracts lots of prostitutes.

**Nakuru Coffee House** (Kenyatta Ave) For a straightforward caffeine fix, this '50s-style cafe sells excellent freshly roasted coffee.

## Entertainment

For a rural town there's actually a choice of evening options.

**Nakuru Players Theatre** (Kipchoge Ave) Four evenings a month this theatre stages entertaining Kenyan plays.

**Odeon** (Geoffrey Kamau Rd; ⏰ 6pm Tue-Sun) It's a bit of a dump, but it usually screens Western movies.

**Lucky Casino** (off Kenyatta Ave) For those who like to be more proactive with their cash.

**XTC Discotheque** (Kenyatta Ave) With strobe lights and a dark dance floor, this is the nearest you'll get to a proper nightclub in Nakuru. It floated our boat because they were playing ABBA when we visited.

## Getting There & Away

Regular buses, matatus and the odd Peugeot (shared taxi) leave the chaotic stands off Mburu Gichua Rd. Check the prices with several different people before handing over your cash, as the ticket touts and even the bus ticket office employees aren't always to be trusted. Naivasha (KSh150, 1¼ hours), Nyahururu (KSh140, 1¼ hours), Kericho (KSh300, two hours), Nyeri (KSh300, 2½ hours), Eldoret (KSh300, 2¾ hours), Nairobi (KSh250, three hours), Kitale (KSh500, 3½ hours), Kisumu (KSh500, 3½ hours) and Kisii (KSh500, 4½ hours).

Matatus for Molo (KSh150, one hour) leave from **Crossland Services** (Mburu Gichua Rd), while services to Kampi ya Samaki (for Lake Baringo) via Marigat (for Lake Bogoria) leave further south on Mburu Gichua Rd. Kampi ya Samaki (KSh250, 2½ hours) costs slightly more and takes 30 minutes longer to reach than Marigat.

**Akamba** (George Morara Rd) buses leave from their depot behind the Kenol petrol station west of town. Destinations include Nairobi (KSh400 to KSh650, three hours), Eldoret (KSh250, 2¾ hours) and Kisumu (KSh800, 3½ hours). **Easy Coach** (Kenyatta Ave) offers the same destinations and a little extra comfort for almost double the cost.

# AROUND NAKURU
## Menengai Crater

From town it doesn't look like much, but the striking red cliffs of Menengai Crater, which radiate outwards and encircle a 90-sq-km cauldron of convoluted black lava flows, is quite something once you've scrambled up to its summit. While lush vegetation is now proliferating on the harsh crater floor, some 480m below, the violent and dramatic volcanic history is easily seen.

A grim local legend states that the plumes of steam rising from the bottom are the souls of defeated Maasai warriors, thrown into the crater after a territorial battle, trying to make their way to heaven.

While hiking to the viewpoint from town offers great views back over Lake Nakuru, it's rather isolated, and tourists have been mugged. To be safe, the 9km walk from town should only be done in groups of at least four or five. Alternatively, you can take a taxi up and back for KSh1000 to KSh1500. There's a small group of *dukas* at the main viewpoint selling drinks and trinkets.

## Hyrax Hill Prehistoric Site

This **archaeological site** (Map p163; ☎ 22171175; adult/child KSh500/250; ⏰ 9am-6pm), 4km outside Nakuru, is a great spot for a peaceful amble away from all the rhinos and tourists. It contains a museum and the remains of three settlements excavated between 1937 and the late 1980s, the oldest being possibly 3000 years old, the most recent only 200 to 300 years old.

You're free to wander the site, but it's rather cryptic and a guide is useful – a tip of KSh100 is plenty. The North-East Village, which is believed to be about 400 years old, sits closest to the museum and once housed 13 enclosures. Only the 1965 excavation of Pit D remains open. It was here that a great number of pottery fragments were found, some of which have been pieced together into complete jars and are displayed in the museum.

From Pit D the trail climbs to the scant remains of the stone-walled hill fort near the top of Hyrax Hill itself. You can continue to the peak, from where there's a fine view of flamingo-filled Lake Nakuru in the distance.

Looking down the other side of the hill, you'll see two 'c'-shaped Iron Age stone hut foundations at the base. Just north of the foundations, a series of Iron Age burial pits containing 19 skeletons was found. The majority were male and lots of them had been decapitated, so a number of colourful explanations have been offered.

Nearby, two Neolithic burial mounds and several other Iron Age burial pits were also discovered. The large collection of items found in these pits included a real puzzle – six Indian coins, one of them 500 years old, and two others dating from 1918 and 1919.

On a more lively note, there's a *bao* (traditional game that's played throughout East Africa) board carved into a rock outcrop between the Iron Age settlements and the museum.

It's now possible to **camp** (camping per tent KSh250) here, though facilities are limited.

Local matatus to Naivasha or Nairobi will take you past the turn-off (about 1km from the site), just south of Nakuru.

## LAKE NAKURU NATIONAL PARK

Just a couple of kilometres from the hustle of central Nakuru an army of flamingos turn a sky-blue lake bright pink and prehistoric-looking horned mammals crash through a landscape of euphorbia trees and acacia forests. With all this and a wealth of other birds and animals, there's little doubt why Lake Nakuru National Park is rivalling Amboseli as Kenya's second-most-visited park.

### Information

The main **park** (adult/child US$60/30, smartcard required) gate is about 2km south of the centre of Nakuru. KWS smartcards and official guidebooks (KSh750) are available at the main gate's **office** ( ☎ 051-2217151), but not at the Lanet or Nderit gates.

### Sights

Alongside the flamingos the star attractions of this park are the rhinos (80 white and 56 black). Sightings of white rhinos, rumbling like steamrollers through the bushes, are now almost a given at the lake's southern end. Since this species was reintroduced some years ago, Lake Nakuru has become far and away the best place in the country to see these animals. By contrast, the shy black rhinos, browsers by nature and much more aggressive, are more

difficult to spot. If you're very, very lucky, you'll catch a glimpse of a rare tree-climbing lion. Warthogs are common all over the park, as are waterbucks, zebras and buffaloes, while Thomson's gazelles and reedbucks can be seen further into the bush, where there's also a good chance of seeing leopards. Around the cliffs you may catch sight of hyraxes and birds of prey amid the countless baboons. A small herd of hippos generally frequents the lake's northern shore.

There's no better view of the park than that seen from atop **Baboon Cliff** as the afternoon sun casts a warm glow over the lake.

Since the 180-sq-km park's creation in 1961, the population of lesser and greater flamingos has risen and fallen with the soda lake's erratic water levels. When the lake dried up in 1962 (happy first birthday!), the population plummeted, as it later did in the 1970s, when heavy rainfall diluted the lake's salinity and affected the lesser flamingos' food source (blue-green algae). Over much of the last decade healthy water levels have seen flamingo numbers blossom again. If future droughts or flooding make them fly the coop again, you'll probably find them at Lake Bogoria.

Sadly, not all is picture-perfect, as in recent years pressures on the lake have increased. Environmental problems including pollution from Nakuru town, pesticide runoff from surrounding farms, and massive deforestation within the water catchment area have all caused concern. A WWF project is making considerable progress in countering these problems, and the local afforestation program continues to plant thousands of indigenous tree seedlings.

### Sleeping & Eating

The top-end lodges have restaurants open to nonguests.

#### BUDGET & MIDRANGE

None of the following options provide any meals, so you'll have to bring your own food. If camping, always make sure your tents are securely zipped, or the vervet monkeys and baboons will make a right mess while cleaning you out.

**Makalia Falls Public Campsite** (camping adult/child US$25/20) While it may be hard to get to and have cruder facilities than Backpackers' Campsite, this is the best place to camp in

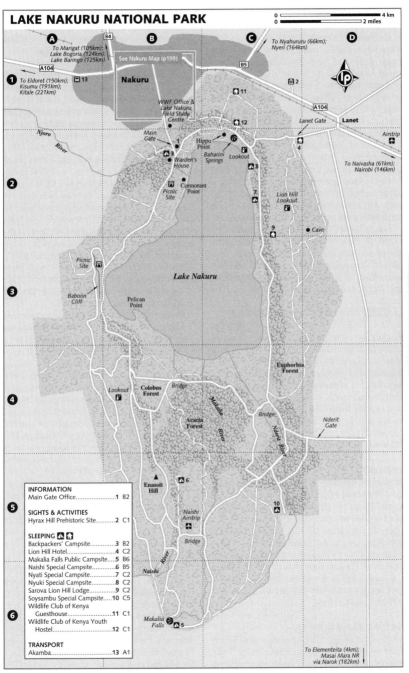

# LAKE NAKURU NATIONAL PARK

0 _____ 4 km
0 _____ 2 miles

To Marigat (105km);
Lake Bogoria (124km);
Lake Baringo (125km)

To Eldoret (150km);
Kisumu (191km);
Kitale (221km)

A104

B4

See Nakuru Map (p159)

**Nakuru**

To Nyahururu (66km);
Nyeri (164km)

B5

A104

WWF Office &
Lake Nakuru
Field Study
Centre

Main
Gate

Hippo
Point

Baharini
Springs

Lookout

Lanet Gate

**Lanet**

Airstrip

Warden's
House

Cormorant
Point

Picnic
Site

Lion Hill
Lookout

To Naivasha (61km);
Nairobi (146km)

Cave

*Lake Nakuru*

Picnic
Site

Baboon
Cliff

Pelican
Point

**Euphorbia
Forest**

**RIFT VALLEY**

Lookout

**Colobus
Forest**

*Bridge*

*Malalia
River*

*Bridge*

*Nderit
River*

*Nderit
Gate*

**Acacia
Forest**

▲
**Enasoit
Hill**

*Naishi
Airstrip*

*Bridge*

*River*

*Naishi*

*Makalia
Falls*

To Elementeita (4km);
Masai Mara NR
via Narok (182km)

## INFORMATION
Main Gate Office.....................**1** B2

## SIGHTS & ACTIVITIES
Hyrax Hill Prehistoric Site..........**2** C1

## SLEEPING
Backpackers' Campsite.............**3** B2
Lion Hill Hotel..........................**4** C2
Makalia Falls Public Campsite...**5** B6
Naishi Special Campsite............**6** B5
Nyati Special Campsite.............**7** C2
Nyuki Special Campsite.............**8** C2
Sarova Lion Hill Lodge.............**9** C2
Soysambu Special Campsite.....**10** C5
Wildlife Club of Kenya
 Guesthouse.......................**11** C1
Wildlife Club of Kenya Youth
 Hostel...............................**12** C1

## TRANSPORT
Akamba.................................**13** A1

the park. It's picturesque and sits next to the seasonal Makalia Falls.

**Backpackers' Campsite** (camping adult/child US$25/20) This large public campsite sits inside the main gate and also has the park's best camping facilities.

**Special Campsites** (camping adult/child US$40/20, plus set-up fee KSh7500) These are dotted all over the park and have no facilities, but offer a true bush experience – just you and the animals.

**Wildlife Club of Kenya Youth Hostel** ( ☎ 0734661463; dm KSh200, bandas KSh400-800) This is a nice, friendly site with clean dorms, simple bandas (whose price depends on the amount of beds contained – some are virtually dorms), cooking areas and plenty of wildlife just around the corner. It's often block-booked by school and university groups but is open to anyone.

**Lion Hill Hotel** ( ☎ 0722802215; camping KSh400, r KSh600; 🏊 ) Just outside the park's Lanet gate, the prison-block-style bungalows might not look too appealing from the outside but once locked in you'll find they are actually simple and pleasant swimming-pool-blue rooms. The campsite, however, is scrappy.

**ourpick** **Wildlife Club of Kenya Guesthouse** ( ☎ 051-851559; PO Box 33, Nakuru; with shared bathroom per person KSh1000) For atmosphere alone this beats anywhere in Nakuru hands down. It's like having your own secluded cottage in the countryside, but instead of a garden full of bunny rabbits it's a garden full of rhinos! There are six comfortable rooms here, as well as an equipped kitchen and a nicely appointed dining room. With advance notice, the guard can cook. There are absolutely no fences between you and the animals, so don't go for a midnight stroll.

### TOP END

**Sarova Lion Hill Lodge** ( ☎ 850235; www.sarovahotels .com; s/d full board US$310/410; 🏊 ) Sitting high up the lake's eastern slopes, this lodge offers first-class service and comfort. The views from the open-air restaurant-bar and from most rooms are great. Rooms are understated but pretty, while the flashy suites are large and absolutely stunning. It's certainly one of the friendlier top-end places, and on quiet days they'll often give you the residents' rate, which is less than half that quoted here.

### Getting There & Away

Walking in the park isn't permitted, so you'll have to rent a taxi, go on a tour or be lucky enough to hitch a ride. A taxi for a few hours

will likely cost KSh2500, though you'll have to bargain hard for it. More enjoyable options can be arranged through **Crater Travel** (Map p159; ☎ 051-2215019; off Kenyatta Ave, Nakuru).

## LAKE BOGORIA NATIONAL RESERVE

Backed by the bleak Siracho Escarpment, moss-green waves roll down Lake Bogoria's rocky, barren shores, **hot springs** and **geysers** spew boiling fluids from the earth's insides and thousands of blood-red flamingos croak and squawk in mournful monotony. This other-worldly place is totally unlike any other Rift Valley lake.

In the late 1990s this reserve's shallow soda lake achieved fame as 'the new home of the flamingo', with a migrant population of up to two million birds. In 2000 it was designated a Ramsar site, establishing it as a wetland of international importance. While lesser flamingo numbers have since dropped significantly (now that Lake Nakuru has recovered from earlier droughts), this **reserve** ( ☎ 051-2211987; PO Box 64, Marigat; adult/child KSh2000/200; 🕐 6am-7pm) is still a fascinating place to visit.

Amazingly, this inhospitable environment is a haven for birdlife and at **Kesubo Swamp**, just north of the park, more than 200 species have been recorded. One lucky soul spotted 96 species in one hour – a Kenyan record.

The lack of dense bush around Lake Bogoria used to make this one of the best places in Kenya to see the greater kudu, but unfortunately bad management and an increase in human activity inside the reserve has meant that it is rarely seen nowadays. The isolated wooded area at the lake's southern end is also home to leopards, klipspringers, gazelles, caracals and buffaloes.

You now have the bonus of being able to explore on foot or bicycle, though stay clear of the small buffalo population. If you'd like a guide (half-/full day KSh500/1000), enquire at Loboi gate.

### Sleeping & Eating

Camping is the only sleeping option within the reserve. If you'd prefer a roof, there's a top-end hotel nearby, but no cheapies that can be recommended.

**Fig Tree Camp** (camping per person KSh500) Nestled beneath a stand of massive fig trees is this fantastic site. Sure, the loos lack doors and baboons can be a nuisance, but there are brilliant views down the lake and a permanent freshwater stream. The

2km drive (4WD only) or hike from the main park road is worth the trip alone.

**Acacia Camp** (camping per person KSh500) A pretty lakeside site shaded by acacias, with some soft grass on which your tent and your bottom can rest. You'll have to bring your own water, though. Acacia and Fig Tree knock the socks off the dismal Hot Springs and VIPS campsites nearby.

**Lake Bogoria Spa Resort** ( ☎ 051-2216867; www .lbogoriasparesort.com; s/d incl breakfast US$70/90; ⚑ ) Set in lovely grounds around 2km before the Loboi gate, the long-standing Lake Bogoria Hotel has been relaunched as a posh-sounding 'spa' resort. However, the money must have run out after they changed the signs, because nobody has invested in the rooms for years, which are bland and so boring you'll fall sleep as soon as you see them (perhaps a bonus). For once, though, the price is about right and the cottages (same price) are slightly better than the rooms. The inviting pool is open to nonguests for KSh200.

The town of Marigat, located nearby, is a good place to buy local produce or to have a local meal. The following places are both located off the B4 Hwy:

**Kamco Hotel** (meals KSh40-150; ☻ lunch & dinner)
**Union Hotel** (meals KSh40-150; ☻ lunch & dinner)

### Getting There & Away

There are three entrance gates to Lake Bogoria: Emsos in the south, Maji Moto in the west and Loboi in the north. The turn-off for Emsos and Maji Moto gates is at Mogotio, which is about 38km past Nakuru on the B4 highway, but both of these routes are poorly signposted and inaccessible without a serious 4WD.

Loboi gate is a far more straightforward point of entry, reached by taking a turn-off shortly before Marigat. It's 20km from here to the actual gate along a good sealed road. The sealed road continues to the hot springs, but is in horrendous shape in this section.

The nearest petrol is found in Marigat.

Without your own vehicle, Loboi gate can be accessed by matatu from Marigat (KSh70, 30 minutes). Regular matatus serve Marigat from Nakuru (KSh200, two hours) and Kabarnet (KSh140, 1¼ hours).

## LAKE BARINGO
☎ 051

This rare freshwater Rift Valley lake, encircled by mountains and with a surface dotted with picturesque islands and hippos batting their eyelids, is probably the most idyllic of the Rift Valley lakes, as well as the most remote. Topping the scenic surrounds is an amazing abundance of birdlife, with over 450 of the 1200 bird species native to Kenya present. For years bird-watchers have come here from all over the world to glimpse the rare and beautiful feathered friends.

Despite being listed as Kenya's fourth Ramsar site in January 2002, Lake Baringo has been plagued with various problems over the past few years. Irrigation dams and droughts caused the water level to drop alarmingly, pulling the shoreline back several hundred metres; severe siltation due to soil erosion around the seasonal *luggas* (dry river beds) has meant that the water is almost always muddy; and the lake has been overfished so badly that any tilapia caught these days is rarely more than 15cm long. The water level has recently risen again, but the situation is still very delicate, and with further droughts expected the ecosystem remains at risk.

Lake access is easiest from **Kampi ya Samaki** on the lake's western shore, some 15km north of Marigat. This small, quiet town used to be a fishing village, but now it depends almost entirely on tourism.

With some of the best-value accommodation in the Kenyan interior, scenery that's little short of poetry, wonderful wildlife and a go-slow vibe this lake is easily one of the undiscovered highlights of Kenya.

### Information

The 'authorities' at Kampi ya Samaki charge a toll (per person/car KSh200/KSh100) to enter the town; make sure you get a receipt to avoid being asked to pay again. The nearest banking facilities are in Kabarnet, about 40km west.

### Sights & Activities
#### BOAT RIDES

The most popular activities around Lake Baringo are **boat rides**. There are boat offices all over town, and literally anyone you talk to will claim to have access to a boat and be able to undercut anyone else's price. Fortunately it's all done in a very leisurely manner and the experience is well worth it. A speciality is a trip to see fish eagles feeding; the birds dive for fish at a whistle.

RIFT VALLEY

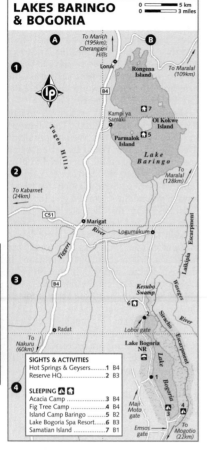

**LAKES BARINGO & BOGORIA**

0 —— 5 km
0 —— 3 miles

**SIGHTS & ACTIVITIES**
Hot Springs & Geysers..........1 B4
Reserve HQ.........................2 B3

**SLEEPING**
Acacia Camp ......................3 B4
Fig Tree Camp ...................4 B2
Island Camp Baringo ..........5 B3
Lake Bogoria Spa Resort......6 B3
Samatian Island .................7 B1

The most reliable trips are organised by the following:

**Community Boats & Excursions** ( ☎ 0722420699; Kampi ya Samaki; per boat per hr KSh3000)

**Lake Baringo Boats Excursions** ( ☎ 0720322113; Kampi ya Samaki; per boat per hr KSh3000) Also organises nature and birding walks (KSh500 to KSh600) and has slow internet (per hr KSh180).

**Roberts' Camp** ( ☎ 072706895; Kampi ya Samaki; per boat per hr KSh3000)

**BIRD WALKS**
Even if you're not an avid twitcher, it's hard to resist setting off on a dawn **bird walk**, when you will have a good chance of seeing hornbills or a magnificent fish eagle in action. Roberts' Camp and Community Boats & Excursions

(see above) lead excellent walks for about KSh400 per person, or a night-time bird walk for KSh700.

**CULTURAL TOURS**
The same players also offer tours to Pokot, Tugen and Njemps villages close to the lake (KSh1200 per person); the Njemps are cousins of the Maasai and live on Ol Kokwe and Parmalok Islands and around the lakeshore, mainly practising pastoralism and fishing.

## Sleeping
**BUDGET & MIDRANGE**
**Bahari Lodge & Hotel** ( ☎ 0726857947; Kampi ya Samaki; r with shared bathroom KSh300) Bahari is popular with the drivers of safari vehicles, which is generally a good sign! The rooms are a little shabby but perfectly good for an undisturbed night.

**Weavers Lodge** ( ☎ 0721556153; Kampi ya Samaki; r KSh500; P ) Down a rocky alley off the town's main drag, you'll find music-filled African fun at this simple lodging, which has incredibly clean rooms with attached bathrooms and solid mattresses. You can't go wrong for this price.

**our pick Roberts' Camp** ( ☎ 072706895, in Nairobi 020-2057718; www.robertscamp.com; Kampi ya Samaki; camping per person KSh350, bandas with shared bathroom per person KSh1500, 4-person cottages KSh7500; P ) As one reader said, 'This place keeps getting better and better', and we couldn't agree more. Right on the lake shore and full of chirping birds, wallowing hippos and toothy crocodiles, it doesn't matter whether you opt for camping in your own tent, a beautifully furnished banda, or an extravagant cottage, what you get for your money here is, quite simply, superb value. You could happily stay here for days and days without a care in the world and, for our money, this is as good as Kenya gets. Numerous excursions are organised here too.

**TOP END**
**Island Camp Baringo** ( ☎ Nairobi 020-4447151; s/d full board US$282/380; ⊠ ) This luxury tented lodge sits on Ol Kokwe Island's southern tip, and it makes a perfect hideaway. It's beautifully conceived, with 23 double tents set among flowering trees, all overlooking the lake. Facilities include two bars and water-sports equipment. The price includes transfers from town. There is talk of doing away with the safari tents and building a handful of divine open-plan cottages.

**ourpick** **Samatian Island** ( ☎ bookings 072706895, in Nairobi 020-2057718; www.samatianislandlodge.com; s/d full board US$570/960) Run by the same delightful couple as Roberts' Camp, this slice of heaven proves they can do top end just as well. Located on a tiny, private island in the middle of the lake, this place, with an infinity pool perched above the hippos and five open-plan cottages stuffed full of antique Zanzibar chests, bookcases and other treasures, just screams 'honeymoon'. What makes this work of art even more amazing is that if you just turn up on a slow day they will do self-catering deals of just KSh1500 per person! There is also talk of reducing the price to somewhere around €100 with full board included. If this happens then this will quite possibly be the best deal in all the country and worth travelling a long way for.

## Eating & Drinking

**Bahari Lodge & Hotel** (meals KSh150-200; ☷ lunch & dinner) Of Kampi ya Samaki's few remaining local restaurants, this is the best place for cheap stodge.

**Thirsty Goat** (Roberts' Camp, Kampi ya Samaki; meals KSh300-450; ☷ lunch & dinner) This lovely open-air restaurant and bar serves a welcome variety of foreign fare. It might seem pricey, but when your nose gets a whiff of the Moroccan meatballs, your taste buds will step on your whingeing wallet's tongue. The veggie lasagne (KSh400) is also worth a bit of your time.

Self-caterers should keep in mind that while some foodstuffs may be available at Roberts' Camp, fresh vegetables and fruit are generally in short supply, and there's only a very limited stock available in Kampi ya Samaki. Bring much of what you need – Marigat usually has a good selection.

## Getting There & Away

A 25-seater bus leaves for Nakuru each morning (KSh250) between 6.30am and 9.30am (it departs when full). Bar that, hop onto one of the regular pick-up trucks heading to Marigat (KSh70, 30 minutes) and catch more frequent matatus from there to Nakuru (KSh200, two hours) or Kabarnet (KSh150, 1¼ hours).

A gravel track connects Loruk at the top end of the lake with the Nyahururu–Maralal road. If you have your own transport, it's a rough but bearable road; there's no public transport along it and hitching is extremely difficult. You can usually buy petrol at Lake Baringo Club; if you're heading northeast, it's worth noting that after Marigat, there's no reliable supply until Maralal.

**RIFT VALLEY**

# Western Kenya

For most people the magic of western Kenya is summed up in two poetic words: Masai Mara. This is understandable. After all, the Mara has fuelled African fantasies for years and, without a shadow of doubt, its wildebeest-spotted savannas are the star attraction of what is a star-studded region. But there is much more to western Kenya than these plains of herbivores and carnivores.

Just like the incredible chameleons inhabiting the dense forests of this region, western Kenya can change its colours from shades of savanna brown to luminous tea-garden green in the rain-soaked hills, or it can fade into deep, Lake Victoria blues speckled with red, yellow and orange fishing boats. And, just as the chameleon's eyes bulge from its body, so too does the land of western Kenya, in a series of mountain peaks that reach far above the clouds and provide a home to elephants searching for salt 100m underground. This region also has humid jungles buzzing with weird and wonderful creatures generally more at home in the forests of the Congo, and tribal groups that are as varied and fascinating as the landscape.

Yes, western Kenya is a perfect place for those who like surprises, contrasts and an ever-changing kaleidoscope of experiences and colours. And the best news of all is that, away from those Masai Mara wildebeest, most of it is virtually untouched by foreign tourists.

**WESTERN KENYA**

## HIGHLIGHTS

- Getting caught up in the swirling wildebeest traffic jams of the **Masai Mara National Reserve** (p171), the greatest animal show on earth

- Scouring the leaf litter for creepy-crawlies and straining your neck muscles searching for the thumbless colobus in the depths of **Kakamega Forest Reserve** (p187)

- Wading through the swampy backwaters of **Saiwa Swamp National Park** (p197) in a hunt for paddling antelope

- Throwing away your watch and making plans to stay forever on the idyllic islands of **Lake Victoria** (p181)

- Learning how to brew a proper cuppa in **Kericho** (p184), the tea capital of Africa

## Climate

Throughout the year the lowlands around Lake Victoria are fairly hot and humid, while the areas around the Western Highlands are decidedly cooler. The heaviest rains fall between March and May, with almost 200mm falling in April. The lesser rains fall in November and December, before things really dry out in January.

## National Parks & Reserves

With the Big Five roaming the savanna of Masai Mara National Reserve (p171), prolific birdlife, primates and flying squirrels soaring through the dense rainforests of Kakamega Forest Reserve (p187) and 4000m peaks beckoning trekkers at Mt Elgon National Park (p195), it is clear western Kenya's parks have it all.

More wildlife and unique surrounds can be found at Ruma National Park (p181), home to Kenya's only roan antelope population, and at Saiwa Swamp National Park (p197), which hosts rare sitatunga antelope and de Brazza's monkeys.

If you want to truly disown the beaten track, hit Lake Kamnarok and Kerio Valley National Reserves (p193).

## Getting There & Away

### AIR

**Kenya Airways** ( ☎ Nairobi 020-3274747; www .kenya-airways.com) connects Nairobi (Wilson Airport) with Kisumu, while both **Airkenya** ( ☎ Nairobi 020-605745; www.airkenya.com) and **Safarilink** ( ☎ Nairobi 020-600777; www.safarilink-kenya .com) link Wilson Airport with Masai Mara National Reserve.

### BUS & MATATU

The road to western Kenya inevitably leads through Nakuru. From there countless buses and matatus run north to all the main centres.

Masai Mara is the one exception, with most transport coming via Narok.

## Getting Around

Being the most densely populated part of the country, the road system is good and there's a multitude of transport plying the routes.

# MASAI MARA

Dream of Africa and you dream of the Masai Mara. This huge expanse of gently rolling grassland, specked with flat-top acacia trees and trampled by thousands-strong herds of zebra and wildebeest, is the ultimate African cliché. But for once the reality lives up to the image, and for many people this reserve is not just the highlight of their Kenyan adventure but the very reason they came.

## NAROK
☎ 050

Three hours west of Nairobi, this ramshackle provincial town is the Masai Mara's main access point and the region's largest – no, only – town. It's a friendly and surprisingly hassle-free place.

## Information

Kenya Commercial Bank is the town's only bank and it has an unreliable ATM (Visa only). Internet is available at Sky Apple Computer Training for KSh2 per minute.

## Sleeping & Eating

**Kim's Dishes Hotel** ( ☎ 22001; s/tw KSh650/1300) Pornstar beds straight out of the disco days of '77 make this a highly memorable place for a night's kip, but alas it's overpriced. The restaurant (meals KSh80 to KSh200) downstairs serves tasty Kenyan dishes.

**Chambai Hotel** ( ☎ 22591; s/d from KSh800/950) The standard rooms out the back are simple, spotless and sport mosquito nets. The new, super rooms in the main building have inviting beds, balconies, large TVs and huge bathrooms – sit on your throne and rule the porcelain kingdom. The bar and restaurant (mains KSh250) are civilised and worth trying.

The **Fast Food Café** (mains from KSh100) is a magic little place with a '50s feel where everyone sits around sipping milky tea and gorging on egg and chips.

Self-caterers should stock up on supplies from the **Jalumat Supermarket** on the road into town from the north.

## Getting There & Away

Frequent matatus run between Narok and Nairobi (KSh400, three hours) and less-frequent departures serve Naivasha (KSh350, 2½ hours) and Kisii (KSh400, three hours).

WESTERN KENYA

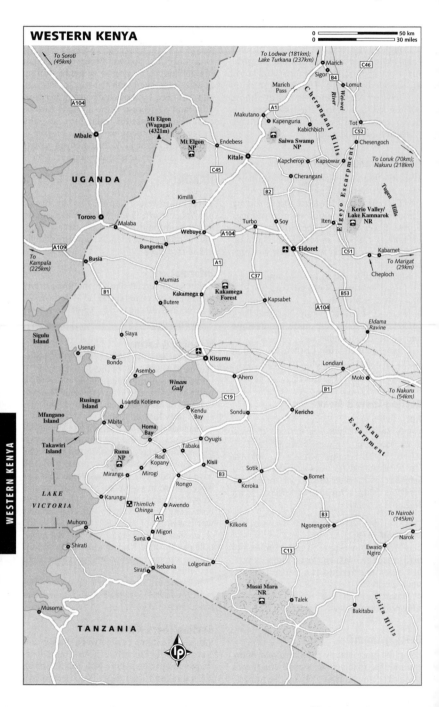

# WESTERN KENYA

0 — 50 km
0 — 30 miles

To Soroti (45km)

To Lodwar (181km); Lake Turkana (237km)

Marich

C46

Sigor

B4

Lomut

Marich Pass

A104

Wei-wei River

Makutano

A1

Kapenguria

Tot

C52

Mbale

Kabichbich

Chesengoch

Mt Elgon (Wagagai) (4321m)

Mt Elgon NP

Endebess

Saiwa Swamp NP

Kapcherop

Kapsowar

To Loruk (70km); Nakuru (218km)

Kitale

C45

Kapsabet

Cherangani

B2

UGANDA

Kimilili

Turbo

Soy

Iten

Kerio Valley/ Lake Kamnarok NR

Tororo

Malaba

Webuye

A104

Eldoret

C51

Kabarnet

To Kampala (225km)

A109

Busia

B1

Bungoma

A1

C37

B53

To Marigat (29km)

Cheploch

Sigulu Island

Mumias

Kakamega

Kakamega Forest

Kapsabet

A104

Eldama Ravine

Butere

Siaya

Usengi

Bondo

Kisumu

Londiani

Molo

Asembo

Ahero

B1

To Nakuru (54km)

Winam Gulf

C19

Rusinga Island

Luanda Kotieno

Kendu Bay

Sondu

Kericho

Mfangano Island

Mbita

Homa Bay

Oyugis

Mau Escarpment

Takawiri Island

Ruma NP

Rod Kopany

Tabaka

Kisii

Sotik

Bomet

Miranga

Mirogi

Rongo

B3

Keroka

LAKE VICTORIA

Thimlich Ohinga

Awendo

A1

Kilkoris

Ngorengore

B3

To Nairobi (145km)

Muhoro

Migori

Suna

Ewaso Ngiro

Narok

Shirati

C13

Sirari

Isebania

Lolgorian

Masai Mara NR

Talek

Loita Hills

Musoma

Bakitabu

TANZANIA

**WESTERN KENYA**

There is also usually daily transport to Sekenani and Talek gates for between KSh300 to KSh400, depending on the condition of the road at the time.

Several petrol stations pump the elixir of vehicular life – fill up, it's much cheaper than in the reserve.

## MASAI MARA NATIONAL RESERVE

Backed by the spectacular Esoit Oloololo (Siria) Escarpment, watered by the Mara River and littered with an astonishing amount of wildlife is the world-renowned Masai Mara. Its 1510 sq km of open rolling grasslands, the northern extension of the equally famous Serengeti Plains, form just a fraction of the immense Narok (managed by Narok County Council) and Transmara National Reserves (managed by Mara Conservancy), all of which is equally stuffed with wildlife.

Although concentrations of wildlife are typically highest in the swampy area around the escarpment on the reserve's western edge, superior roads draw most visitors to the eastern side. Of the big cats, sandy-eyed lions are found in large prides everywhere, and it is not uncommon to see them hunting. Cheetahs and leopards are less visible but still fairly common, and elephants, buffaloes, zebras and numerous other grazers occur in quantities that boggle the mind.

Breathtaking at any time of year, the Mara reaches its pinnacle during the annual wildebeest migration in July and August, when literally millions of the ungainly beasts move north from the Serengeti seeking lusher grass, before turning south again around October.

The Masai Mara's fame means that it can get very busy, and during the migration there seem to be as many minibuses as animals, and many tend to take off, making new tracks wherever they feel fit. This shouldn't be encouraged. In addition the Mara is also very expensive (and prices are continuing to rise out of all proportion to inflation) and little of that money appears to be finding its way into the hands of conservationists.

## Information

Because most of the gates are located inside the **reserve** (adult/child US$40/20) boundary it is easy to enter the Masai Mara unknowingly. Most confusion arises when people camping outside the gates are requested to pay park fees – cue confrontation. For the record,

campsites outside Oloolaimutiek gate are inside the reserve, while Talek gate's sites north of the Talek River are outside it.

Wherever you enter, make sure you ask for a receipt: it is crucial for passage between the reserve's Narok and Transmara sections and your eventual exit. It also ensures your money ends up in the reserve's hands, not elsewhere. Gates also seem to charge KSh800 for all vehicles, instead of KSh300 for ones with less than six seats – be insistent but polite and all will be well.

## Sights & Activities

### WILDLIFE DRIVES & WALKS

Whether you're bouncing over the plains in pursuit of elusive elephant silhouettes or parked next to a pride of lions and listening to their bellowed breaths, wildlife drives are *the* highlight of a trip to the Mara.

All top-end places offer wildlife drives, which can be negotiated into the rate while booking – it's usually cheaper than arranging them on arrival. However, guided walks and activities such as **bush dinners** are booked during your stay.

If you've arrived by matatu, you can organise drives with most lodges, as they're fairly friendly towards independent travellers. Most of the cheaper camps charge around KSh12,000 for a full day's vehicle and driver hire, which can be split between as many of you as there are in a group. If you're arriving solo and are worried about the cost of doing this alone then you can often jump in another group's jeep. Alternatively, walk with a Maasai *moran* (warrior) outside the park (KSh1000 per person), where there is still a large amount of wildlife. Many old Africa hands swear that the best way of experiencing the African bush is on foot, and doing this is a wonderful experience; you'll learn all about the medicinal properties of various plants, see the tell-tale signs of passing animals and have some heart-in-mouth close encounters with the local wildlife. If you do go on a walk be aware that some local Maasai groups may charge you for crossing their land.

If the idea of trotting around lion-infested countryside on the back of a creature that looks remarkably like a zebra sounds appealing then a number of lodges and camps outside the park gates also organise **horse riding** safaris.

WESTERN KENYA

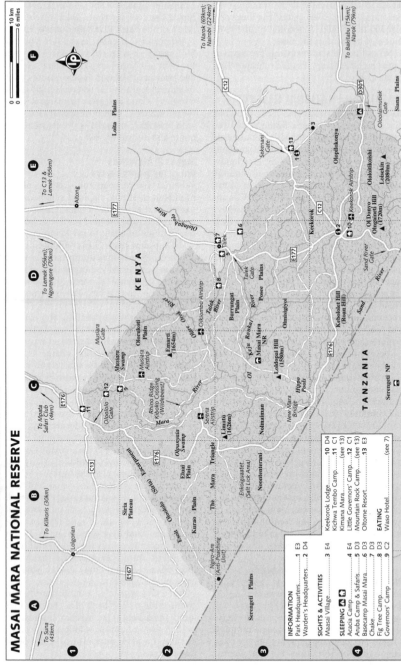

**MASAI MARA NATIONAL RESERVE**

WESTERN KENYA

INFORMATION
Park Headquarters............................1 E3
Warden's Headquarters......................2 D4

SIGHTS & ACTIVITIES
Masai Village..................................3 E4

SLEEPING
Acacia Camp...................................4 E4
Aruba Camp & Safaris........................5 D3
Basecamp Masai Mara.......................6 D3
Chake.........................................7 D3
Fig Tree Camp.................................8 D3
Governors' Camp.............................9 C2
Keekorok Lodge.............................10 D4
Kichwa Tembo Camp.......................11 C1
Kimana Mara...............................(see 13)
Little Governors' Camp....................12 C1
Mountain Rock Camp......................(see 13)
Oltome Resort..............................13 E3

EATING
Waso Hotel................................(see 7)

## BALLOONING

If you can afford US$530 (and yes, that is per person), then balloon safaris are superb and worlds away from the minibus circuit. Trips can be arranged through top-end lodges. See p320 for more details.

## MAASAI VILLAGE

The Maasai village between Oloolaimutiek and Sekenani gates welcomes tourists, though negotiating admission can be fraught – prices start as high as KSh1500 per person, but you should be able to wrangle it down to KSh1000 or a little less. If you're willing to pay this for free rein with the camera, go ahead, but don't expect a genuine cultural experience.

## Sleeping

In general, accommodation in the Masai Mara is insanely overpriced. Don't be at all surprised if you end up paying more for a lacklustre room or tent here than you would for a decent hotel room in a major Western European city. For budget and midrange travellers the situation is especially dire, with only a handful of campsites and a couple of exceedingly overpriced 'lodges'.

### OLOOLAIMUTIEK & SEKENANI GATES
#### Budget & Midrange

While outside the Oloolaimutiek and Sekenani gates, these camps are within the reserve and sleeping here will incur park fees (even if the camps state otherwise).

**Acacia Camp** ( ☎ Nairobi 020-210024; camping US$8, s/tw US$27/47) Thatched roofs shelter closely spaced, spartan semipermanent tents in this quaint camp. They're slightly cheaper (s/tw US$20/40) without bedding. There are numerous cooking areas, a bar and a campfire pit, but no restaurant. Bathrooms are clean and hot water flows in the evening. The only downside for campers is the lack of shade.

**Mountain Rock Camp** ( ☎ 0736149041, 0722511252; www.mountainrockkenya.com; camping per tent KSh500, tents per person KSh1500; s/d full board US$95/165) The simple safari tents here have private bathrooms, cloth wardrobes and firm beds and sit in pretty, individual gardens. The camping area is pleasant and you can use the kitchen to prepare your own food or pay for full board. Also known as the Mara Springs Safari Camp.

**ourpick Kimana Mara** ( ☎ Nairobi 020-217335, 0723052867; www.kimanamara.com; camping KSh500, tents half/full board per person KSh3500/5000) Entirely owned, managed and run by the local community, with profits returning to the community as a whole, this camp has several large, clean self-contained tents nestled under the trees. It's a no-fuss kind of place, the staff is very cool and the food excellent. There's a cosy stone-lined bar and kitchen facilities for campers.

**Oltome Resort** ( ☎ Nairobi 020-3529640; www.oltome resorts.com; s/tw full board US$165/250) A beautifully furnished, brand-spanking-new luxury camp, with below-average prices and above-average standards. There are only 10 spacious tents with plenty of privacy. It was only just opening for business at research time but it looks very promising.

### Top End

**Keekorok Lodge** ( ☎ bookings 020-532329; s/d full board US$350/440; 🏊 ) The oldest lodge in the Mara has over a hundred rooms and chalets kitted out in a modern tribal style. Despite its size it still manages to retain personal service. The crowning glories are the manicured gardens and the hippo pool.

### TALEK GATE
#### Budget & Midrange

**Chake** (r per person KSh300) On the edge of Talek village and very different to all the other accommodation in and around the reserve. Chake is a local hotel with tin-roofed cubicles, comfy beds, clean sheets and friendly management. Foreign guests are rare but quite welcome and it offers not just better value than many of the standard camps but it also immerses you in day-to-day Maasai village life.

**ourpick Aruba Mara Camp** ( ☎ 0723997524; info@aruba -safaris.com; camping KSh450, tents full board/accommodation only per person KSh6000/4200) With only five safari tents available you'll have to fight tooth and nail to get one in high season, but it's a battle well worth fighting as this is one of the few lodges in Kenya where you actually feel as if you're getting value for money. The tents are luxuriously appointed, but not overpowering, have lots of privacy, as well as memorable views over the Talek River. The restaurant is an intimate candlelit affair and the food excellent. The nearby campsite is also decent.

### Top End

**ourpick Basecamp Masai Mara** ( ☎ Nairobi 020-577490; www.basecampexplorer.com; s/d full board US$155/310) 'Eco' is a much-abused word in the tourism industry and sadly some so-called

WESTERN KENYA

'ecofriendly' establishments are often nothing of the sort. To see what an ecofriendly hotel really looks like come to this superb lodge. Everything has been thought through in the finest detail in order to reduce its impact. If all this green scheming makes you worry that the accommodation might be rustic, fear not. The safari tents here fall squarely into the divine luxury bracket and just wait till you get a load of the bathrooms. Basecamp runs the Bush Buck Forestation program and has already planted thousands of trees in the hope of regenerating native woodland (which has been so successful that animals that haven't been seen here for years are re-appearing) – a US$20 donation enables you to plant five trees.

**Fig Tree Camp** ( ☎ Nairobi 020-605328; www.mada hotels.com; s/d full board US$300/400; 🐾 ) Vegetate on your tent's verandah, watching the Talek's waters gently flow by through this sumptuous camp with a colonial-days feel. The gardens are about the most luxurious you'll ever see and the bathrooms about the biggest and most inviting you'll find under canvas. To round things off, there is a small but scenic pool and a trendy treetop bar. One big drawback is that breakfast is only served between 7am and 9am, meaning you can't go on a morning safari and get a feed.

### MUSIARA & OLOOLOLO GATES
Sadly, there are no secure budget or midrange options here.

**Kichwa Tembo Camp** ( ☎ Nairobi 020-3740920; www .kichwatembo.com, full board per person US$475; 🐾 ) Just outside the northern boundary, Kichwa has permanent tents with grass-mat floors, stone bathrooms and tasteful furnishings. Hop in a hammock and take in spectacular savanna views. The food has an excellent reputation.

**Governors' Camp** (Nairobi ☎ 020-2734000; www .governorscamp.com; s/d full board US$596/890; 🐾 ) This camp, and Little Governors' Camp (s/d full board US$652/972, with a swimming pool) are widely regarded as the most magisterial camps in the Mara and offer great service, pleasing riverside locations and activities aplenty. The extraordinary rates include three wildlife drives and someone keen to wash your dirty clothes.

### Eating & Drinking
If you can't afford the lodges' accommodation, drop in for drinks or a meal. Lovely lunches/dinners will set you back US$20/30, but the views and ambience are free.

The **Waso Hotel** in Talek village has cheap meals that keep the Maasai strong for around KSh70. There's also a lively Maasai market.

## Getting There & Away
### AIR
**Airkenya** ( ☎ Nairobi 020-605745; www.airkenya.com) and **Safarilink** ( ☎ Nairobi 020-600777; www.safari link-kenya.com) each have daily flights to Masai Mara. Return flights on Airkenya are US$237, while Safarilink will get you there and back for US$279.

### MATATU, CAR & 4WD
Although it's possible to arrange wildlife drives independently, keep in mind that there are few savings in coming here without transport. That said, it is possible to access Talek and Sekenani gates from Narok by matatu. From Kisii a matatu will get you as far as Kilkoris or Suna on the main A1 Hwy, but you will have problems after this.

For those who drive, the first 52km west of Narok on the B3 and C12 are smooth enough, but after the bitumen runs out you'll find that it gets pretty bumpy. The C13, which connects Oloololo gate with Lolgorian out in the west, is very rough and rocky, and it's poorly signposted – a highway it's not.

Petrol is available (although expensive) at Mara Sarova, Mara Serena and Keekorok Lodges, as well as in Talek village.

# LAKE VICTORIA

Spread over 68,000 sq km, yet never more than 80m deep, Lake Victoria, the source of the White Nile, might well be East Africa's most important geographical feature but is seen by surprisingly few visitors. This is a shame, as its humid shores hide some of the most beautiful and rewarding parts of western Kenya – from untouched national parks to lively cities and tranquil islands, Lake Victoria provides a wealth of sights, sounds and experiences.

The lake's 'evolving' ecosystem has proved to be both a boon and a bane for those living along its shores. For starters, its waters are a haven for mosquitoes and snails, making malaria and bilharzia (schistosomiasis) all too common here. Then there are Nile perch (introduced 50 years ago to combat mosquitoes), which eventually thrived, growing to over 200kg in size and becoming every small fishing boat's dream. Horrifyingly, the ravenous perch have wiped out over 300 species of smaller tropical fish unique to the lake.

Last but not least is the ornamental water hyacinth. First reported in 1986, this 'exotic' pond plant had no natural predators here and quickly reached plague proportions; the Winam Gulf area by Kisumu was worst affected and the fishing industry 'suffocated'. Millions of dollars have been ploughed into solving the problem, with controversial programs including mechanical removal and the introduction of weed-eating weevils. The investment seems to be paying off, with the most recent satellite photos showing hyacinth cover dramatically reduced from the 17,230 hectares it covered at its worst.

## KISUMU
☎ 057
Set on the sloping shore of Lake Victoria's Winam Gulf, the town of Kisumu is the third largest in Kenya. Declared a city during its centenary celebrations in 2001, it still doesn't feel like one; its relaxed atmosphere is a world away from that of places like Nairobi and Mombasa. Amazingly, like much of western Kenya, Kisumu receives relatively few travellers.

Despite the lake being its lifeblood from inception, geographically Kisumu has always had its back to the water, something that now echoes the sentiment and economy of the city today. Until 1977 the port was one of the busiest in Kenya, but decline set in with the demise of the East African Community (Kenya, Tanzania and Uganda), and it sat virtually idle for two decades. Although increasing cooperation between these countries (now known collectively as COMESA) has established Kisumu as an international shipment point for petroleum products, surprisingly the lake plays no part – raw fuel for processing is piped in from Mombasa and the end products are shipped out by truck. With Kisumu's fortunes again rising, and the water hyacinth's impact reduced, it is hoped Lake Victoria will once more start contributing to the local economy.

## Orientation
Kisumu is a fairly sprawling town, but everything you will need is within walking distance. Most shops, banks, cheap hotels and other facilities can be found around Oginga Odinga Rd, while the train station and ferry jetty are short walks from the end of New Station Rd.

Jomo Kenyatta Hwy is the major thoroughfare, connecting the town with the main market and the noisy bus and matatu station, both a 10-minute walk northeast from Oginga Odinga Rd.

The most pleasant access to the lake itself is at Dunga, a small village about 3km south of town along Nzola Rd.

## Information
### EMERGENCY
**Police station** (Uhuru Rd)

### INTERNET ACCESS
**Arcade Cyber Zone** (Mega Plaza, Oginga Odinga Rd; per hr KSh60; ☒ 8am-7pm Mon-Sat, 9am-2pm Sun) Speedy surfing.
**ECL Communications** (Oginga Odinga Rd; per hr KSh60; ☒ 8am-6pm) Fast internet connections.
**Kenshop Cyber Station** (Oginga Odinga Rd; per hr KSh60; ☒ 8am-6pm Mon-Sat) Also includes a cheerful cafe with snacks, cakes and drinks.

### MEDICAL SERVICES
**Aga Khan Hospital** (☎ 2020005; Otiena Oyoo St) A large hospital with modern facilities and 24-hour emergency room.
**Clinipath Laboratory** (☎ 2022363; Mega Plaza, Oginga Odinga Rd; ☒ 8am-5pm Mon-Fri, 8am-1pm Sat, 10am-noon Sun)

### MONEY
**Barclays Bank** (Kampala St) With ATM.
**Kenya Commercial Bank** (Jomo Kenyatta Hwy) With ATM (Visa only).
**Standard Chartered Bank** (Oginga Odinga Rd) With ATM (Visa only).

### POST
**Post office** (Oginga Odinga Rd)

### TOUR GUIDES
**Ibrahim** (☎ 0723083045) is a well-known tour guide to the many sights and sounds of the Kisumu region. He can arrange boat trips, bird-watching tours, nature walks and excursions to Ndere Island National Park. He

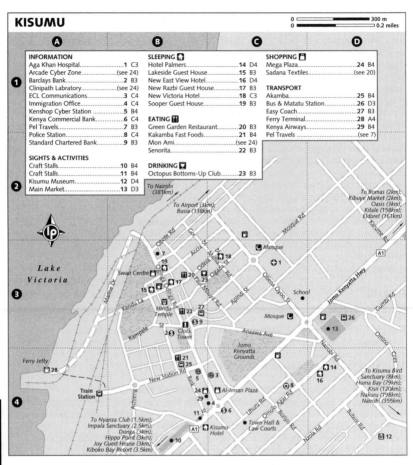

can be contacted through the New Victoria Hotel (p178).

### TRAVEL AGENCIES

**Pel Travels** ( ☎ 2022780; travels@pel.co.ke; Oginga Odinga Rd) The main agent for Kenya Airlines.

## Sights & Activities

### KISUMU MUSEUM

Unlike many local museums, **Kisumu Museum** (Nairobi Rd; admission KSh500; 🕑 6am-6pm) is an interesting delve through the historical and natural delights of the Lake Victoria region.

The displays are wide-ranging and most are well presented, with a good collection of traditional everyday items used by the region's various peoples, includ-ing bird and insect traps, weapons and musical instruments.

The main highlights, though, are the new aquarium (which displays the nearby lake's aquatic assets) and a large snake pit and tortoise pen, as well as separate vivariums displaying all the local snakes you don't want to meet on a dark night.

### HIPPO POINT & BOAT TRIPS

Everyone seems to make the pilgrimage out to Hippo Point, sticking into Lake Victoria at Dunga, about 3km south of town, and though it's pleasant enough there is actually nothing at all to see or do here – except sigh over the sunsets – and you're certainly not guaranteed to see any hippos. Sensibly, most people opt to pass the day living like a lotus eater in the luxurious surrounds of the nearby Kiboko Bay Resort (p178).

If you want virtually guaranteed hippo sightings, you will have to venture onto the lake. As you might imagine, plenty of people offer just such a boat trip. Prices start at KSh2500 but quickly drop to a more sensible KSh1000 to KSh1500. A matatu from Kisumu to Hippo Point is KSh50.

### MARKETS
Kisumu's **main market**, off Jomo Kenyatta Hwy, is one of Kenya's most animated, and certainly one of its largest, now spilling out onto the surrounding roads. If you're curious, or just looking for essentials like suits or wigs, it's worth a stroll around.

Come past the huge **Kibuye Market** (Jomo Kenyatta Hwy) on any quiet weekday and you'll find it as empty as a winter's landscape, but visit on a Sunday and it's transformed into a blossoming spring flower of colour and scents.

The various **craft stalls** near Kisumu Hotel are some of the best places in Kenya for soapstone carvings.

### IMPALA SANCTUARY
On the road to Dunga is the Kenya Wildlife Service (KWS) 1-sq-km **Impala Sanctuary** (adult/child US$15/5; 6am-6pm). Besides being home to a small impala herd, it also provides important grazing grounds for local hippos.

### KISUMU BIRD SANCTUARY
This **sanctuary** ( 6am-6pm), off the A1 Hwy 8km southeast of town, has suffered heavily from human interference and, with many of the birds flapping off to less disturbed sites, local guides in Kisumu now recommend a new 'sanctuary' called **Tako**, about 10km south of Kisumu and only accessed by boat. Around 150 bird species have been recorded here and it's an important breeding ground for herons, storks, cormorants and egrets. The best time to visit is April or May. Boats can be organised in Kisumu for around KSh2000 per hour. You'll need around three hours for the round trip.

### NDERE ISLAND NATIONAL PARK
Gazetted as a **national park** (adult/child US$20/10) back in 1986, tourism to this small 4.2-sq-km island has never taken off. It is forested and

very beautiful, housing a variety of bird species, plus hippos, impalas (introduced) and spotted crocodiles, a lesser-known cousin of the larger Nile crocodile.

Unfortunately there is nowhere to stay and chartered boats are your only option to get there, for which you'll pay around KSh2000 per hour, with typical return trips taking five hours (including three hours on shore) – keep an eye out for hippos en route.

## Sleeping
### BUDGET
After weeding out Kisumu's plethora of dives, we were left with the following options.

**New Razbi Guest House** ( 0721824349; Kendu Lane; s with/without bathroom KSh700/400, d with shared bathroom KSh600) A secure place with small, mosquito-net-clad rooms, some decidedly brighter than others. The shared toilets pass the nostril test and there is a private TV lounge-restaurant upstairs. Unusually, the double rooms are pretty messy in comparison to the singles.

**Lakeside Guest House** ( 2023523, 0722723591; Kendu Lane; r KSh800) With a new extension in progress the former Western Inn (note that at the time of research it was still known by the old name) has more than just a name change underway. Fortunately not everything's changed; the high standards of this lime-green hotel remain undiminished and the balcony is nice to sit on. But the views of the lake are just the same – in other words partial! Hot water is available in the mornings and evenings.

**our pick Sooper Guest House** ( 0725281733; kayamchatur@yahoo.com; Oginga Odinga Rd; s/d/tr KSh800/1000/1500) This spotless ice-cube-white hotel boasts 18 highly sought-after rooms that really are 'sooper'. We've received mountains of positive feedback about this place and the gleaming, spacious rooms with hot showers, informative staff and a low-key traveller vibe are certain to ensure that we receive mountains more. There's a sunny balcony overlooking the street that's perfect for people-watching. Book ahead.

### MIDRANGE
All prices below include breakfast, unless stated otherwise.

**Joy Guest House** ( 0725074837; Dunga; tw with/without bathroom KSh1000/800) Think of a small-town Portuguese pension with a tropical African soundtrack and that's exactly what you get at this charmer located 3km south of town

**OBAMA & THE KENYA CONNECTION** *Matthew D Firestone*

Regardless of your individual politics, it's hard to deny the rock-star qualities of US President Barack Obama.

Following Obama's convincing win in the 2008 election, many around the world erupted in fanfare as the first-ever African American presidential candidate succeeded in his bid for the White House. Indeed, there were perhaps no greater festivities than in Kenya, which saw its own 'native son' ascend to one of the world's highest seats of power.

So what exactly is Obama's Kenya connection?

President Obama is the son of Barack Obama Sr, a Luo from the town of Nyang'oma Kogelo in Nyanza Province. Barack Sr met the president's mother while attending the University of Hawai'i at Mānoa, though the couple separated when young Obama was just two years old. Tragically, Barack Sr only saw his son once more before dying in an automobile accident in 1982.

In 1988, Obama travelled to Kenya for the first time, and spent five weeks in the company of his paternal relatives. He later returned to Africa as a member of the US Senate Foreign Relations Committee, and gave a keynote address at the University of Nairobi, condemning corruption in the Kenyan government.

However, his most high-profile visit came in 2006, when tens of thousands of Kenyans lined the streets of Kisumu and greeted Obama with a hero's welcome. Always the crowd pleaser, the then Senator Obama shouted 'I greet you all!' in the local Luo language.

The 2006 visit was intended to encourage Kenyans to get tested for HIV/AIDS, an action that still carries a deep social stigma in much of Africa. In the spotlight of ordinary Kenyans, Obama and his wife both had their blood drawn and tested for the virus.

At the time, Obama boldly declared: 'I and my wife are personally taking HIV tests. And if someone all the way from America can come and do that, then you have no excuse.'

Considering the fact that an estimated 20% of people in Kisumu are infected, the Obamas' bold act did not go unnoticed. In fact, a local secondary school was later renamed in Barack Obama's honour, as well as a number of newborn babies – this trend has picked up momentum since the outcome of the presidential elections.

At the time of publication, the future of Obama and his Kenya connection was still open to speculation. Given that he has always displayed pride at having African roots, it's likely that President Obama's influence across the continent will be significant.

near Hippo Point's turn-off. It's a great place to escape the city and get a peep into village life. Next door is a chippy, the Pentagon Chips Palace, where you can get a fatty dinner.

**New Victoria Hotel** ( ☎ 2021067; newvictoriahotel @africaonline.co.ke; Gor Mahia Rd; s with shared bathroom KSh800, s/tw/tr KSh1300/1650/2300) This bouncy and fun Yemeni-run hotel has character in abundance and is something of a focal point for the town's small Arab population. Rooms have fans, mossie nets and comfy foam mattresses. The next-door mosque, which will rouse you at 5am, adds to the shades of Arabia.

**New East View Hotel** ( ☎ 0722556721; Omolo Agar Rd; s/tw KSh1200/1600) A converted family home on a peaceful street, the New East View has just enough furniture and decoration to give the rooms a homely feel.

**Hotel Palmers** ( ☎ 2024867; Omolo Agar Rd; s/tw KSh1400/1700) Poky, but fresh and comfortable rooms with enormous double beds. The hotel

also has a comfortable lounge, an outdoor restaurant, secure parking and a nasty old pink paint job.

### TOP END

**Nyanza Club** ( ☎ 2022433; s/tw incl breakfast KSh4000/4500; ⊠ ⊠ ) This recently renovated hotel off Jomo Kenyatta Hwy might feel a little like a Western chain hotel, but after a while in the Kenyan back-blocks that might be no bad thing. It offers great value, well-appointed rooms and some have balconies and lake views. There is a plethora of activities available but since they're strictly for members, you will have to become a temporary one (per day KSh100). It's easily one of western Kenya's cleanest and most modern hotels.

**Kiboko Bay Resort** ( ☎ 2025510; www.kibokobay .com; Dunga; s/d US$90/120; ⊠ ⊠ ) If you couldn't afford the high prices of the Masai Mara's luxury tents then the tightly packed safari tents, huddling under the trees on the banks of the lake, could be a good way of experiencing the African safari dream on a cut price level – though granted you'd have to drink quite a lot to start mistaking a kingfisher for a lion… The restaurant and small pool (nonresidents KSh150) are popular with local expats.

## Eating

The fact that Kisumu sits on Lake Victoria certainly isn't lost on restaurants here and fish is abundant.

If you want an authentic local fish fry, there is no better place than the dozens of smoky tin-shack restaurants siting on the lake's shore at **Railway Beach** at the end of Oginga Odinga Rd. Open flames, a whole lot of mud and dirt and boisterous locals all add to the ultimate Kisumu eating experience. Dive in between 7am and 6pm; a midsized fish served with *ugali* (a staple made from maize or cassava flour, or both) or rice is sufficient for two people and will set you back KSh400.

**Kakamba Fast Foods** (meals KSh100-200; ☺ lunch & dinner) A small, low-key hole in the wall canteen off Oginga Odinga Rd that serves delicious cheap dishes gobbled up by appreciative locals.

**Senorita** (Oginga Odinga Rd; mains KSh150-250; ☺ lunch & dinner) This upmarket locals' restaurant has a great '50s feel and a menu that covers everything that involves chips and other fried food.

**New Victoria Hotel** (Gor Mahia Rd; meals KSh200; ☺ lunch & dinner) Follow the local crowds and descend into the subdued interior of this brightly coloured hotel for a filling Arabian- and Indian-influenced feed. In the mornings you can grab a few cakes from the next-door pastry shop, under the same management, and come here for coffee.

**Mon Ami** (Mega Plaza, Oginga Odinga Rd; meals KSh200-350; ☺ lunch & dinner) A favourite expat pit-stop, with Western standards such as hamburgers, pastas and pizza.

**Our pick Green Garden Restaurant** (☎ 0727738000; Odera St; meals KSh300-400; ☺ 11am-11pm) Tuck into homemade pasta and lasagne surrounded by colourful elephants and baboons at this German-run, Italian-flavoured courtyard restaurant that sits squarely on the top of the town's list of current expat hot spots. It's off Oginga Odinga Rd.

## Drinking & Entertainment

Kisumu's nightlife has a reputation for being even livelier than Nairobi's, but because many of the best parties, live Congolese bands and Kiswahali hip hop crop up at various venues such as **Bomas** and **Oasis** (both on the Jomo Kenyatta Hwy) on the roads out of town, it's harder to find. Check flyers and ask locals who are plugged into the scene. Oasis tends to have live music most nights, whilst Bomas is more of a weekend affair. Entry to both depends on the performer but averages KSh200 for all but the biggest names.

**Mon Ami** (Mega Plaza, Oginga Odinga Rd; ☺ 11am to late) Easy to find and always good for having a drink, this is a lively bar with a pool table, welcoming expat crowd and satellite TV, which blasts European footy in the evenings. Friday evenings might see the odd live act.

**Octopus Bottoms-Up Club** (Ogada St; bar free, club entry KSh200) A short stroll from Oginga Odinga Rd, this heavyweight bar and club rages all night, but be warned that it isn't too pretty. Be careful when leaving, as muggings and worse are not unheard of on the surrounding streets.

## Shopping

**Sadana Textiles** (☎ 073387434; Odera St; ☺ 8am-6pm Mon-Sat) Got a big soirée coming up? Then choose from a huge range of material on offer here and they'll whip up a dapper West African–style outfit in a few hours. About KSh600 to KSh900 should see you looking good. It's off Oginga Odinga Rd.

## Getting There & Away

### AIR

**Kenya Airways** (☎ 2020081; Alpha House, Oginga Odinga Rd) has twice-daily flights to Nairobi (KSh9000, 50 minutes, 9.20am and 6.40pm). Newer, though not necessarily better, airlines serving this route include **Fly540.com**, **East African** and **Jet Link**. Prices start as low as KSh4250 and seats can be booked through **Pel Travels** (☎ 2022780; travels@pel.co.ke; Oginga Odinga Rd).

### BOAT

Despite the reduced hyacinth in the Winam Gulf, ferry services to Tanzania and Uganda haven't restarted. If you're heading to the wilderness islands of Rusinga and Mfangano (p181) then by far the fastest and most comfortable way of getting there is by the regular ferry from Luanda Kotieno, a small village two hours and a KSh300 matatu ride west of Kisumu. Ferries from Luanda Kotieno to Mbita depart (roughly!) at 8am, 11am, 3pm and 6pm. Foot passengers pay KSh100 and a car costs between KSh800 to KSh1000, depending on the size. The journey takes around an hour. Note that there is no accommodation in Luanda Kotieno.

### BUS & MATATU
Most buses, matatus and Peugeots (shared taxis) to destinations within Kenya leave from the large bus and matatu station just north of the main market.

Matatus offer the only direct services to Kakamega (KSh200, 1½ hours) and Eldoret (KSh300, 2½ hours). Plenty of other matatus serve Busia (KSh300, two hours), Kericho (KSh300, two hours), Kisii (KSh300, two hours), Homa Bay (KSh300, three hours), Nakuru (KSh500 to KSh600, 3½ hours), Nairobi (KSh800 to KSh900, 5½ hours) and Isebania (KSh400, four hours), on the Tanzanian border. Peugeots do still serve some destinations, but they cost about 25% more than matatus.

There are very few direct services to Kitale (KSh350, four hours); it is best to take a vehicle to Kakamega or Eldoret and change there.

**Akamba** (off New Station Rd) has its own depot in the town's centre. Besides four daily buses to Nairobi (KSh1100 to KSh1350, seven hours) via Nakuru (KSh800, 4½ hours), Akamba also has daily services to Busia (KSh400, three hours) and Kampala (KSh1350, seven hours). **Easy Coach** (off Mosque Rd) serves similar destinations, as well as Kakamega (KSh250, one hour), with some added comfort and cost.

### TRAIN
At the time of research no trains were running between Kisumu and Nairobi. The latest information is that passenger trains are definitely, maybe, possibly, doubtfully restarting sometime in 2009.

## Getting Around
### BODA-BODA
Bicycle-taxis have proliferated and they are a great way to get around Kisumu. No journey should be more than 20 bob.

### MATATU
Matatus 7 and 9 (KSh25), which travel along Oginga Odinga Rd and Jomo Kenyatta Hwy, are handy to reach the main matatu station,

main market and Kibuye Market – just wave and hop on anywhere you see one.

### TAXI
A taxi around town costs between KSh100 and KSh200, while trips to Dunga range from KSh200 to KSh350, with heavy bargaining.

# LAKE VICTORIA'S SOUTH SHORE
## Kendu Bay
This pint-sized lakeside village, two hours from Kisumu on a superb new road (though no doubt rain and trucks will have rendered it a torn-up mess by the time you read this), has little to offer apart from the strange volcanic **Simbi Lake** a couple of kilometres from town. The circular lake, sunk into the earth like a bomb crater, has a footpath around it and is an excellent twitching spot. The town itself, which is a charming place that feels exactly as you imagine remote Africa would feel, sees very few tourists and the reception is staggeringly warm.

There is no real reason to stay, but if the need arises **Big Five Hotel & Bar** ( ☎ 0722455352, 0724157955; rte C19; s/tw KSh600/700) is, well, how shall we put it, a different and original option! On arrival say 'hi' to the crocodiles, creep carefully past the lion and note that dancing girls sometimes grace the Big Five's bar. Beyond this, you'll find clean, basic and very acceptable rooms set around a courtyard, but Wednesday and weekends can be noisy, thanks to the disco and the extra-curricular activities of the dancing girls.

## Homa Bay
☎ 059
Homa Bay has a slow, tropical, almost Central African vibe, and the near total absence of other tourists means it's extraordinarily and genuinely friendly. There is little to do other than trudge up and down the dusty, music-filled streets, enjoy the seductive lake views, pass the time of day with the locals in one of the rainbow-coloured cafes and climb some of the cartoon-like hills that surround the town. The easiest summit to bag is the unmistakable conical mound of **Asego Hill**, which is just beyond the town and takes about an hour to clamber up. In addition the town also makes a great base from which to visit Ruma National Park (opposite) and Thimlich Ohinga (opposite).

## INFORMATION

Kenya Commercial Bank and Barclays Bank have ATMs. **Reikon Computer Services** (per hr KSh90) has slow internet connections. The **KWS warden's office** ( ☎ 22544) is found up the hill in the district commissioner's compound.

### SLEEPING & EATING

**Bay Lodge** (r with/without bath KSh350/300) This small and manically clean little aquamarine lodging has basic cube rooms and lots of friendly banter. The staff are also embarrassingly polite and greet you with phrases like, 'I'm afraid we have not yet had the opportunity to polish up this room. I hope this does not delay or frustrate you'. No it won't! It's just behind the post office.

**Little Nile Guest House** ( ☎ 0720615941; s/tw incl breakfast KSh600/900) The management of this calm little pension are as gentle and friendly as the rooms, which are kept shiny and bright and have great fishy murals. The only possible downside is that the hounds of the Baskervilles gather outside each night for a howling session.

**Ruma Tourist Lodge** ( ☎ 0727460492; s/d KSh600/900) Lurking behind a messy entrance, Ruma's bungalows offer stuffy but otherwise comfy rooms. Unfortunately the town's best bar – which has cold beers, decent tunes, a pool table and a restaurant (meals KSh80 to KSh160) – also lives here, so noise can be problematic. It is signposted behind the Total station.

### GETTING THERE & AWAY

Akamba's office is just down the hill from the bus station and its buses serve Nairobi (KSh900, nine hours, 7.30pm) via Kericho (KSh450, four hours) and Nakuru (KSh700, six hours). Several other companies and matatus (operating from the bus station) also ply these routes, as well as Mbita (KSh200, 1½ hours) and Kisumu (KSh300, three hours).

## RUMA NATIONAL PARK

Bordered by the dramatic **Kanyamaa Escarpment**, and home to Kenya's only population of roans (one of Africa's rarest and largest antelope), is the surprisingly seldom-visited **Ruma National Park** (adult/child US$20/10). While hot and often wet, it is beautiful and comprises 120 sq km of verdant riverine woodland and savanna grassland within the Lambwe Valley.

Besides roan, other rarities like Bohor's reedbuck, Rothschild giraffe, Jackson's hartebeest and the tiny oribi antelope can be seen. Birdlife is prolific, with 145 different bird species present.

The best thing about this park is its utter seclusion and the fact that you and you alone will have this slab of truly wild Africa all to yourself.

The park is set up for those with vehicles, but contact the **warden** ( ☎ 020-3529119, in Homa Bay 059-22544) and you may be able to organise a hike.

There are two simple **campsites** (US$15) near the main gate and a new guest house (US$100), which is extortionate if there are only two of you but quite good value for groups.

### Getting There & Away

Head a couple of kilometres south from Homa Bay and turn right onto the Mbita road. About 12km west is the main access road, and from there it's another 11km. The park's roads are in decent shape, but require a mega 4WD in the rainy season.

## THIMLICH OHINGA

East of Ruma National Park, this **archaeological site** (admission KSh250) is one of East Africa's most important. The remains of a dry-stone enclosure, 150m in diameter and containing another five smaller enclosures, were discovered here. It's thought to date back as far as the 15th century.

Getting to Thimlich is a problem without your own transport, although not completely impossible (with patience). Head down the Homa Bay–Rongo road for 12km, then turn right at Rod Kopany village, heading southwest through Mirogi to the village of Miranga. The site is signposted from there.

## MBITA & RUSINGA ISLAND

Mbita and Rusinga Island (connected by a causeway) are delightful. Tiny, languid and very rarely visited, they offer a glimpse of an older Africa; an Africa that moves to the gentle sway of the seasons rather than the ticking of a clock. Days easily merge into one here and hundreds of gentle adventures open up on the lightly wooded hills, along the soft sand beaches and in the smoky teashops. This is the sort of place where school children abandon their classes to come out and see you pass by, old women burst into song at your arrival and total strangers offer you a lift on the back of their bicycle.

On the island's north side is **Tom Mboya's mausoleum**. A child of Rusinga and former sanitary inspector in Nairobi, Mboya was one of the few Luo people ever to achieve any kind of political success. He held a huge amount of influence as Jomo Kenyatta's right-hand man and was widely tipped to become Kenya's second president before he was assassinated in 1969.

### Sleeping & Eating

**Viking Hotel** ( ☎ 059-22182; s/tw KSh250/300) The little sister of the Elk offers great value for very low prices. However, it's also suitably lower grade than its sister establishment and all rooms share a common bathroom.

our pick **Elk Guest House** ( ☎ 059-22182; s/tw KSh350/700, with shared toilet KSh300/500) Gleaming isn't the right word for this well-organised guest house in the centre of town. It's so sparklingly clean it actually looks like it has been used in an advert for a cleaning product and it offers easily some of the best budget rooms this side of Lake Victoria.

**Lake Victoria Safari Village** ( ☎ 0721912120; www .safarikenya.net; s/d/tr incl breakfast US$50/65/75) A Lake Victoria beachfront haven if there ever was one. Lovely traditionally thatched roofs tower over comfy beds and impressive bathrooms in each of the pretty cottages. The grassy gardens lead down to a private beach with safe swimming and there's even a 'honeymoon suite' inside a mock lighthouse. It's a couple of kilometres south of town.

For those with the hunger pangs there are a couple of basic shacks in town selling fish for next to nothing, but the best central place to eat is the restaurant at the **Viking Hotel** (meals KSh80-120; ☯ lunch & dinner). Plusher is the restaurant found at the **Lake Victoria Safari Village** (mains KSh300; ☯ lunch & dinner), though meals are very slow in coming (advance orders required) and the service leaves something to be desired.

### Getting There & Away

The best way of getting from Mbita to Kisumu is to take the ferry to Luanda Kotieno on the northern shore of the narrow Winam Gulf. Boats leave Mbita around 7am, 10am, 2pm and 5pm (foot passenger KSh100, vehicle KSh800 to KSh1000). If you get off on being placed inside an airless, hot, sticky room and then beaten and bruised senseless, you'll love the matatu ride between Mbita and Homa Bay and on

to Kisumu. There are two buses to Kisumu (KSh500, five hours) each morning between 6am and 11am. Matatus to Homa Bay are far more frequent (KSh200, 1½ hours). If it has been raining heavily don't even attempt to leave Mbita by land! The odd matatu heads around Rusinga Island to the mausoleum (KSh50).

## MFANGANO ISLAND

If you want to fall totally off the radar then Mfangano Island, sitting out in the placid lake waters, is an idyllic place to get lost. Home to many a monitor lizard, curious locals, intriguing **rock paintings** and the imposing but assailable **Mt Kwitutu** (1694m), Mfangano Island is well worth a day or two. Thanks to the refreshing absence of vehicles, only footpaths criss-cross the island.

The rock paintings, often featuring sun motifs, are both revered and feared by locals (which has hindered vandalism). They are found northwest of Kwitutu towards the village of Ukula. It's thought they were painted by the island's earliest inhabitants, Bantu Pygmies.

Sena village has little more than the post office and the chief's camp (housing the administrator of the island).

### Sleeping & Eating

There are no official guest houses, but it's normally possible to arrange homestays with the local residents – comfort is not guaranteed, but a fantastic insight into local life is. Campers might also stay on the grounds of St Linus' Church (check out the mural inside). One reader reported a small and very basic guest house on the tiny island of **Riringiti**, which sits just off the west coast of Mfangano. Rooms cost KSh100 per person and it's about as off the beaten track as you can get in Kenya. The boats which circle Mfangano (see pbelow) will drop you here.

If you have a bunch of Benjamin Franklins burning a hole in your pocket, there is the **Mfangano Island Camp** ( ☎ bookings 020-2734000; www.governorscamp.com; s/d full board US$596/890) on the north side of the island. Primarily a fishing resort, it's nice, very nice, but possibly not US$900 nice!

### Getting There & Away

Boats ply the lake waves between Mbita and Mfangano Island daily at around 8.30am and noon. They both call in at Takawiri Island en route, stop at Mfangano's 'capital' Sena and then carry on around the island, stopping at most villages on the way. To get back to Mbita the boats head back at a very flexible 2pm. The journey time to Sena is around 1½ hours and costs KSh150. Private boats can be chartered from the Lake Victoria Safari Village for between KSh10,000 to KSh12,000 for a full-day trip.

# WESTERN HIGHLANDS

Despite media impressions depicting a land of undulating savanna stretching to the horizon, the real heart and soul of Kenya, and the area where most of the people live, is the luminous green highlands. Benefiting from reliable rainfall and fertile soil, the Western Highlands are the agricultural powerhouse of Kenya; the south is cash-crop country, with vast patchworks of tea plantations covering the region around Kisii and Kericho, while further north, near Kitale and Eldoret, dense cultivation takes over.

The settlements here are predominantly agricultural service towns, with little of interest unless you need a chainsaw or water barrel. For visitors, the real attractions lie outside these places – the rolling tea fields around Kericho, the tropical beauty of Kakamega Forest, trekking on Mt Elgon, the prolific birdlife in Saiwa Swamp National Park and exploring the dramatic Cherangani Hills.

## KISII
☎ 058
Let's cut straight to the chase. Kisii is a noisy, polluted and congested mess, and most people (quite sensibly) roll right on through without even stopping.

While the feted Kisii soapstone obviously comes from this area, it's not on sale here. Quarrying and carving go on in the village of **Tabaka**, 23km northwest of Kisii, where you can usually visit the workshops.

### Information
**Barclays Bank** (Moi Hwy) With ATM.
**National Bank of Kenya** (cnr Hospital Rd & Sansora Rd) With ATM (Cirrus & Plus cards only).
**Pemo Cyber Café** (Hospital Rd; per hr KSh60) Reasonable internet connections.
**Post office** (Moi Hwy) With cardphones.

### Sleeping & Eating
**Sabrina Lodge** (s/tw with shared bathroom KSh350/600) Just up from Postbank, you'll find real Africa at this friendly hotel. By that we mean basic cubicles, common bathrooms with bucket showers, and toilets that leave you exposed for everyone to see. The staff think foreigners are hilarious – they're probably right.

**Kisii Hotel** ( ☎ 30134; s/tw/ste incl breakfast KSh750/950/1400) Double the price, but triple the pleasure. This is a relaxed place in what

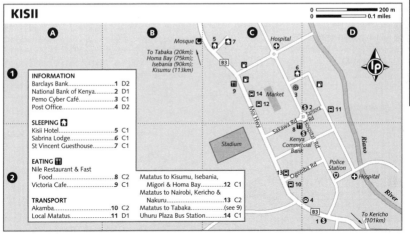

KISII

| INFORMATION | |
|---|---|
| Barclays Bank | 1 D2 |
| National Bank of Kenya | 2 D1 |
| Pemo Cyber Café | 3 C1 |
| Post Office | 4 D2 |

| SLEEPING | |
|---|---|
| Kisii Hotel | 5 C1 |
| Sabrina Lodge | 6 C1 |
| St Vincent Guesthouse | 7 C1 |

| EATING | |
|---|---|
| Nile Restaurant & Fast | |
| Food | 8 C2 |
| Victoria Cafe | 9 C1 |

| TRANSPORT | |
|---|---|
| Akamba | 10 C2 |
| Local Matatus | 11 D1 |

Matatus to Kisumu, Isebania,
 Migori & Homa Bay ............ 12 C1
Matatus to Nairobi, Kericho &
 Nakuru ............................. 13 C2
Matatus to Tabaka ................ (see 9)
Uhuru Plaza Bus Station ........ 14 C1

To Tabaka (20km);
Homa Bay (75km);
Isebania (90km);
Kisumu (113km)

Mosque
Hospital
Market
Stadium
Kenya Commercial Bank
Police Station
Hospital
Moi Hwy
Sakawa Rd
Sansora Rd
Hospital Rd
Oginga Rd
Ogemba Rd
Riana
River
To Kericho (101km)

0 ———— 200 m
0 ———— 0.1 miles

WESTERN KENYA

feels like an old school building off the Moi Hwy. It boasts large gardens and sizeable rooms, each with decent bathrooms. The restaurant (meals KSh150 to KSh300) is deservedly popular.

**St Vincent Guesthouse** ( ☎ 0733650702; s/d/tw incl breakfast KSh1300/1650/2200) This Catholic-run guest house off the Moi Hwy isn't the place for a party but it's perfect for a quiet night's sleep. Rooms are very clean and cosy. Couples travelling together pay a lot less than 'just friends' so, if you are just friends, we'd recommend pushing the beds together and saving 500 bob.

**Victoria Cafe** (Moi Hwy; meals KSh60-160; ⏰ lunch & dinner) A deep-green locals' cafe with fried food on the inside and a music stall adding beats on the outside.

**Nile Restaurant & Fast food** (Hospital Rd; meals KSh150-250) Chicken and chips will set you back KSh250 at this cheeky little restaurant right in the town centre.

### Getting There & Away

Matatus line the length of Moi Hwy – look for the destination placards on their roofs. Regular departures serve Homa Bay (KSh150, one hour), Kisumu (KSh300, two hours), Kericho (KSh300, two hours) and Isebania (KSh250, 1¾ hours) on the Tanzanian border.

Tabaka matatus leave from the Victoria Cafe, while local matatus (and additional Kericho services) leave from the stand at the end of Sansora Rd.

**Akamba** (Moi Hwy) has a daily bus to Nairobi (KSh800, eight hours) via Nakuru (KSh600, 5½ hours) departing at 9pm – it's wise to book a day in advance. International bus departures for Mwanza (KSh1700) in Tanzania also leave from here (see p346).

## KERICHO
☎ 052

The polar opposite of Kisii, Kericho is a haven of tranquillity. Its surrounds are blanketed by a thick patchwork of manicured tea plantations, each seemingly hemmed in by distant stands of evergreens. With a pleasant climate and a number of things to see and do, Kericho makes for a very calming couple of days' rest.

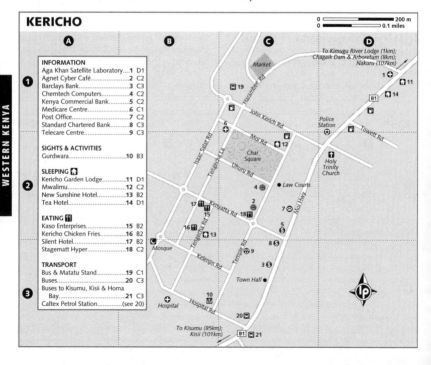

---

**ANYONE FOR TEA?**

Kenya is the world's third-largest tea exporter after India and Sri Lanka, with tea accounting for between 20% and 30% of the country's export income. Tea picking is a great source of employment around Kericho, with mature bushes picked every 17 days and the same worker continually picking the same patch. Good pickers collect their own body weight in tea each day!

The Kenyan tea industry is unique in that its small landholders produce the bulk (60%) of the country's tea. All the leaves used to be sold to the government's Kenya Tea Development Authority (KTDA), which did the processing and supposedly guaranteed farmers 70% of the sale price.

In 2000, the KTDA became the Kenya Tea Development Agency, a private organisation, after local members of parliament argued, among other concerns, that the government system had significant potential for corruption (though there have been recent calls from some farmers to return to government regulation).

Despite Kericho producing some of the planet's best black tea, you will have trouble finding a cup of the finest blends here – most of it's exported.

---

## Information

**Aga Khan Satellite Laboratory** (Moi Hwy)

**Agnet Cyber Café** (Temple Rd; per hr KSh60; ⏰ 7.30am-7.30pm) Connections that will send you to sleep, but they get there eventually.

**Barclays Bank** (Moi Hwy) With ATM.

**Chemtech Computers** (Temple Rd; per hr KSh60; ⏰ 7.45am-6pm Mon-Sat) The attached Bobbies Café puts the cafe into cybercafe.

**Kenya Commercial Bank** (Moi Hwy) With ATM (Visa only).

**Medicare Centre** ( ☎ 21733; Moi Rd) Clinic, pharmacy and X-ray.

**Post office** (Moi Hwy)

**Standard Chartered Bank** (Moi Hwy) With ATM (Visa only).

**Telecare Centre** (Temple Rd) Calling cards and cardphones.

## Sights & Activities

Tea is the reason the English colonialists came to Kericho, and tea is probably the reason you've come too. This is the centre of the most important tea gardens in all of Africa, so you might expect **tea plantation tours** to be touted left, right and centre. Surprisingly, though, they are fairly few and far between. However, the Tea Hotel (p186) does have excellent guided tours (KSh200 per person) to the estates that begin immediately beyond the hotel gardens. Most tours involve walking around the fields and watching the picking in process (note that the pickers don't work on Sundays). If you want to actually see the process through to the end and visit a factory you should book at least a week in advance through the Tea Hotel.

If money's too tight to mention then you can go for a stroll around the fields on your own – the easiest to get to are those sitting behind the Tea Hotel.

Away from tea you can also go for an early-morning romp through the lush countryside in search of colobus, vervet and red-tailed monkeys in the forests that line the Kimugi River; again it's a good idea to take a guide from the Tea Hotel (KSh200 per person).

Seven or eight kilometres east of town, along the Nairobi road, are the gorgeous tropical gardens of **Chagaik Dam** and the **arboretum**, which, with their collection of exotic plants and a lovely pond, are an idyllic slice of picnic-spot heaven.

Finally, if all this natural beauty has left you feeling a little spiritual, head to Africa's largest **Gurdwara** (Sikh place of worship), found on Hospital Rd.

## Sleeping & Eating

**Kericho Garden Lodge** ( ☎ 0722687686; Moi Hwy; s/d from KSh500/600) The single rooms in the main building are something rotten and the plethora of condom machines indicates that rooms might be used more by the hour than by the night. The double rooms, which are actually triples, are much better and will keep any bargain hunters happy. It also houses a busy bar.

**Mwalimu** ( ☎ 036121601; Moi Rd; s/tw KSh500/600) It looks run down from the outside but as long as you don't mind a few scuffed walls you'll find this a decent option. It's secure and has self-contained rooms (with private bathroom) and evening-only hot water.

**New Sunshine Hotel** ( ☎ 0725146601, 0723455516; Tengecha Rd; s/tw KSh1000/1400) The best budget

---

**HARMAN KIRUI**

**How did the recent election violence affect Kericho?**
There wasn't much fighting in Kericho itself compared to elsewhere. I think this is because all the workers on the tea estates are of mixed tribes and have lived together in these mixed communities like brothers and sisters for years.

It hit tourism here badly though. At the time we had some tourists who arrived from Kisumu under a police escort and then they had to be airlifted out of town by helicopter from the hotel grounds. From the end of December until the end of February not a single tourist came to Kericho and all the bookings we had were cancelled. It wasn't until May that things started to pick up again and now they are OK.

For now the coalition seems stable and things are returning to normal, but it was a scary time and we did not know what would happen. I think the violence was just a mad wave that swept over the country, but now I hope it's over for good and that the people are more united than they were before.

*Harman Kirui works as a tea estate guide and waiter for the Tea Hotel in Kericho.*

---

hotel in town, the New Sunshine will put a little sunshine into your life with its well-cared-for rooms, hot showers and management who'll bend over backwards to help. It's NGO-friendly and will often offer groups of NGO workers discounts. There's good security and an equally good attached restaurant (meals KSh100 to KSh200), which serves Western snacks, sandwiches and burgers.

**Tea Hotel** ( ☎ Nairobi 020-2050790; teahotel@africaonline.co.ke; Moi Hwy; camping KSh300, s/d US$65/90; 🖭 ) The rooms are fading fast, but this grand property, built in the 1950s by the Brooke Bond company, is still a fantastic choice full of period charm, vast hallways and dining rooms stuffed full of the mounted heads of animals you just saw in the Masai Mara. The real highlight is the beautiful gardens with a tea-bush backdrop. Even if you can't afford to pay the high rates (though you can normally get resident rates) then it would be silly not to pop round for afternoon tea served with a pile of biscuits. Camping is possible on the edge of the gardens.

**Kaso Enterprises** (Kenyatta Rd) After all that greasy food, make yourself feel a little healthier with one of the wonderful fresh yoghurts or juices available here from KSh20.

**Silent Hotel** ( ☎ 0723338871; Kenyatta Rd; meals KSh80-200; 🍴 lunch & dinner) This purple and white corrugated building is hectically busy with locals downing piles of Kenyan staples, including a tasty beef fry and *ugali* for KSh170.

**Kericho Chicken Fries** (Tengecha Rd; chicken & chips KSh210; 🍴 lunch & dinner) Grab a stall on one of the communal tables and tuck into some excellent chicken and chips. It does a roaring lunchtime trade.

**Stagematt Hyper** (Kenyatta Rd) Perfect for self-caterers to stock up.

## Getting There & Away

While most buses and matatus stop at the main stand in the town's northwest corner, many also pick up passengers on the Moi Hwy near the Caltex petrol station. If you simply state your destination to anyone in town, they'll be happy to point you in the right direction.

Buses to Nairobi (KSh600, 4½ hours) are quite frequent, as are matatus to Kisumu (KSh300, two hours), Kisii (KSh300, two hours), Eldoret (KSh400 to KSh500, 3½ hours) and Nakuru (KSh300, two hours). The odd Peugeot also serves these destinations, but costs about 25% more.

## KAKAMEGA
☎ 056

There is no real reason to stay in this small agricultural town, but if you arrive late in the day it can be convenient to sleep over and stock up with supplies before heading to nearby Kakamega Forest Reserve.

The Kakamega region is part of the traditional Bungoma district (see also p189) and home to the Luhya people (see p41), who are quite Westernised as a community.

## Information

**Barclays Bank** (A1 Hwy) With ATM.
**Kenya Commercial Bank** (Kenyatta Ave) With ATM (Visa only).
**KWS Area Headquarters** ( ☎ 30603; PO Box 88, Kakamega) Kakamega Forest information.

**Post office** (A1 Hwy)
**Telkom Kenya** (A1 Hwy) Calling cards and cardphones.

## Sights & Activities

Perched on a ridge south of town is the **Crying Stone of Ilesi**, a local curiosity that has become a regional emblem. The formation, looking like a solemn head resting on weary shoulders, consists of a large boulder balanced atop a huge column of rock, down which tears are said to flow. There are two legends regarding the reason for this, the first is that the stone is that of a girl who continues to cry after she fell in love with a man her father didn't approve of and, as punishment, he turned her to stone. The second is that the stones weep for the state of humanity in general – and who can blame them!

The town's **market**, a muddle of experiences, is worth poking your nose into. It operates every day but is at its loudest on Saturday and Wednesday mornings when, as if by magic, people appear from all over the surrounding countryside.

## Sleeping & Eating

**Franka Hotel** (Mumias Rd; r KSh500) A maze of dark and dastardly rooms sit above a favourite eating and drinking hole (meals KSh80 to KSh150). Rooms all have bathrooms and come with nets and noise – some of it road-produced, some of it of the baby-making variety.

**Friends Hotel** (☎ 31716; Mumias Rd; s normal/deluxe KSh1000/1300, d normal/deluxe KSh1300/1600) Friends has comfortable rooms that are pleasing to the eye. There's 24-hour hot water, but it's a little overpriced for what you get. The downstairs restaurant is the swankiest place in town to eat.

**Snack Stop Cafe** (Cannon Awori Rd; meals KSh70-150; ☺ lunch & dinner) The restaurant of choice for locals. Simple Kenyan standards, including *ugali wimbi* (*ugali* made from sorghum).

**Pizza Hut Café** (Cannon Awori Rd; meals KSh70-180; ☺ lunch & dinner) What could be better than thin-based pizzas, cooked in a wood-fired oven and dripping in cheese? Is that *ugali* and beef stew we hear you cry? Hope so, because despite the name pizzas are out and *ugali* is in at this basic locals' cafe.

There are several supermarkets for self-caterers.

## Getting There & Around

**Easy Coach** (off Kenyatta Ave) serves Kisumu (KSh400, 1½ hours) at 7.30am and 8pm, Nairobi (KSh1250, 7½ hours) at 8am and 8pm via Nakuru (KSh750, five hours). Nearby, **Akamba** (off Kenyatta Ave) has 7.30am and 8pm buses to Nairobi (KSh1050).

Behind the Total station on the northern edge of the town, matatus leave for Kisumu (KSh200, one hour), Kitale (KSh250, 2½ hours) and Eldoret (KSh250, 2½ hours).

## KAKAMEGA FOREST
☎ 056
Not so long ago much of western Kenya was hidden under a dark veil of jungle and formed a part of the mighty Guineo-Congolian forest ecosystem – even gorillas are rumoured to have played in the mists here. However, the British soon did their best to turn all that lovely virgin forest into tea estates and now all that's left is the superb slab of tropical rainforest surrounding Kakamega. Though seriously degraded, this forest is unique in Kenya and contains plants, animals and birds that occur nowhere else in the country (disappointingly the gorillas died out long, long ago). It's so wild here trees actually kill each other – seriously! Parasitic fig trees grow on top of unsuspecting trees and strangle their hosts to death.

Less murderous is the forest's array of wildlife. An astounding 330 species of birds, including casqued hornbill, Ross's turaco and great blue turaco, have been spotted here. During darkness, hammer-headed fruit bats and flying squirrels take to the air. The best viewing months are June, August and October, when many migrant species arrive. The wildflowers are also wonderful in October, supporting around 400 species of butterfly.

Dancing in the canopy are no less than seven different primate species, one being the exceedingly rare de Brazza's monkey.

The northern section of the forest around Buyangu is both more accessible and more pristine. This makes up the **Kakamega Forest National Reserve**, maintained by the KWS. This area has a variety of habitats but is generally very dense, with considerable areas of primary forest and regenerating secondary forest; there is a total ban on grazing, wood collection and cultivation in this zone.

The southern section, centred on Isecheno, forms the **Kakamega Forest Reserve** and is looked after by the Forest Department. Predominantly forested, this region supports several communities and is under considerable

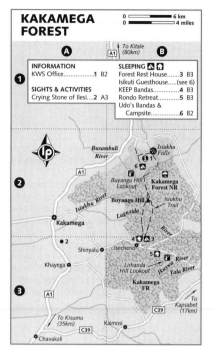

**KAKAMEGA FOREST**

0 —————— 6 km
0 —————— 4 miles

**INFORMATION**
KWS Office..................1 B2

**SIGHTS & ACTIVITIES**
Crying Stone of Ilesi....2 A3

**SLEEPING**
Forest Rest House........3 B3
Isikuti Guesthouse.....(see 6)
KEEP Bandas..............4 B3
Rondo Retreat.............5 B3
Udo's Bandas &
Campsite..................6 B2

pressure from both farming and illegal logging. Despite being more degraded it's to this part of the park that most visitors head, thanks no doubt to having the better accommodation and no entry fees.

Tribal practices in the forest persist: *mugumu* trees are considered sacred, circumcisions are sometimes performed in the forest and bullfights (between bulls not between man and animal) are still held on Sunday mornings in Khayega and Shinyalu. Intervillage wrestling also used to be common, but was eventually banned, as the prize (the victor's pick of the young women present) tended to provoke more fights than the match itself.

## Information
KWS currently only charges admission to the **Kakamega Forest National Reserve** (adult/child US$20/10).

## Sights & Activities
### WALKING TRAILS
The best, indeed the only real, way to appreciate the forest is to walk, and trails radiate from Buyangu and Isecheno areas.

Official **guides** (per person for short/long walk KSh300/600), trained by the Kakamega Biodiversity Conservation and Tour Operators Association, are well worth the money. Not only do they prevent you from getting lost, but most are walking encyclopaedias and will reel off both the Latin and common name of almost any plant or insect you care to point out. They are also able to recognise and imitate any bird call so effectively that you wouldn't be surprised if they suddenly sprouted wings and flew off. They are also highly knowledgeable in the medicinal properties of many of the plants around you, so many of which have some sort of medical value that you can't but help wondering what potential medicines man may already have destroyed through deforestation.

Rangers state that trails vary in length from 1km to 7km. Of the longer walks **Isiukhu Trail**, which connects Isecheno to **Isiukhu Falls**, is one of the most rewarding and takes a minimum of half a day. Short walks to **Buyangu Hill** in the north or **Lirhanda Hill** in the south for sunrise or sunset are highly recommended. As ever, the early morning and late afternoon are the best times to view birds, but night walks can also be a fantastic experience. Though the forest is crawling with life, this isn't the Masai Mara and sightings of animals are fleeting at best (except for the primates, which are normally easy to find). Rather than expecting to see leopards, forest hogs and the like it's better to think small. Concentrate on the birds and the bees – the insect life here is phenomenal (it's said that if you spend one hour rummaging through the leaf litter of a tropical rainforest then you will discover a new species of insect!). However, it's the birds that really steal the show and Kakamega, with its unique collection of species more common to the forests of the Congo, is easily one of the top birding destinations in Kenya.

## Sleeping & Eating
### BUYANGU AREA
If staying at either of the following you will have to pay park entry fees for each night you're here.

**Udo's Bandas & Campsite** ( ☎ 30603, 0727415828; PO Box 879, Kakamega; camping US$5, bandas per person US$10) Named after Udo Savalli, a well-known ornithologist, this lovely site is tidy, well maintained and has seven simple

---

### WHERE BOYS BECOME MEN

The Bungoma/Trans-Nzoia district goes wild in August with the sights and sounds of the Bukusu Circumcision Festival, an annual jamboree dedicated to the initiation of local young boys into manhood.

The tradition was apparently passed to the Bukusu by the Sabaot tribe in the 19th century, when a young hunter cut the head off a troublesome serpent to earn the coveted operation (too symbolic to be true?).

The evening before the ceremony is devoted to substance abuse and sex; in the morning the youngsters are trimmed with a traditional knife in front of their entire village.

Unsurprisingly, this practice has attracted a certain amount of controversy in recent years. Health concerns are prevalent, as the same knife can be used for up to 10 boys, posing a risk of HIV/AIDS and other infections. The associated debauchery also brings a seasonal rush of under-age pregnancies and family rifts that seriously affect local communities.

Education and experience now mean that fewer boys undergo the old method, preferring to take the safe option at local hospitals. However, those wielding the knife are less likely to let go of their heritage. To quote one prominent circumciser: 'Every year at this time it's like a fever grips me, and I can't rest until I've cut a boy' – something passing male tourists might want to bear in mind!

---

thatched bandas; nets are provided, but you will need your own sleeping bag and other supplies. There are long-drop toilets, bucket showers and a communal cooking and dining shelter.

**Isikuti Guesthouse** ( ☎ 30603, 0727415828; per cottage US$50) Hidden in a pretty forest glade close to Udo's are four massive cottages (sleeping up to four), with equipped kitchens and bathrooms. For either the bandas or the cottage it's best to book ahead.

### ISECHENO AREA

**our pick Forest Rest House** ( ☎ 0720700949; camping KSh225, r per person KSh225) The four rooms of this wooden tree house, perched on stilts 2m above the ground and with views straight onto a mass of impenetrable Tarzan jungle, might be as basic as basic gets (no electricity, no bedding and cold-water baths that look like they'd crash through the floor boards if you tried to fill one), but it has to be one of the most atmospheric places to stay in all of Kenya.

**KEEP Bandas** (s/tw KSh500/1000) Even though profits go to the local community, these bandas, which are almost swallowed up by jungle, are a little overpriced, considering that all you get is a scruffy hut, equally scruffy beds, no electricity and communal cold-water showers. Still, you're in the jungle and life isn't supposed to be easy. At either this or the next door Forest Rest House you can normally pay a local to cook for you or self-cater in the basic kitchen.

**our pick Rondo Retreat** ( ☎ 033130268; www.rondo retreat.com; full board adult/child KSh7400/5400) Arrive at the Rondo Retreat, a couple of kilometres on from the Forest Rest House, and you'll be greeted by some dark green gates. These may look like any old gates but they are in fact a magical time portal that whisks you back to 1922 and the height of British rule. Consisting of a series of wooden bungalows filled with a family's clutter, this gorgeous and eccentric place is a wonderful retreat from modern Kenya. The gardens are absolutely stunning and worth visiting even if you're not staying – don't miss the secret garden by the pond, nor the afternoon tea and cake on the veranda. Dinner is a formal affair and you should dress smart (no shorts) and expect old-fashioned English meat-and-two-veg. Profits go to a Christian charity.

## Getting There & Away
### BUYANGU AREA

Matatus heading north towards Kitale can drop you at the access road about 18km north of Kakamega town (KSh70). It is a well signposted 2km walk from there to the park office and Udo's.

### ISECHENO AREA

Regular matatus link Kakamega with Shinyalu (KSh70), but few go on to Isecheno. Shinyalu is also accessed by a rare matatu service from Khayega. From Shinyalu you will probably need to take a *boda-boda* for KSh50 to Isecheno or a rarer motorbike taxi (KSh100).

The improved roads are still treacherous after rain and you may prefer to walk once you've seen the trouble vehicles have. To Shinyalu it's about 7km from Khayega and 10km from Kakamega. From Shinyalu it is 5km to Isecheno.

The dirt road from the rest house continues east to Kapsabet, but transport is rare.

# ELDORET
☎ 053

Mmm…cheese! While the pull of a fine Gouda, Gruyère, Stilton, Brie or Cheddar can vary, depending on how long you've been on your African safari, a stop in Eldoret is a must for all cheese lovers.

For cheese haters, there is little else to draw you to this large service town besides the need of a bank or a good night's sleep before venturing into the nearby Kerio Valley and Kamnarok National Reserves.

## Information
**Barclays Bank** (Uganda Rd) With ATM.
**Cyber Hawk Internet Café** (Nandi Arcade, Nandi Rd; per hr KSh60) Fast connections.
**Cyber World** (Uganda Rd; per hr KSh60) Also burns images to CD.
**Eldoret Hospital** One of Kenya's best hospitals, off Uganda Rd. With 24-hour emergency.
**Kenya Commercial Bank** (Kenyatta St) With ATM (Visa only).
**Post office** (Uganda Rd)
**Standard Chartered Bank** (Uganda Rd) With ATM (Visa only).
**Telkom Kenya** (cnr Kenyatta St & Elijaa Cheruhota St) Calling cards and cardphones.

## Sights & Activities
The only real attraction is an odd (but tasty) one. The **Doinyo Lessos Creameries Cheese Factory** (Kenyatta St; ☒ 8am-6pm) produces over 30 different types of cheese. You can taste most for free and the average price is KSh500 per kg, with a minimum purchase of 250g. The company also makes yummy ice cream (KSh23 for 100mL).

## Sleeping
### BUDGET
**Aya Inn** ( ☎ 2062259; Oginga Odinga St; r with/without bath KSh650/550) The staff will think you're off your head wanting to look at the rooms before hand-

ing over your cash – as if you can't trust them when they say it's like the Hilton! Alas, it's not, but it's also a lot cheaper and for the money it's probably better value. Opt for one of the quieter and secluded rooms with hot water.
**Lincoln Hotel** ( ☎ 22093; Oloo Rd; s/d KSh500/800) The most comfortable of the budget options, this pleasant place has decent rooms spread around its courtyard and seriously go-slow staff who fit well with the overall vibe.
**Mountain View Hotel** ( ☎ 2060728; Uganda Rd; s/tw KSh600/800) It ain't too pretty, but after a few weeks on the road in Kenya you probably aren't looking too hot either, so it could well be a match made in heaven.

### MIDRANGE & TOP END
**White Highlands Inn** ( ☎ 2061541; Elgeyo St; s/d incl breakfast KSh1500/2000) In a quiet corner on the edge of town this is a decent place with clean, spacious rooms with a certain old-fashioned charm. In addition to the hotel, this rambling complex contains a couple of restaurants and a bar with an open fire.
**Klique Hotel** ( ☎ 2060903; www.kliquehotel.com; Oginga Odinga St; s/d US$40/50) A modern and comfortable high-rise with brightly (sometimes garishly) painted rooms and three bathrooms in all of Eldoret. Nonresident rates are a bit steep but if they automatically assume you're a resident you could just go with the flow…
**Sirikwa Hotel** ( ☎ 2063614; Elgeyo Rd; s/d incl breakfast US$66/77; ☒ ) Screams 1977 through and through, and Prince Charles would fall into a faint if he saw how ugly the building is. Its day might be done, but everyone continues to insist it's the top hotel in town; by which they probably mean it's the most expensive. Saving graces are the pool (nonresidents KSh200) and gardens.

## Eating
**Café Delicious** (Oginga Odinga St; meals KSh60-150; ☒ lunch & dinner) Simple fare and cool African sounds are the go in this tidy, bright-green cafe. As well as all the usual suspects you can also pick and choose from a range of gizzards (from KSh60), so that's nice!
**Freddies** (Kenyatta St; meals KSh60-250; ☒ lunch & dinner) You'd better not be on a diet when you come here because it's chips, chips and how about some burger to go with those chips?
**Sizzlers Cafe** (Kenyatta St; meals KSh100-250; ☒ lunch & dinner) Grab a curry and get filled for minimal coinage at this undeniable favourite.

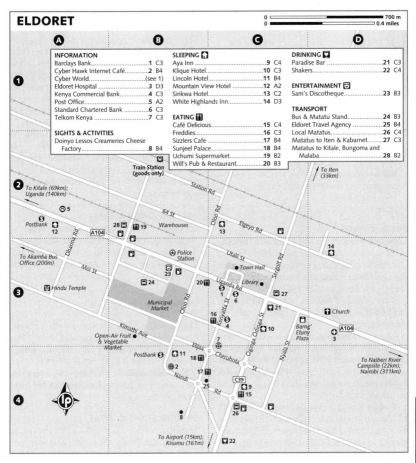

**ELDORET**

0 ____ 700 m
0 ____ 0.4 miles

| INFORMATION | |
|---|---|
| Barclays Bank | 1 C3 |
| Cyber Hawk Internet Café | 2 B4 |
| Cyber World | (see 1) |
| Eldoret Hospital | 3 D3 |
| Kenya Commercial Bank | 4 C3 |
| Post Office | 5 A2 |
| Standard Chartered Bank | 6 C3 |
| Telkom Kenya | 7 C3 |

**SIGHTS & ACTIVITIES**
Doinyo Lessos Creameries Cheese
Factory ........................... 8 B4

| SLEEPING | |
|---|---|
| Aya Inn | 9 C4 |
| Klique Hotel | 10 C3 |
| Lincoln Hotel | 11 B4 |
| Mountain View Hotel | 12 A2 |
| Sirikwa Hotel | 13 C2 |
| White Highlands Inn | 14 D3 |

| EATING | |
|---|---|
| Café Delicious | 15 C4 |
| Freddies | 16 C3 |
| Sizzlers Cafe | 17 B4 |
| Sunjeel Palace | 18 B4 |
| Uchumi Supermarket | 19 B2 |
| Will's Pub & Restaurant | 20 B3 |

| DRINKING | |
|---|---|
| Paradise Bar | 21 C3 |
| Shakers | 22 C4 |

**ENTERTAINMENT**
Sam's Discotheque ............ 23 B3

| TRANSPORT | |
|---|---|
| Bus & Matatu Stand | 24 B3 |
| Eldoret Travel Agency | 25 B4 |
| Local Matatus | 26 C4 |
| Matatus to Iten & Kabarnet | 27 C3 |
| Matatus to Kitale, Bungoma and Malaba | 28 B2 |

**Will's Pub & Restaurant** (Uganda Rd; meals KSh200-450; ☺ lunch & dinner) Looks and feels like an English pub, with similarly heavyweight food. The KSh250 fried breakfast rules.

**Sunjeel Palace** (Kenyatta St; mains KSh300; ☺ lunch & dinner) This formal, dark and spicy Indian restaurant serves superb, real-deal curries. Allow at least half an hour for orders to be prepared.

**Uchumi supermarket**, off Uganda Rd, is well stocked and perfect for self-caterers.

## Drinking & Entertainment

**Shakers** (Oginga Odinga Rd) An atmospheric, albeit isolated, place (take a taxi) just waiting for introductions: arse meet wicker chair. Eyes meet European footy. Beer meet lips.

**Will's Pub** (Uganda St) A tame but lively place for a cold drink. It's a friendly spot for female travellers and has a big-screen TV.

**Paradise Bar** (Oginga Odinga Rd) A rough-and-tumble place that's only paradise if you enjoy hanging with con artists, tough nuts and ladies of the night. As one local said, 'It's hell.'

**Sam's Discotheque** (Uganda Rd; ☺ weekends) Eldoret's energetic dance club is overflowing with students.

## Getting There & Away
### AIR

There are daily flights between Eldoret and Nairobi (KSh6300, one hour) with the little-known Aero Kenya. Bookings are handled by **Eldoret Travel Agency** ( ☎ 2062707; Kenyatta St).

---

**THE TROUBLE WITH MOLO**

On the road between Eldoret and Nakuru to the west, you'll see shocking reminders of the postelection violence that wracked the nation in January 2008. It's most visible around the small farming village of Molo, where it seems every other building is now nothing more than a shattered shell. The violence in this region was intense – even fields of crops were burnt to the ground. What is extraordinary, locals explain, is that while the victims are still huddled in nearby refugee camps, the presumed perpetrators are living amongst the debris of their handiwork.

---

### BUS & MATATU

The main bus and matatu stand is in the centre of town, by the municipal market.

Regular matatus/Peugeots serve Kitale (KSh150/200, 1¼ hours), Kisumu (KSh250/300, 2½ hours), Kericho (KSh250/300, 3½ hours), Nakuru (KSh300/400, 2¾ hours) and Nairobi (KSh600/700, six hours). Buses duplicate these routes.

Local matatus and more Kericho services leave from Nandi Rd. Irregular matatus to Iten and Kabarnet leave opposite Paradise Bar on Uganda Rd. Further west on Uganda Rd, matatus leave for Malaba (KSh400, 2½ hours) on the Uganda border.

**Akamba** (Moi St) buses to Nairobi (KSh500, 10.30am and 9pm) via Nakuru (KSh250) leave from its depot. There is also a 9am and noon service to Kampala (KSh1000; six hours).

### Getting Around

A matatu to or from the airport costs KSh50, and a taxi will cost around KSh1000. *Bodabodas* are rare here, though some linger near the bus stand.

## WEST TO UGANDA
### Malaba
☎ 055

This dusty town sits on the main border crossing to Uganda. The Kenya Commercial Bank (on the A104 Hwy; no ATM) can exchange cash, but almost everybody uses one of the numerous money changers prowling around instead. Rates are generally OK, but count your money carefully!

Crossing the border is generally pain-free, and Ugandan (or Kenyan) visas are available

on the spot for most people for US$50. The Kenyan border is open 24 hours, but we've heard that the Ugandan one runs to a somewhat more 'flexible' timetable, so try and arrive in daylight hours. We've also heard reports that the Ugandan immigration sometimes runs out of visa stamps, but lets you in without one. This might be genuine or it might be just a scam for officials to pocket some money; either way, insist on getting a visa stamp or you'll face untold problems when trying to leave Uganda again.

If for some unfortunate reason you get stuck here for the night then you'll find a couple of not very appetising boardings and lodgings.

### GETTING THERE & AWAY

Sporadic matatus serve Eldoret (KSh400, 2½ hours) and Kitale (KSh400, 2½ hours). If you're going the other way then you'll find plenty of onward connections to Jinja and Kampala.

### Busia
☎ 055

This tiny town links Kisumu with Uganda. There is a Kenya Commercial Bank, but they seem rather unhelpful – use the money changers on the street.

Visas are available on the border and there are a couple of ropy places to put your head down for the night.

### GETTING THERE & AWAY

Matatus make like the wind between Kisumu and Busia (KSh400) and also onward to Kampala.

## KABARNET
☎ 053

With a spectacular location on the eastern edge of the Kerio Valley, Kabarnet is one of many little towns nestled in the Tugen Hills. The journey from Marigat is absolutely stunning, with views right across the arid but tree-covered ridges and the region's valleys. Kabarnet is also the best launching point for treks into the Kerio Valley.

### Information

The Kenya Commercial Bank and Standard Chartered Bank are both in the town centre and have ATMs (Visa only). The local post office, also in the town centre, has cardphones.

## Sleeping & Eating

**Sinkoro Hotel** ( ☎ 22245; s/tw incl breakfast KSh600/1100)
This is a well-run, good value place that
even has a customer care hotline (you
guessed it – nobody answers). Some rooms
have huge views to the plains below and the
downstairs restaurant has all the staples for
KSh100 to KSh250.

**Sportsline Hotel** ( ☎ 21430; r KSh400) This is
a bargain for basic and bright singles. The
attached restaurant is equally bargain-like.

## Getting There & Away

Matatus/Peugeots serve Eldoret (KSh200/250,
two hours), Nakuru (KSh200/250, 2½ hours)
and Marigat (KSh150, 1¼ hours).

## LAKE KAMNAROK & KERIO VALLEY NATIONAL RESERVES

These two little-visited national reserves lie
in the heart of the beautiful Kerio Valley.
Prolific birdlife, crocodiles, wonderful landscapes and the chance to get totally off the
beaten track are the main attractions.

**Lake Kamnarok**, on Kerio River's eastern side,
is the more accessible of the two reserves, although there are absolutely no facilities. At
present you can walk anywhere on foot, but it
is best to take a ranger as a guide. It's possible
to cross into Kerio Valley National Reserve
from Kamnarok, but enquire ahead about
road conditions and access beforehand.

To reach Lake Kamnarok, go 25km north
up the rough dirt track from the village of
Cheploch, which sits just east of the Kerio
River on the Kabarnet–Iten road. A hard-
core 4WD is required in the dry season – an
amphibious tank during the rains.

## KITALE

☎ 054

Agricultural Kitale is a small and friendly
market town with a couple of interesting
museums and a bustling market. For travellers its main purpose is as a base for explor-
ations further afield – Mt Elgon and Saiwa
Swamp National Parks – and as a take-off
point for a trip up to the western side of
Lake Turkana.

## Information

**Barclays Bank** (Bank St) With ATM.
**On the Web Cyber Café** (Kenyatta St; per hr
KSh60; ⊙ 7.30-10.30) Open longer hours than most, this
is one of several reliable internet cafes in the same block.

**Post office** (Post Office Rd)
**Standard Chartered Bank** (Bank St) With ATM
(Visa only).
**Telkom Kenya** (Post Office Rd) Calling cards and
cardphones.

## Sights & Activities

### KITALE MUSEUM

Founded on the collection of butterflies,
birds and ethnographic memorabilia left to
the nation in 1967 by the late Lieutenant
Colonel Stoneham this **museum** ( ☎ 30996;
A1 Hwy; adult/child KSh500/250; ⊙ 8am-6pm) is one
of the more interesting in Kenya. There is
an interesting range of ethnographic displays of the Pokot, Akamba, Marakwet and
Turkana peoples and plenty of stuffed dead
things shot by various colonial types. The
outdoor exhibits include some traditional
tribal homesteads and a collection of snakes,
tortoises and crocodiles, plus an interesting
'Hutchinson Biogas Unit'.

The best thing here is the small **nature trail**
that leads through some not-quite-virgin
rainforest at the back of the museum. The
forest is teeming with birdlife, insects and
the odd colobus monkey.

### OLOF PALME AGROFORESTRY CENTRE

The **Olof Palme Agroforestry Centre** (A1 Hwy; admission free; ⊙ 8am-5pm) is a Swedish-funded
program aimed at educating local people
about protection and rehabilitation of the
environment by integrating trees into farming systems. The project includes a small
demonstration farm and agroforestry plot,
an information centre and an arboretum
containing 46 rare species of indigenous
trees; it's well worth a visit.

### TREASURES OF AFRICA MUSEUM

This private **museum** ( ☎ 30867; toam@multitechweb
.com; A1 Hwy; admission KSh250; ⊙ 9am-12pm & 2-5.30pm
Mon-Sat) is the personal collection of old Africa
hand Mr Wilson, a former colonial officer in
Uganda. Based mainly on the Karamojong of
northern Uganda, it illustrates his theory that
a universal worldwide agricultural culture existed as far back as the last Ice Age – far older
than was currently thought. Guided tours can
be arranged with advance notice.

## Sleeping

### BUDGET

**Hotel Mamboleo** ( ☎ 30850; Moi Ave; s/tw with shared
bathroom KSh300/500) This is the least revolting

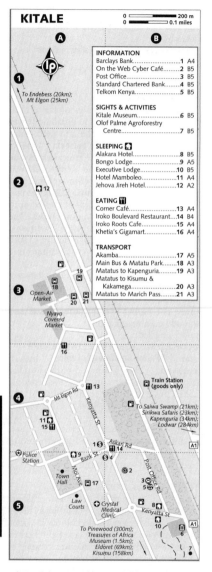

## KITALE

0 —————— 200 m
0 —————— 0.1 miles

**INFORMATION**
Barclays Bank.........................1 A4
On the Web Cyber Café.........2 B5
Post Office.............................3 B5
Standard Chartered Bank......4 B5
Telkom Kenya.........................5 B5

**SIGHTS & ACTIVITIES**
Kitale Museum.......................6 B5
Olof Palme Agroforestry
Centre.................................7 B5

**SLEEPING**
Alakara Hotel.........................8 B5
Bongo Lodge.........................9 A5
Executive Lodge...................10 B5
Hotel Mamboleo...................11 A4
Jehova Jireh Hotel.................12 A2

**EATING**
Corner Café..........................13 A4
Iroko Boulevard Restaurant....14 B4
Iroko Roots Cafe...................15 A4
Khetia's Gigamart.................16 A4

**TRANSPORT**
Akamba................................17 A5
Main Bus & Matatu Park.......18 A3
Matatus to Kapenguria..........19 A3
Matatus to Kisumu &
Kakamega.........................20 A3
Matatus to Marich Pass.........21 A3

To Endebess (20km);
Mt Elgon (25km)

Open-Air
Market

Nyayo
Covered
Market

Train Station
(goods only)

Mt Elgon Rd

Kenyatta St

To Saiwa Swamp (21km);
Sirikwa Safaris (23km);
Kapenguria (34km);
Lodwar (284km)

Askari Rd

A1

Police
Station

Bank St

Moi Ave

Post Office Rd

Town
Hall

Law
Courts

Crystal
Medical
Clinic

Kenyatta St

A1

To Pinewood (300m);
Treasures of Africa
Museum (1.5km);
Eldoret (69km);
Kisumu (158km)

of Kitale's true cheapies. The rooms upstairs are a little brighter than the cell-like options below.

**Executive Lodge** (☎ 31782; Kenyatta St; s/tw KSh500/700) You can't really fault these shockingly cheap rooms situated around a large courtyard. However, get one as far away from the noisy bar as possible.

**Bongo Lodge** (☎ 30972; Moi Ave; s/d/tw KSh600/600/800) Stop wasting time and come straight here if you want to get your hands on the best budget beds in town. All rooms have bathrooms and are scrupulously clean.

### MIDRANGE

**Alakara Hotel** (☎ 31554; Kenyatta St; s with/without bathroom KSh1000/700, d with/without bathroom KSh1300/1000) We came, we saw, we liked. The comfortable rooms have phones, the staff are friendly and prices include breakfast. It has a good bar, restaurant, TV room and parking facilities.

**Jehova Jireh Hotel** (☎ 31752; s/tw KSh1500/1700) A solid midrange choice close to the colourful markets and just off the A1 Hwy. Rooms are spacious, quiet and clean and, don't worry, it's not as God-fearing as it sounds. There's an excellent downstairs restaurant that serves food later than most.

**Pinewood** (☎ 30011; A1 Hwy; s/d/tw KSh1500/2000/2500) The best place to rest weary eyes is in one of the wooden huts on offer here. The quality of the very comfortable rooms actually isn't that far off some of the national park lodges, but unlike those, you won't see any lions from your terrace, although you might see some domestic cats, which if viewed through binoculars look kind of similar.

## Eating & Drinking

**Corner Café** (Kenyatta St; meals KSh60-130; ⏰ lunch & dinner) Bright, cheap and cheerful, this place, located inside a lovely old colonial building, has all the standards for standard prices.

**Iroko Roots Cafe** (Moi Ave; meals KSh100-150; ⏰ lunch & dinner) Feeling more like a coffee shop in the Rocky Mountains, this spotless, unique place serves up great Kenyan dishes and is perfect for breakfast.

**Iroko Boulevard Restaurant** (Askari Rd; meals KSh120-200; ⏰ lunch & dinner) It's got style, it's got glamour, it's got big-city aspirations and it's totally unexpected in Kitale. With cheap dishes that include a different African special every day and an old Morris car hanging from the ceiling this is easily the best (and most popular) place to eat in town. You may even have to queue for a table!

**Pinewood** (A1 Hwy; mains KSh200; ⏰ lunch & dinner) Posh new place for Indian or Chinese fare (complete with fresh ginger). Sit outside with views of Mt Elgon or head inside to the plethora of pine. The pub here has live music at weekends.

**Khetia's Gigamart** ( 7.30am-7pm) Stock up at this massive supermarket.

## Getting There & Away

Matatus, buses and Peugeots are grouped by destination, and spread in and around the main bus and matatu park.

Regular matatus run to Endebess (KSh100 to KSh150, 45 minutes), Kapenguria (KSh100, 45 minutes), Eldoret (KSh150 to KSh200, 1¼ hours) and Kakamega (KSh250, two hours). Less regular services reach Mt Elgon National Park (KSh100, one hour), Nakuru (KSh450, 3½ hours) and Kisumu (KSh450, four hours).

Most bus companies have offices around the bus station and serve Eldoret (KSh150, one hour), Nakuru (KSh400, 3½ hours) and Nairobi (KSh700, six hours).

Several buses now run up to Lodwar (KSh1200, 8½ hours) each day.

**Akamba** (Moi Ave) runs buses from outside its office to Nairobi at 8.30am (KSh1000, nine hours).

## MT ELGON NATIONAL PARK

Peaking with Koitoboss (4187m), Kenya's second-highest peak, and Uganda's Wagagai (4321m), the forested slopes of Mt Elgon, which straddles the border, is a sight indeed and offers superb trekking.

Despite its lower altitude making conditions less extreme than Mt Kenya, Elgon sees a fraction of its bigger cousin's visitors. Not least because of its wetter weather and, recently, a dicey security situation, which even led to the park being closed in the latter half of 2007. Fortunately, the situation has improved considerably and the mountain is once again back open for business.

While rarely seen, the mountain's most famous attractions are the elephants known for their predilection for digging salt out of the lower eastern slopes' caves. Sadly, the number of these saline-loving creatures has declined over the years, mainly due to incursions by Ugandan poachers.

Four main lava tubes (caves) are open to visitors: **Kitum**, **Chepnyalil**, **Mackingeny** and **Rongai**. Kitum holds your best hope for glimpsing elephants (especially before dawn), while Mackingeny, with a waterfall cascading across the entrance, is the most spectacular.

The mountain's fauna and flora are also great attractions. With rainforest at the base,

the vegetation changes as you ascend, to bamboo jungle and finally alpine moorland featuring the giant groundsel and giant lobelia plants. Common animals include buffaloes, bushbucks, olive baboons, giant forest hogs and duikers, while Defassa waterbucks are also present. The lower forests are the habitat of the black-and-white colobus, and blue and de Brazza's monkeys.

There are more than 240 species of birds here, including red-fronted parrots, Ross's turacos and casqued hornbills. On the peaks you may even see a lammergeier raptor gliding through the thin air.

## Information

The **park** (adult/child US$25/10) is wet much of the year, but driest between December and February. As well as bringing waterproof gear, you will need warm clothes, as it gets cold up here at night. Altitude may also be a problem for some people.

Access to the 169-sq-km national park is permitted without a vehicle. Indeed, walking is the best way to get around, as the roads are treacherous.

Due to the odd elephant, a **ranger** (per half/full day KSh500/1000) must escort you on walks on the lower slopes, such as to the caves.

For trekking the higher slopes you will need a tent and all your own camping gear. A **guide** (per day KSh1000) is also essential (see p322 for general advice).

Lonely Planet's *Trekking in East Africa* has more details on the various trekking and walking routes.

## Trekking

Check out the security situation with **KWS headquarters** ( Nairobi 020-600800; kws@kws.org; PO Box 40241, Nairobi) in Nairobi or **Mt Elgon National Park** ( 054-31456; PO Box 753, Kitale) before you plan anything. Crossing into Uganda isn't currently permitted, but ask for the latest at the gate.

Allow at least four days for any round trip and two or three days for any direct ascent of **Koitoboss** if you're walking from the Chorlim gate.

The **Park Route** offers some interesting possibilities and there is a well-worn route from Chorlim gate up to Koitoboss Peak that requires one or two overnight camps.

Descending, you have a number of options. You can descend northwest into the crater to **Suam Hot Springs**. Alternatively you could go

WESTERN KENYA

# MT ELGON NATIONAL PARK

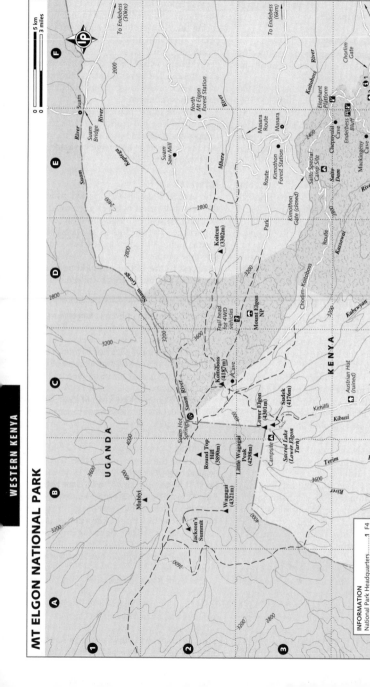

**INFORMATION**
National Park Headquarters.........1  F4

**SLEEPING**
Chorlim Campsite.........................2  F4
Kapkuro Bandas...........................3  F4
Nyati Campsite.............................4  F4
Rongai Campsite...........................5  F4

---

### MT ELGON VIOLENCE

Since 2005 the area around Mt Elgon has seen a violent uprising that has left around 600 people dead and thousands displaced. The Sabot Land Defence Force (SLDF) was formed in 2005 to resist government attempts to evict squatters in the Chebyuk area of Mt Elgon. It quickly resorted to intimidation and widespread violence against those who opposed them. This reportedly included murder, rape, theft and torture – a favourite tactic was cutting the ear off a victim and forcing them to eat it. There have also been many reported incidents of gang rape, as well as the use of child soldiers. In March 2008 the Kenyan military launched a major operation to bring a halt to the insurgency: though initially welcomed by the general populace, they themselves now face widespread accusations of human rights abuses, including murder, rape and torture.

With the killing of the SLDF leader in May 2008 things began to calm down and, at the time of research, major operations appeared to be over, but check the security situation very carefully if travelling to the Mt Elgon area.

---

east around the crater rim and descend the **Masara Route**, which leads to the small village of Masara on the eastern slopes of the mountain (about 25km) and then returns to Endebess. Or you can head southwest around the rim of the crater (some very hard walking) to **Lower Elgon Tarn**, where you can camp before ascending **Lower Elgon Peak** (4301m).

### Sleeping

If you're trekking, your only option is to **camp** (adult/child US$8/5). This fee is the same whether you drop tent in the official campsites or on any old flat spot during your trek.

**Chorlim campsite**, next to the Chorlim gate, has the park's best facilities but is less scenic than the other two public sites, Nyati and Rongai.

**Kapkuro Bandas** (per banda US$30) These excellent stone bandas can sleep three people in two beds and have simple bathrooms and small kitchen areas.

### Getting There & Away

Sporadic matatus and Peugeots now reach the Chorlim gate from Kitale (KSh100, one hour). More regular services reach Endebess (KSh100 to KSh150, 45 minutes), a 9km walk from the gate. Locals will happily point you in the right direction.

## SAIWA SWAMP NATIONAL PARK

This small and rarely visited **park** (adult/child US$20/10) north of Kitale is a real treat. Originally set up to preserve the habitat of the *nzohe*, also known as the sitatunga antelope, the 3-sq-km reserve is also home to blue, vervet and de Brazza's monkeys and some 370 species of birds. The fluffy black-and-white colobus and the impressive crowned crane are both present, and you may see the Cape clawless and spot-throated otters.

The best part is that this tiny park is only accessible on foot. Walking trails skirt the swamp, duckboards go right across it, and there are some extremely rickety observation towers.

### Sleeping

**Public campsite** (adult/child US$15/10) A lovely site with flush toilets, showers and two covered cooking bandas.

**our pick Sirikwa Safaris** ( ☎ 0737133170; sirikwa barnley@swiftkenya.com; camping KSh450, tents KSh900, farmhouse with shared bathroom s/d KSh3000/4000) Owned and run by the family that started Saiwa, this is a beautiful old farmhouse lost in the green hills north of Kitale, a few kilometres from the swamp. You can chose between camping in the grounds, sleeping in a well-appointed safari tent or, best of all, opting for one of the two bedrooms full of piles of National Geographic magazines, old ornaments and antique sinks. The mother and daughter who run it will entertain you for hours with stories from their more than 70 years in Kenya, and equally entertaining are the English country gardens – just sit and smile. Wholesome, though fairly expensive, home-cooked food is available. Excursions can be arranged, including ornithological tours of the Cherangani Hills and Saiwa Swamp (bird guides KSh900 per half-day).

### Getting There & Away

The park is 18km northeast of Kitale; take a matatu towards Kapenguria (KSh100, 30 minutes) and get out at the signposted turn-off,

**WESTERN KENYA**

from where it is a 5km walk or KSh50 *moto-taxi* (motorcycle taxi) ride.

## CHERANGANI HILLS

Northeast of Kitale, forming the western wall of the spectacular **Elgeyo Escarpment**, are the Cherangani Hills. This high plateau has a distinctly pastoral feel, with thatched huts, patchwork *shambas* (small farm plots) and wide rolling meadows cut by babbling brooks. You could easily spend weeks absorbed in the utter beauty of this landscape and never come across a single tourist.

You won't be alone here, though, as the plateau is home to the interesting Marakwet (or 'Markweta') people (part of the greater Kalenjin group), who migrated here from the north (see also p40). The Marakwet settled here because the area was secure and the consistent rainfall and streams were ideal for agriculture.

There are a couple of great five-day **treks**, namely from Kabichbich to Chesengoch and Kapcherop to Sigor. These two treks are detailed in Lonely Planet's *Trekking in East Africa;* for information on some of the shorter hikes in the northern reaches of the Cherangani Hills, see p249.

### Getting There & Away

Kabichbich is best reached from Kapenguria by matatu (KSh150, 1¼ hours), and Kapcherop is accessible from Kitale with patience and a matatu change in Cherangani. You can walk to the northern part of the hills from Marich Pass Field Studies Centre (p249).

# Central Highlands

Cut Kenya and she bleeds soil. It is the land the Mau Mau fought for, that lies at the heart of lingering communal tensions, and captures the dreams of both Nairobi-bound business-men and farmers scratching the earth.

And if the land is this nation's blood, that essence runs deepest in this place of wet air and long shadows. The Central Highlands are the fertile, mist- and rain-fattened breadbasket of a nation, and the green-girt, red-dirt spiritual heartland of that country's largest tribe, the Kikuyu.

In these valleys lay the blessed, best fields of people still tied to agriculture, where the cyclical patterns of nature mirror slow rhythms of movement. The latter is etched into the steps of the highlands' easily identifiable residents: the wobbly lope of twisty-horned cattle over sweet grass, the weary squelch of gumboots in mud as labourers head into the fields and the gossipy bounce of a matron decked in her Sunday best coming home from church.

The prime attraction here is Kirinyaga, the Mountain of Mysteries (or Ostriches, depending on who's translating). Better known as Mt Kenya, this icy massif dominates the small towns and *shambas* (farm plots) scattered in its shadow, which also creeps over some of the nation's most stunning, and least visited, national parks.

This is where queens are crowned, impregnated and overthrown (see boxed text, p201); chewing branches leads to building castles (see p222); water drains in a straight line (see boxed text, p219); boys become men; and people worship God but keep their doors open to the Mountain. Most of all, it's a land the Kikuyu call home, and that's reason enough for you to visit.

## HIGHLIGHTS

- Singing the opening song of *The Lion King* as the sun rises over **Meru National Park** (p222)
- Holding a frozen Kenyan flag in your frozen hands atop the frozen summit of Point Lenana on **Mt Kenya** (p208), 16km from the equator
- Living like a Somali nomad at **Nanyuki River Camel Camp** (p217)
- Playing 'dodge the elephant' in **Aberdare National Park** (p204)
- Eating *githeri* (beans, corns and meat) with the Kikuyu in their homeland

## History

After most likely arriving from West or Central Africa, the ancestors of the Kikuyu, like the *wazungu* (white) settlers who arrived in the 19th century, recognised a good thing when they saw it: the incredibly fertile soil of the slopes of Mt Kenya. Hunter-gathers and pastoralists became farmers who lived fat off the land.

Said land became the ripest plum for colonial picking when European newcomers filtered into East Africa. Failing farms in other parts of Kenya magnetised *wazungu* into the highlands, and in the 1880s the Kikuyu were displaced from their homes to make way for white agriculture and the Mombasa–Uganda railway.

Having born the brunt of colonialism's abuses, the Kikuyu shouldered much of the burden of nationalism's struggle and formed the core of the Mau Mau uprising in the 1950s (see p28). That struggle was largely fought in Highland valleys, and the abuses of the anti-insurgency campaign were largely felt by Highland civilians. While even the staunchest patriot cannot claim the Mau Mau won the uprising, the movement, combined with the general dismantling of the British Empire, forced colonial authorities to reassess their position and eventually abandon Kenya.

It was a Kikuyu, Jomo Kenyatta, who assumed presidency of the new country, and the Kikuyu, widely recognised (even by grudging rivals) as one of the hardest-working, most business-savvy tribes in Kenya, who assumed control of the nation's economy. Incidentally, they also reclaimed their rich fields in the Central Highlands, a move which has been the source of no little tension in Kenya to this day. Many *wazungu* farmers remain, and their huge plots can be seen stretching all along the highways between Timau, Meru and Nanyuki.

## Climate

The Central Highlands might the most agreeable climate in the country. Average temperatures rarely exceed 23°C and nights are pleasantly cool, bordering on kind of cold if you're coming from hotter parts of Africa. Rain falls in two seasons: March to the beginning of June (the 'long rains') and October to the end of November (the 'short rains'). Dry zones are scattered throughout this generally lush land, notably near Thika and Kamburu Dam.

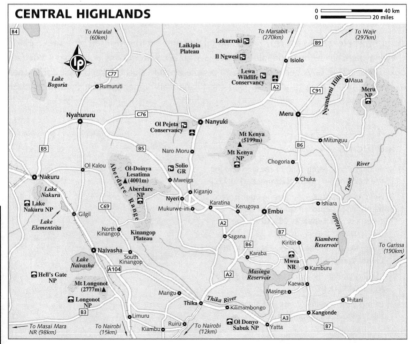

CENTRAL HIGHLANDS

---

**THE NINE-MONTH COUP**

During the colonial period, the appointed leaders of tribal Africa were headmen and, by and large, men they were (and, usually, remain). But there's one exception from the history books, a woman who both reversed the constraints of her sex and, if the unusual story behind her removal from power is to be believed, fell prey to the pitfalls of gender in a way only a woman could appreciate.

These are the facts as we know them: Wangu wa Makeri was a Kikuyu, born in the second half of the 19th century. In 1901 she was appointed headman of Weithaga, the only female ruler in colonial Kenya. Accounts agree she was a rigid and authoritarian ruler, but whether or not this was a good thing seems to have been a matter of opinion, largely determined by the presence or lack of a Y chromosome. Wangu made a point of literally using men as furniture, discarding traditional Kikuyu stools for the backs of Kikuyu males. Perhaps unsurprisingly, stories suggest her rule was warmly approved of by Kikuyu women.

And so the wily (and, more pertinently, fertile) men of the Kikuyu tribe hatched a plot, one of the most unique coups in history (disclaimer: we are now leaving the realm of history and entering the more entertaining, if less reliable, space of tribal folklore). They all did their husbandly duty and impregnated their wives, including Wangu, more or less simultaneously. This ensured that in nine months, the chief and her supporters were either in labour, nursing or too heavily pregnant to prevent the re-ascendancy of male Kikuyu-dom.

Additional rumour holds there was a drastic shortage of pickles in ice cream in Kikuyu-land during this period.

---

## National Parks

Saying you risked frostbite in Africa can definitely score you accolades and drinks at the local pub, and one of the best places to do so (risk frostbite, not score drinks) is Mt Kenya National Park (p208). This is more than Kenya's highest mountain: it's the spiritual compass of many Kikuyu, home of unique alpine flora and fauna and the region's biggest attraction besides. Meru National Park (p222), which contains both riverine jungle and open savanna, is one of Kenya Wildlife Services' (KWS) best-kept (or perhaps worst-publicised) secrets. Aberdare National Park (p204) is similarly packed with wildlife and great natural beauty, but here the landscape veers between dark, clotted jungle and wind-blown moors. The tiny national park of Ol Donyo Sabuk (p225) straddles its namesake hill and plays home to buffaloes, birdlife and primates.

## Getting There & Away

### AIR

Daily **Airkenya** ( ☎ 020-606539; www.airkenya.com) and **Safarilink** ( ☎ 020-600777; www.safarilink.co.ke) services link Nanyuki with Nairobi (Wilson Airport), and Airkenya also flies daily to Meru National Park. See Getting There & Away under the relevant sections for more details.

### BUS & MATATU

The Central Highlands are linked to Nairobi, western Kenya and the southern reaches of northern Kenya by countless matatus (minibuses) and regular bus services. Limited bus services also connect to Mombasa.

## Getting Around

Plenty of buses and matatus ply the routes between all major towns and many minor ones as well, but to get to (and through) the national parks off the beaten track, you'll need your own wheels. Everyone says Central Province has the best roads in Kenya, and the main highways are decent, but they're not the Autobahn a lot of expats seem to describe either. Roads weren't that safe after dark; hold-ups were uncommon but frequent enough to merit caution during our visit. The A2 and B6 highways run a ring around Mt Kenya.

# ABERDARES

The cloud-kissed contours of these brown-and-grey slopes, dubbed Nyandarua (Drying Hide) by the Kikuyu, are deceptively round and inviting. But with an average elevation of 3350m, the Aberdares are no soft foothills.

Stretching 160km from South Kinangop, east of Naivasha, up to the Laikipia Escarpment northwest of Nyahururu, the Aberdares form the solid spine of western Central Province, and were a popular base for Mau Mau fighters during the independence struggle.

The tallest regions of this range can claim some of Kenya's most dramatic up-country scenery, packed with 300m waterfalls, dense forests and serious trekking potential. The fuzzy moors in particular possess a stark, wind-carved beauty, wholly unexpected after driving up from the richly cultivated plots of the eastern Aberdares. In contrast, the western high country has been left to leopards, buffaloes, warthogs, lions and elephants, and remains one of Kenya's best places to spot black rhinos.

European settlers established coffee and tea plantations on the eastern side of the Aberdares and wheat and pyrethrum (chrysanthemum) farms on the western slopes.

## NYERI & AROUND
☎ 061

Nyeri is sort of the epitome of a busy Kikuyu market town, and is as welcoming and bustling as the Central Highlands gets. With that said, there's not much reason to linger for more than a day or two unless you have a thing for chaotic open-air bazaars and the mad energy of Kikuyu and white Kenyans selling maize, bananas, arrowroot, coffee and macadamia nuts. Or if you're like Boy Scout founder Lord Baden-Powell, who died here and once wrote, 'The nearer to Nyeri, the nearer to bliss.'

### Information

There are three post offices, two in the centre of town, and one near the lower bus stand.

**Barclays Bank** (cnr Sulukia & Sharpe Rds) Exchange cash and travellers cheques. With ATM.

**Kenya Commercial Bank** (Kenyatta Rd) With ATM (Visa only).

**Standard Chartered Bank** (Kenyatta Rd) With ATM (Visa only).

**Villa Cyber** (Kanisa Rd) Decently fast connection. It's opposite Central Hotel.

### Sights & Activities
#### SOLIO GAME RESERVE

This family-run, private 17,500-acre **reserve** (☎ 55271; B5 Hwy; adult/child/vehicle KSh1600/free/500),

22km north of Nyeri, is both one of the best places in Kenya to spot black rhinos and an important breeding centre for the species besides. Rhinos are regularly transported from here to other reserves, and most of the horned beasts you see wandering national parks were actually born here. Sadly, rhinos are popular poacher fare; their horns are used in Eastern medicines and for Arabic dagger hilts, but here, at least, they thrive, along with oryxes, gazelles, hartebeests, giraffes, lions, hyenas and buffaloes. The physical contours of the park, which run between clumps of yellow acacia, wide skies and wild marsh, are lovely in and of themselves. Self-drive safaris are permitted, with free maps available at the front gate.

#### BADEN-POWELL MUSEUM

Lord Baden-Powell, the founder of the International Scout Association, spent his last three years at Paxtu cottage in the Outspan Hotel. The ultimate scoutmaster's retirement was somewhat poetic; to 'outspan' is to unhook your oxen at the end of a long journey, and, as Baden-Powell's former home was named 'Pax' (peace) in honour of Armistice Day after WWI, it made sense to dub his second digs 'Paxtu'. Famed tiger-hunter Jim Corbett later occupied the grounds. Baden-Powell's grave, tucked behind **St Peter's Church** (B5 Hwy) faces Mt Kenya and is marked with the Scouts trail sign for 'I have gone home'. Paxtu is now a **museum** (off Map p203; admission KSh300; ☯ 8am-6pm) filled with scouting paraphernalia and great mid-20th-century photos. It's located about 1km west of town.

### Sleeping
#### BUDGET & MIDRANGE

**Paresia Hotel** (☎ 0720986142; off Gakere Rd; s/tw KSh400/700) With its red cement floors and blue linoleum showers, Paresia is as colourful as it is cheap, and a good option if you're willing to go a little cheaper for a little more Third World discomfit. It's located right behind the main market.

**Green Oaks** (☎ 2030093; off Kimathi Way; r KSh500) This is as centrally located as Nyeri sleeps come; not only are you located directly above the main matatu stands and taxi ranks, there's a hopping restaurant on site. You'll need good noise tolerance, but the rooms themselves are clean and comfy.

**Central Hotel** (☎ 2030296; Kanisa Rd; s/tw incl breakfast KSh800/900) The Central has quiet, largish

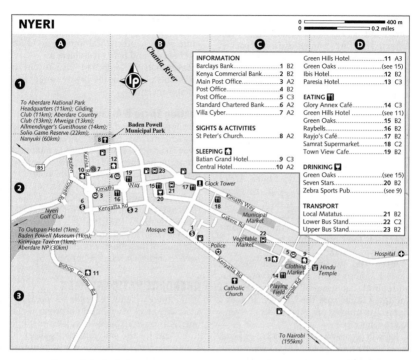

# NYERI

0 ——————— 400 m
0 ——————— 0.2 miles

**INFORMATION**
Barclays Bank..........................1 B2
Kenya Commercial Bank.........2 B2
Main Post Office.....................3 A2
Post Office..............................4 B2
Post Office..............................5 C3
Standard Chartered Bank........6 A2
Villa Cyber.............................7 A2

**SIGHTS & ACTIVITIES**
St Peter's Church....................8 A2

**SLEEPING**
Batian Grand Hotel.................9 C3
Central Hotel........................10 A2

Green Hills Hotel..................11 A3
Green Oaks .......................(see 15)
Ibis Hotel............................12 B2
Paresia Hotel.......................13 C3

**EATING**
Glory Annex Café.................14 C3
Green Hills Hotel ..............(see 11)
Green Oaks..........................15 B2
Raybells...............................16 B2
Rayjo's Café.........................17 B2
Samrat Supermarket.............18 C2
Town View Cafe...................19 B2

**DRINKING**
Green Oaks .......................(see 15)
Seven Stars..........................20 B2
Zebra Sports Pub...............(see 9)

**TRANSPORT**
Local Matatus.......................21 B2
Lower Bus Stand...................22 C2
Upper Bus Stand...................23 B2

rooms with comfy beds, balconies and clean toilets; that's pretty good value for money in this town. There's a desultory on-site restaurant; drunken patrons are thrown in for free.

**Ibis Hotel** ( ☎ 2034858; Kanisa Rd; s/tw KSh800/1000) Located in a building with a surprisingly grand facade (it's not that opulent on the inside), Ibis has comfortable and clean rooms with brilliant power-showers.

**Batian Grand Hotel** ( ☎ 2030743; batianhotel@wanachi.com; Gakere Rd; s/tw KSh1500/2200) This is a bit of a grand title for a fairly mediocre midrange sleep, but the higher up rooms give you a good view of Mt Kenya (on a clear day).

**Green Hills Hotel** ( ☎ 2030604; Bishop Gatimu Rd; s/tw from KSh1900/3300; ☒ ) The best deal in town is actually a little ways out of Nyeri. The small drive is worth it for the palm-lined, poolside ambience and general sense of serenity located a few minutes and several levels of peace from Nyeri's crazy core.

## TOP END
**Allmendinger's Guesthouse** (Sandai; Map p205; ☎ 0721656699; http://africanfootprints.de; s/tw full

board US$98/148) Run by a German couple, Allmendinger's (the homestead is technically called Sandai, but most people in town use the former name) is a pleasantly eccentric and extremely cosy lodge. Inside, the owner's artwork fills the place, and there are locally run horse safaris, which are an excellent way of getting up close and personal with Aberdares' wildlife.

**Aberdare Country Club** (Map p205; ☎ 2055620, in Nairobi 020-3742744; www.choiceswild.com; s/tw full board low season US$87/172, high season US$162/230; ☒ ) Surrounded by its own 500-hectare sanctuary east of Mweiga, the stately stone club sits atop a hill and proffers glorious views. It's one of the more luxurious options in this corner of Kenya.

**Outspan Hotel** (Map p205; ☎ 2032424, 0722207762; www.aberdaresafarihotels.com; r $180-225) This rather gorgeous lodge tries to impart the character of an old-school highland colonial retreat, and does a pretty good job of it, too. Nineteen of the 34 standard rooms have cosy fireplaces, and all have a whiff of historical class. The on-site Kirinyaga club gets pretty crazy on weekends.

## Eating

**Rayjo's Cafe** (Kimathi Way; meals KSh50-140; ☺ lunch & dinner) This tiny canteen is usually packed with customers, including bus and matatu drivers, who are always good judges of cheap places to eat. It's perfect for small snacks and sandwiches.

**Glory Annex Cafe** (Behind clothing market; meals KSh50-170; ☺ lunch & dinner) A cheap and cheerful African restaurant packed with happy customers downing the usual chicken and chips fare.

**Town View Cafe** (Kimathi Way; meals KSh80-200; ☺ 6am-11pm) There's a heavy Mama Africa vibe going on here, both with the menu (*nyama choma* – barbecued meat – galore) and the colourful decor. The dining room ain't open air, but it does, as the cafe's name promises, look out onto a breezy view of 'downtown' Nyeri.

**Green Oaks** (off Kimathi Way; meals KSh80-220; ☺ lunch & dinner) this is the locals' favourite, with a lively bar and good vantage point over the taxi stands from the balcony. It does a mean chai, which is pretty warming on Nyeri's many rainy days.

**Raybells** (Kimathi Way; meals KSh120-380; ☺ lunch & dinner) Pretty much anything you want to eat (well, anything Kenyan or Western), from pizza to *choma,* is available and cooked passably well here. The presence of fresh juice (surprisingly rare in this agricultural town) is very welcome.

**Green Hills Hotel** (Bishop Gatimu Rd; buffets KSh650; ☺ lunch & dinner) As with accommodation, so with food: Green Hills dominates again. The full buffet is an impressive piece of work, with some tasty mixed-grill options done up in a satisfyingly fancy fashion.

**Samrat Supermarket** (off Kimathi Way) The best-stocked supermarket in town.

## Drinking

**Green Oaks** (off Kimathi Way) The friendliest bar in town, usually with European football on the box, but like every other joint in town it gets rowdy as the night wears on.

**Kirinyaga Tavern** (Outspan Hotel) While located behind the posh hotel's gates, Kirinyaga is actually separate from the hotel's bar. It has a bonfire and traditional dancing on Saturday nights and is pretty much the spot for those seeking a little upmarket atmosphere with their Tusker.

**Zebra Sports Pub** (Batian Grand Hotel, Gakere Rd) This self-proclaimed sports bar is pretty much the same as every other local lounge; good for sinking beer and light on ambience.

**Seven Stars** (off Kimathi Way) Next to Green Oaks, this place is of the rowdy variety and suitably messy.

## Getting There & Away

The upper bus stand deals with big buses and sporadic matatus to most places, while the lower stand houses local buses and a multitude of matatus heading in all directions. Some local matatus are also found on Kimathi Way.

Matatus run to Nanyuki (KSh150, one hour), Nyahururu (KSh230, 1¼ hours), Thika (KSh200, two hours), Nakuru (KSh300, 2½ hours), Nairobi (KSh300, 2½ hours) and Eldoret (KSh700, eight hours). Buses duplicate most of these lines; you may occasionally have to change at Karatina for Nairobi.

## ABERDARE NATIONAL PARK

While there's plenty of reason to wax rhapsodic over herds of wildlife thundering over an open African horizon, there's also something to be said for the soil-your-pants shock of seeing an elephant thunder out of bush that was, minutes before, just plants.

And that's why people love Aberdare National Park. Camera reflexes are tested as the abundant wildlife pops unexpectedly out of bushes, including elephants, buffaloes, black rhinos, spotted hyenas, bongo antelope, bush pigs, black servals and rare black leopards.

And baboons. Lots and lots of baboons.

The park has two major environments: an eastern hedge of thick rainforest and waterfall-studded hills known as the Salient, and the Kinangop Plateau, an open tableland of coarse moors that huddles under cold mountain breezes.

## Information

To enter the **park** (adult/child US$50/25) through the Treetops or Ark gates, ask permission at **national park headquarters** (☎ 061-2055465/024; Mweiga, PO Box 753, Nyeri). Smartcard is supposedly required, but enforcement was lax as of our visit. Excellent 1:25,000 maps (KSh450), which are essential if you are on a self-drive safari, are available at the gates. Note that during the rains roads get rough, and the numbered navigation posts in the Salient are often difficult to follow.

## Activities

The high moorland and four main peaks (all 3500m to 4000m) are excellent **trekking** spots; the tallest mountain in the park is Ol Donyo Lesatima, a popular bag for those on the East African mountain circuit. Between Honi Campsite and Elephant Ridge is the site of the hideout of Mau Mau leader Dedan Kimathi, who used these mountains as a base; many of his companions learned the ropes of jungle warfare fighting in Burma in WWII.

To trek the Salient you'll need advance permission from the warden at park headquarters, who'll provide an armed ranger (KSh1500/2500 half day/day) to guide and protect you against inquisitive wildlife.

## Sleeping

### BUDGET & MIDRANGE

The following accommodation must be booked through park headquarters.

**Public campsites** (adult/child US$25/15) Basic sites with minimal facilities – some have water.

**Sapper Hut** (banda US$50) A simple banda, with an open fire, two beds and a hot-water boiler, overlooking a lovely waterfall on the Upper Magura River. It's best to bring your own gear.

**Tusk Camp** (cottages Jan-Jun US$100, Jul-Dec US$120) Four dark and cosy alpine cottages located near Ruhuruini gate sleep eight to 10 people. The lounge area is comfy, there're great views (if the fog hasn't rolled in), and plenty of

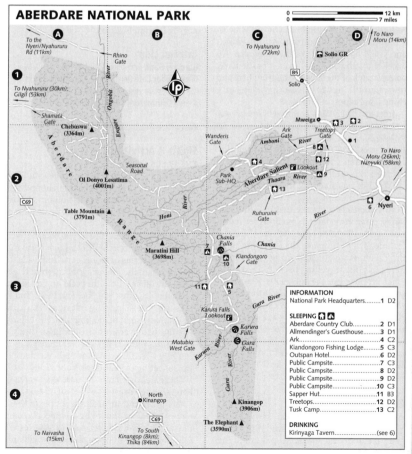

**ABERDARE NATIONAL PARK**

0   12 km
0   7 miles

CENTRAL HIGHLANDS

rhinos around to boot. Hot water, blankets, kerosene lamps, a gas cooker and some utensils are provided, but bring your own equipment (plus water and firewood) to be safe.

**Kiandongoro Fishing Lodge** (cottages Jan-Jun US$200, Jul-Dec US$230) Two large stone houses sleep seven people each and command a good view of the moors that sweep into the Gura River. There are two bathrooms in each house, and all utensils and linens are provided, along with gas-powered kitchens, paraffin cookers and fireplaces.

**TOP END**

**Ark** ( ☎ 0724478058, in Nairobi 020-216940; www.choiceswild.com; s/tw full board low season US$150/210, high season US$180/250) The Ark is more modern (1960s as opposed to 1950s chic) and roomier than Treetops, and has a lounge that overlooks a waterhole. Watch buffalo as you sip wine in a moulded chair lifted from *Austin Powers* and you'll have an idea of the ambience. An excellent walkway leads over a particularly dense stretch of the Salient, and from here and the waterhole lounge you can spot elephants, rhinos, buffaloes and hyenas.

**Treetops** ( ☎ 020-3242425; www.aberdaresafarihotels.com; s/tw with shared bathroom full board mid-Apr–mid-Jun US$168/225, mid-Jun–Nov & late Dec–early Jan US$277/348, all other times US$247/312) Trivia for royal-philes: Treetops isn't actually the spot where Princess Elizabeth became Queen Elizabeth II. Yes: Liz was sleeping in Treetops when George VI died in 1952, but in 1954 Mau Mau guerrillas blew the original lodge to twigs; three years later, a much larger rendition was built on the opposite side of the waterhole. 'Every time like the first time', goes the Treetops slogan, and we agree: sleeping here feels like travelling back to the day the place reopened in the late 1950s. Rooms are small and decorated in mid–20th century wood panelling/floral linens chic, but there is excellent wildlife-viewing and a sense of rusticity (and a little neglect) pervades. High rollers can splurge for the Queen Elizabeth 'suite', which has a picture of the monarch and – wait for it – a *double bed!* Two-hour wildlife drives will run you $45.

## Getting There & Away

Access roads from the B5 Hwy to the Wanderis, Ark, Treetops and Ruhuruini gates are in decent shape. Keep in mind that it takes a few hours to get from the Salient

to the moorlands and vice versa. Regular Nyeri–Mweiga matatus (KSh70, 35 minutes) pass the national park headquarters and the main park gates.

## NYAHURURU (THOMSON'S FALLS)
☎ 065

This unexpectedly attractive town leaps out of the northwest corner of the highlands and makes a decent base for exploring the western edge of the Aberdares. But Nyahururu has its own charms. Its former namesake, Thomson's Falls, are beautiful in their own right and offer an excellent day's worth of trekking options. And at 2360m, this is Kenya's highest major town, with a cool and invigorating climate that lends itself to thorough exploration of the small forested tracks that surround the falls and lead into friendly nearby farming villages.

### Information

**Barclays Bank** (cnr Sulukia & Sharpe Rds) With ATM.
**Clicks Cyber Cafe** (Mimi Centre, Kenyatta Rd; per hr KSh180) Best internet in town, which isn't saying much.
**Kenya Commercial Bank** (Sulukia Rd) With ATM (Visa only).
**Post office** (Sulukia Rd).

### Sights & Activities
**THE FALLS**
Set back in an evergreen river valley studded with sharp rocks and screaming baboons, the white cataracts of **Thomson's Falls** plummet over 72m and are the undeniable main attraction in the area.

The falls are fed by the Ewaso Narok River and can be approached by a fairly straight path over a series of stone steps that leads to the bottom of the ravine. Don't attempt to go down any other way, as the rocks on the side of the ravine are often very loose and wet. You'll be as well (wet), but a bit of drench is worth the dramatic sight of looking up at the falls as baboons pad over the surrounding cliffs. It's 45 minutes there and back, and there's a sign charging KSh100 to take the path, but no one was collecting this fee during our visit.

There are some fantastic **walks** downstream through the forested valley of the Ewaso Narok River and upstream a couple of kilometres to one of the highest hippo pools in Kenya. Guides are fairly easy to find, especially around the souvenir shacks overlooking the falls, but you'll have to bargain hard.

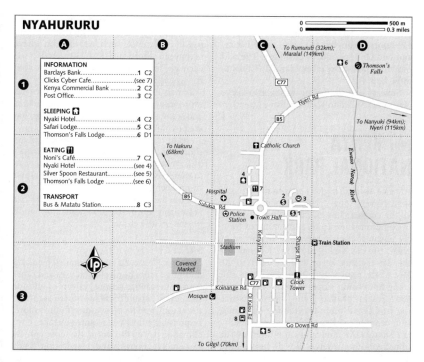

## NYAHURURU

0        500 m
0        0.3 miles

**INFORMATION**
Barclays Bank...................................1 C2
Clicks Cyber Cafe...........................(see 7)
Kenya Commercial Bank ...............2 C2
Post Office........................................3 C2

**SLEEPING**
Nyaki Hotel.....................................4 C2
Safari Lodge....................................5 C3
Thomson's Falls Lodge..................6 D1

**EATING**
Noni's Café......................................7 C2
Nyaki Hotel ...............................(see 4)
Silver Spoon Restaurant..............(see 5)
Thomson's Falls Lodge ...............(see 6)

**TRANSPORT**
Bus & Matatu Station....................8 C3

To Rumuruti (32km);
Maralal (149km)

Thomson's
Falls

C77

Nyeri Rd

B5

To Nanyuki (94km);
Nyeri (115km)

To Nakuru
(68km)

Catholic Church

Ewaso Narok River

Hospital

Sulukia Rd

Police
Station

Town Hall

Train Station

Kenyatta Rd

Shape Rd

Stadium

Covered
Market

C77

Koinange Rd

Clock
Tower

Ol Kalou Rd

Mosque

Go Down Rd

To Gilgil (70km)

## Sleeping

A hotelier's paradise it decidedly isn't, but Nyahururu does have one of the nicest budget options in the Central Highlands.

**Nyaki Hotel** ( ☎ 22313; off Kenyatta Rd; s/tw KSh350/800) This relatively modern five-storey building hosts small but comfy singles and large clean twins. There's hot-water showers and secure parking as well.

**our pick** **Safari Lodge** ( ☎ 22334, 0724485182; Go Down Rd; s/d KSh500/700) Well: clean toilets with *seats*, big, soft beds with couches in the rooms, a nice balcony, TV and a place to charge your phone? What did we do to deserve this luxury? Especially at this price, which makes Safari one of the best budget deals around.

**Thomson's Falls Lodge** ( ☎ 22006; www.tfalls.co.ke; off B5 Hwy; s/d incl breakfast KSh2500/3200) The undisputed nicest splurge in the area sits right above the falls and does a great job of instilling that good old, 'I'm a colonial aristocrat on hill country holiday' vibe. Rooms are spacious but cosy, thanks in no small part to the log fireplaces, and the best evening in Nyahururu is to be had here, enjoying the lounge, a drink and the falls.

## Eating

**Noni's Cafe** (Mimi Centre, Kenyatta Rd; meals KSh40-165; ⏲ breakfast, lunch & dinner) One of the cleanest and most welcoming of Nyahururu's local eateries is a good spot for breakfast and a semibracing coffee (or sticky sweet chai).

**Nyaki Hotel** (off Kenyatta Rd; meals KSh80-250; ⏲ lunch & dinner) Serves standard Kenyan fare in a standard Kenyan setting: bare bones, smiling service and the atmosphere of the moon.

**Silver Spoon Restaurant** (Go Down Rd; meals KSh80-250; ⏲ lunch & dinner) Located on the ground floor of the Safari Lodge, this is a friendly spot that serves up a decent beef curry and chips, along with all the other Central Highland staples.

**Thomson's Falls Lodge** (off B5 Hwy; breakfast/lunch/dinner KSh455/850/900; ⏲ breakfast, lunch & dinner) This is the best (and only) place in town to go for a fancy feast. There's a set buffet for each of the day's three meals, and while they're pricey for this area, you'll walk away well-stuffed and satisfied.

## Getting There & Away

There are numerous matatus that run to Nakuru (KSh120, 1¼ hours) and Nyeri

CENTRAL HIGHLANDS

(KSh230, 1¼ hours) until late afternoon. Less plentiful are services to Naivasha (KSh250, 1½ hours), Nanyuki (KSh300, three hours) and Nairobi (KSh300, three hours). The odd morning matatu reaches Maralal (KSh500, three hours).

Several early-morning buses also serve Nairobi (KSh250 to KsH350, three hours).

# MT KENYA NATIONAL PARK

Africa's second-highest mountain attracts spry trekkers, long, dramatic cloud cover and all the eccentricities of its mother continent in equal measure. Here, mere minutes from the equator, glaciers carve out the throne of Ngai, the old high god of the Kikuyu. To this day the tribe keeps its doors open to the face of the sacred mountain, and some still come to its lower slopes to offer prayers and the foreskins of their young men – this was the traditional place for holding circumcision ceremonies. Besides being venerated by the Kikuyu, Mt Kenya has the rare honour of being both a Unesco World Heritage site and a Unesco Biosphere Reserve.

In the past, 12 glaciers wore Mt Kenya down to 5199m worth of dramatic remnants, but today it is the ice itself that is under threat, disappearing under increased temperatures and taking with them crystalline caves and snowy crevasses. That means the climb up the mountain is easier than it has ever been – but by no means does it mean the ascent is easy.

The highest peaks of Batian (5199m) and Nelion (5188m) can only be reached by mountaineers with technical skills, but Point Lenana (4985m), the third-highest peak, can be reached by trekkers and is the usual goal for most mortals. The views are awe-inspiring – when they're not hemmed in by opaque mist.

If you're going to attempt to climb the king of Central Province, treat it with the utmost respect (see the boxed text, p322). If time is short or you don't want to do all the planning yourself, see p211.

## INFORMATION

The daily fees for the **national park** ( ☎ 061-55645; PO Box 753, Nyeri; adult/child US$55/20) are charged upon entry, so you must estimate the length of your stay. If you overstay, you pay the difference when leaving. You'll have to pay an additional KSh200 per day for each guide and porter you take with you. Always ask for a receipt.

Lonely Planet's *Trekking in East Africa* has more information, details on wilder routes and some of the more esoteric variations that are possible on Mt Kenya.

Technical climbers and mountaineers should get a copy of **Mountain Club of Kenya's** (MCK; ☎ Nairobi 020-602330; www.mck.or.ke) *Guide to Mt Kenya & Kilimanjaro*. This substantial and comprehensive guide is available in bookshops or from the MCK offices (p98). MCK also has reasonably up-to-date mountain information posted on its website.

## SAFETY

Many people ascend the mountain too quickly and suffer from headaches, nausea and other (sometimes more serious) effects of altitude sickness. By spending at least three nights on the ascent, you'll enjoy yourself much more; responsible guides will require you take an acclimation day on the way up the mountain. Be wary of hypothermia and dehydration; fluids and warm clothing go a long way towards preventing both.

Unpredictable weather is another problem. The trek to Point Lenana isn't an easy hike and people die on the mountain every year. Bring proper clothes and equipment; the best time to go is from mid-January to late February or from late Aùgust to September.

Unless you're a seasoned trekker with high-altitude experience and a good knowledge of reading maps and using a compass, you'd be flirting with death by not taking a guide or hiking with someone who isn't qualified. Even those with ample experience should take a guide on the Summit Circuit.

## CLOTHING & EQUIPMENT

Nightly temperatures near the summit often drop to below -10°C, so bring a good sleeping bag and a closed-cell foam mat or Therm-a-Rest if you're camping. A good set of warm clothes (wool or synthetics – never cotton, as it traps moisture) is equally important. As it can rain heavily any time of year, you'll need waterproof clothing (breathable fabric like Gore-Tex is best). A decent pair of boots and sandals or light shoes (for the evening when your boots get wet) are a great idea. At this altitude the sun can do some serious damage to your skin and eyes, so sunblock and sunglasses are also crucial items.

If a porter is carrying your backpack, always keep essential clothing (warm and wet weather gear) in your day pack because you may become separated for hours at a time.

It's not a good idea to sleep in clothes you've worn during the day because the sweat your clothes absorbed keeps them moist at night, reducing their heat-retention capabilities.

If you don't intend to stay in the huts along the way, you'll need a tent, stove, basic cooking equipment, utensils, a 3L water container (per person) and water-purifying tablets. Stove fuel in the form of petrol and kerosene (paraffin) is fairly easily found in towns, and methylated spirits is available in Nairobi, as are gas cartridges. Fires are prohibited in the open except in an emergency; in any case, there's no wood once you get beyond 3300m. If you engage porters, you'll have to supply each of them with a backpack.

If you have a mobile phone, take it along; reception on the mountain's higher reaches is actually very good, and a link to the outside world is invaluable during emergencies.

## GUIDES, COOKS & PORTERS

Having a porter for your gear is like travelling in a chauffeured Mercedes instead of a matatu. A good guide will help set a sustainable pace and hopefully dispense interesting information about Mt Kenya and its flora, fauna and wildlife. With both on your team, your appreciation of this mountain will be enhanced a hundredfold. If you hire a guide or porter who can also cook, you won't regret it.

Considerable effort has been made in recent years to regulate guides and porters operating on the mountain. The KWS now issues vouchers to all registered guides and porters, who should also hold identity cards; they won't be allowed into the park without them.

Female guides are becoming more common. Often, you'll be asked to hire a trekking guide for the first leg of the journey and a more expensive technical guide for the summit.

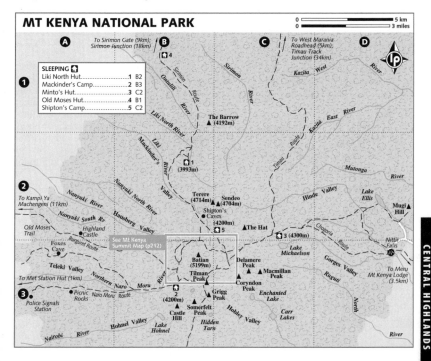

MT KENYA NATIONAL PARK

SLEEPING
Liki North Hut.....................1 B2
Mackinder's Camp................2 B3
Minto's Hut.........................3 C2
Old Moses Hut.....................4 B1
Shipton's Camp....................5 C2

## Costs

The cost of guides varies depending on the qualifications of the guide(s), whatever the last party paid and your own negotiating skills. You should expect to pay a minimum of US$20 per day for a basic guide, while technical climbing guides can cost as much as US$50 per day. Cooks and porters cost US$15 to US$20 per day. Agree on all costs before you depart.

These fees don't include park entry fees and tips, and the latter should only be paid for good service.

## SLEEPING

You can **camp** (adult/child US$15/10) anywhere on the mountain; the nightly fee is payable to KWS at any gate. Most people camp near the huts or bunk-houses, as there are often toilets and water nearby. KWS operates two more upscale lodges on the mountain: the surprisingly comfy stone **Sirimon Bandas** (Map p216; bandas US$80), which are located 9km from the Sirimon gates, and **Batian Guest House** (cottages US$180), a plush, four-bedroom cottage located a kilometre from Naro Moru gate. Reservations for both lodgings must be made through the KWS at ☎ 020-600800 or reservations@kws.org. You can also contact the warden of the national park at ☎ 061-55645 or 061-55201.

Accommodation along the major trekking routes, whether in huts or larger bunk-houses, is described in detail in each route's accommodation section.

## EATING

In an attempt to reduce luggage, many trekkers exist entirely on canned and dried foods. You can do this by keeping up your fluid intake, but it's not a good idea. Keep in mind that your appetite for 'heavy' meals (ie lots of big solids) drops considerably at high altitudes.

Increased altitude creates unique cooking conditions. The major consideration is that the boiling point of water is considerably reduced. At 4500m, for example, water boils at 85°C; this is too low to sufficiently cook rice or lentils (pasta is better) and you won't be able to brew a good cup of tea (instant coffee is the answer). Cooking times and fuel usage are considerably increased as a result, so plan accordingly.

When you're buying dehydrated foods, get the precooked variety to cut down on cooking

time – two-minute noodles are a solution. It's a good idea to bring these from home. Take plenty of citrus fruits and/or citrus drinks as well as chocolate, sweets or dried fruit to keep your blood-sugar level up.

To avoid severe headaches caused by dehydration or altitude sickness, drink at least 3L of fluid per day and bring rehydration sachets. Water purification tablets, available at most chemists, aren't a bad idea either.

## ENVIRONMENT

There are flora, fauna and ecosystems on the slopes of Mt Kenya that cannot be found anywhere else in the country.

This extinct volcano hosts, at various elevations, upland forest, bamboo forest (2500m), high-altitude equatorial heath (3000m to 3500m) and lower alpine moorland (3400m to 3800m), which includes several species of bright everlasting flowers. Some truly surreal plantlife grows in the Afro-Alpine zone (above 3500m) and the upper alpine zone (3800m to 4500m), including hairy carpets of tussock grass, the brushlike giant lobelias, or rosette plants, and the sci-fi-worthy *Senecio Brassica*, or giant groundsel, which looks like a cross between an aloe, a cactus and a dwarf. At the summit it's all rock and ice, a landscape that possesses its own stark beauty, especially this close to the equator.

Unfortunately, there's more rock than ice these days. 'In 15 years I've seen all the glaciers move. I don't need crampons any more', one guide told us. Warmer weather has led to disappearing glaciers, and ice climbing in Mt Kenya is largely finished. We've heard these conditions have led to drier rivers in the region, which makes sense as Mt Kenya is the country's most important permanent watershed.

In lower elevations large wildlife are around; you may need to clap and hoot as you trudge to stave off elephants and buffaloes. Rock hyraxes are common, as are, rather annoyingly, bees. There are also Sykes' monkeys, Mackinder's eagle owls, waterbucks, and (very rarely spotted) leopards, hyenas and servals about, but these animals tend to stay hidden in the thick brush of the lower forests.

Rather than leave supplies out for wildlife, whose feeding patterns are disrupted by foreign food, give extra supplies to your guides. Carry all your litter (including used toilet paper) off the mountain; animals will dig up buried refuse. Bury faeces below 3500m, but above this altitude, leave on the surface of the ground (and scatter them about or scrape them with a stick to speed up decomposition). Hundreds of kilos of waste are removed from the mountain each year via locally run clean-up operations; try not to add to the mess.

## ORGANISED TREKS

If you negotiate aggressively, a package trek may end up costing only a little more than organising each logistical element of the trip separately. As always, you need to watch out for sharks; picking the right company is even more important here than on a regular safari, as an unqualified or inexperienced guide could put you in real danger.

**Mountain Rock Safaris Resorts & Trekking Services** (Map pp104-5; ☎ Nairobi 020-242133, 0722511752; www .mountainrockkenya.com; PO Box 15796-00100, Nairobi), in the Jubilee Insurance Exchange Building in Nairobi, runs the Mountain Rock Lodge (p215) near Naro Moru. A four-day Naro Moru–Sirimon crossover trek, its most popular option, runs to US$960 for a single person, but costs US$560 for groups of three and as low as US$450 for groups of nine or more.

**Naro Moru River Lodge** (Map p216; ☎ 062-31047, 0724082754, in Nairobi 020-4443357; www.alliancehotels .com; PO Box 18, Naro Moru) also runs a range of all-inclusive trips. Its prices are more expensive than most, but it's the only company that can guarantee you beds in the Met Station Hut and Mackinder's Camp on the Naro Moru route (because it owns said lodges!).

**IntoAfrica** ( ☎ UK 0114-255 5610, in Nairobi 722-511752; www.intoafrica.co.uk; 40 Huntingdon Cres, Sheffield, UK) is an environmentally and culturally sensitive company that places an emphasis on fair trade and offers both scheduled and exclusive seven-day trips (six days of trekking) ascending Sirimon route and descending Chogoria. Joining scheduled one-week trips costs US$192 per day (minimum two people), while private treks range from US$77 to US$355 per person per day, depending on the group size.

**KG Mountain Expeditions** ( ☎ 062-62403; www .kenyaexpeditions.com; PO Box 199, Naro Moru), run by a highly experienced mountaineer, offers all-inclusive four-day treks for US$710 for single climbers, which goes down to US$460 for groups of five or more.

**Montana Trek & Information Centre** (Map p218; ☎ 062-32731; Jambo House Hotel, Lumumba Rd, Nanyuki)

are pretty friendly and very knowledgeable about the mountain. A four-day trip will run around US$420 per person for a group of two or more. The centre is particularly useful for Sirimon trekkers.

**EWP** (Executive Wilderness Programmes; ☎ UK 1550-721319, USA/Canada 1800-514-6143; www.ewpnet .com/kenya) employs some knowledgeable local guides; three-day trips cost US$800 per person for a single trekker, down to US$490 per person for groups of three and lower for larger parties.

**Sana Highlands Trekking Expeditions** (Map pp104-5; ☎ 020-227820; www.sanatrekkingkenya.com; Contrust House, Moi Ave, PO Box 5400-00100, Nairobi) operate five-day all-inclusive treks on the Sirimon and Chogoria routes that start at US$325 per person (based on a group of five).

## THE ROUTES

There are at least seven different routes up Mt Kenya. Of those, we cover Naro Moru, the easiest and most popular, as well as Sirimon and Chogoria, which are excellent alternatives. The Burguret and Timau routes are less well known and are described in Lonely Planet's *Trekking in East Africa*.

We also delve into the exciting but demanding Summit Circuit, which circles Batian and Nelion, thus enabling you to mix and match ascending and descending routes.

### Naro Moru Route

Although the least scenic, this is the most straightforward and popular route and is still spectacular. Begin in Naro Moru and allow a minimum of four days for the trek. While possible in three, you risk serious altitude sickness.

#### SLEEPING

There are three good bunk-houses along this route: **Met Station Hut** (Map p216; dm US$12) is at 3000m, **Mackinder's Camp** (Map p209; dm US$15) is at 4160m and **Austrian Hut** (Map p212; dm KSh1000) is at 4790m. Beds in Met Station and Mackinder's are harder to find, as they're booked through **Naro Moru River Lodge** (Map p216; ☎ 062-31047, 0724082754, in Nairobi 020-4443357; www .alliancehotels.com; PO Box 18, Naro Moru). If you're denied beds, you can still climb this route if you camp and carry all the appropriate equipment. Those needing more luxury can doss

**MT KENYA SUMMIT**

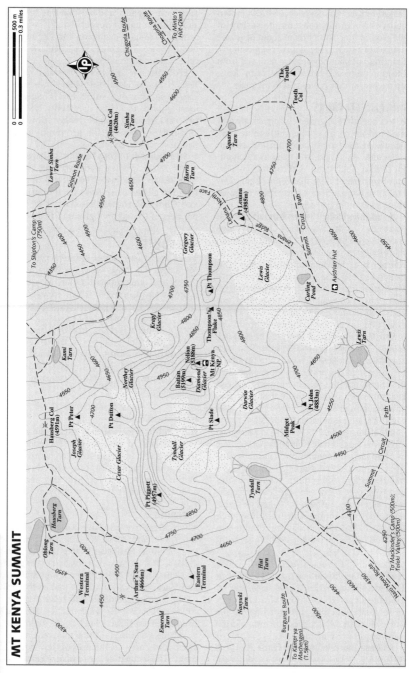

in lovely **Batian Guest House** (Map p216; cottages US$180), a kilometre from Naro Moru gate.

### THE TREK
Starting in Naro Moru town, the first part of the route takes you along a gravel road through farmlands for some 13km (all the junctions are signposted) to the start of the forest. Another 5km brings you to the park entry gate (2400m), from where it's 8km to the road head and the Met Station Hut (3000m), where you stay for the night and acclimatise.

On the second day, set off through the forest (at about 3200m) and Teleki Valley to the moorland around so-called **Vertical Bog**; expect the going here to be, well, boggy. At a ridge the route divides into two. You can either take the higher path, which gives better views but is often wet, or the lower, which crosses the Naro Moru River and continues gently up to Mackinder's Camp (4160m). This part of the trek should take about 4½ hours. Here you can stay in the dormitories or camp.

On the third day you can either rest at Mackinder's Camp to acclimatise or aim for **Point Lenana** (Map p212; 4895m). This stretch takes three to six hours, so it is common to leave around 2am to reach the summit in time for sunrise. From the bunk-house, continue past the ranger station to a fork. Keep right, and go across a swampy area, followed by a moraine, and then up a long scree slope – this is a long, hard slog. KWS's Austrian Hut (4790m) is three to four hours from Mackinder's and about one hour below the summit of Lenana, so it's a good place to rest before the final push.

The section of the trek from Austrian Hut up to Point Lenana takes you up a narrow rocky path that traverses the southwest ridge parallel to the Lewis Glacier, which has shrunk more than 100m since the 1960s. Be careful, as the shrinkage has created serious danger of slippage along the path. A final climb or scramble brings you up onto the peak. In good weather it's fairly straightforward, but in bad weather you shouldn't attempt the summit unless you're experienced in mountain conditions or have a guide. Plenty of inexperienced trekkers have come to grief on this section, falling off icy cliffs or disappearing into crevasses. With all that said the disappearing glacier phenomenon (Gregory Glacier has practically vanished) has made the climb generally easier, although it makes the lives of those who rely on those glaciers for meltwater a hell of a lot more difficult.

From Point Lenana most people return along the same route. Alternatively, you can return to Austrian Hut, then take the Summit Circuit around the base of the main peaks to reach the top of one of the other routes before you descend.

## Sirimon Route
A popular alternative to Naro Moru, Sirimon has better scenery, greater flexibility and a gentler rate of ascent, although it is still easy to climb too fast; allow at least five days for the trek. It's well worth considering combining it with the Chogoria route for a six- to seven-day traverse that really brings out the best of Mt Kenya. Although Naro Moru is the most popular route, Sirimon is probably the easiest for inexperienced trekkers.

Nanyuki (p216) is the best launching point for this route.

### SLEEPING
**Old Moses Hut** (Map p209; dm US$10) at 3300m and **Shipton's Camp** (Map p209; dm US$14) at 4200m serve trekkers on this route. They're both booked through the **Mountain Rock Lodge** (Map p216; ☎ 062-62625; info@mountainrockkenya.com), near Naro Moru. Many trekkers acclimatise by camping at Liki North. If you'd like a little more comfort, book into the KWS's excellent **Sirimon Bandas** (Map p216; bandas US$80).

### THE TREK
It is 23km from Nanyuki to the Sirimon gate, and transport is included with prebooked packages. Otherwise take a matatu towards Timau or Meru, or arrange a lift from town. From the gate it's about 9km through the forest to Old Moses Hut (3300m), where you spend the first night.

On the second day you could head straight through the moorland for Shipton's Camp, but it is worth taking an extra acclimatisation day via **Liki North Hut** (Map p209; 3993m), a tiny place on the floor of a classic glacial valley. The actual hut is a complete wreck and meant for porters, but it's a good campsite with a toilet and stream nearby.

On the third day, head up the western side of Liki North Valley and over the ridge into Mackinder's Valley, joining the direct route about 1½ hours in. After crossing the Liki River, follow the path for another 30 minutes until you reach the bunk-house at Shipton's Camp (4200m), which is set in a fantastic location right below Batian and Nelion.

From Shipton's you can push straight for **Point Lenana** (Map p212; 4895m), a tough 3½- to five-hour slog via Harris Tarn and the tricky north-face approach, or take the Summit Circuit in either direction around the peaks to reach Austrian Hut (4790m), about one hour below the summit. The left-hand (east) route past Simba Col is shorter but steeper, while the right-hand (west) option takes you on the Harris Tarn trail nearer the main peaks.

From Austrian Hut take the standard southwest traverse up to Point Lenana; see p211. If you're spending the night here, it's worth having a wander around to catch the views up to Batian and down the Lewis Glacier into Teleki Valley.

### Chogoria Route

This route crosses some of the most spectacular and varied scenery on Mt Kenya, and is often combined with the Sirimon route (usually as the descent). The only disadvantage is the long distance between Chogoria and the park gate. Allow at least five days for a trek here; many guides will recommend you spend a full week on the trip. As befits its length and difficulty, this is usually the most expensive route up the mountain.

#### SLEEPING

The only option besides camping on this route is **Meru Mt Kenya Lodge** (Map p216; s/tw US$22/44), a group of comfortable cabins administered by **Meru County Council** (Map p221; Kenyatta Hwy, Meru).

#### THE TREK

The main reason this route is more popular as a descent is the 29km bottom stage. While not overly steep, climbing up that distance is much harder than descending it. Either way, it's a beautiful walk through farmland, rainforest and bamboo. You can camp near the Forest Station 6km out of town, but you'll still have 23km to walk the next day. Transport is available from the village, but it'll cost you.

Camping is possible at the gate, or you can stay nearby in Meru Mt Kenya Lodge (3000m), with transport to town available and a small shop selling beer, which is also popular with people coming down.

On the second day, head up through the forest to the trailhead (camping is possible here). From here it's another 7km over rolling foothills to the Hall Tarns area and **Minto's Hut** (Map p209; 4300m). Like Liki North, this place is only intended for porters, but makes for a decent campsite. Don't use the tarns here to wash anything, as they have already been polluted by careless trekkers.

From here follow the trail alongside the stunning **Gorges Valley** (another possible descent for the adventurous) and scramble up steep ridges to meet the Summit Circuit. It is possible to go straight for the north face or southwest ridge of Point Lenana, but stopping at Austrian Hut or detouring to Shipton's Camp is probably a better idea and gives you more time to enjoy the scenery; see Sirimon (p213) and Naro Moru routes (p211) for details.

### Summit Circuit

While everyone who summits Point Lenana gets a small taste of the spectacular Summit Circuit, few trekkers ever grab the beautiful beast by the horns and hike its entire length. The trail encircles the main peaks of Mt Kenya between the 4300m and 4800m contour lines and offers challenging terrain, fabulous views and a splendid opportunity to familiarise yourself with this complex mountain. It is also a fantastic way to acclimatise before bagging Point Lenana.

One of the many highlights along the route is a peek at Mt Kenya's southwest face, with the long, thin Diamond Couloir leading up to the Gates of the Mists between the summits of Batian and Nelion.

Depending on your level of fitness, this route can take between four and nine hours. Some fit souls can bag Point Lenana (from Austrian Hut or Shipton's Camp) and complete the Summit Circuit in the same day.

The trail can be deceptive at times, especially when fog rolls in, and some trekkers have become seriously lost between Tooth Col and Austrian Hut. It is imperative to take a guide.

# AROUND MT KENYA

Mt Kenya forms the hub of a wheel of communities that live, literally and figuratively, in the shadow of its snow-covered bulk, which looms over the land, starkly dark and visible on clear days.

Most of the area is given over to agriculture and the cultivation of staples of both the Kenyan plate and Somali and Yemeni addicts, the latter living for the fields of *miraa* (a leafy shoot chewed for amphetamine-like effects) grown near Meru, to the northeast. Near here as well is Meru National Park, one of the nation's best and most ignored.

Little Naro Moru, embedded in Mt Kenya's western flank, serves as a base for hikers and trekkers. The Laikipia Plateau, home to the friendly town of Nanyuki and one of sub-Saharan Africa's most important wildlife conservation sites, is to the north. Past here are vast northern plains, dotted with volcanic cones and the Matthews Range in the distance. Between Nanyuki and Meru, fields of wheat, sisal and flowers are owned and cultivated by black and white Kenyan farmers, particularly near the small town of Timau.

## NARO MORU
☎ 062

Naro Moru is little more than a string of shops and houses, with a couple of very basic hotels and a market, but it's the most popular starting point for treks up Mt Kenya. There's a post office with internet, but no banks (the nearest are at Nanyuki and Nyeri).

### Sights & Activities

Apart from gawking at Mt Kenya and starting the Naro Moru route up to its summit (p211), there are some fine things to do here. Mt Kenya Hostel & Campsite organises a number of excursions, including **nature walks** and hikes to the **Mau Mau caves**, which are impressive from both a physical and historical perspective. Mountain Rock Lodge and Naro Moru River Lodge also run similar trips, as well as offering **horse riding** and **fishing**.

### Sleeping & Eating

Although there are a number of basic hotels in Naro Moru town, the best options are in the surrounding few kilometres; there's a string of decent lodgings on the bumpy road between Naro Moru and the park gates. Eating options are slim, with only some hotels offering meals. There's a tiny store next to the post office, but you're better off shopping in Nanyuki or Nyeri.

**BUDGET**

Note that both of the midrange and top-end options have great campsites.

**Mt Kenya Guides & Porters Safari Club** (Map p216; ☎ 62015; camping KSh150) If you just need to save money you can camp here, but beware security doesn't inspire much confidence. The club can provide tents (two-person tent KSh600), but the site is rather primitive and the loos are rather grim – showers come in buckets.

**Blue Line Hotel** (Map p216; ☎ 62217; camping KSh150, s/d KSh400/800) This is an excellent budget option; rooms don't get much cleaner or comfortable for such a bargain price. There's a restaurant and bar on the premises that gets pretty busy with locals on weekends, which is either a good thing or a drawback depending on what you're in the mood for. You're about 13km from the park entrance here.

**Mt Kenya Hostel & Campsite** (Map p216; ☎ 62412, 0722598974; wanjaujoseph2000@yahoo.com; camping KSh250, dm KSh500) The closest accommodation to the park is friendly in a youth hostel kind of way, and frequently hosts group tours and treks (and ergo should be booked in advance). The restaurant provides much-needed calories, and there's a kitchen and bar on site as well. It rents limited mountain gear as well as a 4WD vehicle. Mt Kenya treks can be arranged here too.

**Mountain Stop Hotel** (Map p216; s KSh500) Spanking new when we visited, the Mountain Stop has cheerful staff and a similar ambience to Mt Kenya Hostel, which is to say it feels like a friendly, communal kind of place to base yourself before heading up Mt Kenya. The owners organise Mt Kenya treks and other encounters of the hiking, fishing and general outdoorsy kind.

**MIDRANGE & TOP END**

**Mountain Rock Lodge** (Map p216; ☎ 62625, 0722511752, in Nairobi 020-242133; www.mountainrockkenya.com; camping US$5, s/tw standard KSh3000/4000, superior KSh3500/5200) This is one of the major bases for Mt Kenya climbers and all sorts of outdoor activities. It's located 6km north of Naro Moru, tucked away in the woods less than 1km from the Nanyuki road. The standard rooms are decent value, while the 'superiors' rooms have a bit of character to go with their fireplaces (and eerie wooden statues of African tribesmen).

**Naro Moru River Lodge** (Map p216; ☎ 062-31047, 0724082754, in Nairobi 020-4443357; www.alliancehotels .com; PO Box 18, Naro Moru; camping US$10, s/tw half

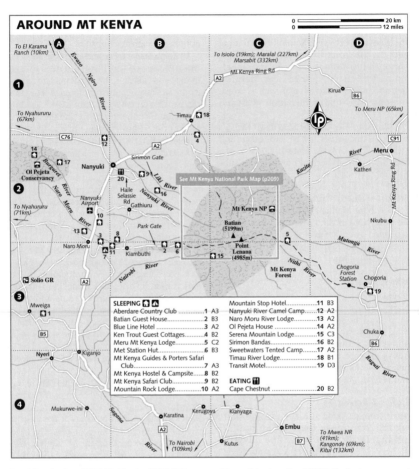

## AROUND MT KENYA

**SLEEPING** 🏠🏕️
Aberdare Country Club ............... 1 A3
Batian Guest House ..................... 2 B3
Blue Line Hotel ........................... 3 A2
Ken Trout Guest Cottages .......... 4 B2
Meru Mt Kenya Lodge ................ 5 C2
Met Station Hut .......................... 6 B3
Mt Kenya Guides & Porters Safari
    Club ........................................ 7 A3
Mt Kenya Hostel & Campsite ..... 8 B2
Mt Kenya Safari Club ................. 9 B2
Mountain Rock Lodge ............... 10 A2

Mountain Stop Hotel .................. 11 B3
Nanyuki River Camel Camp ...... 12 A2
Naro Moru River Lodge ............. 13 A2
Ol Pejeta House ......................... 14 A2
Serena Mountain Lodge ............. 15 C3
Sirimon Bandas .......................... 16 B2
Sweetwaters Tented Camp ......... 17 A2
Timau River Lodge ..................... 18 B1
Transit Motel ............................. 19 D3

**EATING** 🍴
Cape Chestnut ........................... 20 B2

board May-Jun from US$61/90, Mar-Apr US$73/106, rest of year US$99/132; 🏊 ) A bit of a Swiss chalet bordering the equator, the River Lodge is a lovely collection of dark, cosy cottages and rooms embedded into a sloping hillside that overlooks a rushing river. All three classes of room are lovely, but the middle-of-the-road 'superior' option actually seems better than the more expensive 'deluxe' rooms.

### Getting There & Away

There are plenty of buses and matatus heading to Nanyuki (KSh80, 30 minutes), Nyeri (KSh100, 45 minutes) and Nairobi (KSh350, three hours).

Naro Moru River Lodge operates transfers between the lodge and Nairobi (US$120) or Nanyuki airstrip (US$25), but you must book 24 hours in advance.

## NANYUKI & LAIKIPIA
☎ 062

This small but bustling mountain town makes a living off sales, be it of treks to climbers, curios to soldiers of the British Army (which has a training facility nearby) or drinks to pilots of the Kenyan Air Force (this is the site of their main airbase). For all that mercantilism, it's laid back for a market town. And entrepreneurship and conservation have combined in a particularly attractive fashion: the town sits on the edge of the Laikipia Plateau, one of Africa's most important wildlife conservation sites. Private ranches and reserves such as Ol Pejeta Conservancy (p219) are great examples of human business and wildlife preservation occupying the same space; there's more protected species in these camps than many KWS reserves. For an up-to-date list of the ever-changing accommodation and safari options in Laikipia (there were over 40 safari camps here at the time of our research), go to www.laikipia .org. Note that many of the listed properties are located in Northern Province and tend to be visited as parts of prepackaged tours; at the least, you'll want to contact a camp in advance to arrange a stay.

## Information

**Barclays Bank** (Kenyatta Ave) With ATM.
**Kenya Commercial Bank** (Kenyatta Ave) With ATM (Visa only).
**Marina Grill & Restaurant** (Kenyatta Ave) Internet access, cheap international calls and burning images to CD.
**Mt Kenya Cyberworld** (Kenyatta Ave; per hr KSh60) Internet and international calls.
**Post office** (Kenyatta Ave)
**Standard Chartered Bank** (Kenyatta Ave) With ATM.

## Sights & Activities

Besides tackling Mt Kenya's Sirimon (p213) or Burguret routes, you should stroll 3km south to the **equator** (there's a sign) and get a lesson on the Coriolis force from the Mid-World Curio Shop (see p219). 'Graduates' of the course can buy a 'diploma' for KSh300.

About 3km east of town is a **Commonwealth War Cemetery**, a meditative spot which is kept in immaculate shape.

If you ask politely, the stewards of the local **Hindu Temple** (they live behind the building) may let you have a peek inside. There are shrines to Shiva, Rama, Sita and Hanuman and not much else, but you are being afforded a nice peek into the lives what's left of Nanyuki's South Asian community (there are about 29 Indian families left in town).

## Sleeping

### BUDGET
**Joskaki Hotel** ( ☎ 31403; Lumumba Rd; s/tw/d KSh400/500/650) This enormous option is the best of the budget sleeps, offering clean rooms with nice views over town (and Mt Kenya, if you're lucky). Some of the self-contained toilets even have seats (gasp!). The on-site bar and restaurant serves decent food and pleasantly loud good times in the evening.

**Ibis Hotel** ( ☎ 31536; Lumumba Rd; s/tw KSh800/1200) Bright rooms and a brighter covered courtyard lurk behind Ibis Hotel's facade of fresh tiles and woodwork. It's a comfortable, clean place and all rooms have mossie nets. Angle for a room with a Mt Kenya view.

**Nanyuki River Camel Camp** (Map p216; ☎ 0722-361642; camellot@wananchi.com; off C76 Hwy; camping US$6, huts with shared bathroom half board low/high season KSh1500/2500) The most innovative sleep in town (well, 4km outside of it) is this ecocamp, set off in a dry swab of scrub. Inhabited by 200 camels (available for hire) and a pack of friendly dogs, the camp offers lodging in genuine Somali grass huts imported from Mandera. A series of pleasant paths, picnic areas and a tree house are all situated on the nearby Nanyuki River.

### MIDRANGE & TOP END
**Kongoni Camp** (off the A2; camping/huts 600/4000) So new when we arrived it didn't have a phone number, Kongoni Camp was located just off the A2 east of town. Founded by a friendly local-turned-Londoner-turned-local-again, Kongoni combines the rustic, banda ambience of a good safari lodge with pop-punk art that could have been lifted from an East End gallery. After nothing but spartan budget digs or swish safari resorts, Kongoni's dash of hip in the bush is pretty refreshing.

**Equator Chalet** ( ☎ 31480; Kenyatta Ave; theequator chalet@yahoo.com; s/tw/d incl breakfast KSh1300/1700/2000) This is as plush as it gets if you opt to stay inside the Nanyuki town limits, and while it's no four-star hotel, the Equator is welcoming and comfortable. The very fine rooms surround a breezy internal courtyard that opens onto two balcony areas and a roof terrace.

**Sportsman's Arms Hotel** ( ☎ 32348, 0734944077; www.sportsmansarms.com; off Laikipia Rd; s/d/tw incl breakfast KSh3700/4800/5500, 4-person cottages KSh7000; ▨ ) The Sportsman was the meeting point for Nanyuki's elites back in the day, and it still feels frozen in the 1960s school of modish hotel design. Rooms are a little musty but comfy, and the on-site restaurant does great food.

**Serena Mountain Lodge** (Map p216; ☎ 2030785, in Nairobi 020-2842333; www.serenahotels.com; s/d full board Apr-Jun US$175/285, Nov-Christmas US$260/310, Jan, Mar, Jun US$285/360, Feb & Jul-Nov US$320/435; ▨ ) This Treetops-style forest lodge, located within the forest reserve area of Mt Kenya National Park, has a dining room that seemingly floats over the forest, plush if badly decorated cabin-style rooms, open-air terraces and salt licks, and the usual royal amenities Serena is famous for; think post-trek herbal massages.

**Mt Kenya Safari Club** (Map p216; ☎ 30000, in Nairobi 020-216940; www.fairmont.com; full board around US$300-500; ▢ ▣) The Safari Club was undergoing major renovations when we visited and rooms weren't available for viewing, but by the time the dust settles it will probably maintain its position as one of the granddaddy top-end resorts on the slopes of Mt Kenya. It's famous for providing the kind of safari-lodge ambience that requires kicking back with a topi, starched khakis and a pipe. Guests will get access to their own private wildlife sanctuary of rare bongo antelope.

## Eating

**Camcorner** (Kenyatta Ave; meals KSh60-260; ☺ lunch & dinner) If you're in 'downtown' Nanyuki, this is your best option. It serves up the usual stews and steaks, as well as camel products (including camel *biltong* – jerky), but it does wonders with traditional highlands food; the *githeri* (beans, corns and meat) is excellent.

**Marina Grill & Restaurant** (Kenyatta Ave; meals KSh140-420; ☺ lunch & dinner) Popular with trekking groups, British soldiers and Kenyan Air Force officers (the odd cross-section that is Nanyuki), this place does good burgers and pizza and has a nice rooftop eating area for those needing fresh air.

**Ibis Hotel** (Lumumba Rd; meals KSh180-300; ☺ lunch & dinner) Steaks are the claim to fame in this enormous, pleasantly open cafeteria-style dining room, but the other standards of the Kenyan menu won't disappoint.

**George Cafe** (off A2 hwy; meals KSh200-400; ☺ lunch & dinner) A little bit east of town, this is the place to come for outdoor seating, free-flowing beer and excellent *nyama choma*.

**Sportsman's Arms Hotel** (off Laikipia Rd; meals KSh225-550; ☺ lunch & dinner) The Sportsman's Arms has long been heralded as the town's top restaurant. Your mouth will tell you you've splurged, but your wallet is only paying a little above the rate of most town eateries.

**Cape Chestnut** (Map p216; off Kenyatta Ave; meals KSh250-400 ☺ breakfast, lunch & dinner Mon-Sat) This coffee garden caters mostly to white farmers, expats and tourists. If you're in need of a

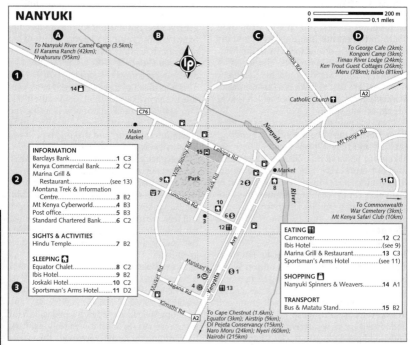

# NANYUKI

0 ————— 200 m
0 ————— 0.1 miles

To Nanyuki River Camel Camp (3.5km);
El Karama Ranch (42km);
Nyahururu (95km)

To George Cafe (2km);
Kongoni Camp (3km);
Timau River Lodge (24km);
Ken Trout Guest Cottages (26km);
Meru (78km); Isiolo (81km)

Catholic Church

Main Market

Market

To Commonwealth
War Cemetery (3km);
Mt Kenya Safari Club (10km)

To Cape Chestnut (1.6km);
Equator (3km); Airstrip (9km);
Ol Pejeta Conservancy (15km);
Naro Moru (24km); Nyeri (60km);
Nairobi (215km)

| INFORMATION | |
|---|---|
| Barclays Bank | 1 C3 |
| Kenya Commercial Bank | 2 C2 |
| Marina Grill & Restaurant | (see 13) |
| Montana Trek & Information Centre | 3 B2 |
| Mt Kenya Cyberworld | 4 B3 |
| Post office | 5 B3 |
| Standard Chartered Bank | 6 C2 |

| SIGHTS & ACTIVITIES | |
|---|---|
| Hindu Temple | 7 B2 |

| SLEEPING | |
|---|---|
| Equator Chalet | 8 C2 |
| Ibis Hotel | 9 B2 |
| Joskaki Hotel | 10 C2 |
| Sportsman's Arms Hotel | 11 D2 |

| EATING | |
|---|---|
| Camcorner | 12 C2 |
| Ibis Hotel | (see 9) |
| Marina Grill & Restaurant | 13 C3 |
| Sportsman's Arms Hotel | (see 11) |

| SHOPPING | |
|---|---|
| Nanyuki Spinners & Weavers | 14 A1 |

| TRANSPORT | |
|---|---|
| Bus & Matatu Stand | 15 B2 |

**GICHIMU JOSEPH**

At the signpost for the equator are the Mid-World Curio Shop and a pitcher of water. As we took a picture in front of the equator, Gichimu Joseph approached us.

'Hello sir. Welcome to the equator! Would you like a demonstration of the Coriolis force?'

'Hello. Sure.'

'Now we are at the centre. On either side is the northern [gestures north] and southern [gestures south] hemisphere. If I pour water from this pitcher into this bowl with a hole inside it [holds up bowl] 15m to the north, it will drain clockwise. Observe!'

He does so, dropping a stick in the water to demonstrate its draining direction.

'Wow.'

'Now, if we go 15m to the south, it will go out in an anticlockwise direction.' He repeats the procedure.

'OK.'

'This whole effect is known as the Coriolis force. It was described by Gaspard de Coriolis in 1835 and is based off Newton's second law of motion. Now, here at zero degrees, when I pour out the water, it will drain out in a straight line. Watch!' (The water drains out in a straight line.)

'Wow! That's pretty impressive, Gichimu.'

'Thank you. I am the professor of the Coriolis force. I am also a carver. Would you like to see my art?'

*Author's note: while the demonstration seems to work, scientists say the Coriolis force doesn't actually cause water to drain in the manner Gichimu depicted.*

great sandwich, some fresh air and a bracing cup of tea or espresso, look no further. It's off Kenyatta Ave, 1km south of town.

## Shopping

There are a number of souvenir stalls and shops around town, catering mostly to the British army – if you have gear to swap, swap it here.

**Nanyuki Spinners & Weavers** (Laikipia Rd) For something less tacky, try this women's craft cooperative that specialises in high-quality woven woollen goods.

## Getting There & Away

**Airkenya** ( ☎ 020-605745; www.airkenya.com) and **Safarilink** ( ☎ 020-600777; www.safarilink.co.ke) fly daily from Wilson Airport in Nairobi to Nanyuki. A return trip on Airkenya/Safarilink costs US$160/195, while one-way fares for northbound and southbound flights are US$80/91 and US$80/117 respectively.

There are daily buses and matatus to Nyeri (KSh150, one hour), Isiolo (KSh200, 1½ hours), Meru (KSh150, 1½ hours) and Nairobi (KSh400, three hours).

## AROUND NANYUKI
### Ol Pejeta Conservancy

This 90,000-acre private **wildlife conservancy** (Map p216; www.olpejetaconservancy.org; adult/child US$25/13), owned by UK-based Fauna and Flora, is home to the full palette of African plains wildlife, including the Big Five, massive eland and a plethora of birdlife. This was once one of the largest cattle ranches in Kenya; as wildlife moved in and stock became less profitable, conservation became a means to both economic and environmental success. An important **chimpanzee sanctuary** ( ☼ 9-10.30am & 3-4.30pm), operated by the Jane Goodall Institute, is also located within the grounds.

### SLEEPING

**Sweetwaters Tented Camp** (Map p216; ☎ 062-31970, 0734699852, in Nairobi 020-2842333; sweetwaters@serena .co.ke; s/d full board low season US$180/295, high season US$295/360, peak season US$445/575), recently purchased by Serena Hotels, sits beside a floodlit waterhole (tent numbers one and two have the best view). Part of its grounds include the beautiful **Ol Pejeta House** (Map p216; ☎ 062-32400, in Nairobi 020-2710511; swtc@kenyaweb.com; s/d Jan-Apr, Jun-Jan US$545/695, other times US$400/495), a massive bush villa that was once home to Lord Delamere.

### GETTING THERE & AWAY

You can visit the reserve independently if you have your own vehicle. Access is off the A2 Hwy south out of Nanyuki.

**CENTRAL HIGHLANDS**

## Timau

Sky-kissed fields of flowers and grain roll in enormous waves all the way to the border of the northern frontiers. This is another major artery of the heart of Kenya's agricultural country, and many of the labourers on local farms base themselves in this tiny town.

### SLEEPING & EATING

**Ken Trout Guest Cottages** (Map p216; ☎ 0720804751; off A2 Hwy; camping KSh300, cottages half board per person KSh2500) This fishing lodge, set back in a pine-clad riverine retreat, is redolent with pastoral isolation and wood smoke. Needless to say, some fine fish is whipped up at the restaurant and there is some good angling about, although you pay for everything you catch. The main house (which sleeps up to eight) is rented exclusively; both it and the on-site cottages are cosy and filled with great old reading material.

**Timau River Lodge** (Map p216; ☎ 062-41230, in Nairobi 020-2034511; timauriverlodge@hotmail.com; off A2 Hwy; camping KSh500, cottages incl breakfast per person KSh3000) Nestled in a skein of cold streams and grassy fields, this beautiful little compound of offbeat log cabins is scattered with wandering chickens, ducks and a few tortoises. The thatched accommodation is warm, slightly funky and enlivened by bouts of electricity in the evening, although it's magic enough to watch the stars with the lights out.

### GETTING THERE & AWAY

Any matatu running between Nanyuki and Isiolo, or Nanyuki and Meru, will drop you in Timau (KSh80, around one hour) or at the turn-off to either sleeping option.

## El Karama Ranch

If you're entertaining a bush-cowboy fantasy of riding across the savanna at a horse's trot (or on a camel's back), come 42km to the northwest of Nanyuki, to **El Karama Ranch** (off Map p216; ☎ 0727532091, Nairobi 020-340331; www.horse backinkenya.com; horse-riding safaris per night $400) on the Ewaso Ngiro River. Although still a working ranch, wildlife conservation is paramount and the 5668 hectares play home to lions, leopards, elephants, Grevy's zebras and reticulated giraffes. It's an old family-run settlers' ranch with a number of basic but comfortable riverside bandas. Bring everything you need, including food.

## MERU

☎ 064

The pick-up trucks race down the highway, screaming through their ancient gears while weighed down with enormous loads of *miraa* twigs (see the boxed text, p222), the basis of this town's economy. Meru is the epicentre of Kenyan production of this amphetamine, and the town itself is like a shot of the stuff: a briefly invigorating, slightly confusing head rush.

This bustling little town, the most likely base for exploring Meru National Park, is worth a day visit in its own right, and is a focal point for the Meru people (see also p41).

## Information

**Barclays Bank** (Tom Mboya St)
**Cafe Candy** (Tom Mboya St; per hr KSh180) Decent internet connections.
**Kenya Commercial Bank** (KCB; Njiru Ncheke St)
**Meru County Council** (Kenyatta Hwy) Bookings for Meru Mt Kenya Lodge on the Chogoria route.
**Post office** (Kenyatta Hwy)
**Standard Chartered Bank** (Moi Ave)

## Sights

The small **Meru National Museum** (☎ 20482; off Kenyatta Hwy; KSh500; ☯ 9.30am-6pm, 1-6pm public holidays) is awfully overpriced. There's a series of faded exhibits, desultory stuffed and mounted wildlife and a small but informative section concerning the clothing, weapons, and agricultural and initiation practices (including clitoridectomies) of the Meru people.

The large compound of a local **Sikh temple** perches over Tom Mboya St. There are only two or three Sikhs left in Meru, and the small shrine to their gurus is a little elegiac when you consider it's the last physical trace of the local Asian community.

## Sleeping

It's pretty slim pickings in town, although there are some decent options a little ways out of the centre. You'll want to watch out for bed bugs wherever you sleep.

**Hotel Royal Prince** (☎ 30567; Angaine Rd; s/d KSh600/1000) A better budget option, the Royal Prince is well-lit and clean and the on-site restaurant and bar keep the atmosphere lively (but not sleazy). Some rooms are smallish, but all of them serve their simple purpose admirably.

CENTRAL HIGHLANDS

**Meru Safari Hotel** ( ☎ 31500, 0724464623; Kenyatta Hwy; s/tw KSh850/1350) At these prices you may as well upgrade to the Pig & Whistle, but if that spot is full the rooms here are clean, fine and functional. We can't give them much more credit than that.

**Pig & Whistle** ( ☎ 31411; off Kenyatta Hwy; s/tw incl breakfast KSh1100/1500) There's a rambling sense of alpine chaos here, offset by friendly staff and truly comfortable cottages set around a sprawling rustic compound. The concrete huts may not look like much from the outside, but they are actually nicely self-contained slices of good-value sleeping pleasure. More memorable stays are to be had in the old (1934) wooden cabins.

**Meru County Hotel** ( ☎ 32432; Kenyatta Hwy; s/tw incl breakfast from KSh1200/1700) This hotel doesn't have the character of the Pig & Whistle, but it does have amiable staff and spick-and-span rooms that are, for Meru, the height of luxury and service.

## Eating & Drinking

**Angie's Café** (Kenyatta Hwy; meals KSh50-150; ☺ lunch & dinner) Sedated goldfish patrol the aquarium and watch over simple menus. Locals recommend the biriani, while other eats include highlands standards including *nyama choma*.

**Cafe Candy** (Tom Mboya St; meals around KSh60-250; ☺ lunch & dinner) This place is perfect for Indian curry, Western-style stews, flaky *sambusas* (deep-fried pastry triangles stuffed with spiced mincemeat) and an awfully impressive menu of offal.

**Meru County Hotel** (Kenyatta Hwy; meals KSh60-280; ☺ lunch & dinner) Thatched umbrellas hover over each table on this pretty *nyama choma* terrace. If you want to give the flaming flesh a rest, try the Western, Kenyan and Indian meals on offer.

**Royal Prince** (Tom Mboya St; meals KSh120-240; ☺ lunch & dinner) There are three stories of bustling eating goodness here, and mobs of locals on the weekend who go gaga for the *choma* and on-site bar.

**Pig & Whistle** (off Kenyatta Hwy; meals KSh150-270; ☺ lunch & dinner) The food (of the Kenyan and Western staples sort) is pretty good and the setting is even better: a lush, lovely garden interspersed with cute lawn-jockey furniture. It's also great for an afternoon beer.

## Entertainment

The Royal Prince gets busier and rowdier as the weekend approaches. Or you can buy some *miraa* and zonk out on its speedy (in every sense of the term) effects.

## Getting There & Away

**Kensilver** (Mosque Hill Rd) has 13 daily departures from 6.45am onwards, covering Embu (KSh300, two hours), Thika (KSh300, 3½ hours) and Nairobi (KSh500, 4½ hours). **Mombasa Raha** (Mosque Hill Rd) has daily 5pm services to Mombasa (KSh1000, 10 hours).

Regular matatus serve the same destinations for similar cost. Matatus also serve Nanyuki (KSh200, 1½ hours) and Isiolo (KSh180, 1½ hours).

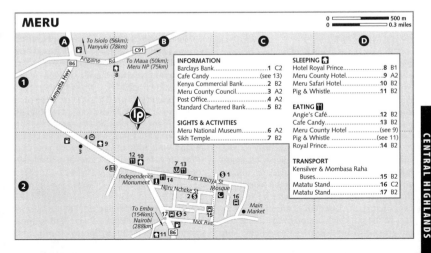

---

**'YOU WILL BUILD CASTLES'**

'What does this stuff do?' we ask our driver.

'It gives you energy. When you chew this thing, you will build castles.'

That was our introduction to *miraa,* the small shoots and leaves of which are chewed throughout the Mt Kenya area and Muslim parts of the country. It's also known as *coas* and *khat,* and by over 40 other names around the world. Chewing *miraa* is an increasingly popular pastime in Kenya, but it's not nearly as important as in places like Yemen or Somalia.

Some of the best *miraa* in the world is grown around Meru. Much of the demand is from Somalia and, since *miraa's* potency is diminished 48 hours after picking, massively overladen pick-up trucks race nightly to Wilson Airport in Nairobi for the morning flight to Mogadishu.

*Miraa* is a mild stimulant. Chewing it predates coffee drinking and is deeply rooted in the cultural traditions of some societies, especially in Muslim countries. It's usually chewed in company to encourage confidence, contentment and a flow of ideas. The active ingredient, cathinone, is closely related to amphetamine, and the euphoric effects can last for up to 24 hours, depending on how much is chewed.

Chewing too much can be habit-forming and has serious consequences, known as 'khat syndrome'. Aggressive behaviour, nightmares and hallucinations are common mental side effects, while reduced appetite, malnourishment, constipation and brown teeth are common physical consequences.

Meru is a good place for curious travellers to give *miraa* a go. It's bitter and gives a brief high, followed by a long come-down. Note that *miraa* is illegal in neighbouring Tanzania, so best leave it out of the suitcase if you're heading that way.

---

# MERU NATIONAL PARK

One of Kenya's best-kept secrets, Meru combines the sun-kissed open savanna of East African dreams with a dark, intensely alive jungle that sprouts along the banks of the crocodile-rich Tana River. Driving into the park, which sits at the end of a long and uninspiring road, you suddenly shift into yellow, sharp-grassed plains pulsing with zebras, waterbucks, buffaloes and elephants, while Hemingway-esque green hills loom like dark, dramatic sentinels in the deep blue distance. It's a pleasantly overwhelming shock to the senses, to say the least.

The park is well worth a few days of your time, not least because it is a fairly sizeable place to explore. Morning, when the dawn breaks over yet another textbook picture of African bush, is the best time to drive, and you'll often feel as if you have the park to yourself; there's no Samburu-style wildlife drive congestion in Meru – yet.

There's an excellent **rhino sanctuary** on site and a bridge across the Tana River at **Adamson's Falls** accessing Kora National Park, and if you're very lucky, you may spot a leopard in the jungle. Elephant and giraffe herds lope over the marshy Bisanadi Plains at the north end of the park, while lions wait under the tall grass, surrounded by oryxes, elands and kudus. Guinea fowl and gazelles hop through the savanna, and every now and then a streaking cheetah leaves ghost tracks across the edge of your eyesight.

The park is the cornerstone of the Meru Conservation Area, a 4000-sq-km expanse that also includes the adjacent Kora National Park, and Bisanadi, Mwingi and North Kitui National Reserves (which are closed), covering the lowland plains east of Meru town.

## Information

Entrance to **Meru National Park** ( ☎ 064-20613, 0733662439; adult/child US$50/25) doesn't entitle you to enter the adjacent **Kora National Park** (adult/child US$50/25). Visits into Kora must be prearranged with Meru's warden at the park headquarters.

At present you need a 4WD or to be on a tour to visit; the 4WD costs an extra KSh800. KWS's *Meru National Park* map (KSh450), sold at the park gates, is essential if you want to find your way around. Even so you may want to hire a guide (four-hour/full-day tour KSh1500/2500).

## Sleeping

**Special campsites** (adult/child US$15/10, plus set-up fee KSh7500) There are about a dozen of these bush campsites (no facilities) located throughout the park. The gate will let you know which are currently open.

**Murera Bandas** (bandas per person US$50) The Murera camp, overflowing with plain wooden cottages and huts, isn't as charming as Kinna's, but it's a fine place to doss if everything is booked up.

**Kinna Bandas** (bandas Apr, Aug & Dec/rest of year US$100/80; ) These four bandas are stocked with kerosene lanterns that add the right romanticism to a star-studded bush night, and you can't get closer to the wildlife without risking being eaten by it.

**Leopard Rock Lodge** ( ☎ 020-600031, 0733333100; www.leopardmico.com; s/d mid-Dec–Mar & Jul-Nov, US$480/570, Apr-Jul & Nov–mid-Dec US$450/490; ) This

beautiful unfenced lodge lets the wildlife right in; little crocodiles wander out of the Murera River to lounge by the pool (don't worry, security is good). This, plus a thatched restaurant and plush rooms, equals top-class, but the Rock's really outmatched by Elsa's Kopje.

**our pick Elsa's Kopje** ( ☎ 020-604053; www.chelipea cock.com/camps/elsas.htm; s/d full board low season US$740-1190, high season US$820-2000; ) Plenty of hotels claim to blend into their environment, but Elsa's did so in such a seamless manner that the bar on chic ecosuites was permanently raised. Carved into Mughwango Hill, these highly individualised 'three-walled' rooms open out onto views *The Lion King* animators would have killed for. Stone-hewn

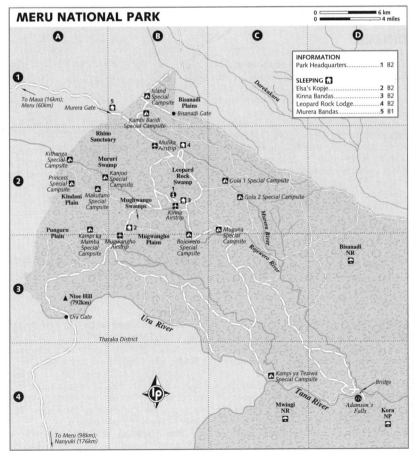

infinity pools plunge over the clifftops, while rock hyraxes play tag in your private garden. These features come with intense luxury pampering, wildlife drives, walking safaris and transfers. Check Elsa's website or email ahead of time for prices, as rates change on a weekly basis.

### Getting There & Away

There's no point reaching the park without a vehicle. If you don't want to join a tour, your cheapest option is to acquire a 4WD (and driver) from a local in Meru or the village of Maua, which is 31km from the gate. Regular matatus service Maua from Meru town (KSh150, one hour).

**Airkenya** ( ☎ 020-605745; www.airkenya.com) has daily flights connecting Meru to Nairobi (one way/round trip US$158/335).

## CHOGORIA

☎ 064

This town shares its name with the most difficult, rewarding route up Mt Kenya (p214). It's a friendly enough place, albeit with little to do besides get coifed in a wooden shack dubbed the Los Angeles Hair Salon.

You can probably arrange local accommodation with one of the many touts offering Mt Kenya climbs; otherwise, head to **Transit Motel** (Map p216; ☎ 22096; PO Box 190, Chogoria; camping per tent KSh500, s/tw incl breakfast KSh1000/1600) 2km south of town. This is a large, friendly lodge with nice rooms and a decent restaurant (meals KSh300 to KSh600) that makes a good base for organising Mt Kenya treks, and a relaxing spot to unwind once the slog is over. Don't believe touts claiming the motel has burnt down – it's a cement structure!

Regular buses and matatus ply the road heading north to Meru (KSh90, 30 minutes) and south to Embu (KSh170, 1½ hours) and Nairobi (KSh350, four hours).

## EMBU

☎ 068

This sleepy town is the unlikely capital of Eastern Province, but despite its local significance there's not a lot to do, and it's a long way from the mountain. It's still a good stopover on the way to (or from) Thika or Nairobi, and if you have your own transport, it's probably the best base for exploring Mwea National Reserve (opposite) or the coffee nurseries off the B6 and A2 highways. If you can, visit

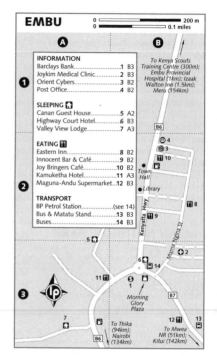

**EMBU**

0 ———— 200 m
0 ———— 0.1 miles

**INFORMATION**
Barclays Bank...................................1 B3
Joykim Medical Clinic.....................2 B3
Orient Cybers...................................3 B2
Post Office.........................................4 B2

**SLEEPING** 🏠
Canan Guest House.........................5 A2
Highway Court Hotel......................6 B3
Valley View Lodge...........................7 A3

**EATING** 🍴
Eastern Inn........................................8 B2
Innocent Bar & Café.......................9 B2
Joy Bringers Café...........................10 B2
Kamuketha Hotel..........................11 A3
Maguna-Andu Supermarket......12 B3

**TRANSPORT**
BP Petrol Station...................(see 14)
Bus & Matatu Stand.....................13 B3
Buses................................................14 B3

To Kenya Scouts Training Centre (300m); Embu Provincial Hospital (1km); Izaak Walton Inn (1.5km); Meru (154km)

Kenyatta Hwy

Mama Ngina St

Town Hall
Library

Morning Glory Plaza

To Thika (94km); Nairobi (134km)
To Mwea NR (51km); Kitui (142km)

around October/November, when the local jacaranda trees are in full, purple bloom; it's a magical sight that must rank as one of the most beautiful foliage shifts in Africa.

### Information

**Barclays Bank** (B6 Hwy) With ATM.
**Embu Provincial Hospital** (Kenyatta Hwy)
**Joykim Medical Clinic** (Mama Ngina St)
**Orient Cybers** (off Mama Ngina St; per hr KSh120) As fast as local internet gets (which is slow).
**Post office** (Kenyatta Hwy)

### Sleeping

**Kenya Scouts Training Centre** ( ☎ 30459; Kenyatta Hwy; camping KSh100, dm/s KSh250/650) It is what the title says: a training facility for the Kenyan Scouts, which happens to rent spotless, well-maintained rooms. It's a real bargain, embellished with shy, friendly service and a *very* strict no drugs, alcohol or tobacco policy. If you can give the above up for a night, this may be the best sleep in town.

**Canan Guest House** ( ☎ 020-20292571; off the B6; s/d KSh500/800) These smallish, green-and-white rooms set off from the main road are immaculate and very good value for money. This place also has a no smoking, toking or boozing policy (this includes *miraa*).

**Highway Court Hotel** ( ☎ 20298, 0720302919; Kenyatta Hwy; s KSh600-800, tw KSh1000-1300, all incl breakfast) The biggest option in town has clean rooms, some of which have TVs, and an energetic restaurant and bar downstairs. You can't beat the trippy mural of crocodiles stalking deer along a riverbank.

**Valley View Lodge** ( ☎ 31714; off B6 Hwy; s/d from KSh650/800) Painted in pea-soup shades of institutional green, this is a decent sleep with clean if slightly faded rooms. We're not sure how much of a valley view you can cop, although the top floors may afford a nice peek down the B6.

**Izaak Walton Inn** ( ☎ 20128; izaakwalton@winnet .co.ke; Kenyatta Hwy; s/d incl breakfast from KSh2500/3500) This rambling series of warm cottages and cabins has an old-school, eccentric air to it, like a hill station operated by a slightly off colonial bureaucrat. You can opt between older, rustic wood lodges or more contemporary cottages. The gardenlike grounds are perfect for an evening beer and some wicker-accented relaxation.

## Eating & Drinking

**Eastern Inn** (Mama Ngina St; meals KSh40-150; ☒ lunch & dinner) Fronted by a shady awning, this Christian restaurant serves up sandwiches, fried chicken and fish.

**Joy Bringers Cafe** (Mama Ngina St; meals KSh70-190; ☒ lunch & dinner) This is a cute little spot where kids run in and out, the food is basic African staples and the tea is surprisingly strong and bracing on a chilly winter morning.

**Innocent Bar & Cafe** (off Kenyatta Hwy; meals KSh80-200; ☒ lunch & dinner) Come here to catch some sports and news on the telly, beers in the spacious back room and good slabs of roast goat and *ugali* (a staple made from maize or cassava flour, or both) when you're hungry.

**Kamuketha Hotel** (B6 Hwy; meals KSh80-200; ☒ lunch & dinner) If you're in the market for some fresh, fried tilapia, the Kamuketha provides nicely.

**Maguna-Andu Supermarket** (B7 Hwy) A well-stocked supermarket.

## Getting There & Away

Regular Kensilver buses heading to Meru (KSh300, two hours) and Nairobi (KSh300,

three hours) pick up passengers at the BP petrol station in the centre of town. There are also express buses to Nairobi (KSh500, 1½ to two hours).

Mombasa Liners leave the BP station for Mombasa (KSh900, 10 hours) each morning at 7.30am.

There are numerous matatus serving Chogoria (KSh170, 1½ hours), Meru (KSh320, two hours), Thika (KSh250, two hours), Nyeri (KSh200, two hours), Nanyuki (KSh300, 2½ hours), Nyahururu (KSh400, three hours), Nairobi (KSh300, three hours) and Nakuru (KSh500, 4½ hours).

## MWEA NATIONAL RESERVE

In contrast to the rich greens that characterise so much of the highlands, this reserve is set in a dry depression that is nonetheless beautiful in a stony-scarp, thornbush and aloe-field kind of way. Kamburu Dam, at the meeting point of the Tana and Thiba Rivers, forms the focus for the 48-sq-km **reserve** (Map p200; adult/child US$20/10). Enclosed by an electric fence, elephants, hippos, buffaloes, lesser kudu and myriad birdlife are present here.

There's a **campsite** (adult/child US$15/10) with basic facilities (no water) close to the reserve headquarters and another site with similar facilities close to Hippo Point. In wet season the nearest formal accommodation is in Embu, while in dry season there's a 14km short cut from the gate southwest to the **Masinga Dam Lodge** ( ☎ Nairobi 020-341781, 0733223831; camping KSh600, s KSh1500-2000, d KSh2800-3500; ☒ ). It's a nice collection of terraced cottages that looks over the dam and plains; the Kenyan national kayaking team occasionally trains here.

Mwea is best accessed from the 11km dirt road that's signposted off the B7 Hwy some 40km south of Embu. There's a signposted 27km dirt track to the park that's 14km south of Embu, but the going is very rough. A 4WD is essential to get to Mwea and around the park.

## OL DONYO SABUK NATIONAL PARK

This tiny **park** (Map p200; ☎ 067-4355257; adult/child US$20/10) is built around the summit and slopes of **Ol Donyo Sabuk** (2146m), known by the Kikuyu as Kilimambongo (Buffalo Mountain). The name fits, as buffaloes are indisputably the dominant animals; this is one of the best places in Kenya to spot these lumbering beasts, which are actually one of the more dangerous members of the Big Five. The rest of the mountain is surrounded by an oasis of dense primeval forest that supports primates like black-and-white colobus and blue monkeys.

It's possible to explore on foot if accompanied by a ranger (per half/full day KSh2500/ KSh1500). It's a 9km hike (three or four hours) to an amazing 360-degree view at the summit, which is crowned with the sort of weird Afro-alpine fauna you'd otherwise have to climb Mt Kenya to see.

There's a pretty **campsite** (adult/child US$10/5) just before the main gate. Facilities include one long-drop toilet, a rusty tap and free firewood. If you want a bit more comfort, **Sabuk House** (US$30) is a lovely lodge that comes at a bargain rate compared to similar KWS bandas. You'll want to bring your own food and water if you're staying at either of these places.

From Thika, take a matatu to the village of Ol Donyo Sabuk (KSh90, 50 minutes), from where it's a 2km walk along a straight dirt road to the gate. You could also take a matatu heading to Kitui and hop off at Kilimambongo (KSh70, 45 minutes), which is 6km from Ol Donyo Sabuk village.

## THIKA
☎ 067

Those famous flame trees aren't around anymore, replaced with the bustle of a highway service town and red-earth-caked pineapple plantations (Del Monte is a big player in these parts). The only true 'attractions' are **Chania Falls** and **Thika Falls**, about 1km north of town on the busy Nairobi–Nyeri road, but mainly Thika is a base for a visit to Ol Donyo Sabuk National Park. You can also visit **Jomo Kenyatta's** house about 40km north of here; you'll need your own transport and it's a KSh100 admission to see…well, just a house, but if you're a Kenyan history buff, you might not want to pass it up.

# Northern Kenya

Situation Vacant: adventurers required to boldly go where few have gone before.

We are searching for daring explorers to challenge themselves against some of the most exciting wilderness in Africa. This role will most suit somebody able to withstand appalling roads that would shake a lesser mortal into submission, searing heat, clouds of dust and sand torn up by relentless winds, primitive food and accommodation, vast distances and more than a hint of danger (see p228).

The generous compensation package includes memories of vast shattered lava deserts, camel herders walking their animals to lost oases, fog-shrouded mountains full of mysterious creatures, prehistoric islands crawling with massive reptiles, jokes shared with traditionally dressed warriors and nights spent in smoky village huts. Additional perks include camel trekking through piles of peachy dunes, elephant encounters in scrubby acacia woodlands, nights spent out in the open wishing upon shooting stars and, of course, the chance to walk barefoot along the fabled shores of a sea of jade.

In our 21st-century world of wireless internet connection, always-on mobile phones and dumbed-down TV, this is a rare opportunity to experience a land and a lifestyle that allows you to leave behind all that is familiar and to fall completely off the radar. This is northern Kenya and it will be completely unlike anywhere else you know.

---

## HIGHLIGHTS

- Blasting over the plains of darkness destined for a sea of jade, **Lake Turkana** (p245)

- Searching for forest elephants lost in an ocean of sand in **Marsabit National Park** (p239)

- Shaking hands with the Samburu, crocodile fishing with the El Molo and passing the time of day with the Turkana in **South Horr** (p245), **Loyangalani** (p246) and **Lodwar** (p251)

- Getting your first taste of *injera* and *wat* and washing it down with an espresso in **Moyale** (p240), the end of one adventure and the gateway to another

- Realising not only do zebras change their stripes in **Samburu National Reserve** (p234) but giraffes change their spots and ostriches their legs

- Leading your camels to water in the remote oases villages of **Kalacha** (p248) and **North Horr** (p248)

**WARNING**

Unfortunately, the strong warrior traditions of northern Kenya's nomadic peoples have led to security problems plaguing the region for years. With an influx of cheap guns from conflict zones surrounding Kenya, minor conflicts stemming from grazing rights and cattle rustling (formerly settled by compensation rather than violence) have quickly escalated into ongoing gun battles that the authorities struggle to contain.

While travellers, who rarely witness any intertribal conflict, may consider the issue exaggerated, the scale of the problem is enormous and growing. Over the past decade hundreds of people are thought to have been killed and more than 160,000 been displaced by intertribal conflicts. To give some scale to the problem, in just the final week of research of this guide 15 people were killed in northern Kenya during cattle raids – a figure that is by no means unusual. Fortunately, security on the main routes in the north, and anywhere a tourist is likely to be, has changed for the better. Convoys and armed guards are no longer used between Marich and Lodwar or between Isiolo and Moyale, on the Ethiopian border.

Sadly, not everything is on the mend, and bloody conflict continues in large parts of the north. The whole northeastern region around Garsen, Garissa, Wajir and Mandera is still *shifta* (bandit) country and you should avoid travelling here. Buses heading to Lamu and between Garissa and Thika have been attacked in the past. Intrepid travellers heading up the Suguta Valley should be aware that armed gangs roam these lands and have assaulted foreigners.

Incidentally, travelling up towards the Somali border (which is currently closed) has been dangerous for years, but with the renewed fighting in that blood-saturated country and US air strikes against suspected Al Qaeda militants along the border, only the most foolhardy would attempt to travel up here.

Improvements or not, security in northern Kenya is a fluid entity, and travellers should seek local advice about the latest developments before travelling and never take unnecessary risks.

## Geography

Northern Kenya's diverse landscapes are truly amazing. Deserts range from large tracts of scrub, dissected by *luggas* (dry river beds that burst into violent life after heavy rains) and peppered with acacia trees, to Chalbi's inhospitable black stones and Karoli's soft sands.

Massive dormant shield volcanos like Mt Kulal and Mt Marsabit climb from barren plains to provide forested havens for humans and animals, while countless steep, Martian-like stratovolcanoes burst from lava fields and Lake Turkana's waters. In other areas, such as South Horr, craggy peaks shelter clear streams that flow through valley oases of lush vegetation.

Lake Turkana is the north's most renowned geographic feature and covers an amazing 6405 sq km, making it earth's largest permanent desert lake.

## Climate

The climate here reflects the landscape's incredible contrasts. Temperatures on the plains can reach 44°C, without a breath of wind, only for the desert's dead calm to be shattered by sudden violent thunderstorms that drench everything in an awe-inspiring pyrotechnics display that disappears as quickly as it comes.

The lone constant is the stifling heat and strong winds around Lake Turkana.

## National Parks & Reserves

From the celebrated African animals of today, thriving along the Ewaso Ngiro River's lush banks in the Samburu, Shaba and Buffalo Springs National Reserves (p234), to the fossilised evidence of early humans and prehistoric animals in the scorching soils of Sibiloi National Park (p247), northern Kenya's national parks and reserves cover a breadth of landscapes, wilderness and history unimaginable elsewhere.

Also intriguing is Marsabit National Park (p239), whose rich forest and shy wildlife rest on the cool slopes of a massive volcano rising gently out of the baking northern plains. Dramatic volcanic landscapes of an entirely different manifestation burst bleakly from Lake Turkana's waters and form South Island (p246) and Central Island (p251) National Parks, which, together with Sibiloi, comprise a Unesco World Heritage site. However, you

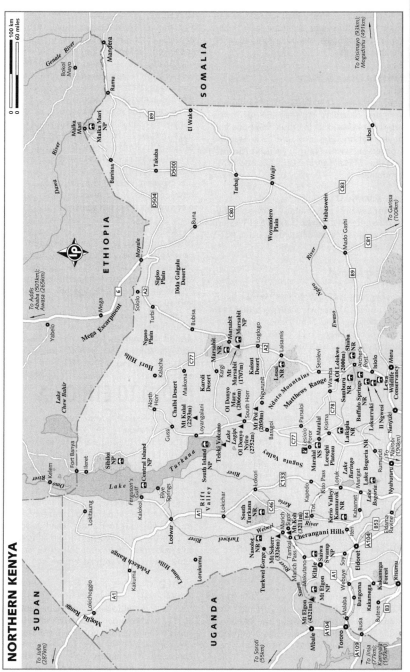

NORTHERN KENYA

needn't enter a national park to see large animals here; numerous antelope, zebras and plenty of elephants can be seen along even the main roads.

## Getting There & Away

### AIR

Daily **Airkenya** ( ☎ Nairobi 020-605745; www.airkenya .com) and **Safarilink** ( ☎ Nairobi 020-600777; www .safarilink-kenya.com) services link Samburu and Shaba National Reserves and Lewa Wildlife Conservancy with Nairobi (Wilson Airport) and the Masai Mara. See p237 and p233 for details.

### BUS & MATATU

Countless bus and matatu services enter northern Kenya from the Central and Western Highlands. They are detailed on p207, p219, p221 and p195.

## Getting Around

### 4WD

Having your own 4WD gives you flexibility but comes with its own challenges, thanks to wide-ranging road conditions. For starters you'll need a large 4WD (a Toyota RAV4 or Suzuki won't do) with high ground clearance and a skid plate to protect the undercarriage. You should have a high-rise jack, sand ladders, a shovel, a long, strong rope or chain (to hitch up to camels or other vehicles) plus enough fuel, water and spare tyres (one is rarely enough). A compass and good map are also invaluable.

Do not underestimate how bad the roads are up here – during a month's research in the far north we ploughed through three large 4WDs. Many car rental companies simply will not allow their vehicles to be taken north of Samburu. If you do come up here it's sensible to take an experienced driver and, if possible, travel in company with another jeep.

Road conditions between destinations are discussed in each town's Getting There & Away section.

### BUS & MATATU

There's regular public transport as far north as Kalokol and Lokichoggio on Turkana's west side, but it's more limited up the lake's east side, only reaching Maralal via Nyahururu or Isiolo. With improved security, buses now run from Isiolo to Moyale on the Ethiopian border via Marsabit.

### HITCHING

For the ultimate Kenyan adventure hop aboard a dusty transport truck with the locals. It's an uncomfortable and dirty, but utterly enchanting, way to travel around northern Kenya. However, improved bus services mean that Loyangalani is the only major destination that still requires hitching.

To enjoy the experience you must throw out your schedule and accept that you'll spend days waiting for rides. Unlike in the West hitching in Kenya is not free, though the per-kilometre rate is less than the equivalent bus fare. Security is another issue, as bandits are more interested in cattle trucks than buses, and for this reason hitching can't be recommended unreservedly.

### SAFARIS

A few organised safaris and overland trucks now go to Lake Turkana's west, but most still stick to the lake's east side. Average trips are seven to 10 days long and they typically follow the same route. See p65 for details and operators.

Other options include camel safaris, although treks down into the Suguta Valley should be approached with caution for security reasons. See p89 for more camel safari information.

# ISIOLO TO ETHIOPIA

For most people this route means two things: the wildlife riches of the Samburu ecosystem or the road to the cultural riches of Ethiopia. But in between and beyond, this area has much more to offer. You can drink tea and track game with the Samburu people, climb mist-shrouded volcanoes in the desert, blaze trails in untrammelled mountains, jeep-surf down sand dunes and get so far off the beaten track you'll start to wonder whether you're still on the same planet. All told, this massive wilderness offers something to everyone whose heart sings with adventure.

## ISIOLO

☎ 064

Isiolo is where anticipation and excitement first start to send your heart a-flutter. This vital pit stop on the long road north is a true frontier town, a place on the edge, torn between the cool, verdant highlands just to the south and the scorching badlands, home of nomads and explorers, to the north. On a more practical note it's also the last place with decent facilities until Maralal or Marsabit.

One of the first things you'll undoubtedly notice is the large Somali population (descendants of WWI veterans who settled here) and the striking faces of Boran, Samburu and Turkana people walking the streets, and it's this mix of people, cultures and religions that is the most interesting thing about Isiolo. Nowhere is this mixture better illustrated than in the hectic market.

## Information

**Barclays Bank** (A2 Hwy) With an ATM. Banks are scarce in the north, so plan ahead.

**District Hospital** (Hospital Rd; 24hr)

**Isiolo Telephone Exchange** (Hospital Rd) Calling cards and card phones.

**Minds Computer Services** (per hr KSh60; 8am-7pm) Reasonable internet connections. Just off the A2 Hwy.

**Post office** (Hospital Rd)

## Sleeping

Isiolo has happy homes for budget and mid-range travellers (and their vehicles), but desperately lacks decent top-end options.

**Jabal-Nur Plaza Boarding & Lodging** (☎ 52460; s with/without bathroom KSh400/300, d KSh500/400) Pleasing budget digs that get frequent fresh licks of paint. The showers have hot water – or at least the facilities for making it!

**Transit Hotel** (s/tw KSh700/1300; P) This multi-storey job is an excellent hangout, with immaculately clean rooms and hot showers in the morning. The central courtyard is a good place to find easy conversations but it can be a little noisy. Breakfast is an additional KSh200.

**Range Land Hotel** (☎ 52099; A2 Hwy; camping KSh200, tw cottages KSh1500; P) About 8km south of town, this is a nice option for campers and families. The sunny campsite has bickering weaver birds in abundance, as well as neat and tidy stone bungalows with hot showers. Many people come to laze around at weekends but in the week it's quiet. Meals can be prepared with advance notice.

**Bomen Hotel** (☎ 52389; s/tw/ste KSh900/1500/2500; P) The NGOs' favourite home, the Bomen Hotel has the town's brightest (ask for one facing outward) and most comfortable rooms. Room prices are steep and you can get much the same at the Transit Hotel for less,

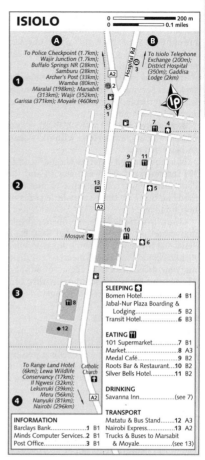

**ISIOLO**

0 ——— 200 m
0 ——— 0.1 miles

To Police Checkpoint (1.7km);
Wajir Junction (1.7km);
Buffalo Springs NR (28km);
Samburu (28km);
Archer's Post (33km);
Wamba (80km);
Maralal (198km); Marsabit
(313km); Wajir (352km);
Garissa (371km); Moyale (460km)

To Isiolo Telephone
Exchange (200m);
District Hospital
(350m); Gaddisa
Lodge (2km)

Mosque

To Range Land Hotel
(6km); Lewa Wildlife
Conservancy (17km);
Il Ngwesi (32km);
Lekurruki (39km);
Meru (56km);
Nanyuki (81km);
Nanyuki (296km)

Catholic
Church

**INFORMATION**
Barclays Bank....................1 B1
Minds Computer Services..2 B1
Post Office.......................3 B1

**SLEEPING** 🏠
Bomen Hotel....................4 B1
Jabal-Nur Plaza Boarding &
Lodging........................5 B2
Transit Hotel...................6 B3

**EATING** 🍴
101 Supermarket..............7 B1
Market............................8 A3
Medal Café......................9 B2
Roots Bar & Restaurant...10 B2
Silver Bells Hotel............11 B2

**DRINKING**
Savanna Inn..................(see 7)

**TRANSPORT**
Matatu & Bus Stand........12 A3
Nairobi Express..............13 A2
Trucks & Buses to Marsabit
& Moyale................(see 13)

but bonus options include TVs and shared terraces with views.

**Gaddisa Lodge** (☎ 724201115; www.gaddisa.com; s/tw KSh3000/4000; P) Around 3km northeast of town is this lonely Dutch-run lodge, where peaceful cottages overlook the fringes of the northern savanna country. There's a pool, though you won't need to pack your bathers, as it's normally empty. It's overpriced for what you get.

## Eating & Drinking

**Medal Café** (meals KSh100; lunch & dinner) A tiny place crammed full of locals seated around a blaring TV eating greasy meals for a handful of shillings. Don't forget to pet the lamb frozen to the spot!

**Silver Bells Hotel** (meals KSh80-200;  lunch & dinner) Decent Kenyan favourites will be brought to your blue-and-white-checked table. It's a good spot for grabbing a cheap predeparture breakfast.

**Transit Hotel** (meals KSh120-250;  lunch & dinner) A rare place serving more than the local usuals, with fried tilapia, pepper steak, goulash and curries up for grabs.

**Bomen Hotel** ( ☎ 52389; meals KSh130-380;  lunch & dinner) Think Transit Hotel with nicer seats and elevated prices.

Northbound self-caterers should head to **101 Supermarket** (  8am-6pm Mon-Sat) and the daily **market** near the mosque to purchase food and drink, as there's very little available beyond here.

Owing to a strong Muslim influence, drinking venues are rare – check out **Roots Bar & Restaurant** where you can chow down on some *nyama choma* (barbecued meat) whilst shaking your dreadlocks to a reggae soundtrack. The **Savanna Inn** is a much more rowdy late-night drinking den near the Bomen.

### Getting There & Away

Although convoys are no longer being used north to Marsabit, check the security situation thoroughly before leaving. This is especially critical if heading towards Garissa, Wajir or Mandera, which are currently considered unsafe for travellers.

#### 4WD

Isiolo marks the tarmac's northern terminus and the start of the corrugated dirt and gravel, which will shake the guts out of you and your vehicle. There are several petrol stations here, so top up, as prices climb and supplies diminish northward. If you're heading south, note that Central Highlands petrol is cheaper.

#### BUS & MATATU

Lots of bus companies serve Nairobi with most buses leaving between 6am and 6.30am (KSh500, 4½ hours) from the main road through town and also stopping at the matatu and bus stand just south of the market. **Nairobi Express** (A2 Hwy) is one of the more reliable operators. Nightly buses creep north to Marsabit (KSh800, nine hours) and Moyale (KSh1500, 20 hours) and, with a bit of luck, you'll get the bus operated by the brilliantly named **Sir Alex Ferguson Bus Company.** Buses pick up passengers from outside the Nairobi Express of-

fice sometime between 11pm and midnight. Tickets cannot be bought in advance, so get there early and shout, push and shove with the best of them.

For Maralal take an early-morning matatu to Wamba (KSh300, 2½ hours), and then a Maralal-bound matatu (KSh400, 2½ hours) from there. Regular matatus leave from a chaotic stand around the market and also serve Archer's Post (KSh120, 45 minutes) and Meru (KSh150, 1½ hours). Peugeots (shared taxis) also service Nanyuki (KSh200, 1¾ hours).

#### HITCHING

Trucks are filthy and uncomfortable but a viable option for the northbound adventurous. Although they pick up passengers at the police checkpoint north of town, better seats are available if you board when they stop near Nairobi Express. Drain your bladder, purchase enough food, water and sunscreen, and hop aboard. Prices are negotiable but reckon on KSh500 to Marsabit and KSh1000 to Moyale.

## LEWA WILDLIFE CONSERVANCY

While the massive 263-sq-km **Lewa Wildlife Conservancy** (LWC; ☎ 064-31405; www.lewa.org; admission incl in accommodation rates), just south of Isiolo, could boast about their luxury lodges, stunning scenery, astounding wildlife activities and having hosted Prince William, they'd rather talk about their community and conservation projects. Founded in 1995, LWC is a nonprofit organisation that invests around 70% of its annual US$2 million–plus budget into healthcare, education and various community projects for surrounding villages, whilst the rest funds further conservation and security projects. To help raise awareness and funds they host one of the world's most rewarding and exhausting marathons (see boxed text, opposite).

The conservation effort has been astounding and 20% of the world's Grevy's zebras, 11% of Kenya's black rhinos, a rare population of aquatic sitatunga antelope and sizeable populations of white rhinos, elephants and buffaloes. Of the predators there are small, but growing, populations of leopards, lions and cheetahs, and it's thought that a pack of wild dogs may still lurk about.

Wildlife drives in private vehicles aren't permitted and only guests of the LWC's lodges are allowed into the conservancy. A plethora of activities, ranging from drives (day and

---

**RUNNING FOR YOUR LIFE**

It's one thing to run a marathon to the encouraging screams of people, it's entirely another to run it sharing the course with elephants, rhinos and the odd antelope! Established in 2000 to raise funds for wildlife conservation and community development, the Safaricom Marathon, run within the Lewa Wildlife Conservancy in late June/early July, attracts world-record holders and is renowned worldwide as one of the planet's toughest marathons. Thanks to experienced rangers, helicopters and spotter planes, your only worry should be the heat and the 1700m average elevation. Visit www.tusk.org for more information and registration details.

---

night) and walks to horse riding and camel rides, are available at most lodges. Guests are encouraged to take part in conservation activities, like tracking and tagging animals.

## Sleeping & Eating

There are a number of very exclusive, expensive places to stay inside the wildlife conservancy. These include the beautiful **Lewa House**, with its three sublime thatched cottages and even more sublime main building, and **Lewa Safari Camp**, which isn't really like camping at all. For both these you must book through **Bush and Beyond** ( ☎ Nairobi 020-600457; www.bush-and-beyond.com) and reckon on a minimum of US$600 per person, per day for full board and lodging.

## Getting There & Away

LWC is only 12km south of Isiolo and is well signposted on the A2 Hwy. **Airkenya** ( ☎ Nairobi 020-605745; www.airkenya.com) as well as **Safarilink** ( ☎ Nairobi 020-600777; www.safarilink-kenya.com) have daily flights to LWC from Nairobi. Return fares on Airkenya/Safarilink are US$234/282, excluding taxes.

## AROUND LEWA WILDLIFE CONSERVANCY

### Il Ngwesi

Il Ngwesi is a project linking wildlife conservation and community development. The Maasai of Il Ngwesi, with help from neighbour LWC, have transformed this undeveloped land, previously used for subsistence pastoralism, into a prime wildlife conservation area hosting white and black rhinos, waterbucks, giraffes and other plains animals. It's truly fitting that Il Ngwesi translates to 'people of wildlife'.

The community now supplements its herding income with tourist dollars gained from their award-winning ecolodge, **Il Ngwesi Group Ranch** ( ☎ Nairobi 020-340331; info@letsgosafari.com; s/d incl all meals US$209/418; ☒ ). Six open-fronted thatched cottages boast views over the dramatic escarpment. The best part is that profits go straight to the Maasai community.

## ARCHER'S POST

This dusty, ramshackle village sits 33km north of Isiolo and is perfect for budget travellers visiting the nearby reserves. There's definitely a forgotten-world feel to the place, with proud Samburu men drifting down the main street trailed by camels, and women in butterfly-beautiful garments. It's the kind of place that will linger in your mind forever.

There's a small **market** (Map p236) off the A2, but little else in the way of services.

There are a number of Samburu villages in the area that welcome paying guests. Probably the best one is **Umoja village**, which was originally founded as a refuge for abused women and has now budded into a viable village in its own right. Admission is KSh500. It's located next to the Umoja campsite (see p234).

Eight kilometres north of Archer's Post is the immense 384-sq-km **Kalama Community Wildlife Conservancy** (admission adult/child US$40/20), which opened in 2004 and hosts wildlife, including Grevy's zebras, elephants and reticulated giraffes, and acts as a vital wildlife corridor for animals migrating between the Samburu and Marsabit area. The road network is still undeveloped, but guides lead walks and hikes up **Kalama Hill**. **Camping** (KSh500) in their three pleasant shady sites is for the hard-core, whilst the **Saruni Samburu Lodge** (www.sarunisamburu.com) is for the hard-core who still like frilly extras and lymphatic drainage massages. This community-run project supports a couple of hundred local families and apparently, once the Italian owner of the lodge has reclaimed the money he has invested, he will hand the lodge over to the community.

About 30km north of town and shrouded in Samburu folklore is the massive mesa of

**STALL TACTICS**

In 1990, 15 women who'd suffered too long from violent husbands abandoned their homes and started the village of Umoja (meaning 'unity' in Kiswahili), just outside Archer's Post. They hoped to survive together by producing and selling traditional Samburu jewellery to tourists. It all proved rather successful and Umoja thrived, even opening a campsite a few years later. Boosted by its success, 33 more women left unhappy situations and now call the women-only village home.

Local men were fairly tolerant initially, but apathy became jealousy among some, which resulted in the establishment of rival trinket stalls nearby. Following the newer stalls' failure and the women's continued success, there have been reports of angry men warning tourist vehicles not to visit Umoja. Worse still are recent raids on Umoja by men threatening these women with violence – something they had hoped to have left behind for good. Find out more about them at www.umojawomen.org.

**Ol Lolokwe**. It's a great day hike (five hours just to climb up it) and, at sunset, light radiating off its rusty bluffs is seen for miles around. It's now managed by the **Namunyak Wildlife Conservation Trust**, which is a locally run community-based conservation effort. It charges US$20 to climb it and US$50 for a guide.

A number of locals can take you on wildlife-tracking walks in the surrounding wilderness. **Mohamed Leeresh** ( ☎ 0724143080) is recommended. He charges US$50 per day, per group.

Don't want to camp with the lions and leopards in the national reserves? Want to save some moolah? Head to the brilliant ourpick **Umoja campsite** (Map p236; ☎ 721659717; www .umojawomen.org; camping KSh300, tent hire KSh500, bandas s/tw KSh1500/2000), which sits on the Ewaso Ngiro's banks between town and Archer's Post gate. It's run by women who've fled abusive husbands (see boxed text, above) and has clean and comfortable bandas, great camping, a chilled cafe (meals available on request) and frequent big-nosed, big-eared visitors coming in from the reserves.

While **Uaso Cafe** (Map p236; A2 Hwy; meals KSh60-150; ☾ lunch & dinner) isn't the only restaurant in town, it's the only place to eat – enough said.

### Getting There & Away

Matatus from Isiolo stop here en route to Wamba (KSh300, 1¾ hours) and those coming from Wamba also pick up for Isiolo (KSh120, 45 minutes). If you rock up in public transport and need a jeep to get into the reserves they can be hired for around US$100 through the Umoja campsite. Expensive fuel is available by the jerry can from several shops in town.

## SAMBURU, BUFFALO SPRINGS & SHABA NATIONAL RESERVES

Blistered with termite skyscrapers, shot through with the muddy Ewaso Ngiro River and heaving with heavyweight animals, the three national reserves of Samburu, Buffalo Springs and Shaba are not as famous as some others, but they have a beauty that is unsurpassed, as well as a population of creatures that occur in no other major Kenyan park. These include the blue-legged Somali ostrich, super-stripy Grevy's zebras, unicorn-like beisa oryxes, ravishing reticulated giraffes and the gerenuk – a gazelle that dearly wishes to be a giraffe. Despite comprising of just 300 sq km, the breadth of vegetation and landscapes here is amazing; Shaba, with its great rocky *kopjes* (isolated hills), natural springs and doum palms, is the most physically beautiful, as well as the least visited. Meanwhile the open savannas, scrub desert and verdant river foliage in Samburu and Buffalo Springs virtually guarantee close encounters with elephants and all the others.

### Information

Conveniently, **Buffalo Springs**, **Shaba** and **Samburu** (admission adult/child US$40/20) entries are interchangeable, so you only pay once, even if you're visiting all three in one day.

If you're driving, Survey of Kenya's map *Samburu & Buffalo Springs Game Reserves* is helpful, but it is hard to find. Getting around isn't difficult but some minor roads are for 4WDs only, and while signage has improved in Samburu, the maze of wayward minibus tracks can be confusing.

Petrol is available at Sarova Shaba Lodge and Samburu Game Lodge, but stock up in Isiolo.

## Sleeping & Eating

Each reserve is blessed with at least one luxury lodge and several campsites. For campers and day visitors, all the luxury lodges have buffet meals (US$25).

### BUFFALO SPRINGS NATIONAL RESERVE

The five **public campsites** (camping US$10) close to Gare Mara gate are overgrown, hard to find and have absolutely no facilities or water. For toilets, showers and less solitude, camp in Samburu.

**Special campsites** (camping US$15) While scenically located by freshwater springs along the Isiolo and Maji ya Chumvi Rivers, there are no facilities here.

**Samburu Serena Lodge** ( ☎ Nairobi 020-2842333; www.serenahotels.com; s/d full board US$285/385; ☒ ) The comfy cottages, with breezy verandas, reed-lined ceilings and canopy beds, feel a little like over-the-top tents and have delightful river views.

### SAMBURU NATIONAL RESERVE

**Beach Camp** ( ☎ 0721252737; camping KSh500, tents for hire KSh500) On the banks of the Ewaso Ngiro River's northern bank, this site has the setting of any of the big-boy lodges but, let's face it, this is much more authentic Africa. It's a good idea to bring your own bedding. Meals can be prepared on request. Vervet monkeys and baboons can be a menace though.

**Samburu public campsite** (camping US$10) Several public campsites can be found close to the Beach Camp, though most lack even basic amenities.

**Special campsites** (camping US$15) Special they're not – bush sites with no facilities or water. They're further west and tricky to find.

**Samburu Intrepids Club** ( ☎ 064-30453, in Nairobi 020-446651; full board s/d US$195/225; ☒ ) Grab a drink, sink into the bar's teak lounges and gaze over the Ewaso Ngiro towards the poor people living in the village just outside the reserve – the ultimate example of the haves and have-nots! While thatched roofs and canopy beds scream luxurious tents scream safari Africa, the refined furniture unfortunately shrieks Fortune 500. The friendly service is unmatched.

**Elephant Watch Camp** ( ☎ Nairobi 020-891112; www.elephantwatchsafaris.com; s/d full board incl guided walks US$550/1000; closed Apr & Nov) Undoubtedly the most unique and memorable place to stay in the reserves. Massive thatched roofs cling to crooked acacia branches and tower over cosy, palatial, eight-sided tents and large grass-mat-clad terraces. Natural materials dominate and the bathrooms are stunning. Owners Iain and Oria Douglas-Hamilton are renowned elephant experts.

### SHABA NATIONAL RESERVE

**Special campsites** (camping US$15) Of the several sites (no facilities), Funan, set in Shaba's core,

---

**REBECCA LOLOSOLI**

Dressed in bright beads and necklaces Rebecca Lolosoli greets us at the entrance to her smoky hut. She seems like every other shy Samburu woman and not at all the sort of person to turn her community on its head. But as the founder of the Umoja village (opposite) that is exactly what she's done.

**What first gave you the idea to start a breakaway 'women only' village?** There were many local women here who were very poor but never had a voice in how the community was run. One day I asked for a chance to speak at a community meeting but was told to keep quiet and not to stand up when speaking to men. Afterwards other women came to speak to me about it. We began to have meetings and decided to make some money of our own by selling handicrafts to tourists. We had many problems from the men because of this; sometimes they'd slap us and push us into the thorns, so that is when we decided to set up our own village. There are now 48 of us living here, and since then we have helped 60 other groups in other areas start their own villages and projects.

**What are you most proud of?** We are proud of how we have marketed this project. We are also proud of our school and our teachers. We asked the government to help us set it up, but they wouldn't, so we built it ourselves and it's free for children to attend. Now many people want their children to attend our school. We even feed the children there for free and at Christmas we have a big party and give the children presents.

NORTHERN KENYA

# SAMBURU & BUFFALO SPRINGS NATIONAL RESERVES

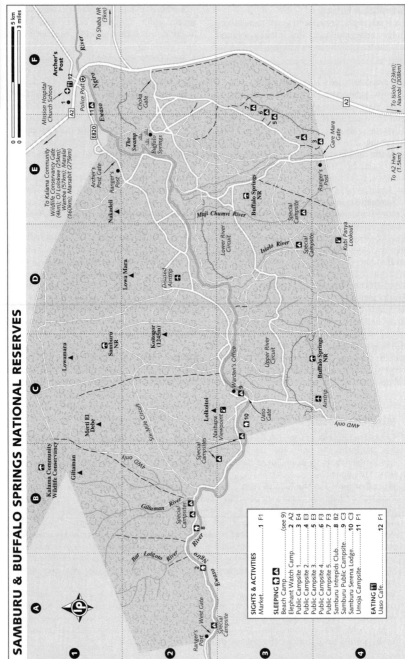

**SIGHTS & ACTIVITIES**

Market.................................1 F1

**SLEEPING**

Beach Camp....................(see 9)
Elephant Watch Camp........2 A2
Public Campsite 1..............3 E4
Public Campsite 2..............4 E3
Public Campsite 3..............5 E3
Public Campsite 4..............6 F3
Public Campsite 5..............7 F3
Samburu Intrepids Club.....8 B2
Samburu Public Campsite...9 C3
Samburu Serena Lodge.....10 C3
Umoja Campsite................11 F1

**EATING**

Uaso Cafe.......................12 F1

takes the cake. Shaded by acacias, it's next to a semipermanent spring, which provides water for visitors and wildlife. A ranger must accompany you to these sites; the cost is included in the fee but a tip is appropriate.

**Shaba Sarova Lodge** ( ☎ Nairobi 020-713333; s/d full board US$270/320; ☎ ) This spectacular place nestles on the Ewaso Ngiro River and its pathways intertwine with frog-filled streams and ponds. Next to the magnificent pool, natural springs flow through the gorgeous open-air bar and beneath the lofty 200-seat restaurant. The rooms? They're pretty lavish too! And the local animals are turned into entertainment by leaving bait out.

### Getting There & Away
The vehicle-less can wrangle a 4WD and driver in Archer's Post for about US$100 per day. **Airkenya** ( ☎ Nairobi 020-605745; www.airkenya.com) and **Safarilink** ( ☎ Nairobi 020-600777; www.safarilink-kenya.com) have frequent flights from Nairobi to Samburu. Return fares on Airkenya/Safarilink are US$253/296.

## MATTHEWS RANGE
West of the remarkable flat-topped mountain Ol Lolokwe and north of Wamba is the Matthews Range. The name might sound tame enough, but rest assured that this is real wilderness Africa, full of a thousand forest-clad adventures. These forests and dramatic slopes support a wealth of wildlife, including elephants, lions, buffaloes and Kenya's most important wild dog population. With few roads and almost no facilities, only those willing to go the extra mile on foot will be rewarded with the spoils.

In 1995 the local Samburu communities collectively formed the **Namunyak Wildlife Conservation Trust**, now one of Kenya's most successful community conservation programs. The trust is unique as it's run by a democratically elected board, each community having one trustee. Now endorsed by the Kenya Wildlife Service (KWS), it oversees 750 sq km and has substantially increased animal populations by successfully combating poaching.

The main base for the mountains is the one-street town of **Wamba**, remarkable only for the amount of drunks that roam around. If you intend to explore the mountains independently and on foot then you will need a guide. Unfortunately, most of the self-appointed guides are in fact the aforementioned drunks, and none of them can really be recommended.

The basic **El-Moran** (s KSh250, with shared bathroom KSh150) in Wamba is the only option besides bush camping. It's very basic indeed, but if it's Africa you want then it's Africa you'll get! If it's full you could try the local mission (which incidentally has northern Kenya's best hospital, a fact worth remembering while in the bush).

### Getting There & Away
While matatus from Isiolo (KSh300; p232) and Maralal (KSh350; p242) do reach Wamba, there's little point in coming without a vehicle.

## NDOTO MOUNTAINS
Climbing from the Korante Plain's sands are the magnificent rusty bluffs and ridges of the Ndoto Mountains. Kept a virtual secret from the travelling world by their remote location, the Ndotos abound with hiking, climbing and bouldering potential. **Mt Poi** (2050m), which resembles the world's largest bread loaf from some angles, is a technical climber's dream, its sheer 800m north face begging to be bagged. If you're fit and have a whole day to spare, it's a great hike to the summit and the views are extraordinary.

The tiny village of **Ngurunit** is the best base for your adventures and is interesting in its own right, with captivating, traditionally dressed Samburu people living in simple, yet elegantly woven, grass huts.

### Getting There & Away
Ngurunit is best accessed from Loglogo, 47km south of Marsabit and 233km north of Archer's Post. From Loglogo it's a tricky 79km drive (1¾ hours), with many forks, through the Kaisut Desert. Offer a lift to someone in Loglogo looking for a ride to Ngurunit – for a cheap (free!) and helpful guide.

To access Ngurunit from Baragoi, head about 40km north towards South Horr and, after descending the first steep paved section and crossing the following *lugga*, look out for Lmerim Nursery School. Found it? The Ngurunit turn-off is 200m behind you!

## MARSABIT
☎ 069
Marsabit is a long way from anywhere. The road from Isiolo will rattle your fillings and

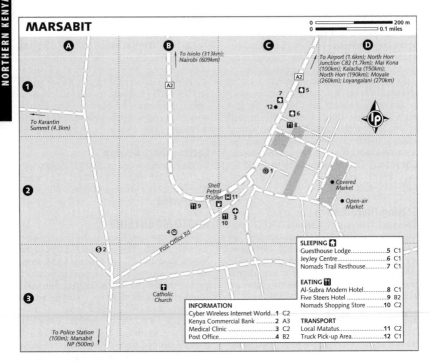

**MARSABIT**

| SLEEPING |
|---|
| Guesthouse Lodge.................**5** C1 |
| JeyJey Centre.......................**6** C1 |
| Nomads Trail Resthouse..........**7** C1 |

| EATING |
|---|
| Al-Subra Modern Hotel............**8** C1 |
| Five Steers Hotel .....................**9** B2 |
| Nomads Shopping Store ........**10** C2 |

| INFORMATION |
|---|
| Cyber Wireless Internet World...**1** C2 |
| Kenya Commercial Bank ..........**2** A3 |
| Medical Clinic ...........................**3** C2 |
| Post Office..............................**4** B2 |

| TRANSPORT |
|---|
| Local Matatus.........................**11** C2 |
| Truck Pick-up Area.................**12** C1 |

shatter your vehicle, and for hour after scorching hour you'll pass an almost unchanging monoscape of scrubby bush, where encounters with wildlife are common and elegant Samburu walk their herds of camels and goats. As the afternoon heats up, and your brain starts to cook, you'll find the world around you sliding in and out of focus, as mirages flicker on the horizon. Then, as evening comes on, one final mirage appears: a massive wall of forested mountains complete with trickling waters and cool nightly fogs providing an unlikely home to mammoth tusked elephants. But this is no mirage, this is Marsabit.

The small town sits on the side of a 6300-sq-km shield volcano, whose surface is peppered with 180 cinder cones and 22 volcanic craters (*gofs* or *maars*), many housing lakes. Mt Marsabit's highest peak, **Karantin** (1707m), is a rewarding 5km hike from town through lush vegetation and moss-covered trees.

While the town is less attractive than its lush surrounds, which comprise the enormous 1500-sq-km **Marsabit National Reserve**, it's an interesting and lively place, thanks to a colourful migrant population of passing no-mads. The best place to take in the cornucopia of culture is the lively **market**.

## Information
**Kenya Commercial Bank** (off Post Office Rd) No ATM.
**Cyber Wireless Internet World** (per hr KSh120; 8am-7pm Mon-Sat) Off the A2.
**Medical clinic** (Post Office Rd; 8am-7pm Mon-Sat, noon-7pm Sun)
**Post office** (Post Office Rd)

## Sleeping
**Guesthouse Lodge** (r with shared bathroom KSh150) Of the real bottom-rung cheapies this one is the best. It doesn't have a name, but look for the terracotta-coloured building next to the hardware shop. There is an air of Sudan to this place, with rooms sat around a sand-blown courtyard. The communal toilets were full of goat shit when we visited, but it could have been worse – it could have been elephant shit.

**JeyJey Centre** ( 2296; A2 Hwy; s KSh400, s/tw/tr with shared bathroom KSh250/400/600, s with bathroom KSh400) Owned by government MP JJ Falana, this mud-brick castle bedecked in flowers is

Book your stay at lonelyplanet.com/hotels     ISIOLO TO ETHIOPIA •• Marsabit National Park **239**

NORTHERN KENYA

something of a travellers' centre and always bursting with road-hardened souls. Basic rooms with mossie nets surround a courtyard, and bathrooms (even shared ones) sport on-demand hot water. There's also a TV room, a decent restaurant and an unattractive campsite (per person KSh150).

**Nomads Trail Resthouse** ( ☎ 2287; A2 Hwy; r incl breakfast from KSh600) The best accommodation in town are the prim and proper rooms in this new guesthouse opposite the JeyJey. All rooms have attached bathrooms that come with, wait for it, real hot water from a real shower!

## Eating & Drinking
While not having as many Michelin Stars as Paris, you at least won't go to bed hungry here.

**Five Steers Hotel** (A2 Hwy; meals KSh70-130; ☺ lunch & dinner) With a wooden fenced-off terrace, this place is the height of Marsabit style. The '½ Federation' meal (a bulging pile of rice, spaghetti, beef, vegetables and chapatti) is filling and tasty.

**Al-Subra Modern Hotel** (meals KSh70-150; ☺ lunch & dinner) You'll probably need someone to point this place out to you as it's tricky to find (it's off the A2), but the hunt is worthwhile, because as well as Kenyan staples it also presents the first flavours of Ethiopia with its *injera* (Ethiopian breadlike staple) and *wat* (spicy stew). It has two TVs, one blasting out Kenyan programs, the other Ethiopian, making either impossible to watch for most guests.

**JeyJey Centre** ( ☎ 2296; A2 Hwy; meals KSh120-250; ☺ lunch & dinner) Inside the popular lodge, JeyJey serves local favourites as well as the odd curry. Elevated prices don't necessarily reflect a higher standard of food.

If you're short of food or supplies check out the market and **Nomads Shopping Store** (Post Office Rd; ☺ Mon-Sat).

## Getting There & Away
Although improved security meant convoys and armed guards weren't being used to Moyale or Isiolo during our research, it's still wise to get the latest security and Ethiopian border information from locals and the police station before leaving town.

### 4WD
The Moyale road is less corrugated than the one to Isiolo, but its sharp stones will de-

vour your tyres and the deep ruts will scrub your undercarriage. The only fuel north is in Moyale, so stock up in Marsabit. As a rule, if buses and trucks travel in a convoy or take armed soldiers on board, you should too! For advice on travel to Loyangalani, see p247.

### BUS
A bus now connects Marsabit to Moyale (KSh600, 8½ hours). There's no designated stop – simply flag it down on the A2 Hwy as it comes through town around 5pm each day (en route from Nairobi!). The same service heads south to Isiolo (KSh800, 8½ hours) at 9am.

### HITCHING
Trucks regularly ply the bus routes for about KSh100 less, but balancing your malnourished and bony arse on a metal bar above discontented cows for eight hours, while simultaneously battling the sun, wind and dust, is one tricky, tiring act. On the flip side, you'll have a lifetime of memories. There are also some very rare trucks to Loyangalani (KSh1000, hours and hours). Most trucks pick up opposite JeyJey Centre.

## MARSABIT NATIONAL PARK
Within the larger national reserve, this small **park** (adult/child US$20/10), nestled on Mt Marsabit's upper slopes and watered by frequent rains and morning fogs, is coated in thick forests and contains a wide variety of wildlife, including lions, leopards, elephants (some with huge tusks) and buffaloes. The dense forest makes spotting wildlife very hard but fortunately help is at hand in the form of a couple of natural clearings (which occasionally become lakes) where animal sightings are almost guaranteed.

You can drive in the park, but the roads are appalling and you won't see much. A better idea is to hire a KWS guide (KSh1200 for half a day) and explore on foot. You'll see thousands of butterflies, birds and other little creatures and almost certainly have some heart-stopping elephant and buffalo encounters.

## Sleeping & Eating
**Public campsite** (camping adult/child US$15/10) This site, which is next to the main gate, has water and firewood, but the facilities, especially the showers, really are in severe need of an overhaul.

NORTHERN KENYA

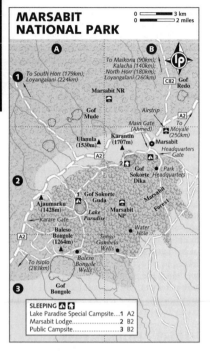

MARSABIT NATIONAL PARK

0 —— 3 km
0 —— 2 miles

**SLEEPING**
Lake Paradise Special Campsite....1  A2
Marsabit Lodge..........................2  B2
Public Campsite..........................3  B2

**Lake Paradise special campsite** (camping adult/child US$15/5, plus set-up fee KSh5000) Although there's nothing except lake water and firewood, this picturesque site is easily the best place to stay in the park. Due to roaming buffalo and elephants, a ranger must be present when you camp here.

**Marsabit Lodge** (s/tw incl breakfast KSh5500/5900) This lodge is in a dreadful state and tremendously overpriced. The whole place is literally falling to bits, however renovations have commenced so perhaps things will have improved by the time you're here. The location, on the edge of the lake occupying Gof Sokorte Dika, is spectacular.

## MOYALE

Let's be honest, nobody comes to Moyale to see Moyale; people come because it's the gateway to one of the world's most fascinating countries, Ethiopia. The drive from Marsabit is long and hard, but immensely rewarding. Leaving the misty highlands of Marsabit you drop onto the bleak by name, bleak by nature **Dida Galgalu Desert** (Plains of Darkness) and trundle for endless hours through a mag-

nificent monotony of black, sunburnt lava rock. The only sign of life, aside from the odd nomad and his camels, is the hamlet of **Bubisa**, a fly-blown place marked on few maps, where bored-looking Gabbra, Somali and Ethiopians sit day after day chewing *miraa* (leaves and shoots that are chewed as a stimulant; see boxed text, p222). It's the kind of place that makes you realise that you aren't in Kansas anymore. Then it's onwards, forever onwards, over a landscape that consists of nothing at all until you reach the tiny village of **Turbi**, sheltered by two small, forested peaks (which can be climbed in half a day, but take a guide, as there is a lot of wildlife and wild people in these parts). If you were to get stuck here for the night there are a couple of very meagre places to stay. For security's sake, however, it's best to push onto Moyale. After Turbi scrubby thorn bushes replace lava desert and, in the distance, the mountain fastness of Ethiopia springs up and tantalises.

In stark contrast to the solitary journey here, Moyale's small, sandy streets burst with activity. The town's Ethiopian half is more developed, complete with sealed roads, and there's a palpable difference in its atmosphere. You will find a small *miraa* market halfway up the main drag on the Ethiopian side.

### Information

If for some bizarre reason you've come here without any intention of continuing into Ethiopia then you can find out what you're missing by entering for the day without a visa, but Ethiopian officials will hold your passport until you return. The border closes at 6pm – don't be late! For those sensible enough to have a visa (they are not available on the border) and to be continuing to Addis Ababa, see p344 for more information on crossing this border. The Commercial Bank of Ethiopia, 2km from the border, changes travellers cheques as well as US dollars and euros. While it doesn't exchange Kenyan shillings, the Tourist Hotel will swap them for Ethiopian Birr.

**Holale Medical Clinic** (A2 Hwy)
**Kenya Commercial Bank** (A2 Hwy) With ATM.
**Post office** (A2 Hwy) With cardphones.

### Sleeping & Eating

When we say that accommodation on both sides of the border is simple, we really do mean it. Also be aware that prostitution here is almost unavoidable as most cheap hotels and bars in this region double as brothels.

### KENYA
**Sherif Guest House** (r with shared bathroom per person KSh150) Sitting above the bank, this guest house has reasonably bright, clean rooms. Some rooms have mossie nets, while others have mattresses too soft for their slat bases, so check out a few before choosing one. The communal toilet is memorable for all the wrong reasons.

**AK Modern Bar** (r with shared bathroom KSh200) It certainly isn't very modern, and the women appear to come with the room. The condom machine on the wall is this establishment's only nod to hygiene and cleanliness. Still, if you're heading to Ethiopia it will be a taste of things to come…

**Sessi Guesthouse** (r per person with shared bathroom KSh400) It's not saying much but this place, a short way out of the centre, is far and away the best place to stay. It's clean, very quiet and the shared bathrooms come with buckets of piping-hot water. The best thing about it is that it's not even a brothel! They are in the process of building both cheaper and pricier rooms (the latter with attached bathroom).

**Baghdad Hotel II** (meals KSh80-150; ☾ lunch & dinner) This is the most popular local restaurant – sit down, swipe some flies and get stuffed.

**Prison Canteen** (meals KSh150-200; ☾ lunch & dinner) It says a lot about the quality of life up here when the best place to eat, drink and party is inside the town jail. Not only do you get a great atmosphere and an excellent *nyama choma*, but you also get to tell your friends that you went to prison in Ethiopia.

### ETHIOPIA
Since prices in the area are quoted in Ethiopian Birr, we've done the same here. The exchange rate is around US$1 to Birr10.

**Fekadu Hotel** (☎ 046-4440049; d Birr25) Simple but efficient self-contained rooms set around an excellent courtyard restaurant and a decent bar.

**Tourist Hotel** (☎ 046-440513; r with shared toilet Birr30) Sheltered behind its cool Rasta-inspired bar, this sleeping option has colourful rooms that include private showers. The shared toilets are nothing to sing about,

but thankfully they're nothing to scream about either.

**Hagos Hotel** (meals Birr8-12; ☾ lunch & dinner) Dig into some *injera* or some spice-laden roasted meat. There's a terrace out back and some shady seating below a flowering tree. It's just up from the border and the Tourist Hotel.

## Getting There & Away
Buses leave town daily at 9am for Marsabit (KSh600, 8½ hours) and Isiolo (KSh1500, 17 hours). Trucks servicing the same destinations on a daily basis pick up passengers near the main intersection in town (Marsabit/Isiolo KSh500/1000). More details about hitching and driving between Moyale and Marsabit are found on p239. Drivers should note that petrol on the Ethiopian side of Moyale is half the cost of that in Kenya.

On the Ethiopian side, a bus leaves for Addis Ababa (Birr95) each morning at around 5am. The two-day journey is broken with a night's sleep at either Awasa or Shashemene.

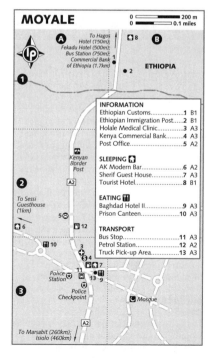

# MARALAL TO TURKANA'S EASTERN SHORE

Journeying to a sea of jade shouldn't be something that is easy to do and this route, the ultimate Kenyan adventure, is certainly not easy. But for the battering you'll take you'll be rewarded a thousand times over with memories of vibrant tribes, camel caravans running into a red sunset, mesmerising volcanic landscapes and, of course, the north's greatest jewel, the Jade Sea, Lake Turkana.

## NORTH TO MARALAL

The 130km drive from Nyahururu to Maralal along the C77 is bumpy but straightforward, despite the tarmac running out at Rumuruti (we do hope you said goodbye, because you won't see it again any time soon). Punctures on this route are common and whilst the scenery isn't special the wildlife is. Don't be at all surprised to see large groups of elephants, giraffes and zebras racing your bus or truck along the edge of the road.

The slightly eccentric Kenyan-/English-run **Bobong Camp and Treefrog Cottage** (☎ 062-32718; olmaisor@africaonline.co.ke; camping per person KSh300, bandas KSh3000), perched on a hill with grand views of the plains below, offers very basic (and overpriced) bandas that will house a family of four. You'd need to be fully self-sufficient as the bandas are empty of everything but beds. Camping is also possible, but it would be a spooky experience staying here alone! A much better reason for dropping by is that they offer some of the cheapest **camel treks** (per day KSh1200 incl guide and ship of the desert) in the north. You must provide all your own camping equipment and food.

If you're not in a hurry, stop by the **Mugie Ranch** (☎ 062-31045; www.mugieranch.com; wildlife drives adult/child US$25/12), a 200-sq-km working ranch, to get a closer look at the local wildlife. One of Kenya's newest rhino sanctuaries (26 rhinos are present) also plays host to all the rest of the Big Five, as well as Grevy's zebras and endangered Jackson's hartebeest.

## MARALAL

☎ 065

Walking down Maralal's dusty streets it wouldn't come as much of a surprise to see Clint Eastwood stride slowly from a bar and proclaim the town not big enough for the two of you. With its swinging cowboy doors and camels tied up outside colourful wooden shopfronts it's impossible not to think that you've somehow been transported to the Wild West.

Maralal has gained an international reputation for its fantastically frenetic **International Camel Derby** (see the boxed text, opposite) and a visit over its duration is truly unforgettable. Less crazy, but almost as memorable, are the year-round camel safaris and treks that are offered here.

Sadly, most visitors don't delve into Maralal, stopping only for a night en route to Lake Turkana. The opposite is true for independent travellers, who often end up spending more time here than planned, simply because transport north is erratic at best. Take it all in your stride: you're an explorer and Maralal is the kind of place where you should spend some time. After all, the town's most famous former resident was one of the greatest explorers of the 20th century, Wilfred Thesiger, and if he decided that Maralal was the perfect place for retirement, then it must be doing something right.

### Information

**Kenya Commercial Bank** Behind the market, with an ATM (the last one going north).

**Maralal Medical Clinic** (🕑 Mon-Sat)

**Links Cyber Café** (per hr KSh120; 🕑 8am-8pm Mon-Sat & 2-8pm Sun)

**Post office** Next to the market.

### Sights & Activities

**Trekking** the Loroghi Hills Circuit, which takes in one of Kenya's most astounding vistas, Lesiolo (p245), is a rewarding five days and 78km. This trek is detailed in Lonely Planet's *Trekking in East Africa*.

**Yare Camel Club & Camp** (☎ 62295) organises guides and camels for independent camel safaris in the region. Self-catered day/overnight trips cost US$20/35 per person.

Surrounding the town is the **Maralal National Sanctuary**, home to zebras, impalas, hyenas, elephants and all the rest. There is no entry fee and you'll probably have the place much to yourself. One of the best ways to take in the animals is with a cold beverage in hand at Maralal Safari Lodge's bar, which also attracts animals after a thirst-quencher from the waterhole just in front.

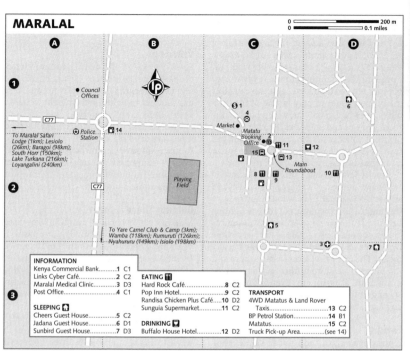

**MARALAL**

## Sleeping

Advance booking is absolutely essential in Maralal during the derby.

**Jadana Guest House** (s/tw KSh250/400; P ) A rare option with secure parking, Jadana is a decent-enough budget option with basic rooms around a central courtyard and tepid morning showers. As an added bonus a fully decked-out Samburu warrior works behind the desk – not something you see every day!

**Sunbird Guest House** ( ☎ 62015; PO Box 74, Maralal; s/d KSh500/700; P ) This shiny and rather friendly place has quiet, clean and comfortable rooms with nice linen, mosquito nets, sparkling bathrooms, 24-hour hot water and sockets to charge your mobile phone. The courtyard has a sunny, garden vibe and if you've been naughty you'll find a Bible in each room.

**Cheers Guest House** ( ☎ 62204; s/tw KSh600/900; P ) An excellent option in the town centre, this slickly run joint has immaculate rooms with hot-water showers, toilets that you'll actually be happy to hang out on and as

---

**MARALAL INTERNATIONAL CAMEL DERBY**

Inaugurated by Yare Safaris in 1990, the annual Maralal International Camel Derby held in early August is one of the biggest events in Kenya, attracting riders and spectators from the world's four distant corners. The races are open to anyone, and the extended after-parties at Yare Camel Club & Camp are notorious – you're likely to bump into some genuine characters here.

Not interested in parties and just want some fast-moving camel action? Then the derby's first race has your name written all over it – it's for amateur camel riders. Pony up KSh1000 for your entry and another KSh3000 for your slobbering steed and get racing! It's a butt-jarring 11km journey. Don't even start feeling sorry for your backside – the professional riders cover 42km.

For further information contact **Yare Safaris** ( ☎ Maralal 065-62295, in Nairobi 020-2163758; www.yaresafaris.co.ke) or Yare Camel Club & Camp in Maralal.

much help and advice as you could need. The secret's out though, so book ahead.

**Yare Camel Club & Camp** ( ☎ 62295, in Nairobi 020-2163758; www.yaresafaris.co.ke; camping KSh200, s/tw/tr US$23/28/35; 🖳 ) This superbly well-run campsite, 3km south of town, is justifiably popular with overlanders. You can camp on the bouncy grass or stay in one of the cosy but dated wooden bandas, which boast bathrooms, towels and hot water. You need to give plenty of notice at the attached restaurant, but fortunately the bar is an ideal spot to waste away time talking rubbish over a pint or two.

**Maralal Safari Lodge** ( ☎ 62220, in Nairobi 020-211124; www.angelfire.com/jazz/maralal; camping KSh500, s/d full board US$165/230; 🖳 ) The wooden cottages are starting to show their age, but the low lighting helps hide the worst of it and, as discounts are as common as impala at the waterhole right outside your window, you can't really moan. The open fireplaces in each room and the views over animal-filled plains provide a romantic atmosphere. Even if you aren't staying at least pop round for a drink in the colonial-style bar.

## Eating

Unless you've got the *ugali* (a staple made from maize or cassava flour, or both) or *nyama choma* itch, few of your tastebuds will be scratched here. That said, a few places hammer out quality local eats.

**Hard Rock Café** (meals KSh60-170; 🕑 lunch & dinner) While the Hard Rock Café chain would cringe at their name's use, this Somali-run restaurant is the town's best restaurant. Enjoy their chapo-fry (spiced beef with chapati and side plate of diced tomatoes, onions and beans) while listening to Rick Astley and being peered over by posters of those Spicy girls – Ginger, Baby, Sporty, David's wife, and can anyone remember the name of the fifth one?

**Pop Inn Hotel** (meals KSh80-150; 🕑 lunch & dinner) This zebra-striped building has decent Kenyan staples but its claim to have the 'best food south of the Sahara' might be pushing it a tad – south of the roundabout seems more realistic.

**Randisa Chicken Plus Café** (meals KSh150; 🕑 lunch & dinner) This new cafe, with tables and stalls running down its walls, is a popular place for chicken in all its various forms – as long as those forms include chips. It also has a few healthy options, such as half-portions of chips and even yoghurt.

Stock up at the Sunguia Supermarket if you're heading north.

## Drinking

Some years ago, the district commissioner ordered Maralal's discos closed due to the region's insecurity. Apparently no one here has thought to fight for their right to party, as this order is still in place.

The Buffalo House Hotel used to be a legendary drinking and partying spot but not so much these days. The bars at Yare Camel Club & Camp and Maralal Safari Lodge are nicer, but if you're staying in town transport back may pose a problem.

## Getting There & Away

Matatus serve Nyahururu (KSh300, three hours), Rumuruti (KSh250, 2½ hours), Wamba (KSh350, 3½ hours) and Nairobi (KSh600, seven hours) on a daily basis, usually in the mornings and early afternoons. Reaching Isiolo involves overnighting in Wamba to catch the early-morning southbound matatu.

During the dry season a few 4WD matatus and Land Rover taxis head north each week to Baragoi (KSh400, three hours). If you're intending to head to Loyangalani and Lake Turkana, you'll have to wait a few days to a week for a truck (KSh1000, nine to 12 hours). Start asking around about transport in this direction as soon as you arrive in town. While breaking the truck journey in Baragoi or South Horr may seem like a good idea, remember that you may have to wait there for a week before another truck trundles through.

Most transport leaves from the main roundabout, while trucks usually pick up passengers at the BP station.

The **BP petrol station** (C77 Hwy) is the town's most reliable. Petrol is cheaper here than further north.

## AROUND MARALAL

There are views and then there are views. **Lesiolo** (meaning 'World's View'), which perches atop an escarpment marking the Loroghi Plateau's dramatic end, offers an outrageous 120km panoramic view over the Rift Valley and serrated Tiati Hills. Lesiolo is part of the Malasso Ecotourism Project and a viewing fee (adult/child KSh500/250) is now charged – pricey, but worth every penny.

The **Lesiolo Loop** (detailed in Lonely Planet's *Trekking in East Africa*) is a spectacular and gruelling 12km trek (eight to 10 hours) that takes you down the escarpment to the Rift Valley floor and then slowly brings you back up again. A local guide (Malasso Ecotourism Project guides cost KSh1000 per day) is essential for this trek.

It's possible to **camp** (adult/child US$10/5) at Lesiolo and the viewing fee is waived if you do so. There's water (collected rain), crude toilets and a whole lot of cow patties to go with the astounding view.

### Getting There & Away

To get here, head north from the town, towards Baragoi; the Malasso Ecotourism Project sign marks the turn-off about 17km from Maralal. Several more signs and helpful locals will point you the rest of the way. Patience and erratic transport can get you to the village of Poror, an easy 9km walk (two to three hours) from Lesiolo. You'll need a 4WD if driving in the wet season.

## BARAGOI

The long descent off the Loroghi Plateau towards Baragoi serves up some sweet vistas and for mile after gorgeous mile you'll literally see nothing but tree-studded grasslands alive with wildlife. It's encouraging to see that so much wilderness still exists outside the national parks. Reaching Baragoi is a bit of an anticlimax though, as the dusty, diminutive town is clearly outdone by its surroundings.

Be careful not to take photos in town, as it's supposedly forbidden and police are keen to enforce the rule.

The **Mt Ngiro General Shop** (C77 Hwy) sells pricey petrol from the barrel and the bougainvillea-dressed **Morning Star Guest House** (C77 Hwy; with shared bathroom per person KSh250) provides a decent place for a night's kip – though they don't supply the peg you'll need to place over your nose before entering the communal toilets. Fine dining (spot the blatant overstatement) is found at the **Widwid Hotel** (C77 Hwy; meals KSh60; ☺ lunch dinner).

### Getting There & Away

The dirt track from Maralal to Baragoi is much improved but still very rocky in places. If there has been any rain it becomes treacherous. The drive takes between 2½ and four hours. See opposite for details

about riding trucks between Maralal, Baragoi and Loyangalani.

## SOUTH HORR

South Horr, surrounded by flowering trees, is the next village north and sits in an acacia-paved valley beneath the towering peaks of **Ol Donyo Nyiro** (2752m) and **Ol Donyo Mara** (2066m). Despite the delightful craggy scenery, your eyes will rarely look up from the enchanting Samburu herders who gather in the wavering trees' shadows.

This is fantastic walking country – easy hikes are possible on the valley's forested lower slopes, while more motivated souls can try to bag Ol Donyo Nyiro's peak. In either case take a guide, because these woodlands are haunted by all manner of large, toothy creatures who'd love to have a passing *mzungu* (white person, foreigner) for lunch.

For such a small place the accommodation options are impressive. Campers will want to stop at the **Lekuka Campsite** (camping KSh250), signposted on the right just south of town. Acacias provide the shade, a stream provides amphibian life and a tin shack provides the long-drop loo at this simple site run by a friendly English woman and her local husband. Canvas enemies will prefer the **Samburu Sports Centre Guesthouse** (per person KSh300), which has well-maintained rondavels (circular African buildings), complete with art on the walls and twisted-branch bookcases and wardrobes. Meals can be prepared on request, but unfortunately few traditionally attired Samburu use the football pitch. There are a couple of basic snack joints; Gunners fans will obviously pick the **Arsenal Inn** (meals KSh40-80; ☺ lunch & dinner).

The road between Baragoi and South Horr is described as being in reasonable shape – what they mean is it's in reasonable shape for northern Kenya.

## NORTH TO LAKE TURKANA

Almost 23km north of South Horr, when the valley opens to the northern plains, you'll see massive Mt Kulal in the distance and Devil's Hand, a large rock outcrop resembling a fist attempting to punch its way out of the earth's surface, to your immediate right. Just north is the eastern turn-off to Marsabit via Kargi, so if you're heading for Turkana keep left. If you get mixed up, just remember that Mt Kulal on your right is good and that Mt Kulal on your

**DID YOU KNOW?**

- Lake Turkana's shoreline is longer than Kenya's entire Indian Ocean coast.

- The lake's water level was over 100m higher some 10,000 years ago and used to feed the mighty Nile.

- The first Europeans to reach the lake were Austrian explorers Teleki and von Höhnel in 1888. They proudly named it Lake Rudolf, after the Austrian Crown Prince at the time. It wasn't until the 1970s that the Kiswahili name Turkana was adopted.

left is very, very bad (unless of course you're heading to Marsabit).

Further north, the scrub desert suddenly scatters and you'll be greeted by vast volcanic armies of shimmering bowling-ball-sized boulders, cinder cones and reddish-purple hues. If this arresting and barren Martian landscape doesn't take your breath away, the first sight of the sparkling Jade Sea a few kilometres north certainly will.

As you descend to the lake, South Island stands proudly before you, while Teleki Volcano's geometrically perfect cone lurks on Turkana's southern shore. Since most of you have probably pulled over for the moment, looking for your swimming kit, we thought we'd warn you that Turkana has the world's largest crocodile population.

## LOYANGALANI

Standing in utter contrast to the dour desert shades surrounding it, tiny Loyangalani assaults all your senses in one crazy explosion of spears, clashing colours, feather headdresses and blood-red robes. Overlooking Lake Turkana and surrounded by small ridges of pillow lava (evidence that this area used to be underwater), the sandy streets of this one-camel town are a meeting point of the great northern tribes, Turkana and Samburu, Gabbra and El Molo. It's easily the most exotic corner of Kenya and a fitting reward after the hard journey here.

The El Molo tribe (see p39), which is one of Africa's smallest, lives on the lake shore just north of here in the villages of **Layeni** and **Komote**. Although outwardly similar to the Turkana, the El Molo are linguistically

linked to the Somali and Rendille people. Unfortunately, the last speaker of their traditional language died before the turn of the millennium.

### Information

Other than the post office and the Catholic mission occasionally selling petrol out of the barrel at exorbitant prices, there's little in the way of services.

### Sights & Activities
#### SOUTH ISLAND NATIONAL PARK

Opened as a public reserve in 1983 and made a World Heritage site by Unesco in 1997, this tiny 39-sq-km purplish volcanic island and **park** (adult/child US$20/10) is completely barren and uninhabited, apart from large populations of crocodiles, poisonous snakes and feral goats. Spending the night at a **special campsite** (camping adult/child US$15/10) makes for an even more eerie trip. All the sites lack water, firewood (there are no trees on the island) and toilets. The southern site is the most sheltered from the wind, so your tent is less likely to take flight here.

In calm weather a speedboat can reach the island in 30 minutes and circumnavigate it in another hour. If winds crop up, trip times can easily double. As speed boats are somewhat limited in number, you will probably end up in something much more sedate: reckon on a six-hour return trip, for which you will pay about KSh3000 per hour. Ask at either the KWS office in town or the Palm Shade Camp about hiring boats.

#### MT KULAL

Mt Kulal dominates Lake Turkana's eastern horizon, and its forested volcanic flanks offer up some serious hiking possibilities. This fertile lost world in the middle of the desert is home to some unique creatures, including the Mt Kulal Chameleon, a beautiful lizard first recorded in only 2003. No matter what the local guides tell you, trekking up to the summit (2293m) from Loyangalani in a day isn't feasible. Plan on several days for a return trip; guides (KSh1000 per day) and donkeys (KSh500 per day) to carry your gear can be hired in Loyangalani, or you can part with substantial sums of cash (KSh8000 to KSh12,000) for a lift up Mt Kulal to the villages of Arapal or Gatab. From there you can head for the summit and spend a long day (eight to 10 hours) hiking back down to Loyangalani. If you pass by Arapal be sure to whistle a tune at the singing wells from where the Samburu gather water (and sing whilst doing so – hence the name).

### LOYANGALANI DESERT MUSEUM
Worth a quick look, this new **museum** (adult/child KSh500/250; 9am-6pm), standing on a bluff above the lake several kilometres north of town, contains lots of photo-heavy displays; but its real use is as an information centre about the surrounding area. You will probably have to track down the man with the key in town.

## Sleeping & Eating
Let's face it; you came north for adventure, not comfort. If you're camping, remember to tie down your tent, as early evening winds pick up tremendously and can be blowing at 60km per hour by 8pm.

**Palm Shade Camp** ( 0726714768; camping KSh450, s/tw rondavels with shared bathroom KSh750/1500) Drop your tent on some grass beneath acacias and doum palms or crash in their tidy domed rondavels. The huts have simple wood beds with foam mattresses and unique walls with meshed cut-outs that let light and heavenly evening breezes in. Throw in the town's best toilets and showers, a cooking shelter and electricity until 10pm and your decision is an easy one.

**Oasis Lodge** ( 0729954672; s/tw KSh3000/4000; ) The German owner doesn't extend the warmest of welcomes and neither do his dated rooms. The best asset is the enticing pool, which nonguests might, if they ask politely and pay KSh500, be allowed to wallow in.

**Cold Drink Hotel** (meals KSh50-110; lunch & dinner) Not just cold drinks but also, according to locals, the finest eating experience in all of Turkana country. The mama who runs it whips up a mean bowl of rice, potatoes and meat for KSh100.

If you ask around, you may find a villager who'll cook up a meal of Nile perch for you in their home.

## Getting There & Away
Trucks, loaded with fish (and soon-to-be-smelly passengers) leave Loyangalani for Maralal (KSh1000 to KSh1500, 10 to 12 hours) around once or twice a week at best.

Trucks heading in any other direction are even rarer.

If you're travelling in your own vehicle, you have two options to reach Marsabit: continue northeast from Loyangalani across the dark stones of the Chalbi Desert towards North Horr, or head 67km south towards South Horr and take the eastern turn-off near Devil's Hand (see p245). The 270km Chalbi route (10 to 12 hours) is hard in the dry season and impossible after rain. It's also wise to ask for directions every chance you get, otherwise it's easy to take the wrong track and not realise until hours later. The 241km southern route (six to seven hours) via Devil's Hand, the Karoli Desert and Kargi is composed of compacted sands and is marginally less difficult in the rainy season.

## SIBILOI NATIONAL PARK
A Unesco World Heritage site and probably Kenya's most remote **national park** (www.sibiloi .com; adult/child US$20/10), Sibiloi is located up the eastern shore of Lake Turkana and covers 1570 sq km. It was here that Dr Richard Leakey discovered the skull of a *Homo habilis* believed to be 2½ million years old, and where others have unearthed evidence of *H erectus*. Despite the area's fascinating prehistory, fossil sites and wonderful arid ecosystem, the difficulties involved in getting this far north tend to discourage visitors, which is a real shame. It seems slightly ironic that the so-called 'Cradle of Mankind' is now almost entirely unpopulated.

The National Museums of Kenya (NMK) maintain a small museum and **Koobi Fora** (www .kfrp.com), a research base that is often home to permanent researchers, visiting scientists and students. It's usually possible to sleep in one of the base's **bandas** (per person KSh1000) or to pitch a tent in one of the **campsites** (camping per person KSh200).

It's best to come in July and August, when the ferocious temperatures break slightly and when activity increases at Koobi Fora. Contact both the staff of the Loyangalani Desert Museum, the **KWS** (kws@kws.org) and **NMK** ( Nairobi 020-3742131; www.museums.or.ke; PO Box 40658, Nairobi) before venturing in this direction.

## Getting There & Away
In the dry season it's a tricky seven-hour drive north from Loyangalani to Sibiloi. You will need a guide from either KWS or the

Loyangalani Desert Museum (Alex Lenapir, ☎ 0726470002, who works at the museum, is a good bet).

## NORTH HORR

On the map North Horr stands out like a beacon from all that surrounding desert, and during the very tough journey here it starts to attain a mythical status akin to Timbuktu. Once you finally drag your weary and battered self onto its sand-washed streets the reality of this drab town is a little disappointing. But if you're travelling this route then you'll almost certainly have to pass through and you might well find yourself stuck here for far longer than you planned. Its one saving grace is the **water source** on the edge of town, where hundreds of camels, goats and weathered nomadic faces come to water each day. Photos not appreciated.

The only place to stay is **Manzigar Lodge** (s/tw KSh150/200). Luxury it's not, authentic it is. Comprising of a dozen or so ropey bandas with no facilities, it can be found on the edge of town near where the camels are taken to drink. You can also camp here but the owner didn't know how much he'd charge for that!

For food you'll find a couple of bare-bones *dukas* (small shops) and cafes in the town.

Trucks and 4WDs very occasionally journey to Loyangalani and Kalacha. There is no set price for this, as transport is so rare that the price completely depends on the whim of the driver. Don't be at all surprised if you get stuck here for more than a week. Even in the dry season the 'roads' are often impassable and after rain it's completely out of the question. Whichever way you're heading it's a road to adventure; blasting over the plains of darkness destined for a sea of jade is nothing short of magical.

## KALACHA

Huddled around a permanent watery oasis in the middle of the Chalbi Desert, the acacia- and doum-palm-pocked village of Kalacha is home to the fascinating Gabbra people. Consisting almost entirely of a mess of domed huts held together with palm fronds and NGO food bags, there's little to see and do, but the sense of isolation is magnificent and the sight of camels, released from their night corrals and kicking up the dust on the way to the grazing

grounds, will remain with you forever. Don't miss the cartoonlike biblical murals in the church, a prelude for those of you heading northward to Ethiopia. Some **rock paintings** and **carvings** can be found near the **Afgaba** waterhole not far from Kalacha – take a guide. The changing colours in the desert at sunset are reason enough alone to stop here, and after dark don't forget to look up at the night sky and drink in the sight of the Milky Way. Go easy with the camera, as the locals don't like it.

**Chalbi Safari Resort Kalacha** ( ☎ 0727218566; camping KSh400, tw bandas per person KSh1000; 🖭 ), managed by the friendly Abdul, is an excellent choice with several immaculate bandas and a sun-battered camping area. With notice they will prepare meals and yes, it really does have a pool!

**Kalacha Camp** ( ☎ Nanyuki 062-32890; PO Box 161, Nanyuki; s/tw US$110/220) is situated beside a permanent water source surrounded by palm trees and has a swimming pool that extends into the shade of the bar. This is a heavenly spot. Unfortunately, if you pay the nonresident rate, the bandas are seriously overpriced. However, if you just turn up unannounced nobody will actually know the nonresident rate and will likely charge you the mere KSh1200-per-person resident rate – a certified bargain.

**Tropic Air** ( ☎ Nanyuki 062-32890; www.tropicair -kenya.com) charter flights from Nanyuki and are your only option of getting here in the wet season. Coming from Marsabit the road winds down off the mountains and sinks into a mass of black lava rocks. Slowly the land becomes ever more barren until finally you hit the blank expanse of the Chalbi Desert, featureless, sandy and blisteringly hot. It's a spectacular ride through a clutter-free world, where the only signs of life are occasional camels heading to the wells of **Maikona**. Don't drive this route without a heavy-duty 4WD and an experienced local guide – that GPS unit you confidently bought before you came to Kenya, and which cannot hope to tell you which is good or bad sand to drive on, or which is currently the best track to use, is worthless here. Good luck if you're travelling by public transport – you'll need it. Trucks might or might not pass by, bound for either or Marsabit (KSh500) or North Horr once a week.

# MARICH TO TURKANA'S WESTERN SHORE

Despite boasting some of northern Kenya's greatest attributes, like copious kilometres of Jade Sea shoreline, striking volcanic landscapes, ample wildlife and vivid Turkana tribes, this remote corner of the country has seen relatively few visitors. With fairly reliable public transport this is definitely the easier side of the lake in which to grab a taste of the northern badlands.

## MARICH TO LODWAR

The spectacular descent from Marich Pass through the lush, cultivated Cherangani Hills leads to arid surroundings, with sisal plants, cactus trees and acacias lining both the road and the chocolate-brown Morun River. Just north, the minuscule village of Marich marks your entrance into northern Kenya. Welcome to adventure!

### Sights & Activities

Although the northern plains may beckon, it's worth heading into the hills for some eye-popping and leg-loving trekking action. **Mt Sekerr** (3326m) is a few kilometres northwest of Marich and can be climbed comfortably in a three-day round trip via the agricultural plots of the Pokot tribe, passing through forest and open moors.

The **Cherangani Hills**, which are the green and lush chalk next to the northern desert's baked cheese, sit immediately south and are also ripe with superb trekking options. In fact, many people consider these intensely farmed and deeply forested hills to be one of the most beautiful corners of the country. Reaching the dome of **Mt Koh** (3211m), which soars some 1524m above the adjacent plains, is a hard but rewarding one-day slog. A more horizontally endowed (13km one way) and vertically challenged (only 300m elevation gain) trek is possible up the **Weiwei Valley** from **Sigor** to **Tamkal**. See p198 for more Cherangani Hills trekking options.

The **Marich Pass Field Studies Centre** (right) offers English-speaking Pokot and Turkana guides for half-day (KSh550), full-day (KSh750) and overnight (KSh1000) treks.

About 15km north of Marich along the A1 Hwy to Lokichar is the turn-off for **Nasolot**

National Reserve (adult/child US$20/10) and **Turkwel Gorge** (admission included with Nasolot NR). Although the reserve is home to many animals, the dense bush means you'll probably only spot the diminutive dikdiks bounding by the roadside. The main attraction is the gorge itself, with towering semidesert rock walls and plenty of pretty precipices. The imposing hydroelectric dam sits about 23km from the reserve gate, which is 6km off the A1. Those without vehicles are allowed to hike in the park with an escort (free with reserve admission).

In the dry, rugged lands further north along the A1 is the **South Turkana National Reserve**. The reserve is still being developed, a campsite is due 'soon', but there is already a guest house, close to the entrance gate. It has no facilities, park staff can't tell you the rates and if you want to stay they must seek approval from 'higher people'. Still, at least the signboard is nice. The roads are in brutal shape (4WD only), and if you want to explore you must take a ranger with you. Entry is free but you'll have to negotiate a fee for the ranger. Despite this, or perhaps because of it, wildlife is abundant but just as likely to be seen crossing the main A1 road. Don't be surprised if you're halted in your tyre tracks by groups of elephants lumbering down the road.

### Sleeping & Eating

The only reasonable accommodation between Marich and Lokichar is at **Marich Pass Field Studies Centre** (www.gg.rhul.ac.uk/MarichPass; PO Box 564, Kapenguria; camping KSh360, dm KSh420, s/tw with private bathroom KSh1450/1950, with shared bathroom KSh900/1240), which is well signposted just north of Marich and the junction of the A1 and the B4. Essentially a residential facility for visiting student groups, it's also a great place for independent travellers to base their adventures. The centre occupies a beautiful site alongside the misty Morun River and is surrounded by dense bush and woodland. The birdlife is prolific, monkeys and baboons have the run of the place, and warthogs, buffaloes, antelope and elephants are occasional visitors. Facilities include a secure campsite with drinking water, toilets, showers and firewood, as well as a tatty dorm and simple, comfortable bandas.

### Getting There & Away

The road from Kitale via Makutano is the oh-so-scenic A1 Hwy, which is often described

**NORTHERN KENYA**

as 'Kenya's most spectacular tarmac road'. The buses plying the A1 between Kitale and Lodwar can drop you anywhere along the route, whether at Marich, the field studies centre or at the turn-off to Nasolot National Reserve. You may be asked to pay the full fare to Lodwar (KSh600), but a smile and some patient negotiating should reduce the cost.

Between Marich and Lokichar the A1 is a bumpy mess of corrugated dirt and lonely islands of tarmac. The first 40km north of Lokichar is better, but you'll still spend more time on the shoulder than on the road. The opposite is true for the remaining 60km to Lodwar, where patches outnumber potholes and driving is straightforward.

The security situation is in a constant state of flux in this area. At the time of research convoys were not required and the situation was considered stable, even though guns were far more visible in civilian hands on this side of the lake than the east side (we even saw a 12-year-old trotting around with his camels and a Kalashnikov!).

## LODWAR
☎ 054

Besides Lokichoggio near the Sudan border, Lodwar is the only town of any size in the northwest. Barren volcanic hills skirted by traditional Turkana dwellings sit north of town and make for impressive early-morning sunrise spots. Lodwar has outgrown its days as just an isolated administrative outpost of the Northern Frontier District, and has now become the major service centre for the region. If you're visiting Lake Turkana, you'll find it convenient to stay here for at least one night.

### Information
The **Kenya Commercial Bank** (no ATM) changes cash and travellers cheques. For internet, surf on over to **Turkana Cyber Café** (per hr KSh180; ☺ 7.30am-7pm Mon-Sat).

### Sights & Activities
There's little to do in the town itself, but the atmosphere is not altogether unpleasant if you can stand the heat, and just listening to the garrulous locals is entertainment in itself. The small **market** is a good place to watch women weaving baskets, and there's an endless stream of Turkana hawkers who wander around town selling the usual souvenirs.

### Sleeping
**Hotel Splash** (☎ 0208017922; PO Box 297, Lodwar; s/tw KSh500/700) Each room at this immaculate hotel has double-swing cowboy doors and is named after a place – choose from Nigeria, Cameroon, Libya, or the slightly oddly named Rumtek.

**Turkwel Lodge** (☎ 0735459530; s/tw KSh500/700, cottages s/d KSh950/1350; **P**) The Turkwel offers spacious rooms containing fans and nets, but lacks the crisp, clean feel of its neighbour, Hotel Splash. Some beds are a bit of an Ikea slat experiment gone horribly wrong. There's secure parking and roomy cottages at the rear, but it's overpriced and the attached bar is noisy.

**Nawoitorong Guest House** (☎ 21208; camping KSh200, s/tw/tr with shared bathroom KSh500/800/900, s/tw cottages from KSh800/1600) Built entirely out of local materials and run by a local women's group, Nawoitorong is an excellent option, and the only one for campers. Thatched roofs alleviate the need for fans and all rooms have mossie nets. The only downside is that the walls between rooms are very thin and you can hear everything your neighbours are up to. There's a pleasant restaurant that needs plenty of notice. Ask here about organising onward transport.

### Eating
**Turkwel Hotel** (meals KSh60-210; ☺ lunch & dinner) The green-lentil curry is particularly good, but you have to get your order in about three hours prior! Oh, and don't forget to order the chapatis at the same time. Their local dishes require less waiting and are some of the best in town.

**Nawoitorong Guest House** (meals KSh150-225; ☺ lunch & dinner) Burgers and toasted sandwiches join local curries and various meaty fries on their menu.

If you're self-catering, there's a well-stocked **Naipa Supermarket** next to the Kobil petrol station.

### Getting There & Away
Several companies have daily buses to Kitale (KSh600, 8½ hours) which depart nightly between 5pm and 7pm (most services pick up passengers near the New Salama Hotel), while erratic matatus serve Kalokol (KSh150, one hour) and Lokichoggio (KSh400, three hours).

## ELIYE SPRINGS

Spring water percolates out of crumbling bluffs and oodles of palms bring a taste of the tropics to the remote sandy shores of Lake Turkana. Down on the slippery shore children play in the lake's warm waters, while Central Island lurks magically on the distant horizon.

Beneath the bluff, the skeleton of an old beach resort (day visitors KSh200) sits half-eaten by its surroundings and makes for an interesting place to drop your tent. Locals now manage the leftovers and charge KSh500 for camping in your own tent, or you can hire one of theirs for an additional KSh400. Besides the spring water there are no facilities, so you'll have to be entirely self-sufficient.

### Getting There & Away

The turn-off for Eliye Springs is signposted a short way along the Lodwar–Kalokol road. The gravel is easy to follow until it suddenly peters out and you're faced with a fork in the road – stay left. The rest of the way is a mix of gravel, deep sand and even deeper sand, which can turn into a muddy nightmare in the wet season. Over the really bad sections locals have constructed a 'road' out of palm fronds, which means that on a good day normal saloon cars can even make it here (though expect to do a bit of pushing and shoving).

If you don't have your own vehicle, you can usually arrange a car and driver in Lodwar for about KSh5000 including waiting time. Very occasionally you might find a truck travelling there, for which a seat on top of the load will set you back about KSh150, but be prepared for a long wait back out again!

## FERGUSON'S GULF

Ferguson's Gulf, while more accessible than Eliye Springs, has none of its southern neighbour's tropical charm. Fishing boats in various states of disrepair litter its grubby western beach and a definite feeling of bleakness pervades.

Birdlife is prolific, particularly in March and April, when thousands of European migratory birds stop here on their way north. There are also hippos and crocodiles so seek local advice before diving in.

If you're planning on visiting Central Island National Park (right) or Sibiloi National Park (p247), this is the best place to arrange a boat.

Set on the eastern shore, **Lake Turkana Lodge** has long since gone to lodge heaven but the remnants are now managed by the local community, who charge KSh500 for camping and an insane KSh1500 to sleep in the shell of the building. There are no facilities whatsoever.

Otherwise you should be able to find some very primitive, but cheaper, accommodation in the nearby village of **Kalokol**.

### Getting There & Away

Few people in Lodwar have heard of Ferguson's Gulf so you need to ask around for transport to nearby Kalokol, which is 75km along a good stretch of tarmac. Ferguson's Gulf is only a few kilometres from there. Matatus to Kalokol cost KSh150 or a taxi direct to Ferguson's Gulf will be around KSh4000 with waiting time.

## CENTRAL ISLAND NATIONAL PARK

Bursting from the depths of Lake Turkana and home to thousands of living dinosaurs is the Jurassic world of Central Island Volcano, last seen belching molten sulphur and steam just over three decades ago. It is one of the most otherworldly places in Kenya. Quiet today, its stormy volcanic history is told by the numerous craters scarring its weathered facade. Several craters have coalesced to form two sizeable lakes, one of which is home to thousands of fish that occur nowhere else.

Both a **national park** (adult/child US$20/10) and Unesco World Heritage site, Central Island is an intriguing place to visit, and budding Crocodile Dundee types will love the 14,000 or so Nile crocodiles, some of which are massive in proportion, who live here.

**Camping** (adult/child US$15/10) is possible and, unlike South Island National Park, there are trees to tie your tent to. But there's no water or any other facilities, so come prepared.

Hiring a boat from Ferguson's Gulf is the only real option to get here. Depending on what you drive up in, locals can ask anywhere from KSh6000 to KSh20,000 for the trip. A fair price is KSh6500 for a motorboat – don't ever think about being cheap and taking a sailboat. The 10km trip and sudden squalls that terrorise the lake's waters aren't to be taken lightly. Once you've found a boat (not as easy as it sounds) you have the additional problem of finding some fuel. You should also visit the KWS office, a couple of kilometres out of Kalokol towards Ferguson's Gulf, to pick up a guide and get the latest lowdown on the island.

# Mombasa & the South Coast

There's something in the air here.

It's not just the salt that fades the streets and sidings of the buildings of Mombasa, *Kisiwa Cha Mvita,* The Island of War. Or the smell of sweat, spice and petrol leaking from a Zanzibar-bound cargo ship. Or the sun's glint off coral castles, ribbons of white sand and the teal break of a vanishing wave.

It enriches the shade cast by thick copses of coconut and banana plantations, their dark recesses concealing the sacred forests of the Nine Homesteads. It amplifies the power of muttered chants echoing over the flagstones of a Jain temple, and the ecstatic passion of the call to prayer pushing a full moon behind the Indian Ocean.

This is the romance of Kenya's coast, one of the great entrepôts of Africa, a land as notable for its history as its pure salt breezes. As different as it may feel from the interior, this region is still Kenyan; the word *Swahili* comes from the Arabic *sawahil* (of the coast). Yet the sea is also, undeniably, separated from the centre. The interplay of Africa, India and Arabia impacted this region hundreds of years before European colonisation and Bantu migration. A distinctive Indian Ocean society evolved here, built on trade (notably of slaves), intermarriage, Arabian poetry, Gujarati sweet stalls, Portuguese castles and Mijikenda tree-tending. This interlaying and interlacing of cultures is exemplified by the Swahili themselves, one of the most distinctively 'blended' ethnicities in Africa. The coast is their beautiful homeland, a land of sugar-powder beaches and a city the poets have embraced for as long as ivory has been traded for iron.

When you arrive, know that you won't be the first visitor in these parts, and be warned: that first trip here is never the last.

## HIGHLIGHTS

- Finding god in the greenery in a **kaya** (p276)
- Discovering Indian sweets and narrow streets in **Mombasa Old Town** (p262)
- Taking a dhow to **Mkwiro village** (p279)
- Strolling the boards and helping the community at **Gazi** (p278)
- Tracking down elusive wildlife in **Shimba Hills National Reserve** (p270) and **Mwaluganje Elephant Sanctuary** (p271)
- Spotting the ocean through the coral walls of **Kongo Mosque** (p274) in Diani Beach

Mwaluganje Elephant Sanctuary ★

★ Mombasa Old Town

★ Diani Beach
★ Kaya Kinondo

Shimba Hills National Reserve ★

★ Gazi

★ Mkwiro

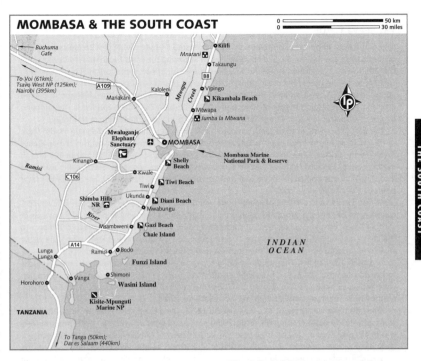

## MOMBASA & THE SOUTH COAST

## History

The coast's history doesn't begin with Arab contact, but written records essentially do. By the 1st century, Yemeni traders were in East Africa, prompting one unidentified Greek observer to write about '…Arab captains and agents, who are familiar with the natives and intermarry with them, and who know the whole coast and understand the language.' Merchants traded spices, timber, gold, ivory, tortoise shell and rhinoceros horn (the last three of which are still smuggled illegally), as well as slaves.

The admixture of Arabs, local Africans and Persian traders gave birth to the Swahili culture and language. But the Swahili were not the only inhabitants of the coast. Of particular note were the Mijikenda, or 'Nine Homesteads', a Bantu tribe whose homeland, according to oral history, was located somewhere in southern Somalia. Six hundred years ago they began filtering into the coast and established themselves in *kayas* (sacred forests), which are dotted from the Tanzanian border to Malindi (see p276).

The riches of this region never failed to attract attention, and in the early 16th century it was the Portuguese who took their turn at conquest. The Swahilis did not take kindly to becoming slaves (even if they traded them), and rebellions were common throughout the 16th and 17th centuries. It's fashionable to portray the Portuguese as villains, but their replacements, the sultans of Oman, were no more popular. Despite their shared faith, the natives of this ribbon of land staged countless rebellions, and passed Mombasa into British hands from 1824 to 1826 to keep it from the sultans. Things only really quietened down after Sultan Seyyid Said moved his capital from Muscat to Zanzibar in 1832.

Said's huge coastal clove plantations created a massive need for labour, and the slave caravans of the 19th century marked the peak of the trade in human cargo. News of massacres and human rights abuses reached Europe, galvanising the British public to demand an end to slavery. Through a mixture of political savvy and implied force, the British government pressured Said's son Barghash to

## THE SLAVE TRADE

One of the most important, controversial, hotly contested and silently-dealt-with topics in African history is the slave trade of the Swahili coast, better known as the East African slave trade. Between the 7th and 19th centuries, Arab and Swahili traders kidnapped some four million slaves from East Africa, selling them for work in households and plantations across the Middle East and Arab-controlled African coastal states. The legacy of the trade is seen today in the chain motifs carved into doors (representing homes of slave traders) in Mombasa Old Town, and felt in the crippling legacy of displacement and ethnic tension caused by a millennium of human trafficking.

The East African slave trade both predated and exceeded the Atlantic Triangle Trade. Slave uprisings in southern Iraqi sugar plantations are reported from the 9th century, while Qatari royalty kept African slaves in their retinue at the coronation of Queen Elizabeth in 1953. Arab merchants on the coast traditionally referred to Africans as *zanj*, meaning 'black', a linguistic clue into the economic backbone of the island of Zanzibar, 'Land of the Blacks', which was the focal point of the coastal slave trade.

At first, slaves were obtained through trade with inland tribes, but as the 'industry' developed, caravans set off into the African interior, bringing back plundered ivory and tens of thousands of captured men, women and children. Of these, fewer than one in five survived the forced march to the coast, most either dying of disease or being executed for showing weakness along the way.

Although some slaves married their owners and gained freedom, the experience for the majority was much harsher. Thousands of African boys were surgically transformed into eunuchs to provide servants for Arabic households, and an estimated 2.5 million young African women were sold as concubines. The impact of a thousand years of warfare, kidnapping, displacement, refugee movement and exploitation has not been measured.

After the trade was brought to a close in the 1870s, the Swahili communities along the coast went into steady decline, although illicit trading continued right up until the 1960s, when slavery was finally outlawed in Oman. These days this dark chapter of African history is seldom discussed by Kenyans and, in a world where awareness of terrorism is heightened, public discussion of the Muslim-dominated coastal slave trade is often politically charged. While the negative legacy of the Triangle Trade is almost universally acknowledged, commentators on the East African slave trade are often either apologists or anti-Islam extremists, with both sides missing the real impacts of this long and painful history. The Swahili themselves were, at different points, the benefactors, facilitators and victims of the slave trade. Their position on the matter remains apologetic, denunciatory and, often, ambiguous.

ban the slave trade, marking the beginning of the end of Arab rule here.

Of course, this 'reform' didn't hurt British interests: as part of the treaty, the British East Africa Company took over administration of the Kenyan interior, taking the opportunity to start construction of the East African Railway. A 16km-wide coastal strip was recognised as the territory of the sultan and leased by the British from 1887. Upon independence in 1963, the last sultan of Zanzibar gifted this land to the new Kenyan government.

The coast remains culturally distinctive via its large Indian minority population and Islamic faith. See the Mombasa history section (opposite) for the story of that city's fascinating role in Kenya's 2007 presidential elections.

## Climate

If you like sultry, skin-kissed humidity and thick, muggy nights, you'll be in heaven. If not, at least the mosquitoes will keep your mind off the weather. The coast maintains tropical temperatures of up to 32°C for most of the year, with humidity levels of around 75% and an average eight hours of sunshine per day between September and March. The coolest time of year is during the rainy season, from April to August. During this time the rains can come unexpectedly and rather heavily. Conditions are also influenced by the monsoon winds, which reverse direction between March and April.

## National Parks & Reserves

Kenya Wildlife Service (KWS) parks in the region include Shimba Hills National Reserve (p270) and Mwaluganje Elephant Sanctuary (p271). Offshore are the Mombasa (p282) and Kisite (p280) Marine National Parks, and Mpunguti Marine National Reserve (p280).

## Getting There & Away
Mombasa is the obvious gateway to the coast, and it takes about seven hours, give or take, to drive there from Nairobi. There are also plenty of buses and an overnight train between Kenya's two largest towns, plus daily flights, which take about 1½ hours. See p268 for details on getting to and from Mombasa.

## Getting Around
This is a pretty easy area to get around, as there's only one main road to speak of and it's flat as a pancake. That would be the coastal highway, which is the A14 south of Mombasa and the B8 north of it. If you're staying in a top-end resort, your hotel should be able to arrange transport to and from your bed. Otherwise, there are frequent matatus and buses between all of the major towns, and drivers can drop you off at any point along the way.

# MOMBASA
☎ 041 / pop 880,000
Mombasa, like the coast it dominates, is both quintessentially African and somehow…not.

If your idea of Africa is roasted meat, toasted maize, beer and cattle and farms and friendliness, those things are here (well, maybe not the cows). But it's all interwoven into the humid peel of plaster from Hindu warehouses, filigreed porches that lost their way in a Moroccan *riad* (traditional town house), spice markets that escaped India's Keralan coast, sailors chewing *miraa* (shoots chewed as a stimulant) next to boats bound for the Yemeni Hadhramaut, and a giant coral castle built by invading Portuguese sailors. Thus, while this city sits perfectly at home in Africa, it could be plopped anywhere on the coast of the Indian Ocean without too many moving pains.

Therein lays Mombasa's considerable charm. But said seduction doesn't hide this town's warts, which include a sleazy under-belly, bad traffic and ethnic tension, the last of which ebbs and flows and is smoothed by the unifying faith of Islam, but it's not entirely sublimated. Overlaying everything is the sweating, tropical lunacy you tend to get in the world's hot zones (and it gets *hot* here). But what would you expect from East Africa's largest port? Cities by the docks always attract mad characters, and Mombasa's come from all over the world.

When the poets sing about this town, they praise it like a beautiful, dangerous woman. We'll let the Swahili describe their largest city in their native tongue with a welcome and an old line of poetry and proverb: *Kongowea nda mvumo, maji maangavu. Male!*

'Mombasa is famous, but its waters are dangerously deep. Beware!'

## History
Unlike Nairobi, Mombasa, which sits over the best deep-water harbour in East Africa, has always been an important town.

Travellers who come here are walking in the footsteps of Ibn Battuta, Marco Polo and Zhang He, which says something of this town's importance to trade rather than tourism. Modern Mombasa traces its heritage back to the Thenashara Taifa (Twelve Nations), a Swahili clan that maintains a contiguous chain of traditions and customs stretching from the city's founding to this day. The date of when those customs began – ie when Mombasa was born – is a little muddy, although it was already a thriving port by the 12th century. Early in its life, Mombasa became a key link on Indian Ocean trade routes.

In 1498, Vasco da Gama became the first Portuguese visitor here. Two years later his countrymen returned and sacked the town, a habit they repeated in 1505 and 1528, when Nuña da Cunha captured Mombasa using what would become a time-honoured tactic: slick 'em up with diplomacy (offering to act as an ally in disputes with Malindi, Pemba and Zanzibar), then slap 'em down by force. Once again Mombasa was burnt to the ground, while the invaders sailed on to Portuguese Goa, although they respected the fighting skills of the locals; a Portuguese saying of the time was *Damas de Melinde; cavalleiros de Mombasa* (Ladies are of Malindi; warriors of Mombasa).

MOMBASA & THE SOUTH COAST

# MOMBASA

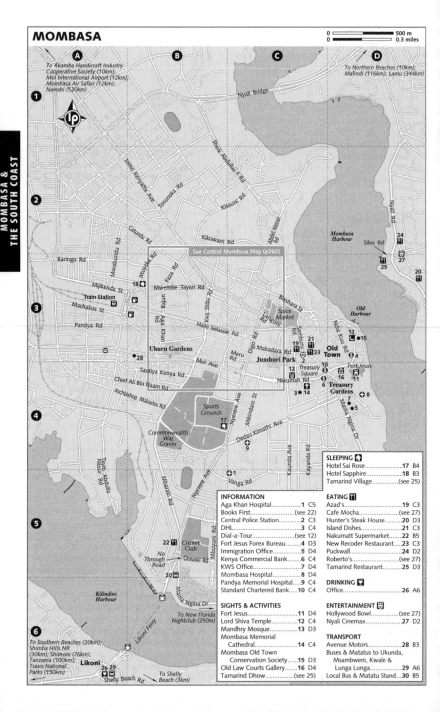

0 — 500 m
0 — 0.3 miles

To Akamba Handicraft Industry
Cooperative Society (10km);
Moi International Airport (12km);
Mombasa Air Safari (12km);
Nairobi (520km)

To Northern Beaches (10km);
Malindi (116km); Lamu (344km)

Nyali Bridge

Sheikh Abdullah Rd

Mombasa
Harbour

Silos Rd

See Central Mombasa Map (p260)

Old
Harbour

Spice
Market

Old
Town

Jumburi Park

Treasury
Square

Treasury
Gardens

Fort Jesus

Sports
Grounds

Commonwealth
War
Graves

Uhuru Gardens

Train Station

Machakos St

Pandya Rd

Baringo Rd

Mijikenda St

Mwembe Tayari Rd

Haile Selassie Rd

Moi Ave

Meru Rd

Nkrumah Rd

Makadara Rd

Sautiya Kenya Rd

Chief Ali Bin Naam Rd

Archbishop Makarios Rd

Nyerere Ave

Dedan Kimathi Ave

Mikindani St

Kaunda Ave

Kayanda Rd

Vanga Rd

Cricket
Club

Oceanic Rd

No
Through
Road

Kilindini
Harbour

Tayib Abdulla
Nassir Rd

Mbaraki Rd

Nyerere Ave

Mtwapa Rd

Mama Ngina Dr

To New Florida
Nightclub (250km)

To Southern Beaches (20km);
Shimba Hills NR
(30km); Shimoni (76km);
Tanzania (100km);
Tsavo National
Parks (150km)

Likoni

Likoni Ferry

To Shelly Beach (3km)

Shelly Beach Rd

### INFORMATION
| | | |
|---|---|---|
| Aga Khan Hospital | 1 | C5 |
| Books First | (see 22) | |
| Central Police Station | 2 | C3 |
| DHL | 3 | C4 |
| Dial-a-Tour | (see 12) | |
| Fort Jesus Forex Bureau | 4 | D3 |
| Immigration Office | 5 | D4 |
| Kenya Commercial Bank | 6 | C4 |
| KWS Office | 7 | D4 |
| Mombasa Hospital | 8 | D4 |
| Pandya Memorial Hospital | 9 | C4 |
| Standard Chartered Bank | 10 | C4 |

### SIGHTS & ACTIVITIES
| | | |
|---|---|---|
| Fort Jesus | 11 | D4 |
| Lord Shiva Temple | 12 | C4 |
| Mandhry Mosque | 13 | D3 |
| Mombasa Memorial Cathedral | 14 | C4 |
| Mombasa Old Town Conservation Society | 15 | D3 |
| Old Law Courts Gallery | 16 | D4 |
| Tamarind Dhow | (see 25) | |

### SLEEPING
| | | |
|---|---|---|
| Hotel Sai Rose | 17 | B4 |
| Hotel Sapphire | 18 | B3 |
| Tamarind Village | (see 25) | |

### EATING
| | | |
|---|---|---|
| Azad's | 19 | C3 |
| Cafe Mocha | (see 27) | |
| Hunter's Steak House | 20 | D3 |
| Island Dishes | 21 | C3 |
| Nakumatt Supermarket | 22 | B5 |
| New Recoder Restaurant | 23 | C3 |
| Puckwall | 24 | D2 |
| Roberto's | (see 27) | |
| Tamarind Restaurant | 25 | D3 |

### DRINKING
| | | |
|---|---|---|
| Office | 26 | A6 |

### ENTERTAINMENT
| | | |
|---|---|---|
| Hollywood Bowl | (see 27) | |
| Nyali Cinemax | 27 | D2 |

### TRANSPORT
| | | |
|---|---|---|
| Avenue Motors | 28 | B3 |
| Buses & Matatus to Ukunda, Msambweni, Kwale & Lunga Lunga | 29 | A6 |
| Local Bus & Matatu Stand | 30 | B5 |

### SWA-WHO-LI?

'So you are a Swahili?' we ask the Mombasa shop owner, who is dressed like all the Swahili in the street and shares their caramel skin colour. 'No! No, I am Kenyan, but my roots are in Gujarat,' he says.

In the village, watching a man walk by, we turn to our guide: 'He's a Digo, right?'

'No!' says the guide. 'His father and his mother are Digo. His mother is so traditional she won't wear shoes. But he was sent to work in a Swahili house when he was young and converted to Islam, married a Muslim girl, made the *haj* (pilgrimage to Mecca) and would be insulted to be called anything but Swahili.'

Just who the Swahili are is a complex question, and not just for anthropologists. For many people on the Kenyan coast, being Swahili is the most important marker of their identity. This is not a unique set of affairs – the same emphasis on tribe can be noted in many groups in Kenya – but what sets the Swahili apart is their connection to the Muslim, particularly Arab, world.

To put it plainly: there are Swahili who believe the presence, real or imagined, of Arab and Persian blood sets them apart – and above – 'black' Africans (this despite the fact many Swahili are as black as any inland Kenyans). This attitude is not shared by all Swahili by any stretch, but it is present. It stems from both good-old racism and a sense of superiority engendered by, among other things, Swahili cosmopolitanism, the Kiswahili language (generally considered to be spoken at its 'purest' on the coast), and the fact the Swahili were the area's original converts to Islam. A stronger link to the Arab world (which may be arbitrarily measured or fancifully concocted, much like white Americans or Australians claiming descent from European nobility) is often taken to mean a weaker tie to black Africa, and by extension, a stronger tie to Islam.

Due to its mixed nature, Swahili identity has been and remains, in some ways, a malleable thing. At its uglier edges, it still draws influence from the Arab imperialism that once dominated the coast. With that said, many thousands of Swahili cheerfully acknowledge they are black and something else – something quintessentially 'coast'.

In 1593, the Portuguese constructed the coral edifice of Fort Jesus as a way of saying, 'We're staying.' This act of architectural hubris led to frequent attacks by rebel forces and the ultimate expulsion of the Portuguese by Omani Arabs in 1698. But the Omanis were never that popular either, and the British, using a series of shifting alliances and brute force turfed them out in 1870. All these power struggles, by the way, are the source of Mombasa's Swahili nickname: The Island of War.

Mombasa subsequently became the railhead for the Uganda railway and the most important city in British East Africa. In 1920, when Kenya became a fully fledged British colony, Mombasa was made capital of the separate British Coast Protectorate. Following independence the city fell into a torpor; it was the most important city in the region and the second-largest in the country, but it was removed from the cut and thrust of Kenyan politics, whose focus had turned inland.

But during the 2007 elections the coast, and Mombasa in particular, provided a rare peek into the policy platforms, rather than communal politics, of Raila Odinga and Mwai Kibaki. Neither politician could rely on a Kikuyu or Luo base here, and both campaigned on ideas, rather than appeals to tribalism. Odinga won the province by promising, in effect, a form of limited federation, which remains a hope of many Mombasan politicians who consider the coast culturally, economically and religiously distinct enough to warrant some form of self-governance.

## Orientation

The town of Mombasa is located on Mombasa island, which is connected to the mainland by Nyali Bridge (from the north), Makupa Causeway (to the west) and the Likoni ferry (to the south). Old Town, which consists of the neighbourhoods of Kibokoni (to the south) and Makadara (west), is squeezed into the eastern edge of the island. The island is only 4km by 7km large, although the city's suburbs extend beyond the island itself.

The main thoroughfare in Mombasa is Digo Rd and its southern extension, Nyerere

Ave, which run north–south through the city to the Likoni ferry. The main east–west road is Moi Ave, where you'll find the tourist office and the famous sculpted 'tusks', two huge pairs of aluminium elephant tusks forming an M over the road.

North of the centre, Digo Rd becomes Abdel Nasser Rd, where you'll find bus stands for Nairobi and the north coast. There's another group of bus offices west of here at the intersection of Jomo Kenyatta Ave and Mwembe Tayari Rd. The train station is at the intersection of Mwembe Tayari and Haile Selassie Rds.

# Information

## BOOKSHOPS
**Bahati Book Centre** (Map p260; ☎ 225010; Moi Ave)
**Books First** (Map p256; ☎ 313482; Nyerere Ave; 💻 ) Well-stocked outlet with separate cafe, in the Nakumatt supermarket.

## EMERGENCY
**AAR Health Services** ( ☎ 312409; 🕑 24hr)
**Central Police Station** (Map p256; ☎ 225501, 999; Makadara Rd)

## INTERNET ACCESS
**Blue Room Cyber Café** (Map p260; ☎ 224021; www .blueroomonline.com; Haile Selassie Rd; per min KSh2; 🕑 9am-10pm)
**Cyber Dome** (Map p260; Moi Ave; per min KSh1; 🕑 8am-9pm Mon-Sat, 9am-6pm Sun)
**FOTech** (Map p260; ☎ 225123; Ambalal House, Nkrumah Rd; per min KSh1)

## INTERNET RESOURCES
**www.hotelsmombasa.com** Good for booking online and checking current contact details.
**www.kenyacoastworld.com** Another clearing house for visitors.
**www.mombasainfo.com** Descriptive tourist information.
**www.mombasanorthcoast.com** More tourist info goodness.

## KENYA WILDLIFE SERVICE
**KWS office** (Map p256; ☎ 312744/5, 222612; Nguua Ct, Mama Ngina Dr; 🕑 6am-6pm) Sells and charges smartcards.

## LIBRARIES
**Mombasa Area Library** (Map p260; ☎ 226380; Msanifu Kombo Rd; 🕑 8am-6.30pm Mon-Thu, to 4pm Fri, to 5pm Sat) Has a fairly extensive English-language section.

## MEDIA
**Coastweek** (www.coastweek.com) Weekly news and features from the coast province.

## MEDICAL SERVICES
All services and medication must be paid for upfront, so have travel insurance details handy.
**Aga Khan Hospital** (Map p256; ☎ 2227710; www .agakhanhospitals.org; Vanga Rd)
**Mombasa Hospital** (Map p256; ☎ 2312191, 2312099, 2228010; www.mombasahosptial.com; off Mama Ngina Dr)
**Pandya Memorial Hospital** (Map p256; ☎ 2313577; Dedan Kimathi Ave)

## MONEY
Outside business hours you can change money at most major hotels, although rates are usually poor. Exchange rates are generally slightly lower here than in Nairobi, especially if you're changing travellers cheques.
**Barclays Bank** Nkrumah Rd (Map p260; ☎ 311660); Digo Rd (Map p260; ☎ 316045)
**Fort Jesus Forex Bureau** (Map p256; ☎ 2230114/6; Ndia Kuu Rd)
**Kenya Commercial Bank** Nkrumah Rd (Map p256; ☎ 312523); Moi Ave (Map p260; ☎ 220978)
**Postbank** (Map p260; ☎ 3434077; Moi Ave) Western Union money transfers.
**Pwani Forex Bureau** (Map p260; ☎ 221727; Digo Rd)
**Standard Chartered Bank** (Map p256; ☎ 224614; Treasury Square, Nkrumah Rd)

## POST
**DHL** (Map p256; ☎ 223933; Nkrumah Rd)
**FedEx** (Map p260; ☎ 228631; Moi Ave)
**Post office** (Map p260; ☎ 227705; Digo Rd)

## TELEPHONE
**Post Global Services** (Map p260; ☎ 230581; inglo bal@africaonline.co.ke; Maungano Rd; 🕑 7.30am-8pm; 💻 ) International calls are around KSh110 per minute.
**Telkom Kenya** (Map p260; ☎ 312811) Locations on Nkrumah Rd and Moi Ave.

## TOURIST INFORMATION
**Mombasa & Coast Tourist Office** (Map p260; ☎ 231159; tourism@fo.ke; Moi Ave; 🕑 8am- 4.30pm) Provides information and can organise accommodation, tours, guides and transport.

## TRAVEL AGENCIES
**Dial-A-Tour** (Map p256; ☎ 221411; dialatour@ikenya .com; Oriental Bldg, Nkrumah Rd)
**Express Travel (Amex)** (Map p260; ☎ 228081; PO Box 90631, Nkrumah Rd) Also an Amex agent – mail can be held here for card-holders.

---

**ANALYSING OSAMA**

There's a lot of pro–Bin Laden graffiti on the Kenyan coast, which causes many travellers to won-der about the nature of local Islam. Here we get into tricky territory. Are most coastal Muslims tolerant individuals? Yes. Has Al Qaeda recruited Kenyans and trained them in camps along the north coast? Yes. Did we see a Muslim shopkeeper in Mombasa cheerfully chat with a Jewish traveller about their respective religions? Yes. Did some people in Lamu publicly celebrate on September 11, 2001? Yes.

A porous border with Somalia, with its heavily armed Islamist militias, a sense of resentment against wealth disparities embodied by luxury hotels, the neglect the Christian central govern-ment has traditionally shown the coast, close ties to the Arab world and, as a result, increasingly intolerant and militant strains of Islam and the physical isolation of the far north coast (especially its islands), have created a haven for Islamic fundamentalists on the Kenyan Indian Ocean. Realise there is no easy line between 'extremist' or 'moderate' – a Kenyan Muslim may decry 9/11 yet praise Al Qaeda's general struggle while serving Italians wine in Malindi. Remember (a) the terrorist threat to tourists on the coast is low (they don't generally like to bomb their backyard, although there have been exceptions), and (b) coastal Muslim thought occupies a complex continuum, rather than easy categories. If you come here, you have a special opportunity to access one side of a complex conflict that is defining the world we travel in. Don't pass it up.

By the way, you may notice another bearded icon depicted all along the coast: Bob Marley. The Godfather of Reggae is primarily invoked by beach boys, but ironically, he is often considered in a similar light to Osama: that is, an antiestablishment and, ergo, anti-Western rebel figure.

---

## Dangers & Annoyances

Mombasa isn't Nairobi, but the streets still clear pretty rapidly after dark so it's a good idea to take taxis rather than walking around alone at night. The Likoni ferry is a bag-snatching hotspot. Visitors should also be aware of anti-Western sentiment among some Kenyan Muslims: hostile graffiti and Osama Bin Laden T-shirts abound, and demonstra-tions against Israel and America are increas-ingly common. Keep a low profile during any escalation of violence in the Middle East or terrorist activity in the West.

Malaria is a big risk on the coast so remem-ber your antimalarial medication (see p361).

## Sights & Activities
### FORT JESUS

All along the coast you'll spot castles and mosques carved out of coral, but the exem-plar of the genre, as it were, is Fort Jesus: Mombasa's most visited site, anchor of Old Town and dominant structure of the city's harbour. The metre-thick walls, frescoed interiors, traces of European graffiti, Arabic inscriptions and Swahili embellishment aren't just evocative – they're a record of the history of Mombasa, and the coast, writ in stone.

The **fort** (Map p256) was built by the Portuguese in 1593 to serve as both symbol and headquarters of their permanent pres-ence in this corner of the Indian Ocean. So it's ironic that the construction of the fort marked the beginning of the end of local Portuguese hegemony. Between Portuguese sailors, Omani soldiers and Swahili rebellions, the fort changed hands at least nine times be-tween 1631 and 1875, when it finally fell under British control and was used as a jail.

The fort was the final project completed by Joao Batista Cairato, whose buildings can be found throughout Portugal's Eastern colonies, from Old Goa to Old Mombasa. The building is an opus of period military design; assuming the structure was well-manned, it would have been impossible to approach its walls without falling under the cone of interlocking fields of fire.

These days the fort houses a **museum** ( ☎ 222425; nmkfortj@swiftmombasa.com; nonresident adult/child KSh800/400; ☉ 8am-6pm), built over the former barracks. The exhibits give good insight into Swahili life and culture, and there's a decent smattering of archaeological artefacts, many of which have been pulled from excavations from the north and south. Of note is the end room's exhibit of Mijikenda culture, particu-larly useful for anyone interested in the sacred *kaya* (see p276).

The area within the compound is just as interesting. In the **Mazrui Hall**, flowery spirals fade across a wall topped with wooden lintels left by the Omani Arabs. In another room,

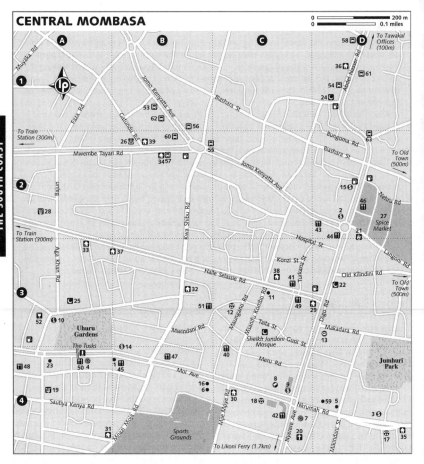

CENTRAL MOMBASA

Portuguese sailors scratched graffiti that illustrates the multicultural naval identity of the Indian Ocean, leaving walls covered with four-pointed European frigates, three-pointed Arabic dhows and the coir-sewn 'camels of the ocean', the elegant Swahili *mtepe* (traditional sailing vessel). Nearby, a pair of whale bones serves in the undignified role of see-saw for Swahili school children. The **Omani house**, in the San Felipe bastion in the northwestern corner of the fort, was built in the late 18th century and houses a small exhibition of Omani jewellery and artefacts. The **eastern wall** includes an Omani audience hall and the **Passage of the Arches**, which leads under the pinkish-brown coral onto a double-azure vista of sea floating under sky.

If you arrive early in the day you may avoid group tours, but the same can't be said of extremely persistent guides, official and unofficial, who will swarm you the minute you approach the fort. Some of them can be quite useful and some can be duds. Unfortunately, you'll have to use your best judgement to suss out which is which. If you don't want a tour, shake off your guide with a firm but polite no; otherwise they'll launch into their spiel and expect a tip at the end. Alternatively, you can buy the *Fort Jesus* guide booklet from the ticket desk and go it alone.

## RELIGIOUS BUILDINGS

In this city of almost a million inhabitants, 70% of whom are Muslim, there are a lot of mosques. Unfortunately, non-Muslims are usually not allowed to enter them, although you can have a look from the outside. **Mandhry Mosque** (Map p256; Sir Mbarak Hinawy Rd) in Old Town is an excellent example of Swahili architecture, which combines the elegant flourishes of Arabic style with the comforting, geometric patterns of African design; note, for example, the gently rounded minaret. More modern examples include the **Sheikh Nurein Islamic Centre** (Map p260) opposite Uhuru Gardens and the **Khonzi Mosque** (Map p260) on Digo Rd.

Mombasa's large Hindu (and smaller Jain) population doesn't lack for places of worship. The enormous **Lord Shiva Temple** (Map p256; Mwinyi Ab Rd) is airy, open and set off by an interesting sculpture garden, while the **Swaminarayan Temple** (Map p260; Haile Selassie Rd) is stuffed with highlighter-bright murals that'll make you feel as if you've been transported to Mumbai. For even more esoteric design, there's a **Sikh Temple** (Map p260; Mwembe Tayari Rd), a **Hare Krishna Temple** (Map p260; Sautiya Kenya Rd) and a lovely **Jain Temple** (Map p260; Langoni Rd) that is only open till noon. The latter services a small religion that believes in total nonviolence, to the point their priests sometimes wrap their mouths with scarves to avoid inhaling insects. Depending on the services

being held, you may not be allowed inside any of these temples.

The two main Christian churches are also worth seeing, for rather different reasons. The **Holy Ghost Cathedral** (Map p260; Nyerere Ave) is a very European hunk of neo-Gothic buttressed architecture, with massive fans in the walls to cool its former colonial congregations. The **Mombasa Memorial Cathedral** (Map p256; Nkrumah Rd), on the other hand, tries almost too hard to fit in, resembling a mosque with its white walls, arches and cupola.

### SPICE MARKET

This **market** (Map p260; Langoni Rd; to sunset), which stretches along Nehru and Langoni Rds west of Old Town, is an evocative, sensory overload; expect lots of jostling, yelling, wheeling, dealing and of course the mind-melting scent of stall upon stall of cardamom, pepper, turmeric, curry powders and everything else that makes eating enjoyable.

### OLD LAW COURTS

The old law courts on Nkrumah Rd have been converted into an informal **gallery** (Map p256; Nkrumah Rd; admission free; 8am-6pm), with regularly changing displays of local art, Kenyan crafts, school competition pieces and votive objects from various tribal groups.

MOMBASA &
THE SOUTH COAST

## Walking Tour

Mombasa may not have the medieval charm of Lamu and Zanzibar, but it does have some of the best balcony-spotting in East Africa.

Balcony-spotting? No, really. These particular architectural embellishments give insight into the inhabitants – the 'porchmanteau' quality, some might say – of Old Town over the years. Some are Indian, others Arab and a few European and all built over beautiful wooden Swahili doors. The filigreed fretwork provided a lookout for Old Town's inhabitants, while protecting the modesty of their women from the outside world. Also be on the lookout for expertly carved doors, many of which carry a chain motif, reference to the slave trading industry that was once part of the city's economy. Both doors and verandahs overlook a network of narrow streets, open-air markets and winding pathways that lead down to the blue waters of the harbour. While many older buildings have been destroyed, there is now a preservation order on the remaining doors and balconies, so further losses should hopefully be prevented. The **Mombasa Old Town Conservation Society** (Map p256; ☎ 312246; Sir Mbarak Hinawy Rd) encourages renovation of many dilapidated buildings. Call for details on helping the society in its mission.

It's worth picking up a copy of *The Old Town Mombasa: A Historical Guide* from the tourist office or the Fort Jesus ticket office, which gives a building-by-building account of the various structures. Or you can take a tour with one of the guides that will inevitably approach you; these guys are generally quite useful, but they'll expect a tip, of course.

This tour can take anywhere from one to two hours, depending on how many stops you make. Don't try to strictly adhere to this route; part of the fun is wandering around slightly lost until you decide you want to go to the next stop. Then, just ask a local for directions. Old Town isn't very big, so you're never that far from anything on the map.

We'll start at **Fort Jesus (1**; p259), the obvious gateway to Old Town. When you've had your fill of ramparts and relics, head past the colonial **Mombasa Club (2)** onto Sir Mbarak Hinawy Rd, once the main access road to the port and now a lively thoroughfare punctuated with shops and football graffiti.

On the left, **Anil's Arcade (3)** is a three-storey building that dates back to 1900, when it was occupied by a British shipping agency.

If you take a quick jaunt to your right you'll hit the water and see the restored facades of old houses; some are garish, but in general the renovations are done tastefully. Back on Sir Mbarak Hinawy, the **Old Town conservation office (4**; not to be confused with the Mombasa Old Town Conservation Society) stands across the street from the 16th-century **Mandhry Mosque (5**; p261), one of the oldest in use in Mombasa.

Turn the corner at the end of the street and you'll enter Government Square, the largest open space in the Old Town, facing towards the harbour. The buildings lining the square used to hold some of the city's key administrative offices, including the **Post Office (6), Customs House (7)**, the **Dhow Registrar's Office (8)**, the

### WALK FACTS

**Start** Fort Jesus
**Finish** Fort Jesus
**Distance** about 2km
**Duration** one to two hours

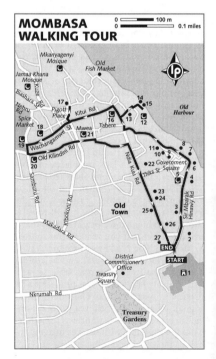

MOMBASA WALKING TOUR
0          100 m
0          0.1 miles

Treasury (9) on Thika St and the Italian Consulate (10). The old Scent Emporium (11), founded in 1850, is used today as a guest house for visiting dignitaries to the Bohra Mosque (12), whose congregants are primarily Indian.

Head past the Bohra and ask for directions to Vasco da Gama's Well. You'll need to bang a right towards the harbour; on the way you'll pass the yellow plaster walls of the Conservation Office (13), set off with original Portuguese-era balconies and a turn-of-the-century-era pillar from a British gazebo. A bit further along are the Leven Steps (14) by the waterfront, site of the former British colonial administration. These lead down past a great view of the ships docking in the harbour to Vasco da Gama's Well (15), a reservoir that supposedly never dries. The well is still used for drinking and washing water; local legend says it is located at the terminus of an underground passage between the slave markets and boats bound for Zanzibar.

Returning to Ndia Kuu Rd, turn left after you pass the Ithna Asheri Mosque (16) and head down Kitui Rd. At the end of the street you'll find Piggot Place, another colonial square. One of the shops fronting the plaza is the Shimla Building (17), which speaks to the traditional Indian dominance of trade in the city; note the large Hindu 'om' sign above the door.

All mosque fans should detour down Wachangamwe St to catch the colourful, modern Memon Mosque (18) and the more traditional Badala (19) and Badri (20) mosques (the latter primarily used by the Swahili community), before heading back down Old Kilindini Rd past the 16th-century Basheikh Mosque (21) to rejoin Ndia Kuu Rd.

Once you're on this straight home-stretch, the final stages of your route can be as direct or as tangential as you wish – diverting into side streets is highly recommended. The winding alleyways linking Old Town to Digo Rd are lively, with market traders selling everything from kangas (wraparounds worn by Swahili women) and mobile-phone accessories to baobab seeds and fried taro root. Or you can light out west, which will eventually land you in the city spice market (p261).

If you do stick to Ndia Kuu Rd, you'll see a lot of nicely restored traditional buildings, mostly occupied by souvenir shops. Heading south, you'll pass Hansing & Co (22), the former German import/export office; the Criterion (23), once a well-known hotel; an Indian-style house known as the Balcony House (24), for obvious reasons; Edward St Rose (25), the former chemist, which retains its original engraved glass panel; and Ali's Curio Market (26), one of the better-preserved balcony houses and formerly Mombasa's police headquarters. Pass the Muslim cemetery (27) and you're back at Fort Jesus, hopefully refreshed and enlivened by a glance into Mombasa's recent past.

## Tours

A number of tour companies offer standard tours of the Old Town and Fort Jesus (per person from US$80), plus safaris to Shimba Hills National Reserve and Tsavo East and Tsavo West National Parks. Most safaris are expensive lodge-based affairs, but there are a few camping safaris to Tsavo East and West. We've received good feedback from travellers on Natural World Tours and Safaris (Map p260; ☎ 2226715, 0720894288; www.naturaltoursandsafaris.com; Jeneyby House, Moi Ave).

### HARBOUR CRUISES

Luxury dhow cruises around the harbour are popular in Mombasa and, notwithstanding the price, they are an excellent way to see the harbour, the Old Town and Fort Jesus and get a slap-up meal at the end of it.

Topping the billing is the Tamarind Dhow (Map p256; ☎ 475074; www.tamarinddhow.com), run by the posh Tamarind restaurant chain. The cruise embarks from the jetty below Tamarind restaurant in Nyali, and includes a harbour tour and fantastic meal. The lunch cruises leave at 1pm and cost US$40/20 per adult/child, or US$80/40 when combined with a city tour. Longer and more splendid evening cruises leave at 6.30pm and cost US$70/35; vegetarians are catered for. Prices include a complimentary cocktail and transport to and from your hotel, and the dhow itself is a beautiful piece of work (you can hire it out exclusively for the day for US$650).

The other big operator is Jahazi Marine ( ☎ 35809770, 0714967717; www.severin-kenya.com), which offers evening trips for €68. The price includes transfers, a sunset cruise, a walk through the Old Town and entry to Fort Jesus for the light show and a five-course meal.

## Festivals & Events

The Mombasa Carnival is the major annual event, held every November. The festival sees

Moi Ave come alive for the day with street parades, floats and lots of music from tribes of the coastal region and the rest of Kenya.

For sporty types or keen spectators, the **Mombasa Triathlon** (www.kenyatriathlon.com) is an open competition with men's, women's and children's races, held in November.

## Sleeping

Many people choose to skip Mombasa and head straight for the beaches to the south (p270) and north (p281), but we'd suggest spending at least one night in town. It's difficult to appreciate Mombasa's energy without waking up to the call to prayer and the honk of the *tuk-tuk* (mini-taxi). All the places listed here have fans and mosquito nets as a minimum requirement.

### BUDGET

Dirt-cheap choices are in the busy area close to the bus stations on Abdel Nasser Rd and Jomo Kenyatta Ave. Lone female travellers might want to opt for something a little further up the price scale.

**Tana Guest House** (Map p260; ☎ 490550; cnr Mwembe Tayari & Gatundu Rds; s/d/tr KSh400/500/600) A simple but friendly place; rooms are small, tidy and pretty much what you'd expect for the price.

**New People's Hotel** (Map p260; Abdel Nasser Rd; s/d KSh600/700, with shared bathroom KSh600/700) At this hotel near the 'Ideal Chicks' poultry building ('Because Chicks is the Boss'), you'll get loads of noise from traffic and the Noor Mosque next door, but rooms are clean and security is good. There's a nice, cheap restaurant downstairs and it's very convenient for buses to Lamu and Malindi.

**New Daba Guest House** (Map p260; Mwembe Tayari Rd; s KSh800) Unfriendly and distinctly functional (ie ugly), the New Daba is nonetheless one of the cleaner options you could go for if you're either on a budget, or have just arrived on a night bus and need a place to crash. Otherwise, look elsewhere.

**Evening Guest House** (Map p260; ☎ 221380; Mnazi Moja Rd; s/d KSh800/1200, with shared bathroom KSh800/1000) If you need a budget doss set off from the bus-stand chaos, this is a good option. The doubles are good value, the singles a bit less so, service is friendly and you'll get a good night's sleep. All rooms have power points 'for mobile phones only'.

**Beracha Guest House** (Map p260; ☎ 0725006228; Haile Selassie Rd; s/d KSh800/1300) This popular

central choice is located in the heart of Mombasa's best eat-streets and has variable but clean rooms in a range of unusual shapes. It's on the 2nd floor of the building it occupies – on the stair landing, turn right into the hotel, and not left into the evangelical church.

### MIDRANGE

**Summerlink Hotel** (Map p260; ☎ 2226178, 0724376849; s/d/tr KSh1550/2200/3150; ❖ ☎) If you can't quite bump up your budget to that next level of comfort, the Summerlink, which hovers (price-wise) at the bottom of the midrange column, might be your best option. It's a clean place with excellent security, good service, a hilariously gaudy terrazzo-columned courtyard and loads of Kenyan businessmen. There's also an on-site gym with daily membership rates (KSh200) and karate classes, which is obviously what you came here for.

**New Palm Tree Hotel** (Map p260; ☎ 311758; Nkrumah Rd; s/d KSh1600/2200) This sociable option has rooms set around a terraced roof, and while the amenities (like hot water) aren't always reliable, service is fine and there's a good vibe about the place.

**Hotel Dorse** (Map p260; ☎ 222252, 31856; hotel dorse@africaonline.co.ke; Kwa Shibu Rd, off Moi Ave; s/d KSh2500/3000) Marketed at a conference clientele, this is a good low-lying building with balconies, big beds and showers designed for very tall people. Knock about KSh500 off the price in low season.

**Hotel Sapphire** (Map p256; ☎ 2494841, 2492257; hotelsapphire@africaonline.co.ke; Mwembe Tayari Rd; s/d/tr KSh2550/3980/4795; ❖ ☎) Come for the saggy beds, stay for the neon palm trees! The Sapphire is a decent option, especially if you want to stay close to the train station. Some of the rooms could do with better lighting, but they're all nicely fitted out with TVs and, yes, squishy beds. The pool is uncomfortably located in the centre of the restaurant terrace.

**Hotel Sai Rose** (Map p256; ☎ 222897; hotelsairose @iconnect.co.ke; Nyerere Ave; s/d/tr KSh3500/4500/6500; ❖) This outrageous hotel is a good example of what happens when Chinese money and design aesthetic meets the Kenyan penchant for going over the top. Rooms resemble the velvet set of a Prince video crossed with a Vietnamese opium den, and the hotel itself is one long, narrow corridor set between two patches of wasteland.

**ourpick** Castle Royal Hotel (Map p260; ☎ 220373, 2222682; www.castlemsa.com; Moi Ave; s/d/tr KSh3500/4500/6000; 🏋 🖳 ) In the West this would be the sort of big boxy but slightly boutique place you stop at after a long drive and wake up to feeling absolutely refreshed. In Mombasa, all of the above equals the best hotel deal in town. Electronic door-locks, TVs, air-con, balconies and rooms that actually have a decent design aesthetic all equal joy. Did we mention the high-speed internet lines (additional US$15)? Oh, and the (included) breakfast buffet is primo: coconut beans and *mandazi* (semi-sweet doughnuts), or bacon and croissants; be you Western, African or dharma bum, the Castle Royal loves 'ya.

### TOP END

**Royal Court Hotel** (Map p260; ☎ 223379; royalcourt @swiftmombasa; Haile Selassie Rd; s US$75-100, d US$85-120, ste US$180; 🏋 🖳 ) The swish lobby is the highlight of this stylish business hotel – executive rooms are reasonably plush, but the standard rooms are beaten by those at the Castle Royal. Still, service and facilities are good, disabled access is a breeze and you get great views and food at the Tawa Terrace restaurant on the roof, which also has a pool.

**Kohinoor Hotel & Apartments** (Map p260; ☎ 2317895; kohinoor@africaonline.co.ke; Haile Selassie Rd; d/apt KSh7200/14,400; 🏋 ) This is a series of nicely outfitted apartments located in the heart of downtown Mombasa. It's a nice place with quite a few thoughtful embellishments, and is very family-friendly to boot, but at this price you could easily stay on the seafront. That is, unless you (a) prefer to be in the thick of the Mombasa city scene, or (b) have a thing for traffic.

**ourpick** Tamarind Village (Map p256; ☎ 474600; www.tamarind.co.ke; Silos Rd, Nyali; apt KSh9500-20,000; 🏋 🖳 🟦 ) This is bar none the best hotel in town, especially if you're going upscale. Located in a modern (and quite elegantly executed) take on a Swahili castle overlooking the blue waters of the harbour, the Tamarind offers crisp, fully serviced apartments with satellite TV, palm-lined balconies and a general sense of white-washed, sun-lathered luxury.

## Eating

Oh thank heaven. If a never-ending parade of chicken, chips, meat and corn roasted beyond palatability, and starch that tastes like…well, nothing, doesn't do it for you, well here comes the coast: flavours! Fresh seafood! Spice! Anything but more *ugali!*

### RESTAURANTS
#### Kenyan & Swahili

Explore the Old Town for cheap, authentic Swahili cuisine; if in doubt, follow the locals to find the best deals. Most places are Muslim-run, so no alcoholic drinks are sold and they're closed until after sunset during Ramadan.

**Recoda Restaurant** (Map p260; Moi Ave; mains around KSh120; 🕐 lunch & dinner) This Muslim eatery is packed in the evenings with locals clamouring for the local take on kebabs, which are grilled to fat-dripping perfection. Service is a bit sharp, but take it with a spoonful of sugar, because the food is worth your patience.

**New Recoder Restaurant** (Map p256; Kibokoni Rd; mains KSh50-180; 🕐 lunch & dinner) This is a local favourite, slightly tattier than Island Dishes, but with much the same coast cuisine. Despite the name similarity, we don't think there's a connection between this place and the Recoda Restaurant (above).

**Qamar Restaurant** (Map p260; Jomo Kenyatta Ave; mains KSh70-200; 🕐 lunch & dinner) This coast-cuisine canteen is generally bustling with activity and radiating a smoky aroma of deliciousness. Located close as it is to the spice market, order anything that's Swahili and spicy, and be pleased.

**Island Dishes** (Map p256; ☎ 0720887311; Kibokoni Rd; mains KSh80-220; 🕐 lunch & dinner) Once your eyes have adjusted to the dazzling strip-lights, feast them on the tasty menu at this whiter-than-white Lamu-themed canteen. *Mishikaki* (marinated, grilled meat kebabs), chicken tikka, fish, fresh juices and all the usual favourites are on offer to eat in or take away, though the biriani (rice with meat or seafood) is only available at lunchtime.

#### Indian

**FH Mithai's** (Map p260; ☎ off Digo Rd; mains KSh70-250; 🕐 lunch & dinner) We had a great time at this cafe set into the spice market, snacking on bhaji, samosas and some of the best sweets this side of Gujarat, while sipping chai and discussing the nature of God with the 'Sugar Daddy', FH Mithai, owner of the establishment, biblical scholar and archaeologist. See p266.

**Singh Restaurant** (Map p260; ☎ 493283; Mwembe Tayari Rd; mains KSh250-320; 🕐 lunch & dinner) This used to be a very simple cafeteria, but it's received an extensive makeover and now looks like

---

## FH MITHAI

This dessert *wallah* (merchant) has an interesting past.

**Where is your family from?** Gujarat, but I am Kenyan. My family has been here for 138 years. We are of the Dawoodi Bohra branch of Islam, and we were here before any Patels! (a traditional Gujarati surname).

**Do you consider yourself Kenyan or Indian?** Kenyan! India is my grandmother, I suppose, but Kenya is my mother. Kenya raised me.

**What did you do before you operated this shop?** I was an archaeologist – a biblical archaeologist. I've dug the graves of Simon and Samuel. I have sought out the grave of Daniel and excavated Fatamid mosques, which are important to the Dawoodi.

**Does working as an archaeologist help your faith?** The prophets are amazing, and they always leave a mark. They knew people would be sceptical, and say such and such a thing about them.

**So you are a seeker of knowledge?** And God. 'Alif la'm mim' – 'Knowledge is not in this book. It is in this book' (he gestures to us). The Quran does not drop from the sky. It comes into the heart of someone. It is nearer to you than your jugular veins. When you find yourself, you have found God.

*FH Mithai is the owner of FH Mithai's (p265), a cafe in central Mombasa.*

---

your standard, dark-wood and Mughal painting–bedecked classy Indian restaurant. With that said, the food is excellent and, thanks to the nearby Sikh temple, this spot serves vegetarians, and well.

**Shehnai Restaurant** (Map p260; ☎ 222847; Fatemi House, Maungano Rd; mains from KSh300; ☽ noon-2pm & 7.30-10.30pm Tue-Sun) Mombasa's classiest curryhouse specialises in tandoori and rich *mughlai* (North Indian) cuisine complemented by nice decor that's been pulled out of Indian restaurants from the world over (pumped-in sitar music thrown in for free). It's very popular with well-heeled Indian families, probably because the food is authentic and very good.

### Chinese

These places double as bars, so you may be the only person eating.

**New Overseas Chinese-Korean Restaurant & Bar** (Map p260; ☎ 230729; Moi Ave; mains KSh220-480; ☽ lunch & dinner) Despite the overblown name and the hilariously clichéd interior design, the New Overseas does actually deliver on its oriental promises and is particularly strong on seafood.

**China Town Restaurant** (Map p260; ☎ 315098; Nyerere Ave; mains KSh400-600; ☽ lunch & dinner) More incredibly chintzy decor, more good Korean and Chinese food. Like the New Overseas, this spot is attracting more and more well-off Chinese businessmen, many of whom snack here before heading to the casinos.

### International

**Little Chef Dinners Pub** (Map p260; ☎ 222740; Moi Ave; mains KSh120-300; ☽ lunch & dinner) This funky, green-hued pub-restaurant has no relation to the British motorway diners of the same name. Little Chef dishes up big, tasty portions of Kenyan and international dishes and also has a pool table. There are a couple more outlets in the area, but this is by far the nicest.

**Perfect Pizza** (Map p260; ☎ 226841; Haile Selassie Rd; pizzas KSh240-660; ☽ lunch & dinner) 'Perfect' might be pushing it, but this is surprisingly good pizza (of the greasy American sort) considering you're in East Africa. There are plenty of topping options, including make-your-own pies.

**Puckwall** (Map p256; ☎ 472896; Nyali Rd, Nyali; mains KSh250-600; ☽ lunch & dinner) Puckwall has to have one of the largest menus in Mombasa, a four-page extravaganza of pizza, curries, *nyama choma* (barbecued meat) and burgers. The execution generally proves the adage 'Jack of all trades, master of none'; what you get here will be decent if not overwhelming. It's quite popular with Mombasa's Indian elite.

**Roberto's** (Map p256; ☎ 476559; Nyali Centre, Nyali Rd, Nyali; mains KSh450-1600; ☽ lunch & dinner) Roberto's caters to the double 'I's of the Kenyan coast: Indians and Italians. The cuisine sources the latter nationality exclusively, and many Italian expats will tell you Roberto's does the best Old Country cooking in town.

**Hunter's Steak House** (Map p256; 'Königsallee', Mkomani Rd, Nyali; mains KSh450-2000; ☽ Wed-Mon)

Where's *die* beef? Here, *meine Freunde*, at this German-run steakhouse, generally regarded as the best purveyors of cooked cow in town (by tourists and expats – Kenyans generally prefer their *choma*). Aimed mainly at visitors, it's often closed for a month or so in June.

**ourpick Tamarind Restaurant** (Map p256; ☎ 474600; Silos Rd, Nyali; mains KSh1100-1800; 🕑 lunch & dinner) If you're entertaining an 'I'm a Swahili sultan overlooking my coastal kingdom with a giant plate of chilli-crab' fantasy, can we recommend the Tamarind? Big Moorish-palace exterior, big jewellery-box dining room, big keyboard music (ugh) and a big menu that concentrates on seafood (but does everything well) equals big satisfaction (and, yeah, a big bill).

### CAFES
**Cafe Mocha** (Map p256; Nyali Centre, Nyali Rd, Nyali; 🕑 lunch & dinner) Mocha is usually brimming with well-heeled Mombasan teeny- and tweeny-boppers and their parents enjoying the good coffee, air-conditioning and lovely cakes and pastries.

**Mombasa Coffee House** (Map p260; Moi Ave; meals from KSh100; 🕑 lunch & dinner; 🖥) An excellent escape from the chaos of Moi Ave that serves excellent locally brewed Kenyan coffee, light pastries and sandwiches.

### QUICK EATS
Mombasa's good for street food: stalls sell cassava, samosas, bhajis, kebabs and the local take on pizza (meat and onions wrapped in soft dough and fried). A few dish out stew and *ugali* (maize- or cassava-based staple). For dessert, vendors ply you with *haluwa* (an Omani version of Turkish delight), fried taro root, sweet baobab seeds and sugared doughnuts. Unless otherwise stated, don't expect to pay more than KSh100 at the following places.

**Blue Room Restaurant** (Map p260; ☎ 224021; www.blueroomonline.com; Haile Selassie Rd; mains KSh170-380; 🕑 lunch & dinner; 🖥) Between the steaks, pizzas, curries and…internet access (no, really), the Blue Room has basically been constructed to serve the needs of every traveller anywhere. OK, maybe not, but this enormous cafeteria is a good option for those who can't make a decision about what kind of feed they need.

**Fayaz Baker & Confectioners** (Map p260; ☎ 220382; Jomo Kenyatta Ave; 🕑 lunch & dinner) Mombasa's 'Master Baker' cooks up excellent cakes and muffins in several locations around town.

**Anglo-Swiss Bakery** (Map p260; Meru Rd; 🕑 lunch & dinner) Perhaps not the obvious entente cordiale, but another good place for cakes.

**Azad's** (Map p256; Makadara Rd; 🕑 lunch & dinner) This tiny spot dominates Mombasa's ice-cream stakes. It gets especially popular during Ramadan, when Muslim parents treat their kids (and themselves) to Azad's fast-breaking icy goodness.

### SELF-CATERING
**Nakumatt supermarket** (Map p256; ☎ 228945; Nyerere Ave) Close to the Likoni ferry, with a good selection of provisions, drinks and hardware items – just in case you need a TV, bicycle or lawnmower to go with your groceries.

**Main market** (Map p260; Digo Rd) Mombasa's dilapidated 'covered' market is packed with stalls selling fresh fruit and vegetables. Roaming produce carts also congregate in the surrounding streets, and dozens of *miraa* (shoots chewed as a stimulant) sellers join the fray when the regular deliveries come in, adding some amphetamine energy to the mix.

## Drinking
There are plenty of good drinking holes in Mombasa, and many restaurants cater primarily to drinkers in the evening.

**Office** (Map p256; ☎ 451700; Shelly Beach Rd, Likoni) Perched above the Likoni ferry jetty and matatu stand, the entirely unaptly named Office is a real locals' hangout with regular massive reggae and dub nights shaking the thatched rafters. Any business that goes on here is definitely not the executive kind.

**Bella Vista** (Map p260; west of Uhuru Gardens) This two-storey beer-o-fest is plenty of fun for those who feel the need to kick back with a cold one, some sports on the tube, a few rounds of pool and a great view of Mombasa's nightlife action unfolding in all it's storied, slightly sleazy glory.

## Entertainment
**New Florida Nightclub** (off Map p256; ☎ 313127; Mama Ngina Dr; 🕑 24hr; 🖥) This vast seafront complex houses Mombasa's liveliest nightclub, which boasts its own open-air swimming pool. It's owned by the same people as the infamous Florida clubs in Nairobi and offers the same atmosphere, clientele and Las Vegas–style floorshows, with the bonus of outdoor bars, table football and German *Currywurst* (curry sausage)! Friday, Saturday and Sunday are the

big party nights. A taxi fare here from central Mombasa is around KSh400.

**Nyali Cinemax** (Map p256; ☎ 470000; www.nyali cinemax.com; Nyali Centre, Nyali Rd, Nyali; tickets KSh250-350) A multiscreen, modern cineplex that's a great air-conditioned escape from the oppressive humidity. It shows a lot of Holly- and Bollywood, although the DVD copyright line in the bottom corner of the show we saw didn't inspire a lot of confidence in ethical royalty practices.

**Hollywood Bowl** (Map p256; ☎ 476056; Nyali Centre, Nyali Rd, Nyali; games KSh199-350) A typical American-style bowling alley.

## Shopping

Biashara St (Map p260), west of its Digo Rd intersection (just north of the spice market), is Kenya's main centre for *kikoi*, brightly coloured woven sarongs for men, and *kangas*, printed wraps worn by women. *Kangas* come as a pair, one for the top half of the body and one for the bottom, and are marked with Swahili proverbs. You may need to bargain, but what you get is generally what you pay for; bank on about KSh350–500 for a pair of *kangas* or a *kikoi*. *Kofia,* the handmade caps worn by Muslim men, are also crafted here; a really excellent one can run you up to KSh2000.

Mombasa has an incredible number of skilled tailors and you can have a safari suit or shirt custom-made in a day or two for an incredible price (less than US$20). There are numerous choices on Nehru Rd, behind the spice market (Map p260).

Moi Ave (Map p260) has loads of souvenir shops, but prices are high and every shop seems to stock exactly the same stuff. There are stalls selling sisal baskets and spices in and around the main market, but you'll rarely pay fair prices as touts loiter here and 'accompany' tourists for a commission.

**Bombolulu Workshops & Cultural Centre** (Map p283; ☎ 471704; www.apdkbombolulu.org; nonresident adult/child KSh360/180; ☑ 8am-6pm Mon-Sat, 10am-3pm Sun) This nonprofit organisation produces crafts of a high standard and gives vocational training to physically disabled people. Visit the workshops and showroom for free to buy jewellery, clothes, carvings and other crafts, or enter the cultural centre to tour mock-ups of traditional homesteads. The turn-off for the centre is on the left about 3km north of Nyali Bridge. Bombolulu matatus run here from Msanifu Kombo Rd, and Bamburi services

also pass the centre (KSh20). It is also accessible from Nyali Beach. The workshops will pick you up from north-coast hotels free of charge. If you're staying on the south coast, you'll need a group of at least four for a pick up (KSh400 per person).

**Akamba Handicraft Industry Cooperative Society** (off Map p256; ☎ 3434396; www.akambahandicraftcoop .com; Port Reitz Rd; ☑ 8am-5pm Mon-Fri, to noon Sun) This cooperative employs an incredible 10,000 people from the local area. It's also a nonprofit organisation and produces fine woodcarvings. Kwa Hola/Magongo matatus run right past the gates from the Kobil petrol station on Jomo Kenyatta Ave. Many coach tours from Mombasa also stop here.

## Getting There & Away
### AIR

**Airkenya** ( ☎ Nairobi 020-605745; www.airkenya.com) doesn't have a ticket office in Mombasa (you can book online), but also flies between Nairobi and Mombasa once a day (one way US$55, one hour); flights leave Nairobi at 9.30am and Mombasa at 11.05am.

**Kenya Airways** (Map p260; ☎ 221251; www.kenya -airways.com; TSS Towers, Nkrumah Rd) flies between Nairobi and Mombasa at least six times daily (one way/return US$130/218, one hour).

**Mombasa Air Safari** (off Map p256; ☎ 433061; www.mombasaairsafari.com; Moi International Airport) flies to Amboseli (US$270, one hour), Tsavo (US$270) and Masai Mara (US$270) National Parks; they can also arrange complete safari packages.

### BOAT

Ask around the docks if you'd like to try to hop a cargo ship to Pemba, Zanzibar or Dar es Salaam in Tanzania. Captains will charge anywhere from KSh2000 to much more. You can also try and get on a dhow, but the chances are significantly smaller (they rarely sail that far) and the fare will likely be much higher. You'll have a better chance down the coast at Shimoni. There were no ferry services at the time of writing.

### BUS & MATATU

Most bus offices are either on Jomo Kenyatta Ave or Abdel Nasser Rd. Services to Malindi and Lamu leave from Abdel Nasser Rd, while buses to destinations in Tanzania leave from the junction of Jomo Kenyatta Ave and Mwembe Tayari Rd.

For buses and matatus to the beaches and towns south of Mombasa, you first need to get off the island via the Likoni ferry (right). Frequent matatus run from Nyerere Ave to the transport stand by the ferry terminal.

### Nairobi

There are dozens of daily departures in both directions (mostly in the early morning and late evening). Companies include the following:

**Akamba** (Map p260; ☎ 490269; Jomo Kenyatta Ave)
**Busscar** (Map p260; ☎ 222854; Abdel Nasser Rd)
**Coastline Safaris** (Map p260; ☎ 220158; Mwembe Tayari St)
**Falcon** (Map p260; Abdel Nasser Rd)
**Mombasa Raha** (Map p260; ☎ 225716) Offices on Abdel Nasser Rd and Jomo Kenyatta Ave.
**Msafiri** (Map p260; ☎ 314691; Aga Khan Rd)

Daytime services take at least six hours, and overnight trips eight to 10 hours and include a meal/smoking break about halfway. The trip isn't particularly comfortable, although it's not bad for an African bus ride. Fares vary from KSh800 to KSh1300. Most companies have at least four departures daily.

All buses to Nairobi travel via Voi (KSh500), which is also served by frequent matatus from the Kobil petrol station on Jomo Kenyatta Ave (KSh200). Several companies go to Kisumu and Lake Victoria, but all go via Nairobi.

### Heading North

There are numerous daily matatus and small lorry-buses up the coast to Malindi, leaving from in front of the Noor Mosque on Abdel Nasser Rd. Buses take up to 2½ hours (KSh100), matatus about two hours (KSh120). You can also catch an 'express' matatu to Malindi (KSh150), which takes longer to fill up but is then supposedly non-stop all the way.

Tawakal, Falcon, Mombasa Raha and TSS Express have buses to Lamu, most leaving at around 7am (report 30 minutes early) from their offices on Abdel Nasser Rd. Buses take around seven hours to reach the Lamu ferry at Mokoke (KSh650 to KSh800), stopping in Malindi (KSh200 to KSh300).

### Heading South

Regular buses and matatus leave from the Likoni ferry terminal and travel along the southern coast.

For Tanzania, Falcon and a handful of other companies have daily departures to Tanga (KSh600, two hours) and Dar es Salaam (KSh1000 to KSh1300, eight hours) from their offices on Jomo Kenyatta Ave, near the junction with Mwembe Tayari Rd. Dubious-looking buses to Moshi and Arusha leave from in front of the Mwembe Tayari Health Centre in the morning or evening.

### TRAIN

Few subjects divided our readers' letters more fiercely than the train from Nairobi to Mombasa. Once one of the most famous rail lines in Africa, the train is today, depending on who you speak to, either a sociable way of avoiding the rutted highway and spotting wildlife from the clackety comfort of a sleeping car, or a ratty, tatty overrated waste of time. The truth lies somewhere in the middle. The train's state could be described as 'faded glory', occasionally bumping up to 'romantically dishevelled', or slipping into 'frustrating mediocrity'. The latter isn't helped by spotty scheduling and lax timetable enforcement.

The 'iron snake' departs Mombasa at 7pm on Tuesday, Thursday and Sunday, arriving in Nairobi the next day somewhere between 8.30am and 11am. Fares are US$65 1st class, US$54 2nd class, including bed and breakfast (you get dinner with 1st class) – reserve as far in advance as possible. The **booking office** (Map p256; ☎ 312220; ⏰ 8am-5pm) is at the station in Mombasa.

## Getting Around

### TO/FROM THE AIRPORT

There is currently no public transport to or from the airport, so you're best taking a taxi – the fare to central Mombasa is around KSh800 to KSh1000. Coming from town, the usual fare is KSh1000, but you have to bargain.

If you don't have much luggage, you can take a Kwa Hola/Magongo matatu from the Kobil petrol station on Jomo Kenyatta Ave to just beyond the Akamba Handicraft Industry Cooperative Society then onto Airport Rd for KSh40 and walk the last few kilometres.

### BOAT

The two Likoni ferries connect Mombasa island with the southern mainland. There's a crossing roughly every 20 minutes between 5am and 12.30am, less frequently outside these times. It's free for pedestrians and KSh50 per car. To get to the jetty from the centre of town, take a Likoni matatu from Digo Rd.

### CAR & MOTORCYCLE
There's not much difference between the car-hire companies in town apart from the possible insurance excesses (see p351). Rates are the same as in Nairobi – about KSh7000 per day for a small jeep and KSh6000 per day for a saloon car. Companies with offices in central Mombasa include the following:

**Avenue Motors** (Map p256; ☎ 225126; Moi Ave)

**Budget** ( ☎ 3433211; www.budget-kenya.com; Moi International Airport)

**Glory Car Hire** (Map p260; ☎ 228063; Moi Ave) Adjacent to the tourist office.

**Hertz** (off Map p256; ☎ 3434020; mombasa@hertz .co.ke; Moi International Airport)

### MATATU, TAXI & TUK-TUK
Matatus charge between KSh10 and KSh20 for short trips. Mombasa taxis are as expensive as those in Nairobi, and harder to find; a good place to look is in front of Express Travel on Nkrumah Rd. Assume it'll cost KSh250 to KSh400 from the train station to the city centre. There are also plenty of three-wheeled *tuk-tuks* about, which run to about KSh70 to KSh150 for a bit of open-air transit.

# SOUTH OF MOMBASA

Why do folks head south of Mombasa? For most people it's all wrapped up in a word: beaches.

And yet there's so much more. We're not saying the sand isn't gorgeous or the ocean isn't lovely, because they are. But there's a depressing amount of package tourists here opting for high-end resorts that only access the above.

Slice into those teal waves and lay out under those coconut fronds, but, while you're at it, can we also recommend walking through the groves of a 600-year-old sacred forest? Or having a homestay with a Swahili family and learning to cook chapatis and *sambusas* (deep-fried pastries stuffed with spiced mincemeat)? How about feeling the breeze over a buffer of mangroves and helping with community-development initiatives? Snorkelling in the jewel-box waters of a marine park? Or feeling the salt wind

curl off a dhow's prow as you light out for a new island?

Enjoy Diani and Tiwi, the beach beauties on the block, but do yourself a favour and go beyond the hotel gates while you're here, because that's where the unique cultural and ecological charms of the coast can be found.

## SHELLY BEACH
Right across the water from Mombasa island, Shelly Beach isn't a bad place to swim if you just want a day trip from Mombasa, though there's lots of seaweed and it's a poor substitute for the northern and southern beaches. To get here take a matatu (KSh30) from the turn-off, just south of the Likoni ferry jetty.

## SHIMBA HILLS NATIONAL RESERVE
If you're in need of traditional African landscapes of the rolling hills variety, this 320-sq-km **reserve** (adult/child US$20/10; ☼ 6am-6pm) is just 30km from Mombasa, directly inland from Diani Beach. Actually, it's a bit more than rolling hills (the Marare and Pengo, to be exact); throw in an escarpment of Triassic rock, riverine valleys dotted with clumps of tropical rainforest, and leopards, sable antelope and elephants, and you've got a national park that holds it own against anything in the hinterland.

The main wildlife attractions are the aforementioned elephants and antelope (the leopards are great too, but much more difficult to spot). In 2005, the elephant population reached an amazing 600 – far too many for this tiny space. Instead of culling the herds, Kenya Widlife Service (KWS) organised an unprecedented US$3.2 million translocation operation to reduce the pressure on the habitat, capturing no fewer than 400 elephants and moving them to Tsavo East National Park. The antelope have made a stunning recovery after their numbers dropped to less than 120 in 1970.

There are over 150km of 4WD tracks that criss-cross the reserve; Marere Dam and the forest of Mwele Mdogo Hill are good spots for birdlife. Highly recommended guided forest walks are run by the **KWS** ( ☎ 040-4159; PO Box 30, Kwale) from the Sheldrick Falls ranger post. Walks are free but a tip would be appropriate.

## Sleeping

The **public campsite** (per person US$8) and **bandas** (per person US$35) are superbly located on the edge of an escarpment close to the main gate, with stunning views down to Diani Beach. Monkeys sit in the trees around the camp, and very tame zebras occasionally warm themselves by your fire.

**Mukurumuji Tented Camp** ( ☎ 040-2412; www .campkenya.com; full board per person US$94) This series of luxury tents does the whole posh African-bush thing quite well, but it's also part of Camp Kenya (see p274), which runs community programs in the area. Some of these projects include managing wildlife–human interactions, landscaping and classroom refurbishment. The campsite is located on a forested hill; there's an outdoor shower with a view over the hills that must be one of the coolest washrooms in Kenya.

**Shimba Rainforest Lodge** ( ☎ 040-4077; Kinango Rd; full board with shared bathroom per person US$170) This is a great lodge of the Treetops genre, the sort of place where you feel like you're Tarzan getting spoilt with a menu of plush amenities. You're so amongst the wildlife that bushbabies will eat out of your hand (don't let them – it's illegal and makes animals less cautious and more susceptible to predators). Children under seven years are not permitted. The floodlit waterhole here attracts quite a lot of wildlife, including leopards and especially buffaloes.

## Getting There & Away

You'll need a 4WD to enter the reserve, but hitching may be possible at the main gate. From Likoni, small lorry-buses to Kwale pass the main gate (KSh50). Mukurumuji Tented Camp can organise transfers from Diani.

## MWALUGANJE ELEPHANT SANCTUARY

This **sanctuary** ( ☎ 040-41121; nonresident adult/child US$15/2, vehicles KSh150-500; ◷ 6am-6pm) is a good example of community-based conservation with local people acting as stakeholders in the project. It was opened in October 1995 to create a corridor along an elephant migration route between Shimba Hills and Mwaluganje Forest Reserve, and comprises 2400 hectares of rugged, beautiful country along the valley of the Cha Shimba River.

More than 150 elephants live in the sanctuary and you're likely to see other fauna and flora, including rare cycads. This primitive, palmlike plant species is over 300 million years old, and all six Kenyan species can be found here; seeing them is kind of like peeking into the Jurassic. There's a good information centre close to the main gate. Don't miss the chance to buy the unique postcards and paper goods as souvenirs for the folks back home – they're all made from recycled elephant dung!

**Mwaluganje Elephant Camp** ( ☎ Mombasa 041-5485121; www.travellersbeach.com; per person US$110) is a rather fine place to stay. There's a waterhole and accommodation is in permanent tents. Most travellers come here on day or overnight packages (US$115/213 per person), which include transfers from the south coast and wildlife drives. **Campsites** (per person KSh300) are located near the main gate and southern end of the park.

The main entrance to the sanctuary is about 13km northeast of Shimba Hills National Reserve, on the road to Kinango. A shorter route runs from Kwale to the Golini gate, passing the Mwaluganje ticket office. It's only 5km but the track is 4WD only.

## TIWI BEACH

☎ 040

The sleepy sister to manic Diani is a string of blissed-out resorts, accessible by dirt tracks, about 20km south of Likoni. It's good for a quiet, cottage-style escape by the sand. One of the best features of Tiwi is Diani reef (which, funnily enough, isn't as evident in Diani), creating a stable, pool-like area between the shore and the coral that's great for swimming. The main drawbacks are the occasional beach boys, who tend to cluster towards the southern end of the beach. Tiwi is a lot less visited than Diani, but you'll still need to book ahead during high season.

Getting to Tiwi requires turning left off the main highway (A14) about 18km south of Mombasa; follow the track until it terminates in a north–south T-intersection. We wouldn't recommend walking between resorts, as the distances can be quite far and if you stroll along the beach, you may get swallowed up by a sudden tide.

## Sleeping & Eating

With a few exceptions, Tiwi doesn't provide the all-in-one package experience of the high-end resorts to the south. The name of the game here is smallish, self-catered cottages, which can be a real joy for groups and

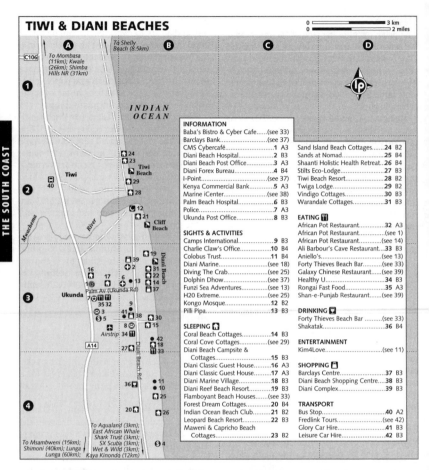

# TIWI & DIANI BEACHES

0 ────── 3 km
0 ────── 2 miles

**INFORMATION**
Baba's Bistro & Cyber Cafe......(see 33)
Barclays Bank............................(see 37)
CMS Cybercafé.............................**1** A3
Diani Beach Hospital....................**2** B3
Diani Beach Post Office................**3** A3
Diani Forex Bureau.......................**4** B3
I-Point.......................................(see 37)
Kenya Commercial Bank...........**5** A3
Marine iCenter..........................(see 38)
Palm Beach Hospital...................**6** B3
Police........................................**7** A3
Ukunda Post Office.....................**8** B3

**SIGHTS & ACTIVITIES**
Camps International......................**9** B3
Charlie Claw's Office...................**10** B4
Colobus Trust.............................**11** B4
Diani Marine.............................(see 18)
Diving The Crab........................(see 25)
Dolphin Dhow............................(see 37)
Funzi Sea Adventures................(see 13)
H20 Extreme.............................(see 25)
Kongo Mosque...........................**12** B2
Pilli Pipa.....................................**13** B3

**SLEEPING**
Coral Beach Cottages.................**14** B3
Coral Cove Cottages.................(see 29)
Diani Beach Campsite &
   Cottages................................**15** B3
Diani Classic Guest House..........**16** A3
Diani Classic Guest House..........**17** A3
Diani Marine Village....................**18** B3
Diani Reef Beach Resort.............**19** B3
Flamboyant Beach Houses........(see 33)
Forest Dream Cottages..............**20** B4
Indian Ocean Beach Club...........**21** B2
Leopard Beach Resort................**22** B3
Maweni & Capricho Beach
   Cottages................................**23** B2

Sand Island Beach Cottages.......**24** B2
Sands at Nomad.........................**25** B4
Shaanti Holistic Health Retreat...**26** B4
Stilts Eco-Lodge.........................**27** B3
Tiwi Beach Resort......................**28** B2
Twiga Lodge..............................**29** B2
Vindigo Cottages.......................**30** B3
Warandale Cottages...................**31** B3

**EATING**
African Pot Restaurant...............**32** A3
African Pot Restaurant...............(see 1)
Ali Barbour's Cave Restaurant....**33** B3
Aniello's....................................(see 13)
Forty Thieves Beach Bar...........(see 33)
Galaxy Chinese Restaurant........(see 39)
Healthy U...................................**34** B3
Rongai Fast Food.......................**35** A3
Shan-e-Punjab Restaurant........(see 39)

**DRINKING**
Forty Thieves Beach Bar ..........(see 33)
Shakatak....................................**36** B4

**ENTERTAINMENT**
Kim4Love..................................(see 11)

**SHOPPING**
Barclays Centre..........................**37** B3
Diani Beach Shopping Centre.....**38** B3
Diani Complex............................**39** B3

**TRANSPORT**
Bus Stop....................................**40** A2
Fredlink Tours...........................(see 42)
Glory Car Hire...........................**41** B3
Leisure Car Hire.........................**42** B3

INDIAN OCEAN

To Shelly Beach (8.5km)

To Mombasa (11km); Kwale (26km); Shimba Hills NR (31km)

Tiwi Beach

Tiwi

Cliff Beach

River

Mwachema

Ukunda

Palm Av (Ukunda Rd)

Diani Beach Rd

Airstrip: 34

To Aqualand (3km); East African Whale Shark Trust (3km); SX Scuba (3km); Wet & Wild (3km); Kaya Kinondo (12km)

To Msambweni (15km); Shimoni (40km); Lunga Lunga (60km);

couples. All of these places are located off the unnamed dirt track that runs parallel to the main highway and the beach.

**Twiga Lodge** ( ☎ 3205126; camping per person KSh300, s/d KSh1100/2000, new wing s/d KSh3000/4000) Twiga is great fun when there's a crowd staying, with the palpable sense of isolation alleviated by the sheer tropical exuberance of the place. The older rooms are set off from the beach and slightly grotty, while the newer wing is much crisper. The on-site restaurant is OK, but having a drink under thatch while stars spill over the sea is as perfect as moments come.

**Sand Island Beach Cottages** ( ☎ 3300043; www .sandislandtiwi.com; cottages low season KSh3500-6500, high season KSh4000-7500) A bunch of dumb, friendly dogs greet you as you enter this gardenlike

strip of lovely cottages fronting an even better beach. It is run by a British expat, and there are all kinds of peaceful serenity awaiting, either here or on pretty Sand Island itself, which lies just off shore.

**Tiwi Beach Resort** ( ☎ 3202801; www.tiwibeachresort .com; s/d half board low season US$46/79, high season US$54/96; ) This is a huge resort complex similar to what you'll find in Diani. It lacks character (not pools, though); it's included here because it is quite family-friendly.

**our pick Coral Cove Cottages** ( ☎ 3300010; www .coralcove.tiwibeach.com; cottages KSh5000-8000) When Doctor Doolittle goes on vacation, he looks no further than this awesome beachfront option. There are dogs, roosters, monkeys, geese, ducks and other fluffy denizens scattered throughout, and they're all tame. We were greeted by a manager cradling a baby, thumb-sucking monkey, and if that doesn't melt your heart, well, you're pretty hard to please. The cottages, by the way, are as lovely and as evocative of paradise as you'd hope for.

**Maweni & Capricho Beach Cottages** ( ☎ 3300012; www.mawenibeach.com; cottages KSh5000-8500; 🖭 ) This is actually three similar groupings of huts (Maweni, Capricho and Moonlight Bay) umbrellaed under one property. All of the options include nicely thatched tropical huts and cottages, and share a lovely restaurant and pretty pool. The grounds are lifted from a Kenya coast postcard. High flyers can opt for the posher 'executive' cottages (KSh12,000 to KSh13,000).

The other group of places is about 2km further south, near the village of Tiwi.

## Getting There & Away

Buses and matatus on the Likoni–Ukunda road can drop you at the start of either track down to Tiwi (KSh30) – keep an eye out for the signs to Capricho Beach Cottages or Tiwi Beach Resort. The southern turn-off, known locally as Tiwi 'spot', is much easier to find.

Although it's only 3.5km to the beach, both access roads are notorious for muggings so take a taxi or hang around for a lift. If you're heading back to the highway, any of the places listed can call ahead for a taxi.

# DIANI BEACH
☎ 040

Diani, the biggest resort town on the Kenyan coast, is a mixed bag. It's got undeniably stunning swathes of white-sand perfection, and if you're looking to party, you're in the right spot. On the other hand, it's rife with the sort of uniform uber-resorts that could be plopped anywhere in the world. We've tried to review the more distinctive places. There's a lot beyond the stale blocks of hotel overdevelopment – visiting coral mosques with archways that overlook the open ocean and sky, sacred forests where guides hug trees that speak in their ancestors' voices, and (well, why not) a monkey reserve are all good ways of experiencing more of the coast than the considerable charms of sun and sand.

## Orientation

The town of Ukunda, which is basically a traffic junction on the main Mombasa–Tanzania

road, is the turn-off point for Diani Beach. There are all sorts of essentials here including post offices, banks and so on. From here a sealed road (officially named Palm Ave, though no one seems to use this title) runs about 2.5km to a T-junction with the beach road, where you'll find everything Diani has to offer.

## Information

### EMERGENCY

**Diani Beach Hospital** ( ☎ 3202435; www.dianibeach hospital.com; Diani Beach Rd; ☼ 24hr)
**Palm Beach Hospital** (www.palmbeach-hospital.com; ☼ 24hr)
**Police** ( ☎ 3202229; Ukunda)

### INTERNET ACCESS

**Baba's Bistro & Cyber Cafe** ( ☎ 3202033; briony @alibarbour.co.ke; Forty Thieves Beach Bar; per min KSh2; ☼ opens 9am)
**CMS Cybercafé** (Palm Ave, Ukunda; per min KSh1.50; ☼ 8am-8pm Mon-Sat, 10.30am-7pm Sun)

### INTERNET RESOURCES

**www.dianibeach.com** Includes information on Tiwi and Funzi Island.

### MONEY

**Barclays Bank** ( ☎ 3202448; Barclays Centre) ATM accepts Visa, MasterCard and Cirrus.
**Diani Forex Bureau** ( ☎ 3203595, 041-226047)
**Kenya Commercial Bank** ( ☎ 3202197; Ukunda) ATM accepts Visa.

### POST

**Diani Beach post office** (Diani Beach Rd)
**Ukunda post office** (Ukunda)

### TOURIST INFORMATION

**i-Point** ( ☎ 3202234; Barclays Centre; ☼ 8.30am-6pm Mon-Fri, 9am-4pm Sat) Private information office with plenty of brochures. Also sells the slightly dated *Diani Beach Tourist-Guide*.
**Marine iCenter** (Diani Beach shopping centre; ☼ 9am-1pm & 2-5.30pm Mon-Fri, 9am-1pm Sat) Information on diving and water sports in the area.

## Dangers & Annoyances

Take taxis at night and try not to be on the beach by yourself after dark. Souvenir sellers are an everyday nuisance, sex tourism is pretty evident and beach boys are a hassle; you will hear a lot of, 'Hey, one love one love' Rastaspeak spouted by guys trying to sell you drugs or scam you into supporting fake charities for 'local schools'.

## Sights & Activities

Package holiday tat seems ubiquitous in Diani, but there's far more waiting to be discovered by independent travellers.

**Kaya Kinondo** ( ☎ 0722344426; www.kaya-kinondo -kenya.com, admission KSh500) is probably the most accessible *kaya* on the Kenyan coast. For more on this incredible ecotourism site, see p276.

Notice the monkeys clambering on rope ladders over the road? That would be the work of the **Colobus Trust** ( ☎ 3203519; www.colobus trust.org; Diani Beach Rd; tours KSh500; ⏰ 8am-5pm Mon-Sat), which works to protect the Angolan black-and-white colobus monkey *(Colobus angolensis palliatus)*, a once-common species now restricted to a few isolated pockets of forest south of Mombasa. Besides being vulnerable to traffic, the monkeys only eat the leaves of certain coastal trees and are particularly vulnerable to habitat destruction, another big problem in this area. The Trust also works to insulate power lines (another serious threat to the monkeys) and reduce poaching, and provides veterinary services and excellent tours of its facilities.

At the far northern end of the beach road (turn right at the three-way intersection where the sealed road ends), the 16th-century **Kongo Mosque** is the last surviving relic of the ancient Swahili civilisations that once controlled the coast, and one of a tiny handful of coral mosques still in use in Kenya. According to the local imam, the mosque is the oldest in use in the country. It's an incredible edifice, fashioned in barrel-vaulted design yet almost organic in its execution, and looks as if it were carved out of a reef by the waves of the nearby ocean. On that note, there's something distinctly magical, dare we say holy, about seeing the breakers crash mere metres from the breezy, pillared main prayer hall. The land also encompasses its own *kaya* (note the enormous baobab tree), although bringing this up may offend some local sensibilities; many Muslims consider *kaya* worship to be heretical.

### DIVING

All the big resorts either have their own dive schools or work with a local operator. Rates run around €70 to €90 for a reef dive. Most dive sites here are under 29m and there's even a purposely sunk shipwreck, the 15m former fishing boat MFV *Alpha Funguo,* at 28m.

**Diani Marine** ( ☎ 3203450/1; www.dianimarine.com; Diani Marine Village) This German-run centre provides its own accommodation (see opposite). Open water courses cost €495. Although nothing seemed amiss when we visited, we've received letters criticising the service here.

**Diving the Crab** ( ☎ 3202003; www.divingthecrab .com; Sands at Nomad) The most commonly used outfit for the big hotels. Open water courses cost €420.

**SX Scuba** ( ☎ 3202720, 0734787336; www.southern crosssscuba.com; Aqualand) Does open-water courses for €348.

### WATER SPORTS

**H2O Extreme** ( ☎ 0721495876; www.h2o-extreme.com; Sands at Nomad)

**Wet & Wild** ( ☎ 0722705350; www.wetandwilddiani .com; Aqualand)

## Tours

Several companies offer dhow trips further down the coast to Funzi (p279) and Wasini Islands (p279). **Pilli Pipa** ( ☎ 3203559; www.pillipipa .com; Colliers Centre, Diani Beach Rd) provides highly rated dhow journeys to Shimoni and diving trips, as does **Dolphin Dhow** ( ☎ 3202144; Barclay's Centre). Day safaris to Shimba Hills and Mwaluganje Elephant Sanctuary typically cost around US$100 to US$150 including lunch and park entry fees.

**Camps International** ( ☎ 0844-8001127; www.camp kenya.com), a British outfit, runs the base of its local operations, Camp Kenya, in Diani. The organisation is primarily aimed at gap-year students, and runs one- to three-month volunteer vacations, costing from UK£1550 to UK£2850. Participants go on snorkelling trips and safari drives as per normal Kenyan vacations, but also get involved in community-building projects such as reef conservation, beach clean-ups, construction, coaching and teaching.

The **East African Whale Shark Trust** ( ☎ 0720293156; www.giantsharks.org; Aqualand) runs excellent, conservation-minded whale shark–spotting safaris; you haven't seen how magnificent this fish can be until you've seen these gentle giants float through the currents. The trips cost US$80 per person, with a minimum of six people needed for a trip. Its offices are located in the Aqualand centre, about 4km south of Diani.

## Festivals & Events

**Diani Rules** (www.dianirules.com) is an entertaining charity sports tournament in aid of the Kwale District Eye Centre, held at Diani Sea Lodge around the first weekend of June. It's more of an expat event than a tourist attraction, but if you're staying locally there's every chance you'll be invited to watch or asked to join a team. Games include football (played with a rugby ball) and blindfold target-throwing, but the real endurance event is the three days of partying that accompanies proceedings.

## Sleeping

### BUDGET

Beach access can be a problem – your best bet is the path by Diani Beach Campsite or through Forty Thieves.

**Diani Classic Guest House** ( ☎ 3203305, 0710267920; Ukunda; s/d KSh700/800) The most budget option in town is, thankfully, excellent: sparkling clean and quite sizeable rooms, en suite toilets with seats (we can't stress how rare this is for the price!), even balconies. Which, OK, look out onto Ukunda junction, but whatever. There are two branches, and both offer the same experience: one just on Ukunda junction and the other a little way down the beach access road.

**Stilts Eco-Lodge** ( ☎ 072252378; Diani Beach Rd; s/d KSh1500/2400) The only dedicated backpacker lodgings as of our research, Stilts offers seven charming stilted tree houses set back in a sandy swathe of coastal forest, located across the street from Forty Thieves. It attracts a young, fun-seeking crowd, has its own thatched lounge/bar area and is all-round enjoyable.

**Diani Beach Campsite & Cottages** ( ☎ 3203192; cottages 1/2/3 bedroom US$40/55/70, camping US$5) This is the only budget choice anywhere near the beach, although, unless you're camping, even the low-season prices are steep. The tent space is a small, simple lawn site with toilets and an eating area.

### MIDRANGE

All of Diani's other accommodation is spread along the beach road. South of the T-junction from Ukunda most places directly front the beach; the further north you go, the steeper the slope to the sand.

#### North of Ukunda Junction

**our pick Warandale Cottages** ( ☎ 3202186; www .warandale.com; cottages low season KSh4000-9000, high season KSh5000-13,000; 🖳 ) These excellent cottages are strung along a pleasant gardenlike retreat that is utterly Edenesque. The rooms are tastefully done in an understated Swahili style, with the right amount of dark wood and white walls to evoke Africa without a steaming surfeit of safari tat. Our picks of the litter are the Mlima and Kipepeo cottages.

**Coral Beach Cottages** ( ☎ 3203662; www.coralbeach cottages.com; cottages KSh5000-8000) These cottages are fine but don't really compare to those at Warandale. There are three-, two- and one-bedroom options, and they get progressively mustier the smaller they go.

#### South of Ukunda Junction

**Diani Marine Village** ( ☎ 3202367; www.dianimarine.com; s/d low season €45/70, high season €50/90) While it's primarily a dive resort, the huge guest rooms here are appealing, with fans, stone floors that give that hint of Swahili style and four-poster mosquito nets. Unlike most places in this class it's not self-catering – rates include breakfast.

**Vindigo Cottages** ( ☎ 3202192; www.vindigocottages .com; cottages low season KSh2800-6700, high season KSh4000-11,200) This is a rather sweet collection of cottages sloping down to the sea, each sleeping between two and eight people. There are no fans but the sea breeze keeps you cool, and all the cottages have nets. The quirky cottage names add to the charm, though we'd rather sleep in a Dhow than a Lobster Pot.

### TOP END

Diani is largely known for its 20-odd high-end resorts, strung out all along the beach. Those listed here are among the best of the bunch, but don't expect a particularly 'authentic Africa' experience. Unless otherwise stated, prices listed are all-inclusive rates for standard rooms. Note that many of these places close for renovation between May and June, and most increase rates during the Christmas holiday up to mid-January.

#### North of Ukunda Junction

**Indian Ocean Beach Club** ( ☎ 3203730; www.jacaranda hotels.com; s/d full board low season from US$98/135, high season from US$105/192; ✗ 🖳 🖳 🖳 ) A great top-end option in Diani, the Beach Club consists of a series of pearl-bright Moorish-style houses along a long, low lawn that slopes into the lovely ocean. Inside, rooms are decorated in a breezy but luxurious spread of polished wood and ornate Swahili details.

---

**ENTERING THE SACRED FOREST**

Entering the sacred forests of the Mijikenda, known as *kaya*, can be one of the crowning experiences of a visit to Kenya. Visiting these groves has elements of wildlife safari, nature walk, historical journey and all-round awe-inspiring experience. Hopefully, more *kaya* will become the focus of responsible tourism initiatives by the time you read this: 11 of the forests were inscribed together as Kenya's fourth World Heritage site in July of 2008.

Currently, the most visited and accessible *kaya* is Kaya Kinondo, near Diani Beach. The irony is extreme: one of the best ecotourism sites in Kenya mere minutes from some of its gaudiest resorts.

Entering *kaya* always requires a certain amount of ritual (such as having a goat killed; see Kaya Kausa, p287), but this is toned down at Kinondo. You have to remove headwear, promise not to kiss anyone inside the grove, wrap a black *kaniki* (sarong) around your waist and go with a guide; ours was Juma Harry, a local *askari* (security guard) and member of the Digo tribe.

The Mijikenda (Nine Homesteads) are actually nine subtribes united, to a degree, by culture, history and language. Yet each of the tribes – Chonyi, Digo, Duruma, Giriama, Jibana, Kambe, Kauma, Rabai and Ribe – remains distinct and speaks its own dialect of the Mijikenda language. Still, there is a binding similarity between the Nine Homesteads, and between the modern Mijikenda and their ancestors: their shared veneration of the *kaya*.

This historical connection becomes concrete when you enter the woods and realise – and there's no other word that fits here – they simply feel *old*, in the dark-scented, green-shaded crackle of twigs and creak of leaves sense of the word. Many trees are 600 years old, which corresponds to the arrival of the first Mijikenda from Singwaya, their semilegendary homeland in

---

**Leopard Beach Resort** ( ☎ 3202721; www.leopard beachresort.com; s/d low season from €78/155, high season from €98/195; ❄ ▢ ▣ ▨ ) Perched on small cliffs huddled above the ocean, Leopard Beach's compound of low *makuti*-thatched buildings, divided by ponds and pools, is gorgeous. 'We welcome you with both hands where lobsters meet leopards' must score points as one of the strangest slogans on the strip.

**Diani Reef Beach Resort** ( ☎ 3202723; www.dianireef .com; s/d half board low season from €80/150, high season from €165/270; ❄ ▢ ▣ ▨ ) Let's face it: when the floor of the lobby is a big aquarium and the centrepiece lighting fixture is a floating, fairy-light-bedecked baobab, you know some crazy pampering and spoiling is going to ensue. This is as over-the-top and excellent as high-end luxury gets on the coast, stuffed with spas, bars, restaurants and very friendly service.

**South of Ukunda Junction**

**Sands at Nomad** ( ☎ 3203643; www.thesandsatnomad .com; s US$157-334, d US$210-608) These nomads have decidedly decked out their digs, with a nicely designed African-village vibe, loads of decorative masks, warm rose-coloured walls, exposed mangrove-beam-studded ceilings and dark wood throughout. It's a beautiful spot and entirely deserving of its African idyll reputation.

**Flamboyant Beach Houses** ( ☎ 720843585; www .dianibeachkenya.com; r US$210; ❄ ▣ ▢ ) Not really – more like 'artsy, cosily quirky beach houses'. Flamboyant, which is owned by nearby Ali Barbours, touts itself as Diani's boutique hotel, and as design goes this is as contemporary as the south coast gets. Which isn't terribly much, but the abstract paintings and vague minimalism are nice touches. Rooms aren't quite as cool as the rest of the hotel, but are perfectly lovely.

**Forest Dream Cottages** ( ☎ 3203223; www.forest dreamcottages.com; cottages half board €220-600; ❄ ▣ ) A fantastic choice set in an actual forest reserve, these six thatched houses are slightly kooky but always plush, and the little open-air rooftop lounge areas are great. Koi ponds, jacuzzis and fully fitted kitchens round out this terrific, tree-clad escape.

**ourpick Shaanti Holistic Health Retreat** ( ☎ 3202064; www.shaantihhr.com; s/d US$300/500; ❄ ▣ ) If you don't have any hippie in you, get some, fast. Actually, let's be fair: while this place offers all sorts of yoga relaxation, ayurvedic activities and spa bliss, it's also a flat-out beautiful resort. The interiors look like Swahili rooms run through a modern art museum, with sculpted curves, airy portholes and beds sunk into the yielding stone. The on-site Moist Oyster bar serves those jewels

MOMBASA &
THE SOUTH COAST

southern Somalia. Cutting vegetation within the *kaya* is strictly prohibited, to the degree that visitors may not even take a stray twig or leaf from the forest.

Harry explained: 'When we are near the trees, we feel close to our ancestors. I know my father, and my grandfather, and his grandfather and so on all cared for this tree.' Here Harry, who is a tough-looking character (and decidedly not a hippie), hugged a tree so large his arms could not encircle it.

'We feel if the tree is old, it is talking. If you hold it and hear the wind,' and there was a pause for breezy effect, 'you can hear it talking.'

The preserved forests do not just facilitate dialogue with the ancestors; they provide a direct link to ecosystems that have been clear-felled out of existence elsewhere. A single *kaya* like Kinondo contains five possible endemic species within its 74 acres. That's five endemic species – ie trees that only grow here – and 140 tree species classified as 'rare' within the space of a suburban residential block.

The main purpose of the *kaya* was to house the villages of the Mijikenda, which were located in a large central clearing. Entering the centre of a *kaya* required ritual knowledge to proceed through concentric circles of sacredness surrounding the node of the village; sacred talismans and spells were supposed to cause hallucinations that disoriented enemies who attacked the forest.

The *kaya* were largely abandoned in the 1940s, and conservative strains of Islam and Christianity have denigrated their value to the Mijikenda, but the recent World Heritage status and a resurgence of interest in the forests will hopefully preserve them for future visitors. The *kaya* have lasted 600 years; with luck, the wind will speak through their branches for much longer.

of the sea raw and delicious, the beach is a skip away and lodging enlightenment is basically achieved at this serene sleep.

## Eating

All of the top-end hotels have on-site restaurants that tend to be pricey if high quality. Otherwise, you're still spoilt for choice.

**African Pot Restaurant** ( ☎ 3203890; Coral Beach Cottages; mains KSh150-230; ☺ lunch & dinner) This place and its culinary siblings (there are two other branches: one about halfway down the beach access road and another at Ukunda junction) does excellent traditional African and Swahili dishes. The title comes from the gimmick of selecting a meat and having it cooked in a variety of sauces and marinades, all of which are highly rated; and the biriani goes down a treat.

**Rongai Fast Food** (Palm Ave, Ukunda; mains KSh200; ☺ lunch & dinner) This rowdy joint is a pretty popular place for *nyama choma*; if you've been missing your roast meat and boiled maize, Rongai's here for you.

**Aniello's** ( ☎ 0733740408; Colliers Centre; mains KSh250-650; ☺ lunch & dinner) It (kind of) looks like an Italian street-cafe, it's filled with Italians and it's run by an Italian; what we're not-so-subtly saying is Aniello's is the place to pop in for pastas, pizzas and osso bucco goodness.

**Forty Thieves Beach Bar** ( ☎ 3203419; mains KSh280-800; ☺ breakfast, lunch & dinner) Part of the Ali Barbour empire, these thieves hawk an expat-oriented menu of grills, curries, roasts and all the other stuff nostalgic Western stomachs have been craving. The bar is a local institution (see p278).

**Galaxy Chinese Restaurant** ( ☎ 3202529; Diani Complex; mains KSh350-800; ☺ noon-6.30pm) A smart Chinese restaurant with an outdoor 'island' pavilion bar and seating area that's as gaudy (and good) as anything you'll come across in Mombasa. Duck will set you back at least KSh1350, while lobster costs KSh200 per 100g. A courtesy bus back to your hotel is available.

**Shan-e-Punjab Restaurant** ( ☎ 3202116; Diani Complex; mains KSh350-800; ☺ lunch & dinner) One of the only dedicated Indian options in town could easily hold its own against any high-class curry house in the world. The food is well-spiced, rich and delicious, but this place is often closed in the low season.

**our pick** **Ali Barbour's Cave Restaurant** ( ☎ 3202033; mains KSh550-1200; ☺ from 7pm) Well, they've got coral mosques and palaces on the coast – why not a restaurant set in a coral cave? The focus here is seafood, done up posh and generally quite tasty, served under stars, jagged rocks and fairy lights.

---

**TAG & BRAG**

While the idea of wrestling a huge marlin on the open sea has macho allure, catches of billfish in the Indian Ocean are getting smaller all the time. The biggest threat to game fish is overfishing by commercial tuna companies, who routinely hook other pelagic fish as so-called 'bycatch'. Pollution and falling stocks of prey are also having a serious knock-on effect. Some large species are believed to have declined by as much as 80% since the 1970s; sharks are particularly vulnerable.

You can do your bit to help sustain shark and billfish populations by tagging your catch and releasing it back into the ocean. Most deep-sea fishing companies provide anglers with a souvenir photo and official recognition of their catch, then release the fish to fight another day, carrying tags that will allow scientists to discover more about these magnificent predators.

---

Self-caterers can stock up at the supermarkets in Diani's shopping centres, or Ukunda. Healthy U, a health-food store, is in Baharini Plaza, south of the T-junction.

## Drinking & Entertainment

Be aware that there are many prostitutes and gigolos here.

**Forty Thieves Beach Bar** ( ☎ 3203419) Of all the phrases you'll hear in Diani, 'Meet you at Forty's?' is probably the most common, and the most welcome – this is easily the best bar on the strip. They've got movie nights, they've got live bands, there's a pub quiz at least once a week and it's open until the last guest leaves.

**Shakatak** ( ☎ 3203124; Diani Beach Rd) The only full-on nightclub in Diani not attached to a hotel, Shakatak is quite hilariously seedy, but can be fun once you know what to expect. Like most big Kenyan clubs, food is served at all hours.

**Kim4Love** (www.kim4love.com) Not a venue but a person, this local DJ and musician puts on regular summer concerts and events to promote tourism. They're usually held at Kim's beach bar, by the former Two Fishes hotel – look out for the sign along Diani Beach Rd.

## Getting There & Around
### BUS & MATATU
Numerous matatus run south from the Likoni ferry directly to Ukunda (KSh60, 30 minutes) and onwards to Msambweni and Lunga Lunga. From the Diani junction in Ukunda, matatus run down to the beach all day for KSh30; check before boarding to see if it's a Reef service (heading north along the strip, then south) or a Neptune one (south beach only).

### CAR & MOTORCYCLE
Motorcycles can be hired from **Fredlink Tours** ( ☎ 3202468; www.motorbike-safari.com; Diani Plaza). Rates have been in a state of flux, but bank on paying around KSh3000 per day. A full motorcycle licence, passport and credit card or cash deposit are required for rental. The company also arranges motorcycle safaris (see p91).

Car rental firms:

**Glory Car Hire** ( ☎ 3203076; Diani Beach shopping centre)

**Leisure Car Hire** ( ☎ 3203225; Diani Sea Resort)

### TAXI
Taxis hang around Ukunda junction and all the main shopping centres; most hotels and restaurants will also have a couple waiting at night. Fares should be between KSh150 and KSh800, depending on the distance.

## GAZI & CHALE ISLAND
About 20km south of Ukunda, down a dirt track branching off the main road, is Gazi, where you'll find a village of friendly Digo Mijikenda and an excellent **Mangrove Boardwalk** (KSh100) run by a local women's group. The boardwalk is a sun-blanched, pleasantly rickety affair that winds back into a wine-dark lagoon webbed over by red, orange, green and grey mangrove species; nearby, the husks of old dhows bake into driftwood on the sand. Previously, the mangroves were cut for timber, which led to extreme beach erosion; today both the shore and the mangroves are being restored, and a glut of entrepreneurial activities has grown around the boardwalk. The fare for the walk goes into improving the boardwalk, buying school textbooks and paying teachers at local schools.

I scream, you scream, we all scream for therapeutic mud. Just north of Gazi is Chale Island, a tropical getaway with the above magic muck, and a fine beach and sulphur springs besides. You'll need a bit of cash to come here, because the place to stay is the **Sands at Chale Island** ( ☎ 040-33000269; www.the sandsatchaleisland.com; s US$157-334, d US$445; 🗶 🖭 ), a private island resort with ayurvedic ponds, yoga retreats, canoe trips into the mangroves, sugary sand and every-tropical-thing else that equals 'sunny paradise'.

You can organise homestays in Gazi, probably for around KSh500 to KSh600 (all based on your bargaining skills) and get much the same tropical mangrove ambience, minus the four-star luxury.

## FUNZI ISLAND

Funzi is a small mangrove island about 35km south of Diani that tends to be visited as part of package tours organised through agencies and hotels to the north. The main attraction (besides the beaches and palm trees) is bird-watching and croc-spotting amidst the surrounding vegetation.

Arranging your own boat trip is easy if you're in a group: boatmen in the mainland village of **Bodo**, west of Funzi, ask around KSh5000 per day per boat (up to eight people), or you can negotiate individual dolphin- and crocodile-spotting trips up the Ramisi River.

**Funzi Sea Adventures** (Map p272; ☎ 0722762656; funzicamp@africaonline.co.ke; office Diani Villas, Diani Beach) runs more luxurious dhow trips to Funzi Island. Trips cost US$70 including food, drink and transfers, or US$80 if you're staying north of Mombasa. It is half-price for children. Staying overnight at their island camp with full board costs US$140 per person.

If you arrive independently, you can generally count on the permanent presence of an accompanying guide from the moment you land, which is actually no bad thing, as they'll show you around the island and can arrange accommodation in the village for around KSh500 to KSh800, with meals available for a further KSh500 (all negotiable).

Or if you're flush, you can stay in the **Funzi Keys Lodge** ( ☎ 0722762656; funzicamp@africaonline.co.ke; r from $216-420; 🗶 🖭 ), usually closed from April to June. This is another series of exclusively done-up Swahili private huts. The property may not seamlessly blend into the beach, but it does manage to strike a harmonious (and luxurious) Zen note with its surroundings.

To get here, take a matatu from Ukunda towards Lunga Lunga and ask for the Bodo turn-off (KSh100). The village is another 2.5km along a sandy track – you can take a *boda-boda* (bicycle taxi), though they'll try and charge you KSh150, or get someone to show you the way.

## SHIMONI & WASINI ISLAND
☎ 040

The final pearls in the tropical beach necklace that stretches south of Mombasa are these villages, located about 76km south of Likoni.

Shimoni and Wasini (the name of the island's main village and the island) are usually visited as legs of package tours that include dhow trips to Kisite Marine National Park. Every morning in high season a convoy of coaches arrives carrying tourists from Diani Beach, and while the trips are well run, you can organise your own excursion directly with the boatmen. Although you wouldn't know it by looking at the group tours, this is a fairly conservative Muslim area, and women travelling independently may want to cover up their legs and shoulders.

Shimoni is lovely after sunset, when the day-trippers go home. The main attraction here are old **slave caves** (adult/child KSh100/25; ⏱ 8.30-10.30am & 1.30-6pm), where a custodian takes you around the dank caverns to illustrate this little-discussed part of East African history. Actual evidence that slaves were kept here is a little thin, but as piles of empty votive rosewater bottles indicate, the site definitely has significance to believing locals.

Wasini Island becomes even more appealing in the peace of the evening. There are no roads or running water and the only electricity comes from generators. It's worth your time to poke about the ancient **Swahili ruins** and the **coral gardens** (adult/child KSh100/20), a bizarre landscape of exposed coral reefs with a boardwalk for viewing.

### Mkwiro

Mkwiro is a small village on the (currently) unvisited end of Wasini Island that is just beginning to market itself as a travellers' destination, primarily via ecotourism projects. It's a lovely, as-of-yet untouched spot that wants to reap the economic benefits of visitors minus the disruption brought by unregulated package tours.

They're new at this in Mkwiro, so there may be some rough folds to iron out as visitors start arriving – which they'll need to do independently by arranging boat trips from Shimoni.

Contact any of the numbers provided below for help doing this, or bargain with a captain yourself (expect to pay KSh2000 to KSh4000 per boat to get to Mkwiro). Prices below are particularly susceptible to change.

Traditional **cooking classes** will get you stuck into the best of coastal cuisine; recipes include chapatis, *sambusas*, potato stew and coconut rice, cooked in a small house over an open fire. Prices are KSh500 per person for minimum groups of two or three, or KSh400 per person for groups of four or five. Contact Faridi Mshamanga ( ☎ 0722438812) or Omari Mshamanga ( ☎ 0710995500) for details, or ask around the village. Of the money raised from the classes, 10% goes into the village fund, which covers infrastructure projects.

The Mkwiro Youth Group was starting a **Cultural Village Tour** when we visited, although it was new enough to not be priced. The goal is to go beyond clichéd singing and dancing and access the day-to-day lives of villagers via visits to the local dispensary, school, orphanage and a small *kaya*. Contact Fadhili Ali ( ☎ 0724990901) or Shafii Vuyaa ( ☎ 0728741098) for tour information.

Friends of Shimoni Forest conduct **eco-walks** (half day KSh400, full-day incl seafood/African lunch KSh1000/1200) into the island interior, which comprises swathes of untouched coastal forest inhabited by monkeys, reptiles, birds and amphibians. Money raised goes towards teacher salaries, medicine, and food for the local deaf population. You can contact Athumani Fadhili ( ☎ 0721114559) or Husseini Chamira ( ☎ 0723847435).

You can arrange homestays in Mkwiro for roughly KSh650, which should include a nice home-cooked coastal dinner. Like Shimoni, this is a conservative Muslim village; women should cover legs and shoulders.

## Kisite Marine National Park

Off the south coast of Wasini, this **marine park** (adult/child US$20/10) is one of the best in Kenya, also incorporating the **Mpunguti Marine National Reserve**. The park covers 28 sq km of pristine coral reefs and offers excellent diving and snorkelling. You have a reasonable chance of seeing dolphins in the Shimoni Channel, and humpback whales are sometimes spotted between August and October.

There are various organised trips to the marine park but these tend to be outside ventures and don't always contribute a great deal to the local community. It's easy to organise your own boat trip with a local captain – the going rate is KSh1500 per person or KSh9500 per boat, including lunch and a walk in the coral gardens on Wasini Island. Masks and snorkels can be hired for KSh200 (fins are discouraged as they may damage the reef).

The best time to dive and snorkel is between October and March. Avoid diving in June, July and August because of rough seas, silt and poor visibility.

## Activities

The Pemba Channel is famous for deep-sea fishing, and Pemba Channel Fishing Club (opposite) holds over 50% of Kenya's marlin-fishing records. Boats cost from US$500 for nine hours (valid for up to four fishers). This company promotes tag and release, which is strongly encouraged (see p278).

## Tours

Various companies offer organised dhow tours for snorkelling, and there are loads of private operators around; using the latter gives you the chance to put your money directly into local pockets. Some reputable captains include Ali Said ( ☎ 0722484191), Athumani Fadhili ( ☎ 0721114559) and Omari Bakari ( ☎ 0725341683). Their tours generally follow the same pattern: leave Shimoni pier at 9am, travel through Kisite, stop for snorkelling and beach time, head for Wasini for a seafood lunch, visit the coral gardens and return to Shimoni around 3pm or 4pm. Prices were KSh2500 at the time of writing.

The Friends of Kenyan Dolphins have set up the **Dolphin Dhow** (Map p272; ☎ 52255, office 3202144; office Barclays Centre, Diani Beach), a dolphin-spotting and snorkelling trip around Wasini Island. The dhow leaves from Shimoni jetty around 8.45am daily and costs US$120. The price includes snorkelling equipment, drinks, a Swahili seafood lunch and marine park fees and, to their credit, they've stopped problematic swim-with-the-dolphin activities.

**Charlie Claw's** (Map p272; ☎ 52224, 0722410599; www .wasini-island.com; office Jadini Beach Hotel, Diani Beach) and **Pilli Pipa** (Map p272; ☎ 3202401; www.pillipipa.com; office Colliers Centre, Diani Beach) are good expat-owned outfits offering well-managed dhow trips that run along similar lines to those listed above. They've also got access to diving equipment locals may not possess. Snorkelling trips cost around US$150 and diving trips US$165.

## Sleeping & Eating

**Mpunguti Lodge** ( ☎ 52288; Wasini Island; campsites per person KSh300, s/d half board per person KSh1500/3500) This funny place is run by local character Masood Abdullah and his many nephews. The rooms are uncomplicated, with mosquito nets and small verandahs; running water is collected in rain barrels and doesn't always look pleasant! The food is excellent, and it's a common lunch-stop for boat trips. You'll need to bring your own towel, soap and booze from the mainland.

**Betty's Camp** ( ☎ 52487, 0720900771; www.bettys-camp.com; Shimoni; bungalows US$90, r/ste US$110/150; 🔊 ) Not really what you'd call a campsite, this Swiss-owned luxury complex right on the waterfront offers a choice of tented bungalows and fancier hotel rooms. Rates include breakfast.

**Pemba Channel Fishing Club** ( ☎ 0722205020; www.pembachannel.com; Shimoni; full board per person low season US$85, high season US$150; 🔊 ) A proper slice of elegant colonial style, with a handful of airy cottages set around a swimming pool and three big daft dogs to make you feel welcome. Deep-sea fishing is almost mandatory (see opposite) and the trophy-studded restaurant and bar is excellent.

**Charlie Claw's** ( ☎ 52224, 0722410599; www.wasini-island.com) These guys seem to have Wasini Island tourism on lockdown – you can visit their website or call for information on other accommodation options, including the playful Sands B&B (US$70 to US$90), pretty Camp Eden bandas (US$10) and quiet Simon's Guesthouse (US$75). They also run every conceivable diving and dhow tour you can imagine and have two restaurants specialising in Swahili cuisine, which are often an obligatory stop for those on group tours.

## Getting There & Around

There are matatus every hour or so between Likoni and Shimoni (KSh120, one hour) until about 6pm. It's best to be at Likoni by 6.30am if you want to get to Shimoni in time to catch one of the dhow sailings.

Getting to Wasini or Mkwiro if you arrive on your own is a problem. The captains on the docks are frankly extortionate, and will demand anywhere from KSh2000 to KSh5000 to get you across. Therefore it's best to arrange some kind of accommodation and transport beforehand, unless you want to spend a very hectic time negotiating.

There are occasional dhows between Shimoni and Pemba in Tanzania; ask at the customs office in Shimoni to see if there are any sailings and expect to pay a lot. There is a small immigration office at Shimoni, but you may have to get your exit stamp back in Mombasa if it's closed.

### LUNGA LUNGA

There isn't much at Lunga Lunga apart from the Tanzanian border crossing, which is open 24 hours. It's 6.5km from the Kenyan border post to the Tanzanian border post at Horohoro – matatus run between the two border posts throughout the day (KSh30). From Horohoro, there are numerous matatus to Tanga (TSh250).

# NORTH OF MOMBASA

From Nyali to Shanzu it's all big-box beach resorts, highway junctions, bottle-green palms and acres of sisal. But there are sights of interest for independent travellers, including the stunning ruins of Jumba la Mtwana, raucous Mtwapa, some nice nature parks and, if you're lucky, one of the best-preserved *kayas* on the coast (see also p276). Beyond that, the high-end resorts are hardly the 'real Kenya' and from December to April, seaweed often clogs the sand. Still, for most of the year this is tropical pleasantness, if not paradise. Expect lots of *makuti* (thatch) chic.

## NYALI BEACH
☎ 041

You won't be on the road for long before the first string of resorts looms off the highway. Nyali Beach is within the orbit of Mombasa's northern suburbs, and it's quite easy to access the city if you're staying here.

The **Nova shopping centre** (Malindi Rd; 🕙 8.30am-10pm Sun-Thu, to midnight Fri & Sat), which also caters for nearby Bamburi Beach, has a big Nakumatt supermarket and the excellent Books First bookshop, with an upstairs **internet cafe** (per min KSh2). **Mamba Village Crocodile Farm** ( ☎ 475180; mambavillage2001@hotmail.com; Links Rd; nonresident adult/child KSh450/250; 🕙 8am-6pm), the largest reptile farm in Kenya, is the big tourist attraction, but be aware that some of the crocodiles here become handbags and fried reptile bites.

Hotels are clearly signposted from relevant roundabouts on Links Rd.

## Sleeping

Unless otherwise stated, all rates here are for half board.

**Reef Hotel** ( ☎ 471771; www.reefhotelkenya.com; Barracks Rd; s/d low season US$61/92, high season US$75/120; 🖳 🖳 🏊 ) If you want access to a four-star beach and the somewhat faded suggestion of a four-star hotel, but can't afford four-star rates, the Reef is a good choice. It's a fine place to stay, with plenty of amenities, bars and restaurants – just not as sparkly as the two hotels below.

**Nyali Beach Hotel** ( ☎ 471551; www.nyalibeach .co.ke; Beach Rd; s/tw low season US$121/187, high season US$165/274; 🖂 🖳 🖳 🏊 ) At the southern end of the beach is the oldest resort in Nyali and Voyager's main competition. It manages to take up even more space and offer even more facilities – you'd have to stay a week just to try all the different restaurants and bars.

**Voyager Beach Resort** ( ☎ 475114; www.heritage -eastafrica.com/voyager_beach-resort.html; Barracks Rd; s/d low season from €200/267, high season from €220/330; 🖂 🖳 🖳 🏊 ) The nautical theme is stretched a bit far, but Voyager can happily cruise through life on its deserved reputation as Nyali's best resort. Facilities are comprehensive, prices are all-inclusive, staff are well drilled, the grounds are huge and the beach is right there – if you have any time for it in between everything else.

## Eating

**Hong Kong Chinese Restaurant** ( ☎ 5485422; Malindi Rd; mains KSh280-595; 🕑 lunch & dinner) The Chinese food in this pavilion-style building, on the main road next to Nova, is a good example of its breed and will definitely fill a hole.

**Minar Restaurant** ( ☎ 471220; Nyali Golf Club, Links Rd; mains KSh280-800; 🕑 lunch & dinner) An Indian restaurant might seem an inspired choice to be located in a classic colonial golf club, but you can't argue with a good curry after 18 holes.

**La Veranda** ( ☎ 5485482; mains KSh350-650; 🕑 lunch & dinner) This reliable Italian restaurant is behind Nova shopping centre, with a big pizza oven, alfresco verandah dining and reasonable prices. It's closed between 3pm and 6pm on weekdays and is child friendly.

## Entertainment

**Mamba International Nightclub** ( ☎ 475180; Mamba Crocodile Village Crocodile Farm, Links Rd; admission KSh100-200)

Who knows what twisted genius thought it was a good idea to have a disco in a crocodile farm, but the result is this totally over-the-top place, now Nyali's main dance floor. It's one of the most popular nightspots around Mombasa – it's a wonder the poor crocs get any sleep.

## Getting There & Away

From Mombasa, Nyali Beach is reached via Nyali Rd, which branches off the main road north just after Nyali Bridge. There are regular matatus to and from Mombasa (KSh30).

## BAMBURI BEACH

☎ 041

Bamburi is a bit of a rarity in these parts in that it's just as popular with Africans as Europeans. The top hotels tend to attract a foreign crowd, while Kenyatta Beach, near the south end of Bamburi, thumps to the beat of hundreds of holidaying Kenyans. Offshore is the **Mombasa Marine National Park & Reserve** ( ☎ 312744; adult/child US$15/10), which has impressive marine life, although it cops some pollution from industry in the area.

There's a branch of **Barclays Bank** ( ☎ 485434; Malindi Rd) here. On land, Bamburi is dominated by Bamburi Cement.

Glass-bottomed boats to the marine park cost from around KSh4000 to KSh5000 per boat (negotiable) for a 2½-hour trip, not including park fees. If you're driving yourself, be aware the roads near Kenyatta beach get *insane* with a combination of matatus and drunk holiday-makers – never a good mix.

## Sights & Activities
### BAOBAB ADVENTURE

Funnily enough, one of the prettiest nature reserves of the immediate Mombasa north coast has been carved out by a cement company. A nice example of environmentalism and entrepreneurship finding common ground, **Baobab Adventure** ( ☎ 5485901; www.bamburicement .com/rehab.htm; Malindi Rd) is the child of seemingly unlikely parents: Bamburi Cement and conservationists. The pair has worked hand in hand to convert industrial slag into a forested sanctuary cut through with animal parks and nature trails.

The main attraction is **Haller Park** (nonresident adult/child KSh450/225; 🕑 8am-5pm), a genuinely lovely escape from the crass commercialism of the resorts. There's a fish farm, reptile park, wildlife sanctuary (in a rehabilitated quarry!)

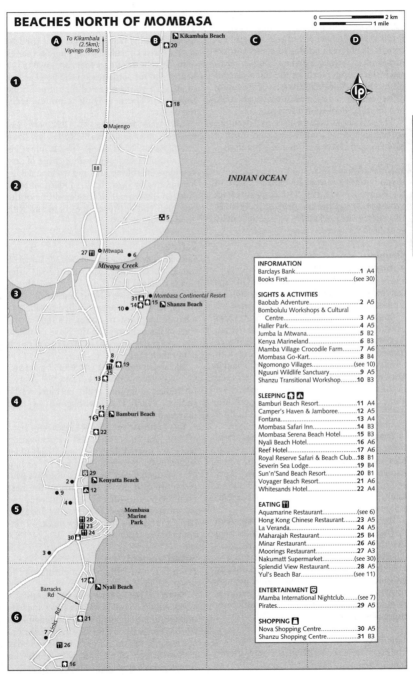

# BEACHES NORTH OF MOMBASA

0 ——————— 2 km
0 ——————— 1 mile

To Kikambala (2.5km); Vipingo (8km)

Kikambala Beach

20

18

Majengo

B8

INDIAN OCEAN

5

27 Mtwapa 6

Mtwapa Creek

31 Mombasa Continental Resort
14 15 Shanzu Beach
10

8
19
25
13

11
16 Bamburi Beach

22

29
2 Kenyatta Beach
9
4 12

Mombasa Marine Park

28
23
24
30

3

17 Nyali Beach

Barracks Rd

21

7 26

16

MOMBASA &
THE SOUTH COAST

and other green goodness. Also here are the **Bamburi Forest Trails** (nonresident adult/child KSh200/100; ⏱6am-5.30pm), a network of walking and cycling trails through reforested cement workings, with a butterfly pavilion and terrace to catch the sunset. North of the main cement plant is **Nguuni Wildlife Sanctuary**, where herds of ostriches, elands and oryxes are farmed. Tours here must be booked in advance.

The various parts of the Baobab Adventure are well signposted from the highway north of Mombasa and have well-marked bus stops.

### MOMBASA GO-KART

If you haven't had your fill of excitement on the Kenyan roads, this 1500ft **go-kart track** (☎ 0721485247; www.mombasa-gokart.com; adult KSh1100-1700, child KSh500; ⏱4-10pm Tue-Sun) should satisfy your need for speed.

## Sleeping

### BUDGET & MIDRANGE

There are no budget choices here, but groups can find some reasonable accommodation for a moderate price.

**Camper's Haven & Jamboree** (☎ 5486954; campers _haven@yahoo.com; camping per tent KSh400-800, r low season KSh2000-3500, high season KSh5500-7500) Jamboree indeed: if you're here from Wednesday to Sunday, know that this place is a disco, and it is loud. We're not sure how anyone can sleep in the rooms (which are lovely, to be fair), let alone the tents given the party raging outside. All that said, if you're looking for fun, it's a good party to join.

**Bamburi Beach Resort** (☎ 0733474482; www.bamburi resort.com; r US$20-90; 🔀 🛌) This tidy little complex has direct access to the beach, and a choice of appealing bamboo-finished hotel rooms and self-catering rooms (with outdoor kitchens). There's a nice beach-front bar with a big shaggy *makuti* thatch.

**Fontana** (☎ 5487493; Malindi Rd; d low/high season KSh2500/3500; 🔀 🛌) Man, we know folks here like their *makuti*, but this is just ridiculous. The lobby is like thatch taken to postmodern heights of hugeness, overlooking an equally enormous restaurant stuffed with all manner of Africana. The beach is 100m beyond the compound, and rooms are good, although toilets are occasionally wanting.

### TOP END

Unless otherwise stated, prices here are for half board.

**Severin Sea Lodge** (☎ 5485212; www.severin-kenya .com; s/d low season US$54/108, high season US$165/206; 🔀 🛌 ♨) This place is so classy it used to have a Swiss consulate in it. There's a series of lovely round cottages that run down to the beach, and for some reason the hotel seems to attract a younger crowd than the average top-ender. The new wing is undoubtedly the nicest.

**Whitesands Sarova Hotel** (☎ 2128000; www.sarova hotels.com; s/d low season from US$100/194, high season from US$198/264; 🔀 🖥 🛌 ♨) The Whitesands is beautiful: a seafront Swahili castle of airy corridors, marble accents and wooden detailing uplifted by every flash, modern amenity you can imagine. It's considered one of the best high-end resorts on the coast, and with good reason.

## Eating

**Splendid View Restaurant** (☎ 5487270; Malindi Rd; mains KSh100-500; ⏱noon-2pm & 7-10pm Tue-Sun) Sister to the original branch in Mombasa, this is the more attractive sibling and has a wider menu, serving customary Indian cuisine and a handful of Western dishes. It's right at the start of the strip, next to the Nova complex; ironically, the views here aren't that much better than in town.

**Maharajah Restaurant** (☎ 5485895; mains from KSh350; ⏱dinner Wed-Mon, lunch Sat & Sun) A stylish Indian restaurant at the entrance to the Indiana Beach Hotel with good veg and nonveg food.

**Yul's Beach Bar** (☎ 2226099; Bamburi Beach Resort; ⏱9am-11pm) Yul's was closed for renovation when we visited, but it's one of the most enthusiastic recommendations we've had on the coast, from locals and tourists who swear up and down that this is the best Bamburi has to offer. The menu runs the gamut from burgers to pizzas to pastas to curries, and they apparently make 60 flavours of ice cream.

## Entertainment

From here to Malindi the nightlife can be pretty dodgy.

**Pirates** (☎ 5486020; Kenyatta Beach; admission Fri & Sat KSh200) A huge complex of water slides and bars transforms into the strip's rowdiest nightclub from Wednesday to Saturday in high season, blazing into the small hours. During the day it's surprisingly wholesome, with family 'fun shows' every Saturday.

## SEX ON THE BEACH

Visitors to Kenya will soon notice that sex tourism is very common on the coast, from petrol stations to high-end restaurants.

There are a fair amount of Western men with younger – sometimes far too young – Kenyan boys and girls. But on that note, there seems to be as many older Western women with young Kenyan men as older Western men with young Kenyan women.

Western women seeking Kenyan boyfriends brings up a different set of issues. Rarely, in this case, is either party engaged in strictly illegal action. The beach boy gets new shoes, shirts and nice nights out; the woman gets…well, we all know. Sometimes romance is sparked, though some beach boys proudly display long lists of girlfriends on their mobile phones, suggesting romance doesn't occur as often as some may hope. It's difficult to judge how many women visitors to Kenya seek brief, beachside affairs; one Reuter's article quotes the figure as one in five.

Many Kenyans are scandalised by the sight of both older Western men with teenage Kenyan girls and the sight of Western women with significantly younger Kenyan men. While they may recognise these relationships are legal, many also find them extremely distasteful and feel that sex tourism destroys the fabric of their society – and that's not counting the enormous STD risks.

Areas like Bamburi, Shanzu and Mtwapa seem particularly bad; be aware that many travellers may feel uncomfortable around the Western clientele – men and women – in many of the bars outside of hotels.

## Getting There & Away

Matatus run from Mombasa to Bamburi for KSh20.

## SHANZU BEACH

Just north of Bamburi is Shanzu Beach. The coastline here is beautiful, but it's pretty much dominated by all-inclusive resorts. Outside of these areas Shanzu is not much more than a highway fuel stop and string of seedy bars.

**Ngomongo Villages** ( ☎ 5486480; www.ngomongo .com; adult/child KSh500/250; ☻ 9am-5pm) is a curious enterprise that attempts to give visitors a glimpse of nine of Kenya's different tribal groups in one place. Although it's touristy, the tours are good fun and you can try your hand at various tribal activities such as Maasai dancing, archery and pounding maize. Nearby, the **Shanzu Transitional Workshop** ( ☻ 8am-12.30pm & 2-4.30pm), run by the Girl Guides Association, provides training for handicapped women and sells their crafts for them.

## Sleeping & Eating

**Mombasa Safari Inn** ( ☎ 5480282, 0733925736; msafa rinn@yahoo.com; s/d KSh700/950) This small, cheerful place has clean rooms painted various hideous shades of yellow and green and a popular bar and restaurant.

**Mombasa Serena Beach Hotel** ( ☎ 485721; www .serenahotels.com; s/d half board low season US$95/190, high season US$200/260; ☒ ☐ ☒ ☒ ) Serena's only Kenyan beach resort is so extensive it's styled on a traditional Swahili village – the pathways around the tree-filled complex even have street names. The split-level rooms are equally impressive, and the design lends an incongruous intimacy.

Most visitors eat at their hotel, but there are several restaurants in the Shanzu shopping centre offering almost identical menus of pizzas and other European favourites for between KSh350 and KSh700.

## Getting There & Away

Public transport plying the route between Mombasa and Malindi or Mtwapa pass the turn-off to Shanzu (KSh30), where a crowd of boda-bodas tout for rides to the hotels (KSh10). Hourly matatus from Mtwapa stop at the resorts (KSh30) before heading to Mombasa. The Metro Mombasa bus 31 to Mtwapa also comes through here; look out for the yellow 'Via Serena' sign in the windscreen.

## MTWAPA
☎ 041

At first glance Mtwapa just looks like a busy roadside service town, but the small fishing village at its heart has a lovely setting with fine views of **Mtwapa Creek**, and makes a great stop for a scenic supper.

Most travellers come for the gourmet meals and dhow tours offered by **Kenya Marineland** ( ☎ 5485248), tucked away on a private estate towards the mouth of Mtwapa Creek. These trips include a visit to the Marineland **aquarium** (admission KSh300), morning and afternoon cruises along the coast with various entertainment, and lunch at the excellent waterside **Aquamarine restaurant** (mains from KSh500).

**Moorings Restaurant** ( ☎ 5485260; mains KSh380-900; ☽ lunch & dinner) is a popular expat hang-out on a floating pontoon on the north shore of Mtwapa Creek, offering prime views of the lofty road bridge. It's a fine place for a beer and serves great seafood. It's a base for various water sports and fishing trips, and sailors have a small chance of finding crewing work or a lift along the coast here. The turn-off is just after the Mtwapa bridge – follow the signs down to the water's edge.

Several companies based in Mtwapa offer deep-sea fishing for marlin and other large billfish. Try **Hallmark Charters** ( ☎ 5485680), **James Adcock** ( ☎ 5485527) or **Howard Lawrence-Brown** ( ☎ 5486394).

## Jumba la Mtwana

These **Swahili ruins** (nonresident adult/child KSh500/100; ☽ 8am-6pm), just north of Mtwapa creek, are easily comparable in terms of archaeological grandeur to the more famous Gede (p294). The remains of buildings, with their exposed foundations for mangrove beam poles, ablution tanks, floors caked with millipedes and swarms of safari ants, and the twisting arms of 600-year-old trees, leftover from what may have been a nearby *kaya*, are quite magical. Jumba la Mtwana means 'Big House of Slaves', and while there is no hard historical evidence to back the theory, locals believe the town was once an important slave port.

Slaves may or may not have been traded here, but turtle shell, rhino horn and ambergris (sperm whale intestinal secretions, used for perfume – mmm) all were. In return, Jumba received goods like Chinese dishes, the fragments of which can be seen in the floors of some buildings today. While here, keep your eyes peeled for the upper-wall holes that mark where mangrove support beams were affixed, the **House of Many Doors**, which is believed to have been a guest house (no breakfast included) and dried out, 40m-deep wells. You'd be remiss to miss the **Mosque by the Sea**, which overlooks a crystal-sharp vista of the Indian Ocean. Notice the Arabic inception on the stela adjacent to the nearby graveyard: 'Every Soul Shall Taste Death'. Underneath is a small hole representing the

opening all humans must pass through on the way to paradise. There are three other mosques on the site, and evidence of extensive sanitation facilities in all the main buildings. A handy guidebook may be available, and the custodian gives excellent tours for a small gratuity.

### Getting There & Away

Regular matatus and buses run from Mtwapa to Mombasa (KSh50) and Malindi (KSh80).

## KIKAMBALA & VIPINGO
☎ 041

These two remote beaches are reached by unsealed roads and both have a peaceful, unspoilt atmosphere. The coast at Vipingo is particularly beautiful and the reef comes right up to the beach.

Despite its 900-head capacity, there's a nice feel to **Sun'n'Sand Beach Resort** ( ☎ 32408; www .sunnsand.info; s/d half board low season US$45/90, high season US$70/100; ✕ 🖳 ⌨ 🏊 ), known as one of the best hotels on the north coast for kids. The mock-mud Moorish buildings are intelligently laid out so it doesn't feel crowded, and the company contributes a lot to the local community, providing drinking water, a health centre and a school.

On the same road, **Royal Reserve Safari & Beach Club** ( ☎ 32022; www.royalreserve.net; apt US$100-260; ✕ 🖳 🏊 ), with its smart, modern apartments, has possibly the best-value self-catering on the coast.

### Getting There & Away

It is possible to come here by public transport (Mombasa–Malindi matatus and buses pass along the highway) but note that all of the places to stay are a long way from the highway and walking isn't recommended on the smaller tracks. Probably the best option is to get off at the clearly marked turn-off to Sun'n'Sand and pick up a taxi in front of the resort.

## KILIFI
☎ 041

Like Mtwapa to its south, Kilifi is a gorgeous river estuary with effortlessly picture-perfect views from its massive road bridge. Many white Kenyans have yachts moored in the creek and there are numerous beach houses belonging to artists, writers and adventurers from around the globe.

The main reasons that most travellers come here are to stay at one of the pleasant beach resorts at the mouth of the creek or to visit the ruins of Mnarani, high on a bluff on the south bank of the creek.

There is also a Barclays Bank on Ronald Ngala St.

## Sights

### MNARANI

The **ruins** (nonresident adult/child KSh100/50; ⊙ 7am-6pm) are high on a bluff just west of the old ferry landing-stage on the southern bank of Kilifi Creek. Only partly excavated, the site was occupied from the end of the 14th century to around the first half of the 17th century, when it was abandoned following sieges by Galla tribespeople from Somalia and the failure of the water supply.

The best preserved ruin is the **Great Mosque** with its finely carved inscription around the mihrab (prayer niche showing the direction of Mecca). A group of **carved tombs** (including a restored pillar tomb), a **small mosque** dating back to the 16th century and parts of the **town wall** are also preserved.

The Kausa Mijikenda are considering opening **Kaya Kausa**, their main *kaya*, to the public, although their visitor policy remained under discussion as of our visit. If the forest does open up, don't miss the chance to go, as this is one of the best-preserved *kaya* in Kenya. We had to pay KSh1000 to tribal elders to enter the site – the money bought a goat, which was sacrificed to purify the area following our visit, proving the Kausa still take the sacred status of these woods very seriously. The forest is about 15km south of Kilifi; if you'd like to visit, contact the **Coastal Forest Conservation Unit** ( ☎ 522140; cfcukilifi@yahoo.com; Kilifi), which manages relations with Kausa elders. For more details on coastal forests in Kenya and Tanzania, check

http://coastalforests.tfcg.org (unrelated to the Coastal Forest Conservation Unit).

### KILIFI CREEK

The **beach** on either side of the creek is lovely and doesn't suffer the seaweed problems of the beaches further south, but most of the frontage is private property. Hotels and local boatmen can arrange **sailing trips** around the creek for about KSh500 per person.

## Sleeping & Eating

The **Dhows Inn** ( ☎ 522028; dhowsinn_kilifi@yahoo .com; Malindi Rd; s/d KSh650/900), on the main road south of Kilifi Creek, is a small, well-maintained hostelry with simple but decent thatched blocks around a garden. The Mnarani ruins are within walking distance, and there's a popular bar and restaurant.

If you need a little more comfort, head to **Kilifi Bay Beach Resort** ( ☎ 522511; www.mada hotels.com; s/d full board €95/125, high season €135/180; ⊠ ⓡ ⓐ), about 5km north of Kilifi on the coast road. It's a pleasant, small resort with a nice beach and plenty of facilities, although the rooms don't quite match the grandeur of the Swahili palace design.

The **Kilifi Members Club** ( ☎ 525258; mains KSh150-400; ⊙ lunch & dinner) is a fantastic spot for sunset, perched on the northern cliff edge with a clear sightline to the creek bridge. There's a good menu with lots of *nyama choma* (up to KSh460 per kg) and the Tusker beer is very reasonable for these parts (KSh70). Despite the name you don't have to be a member.

## Getting There & Away

All buses and matatus travelling between Mombasa (up to 1½ hours) and Malindi (1¼ hours) stop at Kilifi; the fare for either is KSh70. Buses to Mombasa and on to Nairobi leave at around 7.45am and 7.45pm (KSh600).

# The North Coast

> Along this coast live men of piratical habits, very great in stature, and under separate chiefs for each place.
>
> *The Periplus of the Erythraean Sea*

It's hard for us to read those words, written in the 1st century by an unknown merchant, and not thrill to the skin-prickle with wanderlust. The author of the *Periplus* was writing a guide for fellow businessmen, and he describes the places he visits in economic terms, speaking of their goods and services, their products and politics. But when penning this line, he captured something else modern readers may deem distinctly un-PC, yet is inextricably imprinted on the soul of Kenya's north coast: the exotic.

It permeates everything here, blending spice and soul and sense of place, cramming your head with the accents that equal adventure. Here you'll find honey-gathering crocodile hunters; camels of the sea; ghost crabs, tree crabs and elephant shrews; wedding beds strewn with soft blizzards of jasmine blossoms; The Vain Island and The Island of Wailing; and a stone city divided into two halves, the Beauteous and the Fortunate.

The land jukes between dry scrub, spindly jungle, hippo-studded rivers and a skein of mangrove islets and sandbars that breathe in lapping tidal time. And its inhabitants are, as everywhere on the edges of the Indian Ocean, a blend: Cushitic Somalis, Bantu-speaking Mijikenda, cattle-herding Orma, the Bajun, who once sewed their boats together with coconut fibre, and the Swahili, who blend all of the above into a mixed – but not necessarily fixed – identity.

It's these people who inspire the poetry of the place. Their muddy intermingling made this a shore where peoples meet and move and leave stories, so come and add to an adventure that's been writ since the first dhow sailed under the sunset.

## HIGHLIGHTS

- Sailing from **Lamu** (p302) to the coral ruins of once-mighty **Takwa** (p314) on Manda Island
- Finding a slice of pizza even Italians appreciate, eaten by starlight in **Malindi** (p296)
- Discovering the jagged Marscape of the **Marafa Depression** (p298)
- Watching shooting stars tear the sky open while camped at **Mida Creek** (p292)
- Exploring the ruined city of **Gede (p294)**
- Having no electricity, no cars and no worries on **Paté Island** (p314)

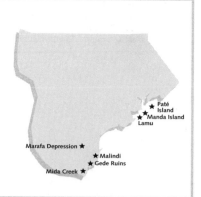

★ Paté Island
★ Manda Island
Lamu

★ Marafa Depression

★ Malindi
★ Gede Ruins
Mida Creek ★

## History

In the ruins of cities like Gede and Shanga, the shards of blue and white still flash when they catch the salt-fattened sunbeams. Its china, from China, is concrete (or porcelain, to be accurate) evidence of the mercantile way of life that shaped the culture of the coast for hundreds of years.

Wind and current naturally bring west-bound ships towards Paté Island, and it was here, and across the Lamu archipelago, that trade centred itself. During pre-Arab contact this area was the preserve of the Bajun, and their interior African features are still prominent in the faces of many Swahili. But the arrival of Arabs and merchants from Greece, Persia, India, China and, later, Portugal, both watered down and enriched local culture.

Settlements in Takwa, Paté, Faza and Siyu (on Paté Island) date back to the 7th and 8th centuries; Lamu was actually a bit of a late starter in this sense, only emerging as a major power in the 16th century. On the mainland, towns like Gede and Malindi also grew into trading city states, although they lacked the natural moat the islands possessed. All these settlements fought, allied, undermined and supported each other, and exported ivory, mangrove poles, tortoiseshell and slaves to Iraq, Oman and Arab colonies on the East African coast.

As one city declined another ascended, but they all became obsolete when the British

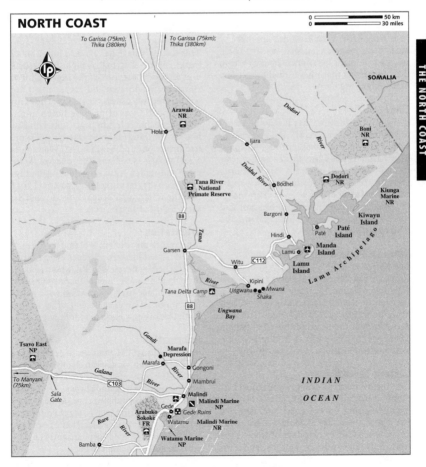

## NORTH COAST

0 — 50 km
0 — 30 miles

SOMALIA

To Garissa (75km);
Thika (380km)

To Garissa (75km);
Thika (380km)

Arawale
NR

Hola

Dodori

Boni
NR

Ijara

River

Tana River
National
Primate Reserve

Dalhaki River

Bodhei

Dodori
NR

Kiunga
Marine
NR

B8

Bargoni

Kiwayu
Island

Tana

Hindi

Paté

Paté
Island

Lamu
Archipelago

Garsen

Lamu

Manda
Island

Witu

C112

Lamu
Island

River

Kipini

Tana Delta Camp

Ungwana

Mwana
Shaka

B8

Ungwana
Bay

Gandi

INDIAN

Tsavo East
NP

Marafa
Depression

Marafa

Gongoni

OCEAN

Galana

River

To Manyani
(75km)

C103

River

Mambrui

Sala
Gate

Malindi

Malindi Marine
NP

Arabuko
Sokoke
FR

Gede

Gede Ruins

Rare

Watamu

Malindi Marine
NR

River

Bamba

Watamu Marine
NP

THE NORTH COAST

effectively ended the slave trade in 1873. The Lamu archipelago was incorporated into British East Africa 1890, and became part of independent Kenya in 1963. Not that anyone noticed much; the islands' heydays seemed long past, and they were generally neglected by the central government.

This obscurity became the travelling world's gain. While mainland coast towns have been extensively developed, in Lamu, buildings weren't knocked down and the indigenous culture only partly assimilated into greater Kenya. A distinct character influenced by architecture and isolation infused the archipelago with travelling cred. Today, only Zanzibar can offer such a feast of uncorrupted traditional Swahili architecture. In 2001 Lamu town was added to Unesco's list of World Heritage sites.

Conflict has flared between the Pokomo and Orma in the Tana River delta in the past, but as of our research this area was safe. You'll see many Somalis here; since the civil war in their homeland many have sought the safety in neighbouring Kenya.

## Climate

If it's raining in Mombasa it may be sunny in Malindi (and vice versa), but general climate patterns are consistent on the coast. The Lamu islands are the exception; although heat and humidity are certainly present, the islands go through dry spells and are buffeted by sea breezes. This makes the weather here a little more pleasant and less prone to extremes than that on the mainland coast.

## National Parks & Reserves

The Kenya Wildlife Service (KWS) operates Arabuko Sokoke Forest Reserve (p293) and Tana River National Primate Reserve (p302). Locally run ecotourism includes the excellent Mida Ecocamp (p292) and Hell's Kitchen, also known as the Marafa Depression (p298). There are marine parks in Malindi (p298), Watamu (opposite) and Kiunga (p316).

## Getting There & Away

Coming overland to Lamu you'll almost certainly arrive via bus from Mombasa. This means bussing up the coast and taking a ferry from the jetties at Mokowe, requiring a day and a half to two days of travel time from Nairobi. While the journey isn't hard

by African standards, it's no roll in the silk sheets either. You can also fly directly to Lamu (see p310).

## Getting Around

There are regular matatus and buses between Watamu and Malindi, and usually about six buses a day between Malindi and Mokowe (where you catch the Lamu ferry). You can get around the Lamu archipelago by boat, although hiring a crewed dhow for yourself is fairly expensive (upwards of at least US$60 per day). Otherwise, there are public ferries that sail between the archipelago's islands; see individual island entries for information. On the islands themselves you can get around by foot, boat and donkey (really).

## WATAMU
☎ 042

This fishing village has evolved into a small expat colony, a string of high-end resorts and a good base for exploring a glut of ruins, national parks and ecosites that are within an easily accessible radius. The main attraction is 7km of pristine beach and a cosy scene that caters to peace, quiet and/or big-game fishing (although there's still some bad behaviour and beach boys). Watamu is a real village as well; on the road you'll see mud-and-thatch houses overlooking family-size *shambas* (farm plots). If you wade out into the water, wear beach shoes or sandals; there's a lot of sharp coral.

## Orientation

Most resorts are south of Watamu on the road to KWS headquarters. Cheaper guest houses are reached by Beach Way Rd, which leads to the old village and is lined with souvenir stalls. The old village itself is something of a maze, with unofficial street names in graffiti, but the main track is easy enough to follow.

## Information

If you need an ATM, your nearest choices are Kilifi or Malindi, or you can change money in hotels. The post office is on Gede Rd. Online information can be found at www.watamu.net or www.discoverwatamu.com. A local charity worth checking out is www.childrenof watamu.net; it provides educational resources, builds 'Happy Houses' (orphanages) and provides bicycles for children etc.

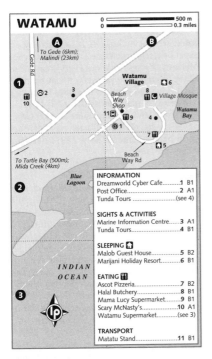

**WATAMU**

0      500 m
0      0.3 miles

To Gede (6km);
Malindi (23km)

Watamu
Village

Beach
Way
Shop

Village Mosque

Watamu
Bay

To Turtle Bay (500m);
Mida Creek (4km)

Beach
Way Rd

Blue
Lagoon

INDIAN
OCEAN

| INFORMATION | |
| --- | --- |
| Dreamworld Cyber Cafe..........1 | B1 |
| Post Office..............................2 | A1 |
| Tunda Tours .........................(see 4) | |

| SIGHTS & ACTIVITIES | |
| --- | --- |
| Marine Information Centre......3 | A1 |
| Tunda Tours............................4 | B1 |

| SLEEPING | |
| --- | --- |
| Malob Guest House.................5 | B2 |
| Marijani Holiday Resort..........6 | B1 |

| EATING | |
| --- | --- |
| Ascot Pizzeria..........................7 | B2 |
| Halal Butchery.........................8 | B1 |
| Mama Lucy Supermarket.........9 | B1 |
| Scary McNasty's....................10 | A1 |
| Watamu Supermarket...........(see 3) | |

| TRANSPORT | |
| --- | --- |
| Matatu Stand........................11 | B1 |

**Dreamworld Cyber Cafe** (Map p291).

**Tunda Tours** (Map p291; ☎ 0733952383; Beach Way Rd; internet access per min KSh5)

## Sights

### BIO KEN SNAKE FARM & LABORATORY

Of some 126 snake species in Kenya, 93 don't pose a threat to humans. The rats and similar species snakes prey on are much more of a health threat than the reptiles themselves. Learn this and other lessons on this excellent research centre and **farm** (Map p293; ☎ 32303; www.bio-ken.com; adult/child KSh700/free; ☒ 10am-noon & 2-5pm), by far the best reptile park on the coast. The nonprofit serves a crucial educational and healthcare role, providing free antivenene wherever it is needed in Kenya, and is located north of Watamu village on the main beach road.

### WATAMU MARINE NATIONAL PARK

The southern part of Malindi Marine National Reserve, this **park** (Map p293; adult/child US$15/10) includes some magnificent coral reefs, abundant fish life and sea turtles (don't try and grab hold of any of these – it's illegal and scares the wildlife). It's about 2km off-

shore from Watamu. To get here you'll need a glass-bottomed boat, which is easy enough to hire at the **KWS office** (Map p293; ☎ 32393), at the end of the coast road, where you pay the park fees. Boat operators ask anywhere from KSh2500 to KSh5000 per person, excluding park fees; it's all negotiable. Many big hotels offer 'goggling' (snorkelling) trips to nonguests as well.

### TURTLES

All credit to the good guys: **Watamu Turtle Watch** (Map p293; www.watamuturtles.com) provides a service, and that is protecting the marine turtles that come here to lay eggs on the beach. Contact the trust's **Marine Information Centre** (Map p291; ☎ 32118; paradise@swiftmalindi.com; ☒ 9.30am-12.30pm & 2-5pm Mon-Sat) if you're interested in seeing this spectacle, volunteering, 'adopting' a turtle or buying medicine for sick turtles; programs run from KSh500 to KSh5000 (see www.adoptaseaturtle.com).

## Activities

### DIVING & DEEP-SEA FISHING

**Aqua Ventures** (Map p293; ☎ 32420; www.diveinkenya .com), at Ocean Sports resort, offers guided dives in the marine park for €28 and a PADI course for €260; they're also good for diving expeditions around Malindi. The best time to be underwater is between October and March. Avoid diving from June to August because of rough seas and poor visibility. Dive trips to **Tewa Caves** (Map p293) at the mouth of Mida Creek are popular, where a group of giant rock cod loiter menacingly at the bottom.

**Tunda Tours** (Map p291; ☎ 0733952383; www.tunda tourssafaris.com; Beach Way Rd) runs fishing safaris (half/full day UK£250/350). A lot of anglers head to **Hemingways Resort** (Map p293; ☎ 32624; www.hemingways.co.ke), where rates run around around UK£550 per boat (high season, up to four anglers). Hemingways is also a luxury lodge, but has been under renovation – it's open now during the main fishing season (mid-July to April).Tag and release is standard procedure (see boxed text, p278).

## Sleeping

### BUDGET & MIDRANGE

**Malob Guest House** (Map p291; ☎ 32260; Beach Way Rd; s KSh800) This is a cute option: a series of simple rooms set around an open courtyard, comfy and friendly and, for this area, incredibly cheap.

THE NORTH COAST

**Mwamba Field Study Centre** (Map p293; ☎ Nairobi 020-2335865, 0720100680; mwamba@arocha.org; Watamu Beach; r KSh2050) This lovely guest house/study centre is run by A Rocha, a Christian conservation society that believes in preserving a world they consider one of 'God's gifts'. African meals are served twice a day and are included in costs, and vegetarians are catered for. The beach is 50m away, and when you're done relaxing you have the option of giving something back to Watamu – Mwamba runs myriad community and environmental programs.

**Marijani Holiday Resort** (Map p291; ☎ 32448; www.marijani-holiday-resort.com; s/d KSh1950/2500, cottages €38.50-52) Best described as a coral villa, Marijani is a friendly, German-owned place that's probably the best sleep in Watamu village. Rooms are airy and elegant, and the grounds are home to several parrots, curious house cats and chillin' tortoises.

**TOP END**

Top-end hotels take up much of the beach frontage along the three coves. Many are closed from at least May to mid-July.

**Turtle Bay Beach Club** (Map p293; ☎ 32003; www.turtlebay.co.ke; s/d/tr KSh5500/6400/7000; ❄ 🖳 🔊 🕹) This is easily one of the best top-end resorts in Watamu, if not the coast: an eco-minded hotel that uses managed tree-cover to hide its environmental imprint, runs enough eco-tourism ventures to fill a book (including bird-watching safaris and turtle protection programs), contributes to local charities and all sorts of other do-gooder stuff. On top of that, it's a pretty plush resort.

**Ocean Sports** (Map p293; ☎ 32624; www.oceansports.net; s/d low season US$135/166, high season US$165/200; 🔊 🕹) Some of the rooms are a bit mildewy (ask to have a sniff), but this is a fine and friendly eccentric fishing lodge. The layout is quite smart, with most rooms commanding a teal vista all the way down to the beach.

## Eating

The better hotels cater for their clients. For local cuisine, try the several tiny stalls lining Beach Way Rd, selling kebabs, chicken, chips, samosas, chapatis and the like.

**Ascot Pizzeria** (Map p291; Ascot Hotel, Beach Way Rd; mains KSh250-750; ❄ lunch & dinner) Many places on the coast hide good Italian joints, and the Ascot is Watamu's noteworthy contribution to the cause.

**Scary McNasty's** (Map p291; ☎ 32500; KSh350-700; ❄ lunch & dinner) With a name like that, how could we not include it? It's owned by an expat Brit, serves genuine black pudding (not McNasty, if scary) and does a very good line in all the other UK-pub greats you may be missing. It's located a little ways out of town.

**Mama Lucy supermarket** (Map p291; ☎ 32584; Beach Way Rd) and Watamu supermarket (Map p291) are handy for self-caterers. There's a good halal butchery (Map p291) near the village mosque.

## Getting There & Around

There are matatus between Malindi and Watamu throughout the day (KSh50, one hour). All matatus pass the turn-off to the Gede ruins (KSh10). For Mombasa, the easiest option is to take a matatu to the B8 highway (KSh10), also known as the Mombasa–Malindi road, and flag down a bus or matatu. A handful of motorised rickshaws ply the village and beach road; a ride to the KWS office should cost around KSh250.

Bicycles can be hired from most hotels or guest houses for KSh60 to KSh80 per hour.

## MIDA CREEK

As Belinda Carlisle so accurately sang, 'Ooh, heaven is a place on earth.'

In this case, it's called Mida Creek, a place hugged by gentle, silver-tinged mudflats flowing with ghost crabs and long tides, the dark, creeping marriage of land and water epitomised by a mangrove forest and the salt-and-fresh sweet scent of wind over an estuary.

Visiting here helps the local Giriama community, which works with A Rocha and Arabuko Sokoke Schools & Eco-Tourism Scheme (ASSETS, which also works in Arabuko Sokoke Forest Reserve) to create the ecotourism projectm **Mida Ecocamp** (Map p293; ☎ 0729213042; www.midaecocamp.com; huts KSh850-1100, camping KSh200), located just off the coast highway (B8) about 6km south of Watamu.

Excellent Giriama guides will take you through the water-laced landscape of the creek to the nearby **mangrove forest** (tickets adult/child KSh150/100, guides KSh200). A bird blind looks out over the surrounding wetlands, while a rope bridge leads back into the mangroves, where giant crabs cling to tree trunks and oysters can be plucked and eaten off the ground.

You can also organise **canoe trips** to the former slaving island of Kirepwe (KSh3000,

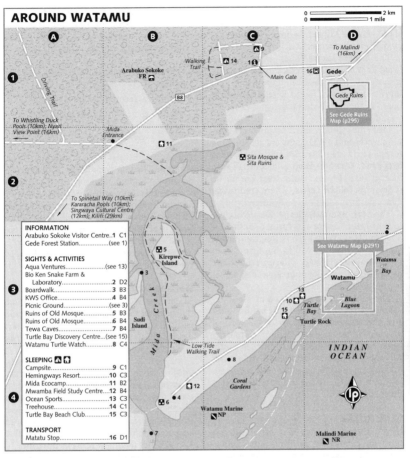

AROUND WATAMU

INFORMATION
Arabuko Sokoke Visitor Centre...1 C1
Gede Forest Station................(see 1)

SIGHTS & ACTIVITIES
Aqua Ventures.....................(see 13)
Bio Ken Snake Farm &
   Laboratory.........................2 D2
Boardwalk................................3 B3
KWS Office...............................4 B4
Picnic Ground.......................(see 3)
Ruins of Old Mosque...............5 B3
Ruins of Old Mosque...............6 B4
Tewa Caves..............................7 B4
Turtle Bay Discovery Centre..(see 15)
Watamu Turtle Watch...............8 C4

SLEEPING
Campsite...................................9 C1
Hemingways Resort................10 C3
Mida Ecocamp........................11 B2
Mwamba Field Study Centre..12 B4
Ocean Sports.........................13 C3
Treehouse...............................14 C1
Turtle Bay Beach Club............15 C3

TRANSPORT
Matatu Stop............................16 D1

THE NORTH COAST

including lunch) or ruins of Gede (KSh2200).
There's no more magical way to approach
that lost city than at a soft paddle, under the
shadow of spider roots via a surrounding network of riverine tree-roofed channels.

At the ecocamp itself is a lovely **restaurant**
(mains KSh250-650), wind-conditioned *makuti*-
topped bar, the opportunity to venture into
nearby villages on culture tours (your money
goes to local schools) and three huts – Giriama,
Swahili and Zanzibari – for sleeping. They're
all lovely – the Giriama is 'rustic' Africa, and
resembles a Native American wigwam, while
the Zanzibari house is as nice as any Swahili
structure you'll find in Lamu, with a rooftop
bed-lounge for eating wind. Nearby campsites
are spacious and simple.

Mida Creek saves its real appeal for evening,
when bonfires are lit and the stars (no exag-
geration) simply rain down on you.

## ARABUKO SOKOKE FOREST RESERVE
Elephants are such an indelibly African
image, but what about the elephant shrew?
Specifically, the golden-rumped elephant
shrew, which is about the size of a rabbit and
cute as a playground full of kittens?

They're only found here, in **Arabuko Sokoke
Forest Reserve** (Map p293; adult/child US$20/10), the
largest tract of indigenous coastal forest remaining in East Africa. But there's way more
than yellow-butted *macroscelidea* – try 240
bird species, including the also completely
endemic Clarke's weaver. Throw in a herd of

forest elephants, the scops owl (only 15cm tall) and 260 species of butterfly and you understand why the Mijikenda preserved their sacred forests, known as *kaya* (see also p276).

The **Arabuko Sokoke Visitor Centre** (Map p293; Malindi Rd; ☎ 042-32462; ⌚ 8am-4pm) is very helpful; it's at Gede Forest Station, with displays on the various species found here. The noticeboard in the centre shows the sites of recent wildlife sightings.

From the visitors centre, nature trails, running tracks and 4WD paths cut through the forest. There are more bird trails at **Whistling Duck Pools**, **Kararacha Pools** and **Spinetail Way**, located 16km further south. Near Kararacha is **Singwaya Cultural Centre**, where traditional dance performances can be arranged.

There are basic **campsites** (per person US$8) close to the visitors centre and further south near Spinetail Way. With permission, camping is also allowed deeper within the forest or at the **tree-house** by Sand Quarry. (Acrobatic nymphomaniacs take note: a painted warning prohibits sex here!)

The forest is just off the main Malindi–Mombasa road. The main gate to the forest and visitors centre is about 1.5km west of the turn-off to Gede and Watamu, while the Mida entrance is about 3km further south. All buses and matatus between Mombasa and Malindi can drop you at either entrance. From Watamu, matatus to Malindi can drop you at the main junction.

## GEDE RUINS

If you thought Kenya was all about nature, you're missing an important component of her charm: lost cities. The remains of medieval Swahili towns dot the coast, and many would say the most impressive of the bunch are the **Gede ruins** (adult/child KSh500/250; ⌚ 7am-6pm).

This series of coral palaces, mosques and townhouses lies quietly in the jungle's green grip, but excavation has unearthed many structures. Within Gede (or Gedi) archaeologists found evidence of the cosmopolitan nature of Swahili society: silver necklaces decorated with Maria Teresa coins (from Europe) and Arabic calligraphy (from the Middle East), vermicelli makers from Asia that would become pasta moulds in the Mediterranean, Persian sabres, Arab coffeepots, Indian lamps, Egyptian or Syrian cobalt glass, Spanish scissors and Ming porcelain.

In *Al Inkishafi,* 'The soul's awakening', written at the beginning of the 19th century, Swahili poet Sayyid Abdalla bin Ali bin Nasir describes Gede at its height:

Their lighted mansions glowed with lamps of brass and crystal

Till night seemed like very day

And in their halls dwelt beauty everywhere…

But the good times were not to last. Gede, which reached its peak in the 15th century, was inexplicably abandoned in the 17th or 18th century. Some theories point to disease and famine; others blame guerrilla attacks by Somalian Gallas and cannibalistic Zimba from near Malawi, or punitive expeditions from Mombasa. Or Gede ran out of water – at some stage the water table here dropped rapidly and the 40m wells dried up.

### Walking Tour

In the early-19th-century poem *Al Inkishafi,* the ruins of Gede, a symbol of the Swahili world the poet believed was falling apart, are described as 'choked with weeds and thorns' and a place where 'men fear today to pass'.

Maybe back then, but today Gede is the most visitor-friendly archaeological site in Kenya. Most of the excavated buildings are concentrated near the entrance, but there are dozens of other ruins scattered through the forest, which is 600 years old and still used for ritual purposes. Guides are available for KSh300 to KSh500; they definitely bring Gede to life.

On your right as you enter the compound is the **Dated Tomb (1)**, so called because of the inscription on the wall, featuring the Muslim date corresponding to 1399. Near it, inside the wall, is the **Tomb of the Fluted Pillar (2)**, which is characteristic of such pillar designs found along the East African coast. The tomb is largely intact and was once decorated with ceramic dishes and coral bosses.

Past the tomb, next to the **House of the Long Court (3)**, the **Great Mosque (4)** is one of Gede's most significant buildings. The mosque is not just typical but exemplary of East African religious architecture. The entranceway was on the side of a long rectangular prayer hall, with the mihrab (prayer niche that faces Mecca) obscured behind rows of stone pillars. Pilasters (slightly projecting flattened columns) separated the six doors that led into the prayer hall; the pilasters themselves were studded with decorative niches. The multilayered mihrab is flanked by decorative bowls. On the edge of the mosque is a ritual washing area, served by a conduit from a nearby well.

Behind the mosque are the ruins of an extensive **palace (5)** spread out over a quarter of an acre. Some of the walls contain square niches used for oil lamps, and there's also a well-preserved Swahili toilet. One of the most interesting things found within the ruins was an earthenware jar containing a *fingo* (charm), thought to attract *djinns* (guardian spirits) who would drive trespassers insane. The palace also has a particularly fine **pillar tomb (6)**; its hexagonal shape is unique to East Africa.

Along the path past the tomb are around 11 old **Swahili houses (7)**. They're each named after particular features of their design or objects found in them by archaeologists, such as the House of Scissors and the House of the Iron Lamp. The **House of the Cistern (8)** is particularly interesting, with ancient illustrations incised into the plaster walls. Like most houses at Gede, these dwellings follow a traditional

Swahili pattern, with a reception court at the front and separate living quarters for the master of the house and his wives.

The other excavations include the **House of the Dhow (9)**, the **House of the Double Court (10)** and the nearby **Mosque of the Three Aisles (11)**, which has the largest well at Gede.

As you head back out past the car park, you'll find a small, excellent **museum (12)** filled with displays of artefacts found on the site.

## Other Attractions

Right by the entrance to the Gede complex is **Kipepeo butterfly farm** ( ☎ 32380; nonresident adult/child KSh100/50; ☻ 8am-5pm), which pays locals to collect live pupae from Arabuko Sokoke, which are hatched into butterflies and sold to collectors and live exhibits in the UK and USA. The

**WALK FACTS**

**Start** Gede ruins
**Finish** Gede ruins
**Distance** 1.5km
**Duration** one to 1½ hours

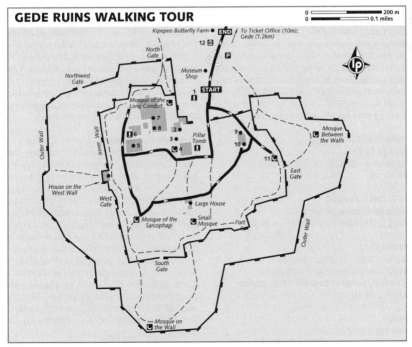

money is then ploughed back into conservation of the forests. It's a lovely place for a stroll.

## Getting There & Away

The ruins lie off the main highway on the access road to Watamu. The easiest way here is via any matatu plying the main highway between Mombasa and Malindi. Get off at the village of Gede and follow the well-signposted dirt road from there – it's about a 10-minute walk.

## MALINDI

☎ 042

Malindi is lot nicer than its haters realise, and probably not quite as nice as its lovers insist. It's easy to bash the place as an Italian beach resort – which it is. But you can't deny it's got a *bella spiaggia* (beautiful beach) and, excuse the stereotype, all those Italians have brought some high gastronomic standards with them. Did we mention a fascinating history that speaks to the great narrative of exploration, Malindi Marine Park and the twisty warren of thatch and whitewash that is Old Town? Throw it all together and you get a lot more character than the beach bums let on.

## Orientation

Old Town, which runs from the bus stands to the ocean-front curio market, is filled with narrow streets and medieval Swahili ambience. It also serves as the closest thing to Malindi's 'city centre'. Tourist services, restaurants and bars run from Uhuru Park up Lamu Rd. To the north and south of town and along the water are high-end resorts and expat palaces.

## Information

**EMERGENCY**
**Ambulance** ( ☎ 30575, 041-3432411, 999)
**Police** ( ☎ 31555, 20486; Kenyatta Rd)

**INTERNET ACCESS**
**Bling Net** (Lamu Rd; per min KSh2)
**Book Café** (Galana Centre, Lamu Rd; per min KSh2)

**MONEY**
**Barclays Bank** ( ☎ 20036; Lamu Rd)
**Dollar Forex Bureau** ( ☎ 30602; Lamu Rd)
**Standard Chartered Bank** ( ☎ 20130; Stanchart Arcade, Lamu Rd)

**POST**
**Post office** (Kenyatta Rd)

**TOURIST INFORMATION**
**Tourist office** ( ☎ 20689; Malindi Complex, Lamu Rd; ☺ 8am-12.30pm & 2-4.30pm Mon-Fri)
**Italian Consulate** ( ☎ 31170, 20502; Sabaki Centre, Lamu Rd)

**TRAVEL AGENCIES**
**North Coast Travel Services** ( ☎ 30312; ncts@ swiftmalindi.com; Lamu Rd)

## Dangers & Annoyances

Being on the beach alone at night is asking for trouble. There are lots of guys selling drugs, so remember: everything from marijuana on up is illegal. Sales of drugs often turn into stings, with the confidante druggie getting a cut of whatever fee police demand from you (if they don't throw you in jail). There's also a lot of prostitution here, unfortunately.

## Sights & Activities
### MALINDI HISTORIC CIRCUIT

National Museums of Kenya has smartly umbrellaed the three major cultural sites of Malindi under the one general ticket of this **circuit** (adult/child KSh500/250; ☺ 8am-6pm).

### Malindi Museum/House of Columns

The most compelling attraction covered in the Malindi Historic Circuit is the **House of Columns** (Mama Ngina Rd). The structure itself is a good example of traditional Swahili architecture and, more pertinently, contains great exhibits of all sorts of archaeological finds dug up around the coast (plus some amusingly interactive areas – don't miss the display on the netting of a coelacanth fish from local waters).

### Vasco da Gama Pillar

This **pillar** is admittedly more impressive for what it represents (the genesis of the Age of Exploration) than the edifice itself. Erected by da Gama as a navigational aid in 1498, the coral column is topped by a cross made of Lisbon stone, which almost certainly dates from the explorer's time. There are good views from here down the coast and out, thousands of kilometres east, to India, where Portugal and eventually Europe would extend its political control. If you can, come at night (the guards may allow it); the rock pools glow with phosphorescence and firefly larvae – all quite magical under an Indian Ocean star-studded sky. To get here turn off Mama Ngina Rd, by Scorpio Villas.

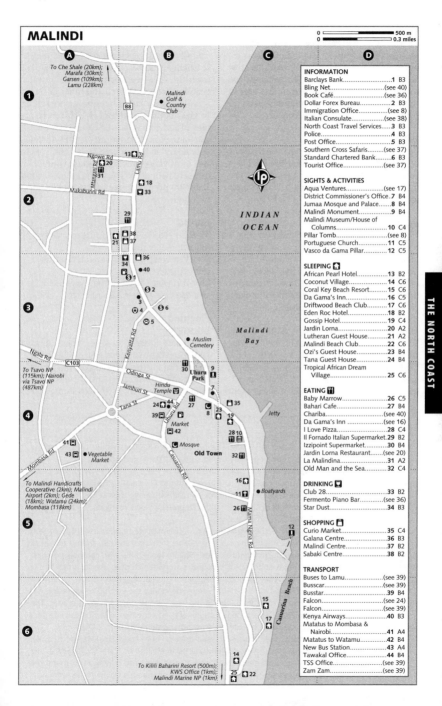

# MALINDI

THE NORTH COAST

## Portuguese Church

This tiny thatched **Portuguese church** (Mama Ngina Rd) is so called because Vasco da Gama is reputed to have erected it, and two of his crew are supposedly buried here. It's certainly true that St Francis Xavier visited on his way to India. The rest of the compound is taken up by the graves of Catholic missionaries.

### JUMAA MOSQUE

Behind the main Malindi mosque are the ruins of **Jumaa Mosque and Palace** (Mama Ngina Rd), but if you're non-Muslim, you can't get inside. The main appeal is a large pillar tomb, which stands incongruously in the centre of Old Town.

### NOTABLE STRUCTURES

The **Malindi Monument** is pretty uninspiring: a white concrete sail erected in 1960 to commemorate Henry the Navigator and Vasco da Gama's Swahili guide, Ahmed Ibn Majid. It was originally visible from the sea (hard to imagine now). The **District Commissioner's Office**, one of the oldest buildings in town, is nearby.

### MALINDI MARINE NATIONAL PARK

The oldest **marine park** (adult/child US$15/10; ☉ 7am-7pm) in Kenya covers 213 sq km of rainbow clouds of powder-blue fish, organ-pipe coral, green sea-turtles and beds of *Thalassia* seagrass. If you're extremely lucky, you may spot mako and whale sharks. Unfortunately, these reefs have suffered (and continue to suffer) extensive damage, evidenced by the piles of seashells on sale in Malindi. Note that silt from the Galana River reduces underwater visibility between March and June.

You'll likely come here on a snorkelling or glass-bottom boat tour, which can be arranged at the **KWS office** ( ☎ 20845; malindimnp@kws .org) on the coast road south of Malindi. Boats only go out at low tide, so it's a good idea to call in advance to check times (your hotel can help with this). The going rate is around KSh4000 per boat (five to ten people) for a two-hour trip.

### DIVING

Most hotels offer diving excursions. Or try the following operators:

**Aqua Ventures** ( ☎ 32420; www.diveinkenya.com; Driftwood Beach Club, Mama Ngina Rd)

**Blue-Fin Diving** ( ☎ 0722261242; www.bluefindiving .com) Operates out of several Malindi resorts.

## Sleeping

### BUDGET

**Tana Guest House** ( ☎ 30940; Jamhuri St; s/d/tr KSh550/550/650, s/d with shared bathroom KSh350/450) If you're scraping the budget barrel, you probably can't come up with a better price and location than this place, right by the bus stops. Rooms

---

### DON'T MISS MARAFA!

Put this geographic phenomenon anywhere else on earth and families would plan vacations around visiting and a glut of shopping malls would surround the approaches.

Instead, the **Marafa Depression** (Map p289), also known as Hell's Kitchen or Nyari ('the place broken by itself') is the most underrated site on the coast (if not Kenya). It's a real natural wonder, an eroded sandstone gorge where jungle, red rock and cliffs upheave themselves into a single stunning Marscape. Going to Malindi and missing the Depression – like many do – is like visiting Arizona and giving the Grand Canyon a pass.

About 30km northeast of Malindi, the Depression is currently managed as a local tourism concern by **Marafa village**. It costs KSh250 (which goes into village programs) to walk around the lip of the gorge, and a bit more (we'd recommend at least KSh200) for a guide who can walk you into the sandstone heart of the ridges and tell Hell's Kitchen's story. Which goes like so: A rich family was so careless with their wealth they bathed themselves in the valuable milk of their cattle. God became angry with this excess and sunk the family homestead into the earth. The white and red walls of the Depression mark the milk and blood of the family painted over the gorge walls. The more mundane explanation? The Depression is a chunk of sandstone that is geologically distinct from the surrounding rock and more susceptible to wind and rain erosion.

Most people visit here on organised tours, with a self-drive car or by taxi (KSh7000). Alternatively, there are one or two morning matatus from Mombasa Rd in Malindi to Marafa village (KSh140, three hours) and from there it's a 30-minute walk to Hell's Kitchen. You may have to spend the night in one of the basic lodges easily found in the area, as all matatus travel in the morning.

---

### LET'S GO SURF A KITE

There are plenty of beach resorts offering kitesurfing classes, which are very popular on the Kenyan coast. A good place to pick up this pastime and experience utter tropical escapism is **Che Shale** ( ☎ 0722230931; www.cheshale.com; s/d €50/90), one of the best-executed sandy retreats we've stumbled across. Located at the end of a long dirt track (you'll need a 4WD, or arrange a pick up with the hotel) about 30 minutes north of Malindi is this village that manages to blend Swahili aesthetics with contemporary flash in a luxurious and tasteful way. There's a huge thatched bar and playfully irreverent riffs on the 'coconut-chic' thing. To top it off, Che Shale's instructors and isolated location make for some of the best kitesurfing on the coast; a full course for beginners runs to €240.

---

are passably clean, with mossie nets, squat toilets and other joys of budget travel life.

**Da Gama's Inn** ( ☎ 31942; Mama Ngina Rd; s/d KSh600/800) Big, bare doubles and smaller singles share this modern block, with a decent Indian restaurant downstairs.

**Gossip Hotel** ( ☎ 0723516602; Mama Ngina Rd; s/d KSh800/1400) You'll either love or hate that World Wrestling Federation is usually playing in the TV lounge/junk pile downstairs. The rooms themselves are decent, if a little dusty, and views from upper-floor balconies onto the water are lovely.

**Lutheran Guest House** ( ☎ 30098; tw KSh1000, tw/tr with shared bathroom KSh800/1200, bungalows KSh1500) If you need quiet, this religious centre (which accepts guests of all stripes) is a nice option. Like most church-run places in Kenya, everything here is a little cleaner, staff are earnestly friendly and alcohol is strictly prohibited.

#### MIDRANGE

**Ozi's Guest House** ( ☎ 20218; ozi@swiftmalindi.com; Mama Ngina Rd; r KSh1500) Popular with backpackers, likely because it perches on the attractive edge of Old Town (next to a mosque), Ozi's runs good tours and has friendly service that knows the needs of independent travellers.

**Jardin Lorna** ( ☎ 30658; harry@swiftmalindi.com; Mtangani Rd; r KSh2500-3500; 🅿 🖳 ) Lorna is very unpretentious, providing accommodation mainly for students of the Hospitality Training and Management Institute. Rooms are endearingly quirky, zebra rugs and local art punctuate the interior, and the large family room even has a panic button!

**African Pearl Hotel** ( ☎ 0733966167; Lamu Rd; s/d from KSh2500/4500; 🅿 🖳 ) This complex is done up with Africana accents, dark-wood sculptures, safari-themed souvenirs and a pleasant pool and lounge area that connects the scattered corners of this large resort.

**Eden Roc Hotel** ( ☎ 20333; www.edenrockenya.com; Lamu Rd; s/d from KSh3000/6000; 🅿 🖳 ) The standard rooms at this conference-style complex are nice by Kenyan standards but overpriced by Western ones. You'll be pretty close to the nighthawk action on Lamu Rd (and get free entrance to the local Star Dust disco, p300).

#### TOP END

The hotels south of town open right onto a wonderful stretch of beach, but those north of the centre are separated from the ocean by a wide swathe of dunes.

Unless otherwise stated, the following rates include breakfast. Note that most of these places close or scale down operations between April and June or July.

**Coral Key Beach Resort** ( ☎ 30717; www.coralkey malindi.com; Mama Ngina Rd; s/d low season from €51/77, high season from €64/90; 🅿 🖳 🖳 🏊 ) If you've ever wondered what would happen if MC Escher designed a top-end Italian beach resort, here's your answer: five themed areas, all a-swaddle in *makuti* (thatch) and enough pools to hold a small Olympics.

**Tropical Beach Resort** ( ☎ 31673; www.planhotel.com; Casuarina Rd; s/d low season from €75/96, high season from €130/161; 🅿 🖳 🖳 🏊 ) Towards the southern end of Malindi are three large hotels umbrellaed under the rather generic title of Tropical Beach Resort. Tropical African Dream Village is a rococo complex of *makuti*-roofed plantation-style houses. Around the corner, Malindi Beach Club has a glorious Swahili doorway and accommodation in stylish Moorish cottages, while the cheaper Coconut Village is a predictable collection of *makuti*-roofed villas.

**Driftwood Beach Club** ( ☎ 20155; www.driftwoodclub.com; Mama Ngina Rd; s/d/tr KSh8750/12,500/18,7500, cottages KSh35,600; 🅿 🖳 🏊 ) One of the best-known resorts in Malindi, Driftwood prides itself on an informal atmosphere and attracts a more independent clientele than many of its peers. The ambience is closer to palm-breezed serenity than the party atmosphere at similar hotels.

**Kilili Baharini Resort** ( ☎ 20169; www.kililibaharini .com; Casuarina Rd; s/d half board from US$153/182; ☒ ☒ ) Italian run and gorgeous, Kilili's options run between breeze-catching Swahili-inspired suites and a new wing inspired by a lush (but elegantly executed) Arabian-nights theme. The beach is particularly fine, as are the restaurants.

## Eating

### KENYAN & SWAHILI
Many cheaper Swahili places close during the month of Ramadan.

**Bahari Cafe** (Mama Ngina Rd; meals KSh80-220; ☽ lunch & dinner) The perfect Swahili cafe, serving bracing chai, good biriani and some sweet roasted goat.

**Chariba** (Lamu Rd; meals KSh80-220; ☽ lunch & dinner) This is a top African option, and by African we mean interior cuisine like grilled meat with *githeri*, *mukimo* and other variations on mashed corn and beans.

### WESTERN/ITALIAN
**Da Gama's Inn** ( ☎ 31942; Mama Ngina Rd; KSh180-420; ☽ lunch & dinner) This slightly seedy seafront joint is the place for all the Wiener schnitzel and other Germanic favourites you may have been missing.

**Jardin Lorna Restaurant** ( ☎ 30658; Mtangani Rd; mains KSh250-550; ☽ lunch & dinner) Who likes creatively concocted French food served in a green garden? The enthusiastic service (staff are students at the local Hospitality Training Institute) is undoubtedly the best feature.

**I Love Pizza** ( ☎ 20672; Mama Ngina Rd; pizzas KSh250-750, mains from KSh600; ☽ lunch & dinner) We do too, and the pizza is done really well here – way better than you might expect this far from Naples. The porch-front and Mediterranean atmosphere tops off this excellent pie.

**Old Man and the Sea** ( ☎ 31106; Mama Ngina Rd; mains KSh400-750, seafood KSh550-1100; ☽ lunch & dinner) This Old Man's been serving elegant, excellent cuisine using a combination of local ingredients and fresh recipes for years. The classy waitstaff and wicker-chic ambience all combine for some nice colonial-style, candle-lit meals under the stars.

**Baby Marrow** ( ☎ 0733542584; Mama Ngina Rd; mains KSh500-2000; ☽ lunch & dinner) Everything about this place is quirkily stylish, from the thatched veranda and plant-horse to the Italian-based menu and tasty seafood (KSh1400 to KSh1800). We're hoping the 'titramisu' is a misprint though.

**La Malindina** ( ☎ 31449; www.malindina.com; Mtangani Rd) This extremely upmarket Italian seafood place serves locally caught, fantastically fresh seafood. It's only open during the season (25 July to 15 April) from around 9pm on; set meals cost around KSh2000.

### SELF-CATERING
Try the following outlets:
**Izzipoint supermarket** ( ☎ 30652; Uhuru Rd)
**Il Fornado Italian Supermarket** (Lamu Rd)

## Drinking
**Fermento Piano Bar** ( ☎ 31780; Galana Centre, Lamu Rd; admission KSh200; ☽ from 10pm Wed, Fri & Sat; ☒ ) Fermento has the town's hippest dance floor, apparently once frequented by Naomi Campbell. It's young and trendy, so try to look as such yourself if you show up here.

The main nightclubs outside the resorts are **Star Dust** (Lamu Rd) and **Club 28** (Lamu Rd), which open erratically out of season but do. Expect lots of working-girl and beach-boy attention.

## Shopping
There are numerous souvenir shops and a large **curio market** along Uhuru Rd and Mama

---

**THE PIT STOP OF HISTORY**

While in Malindi, don't forget, as you enjoy that anchovy pizza and watch the moon breathe on the palm-fringed ocean, that back in 1498 this was the most important rest stop in the world. Here was where Vasco da Gama stopped after rounding the Cape of Good Hope, turned east and aimed for the heart of India, the spice trade, and the dawn of the Age of Exploration. An entire half-millennium narrative of conquest and discovery hinged on this town and its position as a navigational waypoint between Europe, Africa and the East, its role a crux among an interplay of trade, nationalities and religions that has largely resolved itself into today's geopolitical world order.

And did we mention the beaches are great?

Ngina Rd near the Old Town – bargain hard and walk away with the *bao* set (African board game) of your dreams. Avoid shell vendors – the shells are mostly plundered from the national park.

Another good place to buy handicrafts is **Malindi Handicrafts Cooperative** ( ☎ 30248). This community project employs local artisans, and the woodcarvings are of high quality. To get there, turn off the main road to Mombasa near the BP petrol station; the centre is 2km along a dirt road, just opposite the community clinic.

## Getting There & Away

### AIR
**Airkenya** ( ☎ 30646; Malindi Airport) has daily afternoon/evening flights to Nairobi (US$100, two hours). **Kenya Airways** ( ☎ 20237; Lamu Rd) flies the same route at least once a day (US$134).

### BUS & MATATU
There are numerous daily buses to Mombasa (KSh150, two hours). Companies such as Busstar, Busscar, TSS and Falcon have offices opposite the old market in the centre of Malindi. All have daily departures to Nairobi at around 7am and/or 7pm (KSh850 to KSh1100, 10 to 12 hours), via Mombasa. Matatus to Watamu (KSh50, one hour) leave from the old market in town.

There are usually at least six buses a day to Lamu. Tawakal buses leave at 8.30am, Falcon at 8.45am and Zam Zam at 10.30am; the fare is from KSh400 to KSh600. The journey takes at least four hours between Malindi and the jetty at Mokowe. The ferry to Lamu from the mainland costs KSh50 (20 minutes) or KSh100 for a speedboat.

## Getting Around
You can rent bicycles from most hotels or the KWS for KSh200 to KSh500 per day. This is the best way to get around town unless you prefer to walk, which is a great way of exploring the Old Town area (conversely, cycling can be tough in Old Town's narrow streets). Cycling at night is not permitted. *Tuk-tuks* (mini-taxis) are ubiquitous – a trip from town to the KWS office should cost around KSh150 to KSh200.

## TANA RIVER
Once the site of a communal war (see p303), the Tana River delta is regarded by most travellers as an inconvenient stretch of road between Malindi and Lamu. It's true that the delta marks the fall line, as it were, of resorts; past here, David Attenborough might say, the hotels simply cannot survive (well, until Lamu).

But there are some fantastic areas of exploration here for intrepid travellers. The delta country is a long, low marshland dotted with domes of jungle sprouting over a wet prairie. Cooking smoke from the thin houses of the Orma people and mud-and-thatch huts of the Pokomo floats over the sedge while black herons dinosaur-flap over the slow water, and in the tall grass hippos and crocodiles warily circle one another. This is one of those parts of Kenya where hippos are a viable traffic hazard!

If you'd like to explore this region on your own, we suggest disembarking Lamu–Malindi buses at little Witu and catching a matatu (KSh20) to smaller **Kipini**, at the mouth of the delta (when you're ready to leave, you can board Lamu–Malindi buses in Witu up to about 2.30pm). Once in Kipini you'll need to arrange private homestays, which is easy enough – friendly folk will charge KSh400 to KSh700 for a night at their house.

There was no formal tour structure when we arrived in Kipini, but one **Mr Abdallah** ( ☎ 0729503908) offered, it's safe to say, fairly standard services and rates. As more travellers arrive, expect more locals to offer themselves as guides and prices to get more competitive.

A great thing to do here is a **canoe safari** onto the great, greasy, green Tana River. There's no thrill like that of being in a dugout canoe, looking at a tree, then watching said tree slide into the water and realising, 'that's a crocodile!' The guides are utterly unfazed by the crocs but terrified of the local hippos, which are ubiquitous and actually far more dangerous than the crocs (see p81). Canoe safaris are about KSh2000 for the day, or KSh10,000 for an overnight trip into the mangroves and marshes. Mr Abdallah (above) can arrange safaris, or you can enquire with other locals.

About 20km west of here are the Swahili ruins of **Mwana**, **Shaka** and **Ungwana**; none is very well excavated. Ungwana is the most impressive, dotted with the ruins of eight mosques and houses notable for their arched doors. These sites inspired H Rider Haggard, whose brother was British consul in Lamu, to pen *She* and *King Solomon's Mines*. To get here, you'll need to arrange private transport, which can run from KSh1000 on up.

You can also head 40km north of Garsen (on the road to Thika) to the **Tana River National**

**Primate Reserve** ( ☎ 046-2035; adult/child US$20/10), established in 1976 to protect the populations of the endangered crested mangabey and Tana River red colobus. Funded by the World Bank, the **Muchelelo Research Camp** was set up here in 1992 to study these rare primates.

If you've got cash to splash, try Bush Homes of East Africa's **Tana Delta Camp** ( ☎ Nairobi 020-600457; www.bush-homes.co.ke; from US$500). This remote, exclusive lodge sits at the scenic mouth of the Tana River and offers walking and canoe safaris amidst the marshes, where you can spot crocs, hippos, monkeys and buffaloes. Prices vary widely (we've quoted the minimum safari package) but include all meals and activities. It's at least three hours from Malindi by road, or air transfers are available for around US$60.

# LAMU ARCHIPELAGO

The Arabs called them 'The Seven Isles of Eryaya', while sailors called them a welcome port of call when en route to, or from, India. Hundreds of expats who have fallen irrevocably in love with these islands call them home, as do the Swahili, who trace the deepest roots of their culture here.

Few would dispute the Lamu archipelago forms the most evocative destination on the Kenyan coast. In travelling terms, it's the best of several possible worlds: medieval stone towns of narrow streets *and* charming architecture *and* tropical island paradise *and* delicious local cuisine *and* star-heavy nights that are pregnant with the smell of spice and possibility. The Lamu love-struck moment can settle anytime; perhaps when the wind moves through the mangroves as you sail from one coral-castle-dotted island to the next. 'As for being a rider of the sea,' the Swahili proverb goes, 'let ye who choose it, choose it.'

We say: choose it.

## LAMU
☎ 042
Lamu town has that excellent destination quality of immediately standing out as you approach it from the water (and let's face it – everything is better when approached from water). The shop fronts and mosques, faded under the relentless kiss of the salt wind, creep out from behind a forest of dhow masts. Then you take to the streets,

or more accurately, the labyrinth: donkey-wide alleyways; robed children grinning from the alleys; women whispering by in full-length *bui-bui* (black cover-all worn by some Islamic women outside the home); cats casually ruling the rooftops; blue smoke from meat grilling over open fires; and the organic, biting scent of cured wood affixed into a townhouse made of stone and coral. Many visitors call this town, the oldest living one in East Africa, the highlight of their trip to Kenya. Residents call it *Kiwa Ndeo* – The Vain Island – and, to be fair, there's plenty for them to be vain about.

## History
In pre-Arab times the islands were home to the Bajun, but their traditions vanished almost entirely with the arrival of the Arabs. A distinctly nautical culture emerged.

Here, perhaps more than anywhere on the coast, the concept of Arab lineage as aristocracy holds strongest. For years, the word for descendants of Lamu's influential families was *Wa-Arabu* ('Arabs' in Swahili). Another local Lamu word for Arab is *Kijoho* (plural *Zijoho*), *joho* being a term for Arabic ceremonial gowns.

Lamu was also extremely insular. Breaking into the aristocracy, even with polished Arab credentials, was difficult for outsiders. When Ali Habib Saleh, founder of Lamu's mosque college (one of the most respected Islamic institutions in East Africa) arrived here, he initially was not allowed to live in a stone house and was lodged on the outskirts of town.

In the 19th century, the soldiers of Lamu caught the warriors of Paté on open mud at low tide and slaughtered them. This victory, plus the cash cows of ivory and slavery made Lamu a splendidly wealthy place, and most of the fine Swahili houses that survive today were built during this period.

It all came to an end in 1873, when the British forced Sultan Barghash of Zanzibar to close down the slave markets. With the abolition of slavery, the economy went into rapid decline. The city-state was incorporated into the British Protectorate from 1890, and became part of Kenya with independence in 1963.

Until it was 'rediscovered' by travellers in the 1970s, Lamu existed in a state of humble obscurity – which has allowed it to remain well preserved for tourists today.

THE NORTH COAST

---

**TANA TROUBLES**

In 2001 a war was fought in the Tana delta between the Pokomo and Orma peoples.

The Pokomo are honey gatherers, catfish catchers, crocodile hunters and farmers. Once ruled by the Ngadzi (Council of Elders), today they have been split by missionary activity into Muslim and Christian populations, and their traditional culture has waned as a result. The tune of the lullaby Pokomo mothers sing to their children was given new lyrics in 1963 and turned into the Kenyan national anthem.

The Orma are cattle herders. Even the Maasai grudgingly respect their skill as stockmen. Their children play with clay cattle in the crib, and families live in beehive-shaped huts set about with smoke to drive off the tsetse fly. Now Muslim, they once worshipped Waka, who forsook them when the moon waned and blessed them when the moon was full.

These two tribes of the Tana – tillers of the fields and keepers of beasts – fought a vicious war against each other at the turn of this century. The conflict was the most recent bloodshed over one of the oldest communal rivalries in history: pastoralists versus agriculturalists. The Orma need the Tana to water their cattle; the Pokomo used the river for fishing and irrigation. A series of attacks and revenge raids ensued, with the nearby Somali civil war introducing a dangerous variable: small arms. The result was the slaughter of hundreds by cheap firearms, and for years it was not safe to enter the Tana delta.

Thanks to educational programs and initiatives aimed at redressing the local lack of resources, there is peace in the region. Pokomo and Orma children attend school together, and it is hoped by local authorities that an erosion of tribal identity will lead to erasure of tribal tension.

---

## Orientation

Although there are several restaurants and places to stay along the waterfront (Harambee Ave), most of the guest houses are tucked away in the maze of alleys behind. Lamu's main thoroughfare is Kenyatta Rd, a long winding alley known popularly as 'Main St', which runs from the northern end of town, past the fort, and then south to the Muslim cemetery and the inland track to Shela. Heading west, the town peters out in a series of terrace houses, then fields, then nothing. See also p305.

### MAPS

The leaflet-map *Lamu: Map & Guide to the Archipelago, the Island & the Town,* available from the tourist office, is worth buying if you want to explore properly. Or pick up a copy of the magazine *Lamu Chonjo* (KSh200) from their offices.

## Information

### BOOKSHOPS

**Lamu Museum shop** (Harambee Ave) Specialises in Lamu and Swahili culture.

**Mani Books & Stationers** ( ☎ 632238; Kenyatta Rd)

### INTERNET ACCESS

**Cyberwings** (per min KSh2; across from Petley's Inn; ☾ 8am-8pm) Temperamental connection, but friendly service.

**Lynx Infosystems** (per min KSh2; ☾ 8am-10pm) Inside Lamu Fort.

**New Mahrus Internet Café** (Kenyatta Ave; per min KSh2; ☾ 8am-8pm) Decently fast, but only has four computers.

### MEDICAL SERVICES

**King Fadh Lamu District Hospital** ( ☎ 633012) One of the most modern and well-equipped hospitals on the coast.

**Lamu Medical Clinic** ( ☎ 632051; Kenyatta Rd; ☾ 8am-9pm)

**Langoni Nursing Home** ( ☎ 633349; Kenyatta Rd; ☾ 24hr) Offers clinic services.

### MONEY

Local shopkeepers may be able to help with changing money.

**Kenya Commercial Bank** ( ☎ 633327; Harambee Ave) The only bank on Lamu has an ATM.

### POST

**Post office** ( ☎ 633126; Harambee Ave)

### TOURIST INFORMATION

**Tourist information office** ( ☎ 633132; ☾ 9am-1pm & 2-4pm)

## Dangers & Annoyances

Beach boys, beach boys, beach boys. They'll come at you the minute you step off the boat, offering drugs, tours and hotel bookings

# LAMU

0 _____ 200 m
0 _____ 0.1 miles

**INFORMATION**
Cyberwings......................................1 C3
Immigration Office.........................2 D4
Kenya Commercial Bank..............3 D3
Lamu Chonjo..................................4 B2
Lamu Medical Clinic......................5 C2
Lamu Museum Shop.............(see 14)
Langoni Nursing Home.................6 D5
Lynx Infosystems...........................7 C4
Mani Books & Stationers...............8 D4
New Mahrus Internet Café....(see 25)
Post Office.......................................9 D4
Tourist Information Office...........10 C1

**SIGHTS & ACTIVITIES**
Donkey Sanctuary........................11 C2
German Post Office Museum......12 D4
Lamu Fort.....................................13 C4
Lamu Museum.............................14 C3
Swahili House Museum..............15 B2

**SLEEPING**
Amu House...................................16 C3
Bahari Hotel.................................17 C1
Casuarina Rest House.................18 C2
Jannat House................................19 B1
Kilimanjaro House.......................20 C2
Lamu Castle Hotel.......................21 C4
Lamu Guest House......................22 C3
Lamu World..................................23 C1
New Lamu Palace Hotel..............24 D5
New Mahrus Hotel......................25 C4
Pole Pole Guest House................26 B1
Stone House Hotel.......................27 C2
Wildebeeste 1..............................28 C4
Wildebeeste 2..............................29 C3
Yumbe House...............................30 B2

**EATING**
Asilia Bakery...............................31 D5
Bush Gardens Restaurant...........32 D3
Café Nyumbani............................33 C2
Chapati King................................34 D5
Hapa Hapa Restaurant...............35 D3
Main Market................................36 C4
New Minaa Café..........................37 C6
Olympic Restaurant.....................38 D6
Stone House Hotel ...............(see 27)
Tay Ran.......................................39 D6
Whispers Coffeeshop...................40 D5

**DRINKING**
New Lamu Palace Hotel ........(see 24)
Petley's Inn.................................41 C3

**ENTERTAINMENT**
Zinj Cinema................................42 D6

**SHOPPING**
Baraka Gallery........................(see 40)

**TRANSPORT**
Air Kenya...............................(see 40)
Falcon.........................................43 D5
Kenya Airways............................44 C2
Tawakal......................................45 D4
TSS..............................................46 D5
Zam Zam................................(see 43)

Jamaa Mosque

INDIAN OCEAN

To Mokowe
(mainland) (5km)

Main Jetty

Catholic Church

To Manda Island
(Airport)(1km)

To Matondoni
(6km)

Bohora Mosque

Kenyatta Rd

District Commissioner's Office

Main Square

Shiarthna-Asheri Mosque

To Kipungani Village (10km)

Dhow Moorings

To Manda Beach (4km)

To Civil Servants' Club (800m);
Dodo Villas/Talking Trees
Campsite (1km);
King Fadh Lamu
District Hospital
(1.5km); Shela (3km)

To Muslim Cemetery (150m);
Police Administration Club (500m);
Shela (Inland Track) (3.5km)

THE NORTH COAST

---

### LAMU'S LAYOUT

Lamu town realises Swahili urban planning conventions like few other places in the world. Within the seeming random conglomeration of streets are a patchwork of neighbourhoods and districts divided by family hierarchy, social standing and profession.

There are 28 *mitaa* (districts) in Lamu, with names that range from the functional, such as *Madukani* (Place of Shopping), to the esoteric, such as *Makadara* (Eternal Destiny), to the funny, like *Kivundoni* (Smelly Place). In addition, the town is divided into two halves; the north, *Zena* (Beauteous), and the south, *Suudi* (Fortunate).

This division stems from the *Zijoho* (Arab-Swahili elite) traditional contempt for trade. The *Zena* half of town is, to this day, where the grandest houses are to be found, while the main markets, noisy activity and, to be frank, poorer, blacker faces are generally on the *Suudi* side of the tracks. Note that the construction/restoration of grand houses by foreigners has disrupted this dynamic, but it's still present; you'll notice most of these new villas are on the *Zena* side of town.

Also note how the 'front' of a house tends to face north. This may be because of the Muslim concept of kiblah, the direction towards Mecca in which Muslims are supposed to pray (a Swahili term for north is *upande ya kibla*). Or it may be for sunlight protection.

Like most Swahili houses, Lamu homes were built around courtyards. The town's sanitation system was once an engineering marvel, but today it is overtaxed by overpopulation. This can make for some hairy, stinky times of overflow (especially given all the donkey crap lying around) – watch your step here after it rains.

---

(the last can be useful if you're disoriented). Women will find getting a boyfriend is very easy on Lamu. A huge problem with beach boy society is the common occurrence of boys leaving school to work the tourist-hustler circuit.

Lamu has long been popular for its relaxed, tolerant atmosphere, but it does have Muslim views of what is acceptable behaviour. In 1999, a gay couple who planned a public wedding here had to be evacuated under police custody. Whatever your sexuality, it's best to keep public displays of affection to a minimum and respect local attitudes to modesty.

The wealth disparities here are huge. This island generates enormous tourism income, but how much of that money makes it into the pockets of locals is unclear. The general feeling among locals is that if money is not reinvested into Lamu's failing infrastructure, the island will become socially tense, unsanitary (due to overflowing sewers) and unfit for future visitation. Contact the folks at *Lamu Chonjo* magazine ( ☎ 0722859594; lamuchonjo@ yahoo.com) for more information on sustainable tourism in the islands.

## Sights

All of Lamu's museums are open from 8am to 6pm daily. Admission to each is a much overpriced KSh500 for a nonresident adult, KSh250 for a child.

### LAMU MUSEUM

The best museum in town is housed in a grand Swahili warehouse on the waterfront. This is as good a gateway as you'll get into Swahili culture and that of the archipelago in particular. Of note are the displays of traditional women's dress – those who consider the head-to-toe *bui-bui* restrictive might be interested to see the *shiraa* – a tentlike garment (complete with wooden frame to be held over the head), once the respectable dress of local ladies. There are also exhibits dedicated to artefacts from Swahili ruins, the bric-a-brac of local tribes and the nautical heritage of the coast (including the *mtepe,* a traditional coir-sewn boat meant to resemble the Prophet Mohammed's camel – hence the nickname: 'camels of the sea'). Guides will show you around, but their knowledge is hit-and-miss.

The upstairs walk through a Swahili wedding is particularly well done; for more on this incredible rite, see p306.

### SWAHILI HOUSE MUSEUM

This preserved Swahili house, tucked away to the side of Yumbe House hotel, is beautiful, and a great site for those who love Swahili architecture. But the KSh500 entry fee is very hard to justify, especially as half the hotels in Lamu are as well preserved as this small house. Still, the cultural insights are fascinating. Details include the ceremonial

### TODAY IS TODAY IS TODAY

*Leo ni leo ni leo* (Today is today is today)
*Tutaona mpambano* (We will see the engagement)
*Kweli si urongo* (The truth will not be hidden)

This is the song a Swahili mother-in-law traditionally sang to a groom as he performed the *Kutiya Nyumbani* (Entering the House), one of the final links in a long chain of events that constitutes a Swahili wedding. Practically an entire floor of the excellent Lamu Museum is dedicated to this fascinating ceremony, but in case you miss it or don't take notes, here are some details.

In the three days before the ceremony all the bride's hair is waxed using a formulae of melted sugar and lemon juice, decorated with henna, and rubbed with *liwa* (sandalwood), while *udi* (aloe wood) is burnt for incense and also applied to her body. The bridal and groom parties divide the labour in the run-up to the big day: the women sing songs to the bride while beating buffalo horn clackers and keep *kesha* (watch) on her throughout the night. The groomsmen dance and hit each other with sticks.

The *Kutiya Nyumbani* follows, with the groom sometimes having to fake fight or bribe his way into the house. Both the bride's and groom's families give a lunch, while the bride receives her husband decked out in her nicest *bangili* (bangles). The honeymoon goes a marathon seven days, beginning when the groom enters an incense-filled room where his new wife awaits under a *kitanda* (gold-embroidered canopy) on a bed strewn with *asimini* (jasmine blossoms). A supremely romantic image, perhaps slightly marred by what follows – the root of that 'The truth will not be hidden' lyric. The bedsheets are then shown to the women of the bride's family to prove nuptials have occurred. For all that, Swahili weddings are pretty much the ladies' day out: for a brief period the bridal party members get to ignore the chores of everyday life, dress in their finest, dance all night, and generally have the sort of fun Swahili men engage in at their leisure.

deathbed where the deceased lay in state before burial, and the echo chamber, used by women to receive visitors without being seen when their menfolk were away.

### LAMU FORT

Some say this squat castle lords it over other structures on the island, but its distinctive muscularity sets it off from Lamu's elegant Swahili aesthetic. The building was begun by the sultan of Paté in 1810 and completed in 1823. From 1910 right up to 1984 it was used as a prison, and now houses the island's library, which holds one of the best collections of Swahili poetry and Lamu reference work in Kenya. A five-day membership, needed to take out books, costs KSh200.

### GERMAN POST OFFICE MUSEUM

In the late 1800s, before the British decided to nip German expansion into Tanganyika in the bud, the Germans regarded Lamu as an ideal base from which to exploit the interior. As part of their efforts the German East Africa Company set up a post office, and the old building is now a museum exhibiting photographs and memorabilia from that fleeting period when Lamu had the chance of being spelt with umlauts.

### DONKEY SANCTUARY

> A man without a donkey, *is* a donkey.
>
> *Swahili proverb*

With around 3000 donkeys (and two cars) active on Lamu, *Equus asinus* is the main form of transport here, and this **sanctuary** (☎ 633303; Harambee Ave; admission free; ⏰ 9am-1pm Mon-Fri) was established by the International Donkey Protection Trust of Sidmouth, UK, to improve the lot of the island's hard-working beasts of burden. The project provides free veterinary services and tends to injured, sick or worn-out animals; there's even a small ambulance for donkey-mergencies. And, might we add, the lilting cry of all those donkeys is as beautiful as nails scraped over sandpaper.

### Activities

If you want to hit the beach, you'll need to take a 40-minute walk (or quick KSh150 dhow ride) to Shela (p311).

## DHOW TRIPS

More than the bustle of markets or the call to prayer, the pitch of, 'We take dhow trip, see mangroves, eat fish and coconut rice', is the unyielding chorus Lamu's voices offer up when you first arrive. With that said, taking a dhow trip (and seeing the mangroves and eating fish and coconut rice) is almost obligatory and generally fun besides, although this depends to a large degree on your captain. Look out for Captain Buongiorno, who tends to hang out around the docks near Lamu World or Petley's Inn. And yes, they all have ridiculous names – some of our favourites include Captains Reggae, Tarzan and DontWorryBeHappy.

Incompetent crews will lead you on a dreary day of nonstop tacking up Manda Channel and give you disastrously false information about local sites. Good ones are competent seamen and knowledgeable of the area. And the good is, frankly, great. There's a real joy to kicking it on the boards under the sunny sky, with the mangroves drifting by in island time while snacking on spiced fish. More likely than not you will be regaled with songs from your enthusiastic crew, and while we wouldn't want to suggest drug consumption occurs on the boats…who are we kidding – lots of these guys will try to get you stoned as a quarry. Be sensible – you may be safe smoking on a boat, but you never know who's willing to sell you something at sea and call the police on land.

Prices vary depending on where you want to go and how long you go for; with bargaining you could pay around KSh700 per person in a group of four or five people. Make sure you know exactly how much you'll be paying and what that will include. Don't hand over any money until the day of departure, except perhaps a small advance for food. On long trips, it's best to organise your own drinks. A hat and sunscreen are essential.

Most day trips meander around the channel between Lamu and Manda Islands, and the price includes fishing and snorkelling, although the fish tend to hide amongst the coral during the day. Lunch is usually served up on a beach on Manda Island.

## Walking Tour

The best, indeed only, way to see Lamu town is on foot. Few experiences compare with exploring the far back streets, where you can wander amid wafts of cardamom and

**WALK FACTS**

**Start** Lamu main jetty
**Finish** Shiaithna-Asheri Mosque
**Distance** about 1km
**Duration** 45 minutes to one hour

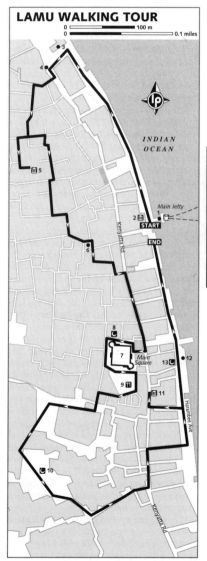

**LAMU WALKING TOUR**

carbolic and watch the town's agile cats scaling the coral walls. This tour will take you past some of the more noteworthy buildings, but don't feel bound to follow too rigidly. In fact, getting slightly lost is a vital part of the process, so take as many detours and digressions as possible! There are so many wonderful Swahili houses that it's pointless for us to recommend specific examples – keep your eyes open wherever you go, and don't forget to look up.

Starting at the **main jetty (1)**, head north past the **Lamu Museum (2**; p305) and along the waterfront until you reach the **door-carving workshops (3)**. Try and find Mr AA Skanda's workshop; the esteemed Skanda was the carver of the doors of Kenya's parliament house.

From here head onto Kenyatta Rd, passing an original Swahili **well (4)**, and into the alleys towards the **Swahili House Museum (5**; p305). Once you've had your fill of domestic insights, take any route back towards the main street – if you hit the road leading towards Matondoni you'll pass a particularly elaborate original carved **door (6)** in the Arabic style. This entire area is the *Zena* (Beauteous) district, and the houses here are particularly fine.

Once you've hit the main square and the **fort (7**; p306), take a right to see the crumbled remains of the 14th-century **Pwani Mosque (8)**, one of Lamu's oldest buildings – an Arabic inscription is still visible on the wall. From here you can head round and browse the covered **market (9)**, then negotiate your way towards the bright Saudi-funded **Riyadha Mosque (10)**, the centre of Lamu's religious scene.

Now you can take as long or as short a route as you like back to the waterfront; this is the *Suudi* (Fortunate) half of town, which is to say, the slightly shabbier, more business-oriented area. Stroll along the promenade, diverting for the **German Post Office Museum (11**; p306) if you haven't already seen it – the door is another amazing example of Swahili carving. If you're feeling the pace, take a rest and shoot the breeze on the **baraza ya wazee (12**; 'old men's bench') outside the stucco minarets of the **Shiaithna-Asheri Mosque (13)**. Benches of this kind were a crucial feature of Swahili homes, providing an informal social setting for men to discuss the issues of the day.

Carrying on up Harambee Ave will bring you back to the main jetty. We suggest you celebrate a hard day's walk with a large juice at one of the seafront restaurants.

## Festivals & Events

The Maulid Festival celebrates the birth of the Prophet Mohammed. Its date shifts according to the Muslim calendar; it will fall on 9 March 2009, and 26 February in 2010. The festival has been celebrated on the island for over 100 years and much singing, dancing and general jollity takes place around this time. Among the cooler traditional dances is the quivering-sword dance, where sword-wielding dancers set up a chorus of vibrating steel. On the final day a procession heads down to the tomb of the man who started it all, Ali Habib Swaleh. The Lamu Cultural Festival is another colourful carnival, held in the last week of August.

## Sleeping

### BUDGET

There's always scope for price negotiation, especially if you plan to stay for over a day or two. Touts will invariably try and accompany you to get commission; the best way to avoid this is to book at least one night in advance, so you know what you'll be paying.

If you plan on staying for a while it's worth making enquiries about renting a house, if you have a group to share the cost.

**Casuarina Rest House** ( ☎ 633123; s/d KSh400/800, s/d/tr with shared bathroom KSh300/500/700) Some of the rooms (notably the triples) are a bit worse for wear, but this is still a budget bargain: a tilted palace with a social lounge rooftop, fun staff and a general sense of that feel-good backpacker-style camaraderie you'd have to be an ogre not to love.

**Lamu Guest House** ( ☎ 633338; Kenyatta Rd; s/d KSh500/1000, s/d/tr with shared bathroom KSh400/800/900) The basic rooms here are very plain, but the upper-floor ones are better and catch the sea breeze. The 'official' rates posted in reception are a good KSh500 more than quoted here and not worth paying. Located behind Petley's Inn.

**Pole Pole Guest House** ( ☎ 0722652477; s/d KSh500/1000) Pole Pole is north of the centre of town and back from the waterfront. One of the tallest buildings in Lamu, it has bright doubles with fans and nets. There's a spacious *makuti*-roofed terrace area with great views and its own mini 'tower'.

**Bahari Hotel** ( ☎ 633172; s/d KSh700/1200) This borderline budget option is set around a neat rectangular courtyard. All rooms have fans, nets and fridges, and when it's busy with guests, this can be quite a fun place to stay.

**Lamu Castle Hotel**, behind the main market, and **New Mahrus Hotel** (Kenyatta Rd) are both pretty tatty, but you can find rooms here for as low as KSh500 if you're truly budget conscious.

### MIDRANGE

Low-season deals here equal some of the best value lodging rates in Kenya. Most of these places are located in well-appointed Swahili houses, and are frankly as beautiful as any high-end option. Prices are usually negotiable.

**our pick** **Yumbe House** ( ☎ 633101; lamuoldtown@ africaonline.co.ke; s/d/tr low season KSh1000/2100/2900, high season KSh1290/2700/3860) As coral castles go, Yumbe's pretty good…wait a minute, did we say coral castle? Yes, it's a coral castle! With spacious rooms decorated with pleasant Swahili accents, verandahs that are open to the stars and the breeze, and a ridiculously romantic top-floor suite that's perfect for couples needing a palace tower retreat, Yumbe's a winner in a field of standouts.

**Kilimanjaro House** (town centre; s/d KSh1500/2600) Another nicely restored Swahili house, this is a smallish place but friendly and cosy. It's across from the Stone House Hotel on a pleasantly quiet side street.

**our pick** **Wildebeeste 1 & 2** ( ☎ 32261, 07236874008; www.wildebeeste.com; apt KSh1500-6000) Locals often call it the 'Wild Beast'; we prefer 'coolest hotel in Lamu'. A combination art gallery and hotel, the Wildebeeste buildings are stuffed with all manner of generally eccentric stuff (including an iron crown, a 19th-century surgeon's handbook and a coconut bong). The Swahili aesthetic is realised in a classy but playful manner while staff is fantastically friendly and in touch with many local artists. The compound is divided into apartments, which sleep from two to six people. If you can score the upstairs rooms, do so – they're often either open-air towers (with thatch roofs that protect from the elements) or 'three-walled' niches, which provide a breezy look onto the rooftops as you fall asleep.

**Amu House** ( ☎ 633420; s/d/tr KSh2200/2800/3500) This restored 16th-century Swahili 'house' feels more like an urban medieval sultan's retreat, set with fine wooden doors, a spacious, red-tiled courtyard and wonderfully carved-out rows of *vidaka* (wall niches). Did we mention the rooms are plush?

**Jannat House** ( ☎ 633414; www.jannathouse.com; s/d KSh3400/5950; 🖭 ) The architects clearly had a field day designing Jannat: it's essentially two houses spliced together around a courtyard, with several levels and multiple terraces. Lower rooms are a little disappointing, but the upper levels are as nice as you'd hope for and the pool is a rare refresher in these parts.

### TOP END

**Stone House Hotel** ( ☎ 633544; half board s US$55-70, d US$90-110) This Swahili mansion is set into a Fez-like alleyway and is notable for its fine, whitewashed walls and fantastic rooftop, which includes a superb restaurant (no alcohol) with excellent views over the town and waterfront.

**New Lamu Palace Hotel** ( ☎ 633272; Harambee Ave; s/d US$70/90) This is a perfectly fine modern-looking hotel, but who comes to Lamu wanting to stay in a modern-looking hotel? In fairness, the rooms are designed in Swahili style, and the on-site restaurant is great.

**Lamu World** ( ☎ 633491; www.lamuworld.com; Harambee Ave; s/d €175/225; 🖭 🖭 ) In a city where every building wants to top the preservation stakes, what are the modern hotels like? In the case of Lamu World: absolutely luxurious. It looks like an old Swahili villa, but it feels like a contemporarily decked out four-star resort, where they've blended the pale, breezy romance of the Greek islands into an African palace, with predictably awesome results. There are 10 rooms in two five-room houses; exclusive hire of each house costs €940, or €1100 with a captained dhow thrown in.

## Eating

It's important to know all the cheap places to eat, and many of the more expensive restaurants, are closed until after sunset during Ramadan. If your hotel doesn't provide breakfast and lunch, you'll have to head to Whispers Coffeeshop, Petley's Inn or New Lamu Palace Hotel, or Peponi Hotel in Shela.

**New Minaa Café** (meals KSh120-200; 🕑 6.30am-midnight) This is the place to eat Swahili food with Swahilis. Their version of fish (grilled or fried) and chips is pretty decent, as is the atmosphere of rowdy locals yelling at the nightly news.

**Café Nyumbani** (Kenyatta Rd; meals KSh150-380; 🕑 lunch & dinner) Does good Swahili and African favourites in an open-air terrace that overlooks an attractive bend of Lamu's main street.

**Hapa Hapa Restaurant** (Harambee Ave; mains KSh150-800; 🕑 breakfast, lunch & dinner) Very much in the same vein as Bush Gardens, and vehemently advocated by its regulars, this waterfront eatery is a bit more informal under its low thatch.

**Bush Gardens Restaurant** ( ☎ 633285; Harambee Ave; mains KSh180-800; ☺ breakfast, lunch & dinner) Bush Gardens is the template for a whole set of restaurants along the waterfront, offering breakfasts, seafood (excellent fish, top-value 'monster crab' and the inevitable lobster in Swahili sauce), and superb juices and shakes mixed up in panelled British pint-mugs.

**Whispers Coffeeshop** (Kenyatta Rd; mains KSh240-750; ☺ 9am-9pm) You know how sometimes you just need that escape into the modern world of magazines and fresh pastries? Welcome to Whispers. For a fresh pizza, real cup of cappuccino or the best desserts in town, this garden cafe, set in the same building as the Baraka gallery, is highly recommended.

our pick **Olympic Restaurant** (Harambee Ave; mains KSh250-700; ☺ lunch & dinner) The family that runs the Olympic makes you feel as if you've come home every time you enter, and their food, particularly the curries and biriani, is excellent. There are few better ways to spend a Lamu night than with a cold mug of passion-fruit juice and the noir-ish view of the docks you get here at the ramshackle end of town.

**Stone House Hotel** ( ☎ 633544; mains KSh250-750; ☺ noon-2pm & 7-9pm) A fine rooftop restaurant that really catches the breeze. The wonderful panorama of the town and seafront is matched by the quality of the food. There are usually several choices for lunch or dinner, and menus often feature crab and grilled barracuda. Only soft drinks are available.

At the south end of Kenyatta Rd are three great cheap eats: **Asilia Bakery**, the most popular bakery in town, **Tay Ran** (which might be spelt Tehran – no one behind the counter seemed to know or care) and an unnamed joint we like to call **Chapati King**. The latter two serve dirt-cheap meals of fish, beans done in several ways (the best is *maharagwe ya chumvi* – with coconut milk) and, of course, chapatis, and are consistently packed with locals. You'll have a hard time filling up for more than KSh100 at any of these places.

At some point most travellers will come across Ali Hippy, who offers meals at his house for around KSh600 and will almost certainly point out his presence in this book. The whole family entertains you while you eat and some people come away quite satisfied, but plenty are put off instantly by the sales pitch!

Self-caterers should head to the main market next to the fort. The fruit and vegetables are cheap and fresh, and there's a slightly gory section where you can get meat and fish.

## Drinking & Entertainment

As a Muslim town, Lamu has few options for drinkers.

**Petley's Inn** ( ☎ 633107; Harambee Ave) and **New Lamu Palace Hotel** ( ☎ 633272; Harambee Ave) both have nice bars where you can sink a cold beer. Petley's has the edge as its terrace catches the breeze and the pool table is well used. Beers cost a steep KSh120.

Even bureaucrats need to let their hair down – the **Civil Servants' Club** (admission KSh100), along the waterfront towards Shela village, is virtually the only reliable spot for a drink and a dance on weekends. It's small, loud and rowdy. Lone women should run for cover, lone men should expect working-girl attention and the harbour wall outside is a potential death-trap after a few Tuskers.

The informal disco at the **Police Administration Club** (admission KSh50; ☺ Fri & Sat), which is on the inland track that leads to Shela, is the only other option, though for some reason it's only open during school terms.

Lamu has several small cinemas, all screening Bollywood blockbusters and big football matches for around KSh20 a seat. The **Zinj Cinema** (Kenyatta Rd) at the southern end of town is easy to find.

## Shopping

There's a huge international market for traditional doors, furniture and window frames; carvers tend to concentrate on the north side of the waterfront. More portable woodwork includes picture frames, *bao* sets, Quran stands and *ito* – round painted 'eyes' from Swahili dhows, originally used as talismans to avoid underwater obstacles and protect against the evil eye. A carver named Ben stations himself on the beach path near the power generators and does particularly fine work. For upmarket Africana, **Baraka Gallery** ( ☎ 633264; Kenyatta Rd) has a fine selection, but stratospheric prices.

Lamu is also a good place to buy *kikois*, the patterned wraps traditionally worn by Swahili men. The standard price is around KSh350, more for the heavier Somali style.

## Getting There & Away
### AIR
**Airkenya** ( ☎ 633445; Baraka House, Kenyatta Rd) offers daily afternoon flights between Lamu

and Wilson Airport in Nairobi (US$142, 1¾ hours). The inbound flights also continue on to Kiwayu Island (US$65, 15 minutes).

**Kenya Airways** ( ☎ 633155; Casuarina House, Harambee Ave) has daily afternoon flights between Lamu and the domestic terminal at Nairobi's Kenyatta International Airport (US$134, 2¼ hours). Fares come down dramatically if you can book in advance. Remember to reconfirm your flights at least 72 hours before flying.

The airport at Lamu is on Manda Island, and the ferry across the channel to Lamu costs KSh100. You will be met by 'guides' at the airport who will offer to carry your bags to the hotel of your choice for a small consideration (about KSh200). Many double as touts, so be cautious about accepting the first price you are quoted when you get to your hotel.

### BUS

There are booking offices for several bus companies on Kenyatta Rd. The going rate for a trip to Mombasa is KSh600 to KSh700; most buses leave between 7am and 8am, so you'll need to be at the jetty at 6.30am to catch the boat to the mainland. Tawakal also has 10am and 1pm bus services. It takes at least four hours to get from Lamu to Malindi, plus another two hours to Mombasa. Book early.

## Getting Around

There are ferries (KSh50) between Lamu and the bus station on the mainland (near Mokowe). Boats leave when the buses arrive at Mokowe; in the reverse direction, they leave at around 6.30am to meet the departing buses. Ferries between the airstrip on Manda Island and Lamu cost KSh100 and leave about half an hour before the flights leave. Expect to pay KSh200 for a custom trip if you miss either of these boats.

Between Lamu village and Shela there are plenty of motorised dhows throughout the day until around sunset; these cost about KSh150 per person and leave when full.

There are also regular ferries between Lamu and Paté Island (see p315).

## AROUND LAMU
### Shela

Shela is sort of like Lamu put through a high-end wringer. It's cleaner and more medievally 'authentic' in spots, mainly because a lot of the houses have been lovingly

done up by expats, who make up a sizeable chunk of the population. There's a long, lovely stretch of beach and a link to a specific slice of coast culture – the locals speak a distinct dialect, which they're quite proud of. Thanks to the expat presence Shela feels somewhere between the East African coast and a swish Greek island, which you'll either find off-putting or appealing.

### SIGHTS & ACTIVITIES

Most people are here for the **beach** – a 12km-long sweep of sand where you're guaranteed an isolated spot to pitch your kit and catch some rays. But as locals say, *Yana vuta kwa kasi* – 'There is a violent current there'. And no lifeguards. Tourists drown every year, so don't swim out too far. Some backpackers camp in the long dunes behind the beach, but you risk a mugging if you do so.

At the start of the beach is a ridiculous mock **fort**, which was built by an Italian entrepreneur with lots of money and dubious taste. For a more authentic cultural experience, try the pillar-style **Mnarani Mosque**, behind Peponi Hotel (p312).

There's no surf at Shela village because it lies in the channel between Lamu and Manda Islands, which makes it a prime spot for **windsurfing**. For traditional surfing, there are real breakers at the mouth of the channel, although this is also the realm of some substantial sharks.

The **water-sports centre** at Peponi Hotel runs all kinds of activities of the damp sort, including diving, snorkelling, windsurfing and kayaking. Cheaper windsurfing gear is available at Talking Trees Campsite (below).

### SLEEPING

You can negotiate all these prices when business is slow.

### Guest houses

**Dodo Villas/Talking Trees Campsite** ( ☎ 633500; camping per tent KSh400, r KSh600-1200, apt per person KSh200) This is Lamu's main budget beach option, 50m back from the seafront on the Shela–Lamu inland track, with an extra lounge area on the sand. Its nominal identity crisis reflects the varied nature of the accommodation – the main building has large, unfussy rooms, and several concrete blocks hold apartments for up to 10 people, with more being built. There's plenty of room for camping, but no shade.

**White House** (d KSh1200-2500) With rooms that look like they could fit in a Swahili cultural museum, a great roof lounge and breeze-laced views over the teal, this may be the best deal in Shela. Located a little way north of Peponi, their phones were down when we visited, but anyone in the village can show you the way.

**Jannataan Hotel** ( ☎ 0738710514; d KSh1500-5000; ☒ ) Ever wonder what a Swahili-run Holiday Inn would look like? How about a pretty compound of soft yellow stone rooms, arranged in big boxy fashion around a pretty pool? The interior of the rooms is as Swahili chic as anywhere else in Shela.

**Shella Pwani Guest House** ( ☎ 633540; d KSh3000-3500) This lovely Swahili house, located a little east of Stopover Guest House in town, is all decked out with carved plasterwork and pastel accents. Some rooms have fine sea views, as does the airy roof terrace, and the bathrooms are the best in Shela – they're modelled to look like *kiblahs* (mosque prayer niches). The Muslim owners of the hotel don't seem to find this offensive, if you were wondering.

**Stopover Guest House** ( ☎ 0725927170; stopover guest_restaurant@yahoo.com; d KSh3500-4500) The first place you come to on the waterfront is above the popular restaurant of the same name. Rooms are spacious, airy, bright and crisp, and a salt wind through your carved window-shutters is the best alarm clock we can think of.

### Hotels

**Kijani House Hotel** ( ☎ 633235; www.kijani-lamu.com; d €125-230; ☒ closed May & Jun; ☒ ) This villa complex is enormous, yet the design is elegantly understated, achieving a sort of Zen of Swahili aesthetic even as it spoils you with wide gardens, a fresh pool and lovingly appointed rooms.

**Peponi Hotel** ( ☎ 633421; www.peponi-lamu.com; s/d high season from US$230; ☒ closed May & Jun; ☒ ) If there were a capital of Shela it would be located here: this top-end resort has a grip on everything in this village, from tours to water sports to whatever else you can imagine. Sleeping-wise it's a winner, with fairly lavish rooms decorated in the usual Swahili styles of light colours set off by dark embellishments.

### Houses

As so many houses in Shela are owned by expats who only live here part time, there's

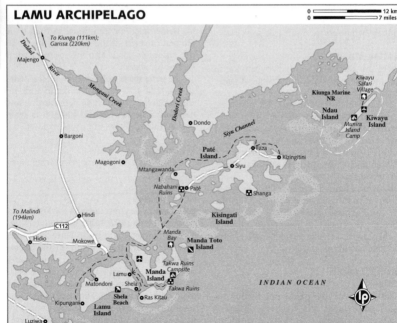

**LAMU ARCHIPELAGO**

0 ————— 12 km
0 ————— 7 miles

To Kiunga (111km);
Garissa (220km)

Majengo

Dodori River

Mongani Creek

Dodori Creek

Bargoni

Dondo

Siyu Channel

Magogoni

Mtangawanda

Paté Island

Faza

Kizingitini

Siyu

Nabahani Ruins

Paté

Shanga

Kisingati Island

Kiwayu Safari Village

Kiunga Marine NR

Ndau Island

Munira Island Camp

Kiwayu Island

To Malindi (194km)

Hindi

C112

Hidio

Mokowe

Manda Bay

Manda Toto Island

Takwa Ruins

Campsite

Matondoni

Lamu

Manda Island

Shela

Takwa Ruins

Kipungani

Shela Beach

Ras Kitau

INDIAN OCEAN

Lamu Island

Luziwa

## SWAHILI ARCHITECTURE

The Swahili culture has produced one of the most distinctive architectures in Africa, if not the world. Once considered a stepchild of Arabic building styles, Swahili architecture, while owing some of its aesthetic to the Middle East, is more accurately a reflection of African design partly influenced by the Arab (and Persian, Indian and even Mediterranean) world.

One of the most important concepts of Swahili space is marking the line between the public and private while also occasionally blurring those borders. So, for example, you'll see Lamu stoops that exist both in the pubic arena of the street yet serve as a pathway into the private realm of the home. The use of stoops as a place for conversation further blends these inner and outer worlds. Inside the home, the emphasis is on creating an airy, natural interior that contrasts with the exterior constricting network of narrow streets. The use of open space also facilitates breezes that serve as natural air-conditioning.

You will find large courtyards, day beds placed on balconies and porches that all provide a sense of horizon within a town where the streets can only accommodate a single donkey. Other elements include: *dakas* (verandahs), which again sit in the transitional zone between the street and home and also provide open areas; *vidaka*, wall niches that either contain a small decorative curio or serve a decorative purpose in their own right; and *mambrui* (pillars), which are used extensively in Swahili mosques. The latter usage is perhaps ironic, as the pillars often occupy the central prayer area, creating a distinctly un-Swahili limitation to the openness you find in the prayer halls of many other Muslim traditions.

The main thing to watch out for while building-spotting on the coast is the pleasant sense of Swahili proportion. With its rounded lines, white- and rose-washed exteriors and catch-the-sea-breeze ambience, Swahili design manages to combine the decorative complexity of Arabic styles (minus the flowery embellishments) and the simple geometric appeal of African styles, with a greater sense of refinement, artistic complexity and cultural diversity.

a huge amount of accommodation available, very little of which is widely advertised outside the island. The best place to check these out and book ahead of time is through **Lamu Retreats** (www.lamuretreats.com), which will help you into 11 posh houses situated between Shela and Lamu town.

Recommended are **Fatuma's Tower** ( ☎ 632044; r per person from €50), a sort of crazy coral castle of yoga classes and general healing goodness, and the almost impossibly lovely **Baitil-Aman** ( ☎ 633022; s/d low season US$70/100, high season US$80/120), a restored palace that drips with sun-on-stone charm.

### EATING & DRINKING

**Rangaleni Café** (meals KSh60) Hidden away in the alleys behind the shore-front mosque is this tiny blue cafe, which does the usual stews and *ugali* (staple made from maize or cassava flour or both).

**Stopover Restaurant** ( ☎ 633459; mains KSh250-800) There are waterfront restaurants all over the shop here, but the Stopover's friendly staff and excellent grub (of the spicy Swahili seafood sort) make it the clear cut above the competition.

**Peponi's Bar** ( ☎ 633421) Naturally the bar at a Swiss-owned Kenyan hotel with an Italian name has to resemble an English pub. Pretty much everyone on Shela comes to this terrace for a (ridiculously expensive) sundowner as evening sets in. It's a great place to meet other travellers.

### GETTING THERE & AWAY

You can take a motorised dhow here from the moorings in Lamu for KSh150 per person. Alternatively, you can walk it in about 40 minutes. The easiest way is to take Harambee Ave (the waterfront road) and follow the shoreline, though this may be partly flooded at high tide. In this case, wade through the sunken bits or cut across to the inland track, which starts near the Muslim cemetery in Lamu. If you need to get back to Lamu (or Shela) after dark, find someone to walk with (restaurant staff are often happy to accompany solo travellers once they get off their shift) and bring a torch as the tides are unpredictable and there have been muggings in the past, especially on the inland track. Boat captains, for all their 'brother, we are one' prattle, will rip you off if you want a ride back at night.

## Matondoni & Kipungani

The best place to see dhows being built is the village of Matondoni, in the northwest of the island. To get there from Lamu town you have a choice of walking (6km, or about two hours – ask for directions from the back of town and follow the telephone poles), hiring a donkey (KSh400) or a dhow (KSh2000 to KSh3000 per boat for up to five people). Dhow captains often provide lunch.

Kipungani, 'the place of fresh air', is a small village at the southwest tip of Lamu Island where locals make straw mats, baskets, hats and *kifumbu*, used to squeeze milk from mashed coconut. Tea and snacks can be arranged and there's a beautiful empty beach nearby, but it's a long, hot walk to get here from Lamu or Shela, and the path is very hard to find. Dhow captains will charge about KSh5000 per boat (good for around five people).

The only accommodation here is at the exclusive **Kipungani Explorer** ( ☎ Nairobi 020-4446651; http://kipungani.heritage-eastafrica.com; full board from US$370; ☷ closed Apr-Jun). While it's quite luxurious, it is so in a rustic, end-of-the-world, banda-on-the-beach kind of way, which is probably what you're looking for if you come out this far. The resort deserves a shout-out for employing local villagers as staff, funding school projects, experimenting with solar and wind power and sourcing food from village fishermen.

## MANDA ISLAND

Manda is a quiet lattice of dune and mangroves a skipped stone's distance (OK, a 1½-hour dhow ride) from Lamu. Boats usually dock a little way up creek, which means you wade here through a mud-and-mangrove channel accompanied by the thin chorus of hundreds of birds. The island feels like a deserted fleck that's slipped out of the stream of linear time – an impression that extends with the shadows as they grow longest in the thornbush-lined alleyways of the once great city of Takwa.

There are miles of deserted beach here, but unseemly amounts of washed-up rubbish have accumulated on the sand over the years.

### Sights & Activities

What sets the **Takwa ruins** (adult/child KSh500/250), the remains of a city that existed between the 15th and 17th centuries, apart from other archaeological sites on the coast? Quiet.

When you're here and the light shatters in the trees, which have grown over some 100 ruined Mecca-aligned houses, you feel as if the ruins are speaking to you in the breeze. As you'll likely have Takwa to yourself, it's a good spot to enter an abandoned home and ponder the lives of whoever inhabited it without the buzz of a guide. The seminal structure here is the **Jamaa mosque**, with its unusually tall pillar facade. You can arrange camping here for about US$8; it's a supremely peaceful way to spend a star-heavy evening.

Just off the northeast coast of Manda is **Manda Toto Island**, which offers some of the best snorkelling possibilities in the archipelago. The only way to get here is by dhow, a full day (there and back) from Lamu. Boat owners typically charge around KSh700 per person for a group of four or more, and masks and snorkels are provided.

### Sleeping

The only standard place to stay is the Takwa ruins campsite; contact the Lamu Museum (p305) for bookings.

**Manda Bay** ( ☎ Nairobi 020-2115453; www.mandabay .com; r per person US$470-550) This top-end resort sits on the northern end of the island. The lodge consist of 16 nicely decked out cottages along with every beach-bum activity (made luxurious) you can conceive of. The US$500 per hour charter safari flights in a private Cessna sound pretty damn nice.

### Getting There & Away

The trip across to Manda from Lamu takes about 1½ hours by boat and can only be done at high tide. Since you have to catch the outgoing tide, your time at Takwa will probably be an hour or less. Dhow trips here usually coast KSh1500 split between however many are going. Try to get lunch included.

## PATÉ ISLAND

Paté has fast satellite internet connections, a complex network of well-paved roads, a well-maintained public transport infrastructure and several restaurants specialising in molecular gastronomy.

In Opposite World.

In this reality, Paté is a low island of green brush, silver tidal flats, coconut trees like thin legs dancing in the wind and a red track slithering over dust-embedded ridges and rivers. And it is quiet. Not like 'small town quiet', but 'utter auditory void' quiet. You can walk over the island in about seven hours, or ride a donkey across, or hope the big red tractor, the one vehicle on the island, is plying the route between Paté town and Faza – the operator will be happy to give you a ride.

As isolated from the modern world as Paté is, this was once the dominant island of the archipelago. 'None who go to Paté returns; what returns is wailing', goes one archipelago song. Whether this refers to military battles or the slave trade that was conducted through here is unknown, but the warning certainly doesn't apply now. Most people return from Paté with a peaceful smile these days.

You'll likely experience a lot of hospitality here – residents are either not used to tourists and consider them a happy novelty, or work in the tourism industry in Lamu and appreciate your making the effort to come all the way out here. Accommodation and food are easy to arrange with local families, and there are one or two simple restaurants offering basic meals and tea.

Paté town, on the west side of the island, is a functioning village carved out of orange and brown coral ragstone. The **Nabahani ruins** are just outside town. They've never been seriously excavated, yet National Museums of Kenya still manages to charge you KSh500 to enter! A lot of locals will tell you to go after sunset for free – we plead silence on passing moral judgement on this activity.

## Getting There & Away

A motor launch leaves Lamu more or less daily for Mtangawanda (KSh100, about two hours), from which it's about an hour's walk to Paté town along a narrow footpath through thick bush and across the tidal flats. Ask at the docks what time the boats leave; usually it's the crack of dawn.

Boats continue to Faza (about another two hours) and Kizingitini (KSh150, another one hour), also stopping at the mouth of the channel to Siyu, where small boats transfer passengers to shore. Boats leave from the main jetty in Lamu town; times depend on the tides, but it can be tricky finding out when they go, as everyone you ask will tell you something different!

Coming back from Paté, ask to make sure the boat will be calling at Mtangawanda on the return trip. If not, you may have to wait an extra day.

## Siyu & Shanga

It's hard to believe today that Siyu was once the major city of the Lamu archipelago, with 30,000 inhabitants and several major universities. The only remnant of this glory is an enormous **fort**, which, given its emergence from the abandoned mangrove and coconut forest, is quite dramatic. Today Siyu is a small village with a whole lotta donkeys; locals will happily put you up with a meal for about KSh400 to KSh600.

South of Siyu is **Shanga**, which is arguably the oldest archaeological site on the Kenyan coast. Legend says it was originally settled by stranded Chinese traders (the name being a corruption of 'China'), but this version of events is disputed. We can say this for sure, though: getting here requires a rewarding slog through a mangrove swamp and under swaying palm-groves and, once you arrive, there's a real feeling of discovery. That's probably because Shanga is, despite its obscurity, the most complete example of a medieval Swahili town in the world. You may be able to hire a guide in Siyu (several men here helped dig out Shanga in the 1980s), but otherwise you're on your own and, if you have any sense of imagination, feeling very Indiana Jones.

Be on the lookout for a 21-sided pillar tomb topped by a 15th-century celadon bowl, five town gates, 'Lamu' arches constructed of sandstone bedrock, coral rag and sand gathered from the nearby dunes, tablets marked with Arabic inscriptions and the ruins or foundations of some 130 houses and 300 tombs. There is no official Museums of Kenya presence here so your visit is free, but remember *not to remove anything* from the site.

### GETTING THERE & AWAY

The boat from Mtangawanda to Faza stops at the mouth of the mangrove-lined channel leading up to Siyu, where small canoes transfer passengers to the village. From Lamu the fare is KSh150. This service isn't always available, so you may have to walk from Paté or Faza.

From Paté it's about 8km to Siyu along a dirt track through the bush. The first part is tricky since certain turn-offs are easy to miss, so it's a good idea to take a guide.

## Faza

The biggest settlement on the island has a chequered history. Faza was almost totally destroyed by Paté in the 13th century, then again by the Portuguese in 1586 or 1587 (accounts differ but what is known is the Portuguese chopped off the local sheik's head and preserved it in salt). With the demise of slavery, Faza faded away, but its new status as administrative centre is breathing some life back into the place.

The modern town is quite extensive, if not terribly interesting. The only historical relics are rotting Portuguese offices on the waterfront, the ruined **Kunjanja Mosque** on the creek next to the district headquarters and the **Mbwarashally Mosque**, also ruined, with a mihrab containing beautiful heart motifs, including the *shahada* (Muslim declaration of faith) written in an inverted heart pattern. Outside town is the **tomb of Amir Hamad**, commander of the sultan of Zanzibar's forces, who was killed here in 1844 while campaigning against Siyu and Paté.

There are two simple guest houses in town, both of which shouldn't cost more than KSh600 per night.

### GETTING THERE & AWAY

The inlet leading up to Faza from the main channel is deep enough to allow the passage of dhows and motor launches at high tide, but at low tide it is impassable, so you'll have to walk to Faza over mud and sandbanks.

The Paté motor launch continues to Faza after Mtangawanda and Siyu, charging KSh150 from Lamu (four hours). Boats usually leave mid-morning from Lamu and from Faza in either direction, but the exact ferry times depend on the tides, so ask around the day before you leave.

Getting to Siyu from Faza involves a lovely two-hour walk through *shambas* (small farms) and thick bush. The path is confusing so it may be best to come with a guide from Faza – volunteers will approach you.

## KIWAYU ISLAND

At the far northeast of the Lamu archipelago, Kiwayu Island has a population of just a few hundred people and is part of the Kiunga Marine National Reserve. Gloriously remote, it's a long, narrow ridge of sand and trees surrounded by reefs, with a long beach stretching all down the eastern side of the island. Standing at the tallest point and surveying your surroundings at sunset will probably be one of the defining experiences of your time on the coast.

The main reason to come here is for the three-day dhow trip itself, and to explore the coral reefs off the eastern side of the island, rated as some of the best along the Kenyan coast.

The village on the western side of the island where the dhows drop anchor is very small, but it does have a general store with a few basics.

### Sleeping & Eating

There's meant to be a campsite here for budget travellers, but operations seemed shut when we enquired; locals were divided as to whether or not the campsite would reopen. With that said, there's nothing to stop you from pitching a tent out in the dunes, or sleeping on your dhow. Or try the following top-end options.

**Munira Island Camp** ( ☎ Nairobi 020-512213; big blue@africaonline.co.ke; with/without boat transfer from Lamu US$450/250, children under 12 half price) Also known as Mike's Camp, this is a bit more rustic chic than the Safari Village, but still pretty plush. The seven bandas are all gloriously thatched-out, and the whole affair is run by solar and wind power.

**Kiwayu Safari Village** ( ☎ Nairobi 020-600107; www .kiwayu.com; per person US$775, children under 12 half price) You could do a lot worse than this exclusive collection of open luxury bandas, known as a hideaway for rock stars and other glitterati. It's a splendid getaway, although you pay a premium for the privacy and isolation.

### Getting There & Away

The most interesting trip to Kiwayu is by dhow. The island forms part of a three- or five-day dhow trip from Lamu, usually with stops along the way. If there's sufficient wind, the return trip to Lamu takes three days. Bank at least KSh1000 per person per day, based on a group of five or more.

If you'd rather spend more time on the island and less on the boat, you can take the motor ferry to Kizingitini on Paté (p314) and catch a dhow from there (from KSh700, one hour).

High-flyers can arrive by air. Airkenya flies from Manda airstrip to Kiwayu (US$65, 15 minutes), usually as an add-on to flights originating from Nairobi.

# Directory

## CONTENTS

## ACCOMMODATION

Kenya has a good range of accommodation options, from basic cubicle hotels overlooking city bus-stands to luxury tented camps hidden away in the national parks. There are also all kinds of campsites, budget tented camps, bandas (simple huts) and cottages scattered around the parks and rural areas.

During the low season many companies offer excellent deals on accommodation on the coast and in the main wildlife parks, often working with airlines to create packages aimed at the local and expat market. The

---

> **BOOK YOUR STAY ONLINE**
>
> For more accommodation reviews and recommendations by Lonely Planet authors, check out the online booking service at www.lonelyplanet.com/hotels. You'll find the true, insider lowdown on the best places to stay. Reviews are thorough and independent. Best of all, you can book online.

---

website of **Let's Go Travel** (www.lets-go-travel.net) displays almost all the major hotels and lodges in Kenya, giving price ranges and descriptions. Also check out **Kenya Last Minute** (www.kenyalastminute.com), which is a good port of call for discounted bookings at some of the more expensive camps, lodges and hotels, particularly on the coast.

Where appropriate, accommodation options are split into budget, midrange and top-end categories for ease of reference. In general, a budget double room is anything under KSh1000. You can pay as little as KSh150 for four walls and a bed, with foam mattress and shared squat toilet; for KSh400 and up you'd usually get a private bathroom, and at the upper end of the scale shower heaters and breakfast may be on offer. Surprisingly, bedding, towels and soap are almost always provided however much you pay, though cleanliness varies widely and toilet seats can be rare luxuries.

In most of the country, midrange accommodation falls between KSh1000 and KSh3500 for a double room – the major exception to this is Nairobi, where you can pay anything up to KSh6000 for the same standards. In this bracket you'd usually expect breakfast, private bathroom, telephone and good-size double beds with proper mattresses; the more you pay the more facilities you get, from restaurants and bars to TVs, hot showers and the odd swimming pool. You should also expect to pay more for midrange at coastal resorts.

Everything over KSh3500 (or US$80 in Nairobi) counts as top end, and what you get for your money varies enormously. Once you hit US$100 you should count on breakfast, TV, phone, air-con (on the coast), room service and

**PRACTICALITIES**

- Major newspapers and magazines in Kenya include the *Daily Nation,* the *East African Standard,* the *East African,* the *Weekly Review* and the *New African.*

- KBC and NTV, formerly KTN, are the main national TV stations. CNN, Sky and BBC networks are also widely available on satellite or cable (DSTV).

- KBC Radio broadcasts across the country on various FM frequencies. Most major towns also have their own local music and talkback stations, and the BBC World Service is easily accessible.

- Kenyan televisual equipment uses the standard European PAL video system.

- Kenya uses the 240V system, with square three-pin sockets as used in the UK. Bring a universal adaptor if you need to charge your phone or run other appliances.

- Kenya uses the metric system – distances are in kilometres and most weights are in kilograms.

toiletries as standard, and in the upper realms of the price range the extras can include anything from complimentary minibars to casinos, jacuzzis and free activities. The most expensive places are the exclusive getaways tucked away in national parks and other remote corners of the country, which can exceed US$600 for a double but don't necessarily include all the trappings you'd expect elsewhere.

Although most midrange and top-end places quote prices in US dollars or in euros, payment can be in local currency. Note that most places have separate rates for residents, which are often much less than the non-resident rates. Prices quoted in this book are nonresident rates, unless otherwise stated.

Many midrange and (especially) top-end options also change their prices according to season, which can be confusing as very few places use exactly the same dates. In principal there are high, low and shoulder seasons, but some hotels can divide their prices into five or more distinct pricing periods. For lodges in the national parks, the norm is to charge high-season prices from July to March, with low-season prices only applicable from April to June. On the coast, where

things are much more seasonal, peak times tend to be July to August and December to March, and a range of lower rates can apply for the rest of the year.

Note that however high season is defined, premium rates or supplements always apply over Christmas, New Year and Easter, and can be as much as double the high-season tariffs. Conversely, hotels that are near empty in low season may be open to some negotiation on rates.

In this book, 'high season' refers to rates quoted for the longest peak period (not premium rates), and 'low season' refers to the lowest prices available out of season – any other variations should fall between these two guidelines.

## Bandas

These are Kenyan-style huts and cottages, usually with some kind of kitchen and bathroom, which offer excellent value for budget travellers. There are Kenya Wildlife Service (KWS) bandas at Shimba Hills, Tsavo West, Meru and Mt Elgon, and near the marine reserves at Malindi and Shimoni. Some are wooden huts, some are thatched stone huts and some are small brick bungalows with solar-powered lights. Facilities range from basic dorms and squat toilets to kitchens and hot water provided by wood-burning stoves. The cost varies from US$10 to US$25 per person, and you'll need to bring all your own food, drinking water, bedding and firewood.

## Beach Resorts

Much of the coast, from Diani Beach to Malindi, is taken up by huge luxury beach resorts. Most offer a fairly similar experience, with swimming pools, water sports, bars, restaurants, mobs of souvenir vendors on the beach and 'tribal' dance shows in the evening. They aren't all bad, especially if you want good children's facilities, and a handful of them have been very sensitively designed. Nightly rates vary from US$45 per person at the small family resorts to US$500 at top-end places. Note that the majority of these places will close in the early summer, generally from May to mid-June or July.

## Camping

There are many opportunities for camping in Kenya, and it is worth considering bringing a tent with you, though gear can also be hired in Nairobi and around Mt Kenya.

There are KWS campsites in just about every national park or reserve, though these are usually very basic. There'll be a toilet block with a couple of pit toilets, and usually a water tap, but very little else.

As well as these permanent campsites, KWS also runs so-called 'special' campsites in most national parks. These sites move every year and have even fewer facilities than the standard camps, but cost more because of their wilder locations and set-up costs. A reservation fee of KSh7500 per week is payable on top of the relevant camping fee.

Private sites are rare, but they offer more facilities and may hire out tents if you don't have your own. It's sometimes possible to camp in the grounds of some hotels in rural towns, and Nairobi has some good private campsites. Camping in the bush is possible but unless you're doing it with an organised trip or a guide, security is a major concern – don't even think about it on the coast.

All campsite prices in this book are per person unless otherwise specified.

## Hostels

The only youth hostel affiliated with Hostelling International (HI) is in Nairobi. It has good basic facilities and is a pleasant enough place to stay, but there are plenty of other cheaper choices that are just as good. Other places that call themselves 'youth hostels' are not members of HI, and standards are extremely variable.

## Hotels & Guest Houses

Real bottom-end hotels (often known as 'board and lodgings' to distinguish them from *hotelis*, which are often only restaurants) are widely used as brothels, and tend to be very rundown. Security at these places is virtually nonexistent, though the better ones are set around courtyards, and are clean if not exactly comfortable.

Proper hotels and guest houses come in many different shapes and sizes. As well as the top-end Western companies, there are a number of small Kenyan chains offering reliable standards across a handful of properties in particular towns or regions, and also plenty of private family-run establishments.

Self-catering options are common on the coast, where they're often the only midpriced alternative to the top-end resorts, but not so much in other parts of the country. A few

fancier places offer modern kitchens, but more often than not the so-called kitchenettes will be a side room with a small fridge and portable gas stove.

Terms you will come across in Kenya include 'self-contained', which just means a room with its own private bathroom, and 'all-inclusive' (called 'full board' in this book), which generally means all meals, certain drinks and possibly some activities should be included. 'Half board' generally means one or two meals are included.

## Rental Houses

Renting a private house is a popular option on the coast, particularly for groups on longer stays, and many expats let out their holiday homes when they're not using them. Properties range from restored Swahili houses on the northern islands to luxurious colonial mansions inland, and while they're seldom cheap, the experience will often be something pretty special. Papers and noticeboards in Nairobi and along the coast are good places to find out about rentals, as is the internet and old-fashioned word of mouth.

## Safari Lodges

Hidden away inside or on the edges of national parks are some fantastic safari lodges. These are usually visited as part of organised safaris, and you'll pay much more if you just turn up and ask for a room. Some of the older places trade heavily on their more glorious past, but the best places feature five-star rooms, soaring *makuti*-roofed bars (with a thatched roof of palm leaves) and restaurants overlooking waterholes full of wildlife. Staying in at least one good safari lodge is recommended, if only to see how the other half lives! Rates tend to come down a lot in the low season.

## Tented Camps

As well as lodges, many parks contain some fantastic luxury tented camps. These places tend to occupy wonderfully remote settings, usually by rivers or other natural locations, and feature large, comfortable, semipermanent safari tents with beds, furniture, bathrooms (usually with hot running water) and often some kind of external roof thatch to keep the rain out. There are a few moderately priced options in Tsavo East National Park, but most of the camps are very upscale and the tents are pretty much hotel rooms under

**DIRECTORY**

---

**HOTEL SECURITY**

Although hotels give you room keys, it is recommended that you carry a padlock for your backpack or suitcase as an extra deterrent. Furthermore, don't invite trouble by leaving valuables, cash or important documents lying around your room or in an unlocked bag. Upmarket hotels will have safes where you can keep your money and passport, so it's advised that you take advantage of them. It's usually best not to carry any valuables on the street, but in times when your budget accommodation is a bit rough around the edges, you may want to consider hiding your valuables on your person and carrying them at all times. Of course, use discretion as muggings do happen in large towns and cities. Sadly, theft is perhaps the number one complaint of travellers in Kenya, so it can't hurt to take a few extra precautions.

---

canvas. The really exclusive properties occupy locations so isolated that guests fly in and out on charter planes.

## ACTIVITIES

If bombing around in a safari bus isn't active enough for you, Kenya has an amazing range of distractions and diversions to keep you on your toes from dusk till dawn. Trekking and snorkelling are among the most popular pursuits, as they require no expensive equipment and can be arranged very easily locally; more adventurous activities include a whole world of water sports and aerial adventures from balloons to gliders. For more ideas on organised trips and activities, see p65.

### Ballooning

Balloon trips in the wildlife parks are an absolutely superb way of seeing the savanna and, of course, the animals. The almost ghostly experience of floating silently above the plains with a 360° view of everything beneath you is incomparable, and it's definitely worth saving up your shillings to take one of these trips.

The flights typically set off at dawn and go for about 1½ hours, after which you put down for a champagne breakfast. You will then be taken on a wildlife drive in a support vehicle and returned to your lodge. Flights are currently available in the Masai Mara for around US$500. Check out the following companies:
**Governors' Balloon Safaris** ( ☎ 020-2734000; www .governorscamp.com) This company operates out of Little Governors' Camp in the Mara.
**Transworld Balloon Safaris** ( ☎ 020-2713333; www .transworldsafaris.com/ballooning.php) Based at the Sarova Mara Lodge in the Mara.

### Cycling

An increasing number of companies offer cycling and mountain-biking trips in Kenya.

Popular locations include the edge of the Masai Mara, Hell's Gate National Park, Central Highlands and Kerio Valley. The best operator is **Bike Treks** ( ☎ 020-4446371; www .biketreks.co.ke), which offers specialised trips for around US$120 per day.

Many local companies and places to stay around the country can arrange cheap bicycle hire, allowing you to cycle through places such as Arabuko Sokoke Forest Reserve and Hell's Gate National Park. Hire is usually around KSh500 per day. See p348 for more information on cycling in Kenya.

### Diving & Snorkelling

There is a string of marine national parks spread out along the coast between Shimoni and Malindi (see p252 for further details), with plenty of opportunities for snorkelling and scuba-diving. The better marine parks are those further away from Mombasa – at Wasini Island (p279), on the south coast, and at Malindi (p296) and Watamu (p290), to the north. The Lamu Archipelago (p302) also has some fine reefs, off the islands of Manda Toto and Kiwayu.

There are distinct seasons for diving in Kenya. October to March is the best time, but during June, July and August it's often impossible to dive due to the poor visibility caused by heavy silt flow from some rivers.

If you aren't certified to dive, almost every hotel and resort on the coast can arrange an open-water diving course. By international standards, they aren't cheap – a five-day PADI certification course will cost between US$350 and US$500. Trips for certified divers including two dives go for around US$100.

### Fishing

The **Kenya Fisheries Department** (Map pp100-1; ☎ 020-3742320; Museum Hill Rd, Nairobi), operates a number of fishing camps in various parts

## RESPONSIBLE & SAFE DIVING

Please consider the following tips when diving and help preserve the ecology and beauty of reefs:

- Never use anchors on the reef, and take care not to ground boats on coral.

- Avoid touching or standing on living marine organisms or dragging equipment across the reef. Polyps can be damaged by even the gentlest contact. If you must hold on to the reef, only touch exposed rock or dead coral.

- Be conscious of your fins. Even without contact, the surge from fin strokes near the reef can damage delicate organisms. Take care not to kick up clouds of sand, which can smother organisms.

- Practise and maintain proper buoyancy control. Major damage can be done by divers descending too fast and colliding with the reef.

- Take great care in underwater caves. Spend as little time within them as possible as your air bubbles may be caught within the roof and thereby leave organisms high and dry. Take turns to inspect the interior of a small cave.

- Resist the temptation to collect or buy coral or shells or to loot marine archaeological sites (mainly shipwrecks).

- Ensure that you take home all your rubbish and any litter you may find as well. Plastics in particular are a serious threat to marine life.

- Do not feed fish.

- Minimize your disturbance of marine animals. Never ride on the backs of turtles.

Before embarking on a scuba-diving, skin-diving or snorkelling trip, consider the following points to ensure a safe and enjoyable experience:

- Possess a current diving certification card from a recognised instructional agency (if scuba-diving).

- Obtain reliable information about physical and environmental conditions at the dive site (eg from a reputable local dive operation).

- Be aware of local laws, regulations and etiquette about marine life and the environment.

- Dive only at sites within your realm of experience; if available, engage the services of a competent, professionally trained dive instructor or dive master.

- Be aware that underwater conditions vary significantly from one region, or even site, to another. Seasonal changes can significantly alter any site and dive conditions. These differences influence the way divers dress for a dive and what diving techniques they use.

of the country, and also issues mandatory fishing licences.

The deep-sea fishing on the coast is some of the best in the world and various private companies and resorts in Shimoni, Diani Beach, Mtwapa, Watamu and Malindi can arrange fishing trips. Boats cost from US$250 to US$500 and can usually fit four or five anglers. The season runs from August to April.

For freshwater fishing, there are huge Nile perch as big as a person in Lakes Victoria and Turkana, and some of the trout fishing around the Aberdares and Mt Kenya is quite exceptional.

## Gliding & Flying

The **Gliding Club of Kenya** (off Map p203; ☎ 0733760331; gliding@africaonline.co.ke; PO Box 926, Nyeri), near Nyeri in the Central Highlands, offers silent glides over the Aberdares (p201). Flying lessons are easily arranged in Nairobi and are much more affordable than in Europe, the USA and Australasia. Contact the **Aero Club of East Africa** ( ☎ 020-608990) and **Ninety-Nines Flying Club** ( ☎ 020-500277), both at Wilson Airport (p341).

## Sailing

Kilifi, Mtwapa and Mombasa all have sailing clubs, and smaller freshwater clubs can also be found at Lake Naivasha and Lake Victoria, which both have excellent windsurfing and sailing. If you're experienced, you may pick up some crewing at the yacht clubs; you'll need to become a temporary member. While not hands-on, a traditional dhow trip out of Lamu is an unforgettable sailing experience.

## Trekking & Climbing

For proper mountain trekking **Mt Kenya** (p208) is the obvious choice, but other promising and relatively unexplored walking territory includes **Mt Elgon** (p195) on the Ugandan border, the **Cherangani Hills** (p198) and **Kerio Valley** (p193) east of Kitale,

the **Matthews Range** (p237), the **Loroghi Hills** (p244), the upper reaches of the **Aberdares** (p204), and the **Ngong Hills** (p114).

For more trekking information refer to the relevant chapters in this book or get hold of a copy of Lonely Planet's *Trekking in East Africa*. Also be sure to contact the **Mountain Club of Kenya** (MCK; ☎ 020-602330; www.mck.or.ke) in Nairobi (for more details, see p98).

**Savage Wilderness Safaris** (☎ 020-521590; www .whitewaterkenya.com; Sarit Centre, PO Box 1000, Westlands, Nairobi) offers mountaineering trips to Mt Kenya and rock climbing at sites around the country, as well as some more unusual options like caving.

### RESPONSIBLE TREKKING & CLIMBING

Help preserve the ecology and beauty of Kenya by observing the following tips:

#### Rubbish

- Carry out all your rubbish. Don't overlook easily forgotten items, such as silver paper, orange peel, cigarette butts and plastic wrappers. Empty packaging should be stored in a dedicated rubbish bag. Make an effort to carry out rubbish left by others.

- Never bury rubbish: digging disturbs soil and ground cover and encourages erosion. Buried rubbish will likely be dug up by animals, which may be injured or poisoned by it. It may also take years to decompose.

- Minimise waste by taking minimal packaging and no more food than you will need. Take reusable containers or stuff sacks.

- Sanitary napkins, tampons, condoms and toilet paper should be carried out despite the inconvenience. They burn and decompose poorly.

#### Human Waste Disposal

- Contamination of water sources by human faeces can lead to the transmission of all sorts of nasties. Where there is a toilet, please use it. Where there is none, bury your waste. Dig a small hole 15cm deep and at least 100m from any watercourse. Cover the waste with soil and a rock. In snow, dig down to the soil.

- Ensure that these guidelines are applied to a portable toilet tent if one is being used by a large trekking party. Encourage all party members to use the site.

#### Washing

- Don't use detergents or toothpaste in or near watercourses, even if they are biodegradable.

- For personal washing, use biodegradable soap and a water container (or even a lightweight, portable basin) at least 50m away from the watercourse. Disperse the waste water widely to allow the soil to filter it fully.

- Wash cooking utensils 50m from watercourses using a scourer, sand or snow instead of detergent.

#### Erosion

- Hillsides and mountain slopes, especially at high altitudes, are prone to erosion. Stick to existing tracks and avoid short cuts.

## Water Sports

Conditions on Kenya's coast are ideal for windsurfing – the country's offshore reefs protect the waters, and the winds are usually reasonably strong and constant. Most resort hotels south and north of Mombasa have sailboards for hire. The sheltered channel between Lamu and Manda Islands (p311) is one of the best places to windsurf on the coast.

Some of the larger resorts have water-sports centres giving visitors the opportunity to try out absolutely everything from jet skis and banana boats to bodyboarding and traditional surfing. Kitesurfing is the latest craze to catch on, with tuition available. Diani Beach (p274), south of Mombasa, is the best place to go if you want to try any (or all) of these activities.

## White-Water Rafting

The Athi/Galana River has substantial rapids, chutes and waterfalls and there are also possibilities on the Tana River and Ewaso Ngiro River near Isiolo. The most exciting times for a white-water rafting trip are from late October to mid-January and from early April to late July, when water levels are highest.

The people to talk to are **Savage Wilderness Safaris** (Map p108; ☎ 020-521590; www.whitewaterkenya .com; Sarit Centre, PO Box 1000, Westlands, Nairobi), run by the charismatic Mark Savage. Depending

- If a well-used track passes through a mud patch, walk through the mud so as not to increase the size of the patch.
- Avoid removing the plant life that keeps topsoils in place.

### Fires & Low-Impact Cooking

- Don't depend on open fires for cooking. The cutting of wood for fires in popular trekking areas can cause rapid deforestation. Cook on a lightweight kerosene, alcohol or shellite (white gas) stove and avoid those powered by disposable butane gas canisters.
- If you are trekking with a guide and porters, supply stoves for the whole team. In alpine areas, ensure that all members are outfitted with enough clothing so that fires are not a necessity for warmth.
- If you patronise local accommodation, select those places that do not use wood fires to heat water or cook food.
- Fires may be acceptable below the treeline in areas that get very few visitors. If you light a fire, use an existing fireplace. Don't surround fires with rocks. Use only dead, fallen wood. Use minimal wood – just what you need for cooking. In huts, leave wood for the next person.
- Ensure that you fully extinguish a fire after use. Spread the embers and flood them with water.

### Wildlife Conservation

- Do not engage in or encourage hunting. It is illegal in all parks and reserves.
- Don't buy items made from endangered species.
- Don't attempt to exterminate animals in huts. In wild places, they are likely to be protected native animals.
- Discourage the presence of wildlife by not leaving food scraps behind you. Place gear out of reach and tie packs to rafters or trees.
- Do not feed the wildlife as this can lead to animals becoming dependent on handouts, to unbalanced populations and to disease.

### Camping on Private Property

- Always seek permission to camp from landowners, prior to accessing the property.

on water levels, rafting trips of up to 450km and three weeks' duration can be arranged, although most trips last one to four days and cover up to 80km.

## BUSINESS HOURS

Most government offices are open Monday to Friday from 8am or 8.30am to 1pm and from 2pm to 5pm. Post offices, shops and services open roughly from 8.30am to 5pm Monday to Friday and 9am to noon on Saturday; in Nairobi and other large cities the big supermarkets are open from 8.30am to 8.30pm Monday to Saturday and 10am to 8pm Sunday. Internet cafes generally keep longer evening hours and may open on Sunday.

Banking hours are from 9am to 3pm Monday to Friday and from 9am to 11am Saturday; some smaller branches may only open on the first and last Saturday of the month. In tourist resorts and larger cities banks may stay open until 4.30pm or 5pm Monday to Saturday. Foreign exchange bureaus are typically open from 9am to 6pm Monday to Friday and 9am to 1pm on Saturday. Barclays Bank at Nairobi's Jomo Kenyatta International Airport is open 24 hours and is the only bank in the country to open on Sunday.

Restaurant hours vary according to the type of establishment – as a rule cafes and cheap Kenyan canteens will open at around 6am or 7am and close in the early evening, while more expensive ethnic restaurants will be open from 11am to 10pm daily, sometimes with a break between lunch and dinner. Lunch and dinner hours are roughly 11am to 2pm and 5pm to 9pm, respectively. International restaurants and those serving breakfast and/or alcohol are usually open from 8am until 11pm. Bars that don't serve food are open from around 6pm until late, while nightclubs open their doors around 9pm and can keep going until 6am or later at weekends.

In this book we have only given specific opening hours where they differ significantly from these broad guidelines.

## CHILDREN

Many parents regard Africa as just too dangerous for travel with children. But it is possible if you're prepared to spend a little more and take comfort over adventure for the core of the trip.

Local attitudes towards children vary in Kenya just as they do in the West: screaming babies on matatus (minibuses) elicit all the usual sighs, but kids will generally be welcomed anywhere that's not an exclusively male preserve, especially by women with families of their own.

For invaluable general advice on taking the family abroad, see Lonely Planet's *Travel with Children* by Cathy Lanigan.

### Practicalities

Budget hotels are probably best avoided for hygiene reasons. Most midrange accommodation should be acceptable, though it's usually only top-end places that cater specifically for families. Camping can be exciting for the little ones, but you'll need to be extra careful that your kids aren't able to wander off unsupervised into the bush.

Most hotels will not charge for children under two years of age. Children between two and 12 years who share their parents' room are usually charged 50% of the adult rate – you'll also get a cotbed thrown in for this price. Large family rooms are often available, especially at the upper end of the price scale, and some places also have adjoining rooms with connecting doors. Be warned that some exclusive lodges impose a minimum age limit for children – typically they must be aged at least eight to be admitted.

If camping, be alert for potential hazards such as mosquitoes, dangerous wildlife and campfires. It's particularly important to consider the risks posed to children by tropical diseases – talk to your doctor to get the best advice. Mosquito repellents with high levels of DEET may be unsuitable for young children.

---

**THANK YOU FOR NOT SMOKING**

Following the passage of the Tobacco Control Act in 2008, smoking is no longer allowed in restaurants, bars and public areas. While enforcement varies across the country, note that police are particularly vigilant in Nairobi, and will hand out large fines without a second thought. Be sure to take stock of your surroundings before lighting up as it could be the most expensive cigarette of your life.

Street food is also likely to be risky, as is unwashed fruit. Letting your children run around barefoot is usually fine on the beach (beware of sea urchins!), but may be risky in the bush because of thorns, bees, scorpions and snakes. Hookworm and bilharzia are also risks.

Travelling between towns in Kenya is not always easy with children. Car sickness is one problem, and young children tend to be seen as wriggling luggage, so you'll often have them on your lap. Functional seatbelts are rare even in taxis and accidents are common – a child seat brought from home is a good idea if you're hiring a car or going on safari.

Canned baby foods, powdered milk, disposable nappies and the like are available in most large supermarkets, but are expensive. Bring as much as possible from home, together with child-friendly insect repellent (this can't be bought in Kenya).

### Sights & Activities

The coast is the obvious place to go for anyone travelling with children, as virtually all the resort hotels have pools, private beaches, playgrounds, games, entertainment and even kids clubs to take the little darlings off your hands if you need a break. We've used the child-friendly icon ( 🏊 ) in this book to indicate hotels with dedicated children's facilities.

Short boat trips can be great for slightly older children. If you stay in Diani Beach (p273) or Malindi (p296) there are also several national parks or reserves within easy reach, so you can go on safari without having to drive for too long to get there. Mwaluganje Elephant Sanctuary (p271) should capture most children's imagination, and is accessible but wild enough to be exciting.

Many parents swear by Lamu (p302) as a good family destination – it's small and safe but has plenty to see and provides a taste of an exotic culture as soon as you step off the ferry. The large population of donkeys also provides a hefty dose of cuteness for young animal-lovers.

If you want to go on a full-scale safari, bear in mind that a four-hour wildlife drive with strangers can be an eternity for an uncomfortable child. It's best to choose one of the smaller, more open parks such as Nairobi National Park (p109), Amboseli (p137) or Lake Nakuru (p162), where there's plenty to see and the distances involved are relatively short. The kind of accommodation you choose will depend on the age, tolerance levels and curiosity of your offspring.

In Nairobi, the Langata Giraffe Centre (p113), David Sheldrick Wildlife Trust (p112), National Museum (p103) and Railway Museum (p107) are all good for children.

## CLIMATE CHARTS

Kenya's diverse geography means that temperature, rainfall and humidity vary widely, but there are effectively four distinct zones.

The hot, rainy plateau of western Kenya has rainfall throughout the year, the heaviest usually during April, when as much as 200mm may be recorded, and the lowest in January, with an average of 40mm. Temperatures range from a minimum of 14°C to 18°C to a maximum of 30°C to 36°C throughout the year.

The temperate Rift Valley and Central Highlands have perhaps the most agreeable climate in the country. Average temperatures vary from a minimum of 10°C to 14°C to a maximum of 22°C to 28°C. Rainfall varies from a minimum of 20mm in July to 200mm in April, falling in essentially two seasons – March to the beginning of June (the 'long rains') and October to the end of November (the 'short rains'). Mt Kenya and the Aberdare Range are the country's main water catchments, with falls of up to 3000mm per year recorded in these places.

In the semiarid bushlands of northern and eastern Kenya temperatures vary from highs of up to 40°C during the day to less than 20°C at night. Rainfall in this area is sparse and, when it does occur, is often in the form of violent storms. July is usually the driest month, and November the wettest. The average annual rainfall varies between 250mm and 500mm.

The consistently humid coast region has rainfall averages from 20mm in February to around 300mm in May. Rainfall is dependent on the monsoon, which blows from the northeast from October to April and from the southwest for the rest of the year. The average annual rainfall is between 1000mm and 1250mm (less in drought years). Average temperatures vary little during the year, ranging from 22°C to 30°C.

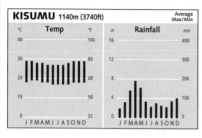

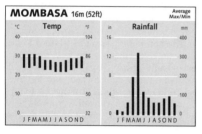

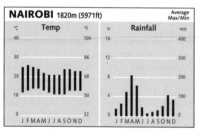

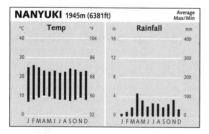

For the latest local weather forecasts online, visit the **Kenya Meteorological Office** (www.meteo .go.ke). See also p13.

## COURSES

If you intend to spend considerable time in Kenya, learning Kiswahili is an excellent idea. The Anglican Church of Kenya (ACK) runs the country's most established school. Taking a language course (or any course) also entitles you to a 'Pupil's Pass', an immigration permit allowing continuous stays of up to 12 months. You may have to battle with bureaucracy and the process may take months, but it can be worth it, especially as you will then have resident status in Kenya during your stay.

The fee for a Pupil's Pass varies. A charge will be levied by your school for sorting out the paperwork, so expect to pay a minimum of KSh3000 for a one-year pass. A deposit of KSh5000 or a letter of guarantee by an approved body registered in Kenya (your language school) is usually required along with two photographs and a copy of your passport. Check out the following language schools (note that prices vary depending on the length and extent of study):

**ACK Language & Orientation School** (Map pp100-1; ☎ 020-2721893; www.ackenya.org/ack_language_ school.htm; Bishops Rd, Upper Hill, PO Box 47429, Nairobi) Full-time courses of varying levels last 14 weeks and take up to five hours a day. More flexible is private tuition, which is available on a part-time schedule.

**Language Center Ltd** (Map p109; ☎ 020-3870610; www.language-cntr.com/welcome.shtml; Ndemi Close, off Ngong Rd, PO Box 40661, Nairobi) Another good centre offering a variety of study options ranging from private hourly lessons to daily group courses.

## CUSTOMS

There are strict laws about taking wildlife products out of Kenya. The export of products made from elephant, rhino and sea turtle are prohibited. The collection of coral is also not allowed. Ostrich eggs will also be confiscated unless you can prove you bought them from a certified ostrich farm. Always check to see what permits are required, especially for the export of any plants, insects and shells.

Usual regulations apply to items you can bring into the country – 50 cigars, 200 cigarettes, 250g of pipe tobacco, 1L of alcohol, 250mL of perfume and other personal items such as cameras, laptop computers and binoculars. Obscene publications are banned, which may extend to some lads' magazines.

You are allowed to take up to KSh100,000 out of the country.

## DANGERS & ANNOYANCES

While Kenya is a comparatively safe African destination, there are still plenty of pitfalls for the unwary or inexperienced traveller, from everyday irritations to more serious threats. A little street sense goes a long way here, and getting the latest local information is essential wherever you intend to travel.

## Banditry

Wars in Somalia, Sudan and Ethiopia have all had their effect on the stability and safety of northern and northeastern Kenya. AK-47s have been flowing into the country for many years, and the newspapers are filled with stories of hold-ups, shoot-outs, cattle rustling and general lawlessness. Bandits and poachers infiltrating from Somalia have made the northeast of the country particularly dangerous, and it has gotten worse in recent years due to a number of complicated factors.

In the northwest, the main problem is armed tribal wars and cattle rustling across the Sudanese border. There are Kenyan *shiftas* (bandits) too, of course, but cross-border problems seem to account for most of the trouble in the north of the country.

Despite all the headlines, tourists are rarely targeted, as much of the violence and robberies take place far from the main tourist routes. Security has also improved considerably in previously high-risk areas such as the Isiolo–Marsabit, Marsabit–Moyale and Malindi–Lamu routes. However, you should check the situation locally before taking these roads, or travelling between Garsen and Garissa or Thika.

The areas along the Sudanese and Ethiopian borders are very risky, so please inquire about the latest security situations if you're heading overland.

## Crime

Even the staunchest Kenyan patriot will readily admit that the country's biggest problem is crime. It ranges from petty snatch theft and mugging to violent armed robbery, carjacking and, of course, white-collar crime and corruption. As a visitor you needn't feel paranoid, but you should always keep your wits about you, particularly at night.

Perhaps the best advice for when you're walking around cities and towns is not to carry anything valuable with you – that includes jewellery, watches, cameras, bumbags, day-packs and money. Most hotels provide a safe or secure place for valuables, although you should also be cautious of the security at some budget places. Cheap digital watches and plastic sunglasses can be bought in Kenya for a few hundred shilling, and you won't miss them if they get taken.

While pickpocketing and bag-snatching are the most common crimes, armed muggings do occur in Nairobi and on the coast. However, they usually occur at night or in remote areas, so always take taxis after dark or along lonely dirt roads. Conversely, snatch-and-run crimes happen more in crowds. If you suddenly feel there are too many people around you, or think you are being followed, dive straight into a shop and ask for help.

Luggage is an obvious signal to criminals that you've just arrived. When arriving anywhere by bus, it's sensible to take a 'ship-to-shore' approach, getting a taxi directly from the bus station to your hotel. You'll have plenty of time to explore once you've safely stowed your belongings. Also, don't read this guidebook or look at maps on the street – it attracts unwanted attention.

In the event of a crime, you should report it to the police, but this can be a real procedure. You'll need to get a police report if you intend to make an insurance claim. In the event of a snatch theft, think twice before yelling 'Thief!' It's not unknown for people to administer summary justice on the spot, often with fatal results for the criminal.

Although crime is a fact of life in Kenya, it needn't spoil your trip. Above all, don't make the mistake of distrusting every Kenyan just because of a few bad apples – the honest souls you meet will far outnumber any crooks who cross your path.

## Money

With street crime a way of life in Nairobi, you should be doubly careful with your money. The safest policy is to leave all your valuables in the hotel safe and just carry enough cash for that day. If you do need to carry larger sums around, a money belt worn under your clothes is the safest option to guard against snatch thefts. However, be aware that muggers will usually be expecting this.

More ingenious tricks include tucking money into a length of elasticised bandage on your arm or leg, or creating a hidden pocket inside your trousers. If you don't actually need your credit card, travellers cheques or cash with you, they'll almost always be safer locked away in your hotel safe. Don't overlook the obvious and leave money lying around your hotel room in plain view. However well you get on with the staff, there will be some unlikely to resist a free month's wages if they've got a family to feed.

## Scams

At some point in Kenya you'll almost certainly come across people who play on the emotions and gullibility of foreigners. Nairobi is a particular hotspot, with 'friendly' approaches a daily, if not hourly, occurrence (see p103 for examples of favourite tricks). People with tales about being refugees or having sick relatives can sound very convincing, but they all end up asking for cash. It's OK to talk to these people if they're not actively hassling you, but you should always ignore any requests for money.

Be sceptical of strangers who claim to recognise you in the street, especially if they're vague about exactly where they know you from – it's unlikely that any ordinary person is going to be *this* excited by seeing you twice. Anyone who makes a big show of inviting you into the hospitality of their home also probably has ulterior motives. The usual trick is to bestow some kind of gift upon the delighted traveller, who is then emotionally blackmailed into reciprocating to the order of several hundred shillings.

Tourists with cars also face potential rip-offs. Don't trust people who gesticulate wildly to indicate that your front wheels are wobbling; if you stop, you'll probably be relieved of your valuables. Another trick is to splash oil on your wheels, then tell you the wheel bearings, differential or something else has failed, and direct you to a nearby garage where their friends will 'fix' the problem – for a substantial fee, of course.

## Terrorism

Kenya has twice been subject to terrorist attacks: in August 1998 the US embassy in Nairobi was bombed, and in November 2002 the Paradise Hotel, north of Mombasa, was car-bombed at the same time as a rocket attack on an Israeli jet. While these events caused a brief panic in the tourist industry, it now seems they were isolated incidents and that Western travellers to Kenya can expect to have a trouble-free time in the country. Visitors to the predominantly Muslim coast region should be aware that anti-American sentiment can run high here (see also the boxed text, p259), but actual violence against foreigners is highly unlikely.

## DISCOUNT CARDS

There's no uniformly accepted discount card scheme in Kenya, but a residence permit entitles you to claim the very favourable resident rates all over the country. Students are eligible for concessionary rates at museums and some other attractions on producing suitable ID – the international ISIC card should be widely recognised. Despite Kenyans' general respect for age and wisdom, there are no concessions or discounts for seniors.

## EMBASSIES & CONSULATES

Kenya has diplomatic representation in many countries. Where there is no Kenyan embassy or high commission, visas can be obtained from the British embassy or high commission.

It's important to understand what your own embassy – the embassy of the country of which you are a citizen – can and can't do to help you if you get into trouble. Generally speaking, it won't be much help in emergencies if the trouble you're in is remotely your own fault. Remember that you are bound by the laws of the country you are in. Your embassy will not be sympathetic if you end up in jail after committing a crime locally, even if such actions are legal in your own country.

In genuine emergencies you might get some assistance, but only if other channels have been exhausted. For example, if you need to get home urgently, a free ticket home is exceedingly unlikely – the embassy would expect you to have insurance. If all your money and documents are stolen, the embassy might assist with getting a new passport, but a loan for onward travel is out of the question.

### Kenyan Embassies & Consulates

**Australia** ( ☎ 02-62474788; www.kenya.asn.au; Manpower Bldg, 33-35 Ainslie Ave, Canberra, ACT 2601)
**Austria** ( ☎ 01-7123919; www.kenyamission-vienna .com; Neulinggasse 29/8, 1030 Vienna)
**Canada** ( ☎ 613-5631773; www.kenyahighcommission .ca; 415 Laurier Ave East, Ottawa, Ontario, K1N 6R4)
**Ethiopia** ( ☎ 01-610033; kengad@telecom.net.et; Fikre Miriam Rd, PO Box 3301, Addis Ababa)
**France** ( ☎ 01-56622525; www.kenyaembassyparis.org; 3 Rue Freycinet, 75116 Paris)
**Germany** ( ☎ 030-2592660; Markgrafenstr 63, 10969 Berlin)
**India** ( ☎ 011-26146537; www.kenyamission-delhi.com; 34 Paschimi Marg, Vasant Vihar, 10057 New Delhi)
**Israel** ( ☎ 03-5754633; 15 Rehov Abba Hillel Silver, Ramat Gan 52522, PO Box 52136, Tel Aviv)
**Italy** ( ☎ 396-8082714; www.embassyofkenya.it; Via Archmede 164, 00197, Rome)

**Japan** ( ☎ 03-37234006; www.kenyarep-jp.com; 3-24-3 Yakumo, Meguro-Ku, Tokyo 152-0023)
**Netherlands** ( ☎ 070-3504215; Niewe Parklaan 21, 2597, The Hague)
**South Africa** ( ☎ 012-3622249; 302 Brooks St, Menlo Park, 0081, Pretoria)
**Sudan** ( ☎ 0155-772801; www.kenembsud.org; Block 1, 516, West Giraif, Street 60, Khartoum)
**Tanzania** ( ☎ 022-2668285; www.kenyahighcomtz.org; 127 Mafinga St, Kinondoni, PO Box 5231, Dar es Salaam)
**Uganda** ( ☎ 041-258235; Plot No 41, Nakasero Rd, PO Box 5220, Kampala)
**UK** ( ☎ 020-76362371; www.kenyahighcommission.net; 45 Portland Pl, London W1B 1AS)
**USA** ( ☎ 202-3876101; www.kenyaembassy.com; 2249 R St NW, Washington DC 20008)

## Embassies & Consulates in Kenya

Many countries around the world maintain diplomatic missions in Kenya; a selection of these is listed here. Missions are located in Nairobi (area code ☎ 020) unless otherwise stated.

**Australia** High Commission (Map pp100-1; ☎ 4445034; www.kenya.embassy.gov.au; Riverside Dr, off Chiromo Rd)
**Austria** (Map pp104-5; ☎ 319076; City House, Wabera St)
**Canada** High Commission (off Map pp100-1; ☎ 3663000; www.kenya.gc.ca; Limuru Rd, Gigiri)
**Ethiopia** (Map pp100-1; ☎ 2732050; State House Rd)
**France** (Map pp104-5; ☎ 2778000; www.ambafrance-ke.org; Barclays Plaza Bldg, Loita St)
**Germany** (off Map pp100-1; ☎ 4262100; www.nairobi.diplo.de; 113 Riverside Dr)
**India** High Commission (Map pp104-5; ☎ 2222566; www.hcinairobi.co.ke; Jeevan Bharati Bldg, Harambee Ave)
**Ireland** Honorary Consulate (off Map pp109; ☎ 556647; www.dfa.ie; ICDL Rd, off Mombasa Rd)
**Israel** (Map pp100-1; ☎ 2722182; http://nairobi.mfa.gov.il; Bishops Rd)
**Italy** Embassy (Map pp104-5; ☎ 2247750; www.ambnairobi.esteri.it; International House, Mama Ngina St); Honorary Consulate (Map p260; ☎ 041-314705; Moi Ave, Mombasa)
**Japan** (Map pp100-1; ☎ 2898000; www.ke.emb-japan.go.jp; Mara Rd, Upper Hill)
**Netherlands** (off Map pp100-1; ☎ 4288000; http://kenia.nlembassy.org; Riverside Lane)
**South Africa** High Commission (off Map pp100-1; ☎ 2827100; Roshanmaer Pl, Lenana Rd)
**Spain** (Map pp104-5; ☎ 26568; International House, Mama Ngina St)
**Sudan** (off Map pp100-1; ☎ 575159; www.sudanembassynrb.org; Kabernet Rd, off Ngong Rd)
**Switzerland** (Map pp104-5; ☎ 2228735; International House, Mama Ngina St)

**Tanzania** High Commission (Map pp104-5; ☎ 331056; Reinsurance Plaza, Aga Khan Walk)
**Uganda** High Commission (off Map pp100-1; ☎ 4445420; Riverside Paddocks); Consular section (Map pp104-5; ☎ 311814; Uganda House, Kenyatta Ave)
**UK** High Commission (Map pp100-1; ☎ 2844000; www.britishhighcommission.gov.uk/kenya; Upper Hill Rd)
**USA** (off Map pp100-1; ☎ 3636000; http://nairobi.usembassy.gov; United Nations Ave)

## FESTIVALS & EVENTS

Major events happening around Kenya include the following:
**Maulid Festival** Falling in February or March for the next few years, this annual celebration of the Prophet Mohammed's birthday is a huge event in Lamu town, drawing hundreds of visitors (see p308).
**Rhino Charge** (www.rhinoark.org) Charity cross-country rally in aid of Rhino Ark, pitting mad motorists against crazy obstacles. Held in June.
**Tusker Safari Sevens** (www.safarisevens.com) International rugby tournament held every June near Nairobi (see p116).
**Kenya Music Festival** ( ☎ 020-2712964) The country's longest-running music festival (see p116), held over 10 days in August.
**Mombasa Carnival** November street festival, with music, dance and other events (see p263).
**East African Safari Rally** (www.eastafricansafarirally.com) Classic car rally more than 50 years old, covering Kenya, Tanzania and Uganda using only pre-1971 vehicles. Held in at the end of November.

## FOOD

You can eat well in Kenya, though outside the major towns variety isn't always a priority – see p51 for a full rundown. In general you should be able to snack for KSh10 to KSh100 on the street and fill up for under KSh500 in any cheap Kenyan cafeteria; an Indian or standard Western meal will cost around KSh500, a Chinese meal anything up to KSh1000, and a top-flight meal in a classy restaurant with wine and all the trimmings can easily exceed KSh2000 per person.

Eating listings in this book are ordered by price (see the inside front cover), and organised by type of cuisine where appropriate.

## GAY & LESBIAN TRAVELLERS

Even today negativity towards homosexuality is still widespread across much of Africa. Of course, people do live homosexual lifestyles covertly, particularly along the coast, but under Kenyan law this is still punishable by up to 14 years in prison. There are very few prosecutions under this law, but it's certainly better to be discreet – some local con artists do a good line in blackmail, picking up foreigners then threatening to expose them to the police.

Awareness is increasing in Kenya, but with the vast majority of churches and mosques maintaining a traditional, conservative position, homosexuality continues to be frowned upon: in 2005, 98% of respondents to a national survey said that same-sex marriage was against their personal and religious principles. Only a third declared themselves totally against homosexuality, but 96% said it was against their beliefs. However, polls of this kind and calls for public debate suggest that the issue may at least cease to be such a taboo subject over coming years.

According to the UN, sex between gay men accounts for only 5% to 10% of HIV/AIDS cases in Kenya. Despite the best efforts of international aid organisations, condoms are still as unpopular with Kenya's gay community as they are in heterosexual circles. Furthermore, due to the secret nature of most gay relationships, some men will also have unprotected sex with women who are unaware of their same-sex partners, increasing the risk factor exponentially.

Although there are probably more gays and lesbians in Nairobi, the coast is more tolerant of gay relationships, at least privately. There is now a Swahili word for gay, coined here: *msenge*. Lamu has long been considered a paradise getaway for gay couples, but it's not as tolerant as it once was. Memories still linger from 1999, when a couple was taken into protective custody in Lamu to shield them from an angry mob of locals opposed to their plans for a gay wedding.

The closest Kenya has to a 'scene' is the tolerant **Gypsy's Car** (see p129) in Westlands, Nairobi. The group **Gay Kenya** (www.gaykenya.com) also organises discreet gay events.

The **Purple Roofs travel directory** (www.purpleroofs .com/africa/kenyata.html) lists a number of gay or gay-friendly tour companies in Kenya and around the world that may be able to help you plan your trip.

For luxury all-inclusive packages, the travel agencies **Atlantis Events** (www.atlantisevents.com) and **David Tours** (www.davidtravel.com) can arrange anything from balloon safaris to luxurious coastal hideaways, all with a gay focus.

For information, **Behind the Mask** (www.mask .org.za) is an excellent website covering gay issues and news from across Africa.

## HOLIDAYS

All government offices and banks close on public holidays, and most shops and businesses will either close or run according to their usual Sunday opening hours. Popular events such as Madaraka Day (celebrating Kenya's attainment of self-rule) can cause a run on accommodation at the lower end of the budget scale, and transport may run less frequently or be more crowded than usual.

Muslim festivals are significant on the coast. Many eateries there close until after sundown during the Muslim fasting month of Ramadan, which runs for 30 days from 21 August 2009, 11 August 2010 and 1 August 2011. The Maulid Festival (see p329), marking the birth of the Prophet Mohammed, is also widely celebrated, especially on Lamu. This runs for five days from 9 March 2009, 26 February 2010 and 15 February 2011.

### Public Holidays

**1 January** New Year's Day
**March/April** Good Friday and Easter Monday
**1 May** Labour Day
**1 June** Madaraka Day
**10 October** Moi Day
**20 October** Kenyatta Day
**12 December** Independence Day
**25 December** Christmas Day
**26 December** Boxing Day

### School Holidays

Kenyan schools run on a three-term system much like the British education establishments on which they were originally modelled, though summer vacations tend to be shorter. Holidays usually fall in April (one month), August (one month) and December (five weeks). As few Kenyan families can afford to stay in tourist hotels, these holidays mostly have little impact on visitors, but more people will travel during these periods and popular public areas like the coastal beaches will be that bit more crowded.

## INSURANCE

Two words: get some! A travel-insurance policy to cover theft, loss and medical problems is a very sensible precaution. The policies handled by STA Travel and other student travel organisations are usually good value. Some policies offer lower and higher medical-expense options, but the higher ones are chiefly for countries such as the USA that have extremely high medical costs. Medical cover is the most vital element of any policy, but make sure you check the small print:

■ Some policies specifically exclude 'dangerous activities', which can even include motorcycling, scuba-diving and trekking. If such activities are on your agenda you'll need a fully comprehensive policy, which may be more expensive. Using a locally acquired motorcycle licence may not be valid under your policy.

■ You may prefer a policy that pays doctors or hospitals direct rather than you having to pay on the spot and claim later. If you have to claim later, make sure you keep all documentation.

■ Some policies ask you to call back (reverse charges) to a centre in your home country where an immediate assessment of your problem is made. Be aware that reverse-charge calls are only possible to certain countries from Kenya (see p336).

■ Check that the policy covers ambulances or an emergency flight home. If you have to stretch out on public transport you will need two seats and somebody has to pay for them!

If you are travelling through Africa for some time or heading to the more remote corners of Kenya, it may be worth signing up with either of the following services.

The **Flying Doctors Service** ( ☎ 020-602495, emergency 020-315454; www.amref.org) is part of the African Medical and Research Foundation (AMREF) and runs a 24-hour air-ambulance service out of Nairobi's Wilson Airport. It will get you from wherever you are to the nearest decent hospital (often Nairobi).

The private **AAR Health Services** (Map pp100-1; ☎ 020-2715319, emergency 020-271737; www.aarhealth .com; Fourth Ngong Ave, Nairobi) is a comprehensive medical network that covers Kenya, Tanzania and Uganda and offers a road and local service as well as emergency air evacuation to any suitable medical facility in East Africa.

Check with your insurance company that you can contact these services direct in the event of a serious emergency without having to confirm it with your company at home first. Worldwide travel insurance is available at www.lonelyplanet.com/travel_services. You can buy, extend and claim online anytime – even if you're already on the road.

## INTERNET ACCESS

Email is firmly established in Kenya, although connection speeds fluctuate wildly, even in Nairobi. Most towns have at least one internet cafe where you can surf freely and access webmail accounts, instant messenger programs and Skype. In Nairobi or Mombasa, you can pay as little as KSh1 per minute for access, but in rural areas and top-end hotels, the rate can be as high as KSh20 per minute.

With the increasing popularity of internet cafes, the national Posta network has stepped in and virtually revolutionised the industry by offering internet access at almost every main post office in the country. It's run on a prepay system – you pay KSh100 for a card with a PIN, which you can then use to log in at any branch as often as you like until the money runs out. While the service can't often compete with the flashier private offices in big cities like Nairobi and Mombasa, it's well worth investigating if you're further afield.

If you're travelling with a notebook or handheld computer, note that plenty of top-end hotels have internet connections or dataports in the rooms, and an increasing number are embracing the world of wi-fi. Establishments with internet access are identified in this book with a computer icon ( 🖳 ).

In any case, unless you've got important work to do, carrying a laptop around can be more trouble than it's worth in Kenya, and with street crime what it is we'd generally recommend leaving expensive bits of kit like this at home.

See also p16 for internet resources.

## LEGAL MATTERS

All drugs except *miraa* (a leafy shoot chewed as a stimulant) are illegal in Kenya. Marijuana (commonly called *bhang*) is widely available but illegal; possession carries a penalty of up to 10 years in prison. Dealers are common on the beaches north and south of Mombasa and frequently set up travellers for sting operations for real or phoney cops to extort money.

African prisons are unbelievably harsh places – don't take the risk! Note that *miraa* is illegal in Tanzania, so if you do develop a taste for the stuff in Kenya you should leave it behind when heading south.

**DIRECTORY**

Rape laws in Kenya currently only protect women, though there have been legislative attempts, such as the Sexual Offences Bill, which aims to make sexual assaults on both men and women criminal offences.

## MAPS

Bookshops, especially the larger ones in Nairobi, are the best places to look for maps in Kenya. The *Tourist Map of Kenya* gives good detail, as does the *Kenya Route Map;* both cost around KSh250. Marco Polo's 1:1,000,000 *Shell Euro Karte Kenya* and Geocenter's *Kenya* (1:1,000,000) are useful overview maps that are widely available in Europe. The scale and clarity are very good, but the locations of some minor features are inaccurate. For those planning a longer trip in southern and East Africa, Michelin's 1:4,000,000 map 955 (Africa Central and South) is very useful.

Macmillan publishes a series of maps to the wildlife parks and these are not bad value at around KSh250 each (three are available in Europe – *Amboseli, Masai Mara* and *Tsavo East & West*). Tourist Maps also publishes a national park series for roughly the same price. They might look a bit flimsy on detail, but they include the numbered junctions in the national parks.

The most detailed and thorough maps are published by the Survey of Kenya, but the majority are out of date and many are also out of print. The better bookshops in Nairobi usually have copies of the most important maps, including *Amboseli National Park* (SK 87), *Masai Mara Game Reserve* (SK 86), *Meru National Park* (SK 65), *Tsavo East National Park* (SK 82) and *Tsavo West National Park* (SK 78). It may be worth a visit to the **Kenya Institute of Surveying & Mapping** ( ☎ 020-861486; http://kism.iconnect.co.ke; Thika Rd, Nairobi), but this can take all day and there's no guarantee it will have any more stock than the bookshops.

## MONEY

The unit of currency is the Kenyan shilling (KSh), which is made up of 100 cents. Notes in circulation are KSh1000, 500, 200, 100, 50 and 20, and there are also new coins of KSh40, 20, 10, five and one in circulation. Old coins are much bigger and heavier, and come in denominations of KSh5 (seven-sided) and KSh1. The old 50¢, 10¢ and 5¢ coins are now pretty rare, as most prices

---

**LEGAL AGE**

- Age of majority –18 years
- Voting age – 18 years
- Age of consent (heterosexual) – 16 years
- Age of criminal responsibility – 8 years
- Drinking age – 18 years

---

are whole-shilling amounts. Note that most public telephones accept only new coins. Locally, the shilling is commonly known as a 'bob', after the old English term for a one-shilling coin.

The shilling has been relatively stable over the last few years, maintaining fairly constant rates against a falling US dollar and a strong British pound. Both these currencies are easy to change throughout the country, as is the euro, which is rapidly replacing the dollar as the currency quoted for hotel prices on the coast. Cash is easy and quick to exchange at banks and foreign exchange bureaus, but carries a higher risk of theft. On the other hand, travellers cheques are replaceable, but are increasingly less widely accepted and often carry high commission charges.

See p13 for information on costs, and the Quick Reference (inside cover) for exchange rates.

### ATMs

Virtually all banks in Kenya now have ATMs at most branches, but their usefulness to travellers varies widely. Barclays Bank has easily the most reliable machines for international withdrawals, with a large network of ATMs covering most major Kenyan towns. They support MasterCard, Visa, Plus and Cirrus international networks.

Standard Chartered and Kenya Commercial Bank ATMs also accept Visa but not the other major providers, and are more likely to decline transactions. Whichever bank you use, the international data link still goes down occasionally, so don't rely on being able to withdraw money whenever you need it.

### Black Market

With deregulation, the black market has almost vanished, and the handful of money-changers who still wander the streets offering 'good rates' are usually involved in scams. The exception is at land border crossings, where moneychangers are often the only option. Most offer reasonable rates, although you should be careful not to get short-changed or scammed during any transaction.

## Cash

While most major currencies are accepted in Nairobi and Mombasa, once away from these two centres you'll run into problems with currencies other than US dollars, pounds sterling and euros. Away from the coast, you may even struggle to change euros. Play it safe and carry US dollars – it makes life much simpler.

## Credit Cards

Credit cards are becoming increasingly popular, with old fraud-friendly, fully manual swipe machines slowly being replaced by electronic systems. While there's less chance of someone making extra copies of chits this way, the connections fail with tedious regularity. Visa and MasterCard are now widely accepted, but it would be prudent to stick to up-market hotels, restaurants and shopping centres to use them.

## Moneychangers

The best places to change money are foreign exchange or 'forex' bureaus, which can be found everywhere and usually don't charge commission. The rates for the main bureaus in Nairobi are published in the *Daily Nation* newspaper. Watch out for differing small bill (US$10) and large bill (US$100) rates; the larger bills usually get the better rates.

Banks also change money, but they charge large commissions and there's a fee per travellers cheque, so you're better off carrying larger denominations. The rates for travellers cheques may be better than at the bureaus, and you'll have the bonus of being able to put your money away in the secure setting of the bank foyer. American Express (Amex) has offices in Mombasa and Nairobi, where you can buy and sell Amex travellers cheques.

### INTERNATIONAL TRANSFERS

Postbank, a branch of the Kenyan Post Office, is the regional agent for Western Union, the global money-transfer company. Using its service is an easy way (if the phones are working) of receiving money in Kenya. Handily, the sender pays all the charges and there's a Postbank in most towns, often in the post office or close by. Senders should contact **Western Union** (USA ☎ 1800-3256000; Australia ☎ 1800-501500; New Zealand ☎ 0800-270000; UK ☎ 0800-833833; www.westernunion.com) to find out the location of their nearest agency.

## Tipping

Tipping is not common practice among Kenyans, but there's no harm in rounding up the bill by a few shillings if you're pleased with the service in a cheap restaurant. In tourist-oriented businesses a service charge of 10% is often added to the bill along with the 16% VAT and 2% catering levy. Most tourist guides and all safari drivers and cooks will expect some kind of gratuity at the end of your tour or trip – see p67. As fares are negotiated in advance, taxi drivers do not need to be tipped unless they provide you with exceptional service.

## Travellers Cheques

Travellers cheques are accepted if they're in US dollars, British pounds or euros. High commission charges are common, and bureaus that charge no commission will often give a rate substantially below the cash rate for cheques. Charges vary widely, from 1% to 3% per transaction, to flat fees of up to US$15.

# PHOTOGRAPHY

Photographing people remains a sensitive issue in Kenya – it is advisable to ask permission first. Some ethnic groups including the Maasai request money for you to take their photo.

You should never get your camera out at border crossings or near government or army buildings – even bridges can sometimes be classed as sensitive areas.

Photography equipment is best purchased at electronics stores in Nairobi or Mombasa, but items are expensive and sometimes of questionable quality. CDs are best burnt at internet cafes.

If you don't have the inclination or resources to buy expensive equipment but do know a bit about photography, it is possible to hire SLR cameras and lenses in Nairobi (see p99).

## Taking Pictures

As the natural light in Kenya can be extremely strong, morning and evening are the best times to take photos. A plain UV filter can also be a good idea to take the harshness out of daylight pictures.

For serious wildlife photography an SLR camera that can take long focal length lenses is necessary. Zoom lenses are best for wildlife photography as it's easier to frame your shot for the best composition. Telephoto (fixed focal length) lenses give better results than zoom lenses, but you're limited by having to carry a separate lens for every focal length.

When using long lenses you'll find that a tripod can be extremely useful. Within the confined space of the hatch of a safari minibus, you may be better off with a folding miniature tripod, which you can then rest on the roof. Remember to ask your driver to switch off the engine to avoid vibrations affecting your photo.

A decent bag is essential to protect your gear from the elements and the rough roads – safari dust gets everywhere, particularly in parks like Samburu and Tsavo. It's also vital to make sure that your travel insurance policy covers your camera gear.

## POST

The Kenyan postal system is run by the government Postal Corporation of Kenya, now rebranded as the dynamic-sounding **Posta** (www.posta.co.ke). Letters sent from Kenya rarely go astray but can take up to two weeks to reach Australia or the USA. Incoming letters to Kenya take anywhere from four days to a week to reach the poste-restante service in Nairobi.

If sent by surface mail, parcels take three to six months to reach Europe, while airmail parcels take around a week. Most things arrive eventually, although there is still a problem with theft within the system. Curios, clothes and textiles will be OK, but if your parcel contains anything of obvious value, send it by courier. Posta has its own courier service, EMS, which is considerably cheaper than the big international courier companies. The best place to send parcels from is the main post office in Nairobi (see p99).

## SENIOR TRAVELLERS

Although there are no tour companies set up specifically for senior travellers, the more expensive tours cater well to seniors' requests and requirements. Before you book, ask the operator what they can do to help

make your trip possible and comfortable. The luxury-tour and safari business is well used to older travellers, and wildlife drives and other safari activities are great for older people. One company with a good reputation for catering to seniors is **Eastern & Southern Safaris** (Map pp104-5; ☎ 020-2242828; www.essafari .co.ke; Finance House, Loita St, PO Box 43332, Nairobi).

You may be able to find other senior-friendly companies on the website of **Wired Seniors** (www.wiredseniors.com), which has travel links from around the world. It's also worth contacting **Holiday Care** (☎ 0845-1249971; www .holidaycare.org.uk), a UK organisation providing advice for travellers of all ages with mobility or health problems.

## SHOPPING

Kenya is an excellent place for souvenirs, although much of the cheap stuff is mass-produced for the tourist trade. Look carefully at what's available before parting with your money. It is illegal to export some wildlife products (see p326).

Nairobi and Mombasa are the main souvenir centres but many of the items come from other regions, so it's often possible to pick them up where they are made. Many top-end hotels have their own stalls or stores and there are dozens of souvenir shops at the airport, but prices are extremely high compared with the rest of the country, and it's better (and more fun) to spend some time shopping around.

It's certainly possible to buy something that will look good in your living room without spending a fortune, but these days something of genuine quality and artistry is going to cost real money. This particularly applies to *makonde* carvings, jewellery and paintings – in some cases you can be talking about thousands of dollars for a single piece.

Posting things of small value home is usually straightforward and secure (for details, see left).

### Bargaining

Haggling is a way of life in Kenya, and prices for everything from taxi fares to hotel rooms may be negotiable. While quibbling over the price of a few bananas is probably going too far, souvenir shopping is one area where you should hold out for the best price. Do plenty of prior research, so you have a clear idea of what an item should cost and how much you're willing to pay before you set foot in the shop you want to buy from. Looking in the more expensive fixed-price outlets is a good way of checking what the real quality items should look like.

When it comes to negotiating, never agree to the first amount offered, but try not to pitch your own first offer too low – this will just make you look clueless about the item's real value, and force you to come up in larger increments than they come down. Once you've reached your desired price, stick to your guns unless they really don't seem to be budging. Remember, they will never sell for a loss, and you can always walk away rather than overpay. Above all, keep it light: Kenyans bargaining among themselves may look like they're arguing, but as a visitor it's much better to stay friendly, avoid antagonism and feel good about the process whatever the outcome.

Local people are occasionally willing to swap their handicrafts for Western clothing, shoes and the like, but it's fair to say that most Kenyans need money more than an old T-shirt. It's worth keeping in mind that paying a fair price can make a real difference to the lives of villagers whose only income comes from selling goods to tourists.

## Baskets

*Kiondos* (sisal baskets) are a very popular Kenyan souvenir. They come in a variety of sizes, colours and styles with many different straps and clasps. Expect to pay a few dollars for a basic basket, and up to US$20 for a large one with leather trim. Some of the finer baskets have baobab bark woven into them, which bumps up the price. Reed baskets, widely used as shopping bags, cost less than KSh50.

## Fabrics & Batik

*Kangas* and *kikois* are the local sarongs and serve many purposes. *Kangas* are colourful prints on thin cotton that are sold in pairs, one to wrap around your waist and one to carry a baby on your back. Each bears a Swahili proverb. Biashara St in Mombasa is the *kanga* centre in Kenya, and you'll pay upwards of KSh500 for a pair, depending on quality. *Kikois,* traditionally worn by men, are made with thicker, striped cotton, and have more basic patterns and brighter colours. They are originally from Lamu, which remains the best place to buy them – prices start at around KSh500 each, more for the thicker Somali fabrics.

Batik cloth is another good buy and there's a tremendous range, but the better prints are not cheap. The tradition was imported from elsewhere. You can expect to pay KSh1000 and upwards for batiks on cotton, and much, much more for batiks on pure silk.

## Jewellery

Most jewellery on sale in Kenya is of tribal origin, although very little is the genuine article. The colourful and distinctive Maasai beaded jewellery is the most striking and the most popular. Necklaces, bangles and wristlets are widely available and beadwork is used on all sorts of knick-knacks, from hair-slides to wallets. Prices are high, but there's lots of work involved in making them. None of the 'elephant hair' bracelets sold by hawkers in Nairobi are the real thing – most are simply plastic wire or reed grass covered in boot polish.

## Soapstone

Easily carved soapstone is used to make popular chess sets, ashtrays or even abstract organic-looking sculptures. Kisumu on Lake Victoria is the best place to buy, although soapstone souvenirs are sold and produced across the country, most notably in Kisii. The only problem is that soapstone is quite fragile and heavy to carry around, so it's probably best to stock up on these souvenirs towards the end of your trip.

## Tribal Art

Traditional tribal art is very popular. Spears are particularly sought-after, and come apart into several sections, making them easy to transport. But, like the painted leather shields, most are mass-produced for the tourist market. Turkana wrist knives and Maasai knives forged from car shock absorbers are also high-kudos souvenirs.

Decorated Maasai calabashes, traditionally used to store *mursik,* a type of drink (see p51), are eye-catching but tend to pong a bit. All sorts of masks are available, although few are used in rituals today. The three-legged African stool is another very popular souvenir, and *shukas* (Maasai blankets) and shoes made from old car tyres are cheap, unusual souvenirs.

## Woodcarvings

These are easily the most popular Kenyan souvenir – a painted wooden giraffe is an instant lonelyplanet.com

marker of a trip to East Africa! Much of the stuff on offer is of dubious taste, but there is some very fine work available.

The most famous woodcarvings found here are the *makonde*-style effigies (made by the Akamba people from around the Tanzanian border), which are traditionally carved from ebony, a very black, heavy wood. They often feature wildlife, towers of thin figures and slender Maasai figurines. However, be aware that ebony is a threatened wood (see p63).

If you buy from one of the many nonprofit handicraft cooperatives around the country rather than souvenir shops, the money goes directly to the artisans. Heavy bargaining is necessary if you buy from market stalls or tourist shops. You can pay anything from KSh250 up to hundreds of dollars for a large and intricate piece.

## SOLO TRAVELLERS

The issues facing solo travellers in Kenya are essentially the same as anywhere else in the world. The biggest drawbacks are not having anyone to watch your back or your bags on the road, and the price of safaris and organised activities, which generally means you have to join a group to make any kind of trip affordable. Advantages include freedom of movement (just try flagging down a matatu when there are eight of you), and a whole different level of contact with local people.

On the whole, men will find travelling alone easier than women, as the level of day-to-day harassment is generally lower for males, especially on the coast. However, lone female travellers are sometimes 'adopted' by local women in a way that seldom happens to men.

## TELEPHONE

The Kenyan fixed-line phone system, run by **Telkom Kenya** (www.telkom.co.ke), is more or less functional, but has been overtaken by the massive popularity of prepaid mobile phones – there are now more than 10 times the number of subscribers than in 2000.

International call rates from Kenya are relatively expensive, though you can save serious cash by using voice over IP programs like Skype. Operator-assisted calls are charged at the standard peak rate, but are subject to a three-minute minimum. You can always dial direct using a phonecard. All public phones should be able to receive incoming calls (the number is usually scrawled in the booth somewhere).

Calls made through a hotel operator from your room will cost an extra 25% to 50% so check before making a call.

Reverse-charge (collect) calls are possible, but only to countries that have set up free direct-dial numbers allowing you to reach the international operator in the country you are calling. Currently these countries include the **UK** ( ☎ 0800-220441), the **USA** ( ☎ 0800-111, 0800-1112), **Canada** ( ☎ 0800-220114, 0800-220115), **New Zealand** ( ☎ 0800-220641) and **Switzerland** ( ☎ 0800-220411).

The minimum charge for a local call from a public phone is KSh5 for around a minute and a half, while long-distance rates vary depending on the distance. When making a local call from a public phone, make sure you put a coin into the slot first. Calls to Tanzania and Uganda are priced as long-distance calls, not international.

The international dialling code for Kenya is ☎ 254.

### Mobile Phones

More than two-thirds of all calls in Kenya are now made on mobile phones, and coverage is good in all but the furthest rural areas. Kenya uses the GSM 900 system, which is compatible with Europe and Australia but not with the North American GSM 1900 system. If you have a GSM phone, check with your service provider about using it in Kenya, and beware of high roaming charges. Remember that you will generally be charged for receiving calls abroad as well as for making them.

Alternatively, if your phone isn't locked into a network, you can pick up a prepaid starter pack from one of the Kenyan mobile-phone companies – the main players are **Safaricom** (www.safaricom.co.ke) and **Celtel** (www.ke.celtel.com). A SIM card costs about KSh100, and you can then buy top-up 'scratchcards' from shops and booths across the country. Cards come in denominations of KSh100 to KSh2000; an international SMS costs around KSh10, and voice charges vary according to tariff, time and destination of call.

You can easily buy a handset anywhere in Kenya, generally unlocked and with SIM card. Prices start around KSh2500 for a very basic model.

### Phonecards

With Telkom Kenya phonecards, any phone can be used for prepaid calls – you just have to dial the **access number** ( ☎ 0844) and enter in the number and passcode on the card. There are booths selling the cards all over the country. Cards come in denominations of KSh200, KSh500, KSh1000 and KSh2000, and call charges are slightly more expensive than for standard lines.

## TIME
Time in Kenya is GMT/UTC plus three hours year-round. You should also be aware of the concept of 'Swahili time', which perversely is six hours out of kilter with the rest of the world. Noon and midnight are 6 o'clock *(saa sita)* Swahili time, and 7am and 7pm are 1 o'clock *(saa moja)*. Just add or subtract six hours from whatever time you are told; Swahili doesn't distinguish between am and pm. You don't come across this often unless you speak Swahili, but you still need to be prepared for it.

## TOILETS
These vary from pits (quite literally) to full-flush, luxury conveniences that can spring up in the most unlikely places. Nearly all hotels sport flushable sit-down toilets, but seats are a rare commodity – either they're a prized souvenir for trophy hunters or there's a vast stockpile of lost lids somewhere… Public toilets in towns are almost equally rare, but there are a few slightly less-than-emetic pay conveniences in Nairobi if you've only got a penny to spend.

In the more up-market bush camps you'll be confronted with a long drop covered with some sort of seating arrangement. Things are less pleasant when camping in the wildlife parks. Squatting on crumbling concrete is common. When trekking it's good practice to take soiled toilet paper out of the park with you (consider carrying sealable bags for this purpose).

## TOURIST INFORMATION
### Local Tourist Offices
Considering the extent to which the country relies on tourism, it's incredible to think that, at the time of writing, there was still no tourist office in Nairobi. There are a handful of information offices elsewhere in the country, ranging from helpful private concerns to underfunded government offices; most can at least provide basic maps of the town and brochures on local businesses and attractions.

**Diani Beach i-point** (Map p272; ☎ 040-3202234; Barclays Centre)
**Lamu** (Map p304; ☎ 042-633449; off Kenyatta Rd)
**Malindi** (Map p297; ☎ 042-20689; Malindi Centre, Lamu Rd)
**Mombasa & Coast Tourist Office** (Map p260; ☎ 041-225428; Moi Ave)

### Tourist Offices Abroad
The Ministry of Tourism maintains a number of overseas offices, including in the UK, USA, Canada and Italy. Most only provide information by telephone, post or email. Visit the ministry website (www.tourism .go.ke) for details.

## TRAVELLERS WITH DISABILITIES
Travelling in Kenya is not easy for physically disabled people, but it's not impossible. Very few tourist companies and facilities are geared up for disabled travellers, and those that are tend to be restricted to the expensive hotels and lodges. However, Kenyans are generally very accommodating and willing to offer whatever assistance they can. Visually or hearing-impaired travellers, though, will find it very hard to get by without an able-bodied companion.

In Nairobi, only the ex-London taxi cabs are spacious enough to accommodate a wheelchair, but many safari companies are accustomed to taking disabled people out on safari. The travel agency **Travel Scene Services** ( ☎ 020-3871530; www.travelsceneafrica.com) has lots of experience with disabled travellers.

Many of the top-end beach resorts on the coast have facilities for the disabled, whether it's a few token ramps or fully equipped rooms with handrails and bathtubs. In Amboseli National Park, **Ol Tukai Lodge** ( ☎ Nairobi 020-4445514; www.oltukailodge.com) has two disabled-friendly cottages.

For further information about disabled travel contact the following:
**Access-Able Travel Source** ( ☎ 303-2322979; www .access-able.com; PO Box 1796, Wheatridge CO, USA)
**Association for the Physically Disabled of Kenya** (APDK; Map pp104-5; ☎ 020-224443; www.apdk.org; APDK House, Lagos Rd, PO Box 46747, Nairobi) This group in Kenya may also be able to help disabled visitors.
**Holiday Care** ( ☎ 0845-1249971, minicom 0845-1249976, outside the UK 208-760072; www.holidaycare .org.uk; Sunley House, 4 Bedford Park, Croydon, Surrey CR0 2AP, UK) Advice for disabled and less-mobile senior travellers.

**DIRECTORY**

# VISAS

Visas are now required by almost all visitors to Kenya, including Europeans, Australians, New Zealanders, Americans and Canadians, although citizens from a few smaller Commonwealth countries are exempt. Visas (US$50/€40/UK£30) are valid for three months from the date of entry and can be obtained on arrival at Jomo Kenyatta International Airport in Nairobi. Tourist visas can be extended for a further three-month period – see below.

It's also possible to get visas from Kenyan diplomatic missions overseas, but you should apply well in advance, especially if you're doing it by mail. Visas are usually valid for entry within three months of the date of issue. Applications for Kenyan visas are simple and straightforward in Tanzania and Uganda, and payment is accepted in local currency. Visas can also be issued on arrival at the land borders with Uganda and Tanzania.

Under the East African partnership system, visiting Tanzania or Uganda and returning to Kenya does not invalidate a single-entry Kenyan visa, so there's no need to get a multiple-entry visa unless you plan to go further afield. The same applies to single-entry Tanzanian and Ugandan visas, though you do still need a separate visa for each country you plan to visit. Always check the latest entry requirements with embassies before travel.

It's always best to smarten up a bit if you're arriving by air; requests for evidence of 'sufficient funds' are usually linked to snap judgments about your appearance. If it's fairly obvious that you aren't intending to stay and work, you'll generally be given the benefit of the doubt.

## Visa Extensions

Visas can be renewed at immigration offices during normal office hours, and extensions are usually issued on a same-day basis. Staff at the immigration offices are generally friendly and helpful, but the process takes a while. You'll need two passport photos for a three-month extension, and prices tend to vary widely depending on the office and the whims of the immigration officials. You also need to fill out a form registering as an alien if you're going to be staying more than 90 days. Immigration offices are only open Monday to Friday; note that the smaller offices may sometimes refer travellers back to Nairobi or Mombasa for visa extensions.

Local immigration offices include the following:

**Kisumu** (Map p176; 1st fl, Reinsurance Plaza, cnr Jomo Kenyatta Hwy & Oginga Odinga Rd)
**Lamu** (Map p304; ☎ 042-633032; off Kenyatta Rd) Travellers are sometimes referred to Mombasa.
**Malindi** (Map p297; ☎ 042-20149; Mama Ngina Rd)
**Mombasa** (Map p256; ☎ 041-311745; Uhuru ni Kari Bldg, Mama Ngina Dr)
**Nairobi** (Map pp104-5; ☎ 020-222022; Nyayo House, cnr Kenyatta Ave & Uhuru Hwy; ⏲ 8.30am-12.30pm & 2-3.30pm Mon-Fri)

## Visas for Onward Travel

Since Nairobi is a common gateway city to East Africa and the city centre is easy to get around, many travellers spend some time here picking up visas for other countries that they intend to visit. If you are going to do this you need to plan ahead and call the embassy to confirm the hours that visa applications are received (these change frequently in Nairobi). Most embassies will want you to pay visa fees in US dollars (see p329 for contact details).

Just because a country has an embassy or consulate here, it doesn't necessarily mean you can get that country's visa. The borders with Somalia and Sudan are both closed, so you'll have to go to Addis Ababa in Ethiopia if you want a Sudanese visa, and Somali visas are unlikely to be available for the foreseeable future.

For Ethiopia, Tanzania and Uganda, three-month visas are readily available in Nairobi and cost US$50 for most nationalities. Two passport photos are required for applications and visas can usually be issued the same day.

# WOMEN TRAVELLERS

Within Kenyan society, women are poorly represented in positions of power, and the few high-profile women in politics run the same risks of violence as their male counterparts. However, in their day-to-day lives, Kenyans are generally respectful towards women, although solo women in bars will attract a lot of interest from would-be suitors. Most are just having a go and will give up if you tell them you aren't interested.

The only place you are likely to have problems is at the beach resorts on the coast, where women may be approached by male prostitutes as well as local aspiring Romeos. It's

---

**STREET KIDS**

Nairobi in particular has huge problems with street children, many of whom are AIDS orphans, who trail foreigners around asking for food or change. It's up to you whether you give, but if you do the word will go around and you won't get a moment's peace. It's also debatable how much your donations will help as the older boys operate like a minima-fia, extorting money from the younger kids. If you want to help out, money might be better donated to a charity, such as the **Consortium for Street Children** (www.street children.org.uk), which works to improve conditions for these children.

---

always best to cover your legs and shoulders when away from the beach so as not to offend local sensibilities.

With the upsurge in crime in Nairobi and along the coast, women should avoid walking around at night. The ugly fact is that while men are likely just to be robbed without violence, rape is a real risk for women. Lone night walks along the beach or through quiet city streets are a recipe for disaster, and criminals usually work in gangs, so take a taxi, even if you're in a group.

Regrettably, black women in the company of white men are often assumed to be prostitutes, and can face all kinds of discrimination from hotels and security guards as well as approaches from Kenyan hustlers offering to help rip off the white 'customer'. Again, the worst of this can be avoided by taking taxis between hotels and restaurants etc.

## WORK

It's difficult, although by no means impossible, for foreigners to find jobs. The most likely areas in which employment might be found are in the safari business, teaching, advertising and journalism. Except for teaching, it's unlikely you'll see jobs advertised, and the only way you'll find out about them is to spend a lot of time with resident expats. As in most countries, the rule is that if a local can be found to do the job, there's no need to hire a foreigner.

The most fruitful area in which to look for work, assuming that you have the relevant skills, is the 'disaster industry'. Nairobi is awash with UN and other aid agencies servicing the famines in Somalia and southern Sudan and the refugee camps along the Kenyan border with those countries. Keep in mind that the work is tough and often dangerous, and pay is usually very low.

Work permits and resident visas are not easy to arrange. A prospective employer may be able to sort the necessary paperwork for you, but otherwise you'll find yourself spending a lot of time and money at the **immigration office** (Map pp104-5; ☎ 020-222022; Nyayo House, cnr Kenyatta Ave & Uhuru Hwy, Nairobi) in Nairobi.

## VOLUNTEERING

There are quite a large number of volunteers in Kenya, which is certainly a cause for celebration as 'voluntourism' is a great way to reduce the ecological footprint of your trip. It's also an amazing forum for self-exploration, especially if you touch a few lives and make friends along the way.

This section provides a list of some of the volunteer programs covered in this book, though our coverage is not exhaustive. These selected programs should give you a head start in finding a position that is perfectly suited to your individual needs and goals.

Keep in mind that there is no such thing as a perfect volunteer placement. Generally speaking, you will get as much out of a program as you are willing to put into it; the vast majority of volunteers in Kenya walk away all the better for the experience.

**Taita Discovery Centre** ( ☎ 020-331191; www.sa vannahcamps.com) is a conservation-based offshoot of Savannah Camps & Lodges. The purpose-built conservation research centre covers 68,000 hectares of the Taita and Rukinga ranches near Tsavo West National Park, forming a vital migration corridor for elephants and other animals between Tsavo and Mt Kilimanjaro. Courses on a huge range of conservation topics are run here along with hands-on projects in conservation and the local community.

Another good organisation is **Kenya Youth Voluntary Development Projects** (Map pp104-5; ☎ 020-225379; kvdakenya@yahoo.com; Gilfillan House, Kenyatta Ave, PO Box 48902, Nairobi), which runs a variety of three- to four-week projects, including road building, health education and clinic construction.

**Inter-Community Development Involvement** (ICODEI; ☎ 0337-30017; www.volunteerkenya.org; Reverend

Reuben Lubanga, PO Box 459, Bungoma), run in conjunction with the University of Indiana in the USA, offers a number of longer community projects focusing on health issues such as AIDS awareness, agriculture and conservation.

Other community-building and environmental projects are run by **Camps International** (p274), offering one- to three-month volunteer vacations; **Watamu Turtle Watch** (p291), which protects the marine turtles that come to Watamu to lay eggs on the beach; **A Rocha** (p292), which operates the Mwamba Field Study Centre at Watamu Beach; and **Arabuko Sokoke Schools & Ecotourism Scheme** (ASSETS; p292), running programs (including Mida Ecocamp) near the Arabuko Sokoke Forest and Mida Creek.

Foreign organisations can also assist with volunteer work. Reliable bodies include the following:

**Coordinating Committee for International Voluntary Service** (www.unesco.org/ccivs)
**Global Volunteers** (www.globalvolunteers.org)
**Voluntary Service Overseas** (VSO; ☎ 020-8780 2266; www.vsointernational.org; 317 Putney Bridge Rd, London SW15 2PN) Placements for professionals.
**Volunteer Work Information Service** (www.workingabroad.com)

# Transport

## CONTENTS

# GETTING THERE & AWAY

Unless you are travelling overland from Southern Africa or Egypt, flying is by far the most convenient way to get to Kenya. Nairobi is a major African hub and flights between Kenya and the rest of Africa are common and relatively cheap. It's important to note that flight availability and prices are highly seasonal. Conveniently for Europeans, the cheapest fares usually coincide with the European summer holidays, from June to September.

It's also worth checking out cheap charter flights to Mombasa from Europe, although these will probably be part of a package deal to a hotel resort on the coast. Prices are often absurdly cheap and there's no obligation to stay at the resort you're booked into.

A few adventurous souls with their own vehicles still travel overland to Kenya from Europe, but most routes pass through several war zones and should only be considered after serious planning and preparation.

Flights, tours and rail tickets can be booked online at www.lonelyplanet.com /travel_services.

## ENTERING THE COUNTRY

Entering Kenya is generally pleasingly straightforward, particularly at the interna-

**THINGS CHANGE...**

The information in this chapter is particularly vulnerable to change. Check directly with the airline or a travel agent to make sure you understand how a fare (and ticket you may buy) works and be aware of the security requirements for international travel. Shop carefully. The details given in this chapter should be regarded as pointers and are not a substitute for your own careful, up-to-date research.

tional airports, which are no different from most Western terminals. Single-entry visas are typically available on arrival for most nationalities (passport photos are not required), and cost US$50/€40/£30/Swiss Fr79. With that said, you should contact your nearest Kenyan diplomatic office to get the most up-to-date information.

### Passport

There are no restrictions on which nationalities can enter Kenya. Citizens of Tanzania, Uganda, Scandinavia, the Republic of Ireland, Rwanda, Sudan and certain Commonwealth countries did not require visas at time of writing; see p338 and check the latest situation before travelling.

## AIR
### Airports & Airlines

Most international flights to and from Nairobi are handled by **Jomo Kenyatta International Airport** (NBO; ☎ 020-825400; www.kenyaairports .co.ke), 15km southeast of the city. By African standards, it's a pretty well-organised place, with two international terminals, a smaller domestic terminal and an incredible number of shops offering duty-free and expensive souvenirs, snacks and internet access. You can walk easily between the terminals.

Some flights between Nairobi and Kilimanjaro International Airport or Mwanza in Tanzania, as well as many domestic flights, use **Wilson Airport** (WIL; ☎ 020-603260), which is about 6km south of the city centre on Langata Rd. The other arrival point in the country is

**Moi International Airport** (MBA; ☎ 041-433211) in Mombasa, 9km west of the centre, but apart from flights to Zanzibar, this is mainly used by charter airlines and domestic flights.

Kenya Airways is the main national carrier, and has a generally good safety record, with just one fatal incident since 1977.

The following are airlines flying to and from Kenya, with offices in Nairobi except where otherwise indicated:

**African Express Airways** (3P; ☎ 020-824333)
**Air India** (AI; Map pp104-5; ☎ 020-340925; www .airindia.com)
**Air Madagascar** (MD; ☎ 020-225286; www.airmada gascar.mg)
**Air Malawi** (QM; ☎ 020-240965; www.airmalawi.com)
**Air Mauritius** (MK; ☎ 020-229166; www.air mauritius.com)
**Air Zimbabwe** (UM; ☎ 020-339522; www.airzim.co.zw)
**Airkenya** (QP; ☎ 020-605745; www.airkenya.com)
**British Airways** (BA; Map pp104-5; ☎ 020-244430; www.british-airways.com)
**Daallo Airlines** (D3; ☎ 020-317318; www.daallo.com)
**Egypt Air** (MS; ☎ 020-226821; www.egyptair.com.eg)
**Emirates** (EK; Map pp104-5; ☎ 020-211187; www.emirates.com)
**Ethiopian Airlines** (ET; Map pp104-5; ☎ 020-330837; www.ethiopianairlines.com)
**Gulf Air** (GF; ☎ 020-241123; www.gulfairco.com)
**Jetlink Express** (J0; ☎ 020-244285; www.jetlink.co.ke)
**Kenya Airways** (KQ; Map pp104-5; ☎ 020-3274100; www.kenya-airways.com)
**KLM** (KL; Map pp104-5; ☎ 020-3274747; www.klm.com)
**Oman Air** (WY; Map p260; ☎ 041-221444; www .oman-air.com)
**Precision Air** (PW; ☎ 020-602561; www.precision airtz.com)
**Qatar Airways** (QR; www.qatarairways.com)
**Rwandair** (WB; ☎ 0733-740703; www.rwandair.com)
**Safarilink Aviation** ( ☎ 020-600777; www.safarilink .co.ke) Kilimanjaro only.
**SN Brussels Airlines** (SN; ☎ 020-4443070; www .flysn.com)
**South African Airways** (SA; ☎ 020-229663; www .flysaa.com)
**Swiss International Airlines** (SR; ☎ 020-3744045; www.swiss.com)

## Tickets

If you enter Nairobi with no onward or return ticket you may incur the wrath of immigration, and be forced to buy one on the spot – an expensive exercise. Note that you can't get a standby flight to Kenya unless you're an airline employee.

The airport departure tax for international flights is included in the cost of your plane ticket.

### INTERCONTINENTAL (RTW) TICKETS

Discount round-the-world (RTW) tickets are a tempting option if you want to include Kenya on a longer journey, but the most common African stop is Johannesburg – if you're coming from Europe any ticket that includes Nairobi is usually much more expensive. If you're coming from Australia or New Zealand the difference may not be so great, but it's still often cheaper to buy an RTW or Australia–Europe ticket, stopover in Johannesburg, and then buy a ticket on to Nairobi from there. Either way you may have to go through several travel agents before you find someone who can put a good deal together.

The following are online agents for RTW tickets:

**Air Treks** (www.airtreks.com)
**Bootsnall** (www.bootsnall.com)
**Round the World Flights** (www.roundtheworld flights.com)
**The Traveller UK** (www.thetravelleruk.com)
**Travel Bag** (www.travelbag.com)

## Africa

**Rennies Travel** (www.renniestravel.com) and **STA Travel** (www.statravel.co.za) have offices throughout Southern Africa. Check its websites for branch locations.

## Asia

STA Travel proliferates in Asia, with branches in **Bangkok** ( ☎ 02-236 0262; www.statravel.co.th), **Singapore** ( ☎ 6737 7188; www.statravel.com.sg), **Hong Kong** ( ☎ 2736 1618; www.statravel.com.hk) and **Japan** ( ☎ 03 5391 2922; www.statravel.co.jp). Another resource in Japan is **No 1 Travel** ( ☎ 03 3205 6073; www.no1-travel.com); in Hong Kong try **Four Seas Tours** ( ☎ 2200 7760; www.fourseastravel.com/english).

## Australia

For the location of STA Travel branches call ☎ 1300 733 035 or visit www.statravel.com .au. **Flight Centre** ( ☎ 133 133; www.flightcentre .au) has offices throughout Australia. For online bookings, try www.travel.com.au.

## Canada

**Travel Cuts** ( ☎ 800-667-2887; www.travelcuts.com) is Canada's national student travel agency. For online bookings try www.expedia.ca and www.travelocity.ca.

## Continental Europe

### FRANCE

Recommended agencies:

**Anyway** ( ☎ 0892 893 892; www.anyway.fr)
**Lastminute** ( ☎ 0892 705 000; www.lastminute.fr)
**NouvellesFrontiéres** ( ☎ 0825 000 747; www
.nouvelles-frontieres.fr)
**OTU Voyages** (www.otu.fr) This agency specialises in student and youth travellers.
**Voyageurs du Monde** ( ☎ 01 40 15 11 15;
www.vdm.com)

### GERMANY

Recommended agencies:

**Expedia** (www.expedia.de)
**Just Travel** ( ☎ 089 747 3330; www.justtravel.de)
**Lastminute** ( ☎ 01805 284 366; www.lastminute.de)
**STA Travel** ( ☎ 01805 456 422; www.statravel.de) For travellers under the age of 26.

### ITALY

One recommended agent is **CTS Viaggi** ( ☎ 06 462 0431; www.cts.it), specialising in student and youth travel.

### THE NETHERLANDS

One recommended agency is **Airfair** ( ☎ 020 620 5121; www.airfair.nl).

### SPAIN

Recommended agencies:

**BarceloViajes** ( ☎ 902 116 226; www.barceloviajes.com)
**NouvellesFrontiéres** ( ☎ 90 217 09 79; www
.nouvelles-frontieres.es)

## New Zealand

Both **Flight Centre** ( ☎ 0800 243 544; www.flightcentre
.co.nz) and **STA Travel** ( ☎ 0508 782 872; www.statravel
.co.nz) have branches throughout the country. The site www.travel.co.nz is recommended for online bookings.

## South America

Recommended agencies:

**ASATEJ** ( ☎ 54-011 4114-7595; www.asatej.com) In Argentina.
**IVI Tours** ( ☎ 0212-993 6082; www.ividiomas.com) In Venezuela.
**Student Travel Bureau** ( ☎ 3038 1555; www.stb.com.br) In Brazil.

## UK & Ireland

Discount air travel is big business in London. Advertisements for many travel agencies appear in the travel pages of the weekend broadsheet newspapers, in *Time Out*, the *Evening Standard* and in the free online magazine **TNT** (www.tntmagazine.com).

Recommended travel agencies:

**Bridge the World** ( ☎ 0870 444 7474; www.b-t-w .co.uk)
**Flight Centre** ( ☎ 0870 890 8099; flightcentre.co.uk)
**Flightbookers** ( ☎ 0870 814 4001; www.ebookers.com)
**North-South Travel** ( ☎ 01245 608 291; www .northsouthtravel.co.uk) North-South Travel donates part of its profit to projects in the developing world.
**Quest Travel** ( ☎ 0870 442 3542; www.questtravel.com)
**STA Travel** ( ☎ 0870 160 0599; www.statravel.co.uk) For travellers under the age of 26.
**Trailfinders** (www.trailfinders.co.uk)
**Travel Bag** ( ☎ 0870 890 1456; www.travelbag.co.uk)

## USA

Discount travel agents in the USA are known as consolidators (although you won't see a sign on the door saying 'Consolidator'). San Francisco is the ticket consolidator capital of America, although some good deals can be found in Los Angeles, New York and other big cities.

The following agencies are recommended for online bookings:

**Cheap Tickets** (www.cheaptickets.com)
**Expedia** (www.expedia.com)
**ITN** (www.itn.net)
**Kayak** (www.kayak.com)
**Lowest Fare** (www.lowestfare.com)
**Orbitz** (www.orbitz.com)
**STA Travel** (www.sta.com) For travellers under the age of 26.
**Travelocity** (www.travelocity.com)

## India

**STIC Travels** (www.stictravel.com) has offices in dozens of Indian cities, including **Delhi** ( ☎ 11-233 57 468) and **Mumbai** ( ☎ 22-221 81 431). Another agency is **Transway International** (www.transwayint ernational.com).

## Middle East

Recommended agencies:

**Al-Rais Travels** (www.alrais.com) In Dubai.
**Egypt Panorama Tours** ( ☎ 2-359 0200; www .eptours.com) In Cairo.
**Israel Student Travel Association** (ISTA; ☎ 02-625 7257) In Jerusalem.
**Orion-Tour** (www.oriontour.com) In Istanbul.

## LAND

### Bus

Entering Kenya by bus is possible on several major routes, and it's generally a breeze;

TRANSPORT

---

**CLIMATE CHANGE & TRAVEL**

Climate change is a serious threat to the ecosystems that humans rely upon, and air travel is the fastest-growing contributor to the problem. Lonely Planet regards travel, overall, as a global benefit, but believes we all have a responsibility to limit our personal impact on global warming.

**Flying & Climate Change**

Pretty much every form of motor travel generates $CO_2$ (the main cause of human-induced climate change) but planes are far and away the worst offenders, not just because of the sheer distances they allow us to travel, but because they release greenhouse gases high into the atmosphere. The statistics are frightening: two people taking a return flight between Europe and the US will contribute as much to climate change as an average household's gas and electricity consumption over a whole year.

**Carbon Offset Schemes**

Climatecare.org and other websites use 'carbon calculators' that allow jet-setters to offset the greenhouse gases they are responsible for with contributions to energy-saving projects and other climate-friendly initiatives in the developing world – including projects in India, Honduras, Kazakhstan and Uganda.

Lonely Planet, together with Rough Guides and other concerned partners in the travel industry, supports the carbon offset scheme run by climatecare.org. Lonely Planet offsets all of its staff and author travel.

---

while you need to get off the bus to sort out any necessary visa formalities, you'll rarely be held up for too long at the border. That said, arranging your visa in advance can save you quite a bit of time and a few angry glares from your fellow passengers.

## Car & Motorcycle

Drivers of cars and riders of motorbikes will need the vehicle's registration papers, liability insurance and an international driving permit in addition to their domestic licence. Beware: there are two kinds of international permits, one of which is needed mostly for former British colonies. You may also need a *Carnet de passage en douane,* which is effectively a passport for the vehicle and acts as a temporary waiver of import duty. The *carnet* may also need to specify any expensive spare parts that you're planning to carry with you, such as a gearbox. This is necessary when travelling in many countries in Africa, and is designed to prevent car-import rackets. Contact your local automobile association for details about all documentation.

Liability insurance is not available in advance for many out-of-the-way countries, but rather has to be bought when crossing the border. The cost and quality of such local insurance varies wildly, and you will find in some countries that you are effectively travelling uninsured.

Petrol, spare parts and repair shops are readily available at all border towns, though if you're coming from Ethiopia you should plan your supplies carefully, as stops are few and far between on the rough northern roads.

If you're planning to ship your vehicle to Kenya, be aware that port charges in the country are very high. For example, a Land Rover shipped from the Middle East to Mombasa is likely to cost more than US$1000 just to get off the ship and out of the port – this is almost as much as the cost of the shipping itself! Putting a vehicle onto a ship in the Mombasa port can cost another US$750 on top of this. There are numerous shipping agents in Nairobi and Mombasa willing to arrange everything for you, but check all the costs in advance.

For road rules and further information, see p349.

## Ethiopia

With ongoing problems in Sudan and Somalia, Ethiopia offers the only viable overland route into Kenya from the north. The security situation around the main entry point at Moyale is changeable – the border is usually open, but security problems often force its closure. Cattle- and goat-rustling are rife, triggering frequent cross-border tribal wars, so check the security situation carefully before attempting this crossing.

From immigration on the Ethiopian side of town it's a 2km walk to the Ethiopian and Kenyan customs posts. A yellow-fever vaccination is required to cross either border at Moyale. Unless you fancy being vaccinated at the border, get your jabs in advance and keep the certificate with your passport. A cholera vaccination may also be required. If you're travelling in the other direction, through Ethiopia to Sudan, you'll have to go to Addis Ababa to get your Sudanese visa.

If you don't have your own transport from Moyale, lifts can be arranged with the trucks from the border to Isiolo for around KSh1000 (or KSh500 to Marsabit).

Those coming to Kenya with their own vehicle could also enter at Fort Banya, on the northeastern tip of Lake Turkana, but it's a risky route with few fuel stops. There's no border post; you must already possess a Kenyan visa and get it stamped on arrival in Nairobi. Immigration are quite used to this, but not having an Ethiopian exit stamp can be a problem if you want to reenter Ethiopia.

## Somalia

There's no way you can pass overland between Kenya and war-ravaged Somalia at present unless you're part of a refugee aid convoy, as the Kenyan government has closed the border to try and stop the flow of poachers, bandits and weapons into Kenya.

## Sudan

There has been some peace progress in recent years, though Kenya's neighbour to the north is still far from untroubled. If things continue to improve, the Kenya–Sudan border may reopen, but at the time of writing it was only possible to travel between the two countries either by air or via Metema on the Ethiopian border (see also opposite).

## Tanzania

The main land borders between Kenya and Tanzania are at Namanga, Taveta, Isebania and Lunga Lunga, and can be reached by public transport. There is also a crossing from the Serengeti to the Masai Mara, which can only be undertaken with your own vehicle, and one at Loitokitok, which is closed to tourists, although you may be able to temporarily cross on a tour (see p347 for more information). Train services between the two countries have been suspended.

Following are the main bus companies serving Tanzania:

**Akamba** (Map pp104-5; ☎ 020-340430)
**Davanu Shuttle** Nairobi (Map pp104-5; ☎ 020-316929) Arusha ( ☎ 057-8142) Arusha/Moshi shuttle buses.
**Easy Coach** (Map pp104-5; ☎ 020-210711; easycoach@wananchi.com)
**Riverside Shuttle** Nairobi (Map pp104-5; ☎ 020-229618) Arusha ( ☎ 057-2639) Arusha/Moshi shuttle buses.
**Scandinavia Express** (www.scandinaviagroup.com)

### MOMBASA TO TANGA/DAR ES SALAAM

Numerous buses run along the coast road from Mombasa to Tanga and Dar es Salaam, crossing the border at Lunga Lunga/Horohoro. Most people travel on direct buses from Mombasa, but it's easy enough to do the journey in stages by local bus or matatu if you'd rather make a few stops along the way.

In Mombasa, buses to Dar es Salaam leave from around Jomo Kenyatta Ave, near the junction with Mwembe Tayari Rd. The average cost is around KSh1000 to Dar (eight hours) and KSh500 to Tanga (two hours), depending on the company you travel with and the standard of the buses.

In Dar es Salaam, buses leave from the Mnazi Mmoja bus stand on Bibi Titi Mohamed Rd, near Uhuru and Lindi Sts, along the southeast side of Mnazi Mmoja Park.

If you want to do the journey in stages, there are frequent matatus to Lunga Lunga from the Mombasa ferry jetty at Likoni. A matatu can then take you the 6.5km between the two border posts. On the Tanzanian side, there are regular matatus from Horohoro to Tanga (see p281 for more details).

### MOMBASA TO ARUSHA/MOSHI

A number of rickety local buses leave Mombasa every evening for Moshi and Arusha in Tanzania. There are occasional morning services, but most buses leave around 7pm from Mombasa or Arusha. Fares are around KSh1000 to Moshi (six hours) and KSh1500 to Arusha (7½ hours). In Mombasa, buses leave from in front of the Mwembe Tayari Health Centre on Jomo Kenyatta Ave.

Buses cross the border at Taveta, which can also be reached by matatu from Voi (see p146 for more details).

### NAIROBI TO ARUSHA/MOSHI

You have the choice of an ordinary bus or a much more comfortable minibus shuttle service between Nairobi and Arusha. Each

**TRANSPORT**

takes about four hours and neither requires a change of service at the border at Namanga.

Riverside Shuttle and Davanu Shuttle both offer convenient shuttle services from central Nairobi, costing roughly US$35 to Arusha and US$40 to Moshi. The big advantage of both these services is being able to board the bus in the comparative sanity of downtown Nairobi. There are often touts at Jomo Kenyatta International Airport in Nairobi advertising a direct shuttle bus service from the airport to Arusha, but they just bring you into Nairobi where you join one of the regular shuttles.

Full-sized buses are much cheaper, but most leave from the hectic River Rd area in Nairobi; thefts are common there so watch your baggage. Easy Coach is a good option, as services leave from its office compound near Nairobi railway station. Buses from Nairobi to Dar es Salaam (see below) also travel via Arusha, and small local buses leave from Accra Rd every morning. The average cost of these services is between KSh700 and KSh1000 to Arusha, and between KSh1000 and KSh1200 to Moshi, more for the real luxury liners.

It's also easy, though less convenient, to do this journey in stages, since the Kenyan and Tanzanian border posts at Namanga are right next to each other and regularly served by public transport. There are a couple of nice places to stay in Namanga if you want to break the journey, for example to visit Amboseli National Park, before heading to Nairobi or Arusha.

### NAIROBI TO DAR ES SALAAM
Several Kenyan companies have buses from Nairobi to Dar es Salaam. Scandinavia Express and Akamba both have reliable daily services, with prices ranging from KSh2000 to real luxury coaches at KSh3000. Journey time is around 16 to 18 hours with stops.

### SERENGETI TO MASAI MARA
Theoretically it's possible to cross between Serengeti National Park and Masai Mara National Reserve with your own vehicle, but you'll need all the appropriate vehicle documentation (including insurance and entry permit).

### NAIROBI/KISUMU TO MWANZA
The road is sealed all the way from Kisumu to just short of Mwanza in Tanzania, offering a convenient route to the Tanzanian

shore of Lake Victoria. From Nairobi, probably the most comfortable way to go is with Scandinavia Express or Akamba; prices range from around KSh1000 to KSh2000, and the journey should take roughly 12 hours.

From Kisumu, regular matatus serve the Tanzanian border at Isebania/Sirari (KSh400, four hours); local services head to Mwanza from the Tanzanian side. Buses going direct to Mwanza (KSh1700, four hours) leave frequently from Kisii.

## Uganda
The main border post for overland travellers is Malaba, with Busia an alternative if you are travelling via Kisumu. Numerous bus companies run between Nairobi and Kampala, or you can do the journey in stages via either of the border towns. **Akamba** (Map pp104–5; ☎ 020-340430), Falcon and Scandinavia Express are the main bus companies that serve Uganda.

### NAIROBI TO KAMPALA
Various companies cover the Nairobi to Kampala route. From Nairobi – and at the top end of the market – Scandinavia Express and Akamba have buses at least once daily, ranging from ordinary buses at around KSh1000 to full-blown luxury services with drinks and movies, hovering around the KSh2500 mark. All buses take about 10 to 12 hours and prices include a meal at the halfway point. Akamba also has a service to Mbale in Uganda for around KSh1000.

Various other companies have cheaper basic services which depart from the Accra Rd area in Nairobi. Prices start at around KSh1000 and journey times are more or less the same as the bigger companies, with a few extra allowances for delays and general tardiness.

If you want to do the journey in stages, Akamba has morning and evening buses from Nairobi to Malaba and a daily direct bus from there to Kampala. There are also regular matatus to Malaba from Cross Rd.

The Ugandan and Kenyan border posts at Malaba are about 1km apart, so you can walk or take a *boda-boda* (bicycle taxi). Once you get across the border, there are frequent matatus until the late afternoon to Kampala, Jinja and Tororo.

Buses and matatus also run from Nairobi or Kisumu to Busia, from where there are regular connections to Kampala and Jinja.

## SEA & LAKE

At the time of writing there were no ferries operating on Lake Victoria, although there's been talk for years of services restarting.

### Tanzania

It's theoretically possible to travel by dhow between Mombasa and the Tanzanian islands of Pemba and Zanzibar, but first of all you'll have to find a captain who's making the journey and then you'll have to bargain hard to pay a reasonable amount for the trip. Perhaps the best place to ask about sailings is at Shimoni (p279). There is a tiny immigration post here, but there's no guarantee they'll stamp your passport so you might have to go back to Mombasa for an exit stamp.

Dhows do sail between small Kenyan and Tanzanian ports along Lake Victoria, but many are involved in smuggling (fruit mostly) and are best avoided.

## TOURS

It's possible to get to Kenya as part of an overland truck tour originating in Europe or other parts of Africa (many also start in Nairobi bound for other places in Africa). See p91 for details of safaris that are specific to Kenya.

Most companies are based in the UK or South Africa, but Flight Centre is a good local operator with offices in Nairobi, Cape Town and Victoria Falls, Zimbabwe. Trips can last from just a few days to epic grand tours of up to 13 weeks.

**Acacia Expeditions** (UK ☎ 020-77064700; www
.acacia-africa.com)

**African Routes** (South Africa ☎ 031-5693911; www
.africanroutes.co.za)

**Dragoman** (UK ☎ 01728-861133; www.dragoman
.co.uk)

**Explore Worldwide** (UK ☎ 01252-760000; www
.exploreworldwide.com)

**Flight Centre** Cape Town ( ☎ 021-3851530; cpt@afri
catravelco.com); Nairobi (Map pp104-5; ☎ 020-210024;
Lakhamshi House, Biashara St); Victoria Falls ( ☎ 013-
40172; vfa@africatravelco.com)

**Gametrackers** (Map pp104-5; ☎ 020-338927; www
.gametrackersafaris.com; Nginyo Towers, cnr Koinange &
Moktar Daddah Sts, Nairobi)

**Guerba Expeditions** (UK ☎ 01373-826611; www
.guerba.co.uk)

# GETTING AROUND

Kenya is home to an incredibly diverse array of landscapes, which can all be traversed by a variety of transport modes. Whether you criss-cross the country by highway bus or hire car, or cruise the clear skies and placid seas by light aircraft or dhow, getting around Kenya is certainly half the fun of travelling here.

Most of Kenya's towns and cities are accessible by local bus, though it's usually necessary to arrange private transport to reach national parks and lodges. If you're a seasoned or aspiring road warrior, hiring a sturdy vehicle can also open up relatively inaccessible corners of the country.

## AIR

### Airlines in Kenya

Including the national carrier, Kenya Airways, four main domestic operators of varying sizes run scheduled flights within Kenya. Destinations served are predominantly around the coast and the popular national parks, where the highest density of tourist activity takes place.

With all these airlines, be sure to book well in advance (this is essential during the tourist high season). You should also remember to reconfirm your return flights 72 hours before departure, especially those that connect with an international flight. Otherwise, you may find that your seat has been reallocated.

The following airlines fly domestically:

**Airkenya** ( ☎ 020-605745; www.airkenya.com) Amboseli, Kiwayu, Lamu, Lewa Downs, Masai Mara, Malindi, Meru, Nanyuki, Samburu.

**Kenya Airways** (Map pp100-1; ☎ 020-3274100; www
.kenya-airways.com) Kisumu, Lamu, Malindi, Mombasa.

**Mombasa Air Safari** ( ☎ 041-433061; www.mombasa
airsafari.com) Amboseli, Ukunda, Lamu, Masai Mara, Malindi, Mombasa, Tsavo.

**Safarilink** ( ☎ 020-600777; www.safarilink-kenya.com) Amboseli, Chyulu Hills, Kiwayu, Lamu, Lewa Downs, Masai Mara, Naivasha, Nanyuki, Samburu, Tsavo West.

#### CHARTER AIRLINES

Chartering a small plane saves you time and is the only realistic way to get to some parts of Kenya. However, it's an expensive affair, and may only be worth considering if you can get a group together.

There are dozens of charter companies operating out of Nairobi's Wilson Airport –

**Excel Aviation** ( ☎ 020-601764), **Z-Boskovic Air Charters** ( ☎ 020-501210) and **Blue Bird Aviation** ( ☎ 020-602338) are worth a look.

A couple of small charter-type airlines run occasional scheduled flights from Diani Beach, Lamu, Mombasa and Eldoret; see the relevant Getting There & Away sections for details.

## BICYCLE

Loads of Kenyans get around by bicycle, and while it can be tough for those who are not used to the roads or the climate, plenty of hardy visiting cyclists do tour the country every year. But whatever you do, if you intend to cycle here, do as the locals do and get off the road whenever you hear a car coming. No matter how experienced you are, it would be tantamount to suicide to attempt the road from Nairobi to Mombasa on a bicycle.

Cycling is easier in rural areas, and you'll usually receive a warm welcome in any villages you pass through. Many local people operate *boda-bodas*, so repair shops are becoming increasingly common along the roadside. Be wary of cycling on dirt roads as punctures from thorn trees are a major problem.

The hills of Kenya are not particularly steep but can be long and hard. You can expect to cover around 80km per day in the hills of the western highlands, somewhat more where the country is flatter. Hell's Gate National Park, near Naivasha, is particularly popular for mountain biking.

It's possible to hire road and mountain bikes in an increasing number of places, usually for less than KSh500 per day. Few places require a deposit, unless their machines are particularly new or sophisticated.

## BOAT

There has been speculation for years that ferry transport will start again on Lake Victoria, but for the foreseeable future the only regular services operating are motorised canoes to Mfangano Island from Mbita Point, near Homa Bay. An occasional ferry service also runs between Kisumu and Homa Bay.

### Dhow

Sailing on a traditional Swahili dhow along the East African coast is one of Kenya's most memorable experiences. And, unlike on Lake Victoria, a good number of traditional routes are very much still in use. Dhows are commonly used to get around the islands in

the Lamu archipelago (p302) and the mangrove islands south of Mombasa (see Funzi Island, p279).

For the most part, these trips operate more like dhow safaris than public transport. Although some trips are luxurious, the trips out of Lamu are more basic. When night comes you simply bed down wherever there is space. Seafood is freshly caught and cooked on board on charcoal burners, or else barbecued on the beach on the surrounding islands.

Most of the smaller boats rely on the wind to get around, so it's quite common to end up becalmed until the wind picks up again. The more commercial boats, however, have been fitted with outboard motors so that progress can be made even when there's no wind. Larger dhows are all motorised and some of them don't even have sails.

## BUS

Kenya has an extensive network of long- and short-haul bus routes, with particularly good coverage of the areas around Nairobi, the coast and the western regions. Services thin out further away from the capital you get, particularly in the north, and there are still plenty of places where you'll be reliant on matatus.

Buses are operated by a variety of private and state-owned companies that offer varying levels of comfort, convenience and roadworthiness. They're considerably cheaper than taking the train or flying, and as a rule services are frequent, fast and often quite comfortable. However, many travellers are put off taking buses altogether by the diabolical state of Kenyan roads.

In general, if you travel during daylight hours, buses are a fairly safe way to get around and you'll certainly be safer in a bus than in a matatu, simply due to its size. The best coaches are saved for long-haul and international routes and offer DVD movies, drinks, toilets and reclining airline-style seats. On the shorter local routes, however, you may find yourself on something resembling a battered school bus.

Whatever kind of conveyance you find yourself in, don't sit at the back (you'll be thrown around like a rag doll on Kenyan roads), or right at the front (you'll be the first to die in a head-on collision, plus you'll be able to see the oncoming traffic, which is usually a terrifying experience). You should also be aware that a Kenyan bus trip is not always the most restful experience – unlike matatus, hawkers can actually board most services to thrust their wares in your face, and it's not unknown for roving preachers, herbalists and just about anyone else to spend entire journeys shouting the odds for the benefit of their fellow passengers. On certain coastal buses you'll even hear the regular Muslim call to prayer broadcast over the loud speaker

Kenya Bus Services (KBS), the government bus line, runs the local buses in Nairobi and also offers long-haul services to most major towns around the country. Its buses tend to be slower than those of the private companies, but are probably safer for this reason. Of the private companies, Akamba has the most comprehensive network, and has a good, but not perfect, safety record. Easy Coach is another private firm quickly establishing a solid reputation for efficiency and comfort.

There are a few security considerations to think about when taking a bus in Kenya. Some routes, most notably the roads from Malindi to Lamu and Isiolo to Marsabit, have been prone to attacks by *shiftas* (bandits) in the past; check things out locally before you travel. Another possible risk is drugged food and drink: it is best to politely refuse any offers of drinks or snacks from strangers.

The following are the main bus companies operating in Kenya:

**Akamba** (Map pp104–5; ☎ 020-340430) Eldoret, Kakamega, Kericho, Kisii, Kisumu, Kitale, Machakos, Mombasa, Nairobi, Namanga.
**Busways** ( ☎ 020-227650) Kilifi, Kisumu, Malindi, Mombasa, Nairobi.
**Coastline Safaris** (Map pp104–5; ☎ 020-217592) Kakamega, Kisumu, Mombasa, Nairobi, Nakuru, Voi.
**Easy Coach** (Map pp104-5; ☎ 020-210711) Eldoret, Kakamega, Kisumu, Kitale, Nairobi.
**Eldoret Express** ( ☎ 020-6766886) Busia, Eldoret, Kakamega, Kisii, Kisumu, Kitale, Malaba, Nairobi.
**Falcon** (Map p260) Kilifi, Lamu, Malindi, Mombasa, Nairobi.
**Kenya Bus Services** (KBS; Map pp104-5; ☎ 020-229707, booking office 020-341250) Busia, Eldoret, Kakamega, Kisii, Kisumu, Kitale, Malaba, Mombasa, Nairobi.
**Mombasa Metropolitan Bus Services** (Metro Mombasa; ☎ 041-2496008) Kilifi, Kwale, Malindi, Mombasa, Mtwapa.

## Costs
Kenyan buses are pretty economical, with fares starting around KSh100 for an hour-long journey between nearby towns. At the other end of the scale, you'll seldom pay more than KSh500 for a standard journey, but so-called 'executive' services on the overnight Nairobi–Mombasa route can command prices of up to KSh1500, almost as much as the equivalent international services.

## Reservations
Most bus companies have offices or ticket agents at important stops along their routes, where you can book a seat. For short trips between towns reservations aren't generally necessary, but for popular longer routes, especially the Nairobi–Kisumu, Nairobi–Mombasa and Mombasa–Lamu routes, buying your ticket at least a day in advance is highly recommended.

## CAR & MOTORCYCLE
Many travellers bring their own vehicles into Kenya as part of overland trips and, expense notwithstanding, it's a great way to see the country at your own pace. Otherwise, there are numerous car-hire companies that can rent you anything from a small hatchback to a 4WD, although hire rates are some of the highest in the world.

A few expats have off-road (trail) motorcycles, but they aren't seen as a serious means of transport, which is a blessing considering the lethal nature of the roads.

## Automobile Associations
**Automobile Association of Kenya** (Map pp100-1; ☎ 020-723195; Hurlingham shopping centre, Nairobi).

## Bribes
Police will stop you everywhere you travel in Kenya, and will more likely than not ask you for a small 'donation'. To prevent being taken advantage of, always ask for an official receipt – this goes a long way in stopping corruption. Also, always ask for their police number and check it against their ID card as there are plenty of con artists running about. If you're ever asked to go to court, always say yes as you just might call their bluff and save yourself a bit of cash.

## Bringing Your Own Vehicle
For information about bringing your own vehicle, see p344.

## ROAD DISTANCES (KM)

| | Busia | Embu | Isiolo | Kakamega | Kericho | Kisumu | Kitale | Lodwar | Malindi | Meru | Mombasa | Nairobi | Nakuru | Namanga | Nanyuki | Nyeri |
|---|---|---|---|---|---|---|---|---|---|---|---|---|---|---|---|---|
| Embu | 610 | | | | | | | | | | | | | | | |
| Isiolo | 569 | 184 | | | | | | | | | | | | | | |
| Kakamega | 95 | 525 | 481 | | | | | | | | | | | | | |
| Kericho | 218 | 395 | 351 | 130 | | | | | | | | | | | | |
| Kisumu | 138 | 475 | 431 | 50 | 80 | | | | | | | | | | | |
| Kitale | 154 | 511 | 467 | 109 | 230 | 158 | | | | | | | | | | |
| Lodwar | 440 | 691 | 735 | 395 | 522 | 443 | 285 | | | | | | | | | |
| Malindi | 1087 | 657 | 877 | 999 | 869 | 949 | 985 | 1141 | | | | | | | | |
| Meru | 565 | 154 | 56 | 477 | 347 | 427 | 463 | 729 | 864 | | | | | | | |
| Mombasa | 969 | 618 | 759 | 881 | 751 | 831 | 867 | 1120 | 118 | 746 | | | | | | |
| Nairobi | 482 | 131 | 272 | 394 | 264 | 368 | 380 | 599 | 605 | 259 | 521 | | | | | |
| Nakuru | 325 | 288 | 244 | 237 | 107 | 211 | 223 | 442 | 762 | 240 | 644 | 157 | | | | |
| Namanga | 661 | 314 | 524 | 596 | 469 | 548 | 563 | 779 | 430 | 468 | 409 | 180 | 337 | | | |
| Nanyuki | 487 | 131 | 84 | 399 | 269 | 349 | 385 | 651 | 795 | 78 | 677 | 190 | 175 | 380 | | |
| Nyeri | 508 | 88 | 140 | 420 | 290 | 370 | 406 | 601 | 752 | 136 | 634 | 150 | 151 | 330 | 58 | |
| Voi | 811 | 460 | 601 | 723 | 593 | 673 | 709 | 960 | 281 | 588 | 160 | 329 | 486 | 249 | 519 | 476 |

### Driving Licence

An international driving licence is not necessary in Kenya, but can be useful. If you have a British photo card licence, be sure to bring the counterfoil, as the date you passed your driving test (something car-hire companies may want to know) isn't printed on the card itself.

### Fuel & Spare Parts

Fuel prices are on the rise the world over, and Kenya certainly isn't an exception. Rates are generally lower outside the capital, but can creep up to frighteningly high prices in remote areas, where petrol stations are often scarce and you may end up buying supplies out of barrels from roadside vendors.

Anyone who is planning to bring their own vehicle with them needs to check in advance what spare parts are likely to be available. Even if it's an older model, local suppliers in Kenya are very unlikely to have every little part you might need. Belt breakages are probably the most common disaster you can expect, so bring several spares. Also note that you can be fined by the police for not having a fire triangle and an extinguisher.

### Hire

Hiring a vehicle to tour Kenya (or at least the national parks) is an expensive way of seeing the country, but it does give you freedom of movement and is sometimes the only way of getting to the more remote parts of the country. However, unless you're sharing with a sufficient number of people, it's likely to cost more than you'd pay for an organised camping safari with all meals.

Unless you're just planning on travelling on the main routes between towns, you'll need a 4WD vehicle. None of the car-hire companies will let you drive 2WD vehicles on dirt roads, including those in the national parks, and if you ignore this proscription and have an accident you will be personally liable for any damage to the vehicle.

A minimum age of between 23 and 25 years usually applies for hirers. Some companies prefer a licence with no endorsements or criminal convictions, and most require you to have been driving for at least two years. You will also need acceptable ID such as a passport.

It's generally true to say that the more you pay for a vehicle, the better condition it will be in. The larger companies are usually in a better financial position to keep their fleet in good order. Whoever you hire from, be sure to check the brakes, the tyres (including the spare), the windscreen wipers and the lights before you set off.

The other factor to consider is what the company will do for you (if anything) if you have a serious breakdown. The major hire companies *may* deliver a replacement vehicle and make arrangements for recovery of the other vehicle at their expense, but with most companies you'll have to get the vehicle fixed and back on the road yourself, and then try to claim a refund.

## COSTS

Starting rates for hire almost always sound very reasonable, but once you factor in mileage and the various types of insurance you'll be lucky to pay less than KSh7500 per day for a saloon car, or KSh10,000 per day for a small 4WD. As elsewhere in the world, rates come down rapidly if you take the car for more than a few days.

Vehicles are usually hired with either an allowance of 100km to 200km per day (you'll pay an extra fee for every kilometre over), or with unlimited kilometres, which is often the best way to go. Rates are usually quoted without insurance, with the option of paying around KSh1000 to KSh2000 per day for insurance against collision damage and theft. It would be financial suicide to hire a car in Kenya without both kinds of insurance. Otherwise you'll be responsible for the full value of the vehicle if it's damaged or stolen.

Even if you have collision and theft insurance, you'll still be liable for an excess of KSh2500 to KSh150,000 (depending on the company) if something happens to the vehicle; always check this before signing. You can usually reduce the excess to zero by paying another KSh1000 to KSh2000 per day for an excess loss waiver. Note that tyres, damaged windscreens and loss of the tool kit are always the hirer's responsibility.

As a final sting in the tail, you'll be charged 16% value added tax (VAT) on top of the total cost of hiring the vehicle. Any repairs that you end up paying for will also have VAT on top. And a final warning: always return the vehicle with a full tank of petrol; if you don't, the company will charge you twice the going rate to fill up.

## Deposits
There's a wide variation in the deposit required on hired vehicles. It can be as much as the total estimated hire charges plus whatever the excess is on the collision damage waiver. You can cover this with cash, signed travellers cheques (returnable) or credit card.

## Drop-Off Rates
If you want to hire a vehicle in one place and drop it off in another there will be additional charges. These vary depending on the vehicle, the company and the pick-up and drop-off locations. In most cases, count on paying KSh10,000 between Nairobi and Mombasa and about KSh5000 between Mombasa and Malindi.

## Driver Rates
While hiring a 'chauffeur' may sound like a luxury, it can actually be a very good idea in Kenya for both financial and safety reasons. Most companies will provide a driver for a few thousand shillings per day – the big advantage of this is that the car is covered by the company's insurance, so you don't have to pay any of the various waivers and won't be liable for any excess in the case of an accident (though tyres, windows etc remain your responsibility).

In addition, having someone in the car who speaks Swahili, knows the roads and is used to Kenyan driving conditions can be absolutely priceless, especially in remote areas. Most drivers will also look after the car at night so you don't have to worry about it, and they'll often go massively out of their way to help you fulfil your travel plans. On the other hand, it will leave one less seat free in the car, reducing the number of people you can have sharing the cost in the first place.

## DRIVING TO TANZANIA & UGANDA
Only the bigger (and more expensive) companies cater for this, and there are large additional charges. With Budget, Hertz or Avis, expect to pay a few hundred dollars for them to sort out all the documentation, insurance, permits etc.

## HIRE AGENCIES
At the top end of the market are some international companies. Most have airport and town offices in Nairobi and Mombasa.

Central Rent-a-Car, which comes highly recommended by readers, is probably the

TRANSPORT

---

**YOUR BEST KIKUYU FRIEND**

If you want to see Kenya through the eyes of a local Kikuyu, contact **Leonard Chege Mwangi** ( ☎ 0721942523, 0714001446), who helped us authors research the latest edition of this guidebook. For an extremely affordable and negotiable price, he can pick you up in Nairobi, and drive you anywhere in the country that you like to go. Chege, as he is known to his friends, is extremely reliable, a very safe and conscientious driver, and knowledgeable about Kenya's tourism scene.

---

best of the local firms. The have a well-maintained fleet of fairly new vehicles and a good back-up service. Adventure Upgrade Safaris also has a good fleet of lean-and-mean 4WDs for tackling the worst of Kenya's roads.

Most safari companies will also hire out their vehicles, though you'll have few of the guarantees that you would with proper hire companies listed here. One notable exception is Let's Go Travel, which organises reliable car hire at favourable rates through partner firms.

On the coast, it is possible to hire motorcycles, scooters and quads at Diani Beach and Bamburi Beach. Fredlink Tours rents out 350cc trail bikes and Yamaha scooters, and also arranges motorcycle safaris. See p91 for information about motorcycle safaris.

The following are local and international hire companies:

**Adventure Upgrade Safaris** ( ☎ 020-228725; www
.adventureupgradesafaris.co.ke)

**Avis** (Map pp104–5; ☎ 020-316061; www.avis.com)

**Budget** (Map pp104–5; ☎ 020-223581; www.budget
.com)

**Central Rent-a-Car** (Map pp104–5; ☎ 020-222888;
www.carhirekenya.com)

**Fredlink Tours** ( ☎ 040-3202647; www.motorbike
-safari.com; Diani Plaza, Diani Beach)

**Hertz** ( ☎ 020-248777; www.hertz.com)

**Let's Go Travel** ( ☎ 020-340331; www.letsgosafari.com)

## Insurance

Driving in Kenya without insurance would be a mind-numbingly idiotic thing to do. It's best to arrange cover before you leave. Liability insurance is not always available in advance for Kenya; you may be required to

purchase some at certain borders if you enter overland, otherwise you will effectively be travelling uninsured.

Most car-hire agencies in Kenya always offer some kind of insurance; see p351 for full details.

## Parking

In small towns and villages parking is usually free, but there's a pay-parking system in Nairobi, Mombasa and other main towns. Attendants issue one-day parking permits for around KSh100, valid anywhere in town. If you don't get a permit you're liable to be wheel-clamped, and getting your vehicle back will cost you a few thousands shillings. With that said, it's always worth staying in a hotel with secure parking if possible.

## Purchase

It's certainly possible to buy a car when you're in Kenya – just look at public noticeboards in expat-rich areas such as the Nairobi suburbs and the coast resorts. However, the practicalities of registering, taxing and keeping your vehicle generally road-legal are quite another matter, and certainly require a fair bit of ground research if you seriously intend to keep the car running for a decent length of time. Also keep in mind that buying or selling a vehicle will give you a bitter taste of Kenyan bureaucracy at its finest, so be sure that you have plenty of time, a mountain of patience and perhaps a bit of luck.

## Road Conditions

Road conditions vary widely in Kenya, from flat smooth highways to dirt tracks and steep rocky pathways. Many roads are severely eroded at the edges, reducing the carriageway to a single lane, which is usually occupied by whichever vehicle is bigger in any given situation. The roads in the north and east of the country are particularly poor. The main Mombasa–Nairobi–Malaba road (A104) is badly worn due to the constant flow of traffic.

Roads in national parks are all made of *murram* (dirt) and have eroded into bone-shaking corrugations through overuse by safari vehicles. Keep your speed down, slowly increasing until you find a suitable speed (when the rattling stops), and be careful when driving after rain. Although some dirt roads can be negotiated in a 2WD vehicle, you're much safer in a 4WD.

## Road Hazards

The biggest hazard on Kenyan roads is simply the other vehicles on them, and driving defensively is essential. Ironically, the most dangerous roads in Kenya are probably the well-maintained ones, which allow drivers to go fast enough to do really serious damage in a crash. On the worse roads, potholes are a dual problem: driving into them can damage your vehicle or cause you to lose control, and sudden avoidance manoeuvres from other vehicles are a constant threat.

On all roads, be very careful of pedestrians and cyclists – you don't want to contribute any more to the death toll on Kenya's roads. Animals are another major hazard in rural areas, be it monkeys, herds of goats and cattle or lone chickens with a death wish.

Acacia thorns are a common problem if you're driving in remote areas, as they'll pierce even the toughest tyres. The slightest breakdown can leave you stranded for hours in the bush, so always carry drinking water, emergency food and, if possible, spare fuel.

Certain routes have a reputation for banditry, particularly the Garsen–Garissa–Thika road, which is still essentially off limits to travellers, and the dirt track from Amboseli National Park to Tsavo West National Park, where you're usually required to join a convoy. The roads from Isiolo to Marsabit and Moyale and from Malindi to Lamu have improved considerably security-wise in the last few years, but you're still advised to seek local advice before using any of these routes.

## Road Rules

You'll need your wits about you if you're going to tackle driving in Kenya. Driving practices here are some of the worst in the world and all are carried out at breakneck speed. Indicators, lights, horns and hand signals can mean anything from 'I'm about to overtake' to 'Hello *mzungu* (white person)!' or 'Let's play chicken with that elephant', and should never be taken at face value.

Kenyans habitually drive on the wrong side of the road whenever they see a pothole, an animal or simply a break in the traffic – flashing your lights at the vehicle hurtling towards you should be enough to persuade the driver to get back into their own lane. Never drive at night unless you absolutely have to, as few cars have adequate headlights and the roads are full of pedestrians and cyclists. Drunk driving is also very common, among expats as much as locals.

Note that foreign-registered vehicles with a seating capacity of more than six people are not allowed into Kenyan national parks and reserves; Jeeps should be fine, but VW Kombis and other campervans may have problems.

## HITCHING

Hitchhiking is never entirely safe in any country, and we don't recommend it. Travellers who hitch should understand they are taking a small but potentially serious risk; it's safer to travel in pairs and let someone know where you are planning to go. Also beware of drunken drivers.

Although it's risky, many locals have no choice but to hitch, so people will know what you're doing if you try to flag down cars. The traditional thumb signal will probably be understood, but locals use a palm-downwards wave to get cars to stop. Many Kenyan drivers expect a contribution towards petrol or some kind of gift from foreign passengers, so make it clear from the outset if you are expecting a free ride.

If you're hoping to hitch into the national parks, dream on! Your chances of coming across tourists with a spare seat who don't mind taking a freeloading stranger along on their expensive safari are slimmer than a starving stick insect, and quite frankly it seems pretty rude to ask. You'll get further asking around for travel companions in Nairobi or any of the gateway towns.

On the other side of the wheel, foreign drivers will be approached all the time by Kenyan hitchers demanding free rides, and giving a lift to a carload of Maasai is certainly a memorable cultural experience.

## LOCAL TRANSPORT
### Boat

The only local boat service in regular use is the Likoni ferry between the mainland and Mombasa island, which runs throughout the day and night and is free for foot passengers (vehicles pay a small toll).

### Boda-boda

*Boda-bodas* (bicycle taxis) are common in areas where standard taxis are harder to find, and also operate in smaller towns and cities

**TRANSPORT**

---

**HAKUNA MATATU?**

The traffic laws implemented in 2003 were not just designed to impact on safety in matatus – they've also had a profound effect on their aesthetic qualities, the very thing that makes them such unique charabancs in the first place.

Matatus, particularly the big 20-seater ones on local Nairobi routes, frequently used to be moving works of street art, daubed with colourful graffiti reflecting whatever was currently hip in Kenya, and blasting out appropriate tuneage on mega-decibel stereos. As part of the regulations, however, strict noise limits are enforced, and every public conveyance must have a yellow stripe down the side displaying the route, vehicle number and capacity, requiring many matatus to be repainted.

Nairobi matatus have taken the change to heart, and most Nissans are now plain white with a few token stickers or paintings in the rear window. Even the names reflect the toned-down image of the transport industry: while there are still plenty of Beyoncés and Homeboyz, you're now just as likely to travel in a bus called Safety Bars, God Never Fails or Rise'n'Shine.

In Mombasa, however, hard-core is alive and well, and while the decorations are kept relatively small, the matatu names are, if anything, more provocative. Look out for Saddam, Blood Fist, Jihad and You Are Lonely When You Are Dead... Our favourite, though, has to be the delightful if slightly baffling 'U Kick My Cat – I Kill Ur Dog'. What better sentiment to keep the spirit of the matatu alive and well?

---

such as Kisumu. There is a particular proliferation on the coast, where the bicycle boys also double as touts, guides and drug dealers in tourist areas. A short ride should cost around 20 or so shillings.

## Bus

Nairobi is the only city with an effective municipal bus service, run by KBS. Routes cover the suburbs and outlying areas during daylight hours and generally cost no more than KSh40. Metro Shuttle and private City Hopper services also run to areas such as Kenyatta Airport and Karen. Due to traffic density, safety is rarely a serious concern.

## Matatu

Local matatus are the main means of getting around for local people, and any reasonably sized city or town will have plenty of services covering every major road and suburb. Fares start at around KSh10 and may reach KSh50 for longer routes in Nairobi. As with buses, roads are usually busy enough for a slight shunt to be the most likely accident, though of course congestion never stops drivers jockeying for position like it's the Kenya Derby.

Minibus transport is not unique to Kenya, but the matatu has raised it into a cultural phenomenon, and most Kenyans use them regularly for both local and intercity journeys. The vehicles themselves can be any-

thing from dilapidated Peugeot 504 pick-ups with a cab on the back to big 20-seater minibuses. The most common are white Nissan minibuses (many local people prefer the name 'Nissans' to matatus).

Matatus used to be notorious for dangerous driving, overcrowding and general shady business, but anyone revisiting Kenya will be stunned at the difference. In 2003 the then transport minister banned all matatus from the roads until they complied with a new set of laws, ensuring amazingly speedy results. Matatus must now be fitted with seatbelts and 80km/h speed governors, drivers must wear clearly identifiable red shirts, route numbers must be clearly displayed and a 14-person capacity applies to vehicles which used to cram in as many as 30 people. Frequent police checks have also been brought in to enforce the rules.

The changes are immediately noticeable and represent an improvement of sorts, but it hasn't taken operators long to find loopholes: most drivers have worked out how to gain extra speed on downhill stretches, conductors memorise the locations of police checkpoints and will scramble extra bodies in and out between them, and passengers seem quite happy only to buckle up when approaching a roadblock. Many drivers still also chew *miraa* (leafy shoots chewed as a stimulant) to stay awake beyond what is a reasonable or safe time.

Apart from in the remote northern areas, where you'll rely on occasional buses or paid lifts on trucks, you can almost always find a matatu going to the next town or further afield, so long as it's not too late in the day. Simply ask around among the drivers at the local matatu stand or 'stage'. Matatus leave when full and the fares are fixed. It's unlikely you will be charged more money than other passengers.

Wherever you go, remember that most matatu crashes are head-on collisions – under no circumstances should you sit in the 'death seat' next to the matatu driver. Play it safe and sit in the middle seats away from the window.

### Shared Taxi (Peugeot)

Shared Peugeot taxis are a good alternative to matatus, though they're not subject to the same speed and safety regulations. The vehicles are usually Peugeot 505 station wagons (hence the local name) that take seven to nine passengers and leave when full.

Peugeots take less time to reach their destinations than matatus as they fill quicker and go from point to point without stopping, and so are slightly more expensive. Many companies have offices around the Accra, Cross and River Rds area in Nairobi, and serve destinations mostly in the north and west of the country.

### Taxi

Even the smallest Kenyan towns generally have at least one banged-up old taxi for easy access to outlying areas or even remoter villages, and you'll find cabs on virtually every corner in the larger cities, especially in Nairobi and Mombasa, where taking a taxi at night is virtually mandatory. Fares are invariably negotiable and start around KSh200 to KSh300 for short journeys. Most people pick up cabs from taxi ranks on the street, but some companies will take phone bookings and most hotels can order you a ride. Since few taxis in Kenya actually have functioning meters (or drivers who adhere to them), it's advisable that you agree on the fare prior to setting out. This will inevitably save you the time and trouble of arguing with your cabbie over the fare.

### Tuk-Tuk

They are an incongruous sight outside Southeast Asia, but several Kenyan towns and cities have these distinctive motorised minitaxis. The highest concentration is in Malindi, but they're also in Nairobi, Mombasa, Machakos and Diani Beach; Watamu has a handful of less sophisticated motorised rickshaws. Fares are negotiable, but should be at least KSh100 less than the equivalent taxi rate for a short journey (you wouldn't want to take them on a long one!).

## SAFARIS

While public transport in Kenya provides ample options for moving between towns and cities, an organised safari is the best way of getting into and around Kenya's national parks and remote areas like Lake Turkana, and they can sidestep many of the day-to-day hassles of travelling independently. See p65 for a full run-down of the many options on offer in Kenya.

## TRAIN

The Uganda Railway was once the main trade artery in East Africa, but these days the network has dwindled to two main routes, Nairobi–Kisumu and Nairobi–Mombasa. At the time of research, however, only the Nairobi–Mombasa train was running, and there remain a few question marks over the comfort and reliability of this route. Indeed, with a night service of around 13 hours, the Nairobi–Mombasa train is much slower and less frequent than going by air or road.

There are three classes on Kenyan trains, but only 1st and 2nd class can be recommended. Fares are US$65 in 1st class, US$54 in 2nd, including bed and breakfast. Note that passengers are divided up by gender.

First class consists of two-berth compartments with a washbasin, wardrobe, drinking water and a drinks service. Second class consists of plainer, four-berth compartments with a washbasin and drinking water. No compartment can be locked from the outside, so remember not to leave any valuables lying around if you leave it for any reason. You might want to padlock your rucksack to something during dinner and breakfast. Always lock your compartment from the inside before you go to sleep. Third class is seats only and security can be a real problem.

Passengers in 1st class on the Mombasa line are treated to a meal typically consisting of stews, curries or roast chicken served with rice and vegetables. Tea and coffee is included;

sodas (soft drinks), bottled water and alcoholic drinks are not, so ask the price before accepting that KSh1500 bottle of wine. Cold beer is available at all times in the dining car and can be delivered to your compartment.

There are booking offices in Nairobi and Mombasa, and it's recommended that you show up in person rather than trying to call.

You must book in advance for 1st and 2nd class, otherwise there'll probably be no berths available. Two to three days is usually sufficient, but remember that these services run just three times weekly in either direction. Note that compartment and berth numbers are posted up about 30 minutes prior to departure.

# Health Dr Caroline Evans

If you stay up-to-date with your vaccinations and take some basic preventive measures, you'd be pretty unlucky to succumb to most of the health hazards covered in this chapter. Africa certainly has an impressive selection of tropical and other diseases, but you're much more likely to get a bout of diarrhoea (in fact, you should bank on it), a cold or an infected mosquito bite rather than an exotic disease. When it comes to injuries (as opposed to illness), the most likely reason for needing medical help in Kenya is as a result of road accidents – vehicles are rarely well maintained, the roads are potholed and poorly lit, and drink-driving is common.

# BEFORE YOU GO

A little planning before departure, particularly for preexisting illnesses, will save you a lot of trouble later. Before a long trip, get a check-up from your dentist, and from your doctor if you use regular medication or have any chronic illness, such as high blood pressure. You should also organise spare contact lenses and glasses (and take your optical prescription with you); get a first-aid and medical kit together (see p358); and arrange necessary vaccinations (p358).

It's tempting to leave all the preparations to the last minute – don't! Many vaccines don't take effect until two weeks after you've been immunised, so visit a doctor four to eight weeks before departure. Ask your doctor for an International Certificate of Vaccination (known in some countries as the yellow booklet), which will list all the vaccinations you've received. This is mandatory for the African countries that require proof of yellow fever vaccination upon entry, which includes Kenya, but it's a good idea to carry it anyway wherever you travel.

Travellers can register with the **International Association for Medical Advice to Travellers** (IAMAT; www.iamat.org). Its website can help travellers find a doctor who has completed recognised training. Those heading off to very remote areas might like to do a first-aid course (contact the Red Cross or St John's Ambulance) or attend a remote medicine first-aid course, such as that offered by the **Royal Geographical Society** (www.wildernessmedicaltraining.co.uk).

If you are bringing medications with you, carry them in their original containers, clearly labelled. A signed and dated letter from your physician describing all medical conditions and medications, including generic names, is also a good idea. If carrying syringes or needles be sure to have a physician's letter documenting their medical necessity.

How do you go about getting the best possible medical help? It's difficult to say – it really depends on the severity of your illness or injury and the availability of local help. If malaria (p361) or another potentially serious disease is suspected, seek medical help as soon as possible or begin self-medicating if you are off the beaten track.

## INSURANCE

Find out in advance whether your insurance plan will make payments directly to providers or will reimburse you later for overseas health expenditures (many doctors expect payment in cash). It's vital to ensure that your travel insurance will cover the emergency transport required to get you to a hospital in a major city, to better medical facilities elsewhere in Africa, or all the way home, by air and with a medical attendant if necessary. Not all insurance covers this, so check the contract carefully. If you need medical help, your insurance company might be able to help locate the nearest hospital or clinic, or you can ask at your hotel. In an emergency, contact your embassy or consulate.

Membership of the **African Medical and Research Foundation** (AMREF; www.amref.org) provides an air evacuation service in medical emergencies in Kenya, as well as air ambulance transfers between medical facilities. Money paid by members for this service goes into providing grass-roots medical assistance for local people.

## RECOMMENDED VACCINATIONS

The **World Health Organization** (www.who.int/en/) recommends that all travellers be covered for diphtheria, tetanus, measles, mumps, rubella and polio, as well as for hepatitis B, regardless of their destination. A great time to ensure that all routine vaccination cover is complete is when you are planning your travel. The consequences of these diseases can be severe, and outbreaks of them do occur.

According to the **Centers for Disease Control and Prevention** (www.cdc.gov), the following vaccinations are recommended for Kenya: hepatitis A, hepatitis B, meningococcal meningitis, rabies and typhoid, and boosters for tetanus, diphtheria, polio and measles. It is also advisable to be vaccinated against yellow fever (see p363).

## MEDICAL CHECKLIST

It is a very good idea to carry a medical and first-aid kit with you, to help yourself in the case of minor illness or injury. Following is a list of items you should consider bringing:

- Acetaminophen (paracetamol) or aspirin
- Acetazolamide (Diamox) for altitude sickness (prescription only)
- Adhesive or paper tape
- Antibacterial ointment (eg Bactroban) for cuts and abrasions (prescription only)
- Antibiotics (prescription only), eg ciprofloxacin (Ciproxin) or norfloxacin (Utinor)
- Antidiarrhoeal drugs (eg loperamide)
- Antihistamines (for hay fever and allergic reactions)
- Anti-inflammatory drugs (eg ibuprofen)
- Antimalaria pills
- Bandages, gauze, gauze rolls
- Insect repellent containing DEET, for the skin
- Iodine tablets (for water purification)
- Oral rehydration salts
- Permethrin-containing insect spray for clothing, tents and bed nets
- Pocket knife
- Scissors, safety pins, tweezers
- Steroid cream or hydrocortisone cream (for allergic rashes)
- Sunscreen
- Syringes, sterile needles and fluids if travelling to remote areas
- Thermometer

If you are travelling through an area where malaria is a problem – particularly an area where *falciparum* malaria predominates – consider taking a self-diagnostic kit that can identify malaria in the blood from a finger prick.

## INTERNET RESOURCES

There is a wealth of travel health advice on the internet. A good place to start is the **Lonely Planet website** (www.lonelyplanet.com). The World Health Organization publishes a superb book called *International Travel and Health,* which is revised annually and available free at www.who.int/ith/. Other useful websites include **MD Travel Health** (www.mdtravelhealth.com), which provides complete travel health recommendations, updated daily, **Centers for Disease Control and Prevention** (www.cdc.gov) and **Fit for Travel** (www.fitfortravel.scot.nhs.uk).

It's also a good idea to consult your government's travel health website before departure, if one is available:

**Australia** www.smartraveller.gov.au
**Canada** www.hc-sc.gc.ca/english/index.html
**UK** www.nhs.uk/Healthcareabroad
**USA** www.cdc.gov/travel/

## FURTHER READING

- *A Comprehensive Guide to Wilderness and Travel Medicine* by Eric A Weiss
- *Healthy Travel* by Jane Wilson-Howarth
- *Healthy Travel Africa* by Isabelle Young
- *How to Stay Healthy Abroad* by Richard Dawood

▪ *Travel in Health* by Graham Fry
▪ *Travel with Children* by Cathy Lanigan

# IN TRANSIT

## DEEP VEIN THROMBOSIS (DVT)

Blood clots can form in the legs during flights, chiefly because of prolonged immobility. This formation of clots is known as deep vein thrombosis (DVT), and the longer the flight, the greater the risk. Although most blood clots are reabsorbed uneventfully, some might break off and travel through the blood vessels to the lungs, where they could cause life-threatening complications.

The chief symptom of DVT is swelling or pain of the foot, ankle or calf, usually but not always on just one side. When a blood clot travels to the lungs, it could cause chest pain and breathing difficulty. Travellers with any of these symptoms should immediately seek medical attention.

To help prevent the development of DVT on long flights you should regularly walk about the cabin, perform isometric compressions of the leg muscles (ie contract the leg muscles while sitting), drink plenty of fluids and avoid alcohol.

## JET LAG & MOTION SICKNESS

If you're crossing more than five time zones you could well suffer jet lag, which results in insomnia, fatigue, malaise or nausea. To minimise the effects, try drinking plenty of fluids (of the nonalcoholic variety) and eating light meals. Upon arrival, get exposure to natural sunlight and readjust your schedule (for meals, sleep etc) as soon as possible.

Antihistamines such as dimenhydrinate (Dramamine) and meclizine (Antivert, Bonine) are usually the first choice for treating motion sickness. The main side effect of these drugs is drowsiness. If you're concerned about taking medication, a herbal alternative is ginger (in the form of ginger tea, biscuits or crystallised ginger), which works like a charm for some people.

# IN KENYA

## AVAILABILITY & COST OF HEALTH CARE

Health care in Kenya is varied: it can be excellent in Nairobi, which generally has well-trained doctors and nurses, but it is often patchy off the beaten track, even in Mombasa. Medicine and even sterile dressings and intravenous fluids might need to be purchased from a local pharmacy. The standard of dental care is equally variable, and there is an increased risk of hepatitis B and HIV transmission from poorly sterilised equipment.

By and large, public hospitals in Kenya offer the cheapest service, but will have the least up-to-date equipment and medications; mission hospitals (where donations are the usual form of payment) often have more reasonable facilities; and private hospitals and clinics are more expensive but tend to have more advanced drugs and equipment and better trained medical staff.

Most drugs can be purchased over the counter without a prescription. Many drugs for sale in Kenya might be ineffective; they might be counterfeit or might not have been stored in the right conditions. The most common examples of counterfeit drugs are malaria tablets and expensive antibiotics, such as ciprofloxacin. Most drugs are available in Nairobi, but remote villages will be lucky to have a couple of paracetamol tablets. It is strongly recommended that you bring all medication from home. Also, the availability and efficacy of condoms cannot be relied upon – bring all the contraception you'll need. Condoms bought in Kenya might not be of the same quality as in Europe, North America or Australia, and they might have been incorrectly stored.

There is a high risk of contracting HIV from infected blood if you receive a blood transfusion in Kenya. The **Blood Care Foundation** (www.bloodcare.org.uk) is a useful source of safe, screened blood, which can be transported to any part of the world within 24 hours.

## INFECTIOUS DISEASES

It's a formidable list but, as we say, a few precautions go a long way…

### Bilharzia (Schistosomiasis)

This disease is spread by flukes (minute worms) that are carried by a species of freshwater snail. The flukes are carried inside the snail, which then sheds them into slow-moving or still water. The parasites penetrate human skin as people paddle or swim and then migrate to the bladder or bowel. They are passed out via stool or urine and could contaminate fresh water, where the cycle starts again. Paddling or swimming in suspect freshwater lakes or slow-running rivers should be avoided. There may be no symptoms. However, there may be a transient fever and rash, and advanced cases may have blood in the stool or in the urine. A blood test can detect antibodies if you might have been exposed, and treatment is then possible in specialist travel or infectious disease clinics. If not treated the infection can cause kidney failure or permanent bowel damage. It is not possible for you to infect others directly.

## Cholera

Cholera is usually only a problem during natural or other disasters, eg war, floods or earthquakes, although small outbreaks can also occur at other times. Travellers are rarely affected. The disease is caused by a bacteria and spread via contaminated drinking water. The main symptom is profuse watery diarrhoea, which causes debilitation if fluids are not replaced quickly. An oral cholera vaccine is available in the USA, but it is not particularly effective. Most cases of cholera can be avoided by drinking only clean water and by avoiding potentially contaminated food. Treatment is by fluid replacement (orally or via a drip), but sometimes antibiotics are needed. Self-treatment is not advised.

## Diphtheria

Found in all of Africa, diphtheria is spread through close respiratory contact. It usually causes a high temperature and a severe sore throat. A membrane can form across the throat, requiring a tracheotomy to prevent suffocation. Vaccination is recommended for those likely to be in close contact with the locals in infected areas. This is more important for long stays than for short-term trips. The vaccine is given as an injection alone or with tetanus, and lasts 10 years.

## Filariasis

Tiny worms migrating in the lymphatic system cause filariasis. The bite from an infected mosquito spreads the infection. Symptoms include localised itching and swelling of the legs and/or genitalia. Treatment is available.

## Hepatitis A

Hepatitis A is spread through contaminated food (particularly shellfish) and water. It causes jaundice and, although it is rarely fatal, it can cause prolonged lethargy. If you're recovering from hepatitis A, you shouldn't drink alcohol for up to six months afterwards, but once you've recovered, there won't be any long-term problems. The first symptoms include dark urine and a yellow colour to the whites of the eyes. Sometimes a fever and abdominal pain might be present. Hepatitis A vaccine (Avaxim, Vaqta, Havrix) is given as an injection: a single dose will give protection for up to a year, and a booster after a year gives 10-year protection. Hepatitis A and typhoid vaccines can also be given as a single-dose vaccine, with hepatyrix or viatim.

## Hepatitis B

Hepatitis B is spread through infected blood, contaminated needles and sexual intercourse. It can also be spread from an infected mother to the baby during childbirth. Hepatitis B affects the liver, which causes jaundice and occasionally liver failure. Most people recover completely, but some people might be chronic carriers of the virus, which could lead eventually to cirrhosis or liver cancer. Those visiting high-risk areas for long periods or those with increased social or occupational risk should be immunised. Many countries now give hepatitis B as part of routine childhood vaccinations. It is given singly or can be given at the same time as hepatitis A (hepatyrix).

A course will give protection for at least five years. It can be given over four weeks or six months.

## HIV

Human immunodeficiency virus (HIV), the virus that causes acquired immune deficiency syndrome (AIDS), is an enormous problem in Kenya, where the infection rate is around 6.7% of the adult population. The virus is spread through infected blood and blood products, by sexual intercourse with an infected partner, and from an infected mother to her baby during childbirth or breastfeeding. It can be spread through 'blood to blood' contacts, such as with contaminated instruments during medical, dental, acupuncture and other body-piercing procedures, and through sharing intravenous needles. At present there is no cure; medication that might keep the disease under control is available, but these drugs are too expensive for the overwhelming majority of Africans, and are not readily available for

**AIDS IN KENYA**

Like most of its neighbours, Kenya is in the grip of a devastating AIDS epidemic. There are more than 2.5 million Kenyans with full-blown AIDS, and more than 750 people die from the disease every day. AIDS is predominantly a heterosexual disease in Kenya and now strikes all classes of people. Close to one million children have been orphaned and many others are infected while in the womb.

Teachers have been badly affected – at least 20 die daily – because they are mostly aged in their 20s, the group that's most affected by HIV/AIDS. Kenya is facing an education crisis as a result, leaving even fewer people to spread the AIDS-awareness message. Around 85% of prostitutes are affected, and young girls in general are especially vulnerable, due to the widespread belief that AIDS can be cured by sleeping with girls who are virgins.

Drug treatments that are available in the West to increase the lifespan of AIDS sufferers and reduce the risk of infection passing to the foetus in HIV-infected women remain well beyond the financial reach of most Kenyans, few of whom have access to even basic health care. The problem is unlikely to improve as long as Western drug companies do not allow developing countries to produce much cheaper generic versions of their products. Currently the cost of treating a single AIDS victim for a year is more than US$35,000, while the annual wage of most people in Kenya is around US$500.

travellers either. If you think you might have been exposed to HIV, a blood test is necessary; a three-month gap after exposure and before testing is required to allow antibodies to appear in the blood.

## Malaria

Malaria is a major health scourge in Kenya. Infection rates vary with season (higher in the rainy season) and climate, so check out the situation before departure. The incidence of malarial transmission at altitudes higher than 2000m is rare.

Malaria is caused by a parasite in the bloodstream spread via the bite of the female anopheles mosquito. There are several types, falciparum malaria being the most dangerous and the predominant form in Kenya. Unlike most other diseases regularly uencountered by travellers, there is no vaccination against malaria (yet). However, several different drugs are used to prevent malaria and new ones are in the pipeline. Up-to-date advice from a travel-health clinic is essential, as some medication is more suitable for some travellers than others. The pattern of drug-resistant malaria is changing rapidly, so what was advised several years ago might no longer be the case.

### SYMPTOMS

Malaria can affect people in several ways. The early stages include headaches, fevers, generalised aches and pains, and malaise, often mistaken for flu. Other symptoms can include abdominal pain, diarrhoea and a cough. Anyone who develops a fever while in a malarial area should assume malarial infection until a blood test proves negative, even if you've been taking antimalarial medication. If not treated, the next stage can develop within 24 hours, particularly if falciparum malaria is the parasite: jaundice, reduced consciousness and coma (known as cerebral malaria), followed by death. Treatment in hospital is essential, and if patients enter this late stage of the disease the death rate may still be as high as 10%, even in the best intensive-care facilities.

### SIDE EFFECTS & RISKS

Many travellers are under the impression that malaria is a mild illness, that treatment is always easy and successful, and that taking antimalarial drugs causes more illness through side effects than actually getting malaria. Unfortunately this is not true. Side effects of the medication depend on the drug being taken. Doxycycline can cause heartburn and indigestion; mefloquine (Larium) can cause anxiety attacks, insomnia and nightmares, and (rarely) severe psychiatric disorders; chloroquine can cause nausea and hair loss; and proguanil can cause mouth ulcers. These side effects are not universal, and can be minimised by taking medication correctly, such as with food.

If you decide that you really do not wish to take antimalarial drugs, you must understand the risks, and be obsessive about avoiding

---

**THE ANTIMALARIAL A TO D**

- A – Awareness of the risk. No medication is totally effective, but protection of up to 95% is achievable with most drugs, as long as other measures have been taken.

- B – Bites: avoid at all costs. Sleep in a screened room, use a mosquito spray or coils; sleep under a permethrin-impregnated net at night. Cover up at night with long trousers and long sleeves, preferably with permethrin-treated clothing. Apply appropriate repellent to all areas of exposed skin in the evenings.

- C – Chemical prevention (ie antimalarial drugs) is usually needed in malaria-infected areas. Expert advice is needed as the resistance patterns of the parasite can change, and new drugs are in development. Not all antimalarial drugs are suitable for everyone. Most antimalarial drugs need to be started at least a week in advance and continued for four weeks after the last possible exposure to malaria.

- D – Diagnosis. If you have a fever or flu-like illness within a year of travel to a malaria-infected area, malaria is a possibility, and immediate medical attention is necessary.

---

mosquito bites. Use nets and insect repellent, and report any fever or flu-like symptoms to a doctor as soon as possible. Some people advocate homeopathic preparations against malaria, such as Demal200, but as yet there is no conclusive evidence that this is effective, and many homeopaths do not recommend their use. Some people should not take a particular antimalarial drug, eg people with epilepsy should avoid mefloquine, and doxycycline should not be taken by pregnant women or children younger than 12. Malaria in pregnancy frequently results in miscarriage or premature labour and the risks to both mother and foetus during pregnancy are considerable. Travel in Kenya when pregnant should be carefully considered.

Adults who have survived childhood malaria develop a resistance and usually only develop mild cases of malaria if it recurs; most Western travellers have no resistance at all. Resistance wanes after 18 months of nonexposure, so even if you have had malaria in the past, you might no longer be resistant.

### STAND-BY TREATMENT
If you are going to be in remote areas or far from major towns, consider taking a stand-by treatment. Emergency stand-by treatments should be seen as emergency treatment aimed at saving the patient's life and not as a routine way of self-medicating. It should be used only if you will be far from medical facilities and have been advised about the symptoms of malaria and how to use the medication. Medical advice should be sought as soon as possible to confirm whether the treatment has been

successful. The type of stand-by treatment used will depend on local conditions, such as drug resistance, and on what antimalarial drugs were being used before stand-by treatment. This is worthwhile because you want to avoid contracting a particularly serious form such as cerebral malaria, which can be fatal within 24 hours. Self-diagnostic kits, which can identify malaria in the blood from a finger prick, are also available in the West.

### Meningococcal Meningitis
Meningococcal infection is spread through close respiratory contact and is more likely to be contracted in crowded situations, such as dormitories, buses and clubs. Infection is uncommon in travellers. Vaccination is recommended for long stays and is especially important towards the end of the dry season. Symptoms include a fever, severe headache, neck stiffness and a red rash. Immediate medical treatment is necessary.

The ACWY vaccine is recommended for all travellers in sub-Saharan Africa. This vaccine is different from the meningococcal meningitis C vaccine given to children and adolescents in some countries; it is safe to be given both types of vaccine.

### Poliomyelitis
Polio is generally spread through contaminated food and water. It is one of the vaccines given in childhood in the West and should be boosted every 10 years, either orally (a drop on the tongue) or as an injection. Polio can be carried asymptomatically (ie showing no symptoms) and could cause a transient fever. In rare cases

it causes weakness or paralysis of one or more muscles, which might be permanent.

## Rabies

Rabies is spread by the bites or licks of an infected animal on broken skin. It is always fatal once the clinical symptoms start (which might be up to several months after an infected bite), so postbite vaccination should be taken as soon as possible. Postbite vaccination (whether or not you've been vaccinated before the bite) prevents the virus from spreading to the central nervous system.

Animal handlers should be vaccinated, as should those travelling to remote areas where a reliable source of post-bite vaccine is not available within 24 hours. To prevent the disease, three injections are needed over a month. If you have not been vaccinated and receive a bite, you will need a course of five injections starting 24 hours or as soon as possible after the injury. If you have been vaccinated, you will need fewer postbite injections, and have more time to seek medical help.

## Rift Valley Fever

This fever is spread occasionally via mosquito bites and is rarely fatal. The symptoms are of a fever and flu-like illness.

## River Blindness (Onchocerciasis)

This is caused by the larvae of a tiny worm, which is spread by the bite of a small fly. The earliest sign of infection is intensely itchy, red, sore eyes. Travellers are rarely severely affected. Treatment should be sought in a specialised clinic.

## Sleeping Sickness (Trypanosomiasis)

Sleeping sickness is spread via the bite of the tsetse fly and causes a headache, fever and eventually coma. There is an effective treatment.

## Tuberculosis (TB)

TB is spread through close respiratory contact and occasionally through infected milk or milk products. BCG vaccination is recommended for anyone who is likely to be mixing closely with the local population, although the vaccination gives only moderate protection against TB. It is more important to be vaccinated for long-term stays than for short stays. The BCG vaccine is not available in all countries, but is given routinely to many children in developing countries. The vaccination is usually given in a specialised chest clinic and causes a small permanent scar at the site of injection. It is a live vaccine and should not be given to pregnant women or immuno-compromised individuals.

TB can be asymptomatic, only being picked up by a routine chest X-ray. Alternatively, it can cause a cough, weight loss or fever, sometimes months or even years after exposure.

## Typhoid

This illness is spread through handling food or drinking water that has been contaminated by infected human faeces. The first symptom of infection is usually a fever or a pink rash on the abdomen. Sometimes septicaemia (blood poisoning) can also occur. A typhoid vaccine (typhim Vi, typherix) will give protection for three years. In some countries, the oral vaccine Vivotif is also available. Antibiotics are usually given as treatment, and death is rare unless septicaemia occurs.

## Yellow Fever

You should carry a certificate as evidence of vaccination against yellow fever if you've recently been in an infected country, to avoid immigration problems. For a full list of countries where yellow fever exists visit the websites of the **World Health Organization** (www.who.int/wer/) or the **Centers for Disease Control and Prevention** (www.cdc.gov/travel/blusheet.htm). A traveller without a legally required up-to-date certificate could possibly be vaccinated and detained in isolation at the port of arrival for up to 10 days, or even repatriated.

Yellow fever is spread by infected mosquitoes. Symptoms range from a flu-like illness to severe hepatitis (liver inflammation), jaundice and death. Vaccination must be given at a designated clinic and is valid for 10 years. It's a live vaccine and must not be given to immuno-compromised or pregnant women. For visitors to Kenya, vaccination is not mandatory but is recommended.

## TRAVELLER'S DIARRHOEA

Although it's not inevitable that you will get diarrhoea while travelling in Kenya, it's certainly likely. Diarrhoea is the most common travel-related illness, and sometimes simply dietary changes, such as increased spices or oils, are the cause. To help prevent diarrhoea, avoid tap water (see p365). You should also only eat fresh fruits or vegetables if cooked or peeled, and be wary of dairy products that might contain unpasteurised milk. Although freshly cooked food can often be safe, plates or serving utensils might be dirty, so be highly selective when eating food from street vendors (ensure that cooked food is piping hot right through).

If you develop diarrhoea, drink plenty of fluids, preferably an oral rehydration solution containing water (lots), and some salt and sugar. A few loose stools don't require treatment but if you start having more than four or five stools a day, you should start taking an antibiotic (usually a quinoline drug, such as ciprofloxacin or norfloxacin) and an anti-diarrhoeal agent (eg loperamide) if you are not within easy reach of a toilet. If diarrhoea is bloody, persists for more than 72 hours or is accompanied by fever, shaking chills or abdominal pain, seek medical attention.

### Amoebic Dysentery

Contracted by eating contaminated food and water, amoebic dysentery causes blood and mucus in the faeces. It can be relatively mild and tends to come on gradually, but seek medical advice if you think you have the illness as it won't clear up without treatment (which is with specific antibiotics).

### Giardiasis

This, like amoebic dysentery, is caused by contaminated food or water. The illness usually appears a week or more after exposure to the parasite. Giardiasis might cause only a short-lived bout of typical traveller's diarrhoea, but may cause persistent diarrhoea. Ideally, seek medical advice if you suspect you have giardiasis, but if you are in a remote area you could start a course of antibiotics.

## ENVIRONMENTAL HAZARDS
### Heat Exhaustion

This condition occurs following heavy sweating and excessive fluid loss with inadequate replacement of fluids and salt, and is particularly common in hot climates when taking unaccustomed exercise before full acclimatisation.

Symptoms include headache, dizziness and tiredness. Dehydration is already happening by the time you feel thirsty – aim to drink sufficient water to produce pale, diluted urine. Self-treatment: fluid replacement with water and/or fruit juice, and cooling by cold water and fans. The treatment of the salt-loss component consists of consuming salty fluids such as soup, and adding a little more salt to foods than usual.

### Heatstroke

Heat exhaustion is a precursor to the much more serious condition of heatstroke. In this case there is damage to the sweating mechanism, with an excessive rise in body temperature; irrational and hyperactive behaviour; and eventually loss of consciousness and death. Rapid cooling by spraying the body with water and fanning is ideal. Emergency fluid and electrolyte replacement is usually also required by intravenous drip.

### Insect Bites & Stings

Mosquitoes might not always carry malaria or dengue fever, but they (and other insects) can cause irritation and infected bites. To avoid these problems, take the same precautions as you would for avoiding malaria (see p362). Use DEET-based insect repellents. Excellent clothing treatments are also available; mosquitoes that land on treated clothing will die.

Bee and wasp stings cause real problems only to those who have a severe allergy to the stings (anaphylaxis). If you are one of these people, carry an EpiPen – an adrenaline (epinephrine) injection, which you can give yourself. This could save your life.

Sandflies are found near many African beaches. They usually only cause a nasty itchy bite but can carry a rare skin disorder called cutaneous leishmaniasis. Prevention of bites with DEET-based repellents is sensible.

Scorpions are frequently found in arid or dry climates. They can cause a painful bite that is sometimes life-threatening. If you are bitten by a scorpion, seek immediate medical assistance.

Bed bugs are often found in hostels and cheap hotels. Bites lead to very itchy, lumpy skin. Spraying the mattress with crawling-insect killer then changing the bedding will get rid of them.

Scabies is also frequently found in cheap accommodation. These tiny mites live in the skin, particularly between the fingers. They cause an intensely itchy rash. The itch is easily treated with malathion and permethrin lotion from a pharmacy; other members of the household also need treatment to avoid spreading scabies, even if they do not show any symptoms.

## Snake Bites

Basically, avoid getting bitten! Don't walk barefoot, and don't stick your hand into holes or cracks. However, 50% of those bitten by venomous snakes are not actually injected with poison (envenomed). If bitten, do not panic. Immobilise the bitten limb with a splint (such as a stick) and apply a bandage over the site, with firm pressure – similar to bandaging a sprain. Do not apply a tourniquet, or cut or suck the bite. Get medical help as soon as possible so antivenene can be given if needed.

## Water

Never drink tap water unless it has been boiled, filtered or chemically disinfected (such as with iodine tablets). Never drink from streams, rivers and lakes. It's also best to avoid drinking from pumps and wells – some do bring pure water to the surface, but the presence of animals can still contaminate supplies.

## TRADITIONAL MEDICINE

At least 80% of the African population relies on traditional medicine, often either because conventional Western-style medicine is too expensive, because of prevailing cultural attitudes and beliefs, or simply because in some cases it works. It might also be because there's often no other choice – a World Health Organization survey found that there is one medical doctor for every 70,000 people in Kenya, but a traditional healer for every 250 people.

Although some traditional African remedies seem to work on illnesses such as malaria, sickle cell anaemia, high blood pressure and some AIDS symptoms, most African healers tend to learn their art by apprenticeship, so education (and consequently the application of knowledge) is inconsistent and unregulated.

Rather than attempting to stamp out traditional practices, or simply pretending they aren't happening, a positive step taken by Kenya is the regulation of traditional medicine by creating healers' associations and offering courses for healers on such topics as sanitary practices.

It remains unlikely in the short term that even a basic level of conventional Western-style medicine will be made available to all the people of Africa. Traditional medicine, on the other hand, will almost certainly continue to be practised widely.

HEALTH

# Language

## CONTENTS

English and Swahili (called *Kiswahili* in the language itself) are the official languages of Kenya and are taught in schools throughout the country. There are also many major indigenous languages (including Kikuyu, Luo, Kikamba, Maasai and Samburu) and a plethora of minor tribal languages. Hindi and Urdu are still spoken by residents of Indian subcontinent origin.

Most urban Kenyans and even tribal people who deal with tourists speak English, so you shouldn't experience too many problems making yourself understood. Italian is almost the second language on the coast, and Kenyans working in the tourist industry may also speak German. Most tourists to the coast also visit the national parks, so safari operators almost always speak some Italian and German.

Swahili is widely spoken in Kenya, but you'll notice more English words creeping into the language the further you get away from the coast. You'll also find that there are more books and newspapers available in English than there are in Swahili. Nonetheless, a working knowledge of Swahili, especially when travelling outside urban areas, is very useful. It will enrich your travel experience and open doors, often enabling you to communicate with people who don't speak English, particularly speakers of different tribal languages.

Another language you may come across in Kenya is Sheng, which is spoken almost exclusively by young people. Essentially a patois, it's a mixture of Swahili and English, with a fair sprinkling of Hindi, Gujarati, Kikuyu and other tribal languages. Unless you can speak reasonable Swahili, you probably won't realise Sheng is being spoken – listen out for the distinctive greeting between friends – *Sassa!*. The response can be *Besht, Mambo* or *Fit* (pronounced almost like 'feet').

# SWAHILI

The Kamusi Project at www.kamusiproject.org is an excellent general online reference to the language and contains a useful audio pronunciation guide. Get a copy of Lonely Planet's *Swahili Phrasebook* for a handy, pocket-sized language guide chock-full of useful Swahili.

## PRONUNCIATION

Perhaps the easiest part of learning Swahili is the pronunciation. Every letter is pronounced, unless it's part of the consonant combinations discussed in the Consonants section below. If a letter is written twice, it is pronounced twice – *mzee* (respected elder) has three syllables: m-ze-e. Note that the 'm' is a separate syllable, and that the double 'e' indicates a lengthened vowel sound. Word stress almost always falls on the second-last syllable.

### Vowels

Correct pronunciation of vowels is the key to making yourself understood in Swahili. If the following guidelines don't work for you, listen closely to how Swahili speakers pronounce their words and spend some time practising.

Remember that if two vowels appear next to each other, each must be pronounced in turn. For example, *kawaida* (usual) is pronounced ka-wa-ee-da.

a    as in 'calm'
e    as the 'ey' in 'they'
i    as the 'ee' in 'keep'
o    as in 'go'
u    as the 'oo' in 'moon'

## Consonants

Most consonants in Swahili have equivalents in English. The sounds **th** and **dh** occur only in words borrowed from Arabic. The **ng** combination is tricky at first but gets easier with practice.

| | |
|---|---|
| **r** | Swahili speakers make only a slight distinction between **r** and **l**; use a light 'd' for **r** and you'll be pretty close. |
| **dh** | as 'th' in 'this' |
| **th** | as in 'thing' |
| **ny** | as in 'canyon' |
| **ng** | as in 'singer' |
| **gh** | like the 'ch' in Scottish *loch* |
| **g** | as in 'get' |
| **ch** | as in 'church' |

## ACCOMMODATION

| Where's a ...? | ... iko wapi? |
|---|---|
| **camping ground** | uwanja wa kambi |
| **guest house** | gesti |
| **hotel** | hoteli |
| **youth hostel** | hosteli ya vijana |

**Can you recommend cheap lodging?**
Unaweza kunipendekezea malazi rahisi?
**What's the address?**
Anwani ni nini?

| Do you have a ... room? | Kuna chumba kwa ...? |
|---|---|
| **single** | mtu mmoja |
| **double** | watu wawili, kitanda kimoja |
| **twin** | watu wawili, vitanda viwili |

**How much is it per day/person?**
Ni bei gani kwa siku/mtu?
**Can I see the room?**
Naomba nione chumba?
**Where's the bathroom?**
Choo iko wapi?
**Where are the toilets?**
Vyoo viko wapi?
**I'll take it.**
Nataka.
**I'm leaving now.**
Naondoka sasa.

## EMERGENCIES

| Help! | Saidia! |
|---|---|
| **There's been an accident!** | Ajali imetokea! |
| **Call the police!** | Waite polisi! |
| **Call a doctor!** | Mwite daktari! |
| **I'm lost.** | Nimejipotea. |
| **Leave me alone!** | Niache! |

## CONVERSATION & ESSENTIALS

It's considered rude to speak to someone without first greeting them, so even if you only want directions, greet the person first. *Jambo* and *salama* can be used as the Swahili equivalents of 'excuse me'. *Shikamoo* is also a respectful greeting used for elders: the reply is *marahaba*.

| Hello. | Jambo or Salama. |
|---|---|
| **Welcome.** | Karibu. |
| **Goodbye.** | Kwa heri. |
| **(Until) tomorrow.** | Kesho. |
| **Goodnight.** | Lala salama. |
| **See you later.** | Tutaonana. |
| **Yes.** | Ndiyo. |
| **No.** | Hapana. |
| **Please.** (if asking a big favour) | Tafadhali. |
| **Thanks (very much).** | Asante (sana). |
| **You're welcome.** | Karibu. |
| **Excuse me.** | Samahani. |
| **Sorry.** | Pole. |
| **How are you?** | Habari? |
| **I'm fine, thanks.** | Nzuri. |
| **What's your name?** | Unaitwa nani? |
| **My name is ...** | Jina langu ni ... |
| **Where are you from?** | Unatoka wapi? |
| **I'm from ...** | Mimi ninatoka ... |
| **Where do you live?** | Unakaa wapi? |
| **I live in ...** | Ninakaa ... |
| **May I take a picture?** | Naomba kupiga picha. |
| **Just a minute.** | Subiri kidogo. |

## DIRECTIONS

| Where's ...? | ... iko wapi? |
|---|---|
| **It's straight ahead.** | Iko moja kwa moja. |
| **near** | karibu na |
| **next to** | jirani ya |
| **opposite** | ng'ambo ya |

| Turn ... | Geuza ... |
|---|---|
| **at the corner** | kwenye kona |
| **at the traffic lights** | kwenye taa za barabarani |

LANGUAGE

| left | kushoto |
| right | kulia |

## HEALTH

| I'm sick. | Mimi ni mgonjwa. |
| It hurts here. | Inauma hapa. |

| I'm allergic to ... | Nina mzio wa ... |
| antibiotics | viuavijasumu |
| aspirin | aspirini |
| bees | nyuki |
| nuts | kokwa |
| peanuts | karanga |

| antiseptic | dawa ya kusafisha jeraha |
| condoms | kondom |
| contraceptives | kingamimba |
| insect repellent | dawa la kufukuza wadudu |
| iodine | iodini |
| painkillers | viondoa maumivu |
| thermometer | pimajoto |
| water purification tablets | vidonge vya kusafisha maji |

## LANGUAGE DIFFICULTIES

**Do you speak (English)?**
Unasema (Kiingereza)?
**Does anyone speak (English)?**
Kuna mtu yeyote kusema (Kiingereza)?
**What does (asante) mean?**
Neno (asante) lina maana gani?
**Yes, I understand.**
Ndiyo, naelewa.
**No, I don't understand.**
Hapana, sielewi.
**Could you please write ... down?**
Tafadhali ... andika?
**Can you show me (on the map)?**
Unaweza kunionyesha (katika ramani)?

## NUMBERS

| 0 | sifuri |
| 1 | moja |
| 2 | mbili |
| 3 | tatu |
| 4 | nne |
| 5 | tano |
| 6 | sita |
| 7 | saba |
| 8 | nane |
| 9 | tisa |
| 10 | kumi |
| 11 | kumi na moja |
| 12 | kumi na mbili |
| 13 | kumi na tatu |
| 14 | kumi na nne |
| 15 | kumi na tano |
| 16 | kumi na sita |
| 17 | kumi na saba |
| 18 | kumi na nane |
| 19 | kumi na tisa |
| 20 | ishirini |
| 21 | ishirini na moja |
| 22 | ishirini na mbili |
| 30 | thelathini |
| 40 | arobaini |
| 50 | hamsini |
| 60 | sitini |
| 70 | sabini |
| 80 | themanini |
| 90 | tisini |
| 100 | mia moja |
| 1000 | elfu |

## ON SAFARI

| Look there. | Tazama pale. |
| What is there? | Iko nini pale? |
| What animal is that? | Huyo ni mnyama gani? |
| electric fence | usiguse sengeni |
| Watch out! | Angalia!/Chunga! |
| Danger (on signs) | Hatari |

| African buffalo | mbogo |
| antelope | pofu/kulungu |
| baboon | nyani |
| bird | ndege |
| bushbaby | komba |
| cheetah | duma |
| crocodile | mamba |
| elephant | ndovu/tembo |
| gazelle | swala/swara/paa |
| giraffe | twiga |
| hippopotamus | kiboko |
| impala | swala pala |
| jackal | mbweha |
| leopard | chui |
| lion | simba |
| mongoose | nguchiro |
| rhinoceros | kifaru |
| snake | nyoka |
| spotted hyena | fisi |
| water buffalo | nyati |
| zebra | punda milia |

## QUESTION WORDS

| Who? | Nani? |
| What? | Nini? |
| When? | Lini? |
| Where? | Wapi? |
| Which? | Gani? |

LANGUAGE

| Why? | Kwa nini? |
| How? | Namna? |

## SHOPPING & SERVICES

| department store | duka lenye vitu vingi |
| general store | duka lenye vitu mbalimbali |
| market | soko |

| I'd like to buy ... | Nataka kununua ... |
| I'm just looking. | Naangalia tu. |
| How much is it? | Ni bei gani? |
| Can I look at it? | Naomba nione. |
| I don't like it. | Sipendi. |
| That's too expensive. | Ni ghali mno. |
| Please lower the price. | Punguza bei, tafadhali. |
| I'll take it. | Nataka. |

| Do you accept ...? | Mnakubali ...? |
| credit cards | kadi ya benki |
| travellers cheques | hundi ya msafiri |

| more | zaidi |
| less | chache zaidi |

| Where's (a/the) ...? | ... iko wapi? |
| bank | benki |
| ... embassy | ubalozi ... |
| hospital | hospitali |
| internet cafe | Intanet Kafe |
| post office | posta |
| public phone | simu ya mtaani |
| public toilet | choo cha hadhara |
| tourist office | maarifa kwa watalii |

## TIME & DATES

| What time is it? | Ni saa ngapi? |
| It's (ten) o'clock. | Ni saa (nne). |
| morning | asubuhi |
| afternoon | mchana |
| evening | jioni |
| today | leo |
| tomorrow | kesho |
| yesterday | jana |

| Monday | Jumatatu |
| Tuesday | Jumanne |
| Wednesday | Jumatano |
| Thursday | Alhamisi |
| Friday | Ijumaa |
| Saturday | Jumamosi |
| Sunday | Jumapili |
| January | mwezi wa kwanza |
| February | mwezi wa pili |
| March | mwezi wa tatu |

| April | mwezi wa nne |
| May | mwezi wa tano |
| June | mwezi wa sita |
| July | mwezi wa saba |
| August | mwezi wa nane |
| September | mwezi wa tisa |
| October | mwezi wa kumi |
| November | mwezi wa kumi na moja |
| December | mwezi wa kumi na mbili |

## TRANSPORT
### Public Transport

**What time is the ... leaving?**
*... inaondoka saa ngapi?*
**Which ... goes to (...)?**
*... ipi huenda (...)?*

| bus | basi |
| minibus | matatu |
| plane | ndege |
| train | treni |

**When's the ... (bus)?**
*(Basi) ... itaondoka lini?*

| first | ya kwanza |
| last | ya mwisho |
| next | ijayo |

**A ... ticket to (...).**
*Tiketi moja ya ... kwenda (...).*

| 1st-class | daraja la kwanza |
| 2nd-class | daraja la pili |
| one-way | kwenda tu |
| return | kwenda na kurudi |

| cancelled | imefutwa |
| delayed | imeche leweshwa |
| platform | stendi |
| ticket window | dirisha la tiketi |
| timetable | ratiba |

### Private Transport

**I'd like to hire a/an ...** *Nataka kukodi ...*

| bicycle | baisikeli |
| car | gari |
| 4WD | forbaifor |
| motorbike | pikipiki |

**Are you willing to hire out your car/motorbike?**
*Unaweza kunikodisha gari/pikipiki yako?*
**(How long) Can I park here?**
*Naweza kuegesha hapa (kwa muda gani)?*
**Is this the road to (Embu)?**
*Hii ni barabara kwenda (Embu)?*
**Where's a petrol station?**
*Kituo cha mafuta kiko wapi?*

LANGUAGE

**Please fill it up.**
*Jaza tangi/tanki.*
**I'd like ... litres.**
*Nataka lita ...*

| diesel | *dizeli* |
| petrol | *mafuta* |
| I need a mechanic. | *Nahitaji fundi.* |
| I've had an accident. | *Nimepata ajali.* |
| I have a flat tyre. | *Nina pancha.* |
| I've run out of petrol. | *Mafuta yamekwisha.* |

**The car/motorbike has broken down (at Chalinze).**
*Gari/pikipiki ime haribika (Chalinze).*
**The car/motorbike won't start.**
*Gari/pikipiki haiwaki.*
**Could I pay for a ride in your truck?**
*Naweza kulipa kwa lifti katika lori lako?*

**Could I contribute to the petrol cost?**
*Naweza kuchangia sehemu ya bei ya mafuta?*
**Thanks for the ride.**
*Asante kwa lifti.*

# TRAVEL WITH CHILDREN

| I need a/an ... | *Nahitaji ...* |
| Is there a/an ...? | *Kuna ...?* |
| baby seat | *kiti cha kitoto* |
| child-minding service | *anayeweza kumlea mtoto* |
| disposable nappies/ diapers | *nepi* |
| (English-speaking) babysitter | *yaya (anayesema Kiingereza)* |
| highchair | *kiti juu cha mtoto* |
| potty | *choo cha mtoto* |
| stroller | *kigari cha mtoto* |

Also available from Lonely Planet:
*Swahili Phrasebook*

# Glossary

The following are some common words you are likely to come across when in Kenya. For a more complete glossary of food terms, see p51.

**abanyamorigo** – medicine man
**askari** – security guard, watchman

**banda** – thatched-roof hut with wooden or earthen walls or simple wood-and-stone accommodation
**bao** – traditional African board game
**beach boys** – self-appointed guides, touts, hustlers and dealers on the coast
**bhang** – marijuana
**boda-boda** – bicycle-taxi
**boma** – village
**bui-bui** – black cover-all garment worn by Islamic women outside the home

**cardphone** – phone that takes a phonecard
**chai** – tea, but also a bribe
**chai masala** – sweet tea with spices
**chakula** – food
**chang'a** – dangerous homemade alcoholic brew containing methyl alcohol
**choo** – toilet; pronounced *cho*

**dhow** – traditional Arabic sailing vessel
**dudu** – a small insect or bug; a creepy-crawly
**duka** – small shop or kiosk selling household basics

**fundi** – repair man or woman who fixes clothing or cars, or is in the building trades; also an expert

**gof** – volcanic crater

**hakuna matata** – no problem; watch out – this often means there is a problem!
**harambee** – the concept of community self-help; voluntary fundraising; a cornerstone of Kenyatta's ideology
**hatari** – danger
**hoteli** – basic local eatery

**ito** – wooden 'eyes' painted on a dhow to allow it to see obstacles in the water

**jinga!** – crazy!; also used as an adjective
**jua kali** – literally 'fierce sun'; usually an outdoor vehicle-repair shop or market

**kali** – fierce or ferocious; eg *hatari mbwa kali* – 'danger fierce dog'
**kanga** – printed cotton wraparound incorporating a Swahili proverb; worn by many women both inside and outside the home
**KANU** – Kenya African National Union
**KC** – Kenya Cowboy, a young white male Kenyan
**kikoi** – striped cotton sarong traditionally worn by men
**kiondo** – woven basket
**kitu kidogo** – 'a little something'; a bribe
**kofia** – cap worn by Muslim men
**KWS** – Kenya Wildlife Service

**lugga** – dry river bed, mainly in northern Kenya

**makonde** – woodcarving style, originally from southern Tanzania
**makuti** – thatch made with palm leaves used for roofing buildings, mainly on the coast
**malaya** – prostitute
**mandazi** – semisweet, flat doughnut
**manyatta** – Maasai or Samburu livestock camp often surrounded by a circle of thorn bushes
**mataha** – mashed beans, potatoes, maize and green vegetables
**matatu** – public minibuses used throughout the country
**matoke** – mashed plantains (green bananas)
**mboga** – vegetables
**miraa** – bundles of leafy shoots that are chewed as a stimulant and appetite suppressant
**mkate mayai** – fried, wheat pancake filled with mincemeat and raw egg; literally 'bread eggs'
**moran** – Maasai or Samburu warrior (plural *morani*)
**murram** – dirt or part-gravel road
**mursik** – milk drink fermented with cow's urine and ashes
**mwananchi** – worker of any kind but usually agricultural (plural *wananchi*, which is also used to refer to 'the people')
**mwizi** – a thief
**mzee** – an old man or respected elder
**mzee kipara** – bald man; literally means 'mosquito airport'
**mzungu** – white person (plural *wazungu*)

**NARC** – National Alliance Rainbow Coalition
**Ng'oroko** – Turkana bandits
**Nissan** – see *matatu*
**nyama choma** – barbecued meat, often goat
**Nyayo** – a cornerstone of Moi's political ideology, meaning 'footsteps'; to follow in the footsteps of Jomo Kenyatta

**panga** – machete, carried by most people in the country-side and often by thieves in the cities
**parking boys** – unemployed youths or young men who will assist in parking a vehicle and guard it while the owner is absent
**pesa** – money
**Peugeot** – shared taxi
**pombe** – Kenyan beer, usually made with millet and sugar

**rafiki** – friend; as in 'my friend, you want safari?'
**rondavel** – circular hut, usually a thatched building with a conical roof

**safari** – 'journey' in Kiswahili
**sambusa** – deep-fried pastry triangles stuffed with spiced mincemeat; similar to Indian samosa
**shamba** – small farm or plot of land
**shifta** – bandit

**shilingi** – money
**shuka** – Maasai blanket
**sigana** – traditional African performance form containing narration, song, music, dance, chant, ritual, mask, movement, banter and poetry
**sis** – white Kenyan slang for 'yuck'
**siwa** – ornately carved ivory wind instrument, unique to the coastal region and often used for fanfare at weddings

**Tusker** – Kenyan beer

**ugali** – staple made from maize or cassava flour, or both
**uhuru** – freedom or independence

**wa benzi** – someone driving a Mercedes-Benz car bought with, it's implied, the proceeds of corruption
**wananchi** – workers or 'the people' (singular *mwananchi*)
**wazungu** – white people (singular *mzungu*)

# The Authors

## MATTHEW D FIRESTONE
**Coordinating Author, Nairobi & Around, Southern Kenya**

Matt is a trained biological anthropologist and epidemiologist who is particularly interested in the health and nutrition of indigenous populations. His first visit to East Africa in 2001 brought him deep into the Tanzanian bush, where he performed a field study on the traditional diet of the Hadzabe hunter-gatherers. Unfortunately, Matt's promising academic career was postponed due to a severe case of wanderlust, though he has relentlessly travelled to over 50 countries in search of a cure. Matt is hoping that this book will help ease the pain of other individuals bitten by the travel bug, though he fears that there is a growing epidemic on the horizon.

## STUART BUTLER
**Environment, Rift Valley, Western Kenya, Northern Kenya**

English-born Stuart Butler has dreamt of Africa ever since he was a child listening to stories of his father's childhood in Kenya. His first glimpses of Africa, staring at the mountains of Morocco from southern Spain, further fuelled this infatuation, and when he finally got to step foot in Africa, it was Kenya he chose. It didn't disappoint. Since that first trip many years ago, he has visited all four corners of the continent and loved every minute of every part of it. Stuart now calls the south of France home, and his travels, for both Lonely Planet and various surfing magazines, have taken him beyond Africa, from the coastal deserts of Pakistan to the jungles of Colombia.

## PAULA HARDY
**History, The Culture**

Born and brought up in Kenya, Paula had an African childhood full of mischief and mayhem. With an architect father, who spent much of his time building wildlife lodges and the like, Paula was snooping around hotels and tented camps at an early age and now considers herself a connoisseur of long-drops and linen. In early 2008 Paula was at home in Kenya during much of the postelection crisis, and despite being shocked by the violence was heartened to see how many everyday Kenyans rallied to help their neighbours and bring the crisis under control. She has much faith in the future.

## ADAM KARLIN
**Central Highlands, Mombasa & the South Coast, The North Coast**

Clichéd as it may sound, Adam Karlin's first trip to Africa, as a student and volunteer, changed his life. It set him on the path of travelling and writing for a living, and seven years later he closed a circle by coming back to the continent to work on this 7th edition of Lonely Planet *Kenya*. In the course of his research, he drove a RAV4 full of elephant poop around Meru National Park, explored the ruins of the Kenyan coast by dhow, and became one of the first Westerners allowed into the *kaya* (sacred forest) of the Kausa Mijikenda.

THE AUTHORS

## CONTRIBUTING AUTHORS

**Dr Caroline Evans** wrote the Health chapter. Having studied medicine at the University of London, Caroline completed general practice training in Cambridge. She is the medical adviser to Nomad Travel Clinic, a private travel-health clinic in London, and is also a GP specialising in travel medicine. Caroline has acted as expedition doctor for Raleigh International and Coral Cay expeditions.

**David Lukas** wrote the Wildlife & Habitat chapter. David teaches and writes about the natural world from his home on the edge of Yosemite National Park. He has contributed Environment and Wildlife chapters for over 25 Lonely Planet guides, including *Tanzania, East Africa, South Africa, Botswana & Namibia,* and *Ethiopia & Eritrea.*

### LONELY PLANET AUTHORS

Why is our travel information the best in the world? It's simple: our authors are passionate, dedicated travellers. They don't take freebies in exchange for positive coverage so you can be sure the advice you're given is impartial. They travel widely to all the popular spots, and off the beaten track. They don't research using just the internet or phone. They discover new places not included in any other guidebook. They personally visit thousands of hotels, restaurants, palaces, trails, galleries, temples and more. They speak with dozens of locals every day to make sure you get the kind of insider knowledge only a local could tell you. They take pride in getting all the details right, and in telling it how it is. Think you can do it? Find out how at **lonelyplanet.com**.

# Behind the Scenes

## THIS BOOK

Hugh Finlay and Geoff Crowther wrote the first three editions of Lonely Planet's *Kenya* and the 4th edition was updated by Matt Fletcher. The 5th edition was revised and updated by Joseph Bindloss and Tom Parkinson, with Sean Pywell contributing the Wildlife Guide. The 6th edition was written by Tom Parkinson, Matt Phillips and Will Gourlay. This 7th edition was coordinated by Matthew D Firestone, who ably led the excellent author team of Stuart Butler, Adam Karlin and Paula Hardy. David Lukas wrote the Wildlife & Habitat chapter.

This guidebook was commissioned in Lonely Planet's Melbourne office, and produced by the following:

**Commissioning Editors** Holly Alexander, Stefanie Di Trocchio, Emma Gilmour, Lucy Monie
**Coordinating Editor** Laura Crawford
**Coordinating Cartographer** Diana Duggan
**Coordinating Layout Designer** Indra Kilfoyle
**Managing Editor** Sasha Baskett
**Managing Cartographers** Shahara Ahmed, Adrian Persoglia, Amanda Sierp
**Managing Layout Designers** Sally Darmody, Laura Jane

**Assisting Editors** Rebecca Chau, Sally O'Brien, Charlotte Orr
**Assisting Cartographer** Bonnie Wintle
**Cover Designer** Kate Slattery
**Colour Designer** Vicki Beale
**Project Managers** Craig Kilburn, Fabrice Rocher
**Language Content Coordinator** Quentin Frayne
**Thanks to** Jessica Boland, Mark Germanchis, James Hardy, Lisa Knights, Lyahna Spencer, Jane Thompson, Marg Toohey

## THANKS
### MATTHEW D FIRESTONE

First to my wonderful family, thank you all for your continued support, even though I've yet to hold down a 'real' job. Second, I'd like to give a big *asante sana* to my editor extraordinaires: Lucy, for giving me the chance to coordinate such an important title, and Holly, for catching up on all-things Africa with incredible speed. The next tip of my safari hat goes to Stuart, who traded a summer of surfing swells and fine dining in Biarritz for the Nile crocodiles and Turkana bandits of northern Kenya. And finally, to Adam, the other half of 2JG – here's to one day figuring out what really goes on in the Somali–Ethiopian–Kenyan border town of El Wak.

### THE LONELY PLANET STORY

Fresh from an epic journey across Europe, Asia and Australia in 1972, Tony and Maureen Wheeler sat at their kitchen table stapling together notes. The first Lonely Planet guidebook, *Across Asia on the Cheap,* was born.

Travellers snapped up the guides. Inspired by their success, the Wheelers began publishing books to Southeast Asia, India and beyond. Demand was prodigious, and the Wheelers expanded the business rapidly to keep up. Over the years, Lonely Planet extended its coverage to every country and into the virtual world via lonelyplanet.com and the Thorn Tree message board.

As Lonely Planet became a globally loved brand, Tony and Maureen received several offers for the company. But it wasn't until 2007 that they found a partner whom they trusted to remain true to the company's principles of travelling widely, treading lightly and giving sustainably. In October of that year, BBC Worldwide acquired a 75% share in the company, pledging to uphold Lonely Planet's commitment to independent travel, trustworthy advice and editorial independence.

Today, Lonely Planet has offices in Melbourne, London and Oakland, with over 500 staff members and 300 authors. Tony and Maureen are still actively involved with Lonely Planet. They're travelling more often than ever, and they're devoting their spare time to charitable projects. And the company is still driven by the philosophy of *Across Asia on the Cheap*: 'All you've got to do is decide to go and the hardest part is over. So go!'

BEHIND THE SCENES

## STUART BUTLER

Special thanks to everyone who helped out who I've forgotten – sorry, but it was appreciated! To my gran, mum and dad for reciting stories of the days when they lived in East Africa, and Paul and Mandy Gosling for giving me a home in Nairobi all those years ago. Fellow authors Matt and Adam for some tough times in Nairobi, George Muriuki of Upgrade Safaris for letting me destroy half his fleet and Simon for his superb driving under trying conditions – thanks a million. Calistus Napulo for the pleasure of meeting you, Ross and Caroline Withey in Baringo – Ross, what were the chances of that?! Shannon Jensen for tips on the north, Kwang Yang Lee for venturing where few dare, George for company whilst writing up, as well as the Binkster, who sadly passed away halfway through this project and to whom I'd like to dedicate my chapters. And finally, once again to Heather for all she has done and continues to do.

## PAULA HARDY

Considering the media storm over the post-election violence, it has been an interesting and thought-provoking time to write about Kenya's turbulent history and culture. I couldn't have done it without the assistance of friends and family, who continue to live through all the highs and lows of Kenya's modern landscape. First and foremost, thanks to David Hardy, my father, for all the stories, adventures and information he has shared. Thanks also to David Hutchison for the useful contacts, to Penny and Brian Nicol for grassroots information on the postelection landscape, and to Wahome Muciri for his perceptive insights on the current political and economic climate. Thanks also go to Lucy Monie for commissioning me to write on a project so close to my heart and to Holly Alexander for taking over so ably when submission loomed. And, finally, to Matt Firestone for his easygoing coordination.

## ADAM KARLIN

*Asante sana* to Chege for being a great driver and a better friend; Matt Phillips and Tom Parkinson for their excellent text; Hugh, Harry and Michael for fun times; all the friends who supported me during the write-up, particularly Phil and Lois; Lucy Monie for giving me this chance; and Matt Firestone for his companionship on the road and advice. And the countless Kenyans who helped wherever I went in their beautiful country. *Safari njema.*

# OUR READERS

**Many thanks to the travellers who used the last edition and wrote to us with helpful hints, useful advice and interesting anecdotes:**

Iris Allen, Francis Argyle, Petra Berkhoff, Caroline Brown, Leanne Brown, Klaus Buchholz, Tina Buckley, Peter Bugge, Chris Burkhart, Carrie Chan, Kate Charlesworth, Beryl Clare, Marco Coduti, Nathan Collett, Nicky Cosens, Richard Currie, Jasper De Vries, Matthew Dunning, Justine Egan, Tessa Finlev, Bouchou Florence, Felicity Fowkes, Robert Fraser, Margaret George, Frederique Georjon, Miranda Gilmore, David Goodick, Margaret Gorman, Cara Grayling, Stephanie Green, Frans Groot, Sarah Harrison, Brian Heeter, Itai Hermelin, Tim Hockham, Ahad I Palland, Jill Jolliff, Dennis And Cynthia Jones, Ronan Kelly, Bill Kenny, Laurin Keto, Jerry Koszednar, John Lantz, Christian Levan, Chuck Ludlam, Amanda Magrath, Sandy Maley, Per Kristian Mathisen, Alan Mccullough, Eric Mein, Nacho Melissis, Robert Miller, Jimba Moffat, Dr Marc-David Munk, Stephen Mustoe, Roxanne Nagel, Sophie Ndngi, Annika Nilsson, Caroline Njeri, Miranda Odam, Funda Ozan, Owen Ozier, Sam Pirbhai, Rita Poker, Ravio Raam, Ellison Richmond, George Ritchie, Richard Rix, Carene Ross, Jan Rybniker, Suessane Sadigh, Angelique Sanders, Amdeep Sanghera, Tom Sansone, Valeska Schaudy, Iris Schwarz, Dana Shokery, Mike Smith, Eric Sone, S J Srinivas, Lesrugg Stewart, Ira Sundberg, Qing Tan, Grant Taplin, Peter Wahome, David Waldman, Mx Weber, Harry Williamson, Susan Winton, Jane Yarham

---

### SEND US YOUR FEEDBACK

We love to hear from travellers – your comments keep us on our toes and help make our books better. Our well-travelled team reads every word on what you loved or loathed about this book. Although we cannot reply individually to postal submissions, we always guarantee that your feedback goes straight to the appropriate authors, in time for the next edition. Each person who sends us information is thanked in the next edition – and the most useful submissions are rewarded with a free book.

To send us your updates – and find out about Lonely Planet events, newsletters and travel news – visit our award-winning website: **lonelyplanet.com/contact**.

Note: we may edit, reproduce and incorporate your comments in Lonely Planet products such as guidebooks, websites and digital products, so let us know if you don't want your comments reproduced or your name acknowledged. For a copy of our privacy policy visit lonelyplanet.com/privacy.

## ACKNOWLEDGMENTS
### Many thanks to the following for the use of their content:

Globe on title page ©Mountain High Maps 1993 Digital Wisdom, Inc.

Internal photographs by Lonely Planet Images, and by Anders Blomqvist p73; Alex Dissanayake p82 (#1); Jason Edwards p79 (#2); Christer Fredriksson p81 (#3), p85 (#3); Dave Hamman p75 (#3); John Hay p76 (#4), p78 (#4); Dennis Jones p86 (#1); Frans Lemmens p83 (#3); Carol Polich p87 (#2); Mitch Reardon p74 (#1), p75 (#2), p81 (#2), p84 (#1), p85 (#2); Andy Rouse p74 (#4), p88 (#1); Philip & Karen Smith p81 (#4); David Tipling p82 (#4), p87 (#4); Ray Tipper p84 (#4); David Wall p76 (#1), p86 (#5); Ariadne Van Zandbergen p77 (#2, #3), p78 (#1), p79 (#3), p80, p83 (#2), p87 (#3), p88 (#2).

All images are the copyright of the photographers unless otherwise indicated. Many of the images in this guide are available for licensing from Lonely Planet Images: www.lonelyplanet images.com.

**BEHIND THE SCENES**

# Index

INDEX

**INDEX**

INDEX

# GreenDex

It seems like everyone's going 'green' these days, but how can you know which businesses are actually ecofriendly and which are simply jumping on the sustainable bandwagon? The following listings have all been selected by Lonely Planet authors because they demonstrate an active sustainable-tourism policy. Some are involved in conservation or environmental education, and many are owned and operated by local and indigenous operators, thereby maintaining and preserving regional identity and culture.

We want to keep developing our sustainable-tourism content. If you think we've omitted someone who should be listed here, or if you disagree with our choices, email us at talk2us@lonelyplanet .com.au. For more information about sustainable tourism and Lonely Planet, see www.lonelyplanet .com/responsibletravel.

## MAP LEGEND

### ROUTES

| | |
|---|---|
| Tollway | One-Way Street |
| Freeway | Street Mall/Steps |
| Primary Road | Tunnel |
| Secondary Road | Walking Tour |
| Tertiary Road | Walking Tour Detour |
| Lane | Walking Trail |
| Under Construction | Walking Path |
| Track | Pedestrian Overpass |
| Unsealed Road | |

### TRANSPORT

| | |
|---|---|
| Ferry | Rail |
| Metro | Rail (Underground) |
| Bus Route | Tram |

### HYDROGRAPHY

| | |
|---|---|
| River, Creek | Canal |
| Intermittent River | Water |
| Swamp | Lake (Dry) |
| Mangrove | Lake (Salt) |
| Reef | Mudflats |

### BOUNDARIES

| | |
|---|---|
| State, Provincial | Regional, Suburb |
| Marine Park | Cliff |

### AREA FEATURES

| | |
|---|---|
| Airport | Mall |
| Area of Interest | Market |
| Beach, Desert | Park |
| Building | Reservation |
| Campus | Rocks |
| Cemetery, Christian | Sports |
| Forest | Urban |
| Land | |

### POPULATION

| | |
|---|---|
| CAPITAL (NATIONAL) | CAPITAL (STATE) |
| Large City | Medium City |
| Small City | Town, Village |

### SYMBOLS

**Sights/Activities**
- Beach
- Castle, Fortress
- Christian
- Diving, Snorkelling
- Islamic
- Jewish
- Monument
- Museum, Gallery
- Point of Interest
- Pool
- Ruin
- Skiing
- Surfing, Surf Beach
- Trail Head
- Winery, Vineyard
- Zoo, Bird Sanctuary

**Eating**
- Eating

**Drinking**
- Drinking
- Cafe

**Entertainment**
- Entertainment

**Shopping**
- Shopping

**Sleeping**
- Sleeping
- Camping

**Transport**
- Airport, Airfield
- Bus Station
- Cycling, Bicycle Path
- General Transport
- Parking Area
- Petrol Station
- Taxi Rank

**Information**
- Bank, ATM
- Embassy/Consulate
- Hospital, Medical
- Information
- Internet Facilities
- Police Station
- Post Office, GPO
- Telephone
- Toilets

**Geographic**
- Lighthouse
- Lookout
- Mountain, Volcano
- National Park
- Pass, Canyon
- Picnic Area
- River Flow
- Waterfall

## LONELY PLANET OFFICES

### Australia
Head Office
Locked Bag 1, Footscray, Victoria 3011
☎ 03 8379 8000, fax 03 8379 8111
talk2us@lonelyplanet.com.au

### USA
150 Linden St, Oakland, CA 94607
☎ 510 250 6400, toll free 800 275 8555
fax 510 893 8572
info@lonelyplanet.com

### UK
2nd fl, 186 City Rd,
London EC1V 2NT
☎ 020 7106 2100, fax 020 7106 2101
go@lonelyplanet.co.uk

**Published by Lonely Planet Publications Pty Ltd**
ABN 36 005 607 983

© Lonely Planet Publications Pty Ltd 2009

© photographers as indicated 2009

Cover photograph: group of young female giraffes, Masai Mara National Reserve, Eastcott Momatiuk/The Image Bank/Getty Images. Many of the images in this guide are available for licensing from Lonely Planet Images: www.lonelyplanetimages.com.

Printed by SNP Security Printing Pte Ltd, Singapore.